THE
SUPREME COURT
AND THE
CONSTITUTION

Readings in
American Constitutional History

SECOND EDITION

THE
SUPREME COURT
AND THE
CONSTITUTION

Readings in
American Constitutional History

SECOND EDITION

EDITED BY
STANLEY I. KUTLER
UNIVERSITY OF WISCONSIN

W · W · NORTON & COMPANY · INC · NEW YORK

Published simultaneously in Canada by George J. McLeod Limited, Toronto.

Library of Congress Cataloging in Publication Data

Kutler, Stanley I   comp.
The Supreme Court and the Constitution.

1. United States—Constitutional law—Cases.
2. United States. Supreme Court. I. Title.
KF4549.K8 1977   347′.73′26   77–934
ISBN 0–393–09140–6

1 2 3 4 5 6 7 8 9 0

For My Students
In Appreciation

PREFACE

★ ★ ★ ★ THIS VOLUME is designed to acquaint the student with the Supreme Court's historical role in American constitutional development. The cases are arranged in chronological fashion, according to traditional historical periods, and further subdivided into pertinent topical categories. The headnotes for each case are designed to familiarize the reader with the historical and constitutional context, the factual background, and the relationship of the case to prior or subsequent ones. While the cases are of course edited, I have sought to provide generous extracts from each so that the reader might more fully understand the legal, political, social, and economic considerations employed in a judicial opinion to reach a "constitutional" decision. When appropriate, I have included portions of dissenting opinions.

It must be emphasized that this volume does not attempt to cover the full range of materials relevant to constitutional and legal history. Judicial decisions are not the exclusive sources for understanding this field. Indeed, I am well aware that all too often there is an overemphasis upon judicial history which deprives us of a more meaningful comprehension of constitutional matters. Political theory, executive and administrative actions, and legislation, too, are the stuff of constitutional history. But many of these documents are readily available in the multitude of source collections generally available for classroom use. Furthermore, the physical limitations of one volume simply do not permit use of divergent materials in great quantity, and in anything other than mere snippet form. For these reasons, then, I have chosen to include only judicial materials in this volume, organized in a manner useful for the historical understanding of constitutional development.

The selection of cases to be included in the volume was difficult. My judgment was based on several criteria. I have used cases which have, or had, long-standing significance for constitutional law. Cases which were only momentarily dramatic or politically controversial, and which were soon overtaken by other decisions and events, have been omitted. Thus, for example, the Marshall Court's first important case on debtor legislation in *Sturges* v. *Crowninshield* (1819) is very significant at a certain point in American history and in the history of the Marshall Court. But eight years later, the opinion was notably modified and superseded by *Ogden* v. *Saunders*. The majority and minority opinions in the latter case offer sufficient insight into the constitutional problems of the debtor-creditor problem of the early nineteenth century. In addition, I have sought to emphasize cases which best depict the Supreme Court's role in the making of public policy, particularly those constitutional decisions which have served as an instrument for reform and change.

★ ★ ★ ★   THIS NEW EDITION includes the major cases of the past decade, particularly the Burger Court's decisions. In doing so, I have not stricken prior decisions which have been overruled or modified. My purpose remains the same: to give the student an opportunity to understand the historical evolution of American constitutional law. In addition, I have added several sections which portray some unique constitutional problems that have been prominent in the past decade. Specifically, the final chapter now includes materials on the military involvement in Indochina, privacy, and the nature of executive power. Again, I have sought to avoid including materials that seem to raise only fleeting issues. But the question of dissent, the relationship between personal behavior and governmental intervention, and the extent of executive power all appear to be of enduring historical significance.

Many friends who share an interest in constitutional history graciously provided advice and criticism for the preparation of this collection. For the first edition, Harold M. Hyman, Maurice Baxter, Herman Belz, Alan D. Harper, Kent Newmyer, Donald Roper, and Philip Stebbins, considered and commented upon preliminary selections and organization. Former graduate students such as George M. Curtis, George Parkinson, and William Wiecek, offered significant suggestions and substantial aid with the collection of documents and preparation of the manuscript. Most important of all, Leonard Levy provided constant encouragement and meaningful criticism of the project from its inception. His suggestions were invaluable and, in many ways, the final results reflect his thinking as well as mine. During the preparation of this edition, he demonstrated a very different kind of care and concern that I will never forget.

I am very grateful to the College Department of W. W. Norton for the opportunity to revise this collection of cases. In particular, I appreciate the faith and interest of James Mairs—and for graciously tolerating a delay in the preparation of the manuscript. Michal Belknap, Harold Kaplan, Mary K. Tachau, and, of course, Stanley N. Katz, kindly contributed thoughtful suggestions and criticisms to my proposed revisions. I suppose I could not have done this book without Louis Bernhardt and Robert Henderson—"real" doctors, as they would be described in my family. And, of course, that family, particularly Sandy, provided very special encouragement and criticism.

Stanley I. Kutler

December 1976
Madison, Wisconsin

CONTENTS

PREFACE   vii

I

The Genesis of Judicial Power: The 1790's

A. The Federal Judiciary and the States
   Chisholm v. Georgia   3

B. State Laws and Vested Rights
   Vanhorne's Lessee v. Dorrance   7
   Calder v. Bull   13

C. National Supremacy
   Ware v. Hylton   17

D. Congressional Power
   Hylton v. United States   20

II

The Marshall Era: 1801–1835

A. Judicial Review
   Marbury v. Madison   25
   Eakin v. Raub   31

B. Federal Judicial Supremacy
   Martin v. Hunter's Lessee   36
   Cohens v. Virginia   41

xi

C. Implied Powers and Federalism

 McCulloch v. *Maryland*   50
 Barron v. *Baltimore*   60

D. The Contract Clause

 Fletcher v. *Peck*   63
 Dartmouth College v. *Woodward*   72
 Ogden v. *Saunders*   79
 Providence Bank v. *Billings*   87

E. The Commerce Clause

 Gibbons v. *Ogden*   90
 Willson v. *Black Bird Creek Marsh Co.*   97

III

The Taney Era: 1837–1864

A. Federal Judicial Power

 Luther v. *Borden*   101
 The Propeller Genesee Chief v. *Fitzhugh*   105
 Ableman v. *Booth*   110

B. The Contract Clause

 Proprietors of the Charles River Bridge v. *Proprietors of the Warren Bridge*   114
 Ohio Life Insurance and Trust Co. v. *Debolt*   120
 Dodge v. *Woolsey*   124

C. The Commerce Clause

 New York v. *Miln*   126
 The Passenger Cases   130
 Cooley v. *Board of Wardens of the Port of Philadelphia*   135

D. Corporations

 Bank of Augusta v. *Earle*   139
 Louisville, Cincinnati and Charlestown Railroad Co. v. *Letson*   142

E. Slavery

Prigg v. Pennsylvania   145
Dred Scott v. Sandford   150

IV

Civil War, Reconstruction, and Racism

A. War Powers

The Prize Cases   161
Ex Parte Milligan   164

B. Reconstruction

Cummings v. Missouri   170
Mississippi v. Johnson   174
Ex Parte McCardle   177
Texas v. White   179

C. Legal Tenders

Hepburn v. Griswold   183
Legal Tender Cases   188

D. The States and Civil Rights

Slaughter-House Cases   192
Hurtado v. California   193

E. The Freedman and the Constitution

United States v. Reese   197
Civil Rights Cases   200
Virginia v. Rives   209
Hall v. DeCuir   213
Plessy v. Ferguson   216

V

The Constitution and the Economy: 1873–1917

A. State Rate Regulation and Due Process

Slaughter-House Cases   225

Munn v. *Illinois*   242

Wabash, St. Louis and Pacific Ry. Co. v. *Illinois*   247

Chicago, Milwaukee, St. Paul Ry. Co. v. *Minnesota*   251

Smyth v. *Ames*   254

B. Federal Transportation Regulation

Interstate Commerce Commission v. *Cinti., New Orleans and
    Tex. Pac. Ry. Co.*   258

Interstate Commerce Commission v. *Illinois Central Railroad Co.*   261

Houston, East and West Texas Ry. Co. v. *United States*   264

C. Problems of Monopoly

United States v. *E. C. Knight Co.*   267

Northern Securities Company v. *United States*   271

Swift and Co. v. *United States*   275

Standard Oil Co. of New Jersey v. *United States*   277

D. The Fourteenth Amendment and Freedom of Contract

Lochner v. *New York*   282

Muller v. *Oregon*   289

Bunting v. *Oregon*   291

E. Labor Problems

In Re Debs   294

Loewe v. *Lawlor*   297

Adair v. *United States*   300

F. Income Tax

Pollock v. *Farmers' Loan and Trust Co.*   304

G. Federal Police Power

Lottery Case   309

McCray v. *United States*   312

VI

War, Radicalism, and Reaction: 1917–1933

A. Conscription and the War Power

Selective Draft Law Cases   321

B. Radicalism and the First Amendment

Schenck v. *United States*   324

Abrams v. *United States*   327
Gitlow v. *New York*   330
Whitney v. *California*   333

C. Economic Regulation and Normalcy

Hammer v. *Dagenhart*   337
Child Labor Tax Case   340
Truax v. *Corrigan*   344
Adkins v. *Children's Hospital*   347
Wolff Packing Co. v. *Court of Industrial Relations*   356
Stafford v. *Wallace*   359

VII

Judicial Power and Constitutional Change: 1933–1964

A. Depression and Constitutional Crisis: 1933–1936

Home Building and Loan Association v. *Blaisdell*   365
Nebbia v. *New York*   369
Schechter Poultry Corp. v. *United States*   373
Carter v. *Carter Coal Co.*   378
United States v. *Butler*   382

B. New Directions in Governmental Regulation

West Coast Hotel Company v. *Parrish*   387
National Labor Relations Board v. *Jones and Laughlin Steel
    Corp.*   394
United States v. *Darby Lumber Company*   402
Wickard v. *Filburn*   406
Steward Machine Company v. *Davis*   412
Ferguson v. *Skrupa*   419
Katzenbach v. *McClung*   422

VIII

Authority and Liberty: Modern Constitutional Tensions

A. The First Amendment: Freedom of Expression,
   Association and Assembly

De Jonge v. *Oregon*   429
Dennis v. *United States*   432

Yates v. *United States*   438

Watkins v. *United States*   445

Barenblatt v. *United States*   453

National Association for the Advancement of Colored People
v. *Alabama*   457

A Book Named [*Fanny Hill*] v. *Attorney General of Massachusetts; Ginzburg* v. *United States; Mishkin* v. *New York*   462

Miller v. *California*   468

Cox v. *Louisiana*   474

Virginia State Board of Pharmacy v. *Virginia Citizens Consumer Council*   477

B. The First Amendment: Freedom of the Press

Near v. *Minnesota*   482

New York Times Co. v. *Sullivan*   486

New York Times Co. v. *United States*   489

C. The First Amendment: Freedom of—and from—Religion

West Virginia Board of Education v. *Barnette*   494

Everson v. *Board of Education of the Township of Ewing*   503

Zorach v. *Clauson*   508

Engel v. *Vitale*   511

Wisconsin v. *Yoder*   516

D. Discrimination and the Search for Equality

Brown v. *Board of Education of Topeka*   522
Cooper v. *Aaron*   527

Swann v. *Charlotte-Mecklenburg Board of Education*   534

Burton v. *Wilmington Parking Authority*   542

Moose Lodge No. 107 v. *Irvis*   546

Heart of Atlanta Motel, Inc. v. *United States*   549

Jones v. *Alfred H. Mayer Co.*   555

Reed v. *Reed, Administrator*   561

McDonald v. *Santa Fe Trail Transportation Co.*   565

Shapiro v. *Thompson*   569

E. Voting Rights

Smith v. *Allwright*   574

South Carolina v. *Katzenbach, Attorney General*   578

Baker v. *Carr*   584

Reynolds v. *Sims*   594

F. Rights of the Accused

Mapp v. *Ohio*   600

Malloy v. *Hogan, Sheriff*   603

Gideon v. *Wainwright*   607

In Re Gault   612

Miranda v. *Arizona*   616

Harris v. *New York*   621

Gregg v. *Georgia*   625

G. Privacy and Personal Relations

Griswold v. *Connecticut*   630

Roe v. *Wade*   633

H. Dissent and the Indochina War

United States v. *O'Brien*   640

Tinker v. *Des Moines School District*   644

Welsh v. *United States*   649

Gillette v. *United States*   653

Massachusetts v. *Laird, Secretary of Defense*   658

I. Executive Power: Prerogatives and Limits

United States v. *Curtiss-Wright Export Corp.*   664

Korematsu v. *United States*   669

Youngstown Sheet & Tube Co. v. *Sawyer*   674

United States v. *United States District Court for the Eastern District of Michigan*   678

United States v. *Nixon*   684

APPENDIXES

The Constitution of the United States   693

The United States Supreme Court, 1789–1977   709

Table of Cases   712

I

The Genesis of Judicial Power:
The 1790's

The Federal Judiciary and the States

Chisholm *v.* Georgia

National Supremacy
Fed over St.

Chisholm v. Georgia *was hardly a promising start for federal judicial power and prestige. Two citizens of South Carolina brought suit against Georgia to recover British-owned property which had been confiscated by Georgia. State officials refused to appear in court and vigorously denied the Court's jurisdiction. The Court's subsequent decision against Georgia provoked widespread criticism. Two days after the opinions were given, the Eleventh Amendment was proposed in Congress to override the decision. It provided that federal judicial power was not to extend to suits against one of the states commenced by citizens of another state or a foreign nation. Despite Federalist opposition, the amendment was ratified in 1798. Through the years, however, the Court has diminished the force of the amendment, particularly by allowing suits against state officials. (See, for example,* Osborn v. Bank of the United States, 9 Wheaton 738 [1824].) *As in most cases of the 1790's, the Court delivered its opinions* seriatim. *Justice Iredell alone disagreed with the decision.*

Chief Justice Jay

The question we are now to decide has been accurately stated, namely, is a State suable by individual citizens of another State?
It is said that Georgia refuses to appear and answer to the plaintiff in this action, because she is a sovereign State, and therefore not liable to such actions. . . .
[A]ny one State in the Union may sue another State in this court, that is, all the people of one State may sue all the people of another State. It is plain, then, that a State may be sued, and hence it plainly follows that suability and state sovereignty are not incompatible. As one State may sue another State in this court, it is plain that no degradation to a State is thought to accompany her appearance in this court. It is not, therefore, to an appearance in this court that the objection points. To

2 Dallas 419 (1793)

what does it point? It points to an appearance at the suit of one or more citizens. But why it should be more incompatible that all the people of a State should be sued by one citizen, than by one hundred thousand, I cannot perceive, the process in both cases being alike, and the consequences of a judgment alike. Nor can I observe any greater inconveniences in the one case than in the other, except what may arise from the feelings of those who may regard a lesser number in an inferior light. But if any reliance be made on this inferiority, as an objection, at least one half of its force is done away by this fact, namely, that it is conceded that a State may appear in this court as plaintiff against a single citizen as defendant; and the truth is that the State of Georgia is at this moment prosecuting an action in this court against two citizens of South Carolina.

The only remnant of objection therefore that remains is, that the State is not bound to appear and answer as a defendant at the suit of an individual. . . . This inquiry naturally leads our attention, 1st. To the design of the constitution. 2d. To the letter and express declaration in it.

Prior to the date of the constitution, the people had not any national tribunal to which they could resort for justice; the distribution of justice was then confined to State judicatories, in whose institution and organization the people of the other States had no participation, and over whom they had not the least control. There was then no general court of appellate jurisdiction by whom the errors of State courts, affecting either the nation at large or the citizens of any other State, could be revised and corrected. Each State was obliged to acquiesce in the measure of justice which another State might yield to her or to her citizens; and that even in cases where State considerations were not always favorable to the most exact measure. There was danger that from this source animosities would in time result; and as the transition from animosities to hostilities was frequent in the history of independent States, a common tribunal for the termination of controversies became desirable, from motives both of justice and of policy.

Prior also to that period the United States had, by taking a place among the nations of the earth, become amenable to the laws of nations, and it was their interest as well as their duty to provide that those laws should be respected and obeyed; in their national character and capacity the United States were responsible to foreign nations for the conduct of each State, relative to the laws of nations, and the performance of treaties; and there the inexpediency of referring all such questions to State courts, and particularly to the courts of delinquent States, became apparent. While all the States were bound to protect each, and the citizens of each, it was highly proper and reasonable that they should be in a capacity not only to cause justice to be done to each, and the citizens of each, but also to cause justice to be done by each, and the citizens of each; and that, not by violence and force, but in a stable, sedate, and regular course of judicial procedure.

These were among the evils against which it was proper for the nation, that is the people of all the United States, to provide by a national judiciary, to be instituted by the whole nation, and to be responsible to the whole nation.

Let us now turn to the constitution. The people therein declare that their design in establishing it comprehended six objects. 1st. To form a more perfect union. 2d. To establish justice. 3d. To insure domestic tranquillity. 4th. To provide for the common defence. 5th. To promote the general welfare. 6th. To secure the blessings of liberty to themselves and their posterity. . . .

The question now before us renders it necessary to pay particular attention to that part of the second section which extends the judicial power "to controversies between a State and citizens of another State." It is contended that this ought to be construed to reach none of these controversies, excepting those in which a State may be plaintiff. The ordinary rules for construction will easily decide whether those words are to be understood in that limited sense.

This extension of power is remedial, because it is to settle controversies. It is, therefore, to be construed liberally. It is politic, wise, and good, that not only the controversies in which a State is plaintiff, but also those in which a State is defendant, should be settled; both cases, therefore, are within the reason of the remedy; and ought to be so adjudged, unless the obvious, plain, and literal sense of the words forbid it. If we attend to the words we find them to be express, positive, free from ambiguity, and without room for such implied expressions: "The judicial power of the United States shall extend to controversies between a State and citizens of another State." If the constitution really meant to extend these powers only to those controversies in which a State might be plaintiff, to the exclusion of those in which citizens had demands against a State, it is inconceivable that it should have attempted to convey that meaning in words not only so incompetent, but also repugnant to it; if it meant to exclude a certain class of these controversies, why were they not expressly excepted; on the contrary, not even an intimation of such intention appears in any part of the constitution. It cannot be pretended that where citizens urge and insist upon demands against a State, which the State refuses to admit and comply with, that there is no controversy between them. If it is a controversy between them, then it clearly falls not only within the spirit, but the very words of the constitution. What is it to the cause of justice, and how can it affect the definition of the word controversy, whether the demands which cause the dispute are made by a State against citizens of another State, or by the latter against the former? When power is thus extended to a controversy, it necessarily, as to all judicial purposes, is also extended to those between whom it subsists.

The exception contended for would contradict and do violence to the great and leading principles of a free and equal national government, one of the great objects of which is to insure justice to all. To the few against the many, as well as to the many against the few. It would be strange, indeed, that the joint and equal sovereigns of this country should, in the very constitution by which they professed to establish justice, so far deviate from the plain path of equality and impartiality, as to give to the collective citizens of one State a right of suing individual citizens of another State, and yet deny to those citizens a right of suing them. . . .

For the reasons before given, I am clearly of opinion that a State is suable by citizens of another State; but lest I should be understood in a latitude beyond my meaning, I think it necessary to subjoin this caution, namely, that such suability may nevertheless not extend to all the demands, and to every kind of action, there may be exceptions. For instance, I am far from being prepared to say that an individual may sue a State on bills of credit issued before the constitution was established, and which were issued and received on the faith of the State, and at a time when no ideas or expectations of judicial interposition were entertained or contemplated. . . .

*land troubles=
Art. of Conf.*

State Laws and Vested Rights

Vanhorne's Lessee *v.* Dorrance (1795)

This was a federal circuit court case in which Justice William Paterson declared a Pennsylvania statute invalid. The state had settled a land claims dispute in 1787 by granting land which it already had vested in others. Three years later, however, the legislature reversed itself and repealed its so-called "Confirmation Act." Nevertheless, Dorrance claimed title under the original act. On a number of grounds, the plaintiff clearly was entitled to a verdict, and Paterson so instructed the jury. His charge to the jury, printed below, went beyond the technicalities of the relevant statutes and grandly theorized on such topics as judicial review, natural rights, the social compact, and constitutional limitations. Significantly, his comments on judicial power and the contract clause of the federal constitution anticipated decisions and developments of the next few decades.

Justice Paterson

To aid you, gentlemen, in forming a verdict, I shall consider:
 I. The constitutionality of the confirming act; or, in other words, whether the legislature had authority to make that act?
 Legislation is the exercise of sovereign authority. High and important powers are necessarily vested in the Legislative body: whose acts, under some forms of government, are irresistible and subject to no control. In England, from whence most of our legal principles and legislative notions are derived, the authority of the Parliament is transcendant, and has no bounds. . . .
 Some of the judges in England, have had the boldness to assert, that an act of parliament, made against natural equity, is void; but this opinion contravenes the general position, that the validity of an act of parliament cannot be drawn into question by the judicial department: It cannot be disputed, and must be obeyed. The power of parliament is absolute and transcendant; it is omnipotent in the scale of political

existence. Besides, in England there is no written constitution, no fundamental law, nothing visible, nothing real, nothing certain, by which a statute can be tested. In America the case is widely different: Every state in the union has its constitution reduced to written exactitude and precision.

What is a constitution? It is the form of government, delineated by the mighty hand of the people, in which certain first principles of fundamental laws are established. The constitution is certain and fixed; it contains the permanent will of the people, and is the supreme law of the land; it is paramount to the power of the legislature, and can be revoked or altered only by the authority that made it.

The life-giving principle and the death-doing stroke must proceed from the same hand. What are legislatures? Creatures of the constitution; they owe their existence to the constitution; they derive their powers from the constitution; it is their commission; and, therefore, all their acts must be conformable to it, or else they will be void. The constitution is the work or will of the people themselves, in their original, sovereign, and unlimited capacity. Law is the work or will of the legislature in their derivative and subordinate capacity. The one is the work of the Creator, and the other of the creature. The constitution fixes limits to the exercise of legislative authority, and prescribes the orbit within which it must move. In short, gentlemen, the constitution is the sun of the political system, around which all legislative, executive and judicial bodies must revolve. Whatever may be the case in other countries, yet in this, there can be no doubt, that every act of the legislature, repugnant to the constitution, is absolutely void. . . .

The constitution of a state is stable and permanent, not to be worked upon by the temper of the times nor to rise and fall with the tide of events: notwithstanding the competition of opposing interests, and the violence of contending parties, it remains firm and immovable, as a mountain amidst the strife of storms, or a rock in the ocean amidst the raging of the waves. I take it to be a clear position: that if a legislative act oppugns a constitutional principle the former must give way, and be rejected on the score of repugnance. I hold it to a position equally clear and sound, that, in such case, it will be the duty of the court to adhere to the constitution, and to declare the act null and void. The constitution is the basis of legislative authority; it lies at the foundation of all law, and is a rule and commission by which both legislators and judges are to proceed. It is an important principle, which in the discussion of questions of the present kind, ought never to be lost sight of, that the judiciary in this country is not a subordinate, but co-ordinate branch of the government.

Having made these preliminary observations, we shall proceed to contemplate the quieting and confirming act, and to bring its validity to the test of the constitution.

In the course of argument, the counsel on sides relied upon certain parts of the late bill of rights and constitution of Pennsylvania, which I shall now read, and then refer to them occasionally in the sequel of the charge. . . .

From these passages it is evident; that the right of acquiring and possessing property and having it protected, is one of the natural inherent and unalienable rights of man. Men have a sense of property: Property is necessary to their subsistence, and correspondent to their natural wants and desires; its security was one of the objects, that induced them to unite in society. No man would become a member of a community, in which he could not enjoy the fruits of his honest labor and industry. The preservation of property then is a primary object of the social compact, and, by the late constitution of Pennsylvania, was made a fundamental law. Every person ought to contribute his proportion for public purposes and public exigencies; but no one can be called upon to surrender or sacrifice his whole property, real and personal, for the good of the community, without receiving a recompence in value. This would be laying a burden upon an individual, which ought to be sustained by the society at large. The English history does not furnish an instance of the kind; the parliament with all their boasted omnipotence, never committed such an outrage on private property; and if they had it would have served only to display the dangerous nature of unlimited authority; it would have been an exercise of power and not of right. Such an act would be a monster in legislation, and shock all mankind. The legislature, therefore, had no authority to make an act divesting one citizen of his freehold, and vesting it in another, without a just compensation. It is inconsistent with the principles of reason, justice, and moral rectitude; it is incompatible with the comfort, peace, and happiness of mankind; it is contrary to the principles of social alliance in every free government; and lastly, it is contrary both to letter and spirit of the constitution. In short, it is what every one would think unreasonable and unjust in his own case. The next step in the line of progression is, whether the legislature had authority to make an act, divesting one citizen of his freehold and vesting it in another, even with compensation. That the Legislature on certain emergencies, had authority to exercise this high power, has been urged from the nature of the social compact, and from the words of [the] constitution, which says, that the house of representatives shall have all other powers necessary for the legislature of a free state or commonwealth; but they shall have no power to add to, alter, abolish, or infringe any part of this constitution. The course of reasoning, on the part of the defendant, may be compromised in a few words. The despotic power, as it is aptly called by some writers, of taking private property, when state necessity requires, exists in every government; the existence of such power is necessary; government could not subsist without it; and if this be the case, it cannot be lodged any where with so much safety as with the legislature,

The presumption is, that they will not call it into exercise except in urgent cases, or cases of the first necessity. There is force in this reasoning. It is, however, difficult to form a case, in which the necessity of a state can be of such a nature, as to authorize or excuse the seizing of landed property belonging to one citizen and giving it to another citizen. It is immaterial to the state, in which of its citizens the land is vested; but it is of primary importance, that, when vested it should be secured, and the proprietor protected in the enjoyment of it. The constitution encircles, and renders it an holy thing. We must, gentlemen, bear constantly in mind, that the present is a case of landed property; vested by law in one set of citizens, attempted to be divested, for the purpose of vesting the same property in another set of citizens. It cannot be assimilated to the case of personal property taken or used in time of war and famine, or other extreme necessity; it cannot be assimilated to the temporary possession of land itself, on a pressing public emergency, or the spur of the occasion. In the latter case there is no change of property, no divestment of right; the title remains, and the proprietor, though out of possession for a while is still proprietor and lord of the soil. The possession grew out of occasion and ceases with it. Then the right of necessity is satisfied and at an end; it does not affect the title, is temporary in its nature, and cannot exist forever. The constitution expressly declares, that the right of acquiring, possessing, and protecting property is natural, inherent, and unalienable. It is a right not *ex gratia* from the legislature, but *ex debito* from the constitution. It is sacred; for, it is further declared, that the legislature shall have no power to add to, alter, abolish, or infringe any part of the constitution. The constitution is the origin and measure of legislative authority. It says to legislators, thus far ye shall go and no further. Not a particle of it should be shaken; not a pebble of it should be removed. Innovation is dangerous. One incroachment leads to another; precedent gives birth to precedent; what has been done may be done again; thus radical principles are generally broken in upon, and the constitution eventually destroyed. Where is the security, where the inviolability of property, if the legislature, by a private act, affecting particular persons only, can take land from one citizen, who acquired it legally, and vest it in another? The rights of private property are regulated, protected, and governed by general, known, and established laws; and decided upon, by general, known, and established tribunals; laws and tribunals not made and created on an instant exigency, on an urgent emergency, to serve a present turn, or the interest of a moment. Their operation and influence are equal and universal; they press alike on all. Hence security and safety, tranquillity and peace. One man is not afraid of another, and no man afraid of the legislature. It is infinitely wiser and safer to risk some possible mischiefs, than to vest in the legislature so unnecessary, dangerous, and enormous a power as that which has been exercised on the present occasion; a power, that, according to the full extent of the argument, is boundless and omnipotent. For, the legislature judged of the necessity of the case, and also of the nature and value of the equivalent.

Such a case of necessity, and judging too of the compensation, can never occur in any nation. Singular, indeed, and untoward must be the state of things, that would induce the legislature, supposing they had the power, to divest one individual of his landed estate merely for the purpose of vesting it in another, even upon full indemnification; unless that indemnification be ascertained in the manner which I shall mention hereafter.

But admitting, that the legislature can take the real estate of A. and give it to B. on making compensation, the principle and reasoning upon it go no further than to show, that the legislature are the sole and exclusive judges of the necessity of the case, in which this despotic power should be called into action. It cannot, on the principles of the social alliance, or of the constitution, be extended beyond the point of judging upon every existing case of necessity. The legislature declare and enact, that such are the public exigencies, or necessities of the state, as to authorize them to take the land of A. and give it to B.; the dictates of reason and the eternal principles of justice, as well as the sacred principles of the social contract, and the constitution, direct, and they accordingly declare and ordain, that A. shall receive compensation for the land. But here the legislature must stop; they have run the full length of their authority, and can go no further: they cannot constitutionally determine upon the amount of the compensation, or value of the land. Public exigencies do not require, necessity does not demand, that the legislature should, of themselves, without the participation of the proprietor, or intervention of a jury, assess the value of the thing, or ascertain the amount of the compensation to be paid for it. . . .

It is contended that the legislature must judge of the necessity of interposing their despotic authority; it is a right of necessity upon which no other power in government can decide: That no civil institution is perfect; and that cases will occur, in which private property must yield to urgent calls of public utility or general danger. Be it so. But then it must be upon complete indemnification to the individual. Agreed: But who shall judge of this? Did there also exist a state necessity, that the legislature, or persons solely appointed by them, must admeasure the compensation, or value of the lands seized and taken, and the validity of the title thereto? Did a third state necessity exist, that the proprietor must take land by way of equivalent for his land? And did a fourth state necessity exist, that the value of this land-equivalent must be adjusted by the board of property, without the consent of the party, or the interference of a jury? Alas! how necessity begets necessity. They rise upon each other and become endless. The proprietor stands afar off, a solitary and unprotected member of the community, and is stripped of his property, without his consent, without a hearing, without notice, the value of that property judged upon without his participation, or the intervention of a jury, and the equivalent therefor in lands ascertained in the same way. If this be the legislature of a republican government, in which the preservation of property is made sacred by the constitution, I ask, wherein it differs from the mandate of an Asiatic prince? Omnipotence in legislation is despotism. According to this doctrine, we have nothing that we can call our own, or are sure of for a moment; we are all tenants at will, and hold our landed property at the mere pleasure of the legislature. Wretched situation, precarious tenure! And yet we boast of property and its security, of laws, of courts, of constitutions, and call ourselves free! In short, gentlemen, the confirming act is void; it never had constitutional existence; it is a dead letter, and of no more virtue or avail, than if it never had been made. . . .

After the opinion delivered on the preceeding questions, it is not necessary to determine upon the validity of the repealing law. But it being my intention in this charge to decide upon all the material points in the cause, in order that the whole may, at once, be carried before the supreme judicature for revision, I shall detain you, gentlemen, a few minutes only, while I just touch upon the constitutionality of the repealing act. . . .

This act was made after the adoption of the Constitution of the United States, and the argument is, that it is contrary to it.

1. Because it is an *ex post facto* law.
2. Because it is a law impairing the obligation of a contract.

1. That it is an *ex post facto* law. But what is the fact? If making a law be a fact within the words of the constitution, then no law, when once made, can ever be repealed. Some of the Connecticut settlers presented their claims to the commissioners, who received and entered them. These are facts. But are they facts of any avail? Did they give any right or vest any estate? No — whether done or not done, they leave the parties just where they were. They create no interest, affect no title, change no property, when done they are useless and of no efficacy. Other acts were necessary to be performed, but before the performance of them, the law was suspended and then repealed.

2. It impairs the obligation of a contract, and is therefore void. If the property to the lands in question had been vested in the state of Pennsylvania, then the legislature would have had the liberty and right of disposing or granting them to whom they pleased, at any time, and in any manner. Over public property they have a disposing and controlling power, over private property they have none, except, perhaps, in certain cases, and those under restrictions, and except also, what may arise from the enactment and operation of general laws respecting property, which

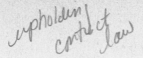

will affect themselves as well as their constituents. But if the confirming act be a contract between the legislature of Pennsylvania and the Connecticut settlers, it must be regulated by the rules and principles, which prevade and govern all cases of contracts; and if so, it is clearly void, because it tends, in its operation and consequences, to defraud the Pennsylvania claimants, who are third persons, of their just rights; rights ascertained, protected, and secured by the constitution and known laws of the land. The plaintiff's title to the land in question, is legally derived from Pennsylvania; how then, on the principles of contract, could Pennsylvania lawfully dispose of it to another? As a contract, it could convey no right, without the owner's consent; without that, it was fraudulent and void. . . .

Calder *v.* Bull

In 1795, the Connecticut legislature set aside a decree of a probate court and granted a new hearing before the same court. The plaintiffs charged that this was an ex post facto *law prohibited by the federal constitution. The Supreme Court, however, followed traditional practice and held that the prohibition applied only to criminal, not civil cases. However, Justice Chase's remarks about vested rights in a separate opinion, revealed a growing judicial impatience with legislative practices which threatened property rights.*

Justice Iredell

If . . . a government, composed of legislative, executive, and judicial departments, were established by a constitution which imposed no limits on the legislative power, the consequence would inevitably be, that whatever the legislative power chose to enact, would be lawfully enacted, and the judicial power could never interpose to pronounce it void. It is true, that some speculative jurists have held, that a legislative act against natural justice must, in itself, be void; but I cannot think, that under such a government any court of justice would possess a power to declare it so. . . .

In order, therefore, to guard against so great an evil, it has been the policy of all the American States, which have, individually, framed their state constitutions since the revolution, and of the people of the United

States, when they framed the federal constitution, to define with precision the objects of the legislative power, and to restrain its exercise within marked and settled boundaries. If any act of congress, or of the legislature of a State, violates those constitutional provisions, it is unquestionably void; though, I admit, that as the authority to declare it void is of a delicate and awful nature, the court will never resort to that authority, but in a clear and urgent case. If, on the other hand, the legislature of the Union, or the legislature of any member of the Union, shall pass a law, within the general scope of their constitutional power, the court cannot pronounce it to be void, merely because it is, in their judgment, contrary to the principles of natural justice. The ideas of natural justice are regulated by no fixed standard; the ablest and the purest men have differed upon the subject; and all that the court could properly say, in such an event, would be, that the legislature, possessed of an equal right of opinion, had passed an act which, in the opinion of the judges, was inconsistent with the abstract principles of natural justice. There are then but two lights in which the subject can be viewed: 1st. If the legislature pursue the authority delegated to them, their acts are valid. 2d. If they transgress the boundaries of that authority, their acts are invalid. In the former case, they exercise the discretion vested in them by the people, to whom alone they are responsible for the faithful discharge of their trust; but in the latter case, they violate a fundamental law, which must be our guide, whenever we are called upon as judges to determine the validity of a legislative act. . . .

The temptation to . . . abuses of power is unfortunately too alluring for human virtue; and, therefore, the framers of the American constitutions have wisely denied to the respective legislatures, federal as well as state, the possession of the power itself. They shall not pass any *ex post facto* law; or, in other words, they shall not inflict a punishment for any act, which was innocent at the time it was committed; nor increase the degree of punishment previously denounced for any specific offence.

The policy, the reason, and humanity, of the prohibition, do not . . . extend to civil cases, to cases that merely affect the private property of citizens. Some of the most necessary and important acts of legislation are, on the contrary, founded upon the principle that private rights must yield to public exigencies. Highways are run through private grounds. Fortifications, light-houses, and other public edifices, are necessarily sometimes built upon the soil owned by individuals. In such, and similar cases, if the owners should refuse voluntarily to accommodate the public, they must be constrained, as far as the public necessities require; and justice is done, by allowing them a reasonable equivalent. Without the possession of this power the operations of government would often be obstructed, and society itself would be endangered. It is not sufficient to urge, that the power may be abused, for such is the nature of all power, — such is the tendency of every human institution; and it might as fairly be said, that the power of taxation, which is only circumscribed by the discretion of the body in which it is vested, ought not to be granted, because the legislature, disregarding its true objects, might, for visionary and useless projects, impose a tax to the amount of nineteen shillings in the pound. We must be content to limit power where we can, and where we cannot, consistently with its use, we must be content to repose a salutary confidence. It is our consolation that there never existed a government, in ancient or modern times, more free from danger in this respect, than the governments of America. . . .

Justice Chase

The effect of the resolution or law of Connecticut . . . is to revise a decision of one of its inferior courts, called the court of probate for Hartford, and to direct a new hearing of the case by the same court of probate that passed the decree against the will of Normand Morrison. By the existing law of Connecticut, a right to recover certain property had vested in Calder and wife (the appellants) in consequence of a decision of a court of justice, but, in virtue of a subsequent resolution or law, and the new hearing thereof, and the decision in consequence, this right to recover certain property was divested, and the right to the property declared to be in Bull and wife, the appellees. The sole inquiry is, whether this resolution or law of Connecticut, having such operation, is an *ex post facto* law, within the prohibition of the federal constitution?

Whether the legislature of any of the States can revise and correct by law, a decision of any of its courts of justice, although not prohibited by the constitution of the State, is a question of very great importance, and not necessary now to be determined, because the resolution or law in question does not go so far. I cannot subscribe to the omnipotence of a state legislature, or that it is absolute and without control, although its authority should not be expressly restrained by the constitution, or fundamental law of the State. The people of the United States erected their constitutions, or forms of government, to establish justice, to promote the general welfare, to secure the blessings of liberty; and to protect their persons and property from violence. The purposes for which men enter into society will determine the nature and terms of the social compact; and as they are the foundation of the legislative power, they will decide what are the proper objects of it. The nature and ends of legislative power will limit the exercise of it. This fundamental principle flows from the very nature of our free republican governments, that no man should be compelled to do what the laws do not require, nor to refrain from acts which the laws permit. There are acts which the federal or state legislature cannot do, without exceeding their authority. There are certain vital principles in our free republican governments, which will determine and overrule an apparent and flagrant abuse of legislative power; as to authorize manifest injustice by positive law; or to take away that security for personal liberty, or private property, for the protection whereof the government was established. An act of the legislature (for I cannot call it a law) contrary to the great first principles of the social compact, cannot be considered a rightful exercise of legislative authority. The obligation of a law in governments established on express compact, and on republican principles, must be determined by the nature of the power on which it is founded. A few instances will suffice to explain what I mean. A law that punished a citizen for an innocent action, or, in other words, for an act, which, when done, was in violation of no existing law; a law that destroys, or impairs, the lawful private contracts of citizens; a law that makes a man a judge in his own cause; or a law that takes property from A. and gives it to B. It is against all reason and justice for a people to intrust a legislature with such powers; and, therefore, it cannot be presumed that they have done it. The genius, the nature, and the spirit of our state governments, amount to a prohibition of such acts of legislation; and the general principles of law and reason forbid them. The legislature may enjoin, permit, forbid and punish; they may declare new crimes, and establish rules of conduct for all its citizens in future cases; they may command what is right, and prohibit what is wrong; but they cannot change innocence into guilt; or punish innocence as a crime; or violate the right of an antecedent lawful private contract; or the right of private property. To maintain that our federal or state legislature possesses such powers, if they had not been expressly restrained, would, in my opinion, be a political heresy altogether inadmissible in our free republican governments. . . .

Ware *v.* Hylton

In Ware *v.* Hylton *the Court struck down a 1777 Virginia statute which sequestered pre-Revolutionary debts of British creditors. The Treaty of Paris of 1783, which ended the Revolutionary War, stipulated that such debts would be honored by the new nation. The Court thus implemented Article VI, Section 2 of the Constitution, providing for the supremacy of treaties over state laws. John Marshall and Patrick Henry argued the cause for the Virginia debtors and contended that state law was controlling. The Court's highly nationalistic decision, coupled with the sensitive issue of British debts, further heightened Anti-Federalist criticism of the judiciary and the national government.*

Justice Chase

The question . . . may be stated thus: Whether the 4th article of the said treaty nullifies the law of Virginia, passed on the 20th of October, 1777; destroys the payment made under it, and revives the debt and gives a right of recovery thereof against the original debtor?

It was doubted by one of the counsel for the defendants in error (Mr. Marshall) whether congress had a power to make a treaty that could operate to annul a legislative act of any of the States, and to destroy rights acquired by, or vested in individuals in virtue of such acts. Another of the defendant's counsel, (Mr. Campbell) expressly, and with great zeal, denied that congress possessed such power.

But a few remarks will be necessary to show the inadmissibility of this objection to the power of congress.

1st. The legislatures of all the States have often exercised the power of taking the property of its citizens for the use of the public, but they uniformly compensated the proprietors. The principle to maintain this right is for the public good, and to that the interest of individuals must yield. The instances are many; and among them are lands taken for

3 Dallas 199 (1796)

forts, magazines, or arsenals, or for public roads, or canals, or to erect towns.

2d. The legislatures of all the States have often exercised the power of devesting rights vested, and even of impairing, and in some instances, of almost annihilating the obligation of contracts, as by tender laws, which made an offer to pay, and a refusal to receive paper money for a specie debt, an extinguishment to the amount tendered.

3d. If the legislature of Virginia could, by a law annul any former law, I apprehend that the effect would be to destroy all rights acquired under the law so nullified.

4th. If the legislature of Virginia could not by ordinary acts of legislation do these things, yet possessing the supreme sovereign power of the State, she certainly could do them by a treaty of peace, if she had not parted with the power of making such treaty. If Virginia had such power before she delegated it to congress, it follows that afterwards that body possessed it. Whether Virginia parted with the power of making treaties of peace, will be seen by a perusal of the ninth article of the confederation (ratified by all the States on the 1st of March, 1781), in which it was declared, "that the United States in congress assembled, shall have the sole and exclusive right and power of determining on peace or war, except in the two cases mentioned in the sixth article, and of entering into treaties and alliances, with a proviso, when made, respecting commerce." This grant has no restriction, nor is there any limitation on the power in any part of the confederation. A right to make peace necessarily includes the power of determining on what terms peace shall be made. A power to make treaties must of necessity imply a power to decide the terms on which they shall be made. A war between two nations can only be concluded by treaty.

Surely the sacrificing [of] public or private property to obtain peace cannot be the cases in which a treaty would be void. . . . It seems to me that treaties made by congress, according to the confederation, were superior to the laws of the States, because the confederation made them obligatory on all the States. They were so declared by congress on the 13th of April, 1787; were so admitted by the legislatures and executives of most of the States; and were so decided by the judiciary of the general government, and by the judiciaries of some of the state governments.

If doubts could exist before the establishment of the present national government, they must be entirely removed by the sixth article of the constitution, which provides "that all treaties made, or which shall be made under the authority of the United States, shall be the supreme law of the land; and the judges in every State shall be bound thereby, any thing in the constitution or laws of any State to the contrary notwithstanding." There can be no limitation on the power of the people of the United States. By their authority the state constitutions were made, and by their authority the constitution of the United States was established; and they had the power to change or abolish the state constitutions, or to make them yield to the general government, and to treaties made by their authority. A treaty cannot be the supreme law of the land, that is, of all the United States, if any act of a state legislature can stand in its way. If the constitution of a State (which is the fundamental law of the State, and paramount to its legislature) must give way to a treaty, and fall before it, can it be questioned whether the less power, an act of the state legislature must not be prostrate? It is the declared will of the people of the United States that every treaty made by the authority of the United States, shall be superior to the constitution and laws of any individual State, and their will alone is to decide. If a law of a State, contrary to a treaty, is not void, but voidable only by a repeal, or nullification by a state legislature, this certain consequence follows, that the will of a small part of the United States may control or defeat the will of the whole. The people of America have been pleased to declare that all treaties made before the establishment of the national constitution, or laws of any of the States, contrary to a treaty, shall be disregarded.

Four things are apparent on a view of this 6th article of the national constitution. 1st. That it is retrospective, and is to be considered in the same light as if the constitution had been established before the making of the treaty of 1783. 2d. That the constitution, or laws, of any of the States, so far as either of them shall be found contrary to that treaty, are, by force of the said article, prostrated before the treaty. 3d. That consequently the treaty of 1783 has superior power to the legislature of any State, because no legislature of any State has any kind of power over the constitution, which was its creator. 4th. That it is the declared duty of the state judges to determine any constitution, or laws of any State, contrary to that treaty, or any other, made under the authority of the United States, null and void. National or federal judges are bound by duty and oath to the same conduct.

The argument, that congress had not power to make the 4th article of the treaty of peace, if its intent and operation was to annul the laws of any of the States, and to destroy vested rights, which the plaintiff's counsel contended to be the object and effect of the 4th article, was unnecessary, but on the supposition that this court possess a power to decide whether this article of the treaty is within the authority delegated to that body, by the articles of confederation. Whether this court constitutionally possess such a power is not necessary now to determine, because I am fully satisfied that congress were invested with the authority to make the stipulation in the 4th article. . . .

★ D ★

Congressional Power

Hylton *v.* United States

This case was the first in which the Supreme Court sitting en banc
*directly confronted an act of Congress. The issue was whether a
1794 carriage tax was an excise or a direct tax. If it were interpreted as a direct tax, it would have been invalid because the
Constitution required such taxes to be apportioned among the states
according to population. The three sitting justices upheld the law,
but clearly assumed the power to void it. The decision narrowing
the meaning of direct taxes paved the way for a broad federal
excise program. With the exception of the income tax cases a
century later, the Court has never classified any federal tax as a
direct one, requiring the rule of apportionment.*

Justice Paterson

By the second section of the first article of the constitution of the
United States, it is ordained that representatives and direct taxes
shall be apportioned among the States, according to their respective numbers, which shall be determined by adding to the whole number of free
persons, including those bound to service for a term of years, and including Indians not taxed, three fifths of all other persons.

The eighth section of the said article declares that congress shall have
power to lay and collect taxes, duties, imposts, and excises; but all duties,
imposts and excises, shall be uniform throughout the United States.

The ninth section of the same article provides, that no capitation or
other direct tax shall be laid, unless in proportion to the census or enumeration before directed to be taken. . . .

The question is, whether a tax upon carriages be a direct tax? If it
be a direct tax, it is unconstitutional, because it has been laid pursuant
to the rule of uniformity, and not to the rule of apportionment. . . .

What are direct taxes within the meaning of the constitution? The
constitution declares that a capitation tax is a direct tax; and both in

---

3 Dallas 171 (1796)

theory and practice, a tax on land is deemed to be a direct tax. In this way, the terms direct taxes, and capitation and other direct tax, are satisfied. It is not necessary to determine, whether a tax on the product of land be a direct or indirect tax. . . . Whether direct taxes, in the sense of the constitution, comprehend any other tax than a capitation tax, and tax on land, is a questionable point. . . . I never entertained a doubt that the principal, I will not say the only objects, that the framers of the constitution contemplated as falling within the rule of apportionment, were a capitation tax and a tax on land. Local considerations, and the particular circumstances and relative situation of the States, naturally lead to this view of the subject. The provision was made in favor of the southern States. They possessed a large number of slaves; they had extensive tracts of territory, thinly settled and not very productive. A majority of the States had but few slaves, and several of them a limited territory, well settled, and in a high state of cultivation. The Southern States, if no provision had been introduced in the constitution, would have been wholly at the mercy of the other States. Congress in such case, might tax slaves, at discretion or arbitrarily, and land in every part of the Union after the same rate or measure; so much a head in the first instance, and so much an acre in the second. To guard them against imposition, in these particulars, was the reason of introducing the clause in the constitution, which directs that representatives and direct taxes shall be apportioned among the States according to their respective numbers. . . .

All taxes on expenses or consumption are indirect taxes. A tax on carriages is of this kind, and of course is not a direct tax. Indirect taxes are circuitous modes of reaching the revenue of individuals, who generally live according to their income. In many cases of this nature the individual may be said to tax himself. . . .

I am, therefore, of opinion that the judgment rendered in the circuit court of Virginia ought to be affirmed.

Justice Iredell

I agree in opinion with my brothers, who have already expressed theirs, that the tax in question is agreeable to the constitution; and the reasons which have satisfied me can be delivered in a very few words, since I think the constitution itself affords a clear guide to decide the controversy.

The congress possess the power of taxing all taxable objects, without limitation, with the particular exception of a duty on exports.

There are two restrictions only on the exercise of this authority —

1. All direct taxes must be apportioned.
2. All duties, imposts, and excises must be **uniform**.

If the carriage tax be a direct tax, within the meaning of the constitution, it must be apportioned.

If it be a duty, impost, or excise, within the meaning of the constitution, it must be uniform.

If it can be considered as a tax, neither direct within the meaning of the constitution, nor comprehended within the term duty, impost, or excise; there is no provision in the constitution, one way or another, and then it must be left to such an operation of the power, as if the authority to lay taxes had been given generally in all instances, without saying whether they should be apportioned or uniform; and in that case, I should presume, the tax ought to be uniform; because the present constitution was particularly intended to affect individuals, and not States, except in particular cases specified; and this is the leading distinction between the articles of confederation and the present constitution.

As all direct taxes must be apportioned, it is evident that the constitution contemplated none as direct but such as could be apportioned.

If this cannot be apportioned, it is, therefore, not a direct tax in the sense of the constitution.

That this tax cannot be apportioned is evident. . . .

There is no necessity or propriety in determining what is, or is not a direct or indirect tax in all cases.

Some difficulties may occur which we do not at present foresee. Perhaps a direct tax, in the sense of the constitution, can mean nothing but a tax on something inseparably annexed to the soil, something capable of apportionment under all such circumstances.

A land or a poll tax may be considered of this description.

The latter is to be considered so particularly under the present constitution, on account of the slaves in the southern States, who give a ratio in the representation in the proportion of three to five.

Either of these is capable of apportionment.

In regard to other articles, there may possibly be considerable doubt.

It is sufficient, on the present occasion, for the court to be satisfied that this is not a direct tax contemplated by the constitution, in order to affirm the present judgment; since, if it cannot be apportioned, it must necessarily be uniform.

I am clearly of opinion this is not a direct tax in the sense of the constitution, and, therefore, that the judgment ought to be affirmed.

II

The Marshall Era:

1801–1835

Marbury *v.* Madison

Marbury v. Madison is the leading precedent for judicial review of congressional acts. It also was a political tour de force *by John Marshall. When Thomas Jefferson became President in 1801, he bitterly complained that the Federalists had retreated to the judiciary to batter down the works of Republicanism. Before the Adams administration had expired in 1801, the Federalists had created a number of new federal courts, and Adams naturally filled the positions with party loyalists. In addition, the Federalist Congress created new Justices of the Peace for the District of Columbia. William Marbury was nominated and confirmed for one such post, but the retiring Secretary of State — none other than John Marshall — failed to deliver his commission. His successor, James Madison, refused to do so and Marbury sought a writ of mandamus from the Supreme Court, directing Madison to serve the commission. Marshall's construction of Section 13 of the Judiciary Act of 1789 was strained; yet he shrewdly denied jurisdiction to serve his larger purpose. It is indicative of the Marshall Court's political standing, however, that it never again declared an act of Congress unconstitutional.*

Chief Justice Marshall delivered the opinion of the Court.

The peculiar delicacy of this case, the novelty of some of its circumstances, and the real difficulty attending the points which occur in it, require a complete exposition of the principles on which the opinion to be given by the court is founded. . . .

In the order in which the court has viewed this subject, the following questions have been considered and decided: 1st. Has the applicant a right to the commission he demands? 2d. If he has a right, and that right has been violated, do the laws of his country afford him a remedy? 3d.

---
1 Cranch 137 (1803)

If they do afford him a remedy, is it a *mandamus* issuing from this court? . . .

It is . . . the opinion of the Court: 1st. That by signing the commission of Mr. Marbury, the President of the United States appointed him a justice of peace for the county of Washington, in the district of Columbia; and that the seal of the United States, affixed thereto by the secretary of state, is conclusive testimony of the verity of the signature, and of the completion of the appointment; and that the appointment conferred on him a legal right to the office for the space of five years. 2d. That, having this legal title to the office, he has a consequent right to the commission; a refusal to deliver which is a plain violation of that right, for which the laws of his country afford him a remedy.

3. It remains to be inquired whether he is entitled to the remedy for which he applies? This depends on — 1st. The nature of the writ applied for; and 2d. The power of this court. . . .

This . . . is a plain case for a *mandamus,* either to deliver the commission, or a copy of it from the record; and it only remains to be inquired, whether it can issue from this court?

The act to establish the judicial courts of the United States authorizes the supreme court, "to issue writs of *mandamus,* in cases warranted by the principles and usages of law, to any courts appointed or persons holding office, under the authority of the United States." [Judiciary Act of 1789, Section 13.]. The secretary of state, being a person holding an office under the authority of the United States, is precisely within the letter of this description; and if this court is not authorized to issue a writ of *mandamus* to such an officer, it must be because the law is unconstitutional, and therefore, absolutely incapable of conferring the authority, and assigning the duties which its words purport to confer and assign.

The constitution vests the whole judicial power of the United States in one supreme court, and such inferior courts as congress shall, from time to time, ordain and establish. This power is expressly extended to all cases arising under the laws of the United States; and consequently, in some form, may be exercised over the present case; because the right claimed is given by a law of the United States.

In the distribution of this power, it is declared, that "the supreme court shall have original jurisdiction, in all cases affecting ambassadors, other public ministers and consuls, and those in which a state shall be a party. In all other cases, the supreme court shall have appellate jurisdiction." It has been insisted, at the bar, that as the original grant of jurisdiction to the supreme and inferior courts, is general, and the clause, assigning original jurisdiction to the supreme court, contains no negative or restrictive words, the power remains to the legislature, to assign original jurisdiction to that court, in other cases than those specified in the article which has been recited; provided those cases belong to the judicial power of the United States.

If it had been intended to leave it in the discretion of the legislature, to apportion the judicial power between the supreme and inferior courts, according to the will of that body, it would certainly have been useless to have proceeded further than to have defined the judicial power, and the tribunals in which it should be vested. The subsequent part of the section is mere surplusage — is entirely without meaning, if such is to be the construction. If congress remains at liberty to give this court appellate jurisdiction, where the constitution has declared their jurisdiction shall be original; and original jurisdiction where the constitution has declared it shall be appellate; the distribution of jurisdiction, made in the constitution, is form without substance. Affirmative words are often, in their operation, negative of other objects than those affirmed; and in this case, a negative or exclusive sense must be given to them, or they have no operation at all.

It cannot be presumed, that any clause in the constitution is intended to be without effect; and therefore, such a construction is inadmissible, unless the words require it. If the solicitude of the convention, respecting our peace with foreign powers, induced a provision that the supreme court should take original jurisdiction in cases which might be supposed to affect them; yet the clause would have proceeded no further than to provide for such cases, if no further restriction on the powers of congress had been intended. That they should have appellate jurisdiction in all other cases, with such exceptions as congress might make, is no restriction; unless the words be deemed exclusive of original jurisdiction.

When an instrument organizing, fundamentally, a judicial system, divides it into one supreme, and so many inferior courts as the legislature may ordain and establish; then enumerates its powers, and proceeds so far to distribute them, as to define the jurisdiction of the supreme court, by declaring the cases in which it shall take original jurisdiction, and that in others it shall take appellate jurisdiction, the plain import of the words seems to be, that in one class of cases, its jurisdiction is original, and not appellate; in the other, it is appellate, and not original. If any other construction would render the clause inoperative, that is an additional reason for rejecting such other construction, and for adhering to their obvious meaning. To enable this court, then, to issue a *mandamus*, it must be shown to be an exercise of appellate jurisdiction, or to be necessary to enable them to exercise appellate jurisdiction.

It has been stated at the bar, that the appellate jurisdiction may be exercised in a variety of forms, and that if it be the will of the legislature that a *mandamus* should be used for that purpose, that will must be obeyed. This is true, yet the jurisdiction must be appellate, not original. It is the essential criterion of appellate jurisdiction, that it revises and corrects the proceedings in a cause already instituted, and does not create that cause. Although, therefore, a *mandamus* may be directed to courts, yet to issue such a writ to an officer, for the delivery of a paper, is, in effect, the same as to sustain an original action for that paper, and therefore, seems not to belong to appellate, but to original jurisdiction. Neither is it necessary in such a case as this, to enable the court to exercise its appellate jurisdiction. The authority, therefore, given to the supreme court by the act establishing the judicial courts of the United States, to issue writs of *mandamus* to public officers, appears not to be warranted by the constitution; and it becomes necessary to inquire, whether a jurisdiction so conferred can be exercised.

The question, whether an act, repugnant to the constitution, can become the law of the land, is a question deeply interesting to the United States; but, happily, not of an intricacy proportioned to its interest. It seems only necessary to recognise certain principles, supposed to have been long and well established, to decide it. That the people have an original right to establish, for their future government, such principles as, in their opinion, shall most conduce to their own happiness, is the basis on which the whole American fabric has been erected. The exercise of this original right is a very great exertion; nor can it, nor ought it, to be frequently repeated. The principles, therefore, so established, are deemed fundamental: and as the authority from which they proceed is supreme, and can seldom act, they are designed to be permanent.

This original and supreme will organizes the government, and assigns to different departments their respective powers. It may either stop here, or establish certain limits not to be transcended by those departments. The government of the United States is of the latter description. The powers of the legislature are defined and limited; and that those limits may not be mistaken or forgotten, the constitution is written. To what purpose are powers limited, and to what purpose is that limitation committed to writing, if these limits may, at any time, be passed by those intended to be restrained? The distinction between a government with limited and unlimited powers is abolished, if those limits do not confine the persons on whom they are imposed, and if acts prohibited and acts allowed, are of equal obligation. It is a proposition too plain to be contested, that the constitution controls any legislative act repugnant to it; or that the legislature may alter the constitution by an ordinary act.

Between these alternatives, there is no middle ground. The constitution is either a superior paramount law, unchangeable by ordinary means, or it is on a level with ordinary legislative acts, and, like other acts, is alterable when the legislature shall please to alter it. If the former part of the alternative be true, then a legislative act, contrary to the constitution, is not law: if the latter part be true, then written constitutions are absurd attempts, on the part of the people, to limit a power, in its own nature, illimitable.

Certainly, all those who have framed written constitutions contemplate them as forming the fundamental and paramount law of the nation, and consequently, the theory of every such government must be, that an act of the legislature, repugnant to the constitution, is void. This theory is essentially attached to a written constitution, and is, consequently, to be considered, by this court, as one of the fundamental principles of our society. It is not, therefore, to be lost sight of, in the further consideration of this subject.

If an act of the legislature, repugnant to the constitution, is void, does it, notwithstanding its invalidity, bind the courts, and oblige them to give it effect? Or, in other words, though it be not law, does it constitute a rule as operative as if it was a law? This would be to overthrow, in fact, what was established in theory; and would seem, at first view, an absurdity too gross to be insisted on. It shall, however, receive a more attentive consideration.

It is, emphatically, the province and duty of the judicial department, to say what the law is. Those who apply the rule to particular cases, must of necessity expound and interpret that rule. If two laws conflict with each other, the courts must decide on the operation of each. So, if a law be in opposition to the constitution; if both the law and the constitution apply to a particular case, so that the court must either decide that case, conformable to the law, disregarding the constitution; or conformable to the constitution, disregarding the law; the court must determine which of these conflicting rules governs the case: this is of the very essence of judicial duty. If then, the courts are to regard the constitution, and the constitution is superior to any ordinary act of the legislature, the constitution, and not such ordinary act, must govern the case to which they both apply.

Those, then, who controvert the principle, that the constitution is to be considered, in court, as a paramount law, are reduced to the necessity of maintaining that courts must close their eyes on the constitution, and see only the law. This doctrine would subvert the very foundation of all written constitutions. It would declare that an act which, according to the principles and theory of our government, is entirely void, is yet, in practice, completely obligatory. It would declare, that if the legislature shall do what is expressly forbidden, such act, notwithstanding the express prohibition, is in reality effectual. It would be giving to the legislature a practical and real omnipotence, with the same breath which professes to restrict their powers within narrow limits. It is prescribing limits, and declaring that those limits may be passed at pleasure. That it thus reduces to nothing, what we have deemed the greatest improvement on political institutions, a written constitution, would, of itself, be sufficient, in America, where written constitutions have been viewed with so much reverence, for rejecting the construction. But the peculiar expressions of the constitution of the United States furnish additional arguments in favor of its rejection. The judicial power of the United States is extended to all cases arising under the constitution. Could it be the intention of those who gave this power, to say, that in using it, the constitution should not be looked into? That a case arising under the constitution should be decided, without examining the instrument under which it arises? This is too extravagant to be maintained. In some cases, then, the constitution must be looked into by the judges. And if they can open it at all, what part of it are they forbidden to read or to obey?

There are many other parts of the constitution which serve to illustrate this subject. It is declared, that "no tax or duty shall be laid on articles exported from any state." Suppose, a duty on the export of cotton, of tobacco or of flour; and a suit instituted to recover it. Ought judgment to be rendered in such a case? ought the judges to close their eyes on the constitution, and only see the law?

The constitution declares "that no bill of attainder or *ex post facto* law shall be passed." If, however, such a bill should be passed, and a person should be prosecuted under it; must the court condemn to death those victims whom the constitution endeavors to preserve?

"No person," says the constitution, "shall be convicted of treason, unless on the testimony of two witnesses to the same *overt* act, or on confession in open court." Here, the language of the constitution is addressed especially to the courts. It prescribes, directly for them, a rule of evidence not to be departed from. If the legislature should change that rule, and declare one witness, or a confession out of court, sufficient for conviction, must the constitutional principle yield to the legislative act?

From these, and many other selections which might be made, it is apparent, that the framers of the constitution contemplated that instrument as a rule for the government of courts, as well as of the legislature. Why otherwise does it direct the judges to take an oath to support it? This oath certainly applies in an especial manner, to their conduct in their official character. How immoral to impose it on them, if they were to be used as the instruments, and the knowing instruments, for violating what they swear to support!

The oath of office, too, imposed by the legislature, is completely demonstrative of the legislative opinion on this subject. It is in these words: "I do solemnly swear, that I will administer justice, without respect to persons, and do equal right to the poor and to the rich; and that I will faithfully and impartially discharge all the duties incumbent on me as ———, according to the best of my abilities and understanding, agreeably to the constitution and laws of the United States." Why does a judge swear to discharge his duties agreeably to the constitution of the United States, if that constitution forms no rule for his government? if it is closed upon him, and cannot be inspected by him? If such be the real state of things, this is worse than solemn mockery. To prescribe, or to take this oath, becomes equally a crime.

It is also not entirely unworthy of observation, that in declaring what shall be the supreme law of the land, the constitution itself is first mentioned; and not the laws of the United States, generally, but those only which shall be made in pursuance of the constitution, have that rank.

Thus, the particular phraseology of the constitution of the United States confirms and strengthens the principle, supposed to be essential to all written constitutions, that a law repugnant to the constitution is void; and that courts, as well as other departments, are bound by that instrument.

The rule must be discharged.– *(see of the Judiciary Act of 1788)*

Eakin *v.* Raub

While John Marshall had his say on judicial review in Marbury v. Madison, *that was a long way from universal acceptance and application of his ideas. The classic judicial refutation to Marshall's position came from Justice John Bannister Gibson of the Pennsylvania Supreme Court. Gibson was one of the great creative figures in early American law, serving on the state court as Associate and Chief Justice for thirty-seven years. Political factionalism within the state unfortunately kept him from a place on the United States Supreme Court. Gibson's opinion can be viewed as a point-by-point refutation of Marshall's rationale and as a rejoinder in logical reasoning. Gibson demonstrated that one result was possible if Marshall's assumptions were granted, but that without his premises another conclusion could be logically reached.*

Justice Gibson dissenting.

I am aware, that a right to declare all unconstitutional acts void, without distinction as to either constitution, is generally held as a professional dogma; but, I apprehend, rather as a matter of faith than of reason. I admit that I once embraced the same doctrine, but without examination, and I shall therefore state the arguments that impelled me to abandon it, with great respect for those by whom it is still maintained. But I may premise, that it is not a little remarkable, that although the right in question has all along been claimed by the judiciary, no judge has ventured to discuss it, except Chief Justice Marshall, . . . and if the argument of a jurist so distinguished for the strength of his ratiocinative powers be found inconclusive, it may fairly be set down to the weakness of the position which he attempts to defend. . . .

I begin, then, by observing that in this country, the powers of the judiciary are divisible into those that are POLITICAL and those that are purely CIVIL. Every power by which one organ of the government is enabled to control another, or to exert an influence over its acts, is a political power. . . . [The judiciary's] civil, are its *ordinary* and *appropriate* powers; being part of its essence, and existing independently of any supposed grant in the constitution. But where the government exists by virtue of a *written* constitution, the judiciary does not necessarily derive from that circumstance, any other than its ordinary and appropriate powers. Our judiciary is constructed on the principles of the common law, which enters so essentially into the composition of our social institutions as to be inseparable from them, and to be, in fact, the basis of the whole scheme of our civil and political liberty. In adopting any organ or instrument of the common law, we take it with just such powers and capacities as were incident to it as the common law, except where these are expressly, or by necessary implication, abridged or enlarged in the act of adoption; and, that such act is a written instrument, cannot vary its consequences or construction. . . . Now, what are the powers of the judiciary at the common law? They are those that necessarily arise out of its immediate business; and they are therefore commensurate only with the judicial execution of the municipal law, or, in other words, with the administration of distributive justice, without extending to anything of a political cast whatever. . . . With us, although the legislature be the depository of only so much of the sovereignty as the people have thought fit to impart, it is nevertheless sovereign within the limit of its powers, and may relatively claim the same pre-eminence here that it may claim elsewhere. It will be conceded, then, that the ordinary and essential powers of the judiciary do not extend to the annulling of an act of the legislature. . . .

The constitution of *Pennsylvania* contains no express grant of political powers to the judiciary. But, to establish a grant by implication, the constitution is said to be a law of superior obligation; and, consequently, that if it were to come into collision with an act of the legislature, the latter would have to give way. This is conceded. But it is a fallacy to suppose that they can come into collision *before the judiciary*. . . .

The constitution and the right of the legislature to pass the act, may be in collision. But is that a legitimate subject for judicial determination? If it be, the judiciary must be a peculiar organ, to revise the proceedings of the legislature, and to correct its mistakes; and in what part of the constitution are we to look for this proud pre-eminence? Viewing the matter in the opposite direction, what would be thought of an act of assembly in which it should be declared that the Supreme Court had, in a particular case, put a wrong construction on the constitution of the United States, and that the judgment should therefore be reversed? It would doubtless be thought a usurpation of judicial power. But it is by no means clear, that to declare a law void which has been enacted according to the forms prescribed in the constitution, is not a usurpation of legislative power. . . .

But it has been said to be emphatically the business of the judiciary, to ascertain and pronounce what the law is; and that this necessarily involves a consideration of the constitution. It does so: but how far? If the judiciary will inquire into anything besides the form of enactment, where shall it stop? There must be some point of limitation to such an inquiry; for no one will pretend, that a judge would be justifiable in calling for the election returns, or scrutinizing the qualifications of those who composed the legislature. . . .

But, in theory, all the organs of the government are of equal capacity; or, if not equal, each must be supposed to have superior capacity only for those things which peculiarly belong to it; and as legislation peculiarly involves the consideration of those limitations which are put on the law-making power, and the interpretation of the laws when made, involves only the construction of the laws themselves, it follows that the construction of the constitution in this particular belong to the legislature, which ought therefore to be taken to have superior capacity to judge of the constitutionality of its own acts. But suppose all to be of equal capacity, in every respect, why should one exercise a controlling power over the rest? That the judiciary is of superior rank, has never been pretended, although it has been said to be co-ordinate. It is not easy, however, to comprehend how the power which gives law to all the rest, can be of no more than equal rank with one which receives it, and is answerable to the former for the observance of its statutes. Legislation is essentially an act of sovereign power; but the execution of the laws by instruments that are governed by prescribed rules, and exercise no power of volition, is essentially otherwise. . . . It may be said, the power of the legislature, also, is limited by prescribed rules: it is so. But it is, nevertheless, the power of the people, and sovereign as far as it extends. It cannot be said, that the judiciary is co-ordinate merely because it is established by the constitution: if that were sufficient, sheriffs, registers of wills, and recorders of deeds, would be so too. Within the pale of their authority, the acts of these officers will have the power of the people for their support; but no one will pretend, they are of equal dignity with the acts of the legislature. Inequality of rank arises not from the manner in which the organ has been constituted, but from its essence and the nature of its functions; and the legislative organ is superior to every other, inasmuch as the power to will and to command, is essentially superior to the power to act and to obey. . . .

[H]ad it been intended to interpose the judiciary as an additional barrier, the matter would surely not have been left in doubt. The judges would not have been left to stand on the insecure and ever-shifting ground of public opinion, as to constructive powers; they would have been placed on the impregnable ground of an express grant; they would not have been compelled to resort to the debates in the convention, or the opinion that was generally entertained at the time. . . . The grant of a power so extraordinary, ought to appear so plain, that he who should run might read. . . .

But what I have in view in this inquiry, is the supposed right of the judiciary to interfere, in cases where the constitution is to be carried into effect through the instrumentality of the legislature, and where that organ must necessarily first decide on the constitutionality of its own act. The oath to support the constitution is not peculiar to the judges, but is taken indiscriminately by every officer of the government, and is designed rather as a test of the political principles of the man, than to bind the officer in the discharge of his duty: otherwise it is difficult to determine what operation it is to have in the case of a recorder of deeds, for instance, who, in the execution of his office, has nothing to do with the constitution. But granting it to relate to the official conduct of the judge, as well as every other officer, and not to his political principles, still it must be understood in reference to supporting the constitution, *only as far as that may be involved in his official duty*; and, consequently, if his official duty does not comprehend an inquiry into the authority of the legislature, neither does his oath. . . .

But do not the judges do a positive act in violation of the constitution, when they give effect to an unconstitutional law? Not if the law has been passed according to the forms established in the constitution. The fallacy of the question is, in supposing that the judiciary adopts the acts of the legislature as its own; whereas the enactment of a law and the interpretation of it are not concurrent acts; and as the judiciary is not required to concur in the enactment, neither is it in the breach of the constitution which may be the consequence of the enactment. The fault is imputable to the legislature, and on it the responsibility exclusively rests. . . .

But it has been said, that this construction would deprive the citizens of the advantages which are peculiar to a written constitution, by at once declaring the power of the legislature in practice to be illimitable. . . . But there is no magic or inherent power in parchment and ink, to command respect and protect principles from violation. In the business of government a recurrence to first principles answers the end of an observation at sea with a view to correct the dead reckoning; and for this purpose, a written constitution is an instrument of inestimable value. It is of inestimable value, also, in rendering its first principles familiar to the mass of people; for, after all, there is no effectual guard against legislative usurpation but public opinion, the force of which, in this country is inconceivably great. . . . Once let public opinion be so corrupt as to sanction every misconstruction of the constitution and abuse of power which the temptation of the moment may dictate, and the party which may happen to be predominant, will laugh at the puny efforts of a dependent power to arrest it in its course.

For these reasons, I am of opinion that it rests with the people, in whom full and absolute sovereign power resides, to correct abuses in legislation, by instructing their representatives to repeal the obnoxious act. . . . On the other hand, the judiciary is not infallible; and an error by it would admit of no remedy but a more distinct expression of the public will, through the extraordinary medium of a convention; whereas, an error by the legislature admits of a remedy by an exertion of the same will, in the ordinary exercise of the right of suffrage, — a mode better calculated to attain the end, without popular excitement. . . .

But in regard to an act of [a state] assembly, which is found to be in collision with the constitution, laws, or treaties of the United States, I take the duty of the judiciary to be exactly the reverse. By becoming parties to the federal constitution, the states have agreed to several limitations of their individual sovereignty, to enforce which, it was thought to be absolutely necessary, to prevent them from giving effect to laws in violation of those limitations, through the instrumentality of their own judges. Accordingly, it is declared in the sixth article and second section of the federal constitution, that "This constitution, and the laws of the United States which shall be made in pursuance thereof, and all treaties made, or which shall be made under the authority of the United States, shall be the *supreme* law of the land; and the *judges* in every *state* shall be BOUND thereby; anything in the *laws* or *constitution* of any *state* to the contrary notwithstanding."

This is an express grant of a political power, and it is conclusive to show that no law of inferior obligation, as every state law must necessarily be, can be executed at the expense of the constitution, laws, or treaties of the United States. . . .

judiciary bound to the law made

Federal Judicial Supremacy

Right of Supreme Ct to review decision of St. Ct

Martin *v.* Hunter's Lessee

The Supreme Court's power to hear cases on appeal from the state courts under Section 25 of the Judiciary Act of 1789 aroused greater contemporary protest and controversy than did judicial review of congressional acts. On two noteworthy occasions, the Marshall Court collided directly with the Virginia Court of Appeals, presided over by Spencer Roane, who allegedly was Jefferson's choice for Chief Justice of the United States. The first case involved the Fairfax lands which had been confiscated by Virginia during the Revolution. Despite the peace treaties, Virginia refused to allow the Fairfax heirs to resume the estate. The Virginia courts upheld the state's action, but the Supreme Court reversed the decision in 1813 (Fairfax's Devisee v. Hunter's Lessee, 7 Cranch 603). The Virginia Court of Appeals thereupon refused to carry out the Supreme Court's mandate and ruled Section 25 unconstitutional. The holding was appealed to the Supreme Court in 1816 by the Fairfax claimants.

Justice Story delivered the opinion of the Court.

The questions involved in this judgment are of great importance and delicacy. Perhaps it is not too much to affirm, that, upon their right decision, rest some of the most solid principles which have hitherto been supposed to sustain and protect the constitution itself. The great respectability, too, of the court whose decisions we are called upon to review, and the entire deference which we entertain for the learning and ability of that court, add much to the difficulty of the task which has so unwelcomely fallen upon us. . . .

The constitution, unavoidably, deals in general language. It did not suit the purposes of the people, in framing this great charter of our liberties, to provide for minute specifications of its powers, or to declare the

1 Wheaton 304 (1816)

means by which those powers should be carried into execution. It was foreseen that this would be a perilous and difficult, if not an impracticable, task. The instrument was not intended to provide merely for the exigencies of a few years, but was to endure through a long lapse of ages, the events of which were locked up in the inscrutable purposes of Providence. . . .

The third article of the constitution is that which must principally attract our attention. . . .

Let this article be carefully weighed and considered. The language of the article throughout is manifestly designed to be mandatory upon the legislature. . . . The object of the constitution was to establish three great departments of government; the legislative, the executive, and the judicial departments. The first was to pass laws, the second to approve and execute them, and the third to expound and enforce them. Without the latter, it would be impossible to carry into effect some of the express provisions of the constitution. How, otherwise, could crimes against the United States be tried and punished? How could causes between two States be heard and determined? The judicial power must, therefore, be vested in some court, by congress; and to suppose that it was not an obligation binding on them, but might, at their pleasure, be omitted or declined, is to suppose that, under the sanction of the constitution, they might defeat the constitution itself. A construction which would lead to such a result cannot be sound. . . .

If, then, it is a duty of congress to vest the judicial power of the United States, it is a duty to vest the whole judicial power. The language, if imperative as to one part, is imperative as to all. If it were otherwise, this anomaly would exist, that congress might successively refuse to vest the jurisdiction in any one class of cases enumerated in the constitution, and thereby defeat the jurisdiction as to all; for the constitution has not singled out any class on which congress are bound to act in preference to others.

The next consideration is as to the courts in which the judicial power shall be vested. It is manifest that a supreme court must be established; but whether it be equally obligatory to establish inferior courts, is a question of some difficulty. If congress may lawfully omit to establish inferior courts, it might follow, that in some of the enumerated cases the judicial power could nowhere exist. . . .

But even admitting that the language of the constitution is not mandatory, and that congress may constitutionally omit to vest the judicial power in courts of the United States, it cannot be denied that when it is vested, it may be exercised to the utmost constitutional extent.

This leads us to the consideration of the great question as to the nature and extent of the appellate jurisdiction of the United States. . . .

As, then, by the terms of the constitution, the appellate jurisdiction is not limited as to the supreme court, and as to this court it may be exercised in all other cases than those of which it has original cognizance, what is there to restrain its exercise over state tribunals in the enumerated cases? The appellate power is not limited by the terms of the third article to any particular courts. The words are, "the judicial power (which includes appellate power) shall extend to all cases," &c.; and "in all other cases before mentioned the supreme court shall have appellate jurisdiction." It is the case, then, and not the court, that gives the jurisdiction. . . .

But it is plain that the framers of the constitution did contemplate that cases within the judicial cognizance of the United States not only might but would arise in the state courts, in the exercise of their ordinary jurisdiction. With this view the sixth article declares, that "this constitution, and the laws of the United States which shall be made in pursuance thereof, and all treaties made, or which shall be made, under the authority of the United States, shall be the supreme law of the land, and the judges in every State shall be bound thereby, any thing in the constitution, or laws of any State to the contrary nothwithstanding." It is obvious that this obligation is imperative upon the state judges in their official, and not merely in their private, capacities. From the very nature of their judicial duties they would be called upon to pronounce the law applicable to the case in judgment. They were not to decide merely according to the laws or constitution of the State, but according to the constitution, laws, and treaties of the United States, "the supreme law of the land."

A moment's consideration will show us the necessity and propriety, of this provision in cases where the jurisdiction of the state courts is unquestionable. . . . Suppose an indictment for a crime in a state court, and the defendant should allege in his defence that the crime was created by an *ex post facto* act of the State, must not the state court, in the exercise of a jurisdiction which has already rightfully attached, have a right to pronounce on the validity and sufficiency of the defence? . . .

It must, therefore, be conceded that the constitution not only contemplated, but meant to provide for cases within the scope of the judicial power of the United States, which might yet depend before state tribunals. It was foreseen that in the exercise of their ordinary jurisdiction, state courts would incidentally take cognizance of cases arising under the constitution, the laws, and treaties of the United States. Yet to all these cases the judicial power, by the very terms of the constitution, is to extend. It cannot extend by original jurisdiction if that was already rightfully and exclusively attached in the state courts, which (as has been already shown) may occur; it must therefore extend by appellate jurisdiction, or not at all. It would seem to follow that the appellate power of the United States must, in such cases, extend to state tribunals; and if in such cases, there is no reason why it should not equally attach upon all others within the purview of the constitution. . . .

Nor can such a right be deemed to impair the independence of state judges. It is assuming the very ground in controversy to assert that they possess an absolute independence of the United States. In respect to the powers granted to the United States, they are not independent; they are expressly bound to obedience by the letter of the constitution; and if they should unintentionally transcend their authority, or misconstrue the constitution, there is no more reason for giving their judgments an absolute and irresistible force, than for giving it to the acts of the other coördinate departments of state sovereignty.

The argument urged from the possibility of the abuse of the revising power, is equally unsatisfactory. It is always a doubtful course, to argue against the use or existence of a power, from the possibility of its abuse. . . . From the very nature of things, the absolute right of decision, in the last resort, must rest somewhere — wherever it may be vested it is susceptible of abuse. In all questions of jurisdiction the inferior, or appellate court must pronounce the final judgment; and common sense, as well as legal reasoning, has conferred it upon the latter. . . .

This is not all. A motive of another kind, perfectly compatible with the most sincere respect for state tribunals, might induce the grant of appellate power over their decisions. That motive is the importance, and even necessity of uniformity of decisions throughout the whole United States, upon all subjects within the purview of the constitution. Judges of equal learning and integrity, in different States, might differently interpret a statute, or a treaty of the United States, or even the constitution itself. If there were no revising authority to control these jarring and discordant judgments, and harmonize them into uniformity, the laws, the treaties, and the constitution of the United States would be different in different States, and might, perhaps, never have precisely the same construction, obligation, or efficacy, in any two States. . . .

There is an additional consideration, which is entitled to great weight. The constitution of the United States was designed for the common and equal benefit of all the people of the United States. The judicial power was granted for the same benign and salutary purposes. It was not to be exercised exclusively for the benefit of parties who might be plaintiffs, and would elect the national forum, but also for the protection of defendants who might be entitled to try their rights, or assert their privileges, before the same forum. Yet, if the construction contended for be correct, it will follow, that as the plaintiff may always elect the state court, the defendant may be deprived of all the security which the constitution intended in aid of his rights. Such a state of things can, in no respect, be considered as giving equal rights. To obviate this difficulty, we are referred to the power which it is admitted congress possess to remove suits from state courts to the national courts; and this forms the second ground upon which the argument we are considering has been attempted to be sustained.

This power of removal is not to be found in express terms in any part of the constitution; if it be given, it is only given by implication, as a power necessary and proper to carry into effect some express power. The power of removal is certainly not, in strictness of language; it presupposes an exercise of original jurisdiction to have attached elsewhere. . . . If, then, the right of removal be included in the appellate jurisdiction, it is only because it is one mode of exercising that power, and as congress is not limited by the constitution to any particular mode, or time of exercising it, it may authorize a removal either before or after judgment. The time, the process, and the manner, must be subject to its absolute legislative control. . . .

The remedy, too, of removal of suits would be utterly inadequate to the purposes of the constitution, if it could act only on the parties, and not upon the state courts. . . .

On the whole, the court are of opinion, that the appellate power of the United States does extend to cases pending in the state courts; and that the 25th section of the Judiciary act, which authorizes the exercise of this jurisdiction in the specified cases, by a writ of error, is supported by the letter and spirit of the constitution. We find no clause in that instrument which limits this power; and we dare not interpose a limitation where the people have not been disposed to create one. . . .

Cohens *v.* Virginia

upholds state polica powers

Story's opinion in the preceding case was a lucid constitutional and legal analysis of the Supreme Court's appellate powers. But criticism of the Court's position persisted and intensified. In a number of anonymous and well-publicized articles, Virginia judge Spencer Roane bitterly protested against the dangers of advancing judicial centralism. Cohens v. Virginia in 1821 gave the Supreme Court another opportunity to assert its powers. The Cohens' had been convicted in a lower Virginia court for selling lottery tickets in violation of state law, although the lottery had been authorized by Congress for support of the District of Columbia. The defendants thereupon appealed directly to the Supreme Court under authority of Section 25 of the Judiciary Act of 1789. The state once again insisted that judgments of its courts were final in cases involving state laws. John Marshall had not participated in Martin v. Hunter's Lessee because of his own interest in the disputed property. But in the Cohens' case, the Chief Justice himself answered the states'-rights arguments of his fellow Virginians. Although his opinion ultimately sustained the state law, Marshall used the controversy as a vehicle to advance constitutional and logical arguments in behalf of federal judicial supremacy. Albert Beveridge, Marshall's biographer, described the opinion as "one of the strongest and most enduring strands of that mighty cable woven by him to hold the American people together as a united and imperishable nation."

Chief Justice Marshall delivered the opinion of the Court.

The first question to be considered is, whether the jurisdiction of this court is excluded by the character of the parties, one of them being a State, and the other a citizen of that State?

The 2d section of the third article of the constitution defines the extent of the judicial power of the United States. Jurisdiction is given to the courts of the Union in two classes of cases. In the first, their jurisdiction depends on the character of the cause, whoever may be the parties. This class comprehends "all cases in law and equity arising under this constitution, the laws of the United States, and treaties made, or which shall be made, under their authority." This clause extends the jurisdiction of the court to all the cases described, without making in its terms

6 Wheaton 264 (1821)

41

any exception whatever, and without any regard to the condition of the party. If there be any exception, it is to be implied against the express words of the article.

In the second class, the jurisdiction depends entirely on the character of the parties. In this are comprehended "controversies between two or more States, between a State and citizens of another State," "and between a State and foreign states, citizens, or subjects." If these be the parties, it is entirely unimportant what may be the subject of controversy. Be it what it may, these parties have a constitutional right to come into the courts of the Union. . . .

The jurisdiction of the court, then, being extended by the letter of the constitution to all cases arising under it, or under the laws of the *United* States, it follows that those would withdraw any case of this description from that jurisdiction, must sustain the exemption they claim on the spirit and true meaning of the constitution, which spirit and true meaning must be so apparent as to overrule the words which its framers have employed.

The counsel for the defendant in error have undertaken to do this; and have laid down the general proposition, that a sovereign independent State is not suable, except by its own consent.

This general proposition will not be controverted. But its consent is not requisite in each particular case. It may be given in a general law. And if a State has surrendered any portion of its sovereignty, the question whether a liability to suit be a part of this portion, depends on the instrument by which the surrender is made. If upon a just construction of that instrument, it shall appear that the State has submitted to be sued, then it has parted with this sovereign right of judging in every case on the justice of its own pretensions, and has intrusted that power to a tribunal in whose impartiality it confides.

The American States, as well as the American people, have believed a close and firm Union to be essential to their liberty and to their happiness. They have been taught by experience, that this Union cannot exist without a government for the whole; and they have been taught by the same experience that this government would be a mere shadow, that must disappoint all their hopes, unless invested with large portions of that sovereignty which belongs to independent States. Under the influence of this opinion, and thus instructed by experience, the American people, in the conventions of their respective States, adopted the present constitution.

If it could be doubted whether, from its nature, it were not supreme in all cases where it is empowered to act, that doubt would be removed by the declaration that "this constitution, and the laws of the United States which shall be made in pursuance thereof, and all treaties made, or which shall be made, under the authority of the United States, shall be the supreme law of the land; and the judges in every State shall be bound thereby, any thing in the constitution or laws of any State to the contrary notwithstanding."

This is the authoritative language of the American people; and, if gentlemen please, of the American States. It marks with lines too strong to be mistaken, the characteristic distinction between the government of the Union and those of the States. The general government, though limited as to its objects, is supreme with respect to those objects. This principle is a part of the constitution; and if there be any who deny its necessity, none can deny its authority. . . .

With the ample powers confided to this supreme government, for these interesting purposes, are connected many express and important limitations on the sovereignty of the States, which are made for the same purposes. The powers of the Union, on the great subjects of war, peace, and commerce, and on many others, are in themselves limitations of the sovereignty of the States; but in addition to these, the sovereignty of the States is surrendered in many instances where the surrender can only operate to the benefit of the people, and where, perhaps, no other power is conferred on congress than a conservative power to maintain the principles established in the constitution. The maintenance of these principles in their purity, is certainly among the great duties of the government. One of the instruments by which this duty may be peaceably performed, is the judicial department. It is authorized to decide all cases, of every description, arising under the constitution or laws of the United States. From this general grant of jurisdiction, no exception is made of those cases in which a State may be a party. When we consider the situation of the government of the Union and of a State, in relation to each other; the nature of our constitution, the subordination of the state governments to that constitution; the great purpose for which jurisdiction over all cases arising under the constitution and laws of the United States, is confided to the judicial department, are we at liberty to insert in this general grant, an exception of those cases in which a State may be a party? Will the spirit of the constitution justify this attempt to control its words? We think it will not. We think a case arising under the constitution or laws of the United States, is cognizable in the courts of the Union, whoever may be the parties to that case. . . .

One of the express objects, then, for which the judicial department was established, is the decision of controversies between States, and between a State and individuals. The mere circumstance that a State is a party, gives jurisdiction to the court. How, then, can it be contended, that the very same instrument, in the very same section, should be so construed, as that this same circumstance should withdraw a case from the jurisdiction of the court, where the constitution or laws of the United States are supposed to have been violated? The constitution gave to every person having a claim upon a State, a right to submit his case to the court of the nation. However unimportant his claim might be, however little the community might be interested in its decision, the framers of our constitution thought it necessary for the purposes of justice, to provide a tribunal as superior to influence as possible, in which that claim might be decided. Can it be imagined, that the same persons considered a case involving the constitution of our country and the majesty of the laws, questions in which every American citizen must be deeply interested, as withdrawn from this tribunal, because a State is a party? . . .

The mischievous consequences of the construction contended for on the part of Virginia, are also entitled to great consideration. It would prostrate, it has been said, the government and its laws at the feet of every State in the Union. And would not this be its effect? What power of the government could be executed by its own means, in any State disposed to resist its execution by a course of legislation? The laws must be executed by individuals acting within the several States. If these individuals may be exposed to penalties, and if the courts of the Union cannot correct the judgments by which these penalties may be enforced, the course of the government may be, at any time, arrested by the will of one of its members. Each member will possess a veto on the will of the whole. . . .

These collisions may take place in times of no extraordinary commotion. But a constitution is framed for ages to come, and is designed to approach immortality as nearly as human institutions can approach it. Its course cannot always be tranquil. It is exposed to storms and tempests, and its framers must be unwise statesmen, indeed, if they have not provided it, as far as its nature will permit, with the means of self-preservation from the perils it may be destined to encounter. No government ought to be so defective in its organization, as not to contain within itself the means of securing the execution of its own laws against other dangers than those which occur every day. Courts of justice are the means most usually employed; and it is reasonable to expect that a government should repose on its own courts, rather than on others. There is certainly nothing in the circumstances under which our constitution was formed; nothing in the history of the times, which would justify the opinion that the confidence reposed in the States was so implicit as to leave in them and their tribunals the power of resisting or defeating, in the form of law, the legitimate measures of the Union. The requisitions of congress, under the confederation, were as constitutionally obligatory as the laws enacted by the present congress. That they were habitually disregarded, is a fact of universal notoriety. With the knowledge of this fact, and under its full pressure, a convention was assembled to change the system. Is it so improbable that they should confer on the judicial department the power of construing the constitution and laws of the Union in every case, in the last resort, and of preserving them from all violation from every quarter, so far as judicial decisions can preserve them, that this improbability should essentially affect the construction of the new system? We are told, and we are truly told, that the great change which is to give efficacy to the present system, is its ability to act on individuals directly, instead of acting through the instrumentality of state governments. But, ought not this ability, in reason and sound policy, to be applied directly to the protection of individuals employed in the execution of the laws, as well as to their coercion? Your laws reach the individual without the aid of any other power; why may they not protect him from punishment for performing his duty in executing them? . . .

It is very true that, whenever hostility to the existing system shall become universal, it will be also irresistible. The people made the constitution, and the people can unmake it. It is the creature of their will, and lives only by their will. But this supreme and irresistible power to make or to unmake resides only in the whole body of the people; not in any subdivision of them. The attempt of any of the parts to exercise it is usurpation, and ought to be repelled by those to whom the people have delegated their power of repelling it.

The acknowledged inability of the government, then, to sustain itself against the public will, and, by force or otherwise, to control the whole nation, is no sound argument in support of its constitutional inability to preserve itself against a section of the nation acting in opposition to the general will. . . .

It is true, that if all the States, or a majority of them, refuse to elect senators, the legislative powers of the Union will be suspended. But if any one State shall refuse to elect them, the senate will not, on that account, be the less capable of performing all its functions. The argument founded on this fact would seem rather to prove the subordination of the parts to the whole, than the complete independence of any one of them. The framers of the constitution were, indeed, unable to make any provisions which should protect that instrument against a general combination of the States, or of the people, for its destruction; and, conscious of this inability, they have not made the attempt. But they were able to provide against the operation of measures adopted in any one State, whose tendency might be to arrest the execution of the laws; and this it was the part of true wisdom to attempt. We think they have attempted it.

It has been also urged, as an additional objection to the jurisdiction of the court, that cases between a State and one of its own citizens, do not come within the general scope of the constitution; and were obviously never intended to be made cognizable in the federal courts. The state tribunals might be suspected of partiality in cases between itself or its citizens and aliens, or the citizens of another State, but not in proceedings by a State against its own citizens. That jealousy which might exist in the first case, could not exist in the last, and therefore the judicial power is not extended to the last. This is very true, so far as jurisdiction depends on the character of the parties; and the argument would have great force if urged to prove that this court could not establish the demand of a citizen upon his State, but is not entitled to the same force when urged to prove that this court cannot inquire whether the constitution or laws of the United States protect a citizen from a prosecution instituted against him by a State. If jurisdiction depended entirely on the character of the parties, and was not given where the parties have not an original right to come into court, that part of the 2d section of the third article, which extends the judicial power to all cases arising under the constitution and laws of the United States, would be mere surplusage. It is to give jurisdiction where the character of the parties would not give it, that this very important part of the clause was inserted. It may be true, that the partiality of the state tribunals, in ordinary controversies between a State and its citizens, was not apprehended, and therefore the judicial power of the Union was not extended to such cases; but this was not the sole nor the greatest object for which this department was created. A more important, a much more interesting object, was the preservation of the constitution and laws of the United States, so far as they can be preserved by judicial authority; and therefore the jurisdiction of the courts of the Union was expressly extended to all cases arising under that constitution and those laws. If the constitution or laws may be violated by proceedings instituted by a State against its own citizens, and if that violation may be such as essentially to affect the constitution and the laws, such as to arrest the progress of government in its constitutional course, why should these cases be excepted from that provision which expressly extends the judicial power of the Union to all cases arising under the constitution and laws? . . .

When, then, the constitution declares the jurisdiction, in cases where a State shall be a party, to be original, and in all cases arising under the constitution or a law, to be appellate — the conclusion seems irresistible, that its framers designed to include in the first class those cases in which jurisdiction is given, because a State is a party; and to include in the second, those in which jurisdiction is given, because the case arises under the constitution or a law.

This reasonable construction is rendered necessary by other considerations.

That the constitution or a law of the United States is involved in a case, and makes a part of it, may appear in the progress of a cause, in which the courts of the Union, but for that circumstance, would have no jurisdiction, and which of consequence could not originate in the supreme court. In such a case the jurisdiction can be exercised only in its appellate form. To deny its exercise in this form, is to deny its existence, and would be to construe a clause dividing the power of the supreme court, in such manner as in a considerable degree to defeat the power itself. All must perceive that this construction can be justified only where it is absolutely necessary. We do not think the article under consideration presents that necessity. . . .

The constitution declares that in cases where a State is a party, the supreme court shall have original jurisdiction; but does not say that its appellate jurisdiction shall not be exercised in cases where, from their nature, appellate jurisdiction is given, whether a State be or be not a party. It may be conceded, that where the case is of such a nature as to admit of its originating in the supreme court, it ought to originate there; but where, from its nature, it cannot originate in that court, these words ought not to be so construed as to require it. There are many cases in which it would be found extremely difficult, and subversive of the spirit of the constitution, to maintain the construction that appellate jurisdiction cannot be exercised where one of the parties might sue or be sued in this court. . . .

It is most true that this court will not take jurisdiction if it should not; but it is equally true, that it must take jurisdiction if it should. The judiciary cannot, as the legislature may, avoid a measure because it approaches the confines of the constitution. We cannot pass it by because it is doubtful. With whatever doubts, with whatever difficulties, a case may be attended, we must decide it, if it be brought before us. We have no more right to decline the exercise of jurisdiction which is given, than to usurp that which is not given. The one or the other would be treason to the constitution. Questions may occur which we would gladly avoid; but we cannot avoid them. All we can do is, to exercise our best judgment, and conscientiously to perform our duty. In doing this on the present occasion, we find this tribunal invested with appellate jurisdiction in all cases arising under the constitution and laws of the United States. We find no exception to this grant, and we cannot insert one. . . .

It is, then, the opinion of the court, that the defendant who removes a judgment rendered against him by a state court into this court, for the purpose of reëxamining the question whether that judgment be in violation of the constitution or laws of the United States, does not commence or prosecute a suit against the State, whatever may be its opinion where the effect of the writ may be to restore the party to the possession of a thing which he demands. . . .

The second objection to the jurisdiction of the court is, that its appellate power cannot be exercised, in any case, over the judgment of a state court.

This objection is sustained chiefly by arguments drawn from the supposed total separation of the judiciary of a State from that of the Union, and their entire independence of each other. The argument considers the federal judiciary as completely foreign to that of a State; and as being no more connected with it, in any respect whatever, than the court of a foreign state. If this hypothesis be just, the argument founded on it is equally so; but if the hypothesis be not supported by the constitution, the argument fails with it. . . .

That the United States form, for many, and for most important purposes, a single nation, has not yet been denied. In war, we are one people. In making peace, we are one people. In all commercial regulations, we are one and the same people. In many other respects, the American people are one; and the government which is alone capable of controlling and managing their interests, in all these respects, is the government of the Union. It is their government, and in that character they have no other. America has chosen to be, in many respects, and to many purposes, a nation; and for all these purposes her government is complete; to all these objects, it is competent. The people have declared, that in the exercise of all powers given for these objects, it is supreme. It can, then, in effecting these objects, legitimately control all individuals or governments within the American territory. The constitution and laws of a State, so far as they are repugnant to the constitution and laws of the United States, are absolutely void. These States are constituent parts of the United States. They are members of one great empire — for some purposes sovereign, for some purposes subordinate.

In a government so constituted, is it unreasonable that the judicial power should be competent to give efficacy to the constitutional laws of the legislature? That department can decide on the validity of the constitution or law of a State, if it be repugnant to the constitution or to a law of the United States. Is it unreasonable that it should also be empowered to decide on the judgment of a state tribunal enforcing such unconstitutional law? Is it so very unreasonable as to furnish a justification for controlling the words of the constitution?

We think it is not. We think that in a government acknowledgedly supreme, with respect to objects of vital interest to the nation, there is nothing inconsistent with sound reason, nothing incompatible with the nature of government, in making all its departments supreme, so far as respects those objects, and so far as is necessary to their attainment. The exercise of the appellate power over those judgments of the state tribunals which may contravene the constitution or laws of the United States, is, we believe, essential to the attainment of those objects.

The propriety of intrusting the construction of the constitution, and laws made in pursuance thereof, to the judiciary of the Union, has not, we believe, as yet, been drawn into question. It seems to be a corollary from this political axiom, that the federal courts should either possess exclusive jurisdiction in such cases, or a power to revise the judgment rendered in them by the state tribunals. If the federal and state courts have concurrent jurisdiction in all cases arising under the constitution, laws, and treaties of the United States; and if a case of this description brought in a state court cannot be removed before judgment, nor revised after judgment, then the construction of the constitution, laws, and treaties of the United States is not confided particularly to their judicial department, but is confided equally to that department and to the state courts, however they may be constituted. "Thirteen independent courts," says a very celebrated statesman, (and we have now more than twenty such courts,) "of final jurisdiction over the same causes, arising upon the same laws, is a hydra in government, from which nothing but contradiction and confusion can proceed."

Dismissing the unpleasant suggestion, that any motives which may not be fairly avowed, or which ought not to exist, can ever influence a State or its courts, the necessity of uniformity, as well as correctness in expounding the constitution and laws of the United States, would itself suggest the propriety of vesting in some single tribunal the power of deciding, in the last resort, all cases in which they are involved.

We are not restrained, then, by the political relations between the general and state governments, from construing the words of the constitution, defining the judicial power, in their true sense. We are not bound to construe them more restrictively than they naturally import. . . .

⋆ C ⋆

Implied Powers and Federalism

McCulloch *v.* Maryland

McCulloch *v.* Maryland *was Marshall's most enduring contribution to broad constitutional construction, the powers of the national government, and its supremacy over the states. The case involved the constitutionality of the Second Bank of the United States and the right of a state to tax an instrumentality of the federal government. The idea of a government-sponsored central bank was an emotion-laden political question during the first half century of the republic. Genuine economic and social differences regarding the Bank, however, were often obfuscated by constitutional arguments. Beginning with Jefferson's cabinet opinion against the Bank in 1792, its opponents contended that the Constitution nowhere provided for such an institution. Hamilton countered with an opinion which rested the Bank's constitutionality upon Congress's implied and resultant powers. In 1819, Marshall picked up Hamilton's argument and engrafted it into constitutional law. The second question, involving state taxation, was chiefly his own contribution.*

Chief Justice Marshall delivered the opinion of the Court.

The first question made in the cause is — has congress power to incorporate a bank? It has been truly said, that this can scarcely be considered as an open question, entirely unprejudiced by the former proceedings of the nation respecting it. The principle now contested was introduced at a very early period of our history, has been recognised by many successive legislatures, and has been acted upon by the judicial department, in cases of peculiar delicacy, as a law of undoubted obligation. . . .

In discussing this question, the counsel for the state of Maryland have deemed it of some importance, in the construction of the constitution, to

---

4 Wheaton 316 (1819)

consider that instrument, not as emanating from the people, but as the act of sovereign and independent states. The powers of the general government, it has been said, are delegated by the states, who alone are truly sovereign; and must be exercised in subordination to the states, who alone possess supreme dominion. It would be difficult to sustain this proposition. The convention which framed the constitution was indeed elected by the state legislatures. But the instrument, when it came from their hands, was a mere proposal, without obligation, or pretensions to it. It was reported to the then existing congress of the United States, with a request that it might "be submitted to a convention of delegates, chosen in each state by the people thereof, under the recommendation of its legislature, for their assent and ratification." This mode of proceeding was adopted: and by the convention, by congress, and by the state legislatures, the instrument was submitted to the *people.* They acted upon it in the only manner in which they can act safely, effectively and wisely, on such a subject, by assembling in convention. It is true, they assembled in their several states — and where else should they have assembled? No political dreamer was ever wild enough to think of breaking down the lines which separate the states, and of compounding the American people into one common mass. Of consequence, when they act, they act in their states. But the measures they adopt do not, on that account, cease to be the measures of the people themselves, or become the measures of the state governments.

From these conventions, the constitution derives its whole authority. The government proceeds directly from the people; is "ordained and established," in the name of the people; and is declared to be ordained, "in order to form a more perfect union, establish justice, insure domestic tranquillity, and secure the blessings of liberty to themselves and to their posterity." The assent of the states, in their sovereign capacity, is implied, in calling a convention, and thus submitting that instrument to the people. But the people were at perfect liberty to accept or reject it; and their act was final. It required not the affirmance, and could not be negatived, by the state governments. The constitution, when thus adopted, was of complete obligation, and bound the state sovereignties. . . .

The government of the Union, then (whatever may be the influence of this fact on the case), is emphatically and truly, a government of the people. In form, and in substance, it emanates from them. Its powers are granted by them, and are to be exercised directly on them, and for their benefit.

This government is acknowledged by all, to be one of enumerated powers. The principle, that it can exercise only the powers granted to it, would seem too apparent, to have required to be enforced by all those arguments, which its enlightened friends, while it was depending before the people, found it necessary to urge; that principle is now universally admitted. But the question respecting the extent of the powers actually granted, is perpetually arising, and will probably continue to arise, so long as our system shall exist. In discussing these questions, the conflicting powers of the general and state governments must be brought into view, and the supremacy of their respective laws, when they are in opposition, must be settled.

If any one proposition could command the universal assent of mankind, we might expect it would be this — that the government of the Union, though limited in its powers, is supreme within its sphere of action. This would seem to result, necessarily, from its nature. It is the government of all; its powers are delegated by all; it represents all, and acts for all. Though any one state may be willing to control its operations, no state is willing to allow others to control them. The nation, on those subjects on which it can act, must necessarily bind its component parts. But this question is not left to mere reason: the people have, in express terms decided it, by saying, "this constitution, and the laws of the United States, which shall be made in pursuance thereof," "shall be the supreme law of the land," and by requiring that the members of the state legislatures, and the officers of the executive and judicial departments of the states, shall take the oath of fidelity to it. The government of the United States, then, though limited in its powers, is supreme; and its laws, when made in pursuance of the constitution, form the supreme law of the land, "anything in the constitution or laws of any state to the contrary notwithstanding."

Among the enumerated powers, we do not find that of establishing a bank or creating a corporation. But there is no phrase in the instrument which, like the articles of confederation, excludes incidental or implied powers; and which requires that everything granted shall be expressly and minutely described. Even the 10th amendment, which was framed for the purpose of quieting the excessive jealousies which had been excited, omits the word "expressly," and declares only, that the powers "not delegated to the United States, nor prohibited to the states, are reserved to the states or to the people;" thus leaving the question, whether the particular power which may become the subject of contest, has been delegated to the one government, or prohibited to the other, to depend on a fair construction of the whole instrument. The men who drew and adopted this amendment had experienced the embarrassments resulting from the insertion of this word in the articles of confederation, and probably omitted it, to avoid those embarrassments. A constitution, to contain an accurate detail of all the subdivisions of which its great powers will admit, and of all the means by which they may be carried into execution, would partake of the prolixity of a legal code, and could scarcely be embraced by the human mind. It would, probably, never be understood by the public. Its nature, therefore, requires, that only its great outlines should be marked, its important objects designated, and the minor ingredients which compose those objects, be deduced from the nature of the objects themselves. That this idea was entertained by the framers of the American constitution, is not only to be inferred from the nature of the instrument, but from the language. Why else were some of the limitations, found in the 9th section of the 1st article, introduced? It is also, in some degree, warranted, by their having omitted to use any restrictive term which might prevent its receiving a fair and just interpretation. In considering this question, then, we must never forget that it is a *constitution* we are expounding.

Although, among the enumerated powers of government, we do not find the word "bank" or "incorporation," we find the great powers, to lay and collect taxes; to borrow money; to regulate commerce; to declare and conduct a war; and to raise and support armies and navies. The sword and the purse, all the external relations, and no inconsiderable portion of the industry of the nation, are intrusted to its government. It can never be pretended, that these vast powers draw after them others of inferior importance, merely because they are inferior. Such an idea can never be advanced. But it may with great reason be contended, that a government, intrusted with such ample powers, on the due execution of which the happiness and prosperity of the nation so vitally depends, must also be intrusted with ample means for their execution. The power being given, it is the interest of the nation to facilitate its execution. It can never be their interest, and cannot be presumed to have been their intention, to clog and embarrass its execution, by withholding the most appropriate means. Throughout this vast republic, from the St. Croix to the Gulf of Mexico, from the Atlantic to the Pacific, revenue is to be collected and expended, armies are to be marched and supported. The exigencies of the nation may require, that the treasure raised in the north should be transported to the south, that raised in the east, conveyed to the west, or that this order should be reversed. Is that construction of the constitution to be preferred, which would render these operations difficult, hazardous and expensive? Can we adopt that construction (unless the words imperiously require it), which would impute to the framers of that instrument, when granting these powers for the public good, the intention of impeding their exercise, by withholding a choice of means? If, indeed, such be the mandate of the constitution, we have only to obey; but that instrument does not profess to enumerate the means by which the powers it confers may be executed; nor does it prohibit the creation of a corporation, if the existence of such a being be essential, to the beneficial exercise of those powers. It is, then, the subject of fair inquiry, how far such means may be employed.

It is not denied, that the powers given to the government imply the ordinary means of execution. That, for example, of raising revenue, and applying it to national purposes, is admitted to imply the power of conveying money from place to place, as the exigencies of the nation may require, and of employing the usual means of conveyance. But it is denied, that the government has its choice of means; or, that it may employ the most convenient means, if, to employ them, it be necessary to erect a corporation. . . .

The government which has a right to do an act, and has imposed on it, the duty of performing that act, must, according to the dictates of reason, be allowed to select the means; and those who contend that it may not select any appropriate means, that one particular mode of effecting the object is excepted, take upon themselves the burden of establishing that exception.

The creation of a corporation, it is said, appertains to sovereignty. This is admitted. But to what portion of sovereignty does it appertain? Does it belong to one more than to another? In America, the powers of sovereignty are divided between the government of the Union, and those of the states. They are each sovereign, with respect to the objects committed to it, and neither sovereign, with respect to the objects committed to the other. We cannot comprehend that train of reasoning, which would maintain, that the extent of power granted by the people is to be ascertained, not by the nature and terms of the grant, but by its date. Some state constitutions were formed before, some since that of the United States. We cannot believe, that their relation to each other is in any degree dependent upon this circumstance. Their respective powers must, we think, be precisely the same, as if they had been formed at the same time. Had they been formed at the same time, and had the people conferred on the general government the power contained in the constitution, and on the states the whole residuum of power, would it have been asserted, that the government of the Union was not sovereign, with respect to those objects which were intrusted to it, in relation to which its laws were declared to be supreme? If this could not have been asserted, we cannot well comprehend the process of reasoning which maintains, that a power appertaining to sovereignty cannot be connected with that vast portion of it which is granted to the general government, so far as it is calculated to subserve the legitimate objects of that government. The power of creating a corporation, though appertaining to sovereignty, is not, like the power of making war, or levying taxes, or of regulating commerce, a great substantive and independent power, which cannot be implied as incidental to other powers, or used as a means of executing them. It is never the end for which other powers are exercised, but a means by which other objects are accomplished. No contributions are made to charity, for the sake of an incorporation, but a corporation is created to administer the charity; no seminary of learning is instituted, in order to be incorporated, but the corporate character is conferred to subserve the purposes of education. No city was ever built, with the sole object of being incorporated, but is incorporated as affording the best means of being well governed. The power of creating a corporation is never used for its own sake, but for the purpose of effecting something else. No sufficient reason is, therefore, perceived, why it may not pass as incidental to those powers which are expressly given, if it be a direct mode of executing them.

But the constitution of the United States has not left the right of congress to employ the necessary means, for the execution of the powers conferred on the government, to general reasoning. To its enumeration of powers is added, that of making "all laws which shall be necessary and proper, for carrying into execution the foregoing powers, and all other powers vested by this constitution, in the government of the United States, or in any department thereof." The counsel for the state of Maryland have urged various arguments, to prove that this clause, though, in terms, a grant of power, is not so, in effect; but is really restrictive of the general right, which might otherwise be implied, of selecting means for executing the enumerated powers. . . .

But the argument on which most reliance is placed, is drawn from that peculiar language of this clause. Congress is not empowered by it to make all laws, which may have relation to the powers conferred on the government, but such only as may be *necessary and proper"* for carrying them into execution. The word *"necessary"* is considered as controlling the whole sentence, and as limiting the right to pass laws for the execution of the granted powers, to such as are indispensable, and without which the power would be nugatory. That it excludes the choice of means, and leaves to congress, in each case, that only which is most direct and simple.

Is it true, that this is the sense in which the word "necessary" is always used? Does it always import an absolute physical necessity, so strong, that one thing to which another may be termed necessary, cannot exist without that other? We think it does not. If reference be had to its use, in the common affairs of the world, or in approved authors, we find that it frequently imports no more than that one thing is convenient, or useful, or essential to another. To employ the means necessary to an end, is generally understood as employing any means calculated to produce the end, and not as being confined to those single means, without which the end would be entirely unattainable. Such is the character of human language, that no word conveys to the mind, in all situations, one single definite idea; and nothing is more common than to use words in a figurative sense. Almost all compositions contain words, which, taken in their rigorous sense, would convey a meaning different from that which is obviously intended. It is essential to just construction, that many words which import something excessive, should be understood in a more mitigated sense — in that sense which common usage justifies. The word "necessary" is of this description. It has not a fixed character, peculiar to itself. It admits of all degrees of comparison; and is often connected with other words, which increase or diminish the impression the mind receives of the urgency it imports. A thing may be necessary, very necessary, absolutely or indispensably necessary. To no mind would the same idea be conveyed by these several phrases. . . . This word, then, like others, is used in various senses; and, in its construction, the subject, the context, the intention of the person using them, are all to be taken into view.

Let this be done in the case under consideration. The subject is the execution of those great powers on which the welfare of a nation essentially depends. It must have been the intention of those who gave these powers, to insure, so far as human prudence could insure, their beneficial execution. This could not be done, by confiding the choice of means to such narrow limits as not to leave it in the power of congress to adopt any which might be appropriate, and which were conducive to the end. This provision is made in a constitution, intended to endure for ages to come, and consequently, to be adapted to the various *crises* of human affairs. To have prescribed the means by which government should, in all future time, execute its powers, would have been to change, entirely, the character of the instrument, and give it the properties of a legal code. It would have been an unwise attempt to provide, by immutable rules, for exigencies which, if foreseen at all, must have been seen dimly, and which can be best provided for as they occur. To have declared, that the best means shall not be used, but those alone, without which the power given would be nugatory, would have been to deprive the legislature of the capacity to avail itself of experience, to exercise its reason, and to accommodate its legislation to circumstances. . . .

The result of the most careful and attentive consideration bestowed upon this clause is, that if it does not enlarge, it cannot be construed to restrain the powers of congress, or to impair the right of the legislature to exercise its best judgment in the selection of measures to carry into execution the constitutional powers of the government. If no other motive for its insertion can be suggested, a sufficient one is found in the desire to remove all doubts respecting the right to legislate on that vast mass of incidental powers which must be involved in the constitution, if that instrument be not a splendid bauble.

We admit, as all must admit, that the powers of the government are limited, and that its limits are not to be transcended. But we think the sound construction of the constitution must allow to the national legislature that discretion, with respect to the means by which the powers it confers are to be carried into execution, which will enable that body to perform the high duties assigned to it, in the manner most beneficial to the people. Let the end be legitimate, let it be within the scope of the constitution, and all means which are appropriate, which are plainly adapted to that end, which are not prohibited, but consist with the letter and spirit of the constitution, are constitutional. . . .

This clause, as construed by the state of Maryland, would abridge, and almost annihilate, this useful and necessary right of the legislature to select its means. That this could not be intended, is, we should think, had it not been already controverted, too apparent for controversy. . . .

If a corporation may be employed, indiscriminately with other means, to carry into execution the powers of the government, no particular reason can be assigned for excluding the use of a bank, if required for its fiscal operations. To use one, must be within the discretion of congress, if it be an appropriate mode of executing the powers of government. That it is a convenient, a useful, and essential instrument in the prosecution of its fiscal operations, is not now a subject of controversy. . . .

But were its necessity less apparent, none can deny its being an appropriate measure; and if it is, the decree of its necessity, as has been very justly observed, is to be discussed in another place. Should congress, in the execution of its powers, adopt measures which are prohibited by the constitution; or should congress, under the pretext of executing its powers, pass laws for the accomplishment of objects not intrusted to the government; it would become the painful duty of this tribunal, should a case requiring such a decision come before it, to say that such an act was not the law of the land. But where the law is not prohibited, and is really calculated to effect any of the objects intrusted to the government, to undertake here to inquire into the decree of its necessity, would be to pass the line which circumscribes the judicial department, and to tread on legislative ground. This court disclaims all pretensions to such a power. . . .

After the most deliberate consideration, it is the unanimous and decided opinion of this court, that the act to incorporate the Bank of the United States is a law made in pursuance of the constitution, and is a part of the supreme law of the land. . . .

It being the opinion of the court, that the act incorporating the bank is constitutional; and that the power of establishing a branch in the state of Maryland might be properly exercised by the bank itself, we proceed to inquire —

Whether the state of Maryland may, without violating the constitution, tax that branch? That the power of taxation is one of vital importance; that it is retained by the states; that it is not abridged by the grant of a similar power to the government of the Union; that it is to be concurrently exercised by the two governments — are truths which have never been denied. But such is the paramount character of the constitution, that its capacity to withdraw any subject from the action of even this power, is admitted. The states are expressly forbidden to lay any duties on imports or exports, except what may be absolutely necessary for executing their inspection laws. If the obligation of this prohibition must be conceded — if it may restrain a state from the exercise of its taxing power on imports and exports — the same paramount character would seem to restrain, as it certainly may restrain, a state from such other exercise of this power, as is in its nature incompatible with, and repugnant to, the constitutional laws of the Union. A law, absolutely repugnant to another, as entirely repeals that other as if express terms of repeal were used.

On this ground, the counsel for the bank place its claim to be exempted from the power of a state to tax its operations. There is no express provision for the case, but the claim has been sustained on a principle which so entirely pervades the constitution, is so intermixed with the materials which compose it, so interwoven with its web, so blended with its texture, as to be incapable of being separated from it, without rending it into shreds. This great principle is, that the constitution and the laws made in pursuance thereof are supreme; that they control the constitution and laws of the respective states, and cannot be controlled by them. From this, which may be almost termed an axiom, other propositions are deduced as corollaries, on the truth or error of which, and on their application to this case, the cause has been supposed to depend. These are, 1st. That a power to create implies a power to preserve: 2d. That a power to destroy, if wielded by a different hand, is hostile to, and incompatible with these powers to create and to preserve: 3d. That where this repugnancy exists, that authority which is supreme must control, not yield to that over which it is supreme. . . .

The power of congress to create, and of course, to continue, the bank, was the subject of the preceeding part of this opinion; and is no longer to be considered as questionable. That the power of taxing it by the states may be exercised so as to destroy it, is too obvious to be denied. But taxation is said to be an absolute power, which acknowledges no other limits than those expressly prescribed in the constitution, and like sovereign power of every other description, is intrusted to the discretion of those who use it. . . .

The argument on the part of the state of Maryland, is, not that the states may directly resist a law of congress, but that they may exercise their acknowledged powers upon it, and that the constitution leaves them this right, in the confidence that they will not abuse it. . . .

That the power to tax involves the power to destroy; that the power to destroy may defeat and render useless the power to create; that there is a plain repugnance in conferring on one government a power to control the constitutional measures of another, which other, with respect to those very measures, is declared to be supreme over that which exerts the control, are propositions not to be denied. But all inconsistencies are to be reconciled by the magic of the word *confidence.* Taxation, it is said, does not necessarily and unavoidably destroy. To carry it to the excess of destruction, would be an abuse, to presume which, would banish that confidence which is essential to all government. But is this a case of confidence? Would the people of any one state trust those of another with a power to control the most insignificant operations of their state government? We know they would not. Why, then, should we suppose, that the people of any one state should be willing to trust those of another with a power to control the operations of a government to which they have confided their most important and most valuable interests? In the legislature of the Union alone, are all represented. The legislature of the Union alone, therefore, can be trusted by the people with the power of controlling measures which concern all, in the confidence that it will not be abused. This, then, is not a case of confidence, and we must consider it is as it really is.

If we apply the principle for which the state of Maryland contends, to the constitution, generally, we shall find it capable of changing totally the character of that instrument. We shall find it capable of arresting all the measures of the government, and of prostrating it at the foot of the states. The American people have declared their constitution and the laws made in pursuance thereof, to be supreme; but this principle would transfer the supremacy, in fact, to the states. If the states may tax one instrument, employed by the government in the execution of its powers, they may tax any and every other instrument. They may tax the mail; they may tax the mint; they may tax patent-rights; they may tax the papers of the custom-house; they may tax judicial process; they may tax all the means employed by the government, to an excess which would defeat all the ends of government. This was not intended by the American people. They did not design to make their government dependent on the states. . . .

The question is, in truth, a question of supremacy; and if the right of the states to tax the means employed by the general government be conceded, the declaration that the constitution, and the laws made in pursuance thereof, shall be the supreme law of the land, is empty and unmeaning declamation. . . .

It has also been insisted, that, as the power of taxation in the general and state governments is acknowledged to be concurrent, every argument which would sustain the right of the general government to tax banks chartered by the states, will equally sustain the right of the states to tax banks chartered by the general government. But the two cases are not on the same reason. The people of all the states have created the general government, and have conferred upon it the general power of taxation. The people of all the states, and the states themselves, are represented in congress, and, by their representatives, exercise this power. When they tax the chartered institutions of the states, they tax their constituents;

and these taxes must be uniform. But when a state taxes the operations of the government of the United States, it acts upon institutions created, not by their own constituents, but by people over whom they claim no control. It acts upon the measures of a government created by others as well as themselves, for the benefit of others in common with themselves. The difference is that which always exists, and always must exist, between the action of the whole on a part, and the action of a part on the whole — between the laws of a government declared to be supreme, and those of a government which, when in opposition to those laws, is not supreme. . . .

The court has bestowed on this subject its most deliberate consideration. The result is a conviction that the states have no power, by taxation or otherwise, to retard, impede, burden, or in any manner control, the operations of the constitutional laws enacted by congress to carry into execution the powers vested in the general government. This is, we think, the unavoidable consequence of that supremacy which the constitution has declared. We are unanimously of opinion, that the law passed by the legislature of Maryland, imposing a tax on the Bank of the United States, is unconstitutional and void. . . .

Barron *v.* Baltimore

Barron v. Baltimore is a case rarely mentioned by Marshall's admirers. Marshall's opinion that the first eight amendments did not apply against state action is indeed difficult to explain in the light of his vigorous, expansionist views of national power. But by 1833, most of Marshall's closest judicial colleagues were gone, and he no longer had the ability to mass the Court. The case involved an action against the city of Baltimore to recover damages to wharf property of the plaintiff arising from acts of the city.

Chief Justice Marshall delivered the opinion of the Court.

The judgment brought up by this writ of error having been rendered by the court of a State, this tribunal can exercise no jurisdiction over it, unless it be shown to come within the provisions of the 25th section of the Judicial Act.

7 *Peters 243 (1833)*

The plaintiff in error contends that it comes within that clause in the 5th amendment to the constitution, which inhibits the taking of private property for public use, without just compensation. He insists that this amendment, being in favor of the liberty of the citizen, ought to be so construed as to restrain the legislative power of a State, as well as that of the United States. If this proposition be untrue, the court can take no jurisdiction of the cause.

The question thus presented is, we think, of great importance, but not of much difficulty.

The constitution was ordained and established by the people of the United States for themselves, for their own government and not for the government of the individual States. Each State established a constitution for itself, and, in that constitution, provided such limitations and restrictions on the powers of its particular government as its judgment dictated. The people of the United States framed such a government for the United States as they supposed best adapted to their situation, and best calculated to promote their interests. The powers they conferred on this government were to be exercised by itself; and the limitations on power, if expressed in general terms, are naturally, and, we think, necessarily applicable to the government created by the instrument. They are limitations of power granted in the instrument itself; not of distinct governments, framed by different persons and for different purposes.

If these propositions be correct, the 5th amendment must be understood as restraining the power of the general government, not as applicable to the States. In their several constitutions they have imposed such restrictions on their respective governments as their own wisdom suggested; such as they deemed most proper for themselves. It is a subject on which they judge exclusively, and with which others interfere no further than they are supposed to have a common interest. . . .

Had the people of the several States, or any of them, required changes in their constitutions; had they required additional safeguards to liberty from the apprehended encroachments of their particular governments; the remedy was in their own hands, and would have been applied by themselves. A convention would have been assembled by the discontented State, and the required improvements would have been made by itself. The unwieldy and cumbrous machinery of procuring a recommendation from two thirds of congress, and the assent of three fourths of their sister States, could never have occurred to any human being as a mode of doing that which might be effected by the State itself. Had the framers of these amendments intended them to be limitations on the powers of the state governments, they would have imitated the framers of the original constitution, and have expressed that intention. Had congress engaged in the extraordinary occupation of improving the constitutions of the several States by affording the people additional protection from the exercise of power by their own governments in matters which concerned themselves alone, they would have declared this purpose in plain and intelligible language.

But it is universally understood, it is a part of the history of the day, that the great revolution which established the constitution of the United States, was not effected without immense opposition. Serious fears were extensively entertained that those powers which the patriot statesmen, who then watched over the interests of our country, deemed essential to union, and to the attainment of those invaluable objects for which union was sought, might be exercised in a manner dangerous to liberty. In almost every convention by which the constitution was adopted, amendments to guard against the abuse of power were recommended. These amendments demanded security against the apprehended encroachments of the general government, not against those of the local governments.

In compliance with a sentiment thus generally expressed to quiet fears thus extensively entertained, amendments were proposed by the required majority in congress, and adopted by the States. These amendments contain no expression indicating an intention to apply them to the state governments. This court cannot so apply them.

We are of opinion that the provision in the 5th amendment to the constitution, declaring that private property shall not be taken for public use without just compensation, is intended solely as a limitation on the exercise of power by the government of the United States, and is not applicable to the legislation of the States. We are therefore of opinion, that there is no repugnancy between the several acts of the general assembly of Maryland, given in evidence by the defendants at the trial of this cause, in the court of that State, and the constitution of the United States. This court, therefore, has no jurisdiction of the cause; and it is dismissed.

* D *

The Contract Clause

Fletcher *v.* Peck

The contract clause, Article I, Section 10, forbidding the states to pass laws impairing the obligation of contracts, was another great object of the Constitution. During the 1790's, the federal judiciary had expressed concern for the protection of vested rights and in the circuit case of Vanhorne's Lessee v. Dorrance, *Justice Paterson applied the clause against a state law. Marshall's opinion in* Fletcher v. Peck *was the first time the high court used it. The case grew out of the infamous Yazoo land frauds in western Georgia in 1795, in which a group of speculators had bribed the state legislature to secure its land claims. The grant became a political issue and most of the corrupt legislators were defeated. The next legislature promptly revoked the grant. In the interim, however, the first grantees had sold some of the lands to speculators around the country. In a collusive case, the latter claimed that they were innocent, bona fide investors and that the state had unconstitutionally impaired the contracts which gave them title to the lands.*

Chief Justice Marshall delivered the opinion of the Court.

That the legislature of Georgia, unless restrained by its own constitution, possesses the power of disposing of the unappropriated lands within its own limits, in such manner as its own judgment shall dictate, is a proposition not to be controverted. The only question, then, presented by this demurrer, for the consideration of the court, is this, did the then constitution of the State of Georgia prohibit the legislature to dispose of the lands, which were the subject of this contract, in the manner stipulated by the contract?

The question, whether a law be void for its repugnancy to the constitution, is, at all times, a question of much delicacy, which ought seldom,

---

6 Cranch 87 (1810)

if ever, to be decided in the affirmative, in a doubtful case. The court, when impelled by duty to render such a judgment, would be unworthy of its station, could it be unmindful of the solemn obligations which that station imposes. But it is not on slight implication and vague conjecture that the legislature is to be pronounced to have transcended its powers, and its acts to be considered as void. The opposition between the constitution and the law should be such that the judge feels a clear and strong conviction of their incompatibility with each other.

In this case the court can perceive no such opposition. In the constitution of Georgia, adopted in the year 1789, the court can perceive no restriction on the legislative power, which inhibits the passage of the act of 1795. They cannot say that, in passing that act, the legislature has transcended its powers, and violated the constitution.

In overruling the demurrer, therefore, to the first plea, the circuit court committed no error.

The 3d covenant is, that all the title which the State of Georgia ever had in the premises had been legally conveyed to John Peck, the grantor.

The 2d count assigns, in substance, as a breach of this covenant, that the original grantees from the State of Georgia promised and assured divers members of the legislature, then sitting in general assembly, that if the said members would assent to, and vote for, the passing of the act, and if the said bill should pass, such members should have a share of, and be interested in, all the lands purchased from the said State by virtue of such law. And that divers of the said members, to whom the said promises were made, were unduly influenced thereby, and, under such influence, did vote for the passing of the said bill; by reason whereof the said law was a nullity, &c., and so the title of the State of Georgia did not pass to the said Peck, &c.

The plea to this count, after protesting that the promises it alleges were not made, avers, that until after the purchase made from the original grantees by James Greenleaf, under whom the said Peck claims, neither the said James Greenleaf, nor the said Peck, nor any of the mesne vendors between the said Greenleaf and Peck, had any notice or knowledge that any such promises or assurances were made by the said original grantees, or either of them, to any of the members of the legislature of the State of Georgia.

To this plea the plaintiff demurred generally, and the defendant joined in the demurrer.

That corruption should find its way into the governments of our infant republics, and contaminate the very source of legislation, or that impure motives should contribute to the passage of a law, or the formation of a legislative contract, are circumstances most deeply to be deplored. How far a court of justice would, in any case, be competent, on proceedings instituted by the State itself, to vacate a contract thus formed, and to annul rights acquired, under that contract, by third persons having no notice of the improper means by which it was obtained, is a question which the court would approach with much circumspection. It may well be doubted how far the validity of a law depends upon the motives of its framers, and how far the particular inducements, operating on members of the supreme sovereign power of a State, to the formation of a contract by that power, are examinable in a court of justice. If the principle be conceded, that an act of the supreme sovereign power might be declared null by a court, in consequence of the means which procured it, still would there be much difficulty in saying to what extent those means must be applied to produce this effect. Must it be direct corruption, or would interest or undue influence of any kind be sufficient? Must the vitiating cause operate on a majority, or on what number of the members? Would the act be null, whatever might be the wish of the nation, or would its obligation or nullity depend upon the public sentiment?

If the majority of the legislature be corrupted, it may well be doubted, whether it be within the province of the judiciary to control their conduct, and, if less than a majority act from impure motives, the principle by which judicial interference would be regulated, is not clearly discerned.

Whatever difficulties this subject might present, when viewed under aspects of which it may be susceptible, this court can perceive none in the particular pleadings now under consideration.

This is not a bill brought by the State of Georgia, to annul the contract, nor does it appear to the court, by this count, that the State of Georgia is dissatisfied with the sale that has been made. The case, as made out in the pleadings, is simply this. One individual who holds lands in the State of Georgia, under a deed covenanting that the title of Georgia was in the grantor, brings an action of covenant upon this deed, and assigns, as a breach, that some of the members of the legislature were induced to vote in favor of the law, which constituted the contract, by being promised an interest in it, and that therefore the act is a mere nullity.

This solemn question cannot be brought thus collaterally and incidentally before the court. It would be indecent, in the extreme, upon a private contract, between two individuals, to enter into an inquiry respecting the corruption of the sovereign power of a State. If the title be plainly deduced from a legislative act, which the legislature might constitutionally pass, if the act be clothed with all the requisite forms of a law, a court, sitting as a court of law, cannot sustain a suit brought by one individual against another founded on the allegation that the act is a nullity, in consequence of the impure motives which influenced certain members of the legislature which passed the law.

The circuit court, therefore, did right in overruling this demurrer.

The 4th covenant in the deed is, that the title to the premises has been, in no way, constitutionally or legally impaired by virtue of any subsequent act of any subsequent legislature of the State of Georgia.

The third count recites the undue means practised on certain members of the legislature, as stated in the second count, and then alleges that, in consequence of these practices and of other causes, a subsequent legislature passed an act annulling and rescinding the law under which the conveyance to the original grantees was made, declaring that conveyance void, and asserting the title of the State to the lands it contained. The count proceeds to recite at large, this rescinding act, and concludes with averring that, by reason of this act, the title of the said Peck in the premises was constitutionally and legally impaired, and rendered null and void.

After protesting, as before, that no such promises were made as stated in this count, the defendant again pleads that himself and the first purchaser under the original grantees, and all intermediate holders of the property, were purchasers without notice.

To this plea there is a demurrer and joinder.

The importance and the difficulty of the questions presented by these pleadings, are deeply felt by the court.

The lands in controversy vested absolutely in James Gunn and others, the original grantees, by the conveyance of the governor, made in pursuance of an act of assembly to which the legislature was fully competent. Being thus in full possession of the legal estate, they, for a valuable consideration, conveyed portions of the land to those who were willing to purchase. If the original transaction was infected with fraud, these purchasers did not participate in it, and had no notice of it. They were innocent. Yet the legislature of Georgia has involved them in the fate of the first parties to the transaction, and, if the act be valid, has annihilated their rights also.

The legislature of Georgia was a party to this transaction; and for a party to pronounce its own deed invalid, whatever cause may be assigned for its invalidity, must be considered as a mere act of power which must find its vindication in a train of reasoning not often heard in courts of justice.

But the real party, it is said, are the people, and when their agents are unfaithful, the acts of those agents cease to be obligatory. It is, however, to be recollected that the people can act only by these agents, and that, while within the powers conferred on them, their acts must be considered as the acts of the people. If the agents be corrupt, others may be chosen, and if their contracts be examinable, the common sentiment, as well as common usage of mankind, points out a mode by which this examination may be made, and their validity determined.

If the legislature of Georgia was not bound to submit its pretensions to those tribunals which are established for the security of property, and to decide on human rights, if it might claim to itself the power of judging in its own case, yet there are certain great principles of justice, whose authority is universally acknowledged, that ought not to be entirely disregarded.

If the legislature be its own judge in its own case, it would seem equitable that its decision should be regulated by those rules which would have regulated the decision of a judicial tribunal. The question was, in its nature, a question of title, and the tribunal which decided it was either acting in the character of a court of justice, and performing a duty usually assigned to a court, or it was exerting a mere act of power in which it was controlled only by its own will.

If a suit be brought to set aside a conveyance obtained by fraud, and the fraud be clearly proved, the conveyance will be set aside, as between the parties; but the rights of third persons, who are purchasers without notice, for a valuable consideration, cannot be disregarded. Titles, which, according to every legal test, are perfect, are acquired with that confidence which is inspired by the opinion that the purchaser is safe. If there be any concealed defect, arising from the conduct of those who had held the property long before he acquired it, of which he had no notice, that concealed defect cannot be set up against him. He has paid his money for a title good at law; he is innocent, whatever may be the guilt of others, and equity will not subject him to the penalties attached to that guilt. All titles would be insecure, and the intercourse between man and man would be very seriously obstructed, if this principle be overturned.

A court of chancery, therefore, had a bill been brought to set aside the conveyance made to James Gunn and others, as being obtained by improper practices with the legislature, whatever might have been its decision as respected the original grantees, would have been bound, by its own rules, and by the clearest principles of equity, to leave unmolested those who were purchasers, without notice, for a valuable consideration.

If the legislature felt itself absolved from those rules of property which are common to all the citizens of the United States, and from those principles of equity which are acknowledged in all our courts, its act is to be supported by its power alone, and the same power may devest any other individual of his lands, if it shall be the will of the legislature so to exert it.

It is not intended to speak with disrespect of the legislature of Georgia, or of its acts. Far from it. The question is a general question, and is treated as one. For although such powerful objections to a legislative grant, as are alleged against this, may not again exist, yet the principle, on which alone this rescinding act is to be supported, may be applied to every case to which it shall be the will of any legislature to apply it. The principle is this: that a legislature may, by its own act, devest the vested estate of any man whatever, for reasons which shall, by itself, be deemed sufficient.

In this case the legislature may have had ample proof that the original grant was obtained by practices which can never be too much reprobated, and which would have justified its abrogation so far as respected those to whom crime was imputable. But the grant, when issued, conveyed an estate in fee-simple to the grantee, clothed with all the solemnities which law can bestow. This estate was transferable; and those who purchased parts of it were not stained by that guilt which infected the original transaction. Their case is not distinguishable from the ordinary case of purchasers of a legal estate without knowledge of any secret fraud which might have led to the emanation of the original grant. According to the well-known course of equity, their rights could not be affected by such fraud. Their situation was the same, their title was the same, with that of every other member of the community who holds land by regular conveyances from the original patentee.

Is the power of the legislature competent to the annihilation of such title, and to a resumption of the property thus held?

The principle asserted is, that one legislature is competent to repeal any act which a former legislature was competent to pass; and that one legislature cannot abridge the powers of a succeeding legislature.

The correctness of this principle, so far as respects general legislation, can never be controverted. But if an act be done under a law, a succeeding legislature cannot undo it. The past cannot be recalled by the most absolute power. Conveyances have been made, those conveyances have vested legal estates, and, if those estates may be seized by the sovereign authority, still, that they originally vested is a fact, and cannot cease to be a fact.

When, then, a law is in its nature a contract, when absolute rights have vested under that contract, a repeal of the law cannot devest those rights; and the act of annulling them, if legitimate, is rendered so by a power applicable to the case of every individual in the community.

It may well be doubted whether the nature of society and of government does not prescribe some limits to the legislative power; and if any be prescribed, where are they to be found, if the property of an individual, fairly and honestly acquired, may be seized without compensation.

To the legislature all legislative power is granted; but the question, whether the act of transferring the property of an individual to the public, be in the nature of the legislative power, is well worthy of serious reflection.

It is the peculiar province of the legislature to prescribe general rules for the government of society; the application of those rules to individuals in society would seem to be the duty of other departments. How far the power of giving the law may involve every other power, in cases where the constitution is silent, never has been, and perhaps never can be, definitely stated.

The validity of this rescinding act, then, might well be doubted, were Georgia a single sovereign power. But Georgia cannot be viewed as a single, unconnected, sovereign power, on whose legislature no other restrictions are imposed than may be found in its own constitution. She is a part of a large empire; she is a member of the American Union; and that union has a constitution the supremacy of which all acknowledge, and which imposes limits to the legislatures of the several States, which none claim a right to pass. The constitution of the United States declares that no State shall pass any bill of attainder, *ex post facto* law, or law impairing the obligation of contracts.

Does the case now under consideration come within this prohibitory section of the constitution?

In considering this very interesting question, we immediately ask ourselves what is a contract? Is a grant a contract?

A contract is a compact between two or more parties, and is either executory or executed. An executory contract is one in which a party binds himself to do, or not to do, a particular thing; such was the law under which the conveyance was made by the governor. A contract executed is one in which the object of contract is performed; and this, says Blackstone, differs in nothing from a grant. The contract between Georgia and the purchasers was executed by the grant. A contract executed, as well as one which is executory, contains obligations binding on the parties. A grant, in its own nature, amounts to an extinguishment of the right of the grantor, and implies a contract not to reassert that right. A party is, therefore, always estopped by his own grant.

Since, then, in fact, a grant is a contract executed, the obligation of which still continues, and since the constitution uses the general term contract, without distinguishing between those which are executory and those which are executed, it must be construed to comprehend the latter as well as the former. A law annulling conveyances between individuals, and declaring that the grantors should stand seized of their former estates, notwithstanding those grants, would be as repugnant to the constitution as a law discharging the vendors of property from the obligation of executing their contracts by conveyances. It would be strange if a contract to convey was secured by the constitution, while an absolute conveyance remained unprotected.

If, under a fair construction of the constitution, grants are comprehended under the term contracts, is a grant from the State excluded from the operation of the provision? Is the clause to be considered as inhibiting the State from impairing the obligation of contracts between two individuals, but as excluding from that inhibition contracts made with itself?

The words themselves contain no such distinction. They are general, and are applicable to contracts of every description. If contracts made with the State are to be exempted from their operation, the exception must arise from the character of the contracting party, not from the words which are employed.

Whatever respect might have been felt for the state sovereignties, it is not to be disguised that the framers of the constitution viewed, with some apprehension, the violent acts which might grow out of the feelings of the moment; and that the people of the United States, in adopting that instrument, have manifested a determination to shield themselves and their property from the effects of those sudden and strong passions to which men are exposed. The restrictions on the legislative power of the States are obviously founded in this sentiment; and the Constitution of the United States contains what may be deemed a bill of rights for the people of each State.

No State shall pass any bill of attainder, *ex post facto* law, or law impairing the obligation of contracts.

A bill of attainder may affect the life of an individual, or may confiscate his property, or may do both.

In this form the power of the legislature over the lives and fortunes of individuals is expressly restrained. What motive, then, for implying, in words which import a general prohibition to impair the obligation of contracts, an exception in favor of the right to impair the obligation of those contracts into which the State may enter?

The State legislatures can pass no *ex post facto* law. An *ex post facto* law is one which renders an act punishable in a manner in which it was not punishable when it was committed. Such a law may inflict penalties on the person, or may inflict pecuniary penalties which swell the public treasury. The legislature is then prohibited from passing a law by which a man's estate, or any part of it, shall be seized for a crime which was not declared, by some previous law, to render him liable to that punishment. Why, then, should violence be done to the natural meaning of words for the purpose of leaving to the legislature the power of seizing, for public use, the estate of an individual in the form of a law annulling the title by which he holds that estate? The court can perceive no sufficient grounds for making that distinction. This rescinding act would have the effect of an *ex post facto* law. It forfeits the estate of Fletcher for a crime not committed by himself, but by those from whom he purchased. This cannot be effected in the form of an *ex post facto* law, or bill of attainder; why, then, is it allowable in the form of a law annulling the original grant?

The argument in favor of presuming an intention to except a case, not excepted by the words of the constitution, is susceptible of some illustration from a principle originally ingrafted in that instrument, though no longer a part of it. The constitution, as passed, gave the courts of the United States jurisdiction in suits brought against individual States. A State, then, which violated its own contract, was suable in the courts of the United States for that violation. Would it have been a defence in such a suit to say that the State had passed a law absolving itself from the contract? It is scarcely to be conceived that such a defence could be set up. And yet, if a State is neither restrained by the general principles of our political institutions, nor by the words of the constitution, from impairing the obligation of its own contracts, such a defence would be a valid one. This feature is no longer found in the constitution; but it aids in the construction of those clauses with which it was originally associated.

It is, then, the unanimous opinion of the court, that, in this case, the estate having passed into the hands of a purchaser for a valuable consideration, without notice, the State of Georgia was restrained, either by general principles which are common to our free institutions, or by the particular provisions of the Constitution of the United States, from passing a law whereby the estate of the plaintiff in the premises so purchased could be constitutionally and legally impaired and rendered null and void.

In overruling the demurrer to the 3d plea, therefore, there is no error. . . .

Dartmouth College *v.* Woodward

The Marshall Court offered its greatest protection to private property interests in the Dartmouth College case. Here the Court held that corporate charters were contracts which could not be impaired by the state government. Although the states retained the right to alter, amend, or repeal charters, the Court held that the reservation had to be clearly expressed. The decision secured private investments from state interference, and in a time of capital scarcity, it encouraged further enterprise. The case arose from an attempt by the New Hampshire legislature to alter a charter granted by George III in 1769, giving the college trustees the right to govern "forever." In 1816 a Republican legislature passed statutes which rescinded the powers of the Federalist-dominated trustees, and placed control in a new board of overseers. The New Hampshire Superior Court sustained the new law and the old trustees appealed to the federal Supreme Court.

Chief Justice Marshall delivered the opinion of the Court.

The title of the plaintiffs originates in a charter, dated the 13th day of December, in the year 1769, incorporating twelve persons therein mentioned, by the name of "The Trustees of Dartmouth College," granting to them and their successors the usual corporate privileges and powers, and authorizing the trustees, who are to govern the college, to fill up all vacancies which may be created in their own body.

The defendant claims under three acts of the legislature of New Hampshire, the most material of which was passed on the 27th of June, 1816, and is entitled, "An act to amend the charter, and enlarge and improve the corporation of Dartmouth College. . . ."

It can require no argument to prove, that the circumstances of this case constitute a contract. An application is made to the crown for a charter to incorporate a religious and literary institution. In the application it is stated, that large contributions have been made for the object, which will be conferred on the corporation, as soon as it shall be created. The charter is granted, and on its faith the property is conveyed. Surely, in this transaction, every ingredient of a complete and legitimate contract is to be found.

The points for consideration are,

4 Wheaton 518 (1819)

1. Is this contract protected by the constitution of the United States?
2. Is it impaired by the acts under which the defendant holds? . . .

That the framers of the constitution did not intend to restrain the States in the regulation of their civil institutions, adopted for internal government, and that the instrument they have given us is not to be so construed, may be admitted. The provision of the constitution never has been understood to embrace other contracts than those which respect property, or some object of value, and confer rights which may be asserted in a court of justice. It never has been understood to restrict the general right of the legislature to legislate on the subject of divorces. Those acts enable some tribunal, not to impair a marriage contract, but to liberate one of the parties because it has been broken by the other. When any State legislature shall pass an act annulling all marriage contracts, or allowing either party to annul it without the consent of the other, it will be time enough to inquire whether such an act be constitutional.

The parties in this case differ less on general principles, less on the true construction of the constitution in the abstract, than on the application of those principles to this case, and on the true construction of the charter of 1769. This is the point on which the cause essentially depends. If the act of incorporation be a grant of political power, if it create a civil institution to be employed in the administration of the government, or if the funds of the college be public property, or if the State of New Hampshire, as a government, be alone interested in its transactions, the subject is one in which the legislature of the State may act according to its own judgment, unrestrained by any limitation of its power imposed by the constitution of the United States.

But if this be a private eleemosynary institution, endowed with a capacity to take property for objects unconnected with government, whose funds are bestowed by individuals on the faith of the charter; if the donors have stipulated for the future disposition and management of those funds in the manner prescribed by themselves; there may be more difficulty in the case, although neither the persons who have made these stipulations, nor those for whose benefit they were made, should be parties to the cause. . . .

Dartmouth College is really endowed by private individuals, who have bestowed their funds for the propagation of the Christian religion among the Indians, and for the promotion of piety and learning generally. From these funds the salaries of the tutors are drawn; and these salaries lessen the expense of education to the students. It is then an eleemosynary . . . and, as far as respects its funds, a private corporation.

Do its objects stamp on it a different character? Are the trustees and professors public officers, invested with any portion of political power, partaking in any degree in the administration of civil government, and performing duties which flow from the sovereign authority?

That education is an object of national concern, and a proper subject of legislation, all admit. That there may be an institution founded by government, and placed entirely under its immediate control, the officers of which would be public officers, amenable exclusively to government, none will deny. But is Dartmouth College such an institution? Is education altogether in the hands of government? Does every teacher of youth become a public officer, and do donations for the purpose of education necessarily become public property, so far that the will of the legislature, not the will of the donor, becomes the law of the donation? These questions are of serious moment to society, and deserve to be well considered.

Doctor Wheelock, as the keeper of his charity school, instructing the Indians in the art of reading, and in our holy religion; sustaining them at his own expense, and on the voluntary contributions of the charitable, could scarcely be considered as a public officer, exercising any portion of those duties which belong to government; nor could the legislature have supposed, that his private funds, or those given by others, were subject to legislative management, because they were applied to the purposes of education. When afterwards, his school was enlarged, and the liberal contributions made in England and in America, enabled him to extend his cares to the education of the youth of his own country, no change was wrought in his own character, or in the nature of his duties. Had he employed assistant tutors with the funds contributed by others, or had the trustees in England established a school, with Dr. Wheelock at its head, and paid salaries to him and his assistants, they would still have been private tutors; and the fact that they were employed in the education of youth, could not have converted them into public officers, concerned in the administration of public duties, or have given the legislature a right to interfere in the management of the fund. The trustees, in whose care that fund was placed by the contributors, would have been permitted to execute their trust, uncontrolled by legislative authority.

Whence, then, can be derived the idea, that Dartmouth College has become a public institution, and its trustees public officers, exercising powers conferred by the public, for public objects? Not from the source whence its funds were drawn; for its foundation is purely private and eleemosynary. Not from the application of those funds; for money may be given for education, and the persons receiving it do not, by being employed in the education of youth, become members of the civil government. Is it from the act of incorporation? Let this subject be considered.

A corporation is an artificial being, invisible, intangible, and existing only in contemplation of law. Being the mere creature of law, it possesses only those properties which the charter of its creation confers upon it, either expressly, or as incidental to its very existence. These are such as are supposed best calculated to effect the object for which it was created.

Among the most important are immortality, and, if the expression may be allowed, individuality; properties by which a perpetual succession of many persons are considered as the same, and may act as a single individual. They enable a corporation to manage its own affairs, and to hold property without the perplexing intricacies, the hazardous and endless necessity of perpetual conveyances, for the purpose of transmitting it from hand to hand. It is chiefly for the purpose of clothing bodies of men, in succession, with these qualities and capacities, that corporations were invented, and are in use. By these means a perpetual succession of individuals are capable of acting for the promotion of the particular object, like one immortal being. But this being does not share in the civil government of the country, unless that be the purpose for which it was created. Its immortality no more confers on it political power, or a political character, than immortality would confer such power or character on a natural person. It is no more a State instrument, than a natural person exercising the same powers would be. If, then, a natural person, employed by individuals in the education of youth, or for the government of a seminary in which youth is educated, would not become a public officer, or be considered as a member of the civil government, how is it that this artificial being, created by law, for the purpose of being employed by the same individuals for the same purposes, should become a part of the civil government of the country? Is it because its existence, its capacities, its powers, are given by law? Because the government has given it the power to take and to hold property in a particular form, and for particular purposes, has the government a consequent right substantially to change that form, or to vary the purposes to which the property is to be applied? This principle has never been asserted or recognized, and is supported by no authority. Can it derive aid from reason?

The objects for which a corporation is created are universally such as the government wishes to promote. They are deemed beneficial to the country; and this benefit constitutes the consideration, and, in most cases, the sole consideration, of the grant. In most eleemosynary institutions, the object would be difficult, perhaps unattainable, without the aid of a charter of incorporation. Charitable, or public spirited individuals, desirous of making permanent appropriations for charitable or other useful purposes, find it impossible to effect their design, securely and certainly, without an incorporating act. They apply to the government, state their beneficent object, and offer to advance the money necessary for its accomplishment, provided the government will confer on the instrument, which is to execute their designs, the capacity to execute them. The proposition is considered and approved. The benefit to the public is considered as an ample compensation for the faculty it confers, and the corporation is created. If the advantages to the public constitute a full compensation for the faculty it gives, there can be no reason for exacting a further compensation, by claiming a right to exercise over this artificial being a power which changes its nature, and touches the fund, for the security and application of which it was created. There can be no reason for implying in a charter, given for a valuable consideration, a power which is not only not expressed, but is in direct contradiction to its express stipulations.

From the fact, then, that a charter of incorporation has been granted, nothing can be inferred which changes the character of the institution, or transfers to the government any new power over it. The character of civil institutions does not grow out of their incorporation, but out of the manner in which they are formed, and the objects for which they are created. The right to change them is not founded on their being incorporated, but on their being the instruments of government, created for its purposes. The same institutions, created for the same objects, though not incorporated, would be public institutions, and, of course, be controllable by the legislature. The incorporating act neither gives nor prevents this control. Neither, in reason, can the incorporating act change the character of a private eleemosynary institution. . . .

[I]t appears, that Dartmouth College is an eleemosynary institution, incorporated for the purpose of perpetuating the application of the bounty of the donors, to the specified objects of that bounty; that its trustees or governors were originally named by the founder, and invested with the power of perpetuating themselves; that they are not public officers, nor is it a civil institution, participating in the administration of government; but a charity school, or a seminary of education, incorporated for the preservation of its property, and the perpetual application of that property to the objects of its creation. . . .

This is plainly a contract to which the donors, the trustees, and the crown (to whose rights and obligations New Hampshire succeeds) were the original parties. It is a contract made on a valuable consideration. It is a contract for the security and disposition of property. It is a contract, on the faith of which, real and personal estate has been conveyed to the corporation. It is then a contract within the letter of the constitution, and within its spirit also, unless the fact that the property is invested by the donors in trustees, for the promotion of religion and education, for the benefit of persons who are perpetually changing, though the objects remain the same, shall create a particular exception, taking this case out of the prohibition contained in the constitution.

It is more than possible that the preservation of rights of this description was not particularly in the view of the framers of the constitution, when the clause under consideration was introduced into that instrument. It is probable that interferences of more frequent recurrence, to which the temptation was stronger, and of which the mischief was more extensive, constituted the great motive for imposing this restriction on the State legislatures. But although a particular and a rare case may not, in itself, be of sufficient magnitude to induce a rule, yet it must be governed by the rule, when established, unless some plain and strong reason for excluding it can be given. It is not enough to say, that this particular case was not in the mind of the convention, when the article was framed, nor of the American people, when it was adopted. It is necessary to go further, and to say that, had this particular case been suggested, the language would have been so varied as to exclude it, or it would have been made a special exception. The case being within the words of the rule, must be within its operation likewise, unless there be something in the literal construction so obviously absurd or mischievous, or repugnant to the general spirit of the instrument, as to justify those who expound the constitution in making it an exception. . . .

The opinion of the court, after mature deliberation, is, that this is a contract, the obligation of which cannot be impaired, without violating the constitution of the United States. This opinion appears to us to be equally supported by reason, and by the former decisions of this court.

We next proceed to the inquiry, whether its obligation has been impaired by those acts of the legislature of New Hampshire, to which the special verdict refers.

From the review of this charter, which has been taken, it appears that the whole power of governing the college, of appointing and removing tutors, of fixing their salaries, of directing the course of study to be pursued by the students, and of filling up vacancies created in their own body, was vested in the trustees. On the part of the crown, it was expressly stipulated that this corporation, thus constituted, should continue forever; and that the number of trustees should forever consist of twelve, and no more. By this contract, the crown was bound, and could have made no violent alteration in its essential terms, without impairing its obligation.

By the Revolution, the duties as well as the powers of government devolved on the people of New Hampshire. It is admitted, that among the latter was comprehended the transcendent power of parliament, as well as that of the executive department. It is too clear to require the support of argument, that all contracts and rights, respecting property, remained unchanged by the Revolution. The obligations, then, which were created by the charter to Dartmouth College, were the same in the new that they had been in the old government. The power of the government was also the same. A repeal of this charter at any time prior to the adoption of the present constitution of the United States, would have been an extraordinary and unprecedented act of power, but one which could have been contested only by the restrictions upon the legislature, to be found in the constitution of the State. But the constitution of the

United States has imposed this additional limitation, that the legislature of a State shall pass no act "impairing the obligation of contracts."

It has been already stated, that the act "to amend the charter, and enlarge and improve the corporation of Dartmouth College," increases the number of trustees to twenty-one, gives the appointment of the additional members to the executive of the State, and creates a board of overseers, to consist of twenty-five persons, of whom twenty-one are also appointed by the executive of New Hampshire, who have power to inspect and control the most important acts of the trustees.

On the effect of this law, two opinions cannot be entertained. Between acting directly, and acting through the agency of trustees and overseers, no essential difference is perceived. The whole power of governing the college is transferred from trustees, appointed according to the will of the founder, expressed in the charter, to the executive of New Hampshire. The management and application of the funds of this eleemosynary institution, which are placed by the donors in the hands of trustees named in the charter, and empowered to perpetuate themselves, are placed by this act under the control of the government of the State. The will of the State is substituted for the will of the donors, in every essential operation of the college. This is not an immaterial change. The founders of the college contracted, not merely for the perpetual application of the funds which they gave, to the objects for which those funds were given; they contracted also, to secure that application by the constitution of the corporation. They contracted for a system, which should, as far as human foresight can provide, retain forever the government of the literary institution they had formed, in the hands of persons approved by themselves. This system is totally changed. The charter of 1769 exists no longer. It is reorganized; and reorganized in such a manner, as to convert a literary institution, moulded according to the will of its founders, and placed under the control of private literary men, into a machine entirely subservient to the will of government. This may be for the advantage of this college in particular, and may be for the advantage of literature in general; but it is not according to the will of the donors, and is subversive of that contract on the faith of which their property was given. . . .

It results from this opinion, that the acts of the legislature of New Hampshire, which are stated in the special verdict found in this cause, are repugnant to the constitution of the United States, and that the judgment on this special verdict ought to have been for the plaintiffs. The judgment of the state court must, therefore, be reversed. . . .

Ogden v. Saunders

*Various economic disturbances after the War of 1812 created wide-
spread financial disorder. Although the Constitution granted Congress the power to pass bankruptcy legislation, there was no federal
statute on the subject at the time. Like the period following the
Revolution, the states responded to tremendous pressures to pass
bankruptcy and insolvency laws. Dissatisfied creditors, however,
challenged such statutes as a violation of the contract clause. In
Sturges v. Crowninshield (4 Wheaton 122 [1819]), the Marshall
Court invalidated a New York bankruptcy law which applied to
debts contracted before passage of the statute. But Marshall also
held that the states could enact bankruptcy laws in the absence of
federal action. In Ogden v. Saunders eight years later, the Court's
fragile unity on the subject became apparent. Here the Court
divided 4–3, upholding bankruptcy provisions for future contracts.
The case marked the only major constitutional decision of the
Marshall Court in which the Chief Justice dissented.*

Justice Washington delivered the opinion of the Court.

The first and most important point to be decided in this cause, turns
essentially upon the question, whether the obligation of a contract is impaired by a State bankrupt or insolvent law, which discharges
the person and the future acquisitions of the debtor from his liability
under a contract entered into in that State after the passage of the
act. . . .

What is it . . . which constitutes the obligation of a contract? The
answer is given by the chief justice, in the case of Sturges v. Crowninshield, to which I readily assent now, as I did then; it is the law which
binds the parties to perform their agreement. The law, then, which has
this binding obligation, must govern and control the contract in every
shape in which it is intended to bear upon it, whether it affects its validity,
construction, or discharge. . . .

The universal law of all civilized nations . . . is simply that all men are
bound to perform their contracts. The injunction is as absolute as the
contracts to which it applies. It admits of no qualification and no
restraint, either as to its validity, construction, or discharge, further than
may be necessary to develop the intention of the parties to the contract.

12 Wheaton 213 (1827)

And if it be true that this is exclusively the law to which the constitution refers us, it is very apparent that the sphere of state legislation upon subjects connected with the contracts of individuals, would be abridged beyond what it can for a moment be believed the sovereign States of this Union would have consented to; for it will be found, upon examination, that there are few laws which concern the general police of a State, or the government of its citizens, in their intercourse with each other or with strangers, which may not in some way or other affect the contracts which they have entered into, or may thereafter form. For what are laws of evidence, or which concern remedies — frauds and perjuries — laws of registration, and those which affect landlord and tenant, sales at auction, acts of limitation, and those which limit the fees of professional men, and the charges of tavern keepers, and a multitude of others which crowd the codes of every State, but laws which may affect the validity, construction, or duration, or discharge of contracts? Whilst I admit, then, that this common law of nations, which has been mentioned, may form in part the obligation of a contract, I must unhesitatingly insist that this law is to be taken in strict subordination to the municipal laws of the land where the contract is made, or is to be executed. The former can be satisfied by nothing short of performance; the latter may affect and control the validity, construction, evidence, remedy, performance, and discharge of the contract. The former is the common law of all civilized nations, and of each of them; the latter is the peculiar law of each, and is paramount to the former whenever they come in collision with each other.

It is, then, the municipal law of the State, whether that be written or unwritten, which is emphatically the law of the contract made within the State, and must govern it throughout, wherever its performance is sought to be enforced.

It forms, in my humble opinion, a part of the contract, and travels with it wherever the parties to it may be found. It is so regarded by all the civilized nations of the world, and is enforced by the tribunals of those nations according to its own forms, unless the parties to it have otherwise agreed, as where the contract is to be executed in, or refers to the laws of, some other country than that in which it is formed, or where it is of an immoral character, or contravenes the policy of the nation to whose tribunals the appeal is made; in which latter cases, the remedy which the comity of nations affords for enforcing the obligation of contracts wherever formed, is denied. Free from these objections, this law, which accompanies the contract as forming a part of it, is regarded and enforced everywhere, whether it affect the validity, construction, or discharge of the contract. It is upon this principle of universal law, that the discharge of the contract, or of one of the parties to it, by the bankrupt laws of the country where it was made, operates as a discharge everywhere. . . .

It is . . . most apparent that, which ever way we turn, whether to laws affecting the validity, construction, or discharges of contracts, or the evidence or remedy to be employed in enforcing them, we are met by this overruling and admitted distinction, between those which operate retrospectively, and those which operate prospectively. In all of them the law is pronounced to be void in the first class of cases, and not so in the second. . . .

To the decision of this court, made in the case of Sturges *v.* Crownin-shield, and to the reasoning of the learned judge who delivered that opinion, I entirely submit; although I did not then, nor can I now bring my mind to concur in that part of it which admits the constitutional power of the state legislatures to pass bankrupt laws, by which I understand those laws which discharge the person and the future acquisitions of the bankrupt from his debts. I have always thought that the power to pass such a law was exclusively vested by the constitution in the legislature of the United States. But it becomes me to believe that this opinion was and is incorrect, since it stands condemned by the decision of a majority of this court, solemnly pronounced.

After making this acknowledgment, I refer again to the above decision with some degree of confidence in support of the opinion, to which I am now inclined to come, that a bankrupt law which operates prospectively, or in so far as it does so operate, does not violate the constitution of the United States. It is there stated "that, until the power to pass uniform laws on the subject of bankruptcies be exercised by congress, the States are not forbidden to pass a bankrupt law, provided it contain no principle which violates the 10th section of the 1st article of the constitution of the United States." The question in that case was, whether the law of New York, passed on the 3d of April, 1811, which liberates not only the person of the debtor, but discharges him from all liability for any debt contracted previous as well as subsequent to his discharge, on his surrendering his property for the use of his creditors, was a valid law under the constitution, in its application to a debt contracted prior to its passage. The court decided that it was not, upon the single ground that it impaired the obligation of that contract. And if it be true that the States cannot pass a similar law to operate upon contracts subsequently entered into, it follows inevitably, either that they cannot pass such laws at all, contrary to the express declaration of the court, as before quoted, or that such laws do not impair the obligation of contracts subsequently entered into; in fine, it is a self-evident proposition that every contract that can be formed, must either precede or follow any law by which it may be affected. . . .

There is nothing unjust or tyrannical in punishing offences prohibited by law, and committed in violation of that law. Nor can it be unjust or oppressive, to declare by law that contracts subsequently entered into, may be discharged in a way different from that which the parties have provided, but which they know, or may know, are liable, under certain circumstances, to be discharged in a manner contrary to the provisions of their contract.

Thinking, as I have always done, that the power to pass bankrupt laws was intended by the authors of the constitution to be exclusive in congress, or, at least, that they expected the power vested in that body would be exercised, so as effectually to prevent its exercise by the States, it is the more probable that, in reference to all other interferences of the state legislatures upon the subject of contracts, retrospective laws were alone in the contemplation of the convention. . . .

But why, it has been asked, forbid the States to pass laws making any thing but gold and silver coin a tender in payment of debts contracted subsequent as well as prior to the law which authorizes it; and yet confine the prohibition to pass laws impairing the obligation of contracts to past contracts, or, in other words, to future bankrupt laws, when the consequence resulting from each is the same, the latter being considered by the counsel as being, in truth, nothing less than tender laws in disguise. . . .

[A]n answer . . . satisfactory to my mind, is this: tender laws . . . are always unjust; and, where there is an existing bankrupt law at the time the contract is made, they can seldom be useful to the honest debtor. They violate the agreement of the parties to it, without the semblance of an apology for the measure, since they operate to discharge the debtor from his undertaking, upon terms variant from those by which he bound himself, to the injury of the creditor, and unsupported, in many cases, by the plea of necessity. They extend relief to the opulent debtor, who does not stand in need of it; as well as to the one who is, by misfortunes, often unavoidable, reduced to poverty, and disabled from complying with his engagements. In relation to subsequent contracts, they are unjust when extended to the former class of debtors, and useless to the second, since they may be relieved by conforming to the requisitions of the state bankrupt law, where there is one. Being discharged by this law from all his antecedent debts, and having his future acquisitions secured to him, an opportunity is afforded him to become once more a useful member of society. . . .

Chief Justice Marshall dissenting.

It is well known that the court has been divided in opinion on this case. Three judges, Mr. Justice Duvall, Mr. Justice Story, and myself, do not concur in the judgment which has been pronounced. . . .

That there is an essential difference in principle between laws which act on past and those which act on future contracts; that those of the first description can seldom be justified, while those of the last are proper subjects of ordinary legislative discretion, must be admitted. A constitutional restriction, therefore, on the power to pass laws of the one class, may very well consist with entire legislative freedom respecting those of the other. Yet, when we consider the nature of our Union, that it is intended to make us, in a great measure, one people, as to commercial objects; that, so far as respects the intercommunication of individuals, the lines of separation between States are, in many respects, obliterated; it would not be matter of surprise if, on the delicate subject of contracts once formed, the interference of state legislation should be greatly abridged or entirely forbidden. . . .

The first paragraph of the tenth section of the first article, which comprehends the provision under consideration, contains an enumeration of those cases in which the action of the state legislature is entirely prohibited. . . .

In all . . . cases, whether the thing prohibited be the exercise of mere political power, or legislative action on individuals, the prohibition is complete and total. There is no exception from it. Legislation of every description is comprehended within it. A State is as entirely forbidden to pass laws impairing the obligation of contracts, as to make treaties, or coin money. The question recurs, what is a law impairing the obligation of contracts?

In solving this question, all the acumen which controversy can give to the human mind, has been employed in scanning the whole sentence, and every word of it. Arguments have been drawn from the context, and from the particular terms in which the prohibition is expressed, for the purpose, on the one part, of showing its application to all laws which act upon contracts, whether prospectively or retrospectively; and, on the other, of limiting it to laws which act on contracts previously formed.

The first impression which the words make on the mind, would probably be that the prohibition was intended to be general. A contract is commonly understood to be the agreement of the parties; and, if it be not illegal, to bind them to the extent of their stipulations. It requires reflection, it requires some intellectual effort, to efface this impression, and to come to the conclusion that the words contract and obligation, as used in the constitution, are not used in this sense. . . .

So much of this prohibition as restrains the power of the States to punish offenders in criminal cases, the prohibition to pass bills of attainder and *ex post facto* laws, is, in its very terms, confined to preexisting cases. A bill of attainder can be only for crimes already committed; and a law is not *ex post facto,* unless it looks back to an act done before its passage. Language is incapable of expressing, in plainer terms, that the mind of the convention was directed to retroactive legislation. The thing forbidden is retroaction. But that part of the clause which relates to the civil transactions of individuals is expressed in more general terms; in terms which comprehend, in their ordinary signification, cases which occur after, as well as those which occur before, the passage of the act. It forbids a State to make any thing but gold and silver coin a tender in payment of debts, or to pass any law impairing the obligation of contracts. These prohibitions relate to kindred subjects. They contemplate legislative interference with private rights, and restrain that interference. In construing that part of the clause which respects tender laws, a distinction has never been attempted between debts existing at the time the law may be passed, and debts afterwards created. The prohibition has been considered as total; and yet the difference in principle between making property a tender in payment of debts, contracted after the passage of the act, and discharging those debts without payment, or by the surrender of property, between an absolute right to tender in payment, and a contingent right to tender in payment, or in discharge of the debt, is not clearly discernible. Nor is the difference in language so obvious, as to denote plainly a difference of intention in the framers of the instrument. "No State shall make any thing but gold and silver coin a tender in payment of debts." Does the word "debts" mean, generally, those due when the law applies to the case, or is it limited to debts due at the passage of the act? The same train of reasoning which would confine the subsequent words to contracts existing at the passage of the law, would go far in confining these words to debts existing at that time. Yet, this distinction has never, we believe, occurred to any person. How soon it may occur is not for us to determine. We think it would unquestionably defeat the object of the clause. . . .

The constitution, we are told, deals not with form, but with substance; and cannot be presumed, if it designed to protect the obligation of contracts from State legislation, to have left it thus obviously exposed to destruction.

The answer is, that if the law goes further, and annuls the obligation without affording the remedy which satisfies it, if its action on the remedy be such as palpably to impair the obligation of the contract, the very case arises which we suppose to be within the constitution. If it leaves the obligation untouched, but withholds the remedy, or affords one which is merely nominal, it is like all other cases of misgovernment, and leaves the debtor still liable to his creditor, should he be found, or should his property be found, where the laws afford a remedy. If that high sense of duty which men selected from the government of their fellow-citizens must be supposed to feel, furnishes no security against a course of legislation which must end in self-destruction; if the solemn oath taken by every member, to support the constitution of the United States, furnishes no security against intentional attempts to violate its spirit while evading its letter; the question how far the constitution interposes a shield for the protection of an injured individual, who demands from a court of justice that remedy which every government ought to afford, will depend on the law itself which shall be brought under consideration. The anticipation of such a case would be unnecessarily disrespectful, and an opinion on it would be, at least, premature. But, however the question might be decided, should it be even determined that such a law would be a successful evasion of the constitution, it does not follow, that an act which operates directly on the contract after it is made, is not within the restriction imposed on the States by that instrument. The validity of a law acting directly on the obligation, is not proved by showing that the constitution has provided no means for compelling the States to enforce it.

We perceive, then, no reason for the opinion that the prohibition "to pass any law impairing the obligation of contracts," is incompatible with the fair exercise of that discretion, which the State legislatures possess in common with all governments, to regulate the remedies afforded by their own courts. We think that obligation and remedy are distinguishable from each other. That the first is created by the act of the parties, the last is afforded by government. The words of the restriction we have been considering, countenance, we think, this idea. No State shall "pass any law impairing the obligation of contracts." These words seem to us to import that the obligation is intrinsic, that it is created by the contract itself, not that it is dependent on the laws made to enforce it. When we advert to the course of reading generally pursued by American statesmen in early life, we must suppose that the framers of our constitution were intimately acquainted with the writings of those wise and learned men, whose treatises on the laws of nature and nations have guided public opinion on the subjects of obligation and contract. If we turn to those treatises, we find them to concur in the declaration that contracts possess an original intrinsic obligation, derived from the acts of free agents, and not given by government. We must suppose that the framers of our constitution took the same view of the subject, and the language they have used confirms this opinion. . . .

We cannot look back to the history of the times when the august spectacle was exhibited of the assemblage of a whole people by their representatives in convention, in order to unite thirteen independent sovereignties under one government, so far as might be necessary for the purposes of union, without being sensible of the great importance which was at that time attached to the 10th section of the 1st article. The power of changing the relative situation of debtor and creditor, of interfering with contracts, a power which comes home to every man, touches the interest of all, and controls the conduct of every individual in those things which he supposes to be proper for his own exclusive management, had been used to such an excess by the state legislatures as to break in upon the ordinary intercourse of society, and destroy all confidence between man and man. The mischief had become so great, so alarming, as not only to impair commercial intercourse, and threaten the existence of credit, but to sap the morals of the people and destroy the sanctity of private faith. To guard against the continuance of the evil was an object of deep interest with all the truly wise as well as the virtuous of this great community, and was one of the important benefits expected from a reform of the government.

To impose restraints on state legislation, as respected this delicate and interesting subject, was thought necessary by all those patriots who could take an enlightened and comprehensive view of our situation; and the principle obtained an early admission into the various schemes of government which were submitted to the convention. In framing an instrument, which was intended to be perpetual, the presumption is strong that every important principle introduced into it is intended to be perpetual also; that a principle expressed in terms to operate in all future time, is intended so to operate. But if the construction, for which the plaintiff's counsel contend, be the true one, the constitution will have imposed a restriction in language, indicating perpetuity, which every State in the Union may elude at pleasure. The obligation of contracts in force, at any given time, is but of short duration; and, if the inhibition be of retrospective laws only, a very short lapse of time will remove every subject on which the act is forbidden to operate, and make this provision of the constitution so far useless. Instead of introducing a great principle, prohibiting all laws of this obnoxious character, the constitution will only suspend their operation for a moment, or except from it preëxisting cases. The object would scarcely seem to be of sufficient importance to have found a place in that instrument. . . .

It is also worthy of consideration, that those laws which had effected all that mischief the constitution intended to prevent, were prospective as well as retrospective, in their operation. They embraced future contracts, as well as those previously formed. There is the less reason for imputing to the convention an intention, not manifested by their language, to confine a restriction intended to guard against the recurrence of those mischiefs, to retrospective legislation. . . .

Providence Bank *v.* Billings

*The Dartmouth College case predictably led to extravagant cor-
porate claims of charter rights. Business interests stressed a broad
construction of legislative charters and franchises to imply maximum
privileges. A few states passed constitutional amendments or
general statutes reserving the right to alter charters, while others incorporated such a provision in specific charters. Strict judicial construction of the charters was another device for limiting some of
the extreme claims. Fittingly, John Marshall led the way in this case.
The Providence Bank, chartered in 1791, balked at paying a bank
tax enacted by Rhode Island in 1822. It claimed that its original
charter did not provide for such taxation and therefore the new law
impaired the obligation of a contract.*

Chief Justice Marshall delivered the opinion of the Court.

It has been settled that a contract entered into between a State
and an individual is as fully protected by the tenth section of
the first article of the constitution as a contract between two individuals, and it is not denied that a charter incorporating a bank
is a contract. Is this contract impaired by taxing the banks of the
State?

This question is to be answered by the charter itself.

It contains no stipulation promising exemption from taxation. The
State, then, has made no express contract which has been impaired by
the act of which the plaintiffs complain. No words have been found in
the charter, which, in themselves, would justify the opinion that the
power of taxation was in the view of either of the parties, and that an
exemption of it was intended, though not expressed. The plaintiffs find
great difficulty in showing that the charter contains a promise, either
express or implied, not to tax the bank. The elaborate and ingenious
argument which has been urged amounts in substance to this. The
charter authorizes the bank to employ its capital in banking transactions,
for the benefit of the stockholders. It binds the State to permit these
transactions for this object. Any law arresting directly the operations of
the bank would violate this obligation, and would come within the
prohibition of the constitution. But, as that cannot be done circuitously
which may not be done directly, the charter restrains the State from

4 Peters 516 (1830)

passing any act which may indirectly destroy the profits of the bank. A power to tax the bank may unquestionably be carried to such an excess as to take all its profits, and still more than its profits, for the use of the State, and consequently destroy the institution. Now, whatever may be the rule of expediency, the constitutionality of a measure depends not on the degree of its exercise, but on its principle. A power, therefore, which may in effect destroy the charter, is inconsistent with it, and is impliedly renounced by granting it. Such a power cannot be exercised without impairing the obligation of the contract. When pushed to its extreme point, or exercised in moderation, it is the same power, and is hostile to the rights granted by the charter. This is substantially the argument for the bank. The plaintiffs cite and rely on several sentiments expressed on various occasions by this court, in support of these positions.

The claim of the Providence Bank is certainly of the first impression. The power of taxing moneyed corporations has been frequently exercised, and has never before, so far as is known, been resisted. Its novelty, however, furnishes no conclusive argument against it.

That the taxing power is of vital importance, that it is essential to the existence of government, are truths which it cannot be necessary to reaffirm. They are acknowledged and asserted by all. It would seem that the relinquishment of such a power is never to be assumed. We will not say that a State may not relinquish it, that a consideration sufficiently valuable to induce a partial release of it may not exist; but, as the whole community is interested in retaining it undiminished, that community has a right to insist that its abandonment ought not to be presumed in a case in which the deliberate purpose of the State to abandon it does not appear.

The plaintiffs would give to this charter the same construction as if it contained a clause exempting the bank from taxation on its stock in trade. But can it be supposed that such a clause would not enlarge its privileges? They contend that it must be implied, because the power to tax may be so wielded as to defeat the purpose for which the charter was granted. And may not this be said with equal truth of other legislative powers? Does it not also apply with equal force to every incorporated company? A company may be incorporated for the purpose of trading in goods as well as trading in money. If the policy of the State should lead to the imposition of a tax on unincorporated companies, could those which might be incorporated claim an exemption, in virtue of a charter which does not indicate such an intention? The time may come when a duty may be imposed on manufactures. Would an incorporated company be exempted from this duty, as the mere consequence of its charter?

The great object of an incorporation is to bestow the character and properties of individuality on a collective and changing body of men.

This capacity is always given to such a body. Any privileges which may exempt it from the burdens common to individuals do not flow necessarily from the charter, but must be expressed in it, or they do not exist.

If the power of taxation is inconsistent with the charter, because it may be so exercised as to destroy the object for which the charter is given, it is equally inconsistent with every other charter, because it is equally capable of working the destruction of the objects for which every other charter is given. . . . Yet the power of taxation may be carried so far as to absorb these profits. Does this impair the obligation of the contract? The idea is rejected by all; and the proposition appears so extravagant, that it is difficult to admit any resemblance in the cases. And yet, if the proposition for which the plaintiffs contend be true, it carries us to this point. That proposition is, that a power which is in itself capable of being exerted to the total destruction of the grant, is inconsistent with the grant, and is therefore impliedly relinquished by the grantor, though the language of the instrument contains no allusion to the subject. If this be an abstract truth, it may be supposed universal. But it is not universal, and therefore its truth cannot be admitted, in these broad terms, in any case. We must look for the exemption in the language of the instrument; and if we do not find it there, it would be going very far to insert it by construction.

The power of legislation, and consequently of taxation, operates on all the persons and property belonging to the body politic. This is an original principle, which has its foundation in society itself. It is granted by all, for the benefit of all. It resides in government as a part of itself, and need not be reserved when property of any description, or the right to use it in any manner, is granted to individuals or corporate bodies. However absolute the right of an individual may be, it is still in the nature of that right that it must bear a portion of the public burdens, and that portion must be determined by the legislature. This vital power may be abused; but the constitution of the United States was not intended to furnish the corrective for every abuse of power which may be committed by the state governments. The interest, wisdom, and justice of the representative body, and its relations with its constituents, furnish the only security where there is no express contract, against unjust and excessive taxation, as well as against unwise legislation generally. . . .

Gibbons *v.* Ogden

*Interstate trade wars and rivalries had been one of the causes of the
weakness and final disruption of the Confederation government.
If America were to realize her potential as a great common market,
individual state impediments and regulations had to be subordinated
to a uniform national authority. To this end, the Constitution empowered Congress to regulate commerce among the several states
and with foreign nations. The grant of power to Congress was
direct, yet vague as to its extent. Was congressional power exclusive? Did the states have any concurrent jurisdiction? What precisely was meant by "commerce"? Despite the widespread interest
in the subject in the 1780's, the nature of the commerce clause was
not tested until this case in 1824. In 1808, New York granted steamboat monopoly privileges on its waters to Robert Livingston and
Robert Fulton. They in turn had leased the right to navigate the
waters between New Jersey and New York to Aaron Ogden. Thomas
Gibbons of Georgia, a onetime partner of Ogden's, started a competitive line in 1818 with a federal license granted under authority
of the Federal Coasting Act of 1793. Ogden secured a restraining
injunction from the state courts the next year which Gibbons subsequently appealed to the Supreme Court.*

Chief Justice Marshall delivered the opinion of the Court.

As preliminary to the very able discussions of the constitution which
we have heard from the bar, and as having some influence on its
construction, reference has been made to the political situation of these
States, anterior to its formation. It has been said that they were sovereign,
were completely independent, and were connected with each other only
by a league. This is true. But, when these allied sovereigns converted their
league into a government, when they converted their congress of am-

9 Wheaton 1 (1824)

bassadors, deputed to deliberate on their common concerns, and to recommend measures of general utility, into a legislature, empowered to enact laws on the most interesting subjects, the whole character in which the States appear underwent a change, the extent of which must be determined by a fair consideration of the instrument by which that change was effected.

This instrument contains an enumeration of powers expressly granted by the people to their government. . . . We know of no rule for construing the extent of such powers, other than is given by the language of the instrument which confers them, taken in connection with the purposes for which they were conferred.

The words are: "Congress shall have power to regulate commerce with foreign nations, and among the several States, and with the Indian tribes."

The subject to be regulated is commerce; and our constitution being, as was aptly said at the bar, one of enumeration, and not of definition, to ascertain the extent of the power, it becomes necessary to settle the meaning of the word. The counsel for the appellee would limit it to traffic, to buying and selling, or the interchange of commodities, and do not admit that it comprehends navigation. This would restrict a general term, applicable to many objects, to one of its significations. Commerce, undoubtedly, is traffic, but it is something more: it is intercourse. It describes the commercial intercourse between nations, and parts of nations, in all its branches, and is regulated by prescribing rules for carrying on that intercourse. The mind can scarcely conceive a system for regulating commerce between nations, which shall exclude all laws concerning navigation, which shall be silent on the admission of the vessels of the one nation into the ports of the other, and be confined to prescribing rules for the conduct of individuals, in the actual employment of buying and selling, or of barter.

If commerce does not include navigation, the government of the Union has no direct power over that subject, and can make no law prescribing what shall constitute American vessels, or requiring that they shall be navigated by American seamen. Yet this power has been exercised from the commencement of the government, has been exercised with the consent of all, and has been understood by all to be a commercial regulation. All America understands, and has uniformly understood, the word "commerce," to comprehend navigation. It was so understood, and must have been so understood, when the constitution was framed. The power over commerce, including navigation, was one of the primary objects for which the people of America adopted their government, and must have been contemplated in forming it. The convention must have used the word in that sense, because all have understood it in that sense; and the attempt to restrict it comes too late. . . .

The word used in the constitution, then, comprehends, and has been always understood to comprehend, navigation, within its meaning; and a power to regulate navigation is as expressly granted as if that term had been added to the word "commerce."

To what commerce does this power extend? The constitution informs us, to commerce "with foreign nations, and among the several States, and with the Indian tribes."

It has, we believe, been universally admitted that these words comprehend every species of commercial intercourse between the United States and foreign nations. No sort of trade can be carried on between this country and any other, to which this power does not extend. It has been truly said that commerce, as the word is used in the constitution, is a unit, every part of which is indicated by the term.

If this be the admitted meaning of the word, in its application to foreign nations, it must carry the same meaning throughout the sentence and remain a unit, unless there be some plain intelligible cause which alters it.

The subject to which the power is next applied, is to commerce "among the several States." The word "among" means intermingled with. A thing which is among others, is intermingled with them. Commerce among the States, cannot stop at the external boundary line of each State, but may be introduced into the interior.

It is not intended to say that these words comprehend that commerce which is completely internal, which is carried on between man and man in a State, or between different parts of the same State, and which does not extend to or affect other States. Such a power would be inconvenient, and is certainly unnecessary.

Comprehensive as the word "among" is, it may very properly be restricted to that commerce which concerns more States than one. The phrase is not one which would probably have been selected to indicate the completely interior traffic of a State, because it is not an apt phrase for that purpose; and the enumeration of the particular classes of commerce to which the power was to be extended, would not have been made, had the intention been to extend the power to every description. The enumeration presupposes something not enumerated; and that something, if we regard the language, or the subject of the sentence, must be the exclusively internal commerce of a State. The genius and character of the whole government seem to be, that its action is to be applied to all the external concerns of the nation, and to those internal concerns which affect the States generally; but not to those which are completely within a particular State, which do not affect other States, and with which it is not necessary to interfere, for the purpose of executing some of the general powers of the government. The completely internal commerce of a State, then, may be considered as reserved for the State itself.

But, in regulating commerce with foreign nations, the power of congress does not stop at the jurisdictional lines of the several States. It would be a very useless power, if it could not pass those lines. The commerce of the United States with foreign nations, is that of the whole United States. Every district has a right to participate in it. The deep streams which penetrate our country in every direction, pass through the interior of almost every State in the Union, and furnish the means of exercising this right. If congress has the power to regulate it, that power must be exercised whenever the subject exists. If it exists within the States, if a foreign voyage may commence or terminate at a port within a State, then the power of congress may be exercised within a State.

This principle is, if possible, still more clear, when applied to commerce "among the several States." They either join each other, in which case they are separated by a mathematical line, or they are remote from each other, in which case other States lie between them. What is commerce "among" them; and how is it to be conducted? Can a trading expedition between two adjoining States, commence and terminate outside of each? And if the trading intercourse be between two States remote from each other, must it not commence in one, terminate in the other, and probably pass through a third? . . .

We are now arrived at the inquiry — what is this power?

It is the power to regulate; that is, to prescribe the rule by which commerce is to be governed. This power, like all others vested in congress, is complete in itself, may be exercised to its utmost extent, and acknowledges no limitations other than are prescribed in the constitution. These are expressed in plain terms, and do not affect the questions which arise in this case, or which have been discussed at the bar. If, as has always been understood, the sovereignty of congress, though limited to specified objects, is plenary as to those objects, the power over commerce with foreign nations, and among the several States, is vested in congress as absolutely as it would be in a single government, having in its constitution the same restrictions on the exercise of the power as are found in the constitution of the United States. . . .

But it has been urged with great earnestness that, although the power of congress to regulate commerce with foreign nations, and among the several States, be coextensive with the subject itself, and have no other limits than are prescribed in the constitution, yet the States may severally exercise the same power, within their respective jurisdictions. In support of this argument, it is said that they possessed it as an inseparable attribute of sovereignty, before the formation of the constitution, and still retain it, except so far as they have surrendered it by that instrument; that this principle results from the nature of the government, and is secured by the tenth amendment; that an affirmative grant of power is not exclusive, unless in its own nature it be such that the continued exercise of it by the former possessor is inconsistent with the grant, and that this is not of that description.

The appellant, conceding these postulates, except the last, contends that full power to regulate a particular subject, implies the whole power, and leaves no *residuum;* that a grant of the whole is incompatible with the existence of a right in another to any part of it.

Both parties have appealed to the constitution, to legislative acts, and judicial decisions; and have drawn arguments from all these sources, to support and illustrate the propositions they respectively maintain. . . .

In our complex system, presenting the rare and difficult scheme of one general government, whose action extends over the whole, but which possesses only certain enumerated powers; and of numerous state governments, which retain and exercise all powers not delegated to the Union, contests respecting power must arise. Were it even otherwise, the measure taken by the respective governments to execute their acknowledged powers, would often be of the same description, and might, sometimes, interfere. This, however, does not prove that the one is exercising, or has a right to exercise, the powers of the other. . . .

It has been contended, by the counsel for the appellant, that, as the word to "regulate" implies in its nature full power over the thing to be regulated, it excludes, necessarily, the action of all others that would perform the same operation on the same thing. That regulation is designed for the entire result, applying to those parts which remain as they were, as well as to those which are altered. It produces a uniform whole, which is as much disturbed and deranged by changing what the regulating power designs to leave untouched, as that on which it has operated.

There is great force in this argument, and the court is not satisfied that it has been refuted.

Since, however, in exercising the power of regulating their own purely internal affairs, whether of trading or police, the States may sometimes enact laws, the validity of which depends on their interfering with, and being contrary to, an act of congress passed in pursuance of the constitution, the court will enter upon the inquiry, whether the laws of New York, as expounded by the highest tribunal of that State, have, in their application to this case, come into collision with an act of congress, and deprive a citizen of a right to which that act entitles him. Should this collision exist, it will be immaterial whether those laws were passed in virtue of a concurrent power "to regulate commerce with foreign nations and among the several States," or, in virtue of a power to regulate their domestic trade and police. In one case and the other, the acts of New York must yield to the law of congress; and the decision sustaining the privilege they confer, against a right given by a law of the Union, must be erroneous.

This opinion has been frequently expressed in this court, and is founded as well on the nature of the government as on the words of the constitution. In argument, however, it has been contended that, if a law passed by a State, in the exercise of its acknowledged sovereignty, comes into conflict with a law passed by congress in pursuance of the constitution, they affect the subject, and each other, like equal opposing powers.

But the framers of our constitution foresaw this state of things, and provided for it by declaring the supremacy not only of itself, but of the laws made in pursuance of it. The nullity of any act, inconsistent with the constitution, is produced by the declaration that the constitution is the supreme law. The appropriate application of that part of the clause which confers the same supremacy on laws and treaties, is to such acts of the state legislatures as do not transcend their powers, but, though enacted in the execution of acknowledged state powers, interfere with, or are contrary to the laws of congress, made in pursuance of the constitution, or some treaty made under the authority of the United States. In every such case, the act of congress, or the treaty, is supreme; and the law of the State, though enacted in the exercise of powers not controverted, must yield to it.

In pursuing this inquiry at the bar, it has been said that the constitution does not confer the right of intercourse between State and State. That right derives its source from those laws whose authority is acknowledged by civilized man throughout the world. This is true. The constitution found it an existing right, and gave to congress the power to regulate it. In the exercise of this power, congress has passed "an act for enrolling or licensing ships or vessels to be employed in the coasting trade and fisheries, and for regulating the same." The counsel for the respondent contend, that this act does not give the right to sail from port to port, but confines itself to regulating a preëxisting right, so far only as to confer certain privileges on enrolled and licensed vessels, in its exercise.

It will at once occur that, when a legislature attaches certain privileges and exemptions to the exercise of a right over which its control is absolute, the law must imply a power to exercise the right. The privileges are gone if the right itself be annihilated. It would be contrary to all reason, and to the course of human affairs, to say that a State is unable to strip a vessel of the particular privileges attendant on the exercise of a right, and yet may annul the right itself; that the State of New York cannot prevent an enrolled and licensed vessel, proceeding from Elizabethtown, in New Jersey, to New York, from enjoying, in her course and on her entrance into port, all the privileges conferred by the act of congress; but can shut her up in her own port, and prohibit altogether her entering the waters and ports of another State. To the court it seems very clear that the whole act on the subject of the coasting trade, according to those principles which govern the construction of statutes, implies, unequivocally, an authority to licensed vessels to carry on the coasting trade. . . .

But all inquiry into this subject seems to the court to be put completely at rest, by the act already mentioned, entitled, "An act for the enrolling and licensing of steam-boats."

This act authorizes a steam-boat employed, or intended to be employed, only in a river or bay of the United States, owned wholly or in part by an alien, resident within the United States, to be enrolled and licensed as if the same belonged to a citizen of the United States.

This act demonstrates the opinion of congress, that steam-boats may be enrolled and licensed, in common with vessels using sails. They are, of course, entitled to the same privileges, and can no more be restrained from navigating waters, and entering ports which are free to such vessels, than if they were wafted on their voyage by the winds, instead of being propelled by the agency of fire. The one element may be as legitimately used as the other, for every commercial purpose authorized by the laws of the Union; and the act of a State inhibiting the use of either to any vessel having a license under the act of congress, comes, we think, in direct collision with that act.

As this decides the cause, it is unnecessary to enter in an examination of that part of the constitution which empowers congress to promote the progress of science and the useful arts. . . .

The conclusion to which we have come depends on a chain of principles which it was necessary to preserve unbroken; and, although some of them were thought nearly self-evident, the magnitude of the question, the weight of character belonging to those from whose judgment we dissent, and the argument at the bar, demanded that we should assume nothing.

Powerful and ingenious minds, taking as postulates that the powers expressly granted to the government of the Union, are to be contracted by construction into the narrowest possible compass, and that the original powers of the States are retained, if any possible construction will retain them, may, by a course of well-digested but refined and metaphysical reasoning founded on these premises, explain away the constitution of our country, and leave it a magnificent structure, indeed, to look at, but totally unfit for use. They may so entangle and perplex the understanding, as to obscure principles which were before thought quite plain, and induce doubts where, if the mind were to pursue its own course, none would be perceived. In such a case, it is peculiarly necessary to recur to safe and fundamental principles to sustain those principles, and, when sustained, to make them the tests of the arguments to be examined.

Willson *v*. Black Bird Creek Marsh Co.

Gibbons v. Ogden left open the question of whether the states had any concurrent jurisdiction over interstate commerce. Five years later, in the case below, Marshall opened the way for state regulation when the federal government had not acted. The defendants had been authorized by the state of Delaware to improve marsh lands, and for that purpose, built a dam across a navigable creek. Willson complained that the creek was a "public and common navigable creek" in which there was "a certain common and public way" for all citizens of the United States to pass at their pleasure. The Court was faced with a typical policy-preference choice: whether to sanction the state's action as a valid exercise of its powers to act for the general welfare, or to expand the latent, yet largely unexploited, powers of the national government. As usual, the decision turned on reality and practicality.

Chief Justice Marshall delivered the opinion of the Court.

The jurisdiction of the court being established, the more doubtful question is to be considered, whether the act incorporating the Black Bird Creek Marsh Company is repugnant to the constitution, so far as it authorizes a dam across the creek. The plea states the creek to be navigable, in the nature of a highway, through which the tide ebbs and flows.

The act of assembly by which the plaintiffs were authorized to construct their dam, shows plainly that this is one of those many creeks, passing through a deep level marsh adjoining the Delaware, up which the tide flows for some distance. The value of the property on its banks must be enhanced by excluding the water from the marsh, and the health of the inhabitants probably improved. Measures calculated to produce these objects, provided they do not come into collision with the powers of the general government, are undoubtedly within those which are reserved to the States. But the measure authorized by this act stops a navigable creek, and must be supposed to abridge the rights of those who have been accustomed to use it. But this abridgment, unless it comes in conflict with the constitution or a law of the United States, is an affair between the government of Delaware and its citizens, of which this court can take no cognizance.

2 *Peters* 245 (1829)

The counsel for the plaintiffs in error insist that it comes in conflict with the power of the United States "to regulate commerce with foreign nations and among the several States."

If congress had passed any act which bore upon the case; any act in execution of the power to regulate commerce, the object of which was to control state legislation over those small navigable creeks into which the tide flows, and which abound throughout the lower country of the middle and southern States; we should feel not much difficulty in saying that a state law coming in conflict with such act would be void. But congress has passed no such act. The repugnancy of the law of Delaware to the constitution is placed entirely on its repugnancy to the power to regulate commerce with foreign nations and among the several States; a power which has not been so exercised as to affect the question.

We do not think that the act empowering the Blackbird Creek Marsh Company to place a dam across the creek, can, under all the circumstances of the case, be considered as repugnant to the power to regulate commerce in its dormant state, or as being in conflict with any law passed on the subject.

There is no error, and the judgment is affirmed.

III

The Taney Era

1837–1864

Federal Judicial Power

Luther *v.* Borden

This case is the chief source for the Court's doctrine that it will not decide political questions. The idea has been invoked from time to time, particularly as a rationalization for the Court's unwillingness or inability to interfere in certain constitutional controversies. Luther v. Borden *grew out of the Dorr Rebellion in Rhode Island in the early 1840's when rival governments vied for control of the state. It was hoped that the case would determine the lawful authority in the state, but the Court declined to interfere. Chief Justice Taney's opinion also was the leading statement on the constitutional clause guaranteeing each state a republican form of government. Ironically, the Republicans of the Reconstruction era, who reviled Taney's memory for his part in the Dred Scott case, used his language in* Luther v. Borden *to justify congressional powers of reconstruction.*

Mr. Chief Justice Taney delivered the opinion of the Court.

This case has arisen out of the unfortunate political differences which agitated the people of Rhode Island in 1841 and 1842.

It is an action of trespass brought by Martin Luther, the plaintiff in error, against Luther M. Borden and others, the defendants, in the Circuit Court of the United States for the District of Rhode Island, for breaking and entering the plaintiff's house. The defendants justify upon the ground that large numbers of men were assembled in different parts of the State for the purpose of overthrowing the government by military force, and were actually levying war upon the State; that, in order to defend itself from this insurrection, the State was declared by competent authority to be under martial law; that the plaintiff was engaged in the insurrection; and that the defendants, being in the military service of the State, by command of their superior officer, broke and entered the house

---

7 Howard 1 (1849)

and searched the rooms for the plaintiff, who was supposed to be there concealed, in order to arrest him, doing as little damage as possible. The plaintiff replied, that the trespass was committed by the defendants of their own proper wrong, and without any such cause; and upon the issue joined on this replication, the parties proceeded to trial. . . .

The existence and authority of the government under which the defendants acted was called in question; and the plaintiff insists, that, before the acts complained of were committed, that government had been displaced and annulled by the people of Rhode Island, and that the plaintiff was engaged in supporting the lawful authority of the State, and the defendants themselves were in arms against it.

This is a new question in this court, and certainly a very grave one; and at the time when the trespass is alleged to have been committed it had produced a general and painful excitement in the State, and threatened to end in bloodshed and civil war.

The evidence shows that the defendants, in breaking into the plaintiff's house and endeavouring to arrest him, as stated in the pleadings, acted under the authority of the government which was established in Rhode Island at the time of the Declaration of Independence, and which is usually called the charter government. For when the separation from England took place, Rhode Island did not, like the other States, adopt a new constitution, but continued the form of government established by the charter of Charles the Second in 1663; making only such alterations, by acts of the legislature, as were necessary to adapt it to their condition and rights as an independent State.

In this form of government no mode of proceeding was pointed out by which amendments might be made. It authorized the legislature to prescribe the qualification of voters, and in the exercise of this power the right of suffrage was confined to freeholders, until the adoption of the constitution of 1843. . . .

The Circuit Court rejected this evidence, and instructed the jury that the charter government and laws under which the defendants acted were, at the time the trespass is alleged to have been committed, in full force and effect as the form of government and paramount law of the State, and constituted a justification of the acts of the defendants as set forth in their pleas.

It is this opinion of the Circuit Court that we are now called upon to review. It is set forth more at large in the exception, but is in substance as above stated; and the question presented is certainly a very serious one. For, if this court is authorized to enter upon this inquiry as proposed by the plaintiff, and it should be decided that the charter government had no legal existence during the period of time above mentioned, — if it had been annulled by the adoption of the opposing government, — then the laws passed by its legislature during that time were nullities; its taxes wrongfully collected; its salaries and compensation to its officers illegally paid; its public accounts improperly settled; and the judgments and sentences of its courts in civil and criminal cases null and void, and the officers who carried their decisions into operation answerable as trespassers, if not in some cases as criminals.

When the decision of this court might lead to such results, it becomes its duty to examine very carefully its own powers before it undertakes to exercise jurisdiction.

Certainly, the question which the plaintiff proposed to raise by the testimony he offered has not heretofore been recognized as a judicial one in any of the State courts. . . .

But the courts uniformly held that the inquiry proposed to be made belonged to the political power and not to the judicial; that it rested with the political power to decide whether the charter government had been displaced or not; and when that decision was made, the judicial department would be bound to take notice of it as the paramount law of the State, without the aid of oral evidence or the examination of witnesses. . . .

Indeed, we do not see how the question could be tried and judicially decided in a State court. Judicial power presupposes an established government capable of enacting laws and enforcing their execution, and of appointing judges to expound and administer them. The acceptance of the judicial office is a recognition of the authority of the government from which it is derived. . . .

The point, then, raised here has been already decided by the courts of Rhode Island. The question relates, altogether, to the constitution and laws of that State; and the well settled rule in this court is, that the courts of the United States adopt and follow the decisions of the State courts in questions which concern merely the constitution and laws of the State.

Upon what ground could the Circuit Court of the United States which tried this case have departed from this rule, and disregarded and overruled the decisions of the courts of Rhode Island? Undoubtedly the courts of the United States have certain powers under the Constitution and laws of the United States which do not belong to the State courts. But the power of determining that a State government has been lawfully established, which the courts of the State disown and repudiate, is not one of them. Upon such a question the courts of the United States are bound to follow the decisions of the State tribunals, and must therefore regard the charter government as the lawful and established government during the time of this contest.

Besides, if the Circuit Court had entered upon this inquiry, by what rule could it have determined the qualification of voters upon the adoption or rejection of the proposed constitution, unless there was some previous law of the State to guide it? It is the province of a court to expound the law, not to make it. And certainly it is no part of the judicial functions of any court of the United States to prescribe the qualification of voters in a State, giving the right to those to whom it is denied by the written and established constitution and laws of the State, or taking it away from those to whom it is given; nor has it the right to determine what political privileges the citizens of a State are entitled to, unless there is an established constitution or law to govern its decision. . . .

Moreover, the Constitution of the United States, as far as it has provided for an emergency of this kind, and authorized the general government to interfere in the domestic concerns of a State, has treated the subject as political in its nature, and placed the power in the hands of that department.

The fourth section of the fourth article of the Constitution of the United States provides that the United States shall guarantee to every State in the Union a republican form of government, and shall protect each of them against invasion; and on the application of the legislature or of the executive (when the legislature cannot be convened) against domestic violence.

Under this article of the Constitution it rests with Congress to decide what government is the established one in a State. For as the United States guarantee to each State a republican government, Congress must necessarily decide what government is established in the State before it can determine whether it is republican or not. And when the senators and representatives of a State are admitted into the councils of the Union, the authority of the government under which they are appointed, as well as its republican character, is recognized by the proper constitutional authority. And its decision is binding on every other department of the government, and could not be questioned in a judicial tribunal. . . . Yet the right to decide is placed there, and not in the courts. . . .

Much of the argument on the part of the plaintiff turned upon political rights and political questions, upon which the court has been urged to express an opinion. We decline doing so. The high power has been conferred on this court of passing judgment upon the acts of the State sovereignties, and of the legislative and executive branches of the federal government, and of determining whether they are beyond the limits of power marked out for them respectively by the Constitution of the United States. This tribunal, therefore, should be the last to overstep the boundaries which limit its own jurisdiction. And while it should always be ready to meet any question confided to it by the Constitution, it is equally its duty not to pass beyond its appropriate sphere of action, and to take care not to involve itself in discussions which properly belong to other forums. No one, we believe, has ever doubted the proposition, that, according to the institutions of this country, the sovereignty in every State resides in the people of the State, and that they may alter and change their form of government at their own pleasure. But whether they have changed it or not by abolishing an old government, and establishing a new one in its place, is a question to be settled by the political power. And when that power has decided, the courts are bound to take notice of its decision, and to follow it.

The judgment of the Circuit Court must therefore be affirmed.

The Propeller Genessee Chief *v.* Fitzhugh

The Constitution granted admiralty and maritime jurisdiction to the federal courts. English and American precedents had always limited admiralty jurisdiction to the tidewaters, and as recently as The Steamboat Thomas Jefferson (10 Wheaton 428 [1825]), *the Supreme Court had confirmed this practice. But the invention of the steamboat, and a growing population base, increased trade on the inland waterways, particularly on the Great Lakes. In 1845, Congress passed legislation extending federal admiralty jurisdiction to certain cases occurring on the inland lakes and navigable streams. There were serious objections to the constitutionality of the measure and Taney's opinion in the* Genesee Chief *case was largely devoted to this problem. As in the* Charles River Bridge *case (see part B below), Taney again reconciled constitutional doctrine with technological change and economic reality.*

Chief Justice Taney delivered the opinion of the Court.

This is a case of collision on Lake Ontario. The libellants were the owners of the schooner Cuba, and the respondents and present appellants the master and owners of the propeller Genesee Chief. The libellants state that on the 6th of May, 1847, as The Cuba was on her voyage from Sandusky, in the State of Ohio, to Oswego, in the State of New York, The Genesee Chief, which was proceeding on a voyage up the lake, ran foul of her and damaged her so seriously that she shortly afterwards sunk, with her cargo on board; and they also allege that the collision was occasioned by the carelessness and mismanagement of the officers and crew of the propeller, without any fault of the officers or crew of The Cuba. The respondents deny that it was occasioned by the fault of the steamboat, and impute it to the carelessness with which the schooner was managed.

The proceeding is *in rem,* and in substance as well as in form, a proceeding in admiralty. It was instituted under the act of February 26, 1845, 5 Stats. at Large, 726, extending the jurisdiction of the district courts to certain cases upon the lakes and navigable waters connecting the same. The district court decreed in favor of the libellants, and the decision was affirmed in the circuit court, from which last mentioned decree this appeal has been taken.

Before, however, we can look into the merits of the dispute, there is a question of jurisdiction which meets us at the threshold. When the act of congress was passed, under which these proceedings were had, serious doubts were entertained of its constitutionality. The language and decision of this court, whenever a question of admiralty jurisdiction had come before it, seemed to imply that under the constitution of the United States, the jurisdiction was confined to tide waters. Yet the conviction that this definition of admiralty powers was narrower than the constitution contemplated, has been growing stronger every day with the growing commerce on the lakes and navigable rivers of the western States. . . .

[I]f the admiralty jurisdiction is confined to tide water, the courts of the United States can exercise over the waters in question nothing more than ordinary jurisdiction in cases at common law and equity. And in cases of this description they have no jurisdiction, if the parties are citizens of the same State. This being an express limitation in the grant of judicial power, no act of congress can enlarge it. . . .

If this law, therefore, is constitutional, it must be supported on the ground that the lakes and navigable waters connecting them are within the scope of admiralty and maritime jurisdiction, as known and understood in the United States when the constitution was adopted.

If the meaning of these terms was now for the first time brought before this court for consideration, there could, we think, be no hesitation in saying that the lakes and their connecting waters were embraced in them. These lakes are in truth inland seas. Different States border on them on one side, and a foreign nation on the other. A great and growing commerce is carried on upon them between different States and a foreign nation, which is subject to all the incidents and hazards that attend commerce on the ocean. Hostile fleets have encountered on them, and prizes been made; and every reason which existed for the grant of admiralty jurisdiction to the general government on the Atlantic seas, applies with equal force to the lakes. . . .

Again. The Union is formed upon the basis of equal rights among all the States. Courts of admiralty have been found necessary in all commercial countries, not only for the safety and convenience of commerce, and the speedy decision of controversies, where delay would often be ruin, but also to administer the laws of nations in a season of war, and to determine the validity of captures and questions of prize or no prize in a judicial proceeding. And it would be contrary to the first principles on which the Union was formed to confine these rights to the States bordering on the Atlantic, and to the tide water rivers connected with it, and to deny them to the citizens who border on the lakes, and the great navigable streams which flow through the western States. Certainly such was not the intention of the framers of the constitution; and if such be the construction finally given to it by this court, it must necessarily produce great public inconvenience, and at the same time fail to accomplish one of the great objects of the framers of the constitution: that is, a perfect equality in the rights and the privileges of the citizens of the different States; not only in the laws of the general government, but in the mode of administering them. That equality does not exist, if the commerce on the lakes and on the navigable waters of the west are denied the benefits of the same courts and the same jurisdiction for its protection which the constitution secures to the States bordering on the Atlantic.

The only objection made to this jurisdiction is that there is no tide in the lakes or the waters connecting them; and it is said that the admiralty and maritime jurisdiction, as known and understood in England and this country at the time the constitution was adopted, was confined to the ebb and flow of the tide.

Now there is certainly nothing in the ebb and flow of the tide that makes the waters peculiarly suitable for admiralty jurisdiction, nor any thing in the absence of a tide that renders it unfit. If it is a public navigable water, on which commerce is carried on between different States or nations, the reason for the jurisdiction is precisely the same. And if a distinction is made on that account, it is merely arbitrary, without any foundation in reason; and, indeed, would seem to be inconsistent with it.

In England, undoubtedly the writers upon the subject, and the decisions in its courts of admiralty, always speak of the jurisdiction as confined to tide water. And this definition in England was a sound and reasonable one, because there was no navigable stream in the country beyond the ebb and flow of the tide; nor any place where a port could be established to carry on trade with a foreign nation, and where vessels could enter or depart with cargoes. In England, therefore, tide water and navigable water are synonymous terms, and tide water, with a few small and unimportant exceptions, meant nothing more than public rivers, as contradistinguished from private ones; and they took the ebb and flow of the tide as the test, because it was a convenient one, and more easily determined the character of the river. Hence the established doctrine in England, that the admiralty jurisdiction is confined to the ebb and flow of the tide. In other words, it is confined to public navigable waters.

At the time the constitution of the United States was adopted, and our courts of admiralty went into operation, the definition which had been adopted in England was equally proper here. In the old thirteen States the far greater part of the navigable waters are tide waters. And in the States which were at that period in any degree commercial, and where courts of admiralty were called on to exercise their jurisdiction, every public river was tide water to the head of navigation. And, indeed, until the discovery of steamboats, there could be nothing like foreign commerce upon waters with an unchanging current resisting the upward passage. The courts of the United States, therefore, naturally adopted the English mode of defining a public river, and consequently the boundary of admiralty jurisdiction. It measured it by tide water. And that definition having found its way into our courts, became, after a time, the familiar mode of describing a public river, and was repeated, as cases occurred, without particularly examining whether it was as universally applicable in this country as it was in England. . . . And under the natural influence of precedents and established forms, a definition originally correct was adhered to and acted on, after it had ceased, from a change in circumstances, to be the true description of public waters. It was under the influence of these precedents and this usage, that the case of The Thomas Jefferson, 10 Wheat. 428, was decided in this court; and the jurisdiction of the courts of admiralty of the United States declared to be limited to the ebb and flow of the tide. . . .

It is the decision in the case of The Thomas Jefferson which mainly embarrasses the court in the present inquiry. We are sensible of the great weight to which it is entitled. But at the same time we are convinced that, if we follow it, we follow an erroneous decision into which the court fell, when the great importance of the question as it now presents itself could not be foreseen; and the subject did not therefore receive that deliberate consideration which at this time would have been given to it by the eminent men who presided here when that case was decided. For the decision was made in 1825 when the commerce on the rivers of the west and on the lakes was in its infancy, and of little importance, and but little regarded compared with that of the present day. . . .

It is evident that a definition that would at this day limit public rivers in this country to tide water rivers, is utterly inadmissible. We have thousands of miles of public navigable water, including lakes and rivers in which there is no tide. And certainly there can be no reason for admiralty power over a public tide water, which does not apply with equal force to any other public water used for commercial purposes and foreign trade. The lakes and the waters connecting them are undoubtedly public waters; and we think are within the grant of admiralty and maritime jurisdiction in the constitution of the United States.

We are the more convinced of the correctness of the rule we have now laid down, because it is obviously the one adopted by congress in 1789, when the government went into operation. For the 9th section of the judiciary act of 1789, by which the first courts of admiralty were established, declares that the district courts "shall have exclusive cognizance of all civil causes of admiralty and maritime jurisdiction, including all seizures under the laws of impost, navigation, or trade of the United States, where the seizures are made on waters which are navigable from the sea by vessels of ten or more tons burden, within their respective districts, as well as upon the high seas."

The jurisdiction is here made to depend upon the navigable character of the water, and not upon the ebb and flow of the tide. If the water was navigable, it was deemed to be public; and if public, was regarded as within the legitimate scope of the admiralty jurisdiction conferred by the constitution. . . .

Ableman *v.* Booth

Sherman Booth, a Wisconsin abolitionist editor, was charged with violating the fugitive slave laws by aiding a runaway Negro. Although technically held by federal authorities, he was placed in a local jail. Booth then secured a writ of habeas corpus from a state judge who also declared the federal laws unconstitutional and the Wisconsin Supreme Court affirmed the order. The federal marshal thereupon appealed the order to the federal Supreme Court. During the appeal, Booth was brought to trial in federal court and found guilty. While held in the Milwaukee jail, the state court again ordered his release on the grounds that the fugitive slave laws were invalid. This aspect of the case also was appealed to Washington. The Supreme Court's decision must be treated on two levels. First, it was an attempt by the southern-dominated bench to secure compliance with the fugitive slave laws. Second, and more important, it was the most significant statement for the supremacy of federal over state courts between Cohens v. Virginia *and the mid-twentieth century conflicts over desegregation.*

Chief Justice Taney delivered the opinion of the Court.

If the judicial power exercised in this instance has been reserved to the States, no offence against the laws of the United States can be punished by their own courts, without the permission and according to the judgment of the courts of the State in which the party happens to be imprisoned; for, if the Supreme Court of Wisconsin possessed the power it has exercised in relation to offences against the act of Congress in question, it necessarily follows that they must have the same judicial authority in relation to any other law of the United States; and, consequently, their supervising and controlling power would embrace the whole criminal code of the United States, and extend to offences against our revenue laws, or any other law intended to guard the different departments of the General Government from fraud or violence. And it would embrace all crimes, from the highest to the lowest; including felonies, which are punished with death, as well as misdemeanors, which are punished by imprisonment. And, moreover, if the power is possessed by the Supreme Court of the State of Wisconsin, it must belong equally to every other State in the Union, when the prisoner is

21 Howard 506 (1859)

within its territorial limits; and it is very certain that the State courts would not always agree in opinion; and it would often happen, that an act which was admitted to be an offence, and justly punished, in one State, would be regarded as innocent, and indeed as praiseworthy, in another.

It would seem to be hardly necessary to do more than state the result to which these decisions of the State courts must inevitably lead. It is, of itself, a sufficient and conclusive answer; for no one will suppose that a Government which has now lasted nearly seventy years, enforcing its laws by its own tribunals, and preserving the union of the States, could have lasted a single year, or fulfilled the high trusts committed to it, if offences against its laws could not have been punished without the consent of the State in which the culprit was found.

The judges of the Supreme Court of Wisconsin do not distinctly state from what source they suppose they have derived this judicial power. There can be no such thing as judicial authority, unless it is conferred by a Government or sovereignty; and if the judges and courts of Wisconsin possess the jurisdiction they claim, they must derive it either from the United States or the State. It certainly has not been conferred on them by the United States; and it is equally clear it was not in the power of the State to confer it, even if it had attempted to do so; for no State can authorize one of its judges or courts to exercise judicial power, by *habeas corpus* or otherwise, within the jurisdiction of another and independent Government. And although the State of Wisconsin is sovereign within its territorial limits to a certain extent, yet that sovereignty is limited and restricted by the Constitution of the United States. And the powers of the General Government, and of the State, although both exist and are exercised within the same territorial limits, are yet separate and distinct sovereignties, acting separately and independently of each other, within their respective spheres. And the sphere of action appropriated to the United States is as far beyond the reach of the judicial process issued by a State judge or a State court, as if the line of division was traced by landmarks and monuments visible to the eye. And the State of Wisconsin had no more power to authorize these proceedings of its judges and courts, than it would have had if the prisoner had been confined in Michigan, or in any other State of the Union, for an offence against the laws of the State in which he was imprisoned. . . .

But, as we have already said, questions of this kind must always depend upon the Constitution and laws of the United States, and not of a State. The Constitution was not formed merely to guard the State against danger from foreign nations, but mainly to secure union and harmony at home; for if this object could be attained, there would be but little danger from abroad; and to accomplish this purpose, it was felt by the statesmen who framed the Constitution, and by the people who adopted it, that it was necessary that many of the rights of sovereignty which the States then possessed should be ceded to the General Government; and that, in the sphere of action assigned to it, it should be supreme, and strong enough to execute its own laws by its own tribunals, without interruption from a State or from State authorities. And it was evident that anything short of this would be inadequate to the main objects for which the Government was established; and that local interests, local passions or prejudices, incited and fostered by individuals for sinister purposes, would lead to acts of aggression and injustice by one State upon the rights of another, which would ultimately terminate in violence and force, unless there was a common arbiter between them, armed with power enough to protect and guard the rights of all, by appropriate laws, to be carried into execution peacefully by its judicial tribunals. . . .

But the supremacy thus conferred on this Government could not peacefully be maintained, unless it was clothed with judicial power, equally paramount in authority to carry it into execution; for it left to the courts of justice of the several States, conflicting decisions would unavoidably take place, and the local tribunals could hardly be expected to be always free from the local influences of which we have spoken. And the Constitution and laws and treaties of the United States, and the powers granted to the Federal Government, would soon receive different interpretations in different States, and the Government of the United States would soon become one thing in one State and another thing in another. It was essential, therefore, to its very existence as a Government, that it should have the power of establishing courts of justice, altogether independent of State power, to carry into effect its own laws; and that a tribunal should be established in which all cases which might arise under the Constitution and laws and treaties of the United States, whether in a State court or a court of the United States, should be finally and conclusively decided. Without such a tribunal, it is obvious that there would be no uniformity of judicial decision; and that the supremacy, (which is but another name for independence,) so carefully provided in the clause of the Constitution above referred to, could not possibly be maintained peacefully, unless it was associated with this paramount judicial authority. . . .

This judicial power was justly regarded as indispensable, not merely to maintain the supremacy of the laws of the United States, but also to guard the States from any encroachment upon their reserved rights by the General Government. And as the Constitution is the fundamental and supreme law, if it appears that an act of Congress is not pursuant to and within the limits of the power assigned to the Federal Government, it is the duty of the courts of the United States to declare it unconstitutional and void. The grant of judicial power is not confined to the administration of laws passed in pursuance to the provisions of the Constitution, nor confined to the interpretation of such laws; but, by the very terms of the grant, the Constitution is under their view when any act of Congress is brought before them, and it is their duty to declare the law void, and refuse to execute it, if it is not pursuant to the legislative powers conferred upon Congress. And as the final appellate power in all such questions is given to this court, controversies as to the respective powers of the United States and the States, instead of being determined by military and physical force, are heard, investigated, and finally settled, with the calmness and deliberation of judicial inquiry. And no one can fail to see, that if such an arbiter had not been provided, in our complicated system of government, internal tranquillity could not have been preserved; and if such controversies were left to arbitrament of physical force, our Government, State and National, would soon cease to be Governments of laws, and revolutions by force of arms would take the place of courts of justice and judicial decisions. . . .

But although we think it unnecessary to discuss these questions, yet, as they have been decided by the State court, and are before us on the record, and we are not willing to be misunderstood, it is proper to say that, in the judgment of this court, the act of Congress commonly called the fugitive slave law is, in all of its provisions, fully authorized by the Constitution of the United States. . . .

The Contract Clause

Proprietors of the Charles River Bridge
v.
Proprietors of the Warren Bridge

The Charles River Bridge Case is often cited to show a significant difference between Chief Justices Marshall and Taney. But this may be exaggerated. Although the case had been argued first in 1831, illness and vacancies prevented a majority of the Marshall Court from reaching a decision. The justices were divided, and we cannot be entirely sure of Marshall's own views. When Taney and the other new Jacksonian appointees came to the bench in 1837, the controversy was settled quickly. In 1786, Massachusetts had chartered the Charles River Bridge between Charlestown and Boston. The proprietors were given the right to charge tolls for forty years, later extended to seventy years. In 1828, as a result of widespread agitation, the legislature chartered a new bridge, to be built alongside the old, and which was to become a free avenue after six years. The proprietors of the first bridge charged that the state had impaired the obligation of its contract, which they interpreted as implying an exclusive privilege for the collection of tolls. Taney's majority opinion reaffirmed the ideas of strict charter construction developed by Marshall in the Providence Bank case. It also is a model for observing the impact of technology upon law and the law's relation to economic development.

Chief Justice Taney delivered the opinion of the Court.

The questions involved in this case are of the gravest character, and the court have given to them the most anxious and deliberate consideration. The value of the right claimed by the plaintiffs is large in amount; and many persons may no doubt be seriously affected in

---

11 Peters 420 (1837)

their pecuniary interests by any decision which the court may pronounce; and the questions which have been raised as to the power of the several States, in relation to the corporations they have charted, are pregnant with important consequences; not only to the individuals who are concerned in the corporate franchises, but to the communities in which they exist. The court are fully sensible that it is their duty, in exercising the high powers conferred on them by the constitution of the United States, to deal with these great and extensive interests with the utmost caution; guarding, as far as they have the power to do so, the rights of property, and at the same time carefully abstaining from any encroachment on the rights reserved to the States. . . .

Borrowing, as we have done, our system of jurisprudence from the English law; and having adopted, in every other case, civil and criminal, its rules for the construction of statutes; is there any thing in our local situation, or in the nature of our political institutions, which should lead us to depart from the principle where corporations are concerned? Are we to apply to acts of incorporation, a rule of construction differing from that of the English law, and, by implication, make the terms of a charter in one of the States, more unfavorable to the public, than upon an act of parliament, framed in the same words, would be sanctioned in an English court? Can any good reasons be assigned for excepting this particular class of cases from the operation of the general principle; and for introducing a new and adverse rule of construction in favor of corporations, while we adopt and adhere to the rules of construction known to the English common law, in every other case, without exception? We think not; and it would present a singular spectacle, if, while the courts in England are restraining, within the strictest limits, the spirit of monopoly, and exclusive privileges in nature of monopolies, and confining corporations to the privileges plainly given to them in their charter; the courts of this country should be found enlarging these privileges by implication; and construing a statute more unfavorably to the public, and to the rights of the community, than would be done in a case in an English court of justice.

But we are not now left to determine, for the first time, the rules by which public grants are to be construed in this country. The subject has already been considered in this court; and the rule of construction, above stated, fully established. In the case of the United States *v.* Arredondo, 6 Pet. 738, the leading cases upon this subject are collected together by the learned judge who delivered the opinion of the court; and the principle recognized, that in grants by the public, nothing passes by implication. . . .

But the case most analogous to this, and in which the question came more directly before the court, is the case of the Providence Bank *v.* Billings. . . .

It may, perhaps, be said, that in the case of the Providence Bank, this court were speaking of the taxing power; which is of vital importance to the very existence of every government. But the object and end of all government is to promote the happiness and prosperity of the community by which it is established; and it can never be assumed, that the government intended to diminish its power of accomplishing the end for which it was created. And in a country like ours, free, active, and enterprising, continually advancing in numbers and wealth, new channels of communication are daily found necessary, both for travel and trade; and are essential to the comfort, convenience, and prosperity of the people. A State ought never to be presumed to surrender this power, because, like the taxing power, the whole community have an interest in preserving it undiminished. And when a corporation alleges, that a State has surrendered for seventy years, its power of improvement and public accommodation, in a great and important line of travel, along which a vast number of its citizens must daily pass; the community have a right to insist, in the language of this court above quoted, "that its abandonment ought not to be presumed, in a case, in which the deliberate purpose of the State to abandon it does not appear." The continued existence of a government would be of no great value, if by implications and presumptions, it was disarmed of the powers necessary to accomplish the ends of its creation; and the functions it was designed to perform, transferred to the hands of privileged corporations. The rule of construction announced by the court, was not confined to the taxing power; nor is it so limited in the opinion delivered. On the contrary, it was distinctly placed on the ground that the interests of the community were concerned in preserving, undiminished, the power then in question; and whenever any power of the State is said to be surrendered or diminished, whether it be the taxing power or any other affecting the public interest, the same principle applies, and the rule of construction must be the same. No one will question that the interests of the great body of the people of the State, would, in this instance, be affected by the surrender of this great line of travel to a single corporation, with the right to exact toll, and exclude competition for seventy years. While the rights of private property are sacredly guarded, we must not forget that the community also have rights, and that the happiness and well being of every citizen depends on their faithful preservation.

Adopting the rule of construction above stated as the settled one, we proceed to apply it to the charter of 1785, to the proprietors of the Charles River Bridge. This act of incorporation is in the usual form, and the privileges such as are commonly given to corporations of that kind. It confers on them the ordinary faculties of a corporation, for the purpose of building the bridge; and establishes certain rates of toll, which the company are authorized to take. This is the whole grant. There is no exclusive privilege given to them over the waters of Charles River, above or below their bridge. No right to erect another bridge themselves, nor to prevent other persons from erecting one. No engagement from the State that another shall not be erected; and no undertaking not to sanction competition, nor to make improvements that may diminish the amount of its income. Upon all these subjects the charter is silent; and nothing is said in it about a line of travel, so much insisted on in the argument, in which they are to have exclusive privileges. No words are used, from which an intention to grant any of these rights can be inferred. If the plaintiff is entitled to them, it must be implied, simply, from the nature of the grant; and cannot be inferred from the words by which the grant is made.

The relative position of the Warren Bridge has already been described. It does not interrupt the passage over the Charles River Bridge, nor make the way to it or from it less convenient. None of the faculties or franchises granted to that corporation have been revoked by the legislature, and its right to take the tolls granted by the charter remains unaltered. In short, all the franchises and rights of property enumerated in the charter, and there mentioned to have been granted to it, remain unimpaired. But its income is destroyed by the Warren Bridge; which, being free, draws off the passengers and property which would have gone over it, and renders their franchise of no value. This is the gist of the complaint. For it is not pretended that the erection of the Warren Bridge would have done them any injury, or in any degree affected their right of property, if it had not diminished the amount of their tolls. In order then to entitle themselves to relief, it is necessary to show that the legislature contracted not to do the act of which they complain, and that they impaired, or, in other words, violated that contract by the erection of the Warren Bridge.

The inquiry then is, Does the charter contain such a contract on the part of the State? Is there any such stipulation to be found in that instrument? It must be admitted on all hands that there is none, — no words that even relate to another bridge, or to the diminution of their tolls, or to the line of travel. If a contract on that subject can be gathered from the charter, it must be by implication, and cannot be found in the words used. Can such an agreement be implied? The rule of construction before stated is an answer to the question. In charters of this description, no rights are taken from the public, or given to the corporation, beyond those which the words of the charter, by their natural and proper construction, purport to convey. There are no words which import such a contract as the plaintiffs in error contend for, and none can be implied; and the same answer must be given to them that was given by this court to the Providence Bank. 4 Pet. 514. The whole community are interested in this inquiry, and they have a right to require that the power of promoting their comfort and convenience, and of advancing the public prosperity, by providing safe, convenient, and cheap ways for the transportation of produce and the purposes of travel, shall not be construed to have been surrendered or diminished by the State, unless it shall appear by plain words that it was intended to be done. . . .

Can the legislature be presumed to have taken upon themselves an implied obligation, contrary to its own acts and declarations contained in the same law? It would be difficult to find a case justifying such an implication, even between individuals; still less will it be found where sovereign rights are concerned, and where the interests of a whole community would be deeply affected by such an implication. It would, indeed, be a strong exertion of judicial power, acting upon its own views of what justice required, and the parties ought to have done, to raise, by a sort of judicial coercion, an implied contract, and infer from it the nature of the very instrument in which the legislature appear to have taken pains to use words which disavow and repudiate any intention, on the part of the State, to make such a contract.

Indeed, the practice and usage of almost every State in the Union, old enough to have commenced the work of internal improvements, is opposed to the doctrine contended for on the part of the plaintiffs in error. Turnpike roads have been made in succession on the same line of travel; the later one interfering materially with the profits of the first. These corporations have, in some instances, been utterly ruined by the introduction of newer and better modes of transportation and travelling. In some cases, railroads have rendered the turnpike roads on the same line of travel so entirely useless, that the franchise of the turnpike corporation is not worth preserving. Yet in none of these cases have the corporation supposed that their privileges were invaded, or any contract violated on the part of the State. Amid the multitude of cases which have occurred, and have been daily occurring for the last forty or fifty years, this is the first instance in which such an implied contract has been contended for, and this court called upon to infer it from an ordinary act of incorporation, containing nothing more than the usual stipulations and provisions to be found in every such law. The absence of any such controversy, when there must have been so many occasions to give rise to it, proves that neither States, nor individuals, nor corporations, ever imagined that such a contract could be implied from such charters. It shows that the men who voted for these laws, never imagined that they were forming such a contract; and if we maintain that they have made it, we must create it by a legal fiction, in opposition to the truth of the fact, and the obvious intention of the party. We cannot deal thus with the rights reserved to the States, and by legal intendments and mere technical reasoning, take away from them any portion of that power over their own internal police and improvement, which is so necessary to their well being and prosperity.

And what would be the fruits of this doctrine of implied contracts on the part of the States, and of property in a line of travel by a corporation, if it should now be sanctioned by this court? To what results would it lead us? If it is to be found in the charter to this bridge, the same process of reasoning must discover it in the various acts which have been passed, within the last forty years, for turnpike companies. And what is to be the extent of the privileges of exclusion on the different sides of the road? The counsel who have so ably argued this case, have not attempted to define it by any certain boundaries. How far must the new improvement be distant from the old one? How near may you approach without invading its rights in the privileged line? If this court should establish the principles now contended for, what is to become of the numerous railroads established on the same line of travel with turnpike companies; and which have rendered the franchises of the turnpike corporations of no value? Let it once be understood that such charters carry with them these implied contracts, and give this unknown and undefined property in a line of travelling, and you will soon find the old turnpike corporations awakening from their sleep, and calling upon this court to put down the improvements which have taken their place. The millions of property which have been invested in railroads and canals, upon lines of travel which had been before occupied by turnpike corporations, will be put in jeopardy. We shall be thrown back to the improvements of the last century, and obliged to stand still, until the claims of the old turnpike corporations shall be satisfied, and they shall consent to permit these States to avail themselves of the lights of modern science, and to partake of the benefit of those improvements which are now adding to the wealth and prosperity, and the convenience and comfort of every other part of the civilized world. Nor is this all. This court will find itself compelled to fix, by some arbitrary rule, the width of this new kind of property in a line of travel; for if such a right of property exists, we have no lights to guide us in marking out its extent, unless, indeed, we resort to the old feudal grants, and to the exclusive rights of ferries, by prescription, between towns; and are prepared to decide that when a turnpike road from one town to another had been made, no railroad or canal, between these two points, could afterwards be established. This court are not prepared to sanction principles which must lead to such results. . . .

Ohio Life Insurance & Trust Co. *v.* Debolt

The Taney Court justices did not undermine the contract clause doctrines of their predecessors, the Charles River Bridge Case notwithstanding. They consistently insisted, however, that public charters and contracts could carry nothing by implication. But this development may have been a blessing in disguise for new investors and entrepreneurs as it prompted them to secure charters carefully spelling out corporate privileges. Taney's noble sentiments on "community rights" versus "property rights" had only limited meaning. His opinion in the case below made it clear that the courts would recognize charter rights expressly granted, even though they might be "ruinous or injurious" to the state. In this case, the plaintiff claimed that an 1851 state bank tax law impaired the obligation of contracts previously made between the state and the corporation. The Court agreed on its decision, but the majority was divided in its reasoning.

Chief Justice Taney

It will be admitted on all hands that, with the exception of the powers surrendered by the constitution of the United States, the people of several States are absolutely and unconditionally sovereign within their respective territories. It follows that they may impose what taxes they think proper upon persons or things within their dominion and may apportion them according to their discretion and judgment. They may, if they deem it advisable to do so, exempt certain descriptions of property from taxation, and lay the burden of supporting the government elsewhere. And they may do this in the ordinary forms of legislation or by contract, as may seem best to the people of the State. There is nothing in the constitution of the United States to forbid it, nor any authority given to this court to question the right of a State to bind itself by such contracts, whenever it may think proper to make them.

There are undoubtedly fixed and immutable principles of justice, sound policy, and public duty, which no State can disregard without serious injury to the community, and to the individual citzens who compose it. And contracts are sometimes incautiously made by States, as well as individuals; and franchises, immunities, and exemptions from public burdens improvidently granted. But whether such contracts should be made or not, is exclusively for the consideration of the State.

16 Howard 416 (1854)

It is the exercise of an undoubted power of sovereignty which has not been surrendered by the adoption of the constitution of the United States, and over which this court has no control. For it can never be maintained in any tribunal in this country, that the people of a State, in the exercise of the powers of sovereignty, can be restrained within narrower limits than those fixed by the constitution of the United States, upon the ground that they may make contracts ruinous or injurious to themselves. The principle that they are the best judges of what is for their own interest, is the foundation of our political institutions.

It is equally clear, upon the same principle, that the people of a State may, by the form of government they adopt, confer on their public servants and representatives all the powers and rights of sovereignty which they themselves possess; or may restrict them within such limits as may be deemed best and safest for the public interest. They may confer on them the power to charter banks or other companies, and to exempt the property vested in them from taxation by the State for a limited time during the continuance of their charters, or accept a specified amount less than its fair share of the public burdens. This power may be indiscreetly and injudiciously exercised. Banks and other companies may be exempted, by contract, from their equal share of the taxes, under the belief that the corporation will prove to be a public benefit. Experience may prove that it is a public injury. Yet, if the contract was within the scope of the authority conferred by the constitution of the State, it is like any other contract made by competent authority, binding upon the parties. Nor can the people or their representatives, by any act of theirs afterwards, impair its obligation. When the contract is made, the constitution of the United States acts upon it, and declares that it shall not be impaired, and makes it the duty of this court to carry it into execution. That duty must be performed.

This doctrine was recognized in the case of Billings *v.* The Providence Bank, . . . and again in the case of The Charles River Bridge Company. . . . The powers of sovereignty confided to the legislative body of a State are undoubtedly a trust committed to them, to be executed to the best of their judgment for the public good; and no one legislature can, by its own act, disarm their successors of any of the powers or rights of sovereignty confided by the people to the legislative body, unless they are authorized to do so by the constitution under which they are elected. They cannot, therefore, by contract, deprive a future legislature of the power of imposing any tax it may deem necessary for the public service — or of exercising any other act of sovereignty confided to the legislative body, unless the power to make such a contract is conferred upon them by the constitution of the State. And in every controversy on this subject, the question must depend on the constitution of the State, and the extent of the power thereby conferred on the legislative body.

This brings me to the question more immediately before the court:

Did the constitution of Ohio authorize its legislature, by contract, to exempt this company from its equal share of the public burdens during the continuance of its charter? The supreme court of Ohio, in the case before us, has decided that it did not. But this charter was granted while the constitution of 1802 was in force; and it is evident that this decision is in conflict with the uniform construction of that constitution during the whole period of its existence. It appears, from the acts of the legislature, that the power was repeatedly exercised while that constitution was in force, and acquiesced in by the people of the State. It was directly and distinctly sanctioned by the supreme court of the State. . . .

And when the constitution of a State, for nearly half a century, has received one uniform and unquestioned construction by all the departments of the government, legislative, executive, and judicial, I think it must be regarded as the true one. It is true that this court always follows the decision of the state courts in the construction of their own constitution and laws. But where those decisions are in conflict, this court must determine between them. And certainly a construction acted on as undisputed for nearly fifty years by every department of the government, and supported by judicial decision, ought to be regarded as sufficient to give to the instrument a fixed and definite meaning. Contracts with the state authorities were made under it. And upon a question as to the validity of such a contract, the court, upon the soundest principles of justice, is bound to adopt the construction it received from the state authorities at the time the contract was made. . . .

The rule of construction, in cases of this kind, has been well settled by this court. The grant of privileges and exemptions to a corporation are strictly construed against the corporation, and in favor of the public. Nothing passes but what is granted in clear and explicit terms. And neither the right of taxation nor any other power of sovereignty which the community have an interest in preserving, undiminished, will be held by the court to be surrendered, unless the intention to surrender is manifested by words too plain to be mistaken. This is the rule laid down in the case of Billings *v.* The Providence Bank, and reaffirmed in the case of The Charles River Bridge Company.

Nor does the rule rest merely on the authority of adjudged cases. It is founded in principles of justice, and necessary for the safety and well-being of every State in the Union. For it is a matter of public history, which this court cannot refuse to notice, that almost every bill for the incorporation of banking companies, insurance and trust companies, railroad companies, or other corporations, is drawn originally by the parties who are personally interested in obtaining the charter; and that they are often passed by the legislature in the last days of its session, when, from the nature of our political institutions, the business is unavoidably transacted in a hurried manner, and it is impossible that every member can deliberately examine every provision in every bill upon which he is called on to act.

On the other hand, those who accept the charter have abundant time to examine and consider its provisions, before they invest their money. And if they mean to claim under it any peculiar privileges, or any exemption from the burden of taxation, it is their duty to see that the right or exemption they intend to claim is granted in clear and unambiguous language. The authority which this court is bound, under the constitution of the United States, to exercise, in cases of this kind, is one of its most delicate and important duties. And if individuals choose to accept a charter in which the words used are susceptible of different meanings, — or might have been considered by the representatives of the State as words of legislation only, and subject to future revision and repeal, and not as words of contract, — the parties who accept it have no just right to call upon this court to exercise its high power over a State upon doubtful or ambiguous words, nor upon any supposed equitable constitution, or inferences made upon other provisions in the act of incorporation. If there are equitable considerations in their favor, the application should be made to the State, and not to this court. If they come here to claim an exemption from their equal share of the public burdens, or any peculiar exemption or privilege, they must show their title to it; and that title must be shown by plain and unequivocal language. . . .

not in the cts jurisdiction

Taney then concluded that the plaintiff's claim of a tax exemption was not plainly expressed in its charter, and therefore the state law did not impair the obligation of the contract.

Dodge *v.* Woolsey

Dodge *v.* Woolsey *gave the Taney Court its opportunity to implement the ideas expressed by the Chief Justice in the previous case.
The 1845 charter of the State Bank of Ohio stipulated that the
bank would pay six per cent of its profits to the state in lieu of
taxes. Six years later, however, a new state constitution required
all banks to pay property taxes. The legislature followed this
with a new tax law making the bank liable for taxes of about $7,000
more than it had paid under the previous arrangement. Woolsey,
a stockholder, sought to enjoin the state from collecting the tax on
the grounds that the new law impaired the obligation of an existing
contract.*

Mr. Justice Wayne delivered the opinion of the Court.

The law of 1845 was an agreement with the bank, *quasi ex contractu*
— and also an agreement separately with the shareholders, *quasi
ex contractu* — that neither the bank as such, nor the shareholders as
such, should be liable to any other tax larger than that which was to be
levied under the 60th section of the act of 1845.

That 60th section is, "that each banking company under the act, on
accepting thereof and complying with its provisions, shall semi-annually,
on the days designated for declaring dividends, set off to the State six
per cent. on the profits, deducting therefrom the expenses and ascertained
losses of the company for the six months next preceding, which sum or
amount so set off shall be in lieu of all taxes to which the company, or
the stockholders therein, would otherwise be subject. The sum so set off
to be paid to the treasurer, on the order of the auditor of the State." The
act under which the tax of 1853 has been assessed is: "That the president
and cashier of every bank and banking company that shall have been, or
may hereafter be, incorporated by the laws of this State, and having the
right to issue bills of circulation as money, shall make and return, under
oath, to the auditor of the county in which such bank or banking company
may be situated, in the month of May annually, a written statement containing, first, the average amount of notes and bills discounted or purchased, which amount shall include all the loans or discounts, whether
originally made or renewed during the year aforesaid, or at any previous
time, whether made on bills of exchange, notes, bonds, or mortgages, or
any other evidences of indebtedness, at their actual cost value in money,

18 Howard 331 (1856)

whether due previous to, during, or after the period aforesaid, and on which such banking company has at any time reserved or received, or is entitled to receive, any profit or other consideration whatever; and, secondly, the average amount of all other moneys, effects, or dues of every description belonging to the bank or banking company, loaned, invested, or otherwise used with a view to profit, or upon which the bank, &c., receives, or is entitled to receive, interest."

The two acts have been put in connection, that the difference between the modes of taxation may be more obvious; and it will be readily seen, that the second is not intended to tax the profits of the bank, but its entire business, capital, circulation, credits, and debts due to it, being professed to be intended to equalize the tax to be paid by the bank with that required to be paid upon personal property. A careful examination of the two acts, and of the tabular returns annexed to this opinion, will prove that such equality of taxation has not been attained. It will show that the bank is taxed more than three times the number of mills upon the dollars that is assessed upon personal property, whatever may be comprehended under that denomination by the act of the 13th April, 1852. But if it did not, it could make no difference in our conclusion. For the tax to be paid by the bank under the act of 24th February, 1824, is a legislative contract, equally operative upon the State and upon the bank, and the stockholders of the bank, until the expiration of its charter, which will be in 1866. No critical examination of the words, "that on the days designated for declaring dividends, to wit, on the first Monday in May and November of each year, the bank shall set off to the said State of Ohio six per cent. on the profits, deducting therefrom the expenses and ascertained losses of said company for six months next preceding each dividend day, and that the sums or amounts so set off shall be in lieu of all taxes to which said company or the stockholders thereof, on account of stock owned therein, would otherwise be subject," could make them more exact in meaning than they are. The words "would otherwise be subject," relate to the legislative power to tax, and is a relinquishment of it, binding upon that legislature which passed the act, and upon succeeding legislatures as a contract not to tax the bank during its continuance with more than six per cent. upon its semi-annual profits. A change of constitution cannot release a State from contracts made under a constitution which permits them to be made. The inquiry is, is the contract permitted by the existing constitution? If so, and that cannot be denied in this case, the sovereignty which ratified it in 1802 was the same sovereignty which made the constitution of 1851, neither having more power than the other to impair a contract made by the State legislature with individuals. The moral obligations never die. If broken by states and nations, though the terms of reproach are not the same with which we are accustomed to designate the faithlessness of individuals, the violation of justice is not the less. . . .

⋆ C ⋆

The Commerce Clause

New York *v.* Miln

In Gibbons *v.* Ogden, *Marshall had implied that federal power over interstate commerce was exclusive. But his obvious retreat in the Delaware dam case was an indication of things to come. Under Taney, the Court was deeply divided over the precise lines between national and state authority over commerce.* New York *v.* Miln, *a case carried over from the Marshall period, opened the debate in 1837. At issue was a New York law which required ship captains to offer detailed reports concerning the background and health of every immigrant carried on their ships. The statute was designed to protect the state from increasing numbers of foreign paupers. When it was challenged as an unconstitutional regulation of foreign commerce, a majority of the court skirted the constitutional question and treated the statute as a police regulation. Justice Story, however, disagreed and found the law to be an invalid interference with federal power. Justice Thompson concurred with the majority, but insisted that the states had a right to regulate commerce in the absence of federal action.*

Justice Barbour delivered the opinion of the Court.

It is contended by the counsel for the defendant, that the act in question is a regulation of commerce; that the power to regulate commerce is, by the constitution of the United States, granted to congress; that this power is exclusive, and that consequently the act is a violation of the constitution of the United States.

On the part of the plaintiff it is argued, that an affirmative grant of power previously existing in the States to congress, is not exclusive; except, 1st, where it is so expressly declared in terms, by the clause giving the power; or 2dly, where a similar power is prohibited to the States; or 3dly, where the power in the States would be repugnant to, and in-

---

11 Peters 102 (1837)

compatible with, a similar power in congress; that this power falls within neither of these predicaments; that it is not, in terms, declared to be exclusive; that it is not prohibited to the States; and that it is not repugnant to, or incompatible with, a similar power in congress; and that having preexisted in the States, they therefore have a concurrent power in relation to the subject; and that the act in question would be valid, even if it were a regulation of commerce, it not contravening any regulation made by congress.

But they deny that it is a regulation of commerce; on the contrary, they assert that it is a mere regulation of internal police, a power over which is not granted to congress; and which therefore, as well upon the true construction of the constitution, as by force of the tenth amendment to that instrument, is reserved to, and resides in the several States.

We shall not enter into any examination of the question whether the power to regulate commerce, be or be not exclusive of the States, because the opinion which we have formed renders it unnecessary; in other words, we are of opinion that the act is not a regulation of commerce, but of police; and that being thus considered, it was passed in the exercise of a power which rightfully belonged to the States.

That the State of New York possessed power to pass this law before the adoption of the constitution of the United States, might probably be taken as a truism, without the necessity of proof. . . .

If, as we think, it be a regulation, not of commerce, but police, then it is not taken from the States. To decide this, let us examine its purpose, the end to be attained, and the means of its attainment.

It is apparent, from the whole scope of the law, that the object of the legislature was to prevent New York from being burdened by an influx of persons brought thither in ships, either from foreign countries, or from any other of the States; and for that purpose a report was required of the names, places of birth, &c., of all passengers, that the necessary steps might be taken by the city authorities, to prevent them from becoming chargeable as paupers.

Now, we hold that both the end and the means here used, are within the competency of the States, since a portion of their powers were surrendered to the federal government. Let us see what powers are left with the States. The Federalist, in the 45th number, speaking of this subject, says; the powers reserved to the several States will extend to all the objects which, in the ordinary course of affairs, concern the lives, liberties, and properties of the people; and the internal order, improvement, and prosperity of the State.

And this court, in the case of Gibbons v. Ogden, . . . in speaking of the inspection laws of the States, say; they form a portion of that immense mass of legislation which embraces every thing within the territory of a State, not surrendered to the general government, all which can be most advantageously exercised by the States themselves. Inspection laws, quarantine laws, health laws of every description, as well as laws for regulating the internal commerce of a State, and those which respect turn-pike roads, ferries, &c., are component parts of this mass. . . .

If we look at the persons for whose benefit it was passed, they are the people of New York, for whose protection and welfare the legislature of that State are authorized and in duty bound to provide.

If we turn our attention to the purpose to be attained, it is to secure that very protection, and to provide for that very welfare. . . .

The act of 1819 contains regulations obviously designed for the comfort of the passengers themselves; for this purpose, it prohibits the bringing more than a certain number proportioned to the tonnage of the vessel, and prescribes the kind and quality of provisions, or sea stores, and their quantity, in a certain proportion to the number of the passengers.

Another section requires the master to report to the collector a list of all passengers, designating the age, sex, occupation, the country to which they belong, &c.; which list is required to be delivered to the secretary of state, and which he is directed to lay before congress.

The object of this clause, in all probability, was to enable the government of the United States to form an accurate estimate of the increase of population by emigration; but whatsoever may have been its purpose, it is obvious that these laws only affect, through the power over navigation, the passengers whilst on their voyage, and until they shall have landed. After that, and when they have ceased to have any connection with the ship, and when, therefore, they have ceased to be passengers, we are satisfied that acts of congress, applying to them as such, and only professing to legislate in relation to them as such, have then performed their office, and can, with no propriety of language, be said to come into conflict with the law of a State, whose operation only begins when that of the laws of congress ends; whose operation is not even on the same subject, because, although the person on whom it operates is the same, yet, having ceased to be a passenger, he no longer stands in the only relation in which the laws of congress either professed or intended to act upon him.

There is, then, no collision between the law in question and the acts of congress just commented on; and, therefore, if the state law were to be considered as partaking of the nature of a commercial regulation, it would stand the test of the most rigid scrutiny, if tried by the standard laid down in the reasoning of the court, quoted from the case of Gibbons v. Ogden.

But we do not place our opinion on this ground. We choose rather to plant ourselves on what we consider impregnable positions. They are these: That a State has the same undeniable and unlimited jurisdiction over all persons and things within its territorial limits, as any foreign nation, where that jurisdiction is not surrendered or restrained by the constitution of the United States. That, by virtue of this, it is not only the right, but the bounden and solemn duty of a State to advance the safety, happiness, and prosperity of its people, and to provide for its general welfare, by any and every act of legislation, which it may deem to be conducive to these ends, where the power over the particular subject, or the manner of its exercise, is not surrendered or restrained, in the manner just stated. That all those powers which relate to merely municipal legislation, or what may, perhaps, more properly be called internal police, are not thus surrendered or restrained; and that, consequently, in relation to these, the authority of a State is complete, unqualified, and exclusive. . . .

Now, in relation to the section in the act immediately before us, that is obviously passed with a view to prevent her citizens from being oppressed by the support of multitudes of poor persons, who come from foreign countries without possessing the means of supporting themselves. There can be no mode in which the power to regulate internal police could be more appropriately exercised. New York, from her particular situation, is, perhaps, more than any other city in the Union, exposed to the evil of thousands of foreign emigrants arriving there, and the consequent danger of her citizens being subjected to a heavy charge in the maintenance of those who are poor. It is the duty of the State to protect its citizens from this evil; they have endeavored to do so, by passing, amongst other things, the section of the law in question. We should, upon principle, say that it had a right to do so. . . .

We think it as competent and as necessary for a State to provide precautionary measures against the moral pestilence of paupers, vagabonds, and possibly convicts, as it is to guard against the physical pestilence which may arise from unsound and infectious articles imported, or from a ship, the crew of which may be laboring under an infectious disease. . . .

We are therefore of opinion . . . that so much of the section of the act of the legislature of New York, as applies to the breaches assigned in the declaration, does not assume to regulate commerce between the port of New York and foreign ports, and that so much of said section is constitutional. . . .

The Passenger Cases

By 1849 the justices were still split over the problem of concurrent regulation of commerce. The Passenger Cases involved head taxes levied on passengers arriving in New York and Massachusetts ports. The states alleged that the taxes were not designed to regulate immigration, but only to raise money for the support and care of foreign paupers. Numerous federal laws and treaties concerning immigration existed at the time. The Court divided 5–4, holding the laws invalid as an interference with federal power. All majority justices wrote separate opinions, and three of the four dissenters contributed their own opinions. Justice McLean spoke for the more nationalistic wing of the Court, while Chief Justice Taney advanced the most lucid concurrent power arguments.

Justice McLean

I will consider the case under two general heads: —
    1. Is the power of congress to regulate commerce an exclusive power?
    2. Is the statute of New York a regulation of commerce? . . .

A concurrent power in the States to regulate commerce is an anomaly not found in the constitution. If such power exists, it may be exercised independently of the federal authority.

It does not follow, as is often said, with little accuracy, that, when a state law shall conflict with an act of congress, the former must yield. On the contrary, except in certain cases named in the federal constitution, this is never correct when the act of the State is strictly within its powers. . . .

A concurrent power excludes the idea of a dependent power. The general government and a State exercise concurrent powers in taxing the people of the State. The objects of taxation may be the same, but the motives and policy of the tax are different, and the powers are distinct and independent. A concurrent power in two distinct sovereignties, to regulate the same thing, is as inconsistent in principle as it is impracticable in action. It involves a moral and physical impossibility. A joint action is not supposed, and two independent wills cannot do the same thing. The action of one, unless there be an arrangement, must necessarily

7 Howard 283 (1849)

130

precede the action of the other; and that which is first, being competent, must establish the rule. If the powers be equal, as must be the case, both being sovereign, one may undo what the other does, and this must be the result of their action.

But the argument is, that a State, acting in a subordinate capacity, wholly inconsistent with its sovereignty, may regulate foreign commerce until congress shall act on the same subject, and that the State must then yield to the paramount authority. A jealousy of the federal powers has often been expressed, and an apprehension entertained that they would impair the sovereignty of the States. But this argument degrades the States by making their legislation, to the extent stated, subject to the will of congress. State powers do not rest upon this basis. Congress can in no respect restrict or enlarge state powers, though they may adopt a state law. State powers are, at all times and under all circumstances, exercised independently of the general government, and are never declared void or inoperative except when they transcend state jurisdiction. And, on the same principle, the federal authority is void when exercised beyond its constitutional limits. . . .

It has been well remarked that the regulation of commerce consists as much in negative as in positive action. There is not a federal power which has been exerted in all its diversified means of operation. And yet it may have been exercised by congress, influenced by a judicious policy and the instruction of the people. Is a commercial regulation open to state action because the federal power has not been exhausted? No ingenuity can provide for every contingency; and if it could, it might not be wise to do so. Shall free goods be taxed by a State because congress have not taxed them? Or shall a State increase the duty, on the ground that it is too low? Shall passengers, admitted by act of congress without a tax, be taxed by a State? The supposition of such a power in a State is utterly inconsistent with a commercial power, either paramount or exclusive, in congress.

That it is inconsistent with the exclusive power will be admitted; but the exercise of a subordinate commercial power by a State is contended for. When this power is exercised, how can it be known that the identical thing has not been duly considered by congress? And how can congress, by any legislation, prevent this interference? A practical enforcement of this system, if system it may be called, would overthrow the federal commercial power. . . .

I come now to inquire, under the second general proposition, Is the statute of New York a regulation of foreign commerce? . . .

Commerce is defined to be "an exchange of commodities." But this definition does not convey the full meaning of the term. It includes "navigation and intercourse." That the transportation of passengers is a part of commerce, is not now an open question. . . .

Except to guard its citizens against diseases and paupers, the municipal power of a State cannot prohibit the introduction of foreigners brought to this country under the authority of congress. . . .

The police power of the State cannot draw within its jurisdiction objects which lie beyond it. It meets the commercial power of the Union in dealing with subjects under the protection of that power, yet it can only be exerted under peculiar emergencies, and to a limited extent. In guarding the safety, the health, and morals of its citizens, a State is restricted to appropriate and constitutional means. If extraordinary expense be incurred, an equitable claim to an indemnity can give no power to a State to tax objects not subject to its jurisdiction. . . .

A tax or duty upon tonnage, merchandise, or passengers is a regulation of commerce, and cannot be laid by a State, except under the sanction of congress and for the purposes specified in the constitution. On the subject of foreign commerce, including the transportation of passengers, congress have adopted such regulations as they deemed proper, taking into view our relations with other countries. And this covers the whole ground. The act of New York which imposes a tax on passengers of a ship from a foreign port, in the manner provided, is a regulation of foreign commerce, which is exclusively vested in congress; and the act is, therefore, void. . . .

Chief Justice Taney dissenting.

[T]he first inquiry is, whether, under the constitution of the United States, the federal government has the power to compel the several States to receive, and suffer to remain in association with its citizens, every person or class of persons whom it may be the policy or pleasure of the United States to admit. In my judgment, this question lies at the foundation of the controversy in this case. I do not mean to say that the general government have, by treaty or act of congress, required the State of Massachusetts to permit the aliens in question to land. I think there is no treaty or act of congress which can justly be so construed. But it is not necessary to examine that question until we have first inquired whether congress can lawfully exercise such a power, and whether the States are bound to submit to it. For if the people of the several States of this Union reserved to themselves the power of expelling from their borders any person, or class of persons, whom it might deem dangerous to its peace, or likely to produce a physical or moral evil among its citizens, then any treaty or law of congress invading this right, and authorizing the introduction of any person or description of persons against the consent of the State, would be an usurpation of power which this court could neither recognize nor enforce. . . .

[I]t is equally clear, that, if it may remove from among its citizens any person or description of persons whom it regards as injurious to their welfare, it follows that it may meet them at the threshold and prevent them from entering. . . .

Neither can this be a concurrent power, and whether it belongs to the general or to the state government, the sovereignty which possesses the right must in its exercise be altogether independent of the other. If the United States have the power, then any legislation by the State in conflict with a treaty or act of congress would be void. And if the States possess it, then any act on the subject by the general government, in conflict with the state law, would also be void, and this court bound to disregard it. It must be paramount and absolute in the sovereignty which possesses it. A concurrent and equal power in the United States and the States, as to who should and who should not be permitted to reside in a State, would be a direct conflict of powers repugnant to each other, continually thwarting and defeating its exercise by either, and could result in nothing but disorder and confusion.

Again: if the State has the right to exclude from its borders any person or persons whom it may regard as dangerous to the safety of its citizens, it must necessarily have the right to decide when and towards whom this power is to be exercised. It is in its nature a discretionary power, to be exercised according to the judgment of the party which possesses it. And it must, therefore, rest with the State to determine whether any particular class or description of persons are likely to produce discontents or insurrection in its territory, or to taint the morals of its citizens, or to bring among them contagious diseases, or the evils and burdens of a numerous pauper population. For if the general government can in any respect, or by any form of legislation, control or restrain a State in the exercise of this power, or decide whether it has been exercised with proper discretion, and towards proper persons, and on proper occasions, then the real and substantial power would be in congress, and not in the States. In the cases decided in this court, and herein before referred to, the power of determining who is or who is not dangerous to the interests and well-being of the people of the State has been uniformly admitted to reside in the State. . . .

Most evidently, this court cannot supervise the exercise of such a power by the State, nor control or regulate it, nor determine whether the occasion called for it, nor whether the funds raised have been properly administered. This would be substituting the discretion of the court for the discretionary power reserved to the State. . . .

Undoubtedly, vessels engaged in the transportation of passengers from foreign countries, may be regulated by congress, and are a part of the commerce of the country. Congress may prescribe how the vessel shall be manned, and navigated, and equipped, and how many passengers she may bring, and what provision shall be made for them, and what tonnage she shall pay. But the law of Massachusetts now in question does not in any respect attempt to regulate this trade, or impose burdens upon it. I do not speak of the duty enjoined upon the pilot, because that provision is not now before us, although I see no objection to it. But this law imposes no tonnage duty on the ship, or any tax upon the captain or passengers for entering its waters. It merely refuses permission to the passengers to land until the security demanded by the State for the protection of its own people from the evils of pauperism has been given. If, however, the treaty or act of congress above referred to had attempted to compel the State to receive them without any security, the question would not be on any conflicting regulations of commerce, but upon one far more important to the States, that is, the power of deciding who should or should not be permitted to reside among its citizens. Upon that subject I have already stated my opinion. I cannot believe that it was ever intended to vest in congress, by the general words in relation to the regulation of commerce, this overwhelming power over the States. For if the treaty stipulation before referred to, can receive the construction given to it in the argument, and has that commanding power claimed for it over the States, then the emancipated slaves of the West Indies have at this hour the absolute right to reside, hire houses, and traffic and trade throughout the southern States, in spite of any state law to the contrary; inevitably producing the most serious discontent, and ultimately leading to the most painful consequences. . . .

I may, therefore, safely assume, that, according to the true construction of the constitution, the power granted to congress to regulate commerce, did not in any degree abridge the power of taxation in the States; and that they would at this day have the right to tax the merchandise brought into their ports and harbors by the authority and under the regulations of congress, had they not been expressly prohibited. . . .

Cooley

v.

Board of Wardens of the Port of Philadelphia

In 1851, the Taney Court finally offered a viable doctrine to settle some cases involving concurrent authority. The Cooley case concerned state pilotage regulations enacted in 1803 for the port of Philadelphia. An earlier federal statute had provided that the states might continue their individual regulations until such time as Congress might act. Cooley challenged the 1803 state act as an interference with foreign commerce over which Congress had exclusive jurisdiction. But Congress's own position gave the Court a convenient means for allowing local diversity, or "selective exclusiveness," as the doctrine has come to be called. The Court first rejected contentions that the law was invalid as a duty on imports, exports, or tonnage, or constituted a preference to a port.

Justice Curtis delivered the opinion of the Court.

I t remains to consider the objection, that it [the 1803 state law] is repugnant to the third clause of the eighth section of the first article [of the Constitution]: "The congress shall have power to regulate commerce with foreign nations and among the several States, and with the Indian tribes."

That the power to regulate commerce includes the regulation of navigation, we consider settled. And when we look to the nature of the service performed by pilots, to the relations which that service and its compensations bear to navigation between the several States, and between the ports of the United States and foreign countries, we are brought to the conclusion, that the regulation of the qualifications of pilots, of the modes and times of offering and rendering their services, of the responsibilities which shall rest upon them, of the powers they shall possess, of the compensation they may demand, and of the penalties by which their rights and duties may be enforced, do constitute regulations of navigation, and consequently of commerce, within the just meaning of this clause of the constitution. . . .

The act of 1789 . . . contains a clear legislative exposition of the constitution by the first congress, to the effect that the power to regulate pilots was conferred on congress by the constitution; as does also the act of March the 2d, 1837. . . . The weight to be allowed to this contemporaneous construction, and the practice of congress under it, has, in another connection, been adverted to. And a majority of the court are of opinion, that a regulation of pilots is a regulation of commerce, within the grant to congress of the commercial power, contained in the third clause of the eighth section of the first article of the constitution.

It becomes necessary, therefore, to consider whether this law of Pennsylvania, being a regulation of commerce, is valid.

The act of congress of the 7th of August, 1789, § 4, is as follows: —

"That all pilots in the bays, inlets, rivers, harbors, and ports of the United States shall continue to be regulated in conformity with the existing laws of the States, respectively, wherein such pilots may be, or with such laws as the States may respectively hereafter enact for the purpose, until further legislative provision shall be made by congress."

If the law of Pennsylvania, now in question, had been in existence at the date of this act of congress, we might hold it to have been adopted by congress, and thus made a law of the United States, and so valid. Because this act does, in effect, give the force of an act of congress, to the then existing state laws on this subject, so long as they should continue unrepealed by the State which enacted them.

But the law on which these actions are founded, was not enacted till 1803. What effect then can be attributed to so much of the act of 1789, as declares, that pilots shall continue to be regulated in conformity, "with such laws as the States may respectively hereafter enact for the purpose, until further legislative provision shall be made by congress?"

If the States were divested of the power to legislate on this subject by the grant of the commercial power to congress, it is plain this act could not confer upon them power thus to legislate. If the constitution excluded the States from making any law regulating commerce, certainly congress cannot regrant, or in any manner reconvey to the States that power. And yet this act of 1789 gives its sanction only to laws enacted by the States. This necessarily implies a constitutional power to legislate; for only a rule created by the sovereign power of a State acting in its legislative capacity, can be deemed a law, enacted by a State; and if the State has so limited its sovereign power that it no longer extends to a particular subject, manifestly it cannot, in any proper sense, be said to enact laws thereon. Entertaining these views, we are brought directly and unavoidably to the consideration of the question, whether the grant of the commercial power to congress, did *per se* deprive the States of all power to regulate pilots. This question has never been decided by this court, nor, in our judgment, has any case depending upon all the considerations which must govern this one, come before this court. The grant of commercial power to congress does not contain any terms which expressly exclude the States from exercising an authority over its subject-matter. If they are excluded, it must be because the nature of the power, thus granted to congress, requires that a similar authority should not exist in the States. If it were conceded on the one side, that the nature of this power, like that to legislate for the District of Columbia, is absolutely and totally repugnant to the existence of similar power in the States, probably no one would deny that the grant of the power to congress, as effectually and perfectly excludes the States from all future legislation on the subject, as if express words had been used to exclude them. And on the other hand, if it were admitted that the existence of this power in congress, like the power of taxation, is compatible with the existence of a similar power in the States, then it would be in conformity with the contemporary exposition of the constitution (Federalist, No. 32) and with the judicial construction, given from time to time by this court, after the most deliberate consideration, to hold that the mere grant of such a power to congress, did not imply a prohibition on the States to exercise the same power; that it is not the mere existence of such a power, but its exercise by congress, which may be incompatible with the exercise of the same power by the States, and that the States may legislate in the absence of congressional regulations. . . .

The diversities of opinion, therefore, which have existed on this subject, have arisen from the different views taken of the nature of this power. But when the nature of a power like this is spoken of, when it is said that the nature of the power requires that it should be exercised exclusively by congress, it must be intended to refer to the subjects of that power, and to say they are of such a nature as to require exclusive legislation by congress. Now, the power to regulate commerce, embraces a vast field, containing not only many, but exceedingly various subjects, quite unlike in their nature; some imperatively demanding a single uniform rule, operating equally on the commerce of the United States in every port; and some, like the subject now in question, as imperatively demanding that diversity, which alone can meet the local necessities of navigation.

Either absolutely to affirm, or deny that the nature of this power requires exclusive legislation by congress, is to lose sight of the nature of the subjects of this power, and to assert concerning all of them, what is really applicable but to a part. Whatever subjects of this power are in their nature national, or admit only of one uniform system, a plan of regulation, may justly be said to be of such a nature as to require exclusive legislation by congress. That this cannot be affirmed of laws for the regulation of pilots and pilotage, is plain. The act of 1789 contains a clear and authoritative declaration by the first congress, that the nature of this subject is such, that until congress should find it necessary to exert its power, it should be left to the legislation of the States; that it is local and not national; that it is likely to be the best provided for, not by one system, or plan of regulations, but by as many as the legislative discretion of the several States should deem applicable to the local peculiarities of the ports within their limits.

Viewed in this light, so much of this act of 1789, as declares that pilots shall continue to be regulated "by such laws as the States may respectively hereafter enact for that purpose," instead of being held to be inoperative, as an attempt to confer on the States a power to legislate, of which the constitution had deprived them, is allowed an appropriate and important signification. It manifests the understanding of congress, at the outset of the government, that the nature of this subject is not such as to require its exclusive legislation. The practice of the States, and of the national government, has been in conformity with this declaration, from the origin of the national government to this time; and the nature of the subject when examined, is such as to leave no doubt of the superior fitness and propriety, not to say the absolute necessity, of different systems of regulation, drawn from local knowledge and experience, and conformed to local wants. How, then, can we say, that by the mere grant of power to regulate commerce, the States are deprived of all the power to legislate on this subject, because from the nature of the power the legislation of congress must be exclusive. . . .

It is the opinion of a majority of the court that the mere grant to congress of the power to regulate commerce, did not deprive the States of power to regulate pilots, and that although congress has legislated on this subject, its legislation manifests an intention, with a single exception, not to regulate this subject, but to leave its regulation to the several States. To these precise questions, which are all we are called on to decide, this opinion must be understood to be confined. It does not extend to the question what other subjects, under the commercial power, are within the exclusive control of congress, or may be regulated by the States in the absence of all congressional legislation; nor to the general questions, how far any regulation of a subject by congress, may be deemed to operate as an exclusion of all legislation by the States upon the same subject. We decide the precise questions before us, upon what we deem sound principles, applicable to this particular subject in the State in which the legislation of congress has left it. We go no further. . . .

* D *

Corporations

(handwritten: have either state regulation or none)

Bank of Augusta *v.* Earle

The corporate form of business has periodically aroused great fears and animosity. In the 1830's corporations were denounced as "soulless monsters," yet they grew apace. Particular questions were raised concerning their growing interstate activities and the rights of states to regulate them. This case resulted from Alabama's attempt to exclude out-of-state banks from doing business in the state, after it had assumed ownership of all the banks within the state. The Court divided three ways. The extreme states'-rights advocates held that this was a valid regulation. Others, assuming the importance of the national market believed that such a course would be disastrous to business enterprise. Taney and a majority, however, found a viable middle way which allowed for interstate corporate activity, but approved of the state's right to regulate corporations doing business within its own borders.

Chief Justice Taney delivered the opinion of the Court.

It will at once be seen that the questions brought here for decision are of a very grave character, and they have received from the court an attentive examination. A multitude of corporations for various purposes have been chartered by the several States; a large portion of certain branches of business has been transacted by incorporated companies, or through their agency; and contracts to a very great amount have undoubtedly been made by different corporations out of the jurisdiction of the particular State by which they were created. In deciding the case before us, we in effect determine whether these numerous contracts are valid or not. And if, as has been argued at the bar, a corporation, from its nature and character, is incapable of making such contracts, or if they are inconsistent with the rights and sovereignty of the States in which they are made, they cannot be enforced in the courts of justice. . . .

(handwritten margin note: ISSUES)

But it has been urged in the argument, that notwithstanding the powers thus conferred by the terms of the charter, a corporation, from the very nature of its being, can have no authority to contract out of the limits of the State; that the laws of a State can have no extra-territorial operation; and that, as a corporation is the mere creature of a law of the State, it can have no existence beyond the limits in which that law operates; and that it must necessarily be incapable of making a contract in another place.

It is very true that a corporation can have no legal existence out of the boundaries of the sovereignty by which it is created. It exists only in contemplation of law, and by force of the law; and where that law ceases to operate, and is no longer obligatory, the corporation can have no existence. It must dwell in the place of its creation, and cannot migrate to another sovereignty. But although it must live and have its being in that State only, yet it does not by any means follow that its existence there will not be recognized in other places; and its residence in one State creates no insuperable objection to its power of contracting in another. It is indeed a mere artificial being, invisible and intangible; yet it is a person, for certain purposes in contemplation of law, and has been recognized as such by the decisions of this court. It was so held in the case of The United States *v.* Amedy, 11 Wheat. 412, and in Beaston *v.* The Farmer's Bank of Delaware, 12 Pet. 135. Now natural persons, through the intervention of agents, are continually making contracts in countries in which they do not reside; and where they are not personally present when the contract is made; and nobody has ever doubted the validity of these agreements. And what greater objection can there be to the capacity of an artificial person, by its agents, to make a contract within the scope of its limited powers, in a sovereignty in which it does not reside; provided such contracts are permitted to be made by them by the laws of the place?

The corporation must no doubt show that the law of its creation gave it authority to make such contracts, through such agents. Yet, as in the case of a natural person, it is not necessary that it should actually exist in the sovereignty in which the contract is made. It is sufficient that its existence as an artificial person, in the State of its creation, is acknowledged and recognized by the law of the nation where the dealing takes place; and that it is permitted by the laws of that place to exercise there the powers with which it is endowed.

Every power, however, of the description of which we are speaking, which a corporation exercises in another State, depends for its validity upon the laws of the sovereignty in which it is exercised; and a corporation can make no valid contract without their sanction, express or implied. . . .

[W]e proceed to inquire whether, by the comity of nations, foreign corporations are permitted to make contracts within their jurisdiction; and we can perceive no sufficient reason for excluding them, when they are not contrary to the known policy of the State, or injurious to its interests. . . .

We think it is well settled, that by the law of comity among nations, a corporation created by one sovereignty is permitted to make contracts in another, and to sue in its courts; and that the same law of comity prevails among the several sovereignties of this Union. The public and well known and long continued usage of trade; the general acquiescence of the States; the particular legislation of some of them, as well as the legislation of congress; all concur in proving the truth of this proposition.

But we have already said that this comity is presumed from the silent acquiescence of the State. Whenever a State sufficiently indicates that contracts which derive their validity from its comity are repugnant to its policy, or are considered as injurious to its interests; the presumption in favor of its adoption can no longer be made. . . .

Louisville, Cincinnati, and Charlestown Railroad Co.

v.

Letson

Throughout the nineteenth century, corporations steadily fought to gain federal court jurisdiction for their litigation because of the widespread hostility of state courts toward the claims of foreign corporations. But in 1806, the Supreme Court had held in Straw-bridge v. Curtiss that federal courts could have jurisdiction only when all the stockholders of a corporation were citizens of states different from the state of the other litigants (3 Cranch 267). As corporations grew in size, with their stockholders scattered throughout the nation, the Strawbridge ruling proved an almost insurmountable barrier to federal jurisdiction. The Letson case in 1844 gave the Taney Court an opportunity to reconsider that holding in the light of the expansion of the corporation and interstate business. The controversy involved the right of a New York citizen to sue a South Carolina corporation, in which stock was held by the state and persons from a number of states.

Justice Wayne delivered the opinion of the Court.

The jurisdiction of the court is denied in this case upon the grounds that two members of the corporation sued are citizens of North Carolina; that the State of South Carolina is also a member, and that two other corporations in South Carolina are members, having in them members who are citizens of the same State with the defendant in error. . . .

The objection is equivalent to this proposition, that a corporation in a State cannot be sued in the circuit courts of the United States, by a citizen of another State, unless all the members of the corporation are citizens of the State in which the suit is brought. . . .

A suit brought by a citizen of one State against a corporation by its corporate name, in the State of its locality, by which it was created, and where its business is done by any of the corporators who are chosen to manage its affairs, is a suit, so far as jurisdiction is concerned, between citizens of the State where the suit is brought and a citizen of another State. The corporators, as individuals, are not defendants in the suit, but they are parties having an interest in the result, and some of them

2 Howard 497 (1844)

142

being citizens of the State where the suit is brought, jurisdiction attaches over the corporation; nor can we see how it can be defeated by some of the members, who cannot be sued, residing in a different State. It may be said that the suit is against the corporation, and that nothing must be looked at but the legal entity, and then that we cannot view the members except as an artificial aggregate. This is so, in respect to the subject-matter of the suit and the judgment which may be rendered; but if it be right to look to the members to ascertain whether there be jurisdiction or not, the want of appropriate citizenship in some of them to sustain jurisdiction, cannot take it away, when there are other members who are citizens, with the necessary residence to maintain it.

But we are now met and told that the cases of Strawbridge and Curtis, 3 Cranch, 267, and that of The Bank of the United States and Deveaux, 5 Cranch, 84, hold a different doctrine.

We do not deny that the language of those decisions do not justify in some degree the inferences which have been made from them, or that the effect of them has been to limit the jurisdiction of the circuit courts in practice to the cases contended for by the counsel for the plaintiff in error. The practice has been, since those cases were decided, that if there be two or more plaintiffs and two or more joint defendants, each of the plaintiffs must be capable of suing each of the defendants in the courts of the United States in order to support the jurisdiction, and in cases of corporation to limit jurisdiction to cases in which all the corporators were citizens of the State in which the suit is brought. The case of Strawbridge and Curtis was decided without argument. That of the Bank and Deveaux, after argument of great ability. But never since that case has the question been presented to this court, with the really distinguished ability of the arguments of the counsel in this, in no way surpassed by those in the former. And now we are called upon in the most imposing way to give our best judgments to the subject, yielding to decided cases every thing that can be claimed for them on the score of authority, except the surrender of conscience.

After mature deliberation, we feel free to say, that the cases of Strawbridge and Curtis, and that of the Bank and Deveaux, were carried too far, and that consequences and inferences have been argumentatively drawn from the reasoning employed in the latter which ought not to be followed. . . . A corporation, created by a State, to perform its functions under the authority of that State, and only suable there, though it may have members out of the State, seems to us to be a person, though an artificial one, inhabiting and belonging to that State, and therefore entitled, for the purpose of suing and being sued, to be deemed a citizen of that State. We remark, too, that the cases of Strawbridge and Curtis, and the Bank and Deveaux, have never been satisfactory to the bar, and that they were not, especially the last, entirely satisfactory to the court that made them. They have been followed always most reluctantly and with dissatisfaction. By no one was the correctness of them more questioned than by the late chief justice who gave them. It is within the knowledge of several of us, that he repeatedly expressed regret that those decisions had been made, adding, whenever the subject was mentioned, that if the point of jurisdiction was an original one, the conclusion would be different. We think we may safely assert, that a majority of the members of this court have at all times partaken of the same regret, and that, whenever a case has occurred on the circuit, involving the application of the case of the Bank and Deveaux, it was yielded to, because the decision had been made, and not because it was thought to be right. We have already said that the case of The Bank of Vicksburgh and Slocomb, 14 Pet. 60, was most reluctantly given, upon mere authority. We are now called upon, upon the authority of those cases alone, to go further in this case than has yet been done. It has led to a review of the principles of all the cases. We cannot follow further, and upon our maturest deliberation we do not think that the cases relied upon for a doctrine contrary to that which this court will here announce, are sustained by a sound and comprehensive course of professional reasoning. Fortunately, a departure from them involves no change in a rule of property. Our conclusion, too, if it shall not have universal acquiescence, will be admitted by all to be coincident with the policy of the constitution and the condition of our country. It is coincident also with the recent legislation of congress, as that is shown by the act of the 28th of February, 1839, in amendment of the acts respecting the judicial system of the United States. We do not hesitate to say, that it was passed exclusively with an intent to rid the courts of the decision in the case of Strawbridge and Curtis. . . .

Our conclusion makes it unnecessary for us to consider that averment in the plea which denies jurisdiction on the ground that citizens of the same State with the plaintiff, are members of corporations in South Carolina, which are members of The Louisville, Cincinnati, and Charleston Railroad Company.

The judgment of the circuit court below is affirmed.

Prigg *v.* Pennsylvania

Article IV, Section 2 of the Constitution provided for the return of fugitive slaves. In 1793, Congress implemented this provision and spelled out certain procedures for recovery. But in the next century, growing abolitionist pressures in the northern states resulted in the so-called "personal liberty" laws which thrust the burden of proof upon the masters. Hostile local magistrates increasingly rejected the proof offered by slaveowners. The Prigg case was a collusive one challenging such a Pennsylvania statute. In his usual nationalistic vein, Justice Story spoke for a majority this time and held that the federal government had preempted the subject of fugitive slaves, and the states were forbidden to legislate on it. But he also suggested that state officers were not required to enforce the federal laws. Taney led the alert southerners in dissenting from this part of the Court's opinion.

Justice Story delivered the opinion of the Court.

There are two clauses in the constitution upon the subject of fugitives, which stand in juxtaposition with each other, and have been thought mutually to illustrate each other. They are both contained in the 2d section of the 4th article, and are in the following words:

A person charged in any State with treason, felony, or other crime, who shall flee from justice, and be found in another State, shall, on demand of the executive authority of the State from which he fled, be delivered up, to be removed to the State having jurisdiction of the crime.

No person held to service or labor in one State under the laws thereof, escaping into another, shall in consequence of any law or regulation therein, be discharged from such service or labor; but shall be delivered up, on claim of the party to whom such service or labor may be due.

The last clause is that, the true interpretation whereof is directly in judgment before us. Historically, it is well known that the object of this clause was to secure to the citizens of the slaveholding States the complete right and title of ownership in their slaves, as property, in every State in the Union into which they might escape from the State where they were held in servitude. The full recognition of this right and title was indispensable to the security of this species of property in all the slaveholding States; and, indeed, was so vital to the preservation of their domestic interests and institutions, that it cannot be doubted that it constituted a fundamental article, without the adoption of which the Union could not have been formed. . . .

[U]nder and in virtue of the constitution, the owner of a slave is clothed with entire authority, in every State in the Union, to seize and recapture his slave, whenever he can do it without any breach of the peace or any illegal violence. In this sense, and to this extent this clause of the constitution may properly be said to execute itself, and to require no aid from legislation, State or national. . . .

If, indeed, the constitution guarantees the right, and if it requires the delivery upon the claim of the owner, (as cannot well be doubted,) the natural inference certainly is, that the national government is clothed with the appropriate authority and functions to enforce it. The fundamental principle, applicable to all cases of this sort, would seem to be, that where the end is required, the means are given; and where the duty is enjoined, the ability to perform it is contemplated to exist on the part of the functionaries to whom it is intrusted. The clause is found in the national constitution, and not in that of any State. It does not point out any state functionaries, or any state action to carry its provisions into effect. The States cannot, therefore, be compelled to enforce them; and it might well be deemed an unconstitutional exercise of the power of interpretation, to insist that the States are bound to provide means to carry into effect the duties of the national government, nowhere delegated or intrusted to them by the constitution. On the contrary, the natural, if not the necessary conclusion is, that the national government, in the absence of all positive provisions to the contrary, is bound, through its own proper departments, legislative, judicial, or executive, as the case may require, to carry into effect all the rights and duties imposed upon it by the constitution. . . .

The remaining question is, whether the power of legislation upon this subject is exclusive in the national government, or concurrent in the States, until it is exercised by congress. In our opinion it is exclusive; and we shall now proceed briefly to state our reasons for that opinion. The doctrine stated by this court, in Sturges v. Crowninshield, 4 Wheat. 122, 193, contains the true, although not the sole rule or consideration, which is applicable to this particular subject. "Wherever," said Mr. Chief Justice Marshall, in delivering the opinion of the court, "the terms in which a power is granted to congress, or the nature of the power, require that it should be exercised exclusively by congress, the subject is as completely taken from the state legislatures as if they had been forbidden to act." The nature of the power, and the true objects to be attained by it, are then as important to be weighed, in considering the question of its exclusiveness, as the words in which it is granted.

In the first place, it is material to state, (what has been already incidentally hinted at,) that the right to seize and retake fugitive slaves, and the duty to deliver them up, in whatever State of the Union they may be found, and of course the corresponding power in congress to use the appropriate means to enforce the right and duty, derive their whole validity and obligation exclusively from the constitution of the United States, and are there for the first time, recognized and established in that peculiar character. Before the adoption of the constitution, no State had any power whatsoever over the subject, except within its own territorial limits, and could not bind the sovereignty or the legislation of other States. Whenever the right was acknowledged or the duty enforced in any State, it was as a matter of comity and favor, and not as a matter of strict moral, political, or international obligation or duty. . . .

In the next place, the nature of the provision and the objects to be attained by it, require that it should be controlled by one and the same will, and act uniformly by the same system of regulations throughout the Union. If, then, the States have a right, in the absence of legislation by congress, to act upon the subject, each State is at liberty to prescribe just such regulations as suit its own policy, local convenience, and local feelings. The legislation of one State may not only be different from, but utterly repugnant to and incompatible with that of another. The time, and mode, and limitation of the remedy, the proofs of the title, and all other incidents applicable thereto, may be prescribed in one State, which are rejected or disclaimed in another. One State may require the owner to sue in one mode, another in a different mode. One State may make a statute of limitations as to the remedy, in its own tribunals, short and summary; another may prolong the period, and yet restrict the proofs. Nay, some States may utterly refuse to act upon the subject at all; and others may refuse to open its courts to any remedies *in rem*, because they would interfere with their own domestic policy, institutions, or habits. The right, therefore, would never, in a practical sense, be the same in all the States. It would have no unity of purpose, or uniformity of operation. The duty might be enforced in some States; retarded or limited in others; and denied, as compulsory in many, if not in all. Consequences like these must have been foreseen as very likely to occur in the nonslaveholding States, where legislation, if not silent on the subject, and purely voluntary, could scarcely be presumed to be favorable to the exercise of the rights of the owner. . . .

To guard, however, against any possible misconstruction of our views, it is proper to state, that we are by no means to be understood in any manner whatsoever to doubt or to interfere with the police power belonging to the States, in virtue of their general sovereignty. That police power extends over all subjects within the territorial limits of the States, and has never been conceded to the United States. It is wholly distinguishable from the right and duty secured by the provision now under consideration, which is exclusively derived from and secured by the constitution of the United States, and owes its whole efficacy thereto. We entertain no doubt whatsoever, that the States, in virtue of their general police power, possess full jurisdiction to arrest and restrain runaway slaves, and remove them from their borders, and otherwise to secure themselves against their depredations and evil example, as they certainly may do in cases of idlers, vagabonds, and paupers. The rights of the owners of fugitive slaves are in no just sense interfered with, or regulated by such a course; and in many cases, the operations of this police power, although designed generally for other purposes, for the protection, safety, and peace of the State, may essentially promote and aid the interests of the owners. But such regulations can never be permitted to interfere with or to obstruct the just rights of the owner to reclaim his slave, derived from the constitution of the United States, or with the remedies prescribed by congress to aid and enforce the same. . . .

Chief Justice Taney

I concur in the opinion pronounced by the court, that the law of Pennsylvania, under which the plaintiff in error was indicted, is unconstitutional and void; and that the judgment against him must be reversed. But as the questions before us arise upon the construction of the constitution of the United States, and as I do not assent to all the principles contained in the opinion just delivered, it is proper to state the points on which I differ. . . .

The opinion of the court maintains that the power over this subject is so exclusively vested in congress, that no State, since the adoption of the constitution, can pass any law in relation to it. In other words, according to the opinion just delivered, the state authorities are prohibited from interfering for the purpose of protecting the right of the master, and aiding him in the recovery of his property. I think the States are not prohibited; and that, on the contrary, it is enjoined upon them, as a duty, to protect and support the owner when he is endeavoring to obtain possession of his property found within their respective territories.

The language used in the constitution does not, in my judgment, justify the construction given to it by the court. It contains no words prohibiting the several states from passing laws to enforce this right. They are in express terms forbidden to make any regulation that shall impair it. But there the prohibition stops. And according to the settled rules of construction for all written instruments, the prohibition being confined to laws injurious to the right, the power to pass laws to support and enforce it, is necessarily implied. And the words of the article which direct that the fugitive "shall be delivered up," seem evidently designed to impose it as a duty upon the people of the several States to pass laws to carry into execution, in good faith, the compact into which they thus solemnly entered with each other. The constitution of the United States, and every article and clause in it, is a part of the law of every State in the Union; and is the paramount law. The right of the master, therefore, to seize his fugitive slave, is the law of each State; and no State has the power to abrogate or alter it. And why may not a State protect a right of property, acknowledged by its own paramount law? Besides, the laws of the different States, in all other cases, constantly protect the citizens of other States in their rights of property, when it is found within their respective territories; and no one doubts their power to do so. And in the absence of any express prohibition, I perceive no reason for establishing, by implication, a different rule in this instance; where, by the national compact, this right of property is recognized as an existing right in every State of the Union. . . .

I dissent therefore, upon these grounds, from that part of the opinion of the court which denies the obligation and the right of the state authorities to protect the master, when he is endeavoring to seize a fugitive from his service, in pursuance of the right given to him by the constitution of the United States; provided the state law is not in conflict with the remedy provided by congress.

Dred Scott *v.* Sandford

The most nagging constitutional question involving slavery con-
cerned the right of the federal government to bar slavery in the
territories. The Missouri Compromise of 1820 tried to settle the
matter by partitioning the Louisiana Purchase area. But a decade
later, the South rigidly adopted the position that the federal gov-
ernment had no right to exclude slavery in any part of the terri-
tories. The argument was based on state sovereignty theories which
contended that the federal government held the territories in trust
for all the states. Although Taney had earlier advanced the idea
that the Court should not intervene in political questions, he and
the other justices nevertheless tried to formulate a definitive con-
stitutional solution to the problem. The Court responded, in large
part, to increasing demands that it resolve what the stalemated
political system could not. Although Taney's opinion is the leading
one, it is difficult to classify it as the "opinion of the Court" for
there was widespread division on most of the issues. Each justice
wrote a separate opinion, and Curtis and McLean dissented from
the pro-southern position of their colleagues. Few Supreme Court
decisions have had more political impact than this one. It at once
legitimated the South's canons for the expansion of slavery, and
it afforded the Republican party the sinister glamour of a Cassan-
dra.

Mr. Chief Justice Taney delivered the opinion of the Court.

The question is simply this: Can a negro, whose ancestors were imported into this country, and sold as slaves, become a member of
the political community formed and brought into existence by the constitution of the United States, and as such become entitled to all the
rights, and privileges, and immunities, guarantied by that instrument to
the citizen? One of which rights is the privilege of suing in a court of
the United States in the cases specified in the constitution.

It will be observed, that the plea applies to that class of persons only
whose ancestors were negroes of the African race, and imported into
this country, and sold and held as slaves. The only matter in issue before
the court, therefore, is, whether the descendants of such slaves, when
they shall be emancipated, or who are born of parents who had become

19 Howard 393 (1857)

free before their birth, are citizens of a State, in the sense in which the word citizen is used in the constitution of the United States. And this being the only matter in dispute on the pleadings, the court must be understood as speaking in this opinion of that class only, that is, of those persons who are the descendants of Africans who were imported into this country, and sold as slaves. . . .

The words "people of the United States" and "citizens" are synonymous terms, and mean the same thing. They both describe the political body who, according to our republican institutions, form the sovereignty, and who hold the power and conduct the government through their representatives. They are what we familiarly call the "sovereign people," and every citizen is one of this people, and a constituent member of this sovereignty. The question before us is, whether the class of persons described in the plea in abatement compose a portion of this people, and are constituent members of this sovereignty? We think they are not, and that they are not included, and were not intended to be included, under the word "citizens" in the constitution, and can therefore claim none of the rights and privileges which that instrument provides for and secures to citizens of the United States. On the contrary, they were at that time considered as a subordinate and inferior class of beings, who had been subjugated by the dominant race, and, whether emancipated or not, yet remained subject to their authority, and had no rights or privileges but such as those who held the power and the government might choose to grant them.

It is not the province of the court to decide upon the justice or injustice, the policy or impolicy, of these laws. The decision of that question belonged to the political or law-making power; to those who formed the sovereignty and framed the constitution. The duty of the court is, to interpret the instrument they have framed, with the best lights we can obtain on the subject, and to administer it as we find it, according to its true intent and meaning when it was adopted.

In discussing this question, we must not confound the rights of citizenship which a State may confer within its own limits, and the rights of citizenship as a member of the Union. It does not by any means follow, because he has all the rights and privileges of a citizen of a State, that he must be a citizen of the United States. He may have all of the rights and privileges of the citizen of a State, and yet not be entitled to the rights and privileges of a citizen in any other State. For, previous to the adoption of the constitution of the United States, every State had the undoubted right to confer on whomsoever it pleased the character of citizen, and to endow him with all its rights. But this character of course was confined to the boundaries of the State, and gave him no rights or privileges in other States beyond those secured to him by the laws of nations and the comity of States. Nor have the several States surrendered the power of conferring these rights and privileges by adopting the constitution of the United States. . . .

It is very clear, therefore, that no State can, by any act or law of its own, passed since the adoption of the constitution, introduce a new member into the political community created by the constitution of the United States. It cannot make him a member of this community by making him a member of its own. And for the same reason it cannot introduce any person, or description of persons, who were not intended to be embraced in this new political family, which the constitution brought into existence, but were intended to be excluded from it.

The question then arises, whether the provisions of the constitution, in relation to the personal rights and privileges to which the citizen of a State should be entitled, embraced the negro African race, at that time in this country, or who might afterwards be imported, who had then or should afterwards be made free in any State; and to put it in the power of a single State to make him a citizen of the United States, and endue him with the full rights of citizenship in every other State without their consent? Does the constitution of the United States act upon him whenever he shall be made free under the laws of a State, and raised there to the rank of a citizen, and immediately clothe him with all the privileges of a citizen in every other State, and in its own courts?

The court think the affirmative of these propositions cannot be maintained. And if it cannot, the plaintiff in error could not be a citizen of the State of Missouri, within the meaning of the constitution of the United States, and, consequently, was not entitled to sue in its courts.

It is true, every person, and every class and description of persons, who were at the time of the adoption of the constitution recognized as citizens in the several States, became also citizens of this new political body; but none other; it was formed by them, and for them and their posterity, but for no one else. And the personal rights and privileges guaranteed to citizens of this new sovereignty were intended to embrace those only who were then members of the several State communities, or who should afterwards by birthright or otherwise become members, according to the provisions of the constitution and the principles on which it was founded. It was the union of those who were at that time members of distinct and separate political communities into one political family, whose power, for certain specified purposes, was to extend over the whole territory of the United States. And it gave to each citizen rights and privileges outside of his State which he did not before possess, and placed him in every other State upon a perfect equality with its own citizens as to rights of person and rights of property; it made him a citizen of the United States. . . .

In the opinion of the court, the legislation and histories of the times, and the language used in the declaration of independence, show, that neither the class of persons who had been imported as slaves, nor their descendants, whether they had become free or not, were then acknowledged as a part of the people, nor intended to be included in the general words used in that memorable instrument. . . .

They had for more than a century before been regarded as beings of an inferior order, and altogether unfit to associate with the white race, either in social or political relations; and so far inferior, that they had no rights which the white man was bound to respect; and that the negro might justly and lawfully be reduced to slavery for his benefit. . . .

The legislation of the different colonies furnishes positive and indisputable proof of this fact. . . .

The language of the declaration of independence is equally conclusive. . . .

But it is too clear for dispute, that the enslaved African race were not intended to be included, and formed no part of the people who framed and adopted this declaration; for if the language, as understood in that day, would embrace them, the conduct of the distinguished men who framed the declaration of independence would have been utterly and flagrantly inconsistent with the principles they asserted; and instead of the sympathy of mankind, to which they so confidently appealed, they would have deserved and received universal rebuke and reprobation. . . .

This state of public opinion had undergone no change when the constitution was adopted, as is equally evident from its provisions and language. . . .

But there are two clauses in the constitution which point directly and specifically to the negro race as a separate class of persons, and show clearly that they were not regarded as a portion of the people or citizens of the government then formed.

One of these clauses reserves to each of the thirteen States the right to import slaves until the year 1808, if it thinks proper. . . . And by the other provision the States pledge themselves to each other to maintain the right of property of the master, by delivering up to him any slave who may have escaped from his service, and be found within their respective territories. . . .

The only two provisions which point to them and include them, treat them as property, and make it the duty of the government to protect it; no other power, in relation to this race, is to be found in the constitution; and as it is a government of special, delegated, powers, no authority beyond these two provisions can be constitutionally exercised. The government of the United States had no right to interfere for any other purpose but that of protecting the rights of the owner, leaving it altogether with the several States to deal with this race, whether emancipated or not, as each State may think justice, humanity, and the interests and safety of society, require. The States evidently intended to reserve this power exclusively to themselves. . . .

[U]pon a full and careful consideration of the subject, the court is of opinion, that, upon the facts stated . . . , Dred Scott was not a citizen of Missouri within the meaning of the constitution of the United States, and not entitled as such to sue in its courts; and, consequently, that the circuit court had no jurisdiction of the case, and that the judgment on the plea in abatement is erroneous. . . .

couldn't sue because he wasn't a citizen

We proceed . . . to inquire whether the facts relied on by the plaintiff entitled him to his freedom. . . .

The act of Congress, upon which the plaintiff relies, declares that slavery and involuntary servitude, except as a punishment for crime, shall be forever prohibited in all that part of the territory ceded by France, under the name of Louisiana, which lies north of thirty-six degrees thirty minutes north latitude and not included within the limits of Missouri. And the difficulty which meets us at the threshold of this part of the inquiry is whether Congress was authorized to pass this law under any of the powers granted to it by the Constitution; for, if the authority is not given by that instrument, it is the duty of this Court to declare it void and inoperative and incapable of conferring freedom upon anyone who is held as a slave under the laws of any one of the states.

The counsel for the plaintiff has laid much stress upon that article in the Constitution which confers on Congress the power "to dispose of and make all needful rules and regulations respecting the territory or other property belonging to the United States"; but, in the judgment of the Court, that provision has no bearing on the present controversy. and the power there given, whatever it may be, is confined, and was intended to be confined, to the territory which at that time belonged to, or was claimed by, the United States and was within their boundaries as settled by the treaty with Great Britain and can have no influence upon a territory afterward acquired from a foreign government. It was a special provision for a known and particular territory, and to meet a present emergency, and nothing more. . . .

We do not mean, however, to question the power of Congress in this respect. The power to expand the territory of the United States by the admission of new states is plainly given; and in the construction of this power by all the departments of the government, it has been held to authorize the acquisition of territory, not fit for admission at the time, but to be admitted as soon as its population and situation would entitle it to admission. It is acquired to become a state and not to be held as a colony and governed by Congress with absolute authority; and, as the propriety of admitting a new state is committed to the sound discretion of Congress, the power to acquire territory for that purpose, to be held by the United States until it is in a suitable condition to become a state upon an equal footing with the other states, must rest upon the same discretion. It is a question for the political department of the government, and not the judicial; and whatever the political department of the government shall recognize as within the limits of the United States, the judicial department is also bound to recognize, and to administer in it the laws of the United States, so far as they apply, and to maintain in the territory the authority and rights of the government, and also the personal rights and rights of property of individual citizens, as secured by the Constitution. All we mean to say on this point is that, as there is no express regulation in the Constitution defining the power which the general government may exercise over the person or property of a citizen in a territory thus acquired, the Court must necessarily look to the provisions and principles of the Constitution, and its distribution of powers, for the rules and principles by which its decision must be governed.

Taking this rule to guide us, it may be safely assumed that citizens of the United States who migrate to a territory belonging to the people of the United States cannot be ruled as mere colonists, dependent upon the will of the general government, and to be governed by any laws it may think proper to impose. The principle upon which our governments rest, and upon which alone they continue to exist, is the union of states, sovereign and independent within their own limits in their internal and domestic concerns, and bound together as one people by a general government, possessing certain enumerated and restricted powers, delegated to it by the people of the several states, and exercising supreme authority within the scope of the powers granted to it, throughout the dominion of the United States. A power, therefore, in the general government to obtain and hold colonies and dependent territories, over which they might legislate without restriction, would be inconsistent with its own existence in its present form. Whatever it acquires, it acquires for the benefit of the people of the several states who created it. It is their trustee acting for them and charged with the duty of promoting the interests of the whole people of the Union in the exercise of the powers specifically granted. . . .

But the power of Congress over the person or property of a citizen can never be a mere discretionary power under our Constitution and form of government. The powers of the government and the rights and privileges of the citizen are regulated and plainly defined by the Constitution itself. And, when the territory becomes a part of the United States, the federal government enters into possession in the character impressed upon it by those who created it. It enters upon it with its powers over the citizen strictly defined and limited by the Constitution, from which it derives its own existence, and by virtue of which alone it continues to exist and act as a government and sovereignty. It has no power of any kind beyond it; and it cannot, when it enters a territory of the United States, put off its character and assume discretionary or despotic powers which the Constitution has denied to it. It cannot create for itself a new character separated from the citizens of the United States and the duties it owes them under the provisions of the Constitution. The territory, being a part of the United States, the government and the citizen both enter it under the authority of the Constitution, with their respective rights defined and marked out; and the federal government can exercise no power over his person or property, beyond what that instrument confers, nor lawfully deny any right which it has reserved. . . .

These powers, and others, in relation to rights of person, which it is not necessary here to enumerate, are, in express and positive terms, denied to the general government; and the rights of private property have been guarded with equal care. Thus the rights of property are united with the rights of person and placed on the same ground by the Fifth Amendment to the Constitution, which provides that no person shall be deprived of life, liberty, and property without due process of law. And an act of Congress which deprives a citizen of the United States of his liberty or property, without due process of law, merely because he came himself or brought his property into a particular territory of the United States, and who had committed no offense against the laws, could hardly be dignified with the name of due process of law. . . .

The powers over person and property of which we speak are not only not granted to Congress but are in express terms denied, and they are forbidden to exercise them. And this prohibition is not confined to the states, but the words are general and extend to the whole territory over which the Constitution gives it power to legislate, including those portions of it remaining under territorial government as well as that covered by states. . . .

It seems, however, to be supposed that there is a difference between property in a slave and other property and that different rules may be applied to it in expounding the Constitution of the United States. And the laws and usages of nations, and the writings of eminent jurists upon the relation of master and slave and their mutual rights and duties, and the powers which governments may exercise over it, have been dwelt upon in the argument.

But, in considering the question before us, it must be borne in mind that there is no law of nations standing between the people of the United States and their government and interfering with their relation to each other. The powers of the government and the rights of the citizen under it are positive and practical regulations plainly written down. The people of the United States have delegated to it certain enumerated powers and forbidden it to exercise others. It has no power over the person or property of a citizen but what the citizens of the United States have granted. And no laws or usages of other nations, or reasoning of statesmen or jurists upon the relations of master and slave, can enlarge the powers of the government or take from the citizens the rights they have reserved. And if the Constitution recognizes the right of property of the master in a slave, and makes no distinction between that description of property and other property owned by a citizen, no tribunal, acting under the authority of the United States, whether it be legislative, executive, or judicial, has a right to draw such a distinction or deny to it the benefit of the provisions and guaranties which have been provided for the protection of private property against the encroachments of the government.

Now, as we have already said in an earlier part of this opinion, upon a different point, the right of property in a slave is distinctly and expressly affirmed in the Constitution. The right to traffic in it, like an ordinary article of merchandise and property, was guaranteed to the citizens of the United States, in every state that might desire it, for twenty years. And the government in express terms is pledged to protect it in all future time if the slave escapes from his owner. That is done in plain words — too plain to be misunderstood. And no word can be found in the Constitution which gives Congress a greater power over slave property or which entitles property of that kind to less protection than property of any other description. The only power conferred is the power coupled with the duty of guarding and protecting the owner in his rights.

Upon these considerations it is the opinion of the Court that the act of Congress which prohibited a citizen from holding and owning property of this kind in the territory of the United States north of the line therein mentioned is not warranted by the Constitution and is therefore void; and that neither Dred Scott himself, nor any of his family, were made free by being carried into this territory; even if they had been carried there by the owner with the intention of becoming a permanent resident. . . .

IV

Civil War,
Reconstruction,
and Racism

War Powers

The Prize Cases

President Lincoln proclaimed a blockade of southern ports one week after the outbreak of the Civil War. Congress confirmed his action the following July. But the legal right to capture ships as prizes existed only during a state of war. The problem thus was whether the conflict was a mere insurrection or a war. The question was complicated by the fact that the Lincoln Administration usually insisted that the rebellion was only an insurrection and denied any legal existence to the so-called Confederate States of America. Yet the Union government found it necessary to assume belligerent rights and responsibilities for itself in order to prevent neutrals from aiding the Confederacy. The Court's decision in the Prize Cases served the immediate convenience of the Union side, but for domestic political reasons, the government continued to treat the conflict as an insurrection. Chief Justice Taney and the other Democrats on the Court, with the exception of Grier, dissented from the decision.

Justice Grier delivered the opinion of the Court.

Had the President a right to institute a blockade of ports in possession of persons in armed rebellion against the government, on the principles of international law, as known and acknowledged among civilized States? . . .

Neutrals have a right to challenge the existence of a blockade *de facto*, and also the authority of the party exercising the right to institute it. They have a right to enter the ports of a friendly nation for the purposes of trade and commerce, but are bound to recognize the rights of a belligerent engaged in actual war, to use this mode of coercion, for the purpose of subduing the enemy.

That a blockade *de facto* actually existed, and was formally declared and notified by the President on the 27th and 30th of April, 1861, is an admitted fact in these cases.

2 Black 635 (1863)

That the President, as the Executive Chief of the Government and Commander-in-Chief of the Army and Navy, was the proper person to make such notification, has not been, and cannot be disputed.

The right of prize and capture has its origin in the *"jus belli,"* and is governed and adjudged under the laws of nations. To legitimate the capture of a neutral vessel or property on the high seas, a war must exist *de facto*, and the neutral must have a knowledge or notice of the intention of one of the parties belligerent to use this mode of coercion against a port, city or territory, in possession of the other.

Let us inquire whether, at the time this blockade was instituted, a state of war existed which would justify a resort to these means of subduing the hostile force.

War has been well defined to be, "That state in which a nation prosecutes its right by force."

The parties belligerent in a public war are independent nations. But it is not necessary, to constitute war, that both parties should be acknowledged as independent nations or sovereign States. A war may exist where one of the belligerents claims sovereign rights as against the other.

Insurrection against a government may or may not culminate in an organized rebellion, but a civil war always begins by insurrection against the lawful authority of the government. A civil war is never solemnly declared; it becomes such by its accidents — the number, power, and organization of the persons who originate and carry it on. When the party in rebellion occupy and hold in a hostile manner a certain portion of territory; have declared their independence; have cast off their allegiance; have organized armies; have commenced hostilities against their former Sovereign, the world acknowledges them as belligerents, and the contest a war. They claim to be in arms to establish their liberty and independence, in order to become a sovereign State, while the sovereign party treats them as insurgents and rebels who owe allegiance, and who should be punished with death for their treason. . . .

As a civil war is never publicly proclaimed, *eo nomine* against insurgents, its actual existence is a fact in our domestic history which the court is bound to notice and to know. . . .

By the Constitution, Congress alone has the power to declare a national or foreign war. It cannot declare war against a State or any number of States, by virtue of any clause in the Constitution. The Constitution confers on the President the whole executive power. He is bound to take care that the laws be faithfully executed. He is Commander-in-Chief of the Army and Navy of the United States, and of the militia of the several States when called into the actual service of the United States. He has no power to initiate or declare a war either against a foreign nation or a domestic State. But by the Acts of Congress . . . he is authorized to call out the militia and use the military and naval forces of the United States in case of invasion by foreign nations, and to suppress insurrection against the government of a State or of the United States.

If a war be made by invasion of a foreign nation, the President is not only authorized but bound to resist force, by force. He does not initiate the war, but is bound to accept the challenge without waiting for any special legislative authority. And whether the hostile party be a foreign invader, or States organized in rebellion, it is none the less a war, although the declaration of it be *"unilateral."* . . .

This greatest of civil wars was not gradually developed by popular commotion, tumultuous assemblies, or local unorganized insurrections. However long may have been its previous conception, it nevertheless sprung forth suddenly from the parent brain, a Minerva in the full panoply of war. The President was bound to meet it in the shape it presented itself, without waiting for Congress to baptize it with a name; and no name given to it by him or them could change the fact.

It is not the less a civil war, with belligerent parties in hostile array, because it may be called an "insurrection" by one side, and the insurgents be considered as rebels or traitors. It is not necessary that the independence of the revolted province or State be acknowledged in order to constitute it a party belligerent in a war according to the law of nations. Foreign nations acknowledge it as war by a declaration of neutrality. The condition of neutrality cannot exist unless there be two belligerent parties. . . .

Whether the President in fulfilling his duties, as Commander-in-Chief, in suppressing an insurrection, has met with such armed hostile resistance, and a civil war of such alarming proportions as will compel him to accord to them the character of belligerents, is a question to be decided by him, and this court must be governed by the decisions and acts of the Political Department of the government to which this power was intrusted. "He must determine what degree of force the crisis demands." The proclamation of blockade is, itself, official and conclusive evidence to the court that a state of war existed which demanded and authorized a recourse to such a measure, under the circumstances peculiar to the case. . . .

If it were necessary to the technical existence of a war, that it should have a legislative sanction, we find it in almost every Act passed at the extraordinary session of the Legislature of 1861, which was wholly employed in enacting laws to enable the government to prosecute the war with vigor and efficiency. And finally, in 1861, we find Congress *"ex majore cautela"* and in anticipation of such astute objections, passing an Act "approving, legalizing and making valid all the acts, proclamations, and orders of the President, &c., as if they had been *issued and done under the previous express authority* and direction of the Congress of the United States." . . .

On this first question, therefore, we are of the opinion that the President had a right, *jure belli*, to institute a blockade of ports in possession of the States in rebellion which neutrals are bound to regard. . . .

Ex Parte Milligan

In 1862, Lincoln issued a proclamation suspending the writ of habeas corpus in certain cases. He announced that henceforth all civilians interfering with conscription, or engaging in any other disloyal activity, would be liable to trial and punishment by military commissions. Congress confirmed the suspension of the writ in March 1863. Milligan was an officer in a Confederate paramilitary organization operating in Indiana during the war. He was arrested along with others for inciting insurrection and giving aid and comfort to the enemy, among other charges. He was tried before a military commission and sentenced to hang. After his conviction, a federal grand jury met and refused to indict him. Lincoln held the executions in abeyance for four months, but his successor approved the death sentences two weeks after assuming office. Milligan then applied for a writ of habeas corpus in the federal courts, charging that he had been unconstitutionally tried by a military tribunal. The Supreme Court unanimously agreed that the presidentially-authorized military commissions were illegal. The Court emphasized that martial law was inapplicable in states where the civil courts were open and functioning. Although the question of congressional power was not before the Court, five of the nine justices held that Congress similarly could not authorize such commissions. Chief Justice Chase led the other justices in dissent on this point.

Justice Davis delivered the opinion of the Court.

During the late wicked Rebellion, the temper of the times did not allow that calmness in deliberation and discussion so necessary to a correct conclusion of a purely judicial question. *Then,* considerations of safety were mingled with the exercise of power; and feelings and interests prevailed which are happily terminated. *Now* that the public

---

safety is assured, this question, as well as all others, can be discussed and decided without passion or the admixture of any element not required to form a legal judgment. We approach the investigation of this case fully sensible of the magnitude of the inquiry and the necessity of full and cautious deliberation. . . .

The controlling question in the case is this: Upon the *facts* stated in Milligan's petition, and the exhibits filed, had the military commission mentioned in it *jurisdiction*, legally, to try and sentence him? Milligan, not a resident of one of the rebellious states, or a prisoner of war, but a citizen of Indiana for twenty years past, and never in the military or naval service, is, while at his home, arrested by the military power of the United States, imprisoned, and, on certain criminal charges preferred against him, tried, convicted, and sentenced to be hanged by a military commission, organized under the direction of the military commander of the military district of Indiana. Had this tribunal the *legal* power and authority to try and punish this man?

No graver question was ever considered by this Court, nor one which more nearly concerns the rights of the whole people; for it is the birthright of every American citizen, when charged with crime, to be tried and punished according to law. The power of punishment is alone through the means which the laws have provided for that purpose, and, if they are ineffectual, there is an immunity from punishment, no matter how great an offender the individual may be, or how much his crimes may have shocked the sense of justice of the country or endangered its safety. By the protection of the law human rights are secured; withdraw that protection, and they are at the mercy of wicked rulers or the clamor of an excited people. If there was law to justify this military trial, it is not our province to interfere; if there was not, it is our duty to declare the nullity of the whole proceedings. The decision of this question does not depend on argument or judicial precedents, numerous and highly illustrative as they are. These precedents inform us of the extent of the struggle to preserve liberty and to relieve those in civil life from military trials. The founders of our government were familiar with the history of that struggle and secured in a written constitution every right which the people had wrested from power during a contest of ages. By that Constitution and the laws authorized by it this question must be determined. The provisions of that instrument on the administration of criminal justice are too plain and direct to leave room for misconstruction or doubt of their true meaning. Those applicable to this case are found in that clause of the original Constitution which says, "That the trial of all crimes, except in case of impeachment, shall be by jury"; and in the fourth, fifth, and sixth articles of the amendments. . . .

The Constitution of the United States is a law for rulers and people, equally in war and in peace, and covers with the shield of its protection all classes of men, at all times, and under all circumstances. No doctrine, involving more pernicious consequences, was ever invented by the wit of man than that any of its provisions can be suspended during any of the great exigencies of government. Such a doctrine leads directly to anarchy or despotism, but the theory of necessity on which it is based is false; for the government, within the Constitution, has all the powers granted to it which are necessary to preserve its existence; as has been happily proved by the result of the great effort to throw off its just authority.

Have any of the rights guaranteed by the Constitution been violated in the case of Milligan? And, if so, what are they?

Every trial involves the exercise of judicial power; and from what source did the military commission that tried him derive their authority? Certainly no part of the judicial power of the country was conferred on them, because the Constitution expressly vests it "in one supreme court and such inferior courts as the Congress may from time to time ordain and establish," and it is not pretended that the commission was a court ordained and established by Congress. They cannot justify on the mandate of the President; because he is controlled by law and has his appropriate sphere of duty, which is to execute, not to make, the laws; and there is "no unwritten criminal code to which resort can be had as a source of jurisdiction."

But it is said that the jurisdiction is complete under the "laws and usages of war."

It can serve no useful purpose to inquire what those laws and usages are, whence they originated, where found, and on whom they operate; they can never be applied to citizens in states which have upheld the authority of the government, and where the courts are open and their process unobstructed. This Court has judicial knowledge that in Indiana the federal authority was always unopposed, and its courts always open to hear criminal accusations and redress grievances; and no usage of war could sanction a military trial there for any offense whatever of a citizen in civil life, in nowise connected with the military service. Congress could grant no such power; and to the honor of our national legislature be it said, it has never been provoked by the state of the country even to attempt its exercise. One of the plainest constitutional provisions was, therefore, infringed when Milligan was tried by a court not ordained and established by Congress and not composed of judges appointed during good behavior. . . .

Another guarantee of freedom was broken when Milligan was denied a trial by jury. . . .

It is claimed that martial law covers with its broad mantle the proceedings of this military commission. The proposition is this: that in a time of war the commander of an armed force (if in his opinion the exigencies of the country demand it, and of which he is to judge) has the power, within the lines of his military district, to suspend all civil rights and their remedies and subject citizens as well as soldiers to the rule of *his will*; and in the exercise of his lawful authority cannot be restrained, except by his superior officer or the President of the United States.

If this position is sound to the extent claimed, then when war exists, foreign or domestic, and the country is subdivided into military departments for mere convenience, the commander of one of them can, if he chooses, within his limits, on the plea of necessity, with the approval of the Executive, substitute military force for and to the exclusion of the laws and punish all persons, as he thinks right and proper, without fixed or certain rules.

The statement of this proposition shows its importance; for, if true, republican government is a failure, and there is an end of liberty regulated by law. Martial law, established on such a basis, destroys every guarantee of the Constitution and effectually renders the "military independent of and superior to the civil power" — the attempt to do which by the king of Great Britain was deemed by our fathers such an offense that they assigned it to the world as one of the causes which impelled them to declare their independence. Civil liberty and this kind of martial law cannot endure together; the antagonism is irreconcilable; and, in the conflict, one or the other must perish.

This nation, as experience has proved, cannot always remain at peace and has no right to expect that it will always have wise and humane rulers, sincerely attached to the principles of the Constitution. Wicked men, ambitious of power, with hatred of liberty and contempt of law, may fill the place once occupied by Washington and Lincoln; and if this right is conceded, and the calamities of war again befall us, the dangers to human liberty are frightful to contemplate. . . . For this, and other equally weighty reasons, [the Founding Fathers] secured the inheritance they had fought to maintain, by incorporating in a written constitution the safeguards which *time* had proved were essential to its preservation. Not one of these safeguards can the President, or Congress, or the Judiciary disturb, except the one concerning the writ of habeas corpus.

It is essential to the safety of every government that, in a great crisis, like the one we have just passed through, there should be a power somewhere of suspending the writ of habeas corpus. In every war there are men of previously good character wicked enough to counsel their fellow-citizens to resist the measures deemed necessary by a good government to sustain its just authority and overthrow its enemies; and their influence may lead to dangerous combinations. In the emergency of the times, an immediate public investigation according to law may not be possible; and yet the peril to the country may be too imminent to suffer such persons to go at large. Unquestionably, there is then an exigency which demands

that the government, if it should see fit in the exercise of a proper discretion to make arrests, should not be required to produce the persons
arrested in answer to a writ of habeas corpus. The Constitution goes no
further. It does not say after a writ of habeas corpus is denied a citizen
that he shall be tried otherwise than by the course of the common law;
if it had intended this result, it was easy by the use of direct words to
have accomplished it. The illustrious men who framed that instrument
were guarding the foundations of civil liberty against the abuses of unlimited power; they were full of wisdom, and the lessons of history informed them that a trial by an established court, assisted by an impartial
jury, was the only sure way of protecting the citizen against oppression
and wrong. Knowing this, they limited the suspension to one great
right and left the rest to remain forever inviolable. But it is insisted that
the safety of the country in time of war demands that this broad claim
for martial law shall be sustained. If this were true, it could be well said
that a country, preserved at the sacrifice of all the cardinal principles of
liberty, is not worth the cost of preservation. Happily, it is not so.

It will be borne in mind that this is not a question of the power to
proclaim martial law, when war exists in a community and the courts
and civil authorities are overthrown. Nor is it a question what rule a
military commander, at the head of his army, can impose on states in
rebellion to cripple their resources and quell the insurrection. The jurisdiction claimed is much more extensive. The necessities of the service,
during the late Rebellion, required that the loyal states should be placed
within the limits of certain military districts and commanders appointed
in them; and, it is urged, that this, in a military sense, constituted them
the theater of military operations; and, as in this case, Indiana had been
and was again threatened with invasion by the enemy, the occasion was
furnished to establish martial law. The conclusion does not follow from
the premises. If armies were collected in Indiana, they were to be employed in another locality, where the laws were obstructed and the national authority disputed. On *her* soil there was no hostile foot; if once
invaded, that invasion was at an end, and with it all pretext for martial
law. Martial law cannot arise from a *threatened* invasion. The necessity
must be actual and present; the invasion real, such as effectually closes
the courts and deposes the civil administration.

It is difficult to see how the *safety* of the country required martial law
in Indiana. If any of her citizens were plotting treason, the power of
arrest could secure them, until the government was prepared for their
trial, when the courts were open and ready to try them. It was as easy
to protect witnesses before a civil as a military tribunal; and as there
could be no wish to convict, except on sufficient legal evidence, surely an
ordained and established court was better able to judge of this than a

military tribunal composed of gentlemen not trained to the profession of the law. . . .

Chief Justice Chase delivered the following opinion.

Four members of the Court, concurring with their brethren in the order heretofore made in this cause, but unable to concur in some important particulars with the opinion which has just been read, think it their duty to make a separate statement of their views of the whole case.

We do not doubt that the Circuit Court for the District of Indiana had jurisdiction of the petition of Milligan for the writ of habeas corpus. . . .

But the opinion which has just been read goes further and, as we understand it, asserts not only that the military commission held in Indiana was not authorized by Congress but that it was not in the power of Congress to authorize it; from which it may be thought to follow that Congress has no power to indemnify the officers who composed the commission against liability in civil courts for acting as members of it.

We cannot agree to this. . . .

Congress has the power not only to raise and support and govern armies but to declare war. It has, therefore, the power to provide by law for carrying on war. This power necessarily extends to all legislation essential to the prosecution of war with vigor and success, except such as interferes with the command of the forces and the conduct of campaigns. That power and duty belong to the President as commander-in-chief. Both these powers are derived from the Constitution, but neither is defined by that instrument. Their extent must be determined by their nature and by the principles of our institutions. . . .

We cannot doubt that, in such a time of public danger, Congress had power, under the Constitution, to provide for the organization of a military commission and for trial by that commission of persons engaged in this conspiracy. The fact that the federal courts were open was regarded by Congress as a sufficient reason for not exercising the power; but that fact could not deprive Congress of the right to exercise it. Those courts might be open and undisturbed in the execution of their functions, and yet wholly incompetent to avert threatened danger, or to punish, with adequate promptitude and certainty, the guilty conspirators. . . .

We have confined ourselves to the question of power. It was for Congress to determine the question of expediency. . . .

Reconstruction

Cummings *v*. Missouri

The Court began the postwar period by boldly invalidating state and federal test oaths. In Ex parte Garland (4 Wallace 333), a companion case to this one, the Court voided a requirement that federal attorneys subscribe to a test oath. Missouri's oath stipulated that all persons living in the state had to swear to support the Constitution and laws of the United States in order to engage in numerous occupations. In addition, such persons had to affirm their past loyalty. Cummings, a Roman Catholic priest, was indicted and convicted for preaching without having taken the oath. The Court divided 5-4, with only Justice Field of the Lincoln appointees supporting the majority position. Field's opinion largely was concerned with the meaning and nature of ex post facto laws. But his remarks on individual freedom anticipated some of his later laissez faire doctrines, particularly the right to pursue a lawful calling without interference by government.

Justice Field delivered the opinion of the Court.

This case comes before us on a writ of error to the Supreme Court of Missouri, and involves a consideration of the test oath imposed by the constitution of that State. The plaintiff in error is a priest of the Roman Catholic Church, and was indicted and convicted in one of the circuit courts of the State of the crime of teaching and preaching as a priest and minister of that religious denomination without having first taken the oath, and was sentenced to pay a fine of five hundred dollars, and to be committed to jail until the same was paid. On appeal to the Supreme Court of the State, the judgment was affirmed. . . .

The oath thus required is, for its severity, without any precedent that we can discover. In the first place, it is retrospective; it embraces all the past from this day; and, if taken years hence, it will also cover all the intervening period. In its retrospective feature we believe it is peculiar

---

4 Wallace 277 (1867)

to this country. In England and France there have been test oaths, but they were always limited to an affirmation of present belief, or present disposition towards the government, and were never exacted with reference to particular instances of past misconduct. In the second place, the oath is directed not merely against overt and visible acts of hostility to the government, but is intended to reach words, desires, and sympathies, also. And, in the third place, it allows no distinction between acts springing from malignant enmity and acts which may have been prompted by charity, or affection, or relationship. If one has ever expressed sympathy with any who were drawn into the Rebellion, even if the recipients of that sympathy were connected by the closest ties of blood, he is as unable to subscribe to the oath as the most active and the most cruel of the rebels, and is equally debarred from the offices of honor or trust, and the positions and employments specified.

But, as it was observed by the learned counsel who appeared on behalf of the State of Missouri, this court cannot decide the case upon the justice or hardship of these provisions. Its duty is to determine whether they are in conflict with the Constitution of the United States. On behalf of Missouri, it is urged that they only prescribe a qualification for holding certain offices, and practising certain callings, and that it is therefore within the power of the State to adopt them. On the other hand, it is contended that they are in conflict with that clause of the Constitution which forbids any State to pass a bill of attainder or an *ex post facto* law. . . .

Qualifications relate to the fitness or capacity of the party for a particular pursuit or profession. . . . It is evident from the nature of the pursuits and professions of the parties, placed under disabilities by the constitution of Missouri, that many of the acts, from the taint of which they must purge themselves, have no possible relation to their fitness for those pursuits and professions. There can be no connection between the fact that Mr. Cummings entered or left the State of Missouri to avoid enrolment or draft in the military service of the United States and his fitness to teach the doctrines or administer the sacraments of his church; nor can a fact of this kind or the expression of words of sympathy with some of the persons drawn into the Rebellion constitute any evidence of the unfitness of the attorney or counsellor to practice his profession, or of the professor to teach the ordinary branches of education, or of the want of business knowledge or business capacity in the manager of a corporation, or in any director or trustee. It is manifest upon the simple statement of many of the acts and of the professions and pursuits, that there is no such relation between them as to render a denial of the commission of the acts at all appropriate as a condition of allowing the exercise of the professions and pursuits. The oath could not, therefore, have been required as a means of ascertaining whether parties were qualified or not for their respective callings or the trusts with which they were charged. It was required in order to reach the person, not the calling. It was exacted, not from any notion that the several acts designated indicated unfitness for the callings, but because it was thought that the several acts deserved punishment, and that for many of them there was no way to inflict punishment except by depriving the parties, who had committed them, of some of the rights and privileges of the citizen.

The disabilities created by the constitution of Missouri must be regarded as penalties — they constitute punishment. . . .

The theory upon which our political institutions rest is, that all men have certain inalienable rights — that among these are life, liberty, and the pursuit of happiness; and that in the pursuit of happiness all avocations, all honors, all positions, are alike open to every one, and that in the protection of these rights all are equal before the law. Any deprivation or suspension of any of these rights for past conduct is punishment, and can be in no otherwise defined. . . .

" 'No State shall pass any bill of attainder, *ex post facto* law, or law impairing the obligation of contracts.' "

A bill of attainder is a legislative act which inflicts punishment without a judicial trial.

If the punishment be less than death, the act is termed a bill of pains and penalties. Within the meaning of the Constitution, bills of attainder include bills of pains and penalties. In these cases the legislative body, in addition to its legitimate functions, exercises the powers and office of judge; it assumes, in the language of the text-books, judicial magistracy; it pronounces upon the guilt of the party, without any of the forms or safeguards of trial; it determines the sufficiency of the proofs produced, whether conformable to the rules of evidence or otherwise; and it fixes the degree of punishment in accordance with its own notions of the enormity of the offence. . . .

If the clauses of the second article of the constitution of Missouri, to which we have referred, had in terms declared that Mr. Cummings was guilty, or should be held guilty, of having been in armed hostility to the United States, or of having entered that State to avoid being enrolled or drafted into the military service of the United States, and, therefore, should be deprived of the right to preach as a priest of the Catholic Church, or to teach in any institution of learning, there could be no question that the clauses would constitute a bill of attainder within the meaning of the Federal Constitution. If these clauses, instead of mentioning his name, had declared that all priests and clergymen within the State of Missouri were guilty of these acts, or should be held guilty of them, and hence be subjected to the like deprivation, the clauses would be equally open to objection. And, further, if these clauses had declared that all such priests and clergymen should be so held guilty, and be thus deprived, provided they did not, by a day designated, do certain specified acts, they would be no less within the inhibition of the Federal Constitution.

In all these cases there would be the legislative enactment creating the deprivation without any of the ordinary forms and guards provided for the security of the citizen in the administration of justice by the established tribunals.

The results which would follow from clauses of the character mentioned do follow from the clauses actually adopted. The difference between the last case supposed and the case actually presented is one of form only, and not of substance. The existing clauses presume the guilt of the priests and clergymen, and adjudge the deprivation of their right to preach or teach unless the presumption be first removed by their expurgatory oath — in other words, they assume the guilt and adjudge the punishment conditionally. The clauses supposed differ only in that they declare the guilt instead of assuming it. . . .

By an *ex post facto* law is meant one which imposes a punishment for an act which was not punishable at the time it was committed; or imposes additional punishment to that then prescribed; or changes the rules of evidence by which less or different testimony is sufficient to convict than was then required. . . .

The clauses in the Missouri constitution, which are the subject of consideration, do not, in terms, define any crimes, or declare that any punishment shall be inflicted, but they produce the same result upon the parties, against whom they are directed, as though the crimes were defined and the punishment was declared. They assume that there are persons in Missouri who are guilty of some of the acts designated. They would have no meaning in the constitution were not such the fact. They are aimed at past acts, and not future acts. They were intended especially to operate upon parties who, in some form or manner, by action or words, directly or indirectly, had aided or countenanced the Rebellion, or sympathized with parties engaged in the Rebellion, or had endeavored to escape the proper responsibilities and duties of a citizen in time of war; and they were intended to operate by depriving such persons of the right to hold certain offices and trusts, and to pursue their ordinary and regular avocations. This deprivation is punishment; nor is it any less so because a way is opened for escape from it by the expurgatory oath. The framers of the constitution of Missouri knew at the time that whole classes of individuals would be unable to take the oath prescribed. To them there is no escape provided; to them the deprivation was intended to be, and is, absolute and perpetual. To make the enjoyment of a right dependent upon an impossible condition is equivalent to an absolute denial of the right under any condition, and such denial, enforced for a past act, is nothing less than punishment imposed for that act. It is a misapplication of terms to call it anything else. . . .

The judgment of the Supreme Court of Missouri must be reversed, and the cause remanded, with directions to enter a judgment reversing the judgment of the Circuit Court, and directing that court to discharge the defendant from imprisonment, and suffer him to depart without day.

The Chief Justice, and Justices Swayne, Davis, and Miller dissented.

Mississippi *v.* Johnson

Once the Republican party committed itself to a program of military reconstruction, the South turned to the Supreme Court for a last-ditch defense. The Milligan decision apparently gave some hope for relief. But that opinion was vague as to reconstruction, and Justice Davis, who wrote it, did not believe that it applied to the reconstruction program. The first court test came a few weeks after passage of the 1867 acts when Mississippi attempted to enjoin the President from executing and enforcing the laws. This was therefore more than a challenge against the constitutionality of the acts; it also was a challenge against the authority, power, and duty of the chief executive. It is revealing that Johnson sent his attorney general to the Court to oppose Mississippi's request. Whatever his opinion of the Reconstruction Acts, Johnson vigorously opposed any infringement on what he regarded as his proper constitutional powers.

Chief Justice Chase delivered the opinion of the Court.

A motion was made, some days since, in behalf of the State of Mississippi, for leave to file a bill in the name of the State, praying this court perpetually to enjoin and restrain Andrew Johnson, President of the United States, and E. O. C. Ord, general commanding in the District of Mississippi and Arkansas, from executing, or in any manner carrying out, certain acts of Congress therein named.

The acts referred to are those of March 2d and March 23d, 1867, commonly known as the Reconstruction Acts.

The Attorney-General objected to the leave asked for, upon the ground that no bill which makes a President a defendant, and seeks an injunction against him to restrain the performance of his duties as President, should be allowed to be filed in this court.

---

4 Wallace 475 (1867)

This point has been fully argued, and we will now dispose of it.

We shall limit our inquiry to the question presented by the objection, without expressing any opinion on the broader issues discussed in argument, whether, in any case, the President of the United States may be required, by the process of this court, to perform a purely ministerial act under a positive law, or may be held amenable, in any case, otherwise than by impeachment for crime.

The single point which requires consideration is this: Can the President be restrained by injunction from carrying into effect an act of Congress alleged to be unconstitutional?

It is assumed by the counsel for the State of Mississippi, that the President, in the execution of the Reconstruction Acts, is required to perform a mere ministerial duty. In this assumption there is, we think, a confounding of the terms ministerial and executive, which are by no means equivalent in import.

A ministerial duty, the performance of which may, in proper cases, be required of the head of a department, by judicial process, is one in respect to which nothing is left to discretion. It is a simple, definite duty, arising under conditions admitted or proved to exist, and imposed by law.

The case of *Marbury* v. *Madison, Secretary of State,* furnishes an illustration. A citizen had been nominated, confirmed, and appointed a justice of the peace for the District of Columbia, and his commission had been made out, signed, and sealed. Nothing remained to be done except delivery, and the duty of delivery was imposed by law on the Secretary of State. It was held that the performance of this duty might be enforced by *mandamus* issuing from a court having jurisdiction. . . .

Very different is the duty of the President in the exercise of the power to see that the laws are faithfully executed, and among these laws the acts named in the bill. By the first of these acts he is required to assign generals to command in the several military districts, and to detail sufficient military force to enable such officers to discharge their duties under the law. By the supplementary act, other duties are imposed on the several commanding generals, and these duties must necessarily be performed under the supervision of the President as commander-in-chief. The duty thus imposed on the President is in no just sense ministerial. It is purely executive and political.

An attempt on the part of the judicial department of the government to enforce the performance of such duties by the President might be justly characterized, in the language of Chief Justice Marshall, as "an absurd and excessive extravagance." . . .

It was admitted in the argument that the application now made to us is without a precedent; and this is of much weight against it. . . .

The fact that no such application was ever before made in any case indicates the general judgment of the profession that no such application should be entertained.

It will hardly be contended that Congress can interpose, in any case, to restrain the enactment of an unconstitutional law; and yet how can the right to judicial interposition to prevent such an enactment, when the purpose is evident and the execution of that purpose certain, be distinguished, in principle, from the right to such interposition against the execution of such a law by the President?

The Congress is the legislative department of the government; the President is the executive department. Neither can be restrained in its action by the judicial department; though the acts of both, when performed, are, in proper cases, subject to its cognizance.

The impropriety of such interference will be clearly seen upon consideration of its possible consequences.

Suppose the bill filed and the injunction prayed for allowed. If the President refuse obedience, it is needless to observe that the court is without power to enforce its process. If, on the other hand, the President complies with the order of the court and refuses to execute the acts of Congress, is it not clear that a collision may occur between the executive and legislative departments of the government? May not the House of Representatives impeach the President for such refusal? And in that case could this court interfere, in behalf of the President, thus endangered by compliance with its mandate, and restrain by injunction the Senate of the United States from sitting as a court of impeachment? Would the strange spectacle be offered to the public world of an attempt by this court to arrest proceedings in that court?

These questions answer themselves.

It is true that a State may file an original bill in this court. And it may be true, in some cases, that such a bill may be filed against the United States. But we are fully satisfied that this court has no jurisdiction of a bill to enjoin the President in the performance of his official duties; and that no such bill ought to be received by us.

It has been suggested that the bill contains a prayer that, if the relief sought cannot be had against Andrew Johnson, as President, it may be granted against Andrew Johnson as a citizen of Tennessee. But it is plain that relief as against the execution of an act of Congress by Andrew Johnson, is relief against its execution by the President. A bill praying an injunction against the execution of an act of Congress by the incumbent of the presidential office cannot be received, whether it describes him as President or as a citizen of a State. . . .

Ex Parte McCardle

After the Court dismissed Mississippi's injunction plea, Georgia filed a bill against Secretary of War Stanton and General Grant. The Court, however, refused to make any distinction between responsibilities of the President or those of his subordinate officers (Georgia v. Stanton, 6 Wallace 50 [1868]). But shortly afterward, the Court agreed to hear a private citizen's plea for a writ of habeas corpus, alleging that he had been unconstitutionally held for trial by a military commission. Convinced that the Court would proceed against the Reconstruction Acts, the congressional Republicans hastily repealed the statute giving the Supreme Court jurisdiction in such cases. The Constitution granted Congress the power to make exceptions and regulations of the Court's appellate jurisdiction as it pleased. The Court acquiesced in 1869 and dismissed McCardle's plea, but Chief Justice Chase's concluding remarks made it clear that the Court still possessed the power to issue writs of habeas corpus. Six months later, in a similar case, the Court accepted jurisdiction on the basis of the Judiciary Act of 1789 (Ex parte Yerger, 8 Wallace 85 [1869]).

Chief Justice Chase delivered the opinion of the Court.

The first question necessarily is that of jurisdiction; for, if the act of March, 1868, takes away the jurisdiction defined by the act of February, 1867, it is useless, if not improper, to enter into any discussion of other questions.

It is quite true, as was argued by the counsel for the petitioner, that the appellate jurisdiction of this court is not derived from acts of Congress. It is, strictly speaking, conferred by the Constitution. But it is conferred "with such exceptions and under such regulations as Congress shall make." . . .

The exception to appellate jurisdiction in the case before us . . . is not an inference from the affirmation of other appellate jurisdiction. It is made in terms. The provision of the act of 1867, affirming the appellate jurisdiction of this court in cases of *habeas corpus* is expressly repealed. It is hardly possible to imagine a plainer instance of positive exception.

We are not at liberty to inquire into the motives of the legislature.

7 Wallace 506 (1869)

We can only examine into its power under the Constitution; and the power to make exceptions to the appellate jurisdiction of this court is given by express words.

What, then, is the effect of the repealing act upon the case before us? We cannot doubt as to this. Without jurisdiction the court cannot proceed at all in any cause. Jurisdiction is power to declare the law, and when it ceases to exist, the only function remaining to the court is that of announcing the fact and dismissing the cause. And this is not less clear upon authority than upon principle.

Several cases were cited by the counsel for the petitioner in support of the position that jurisdiction of this case is not affected by the repealing act. But none of them, in our judgment, afford any support to it. They are all cases of the exercise of judicial power by the legislature, or of legislative interference with courts in the exercising of continuing jurisdiction.

On the other hand, the general rule, supported by the best elementary writers, is, that "when an act of the legislature is repealed, it must be considered, except as to transactions past and closed, as if it never existed." And the effect of repealing acts upon suits under acts repealed, has been determined by the adjudications of this court. . . .

It is quite clear, therefore, that this court cannot proceed to pronounce judgment in this case, for it has no longer jurisdiction of the appeal; and judicial duty is not less fitly performed by declining ungranted jurisdiction than in exercising firmly that which the Constitution and the laws confer.

Counsel seem to have supposed, if effect be given to the repealing act in question, that the whole appellate power of the court, in cases of *habeas corpus,* is denied. But this is an error. The act of 1868 does not except from that jurisdiction any cases but appeals from Circuit Courts under the act of 1867. It does not affect the jurisdiction which was previously exercised. . . .

Texas *v.* White

Texas v. White gave the Court its opportunity to comment on the nature of the Union, secession, and the control of reconstruction policy. The case arose out of an attempt by the postwar Texas state government to recover United States bonds which has been sold by the Confederate state government during the war. Chase's views on reconstruction are often seen as another example of the Court's submissiveness to Congress. But his opinion was consistent with the views of the Lincoln Administration throughout the Civil War, and with the comments he had made as early as 1865. Justices Grier, Swayne, and Miller dissented. Grier discounted Chase's contention that Texas had never really seceded as a legal fiction. "Politically," he wrote, "Texas is not a state in this Union."

Chief Justice Chase delivered the opinion of the Court.

The first inquiries to which our attention was directed by counsel, arose upon the allegations . . . that the State, having severed her relations with a majority of the States of the Union, and having by her ordinance of secession attempted to throw off her allegiance to the Constitution and government of the United States, has so far changed her status as to be disabled from prosecuting suits in the National courts. . . .

If, therefore, it is true that the State of Texas was not at the time of filing this bill, or is not now, one of the United States, we have no jurisdiction of this suit, and it is our duty to dismiss it. . . .

In the Constitution the term state most frequently expresses the combined idea just noticed, of people, territory, and government. A state, in the ordinary sense of the Constitution, is a political community of free citizens, occupying a territory of defined boundaries, and organized under a government sanctioned and limited by a written constitution, and established by the consent of the governed. It is the union of such states, under a common constitution, which forms the distinct and greater political unit, which that Constitution designates as the United States, and makes of the people and states which compose it one people and one country. . . .

The Republic of Texas was admitted into the Union, as a State, on the 27th of December, 1845. By this act the new State, and the people of

7 *Wallace* 700 (1869)

the new State, were invested with all the rights, and became subject to all the responsibilities and duties of the original States under the Constitution.

From the date of admission, until 1861, the State was represented in the Congress of the United States by her senators and representatives, and her relations as a member of the Union remained unimpaired. In that year, acting upon the theory that the rights of a State under the Constitution might be renounced, and her obligations thrown off at pleasure, Texas undertook to sever the bond thus formed, and to break up her constitutional relations with the United States. . . .

The position thus assumed could only be maintained by arms, and Texas accordingly took part, with the other Confederate States, in the war of the rebellion, which these events made inevitable. During the whole of that war there was no governor, or judge, or any other State officer in Texas, who recognized the National authority. Nor was any officer of the United States permitted to exercise any authority whatever under the National government within the limits of the State, except under the immediate protection of the National military forces.

Did Texas, in consequence of these acts, cease to be a State? Or, if not, did the State cease to be a member of the Union?

It is needless to discuss, at length, the question whether the right of a State to withdraw from the Union for any cause, regarded by herself as sufficient, is consistent with the Constitution of the United States.

The Union of the States never was a purely artificial and arbitrary relation. It began among the Colonies, and grew out of common origin, mutual sympathies, kindred principles, similar interests, and geographical relations. It was confirmed and strengthened by the necessities of war, and received definite form, and character, and sanction from the Articles of Confederation. By these the Union was solemnly declared to "be perpetual." And when these Articles were found to be inadequate to the exigencies of the country, the Constitution was ordained "to form a more perfect Union." It is difficult to convey the idea of indissoluble unity more clearly than by these words. What can be indissoluble if a perpetual Union, made more perfect, is not?

But the perpetuity and indissolubility of the Union, by no means implies the loss of distinct and individual existence, or of the right of self-government by the States. Under the Articles of Confederation each State retained its sovereignty, freedom, and independence, and every power, jurisdiction, and right not expressly delegated to the United States. Under the Constitution, though the powers of the States were much restricted, still, all powers not delegated to the United States, nor prohibited to the States, are reserved to the States respectively, or to the people. And we have already had occasion to remark at this term, that "the people of each State compose a State, having its own government, and endowed with all the functions essential to separate and independent existence," and that "without the States in union, there could be no such political body as the United States." Not only, therefore, can there be no loss of separate and independent autonomy to the States, through their union under the Constitution, but it may be not unreasonably said that the preservation of the States, and the maintenance of their governments, are as much within the design and care of the Constitution as the preservation of the Union and the maintenance of the National government. The Constitution, in all its provisions, looks to an indestructible Union, composed of indestructible States.

When, therefore, Texas became one of the United States, she entered into an indissoluble relation. All the obligations of perpetual union, and all the guaranties of republican government in the Union, attached at once to the State. The act which consummated her admission into the Union was something more than a compact; it was the incorporation of a new member into the political body. And it was final. The union between Texas and the other States was as complete, as perpetual, and as indissoluble as the union between the original States. There was no place for reconsideration, or revocation, except through revolution, or through consent of the States.

Considered therefore as transactions under the Constitution, the ordinance of secession, adopted by the convention and ratified by a majority of the citizens of Texas, and all the acts of her legislature intended to give effect to that ordinance, were absolutely null. They were utterly without operation in law. The obligations of the State, as a member of the Union, and of every citizen of the State, as a citizen of the United States, remained perfect and unimpaired. It certainly follows that the State did not cease to be a State, nor her citizens to be citizens of the Union. If this were otherwise, the State must have become foreign, and her citizens foreigners. The war must have ceased to be a war for the suppression of rebellion, and must have become a war for conquest and subjugation.

Our conclusion therefore is, that Texas continued to be a State, and a State of the Union, notwithstanding the transactions to which we have referred. And this conclusion, in our judgment, is not in conflict with any act or declaration of any department of the National government, but entirely in accordance with the whole series of such acts and declarations since the first outbreak of the rebellion.

But in order to the exercise, by a State, of the right to sue in this court, there needs to be a State government, competent to represent the State in its relations with the National government, so far at least as the institution and prosecution of a suit is concerned.

And it is by no means a logical conclusion, from the premises which we have endeavored to establish, that the governmental relations of

Texas to the Union remained unaltered. . . . No one has been bold enough to contend that, while Texas was controlled by a government hostile to the United States, and in affiliation with a hostile confederation, waging war upon the United States, senators chosen by her legislature, or representatives elected by her citizens, were entitled to seats in Congress; or that any suit, instituted in her name, could be entertained in this court. All admit that, during this condition of civil war, the rights of the State as a member, and of her people as citizens of the Union, were suspended. The government and the citizens of the State, refusing to recognize their constitutional obligations, assumed the character of enemies, and incurred the consequences of rebellion. . . .

When the war closed there was no government in the State except that which had been organized for the purpose of waging war against the United States. That government immediately disappeared. . . .

There being then no government in Texas in constitutional relations with the Union, it became the duty of the United States to provide for the restoration of such a government. . . .

It is not important to review, at length, the measures which have been taken, under this power, by the executive and legislative departments of the National government. It is proper, however, to observe that almost immediately after the cessation of organized hostilities, and while the war yet smouldered in Texas, the President of the United States issued his proclamation appointing a provisional governor for the State, and providing for the assembling of a convention, with a view to the re-establishment of a republican government, under an amended constitution, and to the restoration of the State to her proper constitutional relations. A convention was accordingly assembled, the constitution amended, elections, held, and a State government, acknowledging its obligations to the Union, established.

Whether the action then taken was, in all respects, warranted by the Constitution, it is not now necessary to determine. The power exercised by the President was supposed, doubtless, to be derived from his constitutional functions, as commander-in-chief; and, so long as the war continued, it cannot be denied that he might institute temporary government within insurgent districts, occupied by the National forces, or take measures, in any State, for the restoration of State government faithful to the Union, employing, however, in such efforts, only such means and agents as were authorized by constitutional laws.

But, the power to carry into effect the clause of guaranty is primarily a legislative power, and resides in Congress. . . .

Nothing in the case before us requires the court to pronounce judgment upon the constitutionality of any particular provision of [the Reconstruction] acts. . . .

⋆ C ⋆

Legal Tenders

Hepburn *v.* Griswold

As President Lincoln prepared to appoint a new Chief Justice in 1864, he is reputed to have said that he wished for a man who would be "right" on emancipation and legal tenders. Salmon P. Chase was an appropriate choice. He was one of the earliest and most prominent political anti-slavery leaders and, as Secretary of the Treasury, he sponsored and promoted the wartime legal tender program. Predicting judicial behavior is a tricky business, and Chase is an obvious case in point. Apparently he believed in legal tender only as a wartime expedient, and after the war, he seized the opportunity to undo his own handiwork. Although his views on legal tender were soon overturned, Chase's bold statements on the nature and extent of judicial power are significant. They testify to the Court's institutional vitality at a time when its prestige was allegedly at a low ebb, and they anticipate the judicial activism which became so prevalent later in the century.

Chief Justice Chase delivered the opinion of the Court.

The case before us is one of private right. The plaintiff in the court below sought to recover of the defendants a certain sum expressed on the face of a promissory note. The defendants insisted on the right, under the act of February 25th, 1862, to acquit themselves of their obligation by tendering in payment a sum nominally equal in United States notes. But the note had been executed before the passage of the act, and the plaintiff insisted on his right under the Constitution to be paid the amount due in gold and silver. And it has not been, and cannot be, denied that the plaintiff was entitled to judgment according to his claim, unless bound by a constitutional law to accept the notes as coin.

Thus two questions were directly presented: Were the defendants relieved by the act from the obligation assumed in the contract? Could the plaintiff be compelled, by a judgment of the court, to receive in pay-

---

8 Wallace 603 (1870)

ment a currency of different nature and value from that which was in the contemplation of the parties when the contract was made?

The Court of Appeals resolved both questions in the negative, and the defendants, in the original suit, seek the reversal of that judgment by writ of error.

It becomes our duty, therefore, to determine whether the act of February 25th, 1862, so far as it makes United States notes a legal tender in payment of debts contracted prior to its passage, is constitutional and valid or otherwise. . . .

It is not necessary . . . in order to prove the existence of a particular authority to show a particular and express grant. The design of the Constitution was to establish a government competent to the direction and administration of the affairs of a great nation, and, at the same time, to mark, by sufficiently definite lines, the sphere of its operations. To this end it was needful only to make express grants of general powers, coupled with a further grant of such incidental and auxiliary powers as might be required for the exercise of the powers expressly granted. These powers are necessarily extensive. It has been found, indeed, in the practical administration of the government, that a very large part, if not the largest part, of its functions have been performed in the exercise of powers thus implied.

But the extension of power by implication was regarded with some apprehension by the wise men who framed, and by the intelligent citizens who adopted, the Constitution. This apprehension is manifest in the terms by which the grant of incidental and auxiliary powers is made. All powers of this nature are included under the description of "power to make all laws necessary and proper for carrying into execution the powers expressly granted to Congress or vested by the Constitution in the government or in any of its departments or officers." . . .

It has not been maintained in argument, nor, indeed, would any one, however slightly conversant with constitutional law, think of maintaining that there is in the Constitution any express grant of legislative power to make any description of credit currency a legal tender in payment of debts.

We must inquire then whether this can be done in the exercise of an implied power.

The rule for determining whether a legislative enactment can be supported as an exercise of an implied power was stated by Chief Justice Marshall, speaking for the whole court, in the case of *McCullough* [*sic*] v. *The State of Maryland;* and the statement then made has ever since been accepted as a correct exposition of the Constitution. His words were these: "Let the end be legitimate, let it be within the scope of the Constitution, and all means which are appropriate, which are plainly adapted to that end, which are not prohibited, but consistent with the letter and spirit of the Constitution, are constitutional." And in another part of the same opinion the practical application of this rule was thus illustrated: "Should Congress, in the execution of its powers, adopt measures which are prohibited by the Constitution, or should Congress, under the pretext of executing its powers, pass laws for the accomplishment of objects not intrusted to the government, it would be the painful duty of this tribunal, should a case requiring such a decision come before it, to say that such an act was not the law of the land. But where the law is not prohibited, and is really calculated to effect any of the objects intrusted to the government, to undertake here to inquire into the degree of its necessity would be to pass the line which circumscribes the judicial department, and tread on legislative ground."

It must be taken then as finally settled, so far as judicial decisions can settle anything, that the words "all laws necessary and proper for carrying into execution" powers expressly granted or vested, have, in the Constitution, a sense equivalent to that of the words, laws, not absolutely necessary indeed, but appropriate, plainly adapted to constitutional and legitimate ends; laws not prohibited, but consistent with the letter and spirit of the Constitution; laws really calculated to effect objects intrusted to the government.

The question before us, then, resolves itself into this: "Is the clause which makes United States notes a legal tender for debts contracted prior to its enactment, a law of the description stated in the rule?"

It is not doubted that the power to establish a standard of value by which all other values may be measured, or, in other words, to determine what shall be lawful money and a legal tender, is in its nature, and of necessity, a governmental power. It is in all countries exercised by the government. In the United States, so far as it relates to the precious metals, it is vested in Congress by the grant of the power to coin money. But can a power to impart these qualities to notes, or promises to pay money, when offered in discharge of pre-existing debts, be derived from the coinage power, or from any other power expressly given? . . .

[I]t has been maintained in argument that the power to make United States notes a legal tender in payment of all debts is a means appropriate and plainly adapted to the execution of the power to carry on war, of the power to regulate commerce, and of the power to borrow money. If it is, and is not prohibited, nor inconsistent with the letter or spirit of the Constitution, then the act which makes them such legal tender must be held to be constitutional. . . .

It is difficult to say to what express power the authority to make notes a legal tender in payment of pre-existing debts may not be upheld as incidental, upon the principles of this argument. Is there any power which does not involve the use of money? . . .

We are unable to persuade ourselves that an expedient of this sort is an appropriate and plainly adapted means for the execution of the power to declare and carry on war. If it adds nothing to the utility of the notes, it cannot be upheld as a means to the end in furtherance of which the notes are issued. Nor can it, in our judgment, be upheld as such, if, while facilitating in some degree the circulation of the notes, it debases and injures the currency in its proper use to a much greater degree. And these considerations seem to us equally applicable to the powers to regulate commerce and to borrow money. Both powers necessarily involve the use of money by the people and by the government, but neither, as we think, carries with it as an appropriate and plainly adapted means to its exercise, the power of making circulating notes a legal tender in payment of pre-existing debts.

But there is another view, which seems to us decisive, to whatever express power the supposed implied power in question may be referred. In the rule stated by Chief Justice Marshall, the words appropriate, plainly adapted, really calculated, are qualified by the limitation that the means must be not prohibited, but consistent with the letter and spirit of the Constitution. Nothing so prohibited or inconsistent can be regarded as appropriate, or plainly adapted, or really calculated means to any end.

Let us inquire, then, first, whether making bills of credit a legal tender, to the extent indicated, is consistent with the spirit of the Constitution.

Among the great cardinal principles of that instrument, no one is more conspicuous or more venerable than the establishment of justice. And what was intended by the establishment of justice in the minds of the people who ordained it is, happily, not a matter of disputation. It is not left to inference or conjecture, especially in its relations to contracts. . . .

The . . . principle found . . . expression in that most valuable provision of the Constitution of the United States, ever recognized as an efficient safeguard against injustice, that "no State shall pass any law impairing the obligation of contracts."

It is true that this prohibition is not applied in terms to the government of the United States. Congress has express power to enact bankrupt laws, and we do not say that a law made in the execution of any other express power, which, incidentally, only impairs the obligation of a contract, can be held to be unconstitutional for that reason.

But we think it clear that those who framed and those who adopted the Constitution, intended that the spirit of this prohibition should pervade the entire body of legislation, and that the justice which the Constitution was ordained to establish was not thought by them to be compatible with legislation of an opposite tendency. In other words, we cannot doubt that a law not made in pursuance of an express power, which necessarily and in its direct operation impairs the obligation of contracts, is inconsistent with the spirit of the Constitution.

Another provision, found in the fifth amendment, must be considered in this connection. We refer to that which ordains that private property shall not be taken for public use without compensation. This provision is kindred in spirit to that which forbids legislation impairing the obligation of contracts; but, unlike that, it is addressed directly and solely to the National government. It does not, in terms, prohibit legislation which appropriates the private property of one class of citizens to the use of another class; but if such property cannot be taken for the benefit of all, without compensation, it is difficult to understand how it can be so taken for the benefit of a part without violating the spirit of the prohibition.

But there is another provision in the same amendment, which, in our judgment, cannot have its full and intended effect unless construed as a direct prohibition of the legislation which we have been considering. It is that which declares that "no person shall be deprived of life, liberty, or property, without due process of law."

It is not doubted that all the provisions of this amendment operate directly in limitation and restraint of the legislative powers conferred by the Constitution. The only question is, whether an act which compels all those who hold contracts for the payment of gold and silver money to accept in payment a currency of inferior value deprives such persons of property without due process of law.

It is quite clear, that whatever may be the operation of such an act, due process of law makes no part of it. Does it deprive any person of property? A very large proportion of the property of civilized men exists in the form of contracts. These contracts almost invariably stipulate for the payment of money. And we have already seen that contracts in the United States, prior to the act under consideration, for the payment of money, were contracts to pay the sums specified in gold and silver coin. And it is beyond doubt that the holders of these contracts were and are as fully entitled to the protection of this constitutional provision as the holders of any other description of property. . . .

We are obliged to conclude that an act making mere promises to pay dollars a legal tender in payment of debts previously contracted, is not a means appropriate, plainly adapted, really calculated to carry into effect any express power vested in Congress; that such an act is inconsistent with the spirit of the Constitution; and that it is prohibited by the Constitution. . . .

Legal Tender Cases
Knox *v.* Lee; Parker *v.* Davis

While the Court was preparing its opinions in the first legal tender cases, President Grant was selecting two new justices. One was to replace Justice Grier, who had announced his retirement but nevertheless voted with the majority in the first case. The other was to fill a new place recently created by Congress. It is unlikely that Grant's appointees, William Strong and Joseph Bradley, gave the President any assurances as to their legal tender views. But Strong had voted to sustain the laws while on the Pennsylvania Supreme Court and Bradley had close ties to the business community which favored retention of the laws. In the first case, the Court divided 4–3 against the acts. But with the two additions to the bench, a new case was accepted. In an unprecedented action, the Court immediately reversed itself, with Strong and Bradley joining the dissenters in the earlier case to form a new majority. Incidentally, Strong's opinion in no way refuted the bold assumptions of judicial power and constitutional interpretation advanced by Chase in the preceding case.

Justice Strong delivered the opinion of the Court.

Are the acts of Congress, known as the legal tender acts, constitutional when applied to contracts made before their passage; and, secondly, are they valid as applicable to debts contracted since their enactment? These questions have been elaborately argued, and they have received from the court that consideration which their great importance demands. It would be difficult to overestimate the consequences which must follow our decision. They will affect the entire business of the country, and take hold of the possible continued existence of the government. If it be held by this court that Congress has no constitutional power, under any circumstances, or in any emergency, to make treasury notes a legal tender for the payment of all debts (a power confessedly possessed by every independent sovereignty other than the United States), the government is without those means of self-preservation which, all must admit, may, in certain contingencies, become indispensable, even if they were not when the acts of Congress now called in question were enacted. It is also clear that if we hold the acts invalid as applicable to debts incurred, or transactions which have taken place since their enactment,

12 Wallace 457 (1871)

our decision must cause, throughout the country, great business derangement, widespread distress, and the rankest injustice. . . . And there is no well-founded distinction to be made between the constitutional validity of an act of Congress declaring treasury notes a legal tender for the payment of debts contracted after its passage and that of an act making them a legal tender for the discharge of all debts, as well as those incurred before as those made after its enactment. There may be a difference in the effects produced by the acts, and in the hardship of their operation, but in both cases the fundamental question, that which tests the validity of the legislation, is, can Congress constitutionally give to treasury notes the character and qualities of money? Can such notes be constituted a legitimate circulating medium, having a defined legal value? If they can, then such notes must be available to fulfil all contracts (not expressly excepted) solvable in money, without reference to the time when the contracts were made. . . .

The consequences of which we have spoken, serious as they are, must be accepted, if there is a clear incompatibility between the Constitution and the legal tender acts. But we are unwilling to precipitate them upon the country unless such an incompatibility plainly appears. A decent respect for a co-ordinate branch of the government demands that the judiciary should presume, until the contrary is clearly shown, that there has been no transgression of power by Congress — all the members of which act under the obligation of an oath of fidelity to the Constitution. . . .

Nor can it be questioned that, when investigating the nature and extent of the powers conferred by the Constitution upon Congress, it is indispensable to keep in view the objects for which those powers were granted. This is a universal rule of construction applied alike to statutes, wills, contracts, and constitutions. If the general purpose of the instrument is ascertained, the language of its provisions must be construed with reference to that purpose and so as to subserve it. . . . [T]he powers conferred upon Congress must be regarded as related to each other, and all means for a common end. Each is but part of a system, a constituent of one whole. No single power is the ultimate end for which the Constitution was adopted. It may, in a very proper sense, be treated as a means for the accomplishment of a subordinate object, but that object is itself a means designed for an ulterior purpose. Thus the power to levy and collect taxes, to coin money and regulate its value, to raise and support armies, or to provide for and maintain a navy, are instruments for the paramount object, which was to establish a government, sovereign within its sphere, with capability of self-preservation, thereby forming a union more perfect than that which existed under the old Confederacy.

The same may be asserted also of all the non-enumerated powers included in the authority expressly given "to make all laws which shall be necessary and proper for carrying into execution the specified powers vested in Congress, and all other powers vested by the Constitution in the government of the United States, or in any department or officer thereof." . . .

And here it is to be observed it is not indispensable to the existence of any power claimed for the Federal government that it can be found specified in the words of the Constitution, or clearly and directly traceable to some one of the specified powers. Its existence may be deduced fairly from more than one of the substantive powers expressly defined, or from them all combined. It is allowable to group together any number of them and infer from them all that the power claimed has been conferred. . . .

And it is of importance to observe that Congress has often exercised, without question, powers that are not expressly given nor ancillary to any single enumerated power. Powers thus exercised are what are called by Judge Story in his Commentaries on the Constitution, resulting powers, arising from the aggregate powers of the government. He instances the right to sue and make contracts. Many others might be given. The oath required by law from officers of the government is one. So is building a capitol or a presidential mansion, and so also is the penal code. . . .

Indeed the whole history of the government and of congressional legislation has exhibited the use of a very wide discretion, even in times of peace and in the absence of any trying emergency, in the selection of the necessary and proper means to carry into effect the great objects for which the government was framed, and this discretion has generally been unquestioned, or, if questioned, sanctioned by this court. This is true not only when an attempt has been made to execute a single power specifically given, but equally true when the means adopted have been appropriate to the execution, not of a single authority, but of all the powers created by the Constitution. . . .

We do not propose to dilate at length upon the circumstances in which the country was placed, when Congress attempted to make treasury notes a legal tender. They are of too recent occurrence to justify enlarged description. Suffice it to say that a civil war was then raging which seriously threatened the overthrow of the government and the destruction of the Constitution itself. It demanded the equipment and support of large armies and navies, and the employment of money to an extent beyond the capacity of all ordinary sources of supply. . . .

It was at such a time and in such circumstances that Congress was called upon to devise means for maintaining the army and navy, for securing the large supplies of money needed, and, indeed, for the preservation of the government created by the Constitution. It was at such a time and in such an emergency that the legal tender acts were passed. Now, if it were certain that nothing else would have supplied the absolute necessities of the treasury, that nothing else would have enabled the government to maintain its armies and navy, that nothing else would have saved the government and the Constitution from destruction, while the legal tender acts would, could any one be bold enough to assert that Congress transgressed its powers? . . .

Concluding, then, that the provision which made treasury notes a legal tender for the payment of all debts other than those expressly excepted, was not an inappropriate means for carrying into execution the legitimate powers of the government, we proceed to inquire whether it was forbidden by the letter or spirit of the Constitution. It is not claimed that any express prohibition exists, but it is insisted that the spirit of the Constitution was violated by the enactment. Here those who assert the unconstitutionality of the acts mainly rest their argument. . . . To assert . . . that the clause enabling Congress to coin money and regulate its value tacitly implies a denial of all other power over the currency of the nation, is an attempt to introduce a new rule of construction against the solemn decisions of this court. So far from its containing a lurking prohibition, many have thought it was intended to confer upon Congress that general power over the currency which has always been an acknowledged attribute of sovereignty in every other civilized nation than our own, especially when considered in connection with the other clause which denies to the States the power to coin money, emit bills of credit, or make anything but gold and silver coin a tender in payment of debts. . . .

We come next to the argument much used, and, indeed, the main reliance of those who assert the unconstitutionality of the legal tender acts. It is that they are prohibited by the spirit of the Constitution because they indirectly impair the obligation of contracts. . . .

That discovery calls for a new reading of the Constitution.

If . . . the legal tender acts were justly chargeable with impairing contract obligations, they would not, for that reason, be forbidden, unless a different rule is to be applied to them from that which has hitherto prevailed in the construction of other powers granted by the fundamental law. But . . . the objection misapprehends the nature and extent of the contract obligation spoken of in the Constitution. As in a state of civil society property of a citizen or subject is ownership, subject to the lawful demands of the sovereign, so contracts must be understood as made in reference to the possible exercise of the rightful authority of the government, and no obligation of a contract can extend to the defeat of legitimate government authority. . . .

We are not aware of anything else which has been advanced in support of the proposition that the legal tender acts were forbidden by either the letter or the spirit of the Constitution. If, therefore, they were, what we have endeavored to show, appropriate means for legitimate ends, they were not transgressive of the authority vested in Congress. . . .

★ D ★

The States and Civil Rights

Slaughter-House Cases

In Barron *v.* Baltimore *the Marshall Court had held the provisions of Amendments IV-VIII applicable only to the actions of the federal government. During the congressional debates in 1866 on the pending Fourteenth Amendment, John Bingham, one of its principal authors, remarked that he and others were anxious to extend the "sacred bill of rights" against state action. The aim was, he said, to "protect by national law the privileges and immunities of all the citizens . . . whenever the same shall be abridged or denied by the unconstitutional acts of any state." But seven years later in the* Slaughter-House Cases, *the Supreme Court flatly rejected the idea that the new amendment incorporated the Bill of Rights. The decision is reprinted below, Chap. V, Sec. A.*

16 Wallace 36 (1873)

Hurtado *v.* California

In Slaughter-House *the Court's opinion focused on the privileges and immunities clause of the Fourteenth Amendment. Litigants subsequently sought to exploit the due process clause of the amendment as a protection for procedural as well as substantive rights. The* Hurtado *case found the Court still reluctant to give broad scope to the amendment.* Hurtado *had been brought to trial for murder after examination by a magistrate, pursuant to the California constitution. He contended that the lack of a grand jury indictment deprived him of due process of law. Justice Harlan alone supported Hurtado's plea. Here, as in other similar Fourteenth Amendment cases, he contended that the amendment was designed "to impose upon the States the same restrictions, in respect of proceedings involving life, liberty and property, which had been imposed upon the general government."*

Justice Matthews delivered the opinion of the Court.

It is claimed on behalf of the prisoner that the conviction and sentence are void, on the ground that they are repugnant to [the due process] clause of the Fourteenth Article of Amendment of the Constitution of the United States. . . .

The Constitution of the United States was ordained, it is true, by descendants of Englishmen, who inherited the traditions of English law and history; but it was made for an undefined and expanding future, and for a people gathered and to be gathered from many nations and of many tongues. And while we take just pride in the principles and institutions of the common law, we are not to forget that in lands where other systems of jurisprudence prevail, the ideas and processes of civil justice are also not unknown. Due process of law, in spite of the absolutism of continental governments, is not alien to that code which survived the Roman Empire as the foundation of modern civilization in Europe, and which has given us that fundamental maxim of distributive justice — *suum cuique tribuere*. There is nothing in Magna Charta, rightly construed as a broad charter of public right and law, which ought to exclude the best ideas of all systems and of every age; and as it was the characteristic principle of the common law to draw its inspiration

110 U.S. 516 (1884)

from every fountain of justice, we are not to assume that the sources of its supply have been exhausted. On the contrary, we should expect that the new and various experiences of our own situation and system will mould and shape it into new and not less useful forms.

The concessions of Magna Charta were wrung from the King as guaranties against the oppressions and usurpations of his prerogative. It did not enter into the minds of the barons to provide security against their own body or in favor of the Commons by limiting the power of Parliament; so that bills of attainder, *ex post facto* laws, laws declaring forfeitures of estates, and other arbitrary acts of legislation which occur so frequently in English history, were never regarded as inconsistent with the law of the land; for notwithstanding what was attributed to Lord Coke in *Bonham's Case*, 8 Rep. 115, 118 *a*, the omnipotence of Parliament over the common law was absolute, even against common right and reason. The actual and practical security for English liberty against legislative tyranny was the power of a free public opinion represented by the Commons.

In this country written constitutions were deemed essential to protect the rights and liberties of the people against the encroachments of power delegated to their governments, and the provisions of Magna Charta were incorporated into Bills of Rights. They were limitations upon all the powers of government, legislative as well as executive and judicial.

It necessarily happened, therefore, that as these broad and general maxims of liberty and justice held in our system a different place and performed a different function from their position and office in English constitutional history and law, they would receive and justify a corresponding and more comprehensive interpretation. Applied in England only as guards against executive usurpation and tyranny, here they have become bulwarks also against arbitrary legislation; but, in that application, as it would be incongruous to measure and restrict them by the ancient customary English law, they must be held to guarantee not particular forms of procedure, but the very substance of individual rights to life, liberty, and property. . . .

We are to construe this phrase in the Fourteenth Amendment by the *usus loquendi* of the Constitution itself. The same words are contained in the Fifth Amendment. That article makes specific and express provision for perpetuating the institution of the grand jury, so far as relates to prosecutions for the more aggravated crimes under the laws of the United States. It declares that:

> No person shall be held to answer for a capital or otherwise infamous crime, unless on a presentment or indictment of a grand jury, except in cases arising in the land or naval forces, or in the militia when in actual service in time of war or public danger; nor shall any person be subject for the same offence to be twice put in jeopardy of life or limb; nor

shall he be compelled in any criminal case to be witness against himself.
[It then immediately adds]: Nor be deprived of life, liberty, or property,
without due process of law.

According to a recognized canon of interpretation, especially applicable to formal and solemn instruments of constitutional law, we are forbidden to assume, without clear reason to the contrary, that any part of
this most important amendment is superfluous. The natural and obvious
inference is, that in the sense of the Constitution, "due process of law"
was not meant or intended to include, *ex vi termini*, the institution and
procedure of a grand jury in any case. The conclusion is equally irresistible, that when the same phrase was employed in the Fourteenth
Amendment to restrain the action of the States, it was used in the same
sense and with no greater extent; and that if in the adoption of that
amendment it had been part of its purpose to perpetuate the institution
of the grand jury in all the States, it would have embodied, as did the
Fifth Amendment, express declarations to that effect. . . .

But it is not to be supposed that these legislative powers are absolute
and despotic, and that the amendment prescribing due process of law
is too vague and indefinite to operate as a practical restraint. It is not
every act, legislative in form, that is law. Law is something more than
mere will exerted as an act of power. It must be not a special rule for a
particular person or a particular case, but, in the language of Mr. Web-
ster, in his familiar definition, "the general law, a law which hears before
it condemns, which proceeds upon inquiry, and renders judgment only
after trial," so "that every citizen shall hold his life, liberty, property and
immunities under the protection of the general rules which govern society," and thus excluding, as not due process of law, acts of attainder,
bills of pains and penalties, acts of confiscation, acts reversing judgments,
and acts directly transferring one man's estate to another, legislative
judgments and decrees, and other similar special, partial and arbitrary
exertions of power under the forms of legislation. Arbitrary power, enforcing its edicts to the injury of the persons and property of its subjects,
is not law, whether manifested as the decree of a personal monarch or
of an impersonal multitude. And the limitations imposed by our constitutional law upon the action of the governments, both State and national,
are essential to the preservation of public and private rights, notwithstanding the representative character of our political institutions. The
enforcement of these limitations by judicial process is the device of self-
governing communities to protect the rights of individuals and minorities,
as well against the power of numbers, as against the violence of public
agents transcending the limits of lawful authority, even when acting in
the name and wielding the force of the government. . . .

It follows that any legal proceeding enforced by public authority,
whether sanctioned by age and custom, or newly devised in the discre-

tion of the legislative power, in furtherance of the general public good, which regards and preserves these principles of liberty and justice, must be held to be due process of law. . . .

Tried by these principles, we are unable to say that the substitution for a presentment or indictment by a grand jury of the proceeding by information, after examination and commitment by a magistrate, certifying to the probable guilt of the defendant, with the right on his part to the aid of counsel, and to the cross-examination of the witnesses produced for the prosecution, is not due process of law. It is, as we have seen, an ancient proceeding at common law, which might include every case of an offence of less grade than a felony, except misprison of treason; and in every circumstance of its administration, as authorized by the statute of California, it carefully considers and guards the substantial interest of the prisoner. It is merely a preliminary proceeding, and can result in no final judgment, except as the consequence of a regular judicial trial, conducted precisely as in cases of indictments. . . .

The Freedman and the Constitution

United States *v.* Reese

Despite the Slaughter-House *opinion that the postwar amendments were designed to protect the ex-slaves from their former masters and guarantee their freedom, the Court soon followed the general public and political reaction against racial equality. In the* Reese *case it severely restricted the scope of the Fifteenth Amendment and the ability of Congress to enforce it. Acting under authority of the Enforcement Act of 1870, the federal government indicted two Kentucky election inspectors for refusing to receive and count the vote of a Negro citizen. The Court was called upon to decide whether the 1870 law was "appropriate legislation" according to Section 2 of the Fifteenth Amendment.*

Chief Justice Waite delivered the opinion of the Court.

Rights and immunities created by or dependent upon the Constitution of the United States can be protected by Congress. The form and the manner of the protection may be such as Congress, in the legitimate exercise of its legislative discretion, shall provide. These may be varied to meet the necessities of the particular right to be protected.

The Fifteenth Amendment does not confer the right of suffrage upon any one. It prevents the States, or the United States, however, from giving preference, in this particular, to one citizen of the United States over another on account of race, color, or previous condition of servitude. Before its adoption, this could be done. It was as much within the power of a State to exclude citizens of the United States from voting on account of race, &c., as it was on account of age, property, or education. Now it is not. If citizens of one race having certain qualifications are permitted by law to vote, those of another having the same qualifications must be. Previous to this amendment, there was no constitutional guaranty against this discrimination: now there is. It follows that the

---

92 U.S. 214 (1876)

amendment has invested the citizens of the United States with a new constitutional right which is within the protecting power of Congress. That right is exemption from discrimination in the exercise of the elective franchise on account of race, color, or previous condition of servitude. This, under the express provisions of the second section of the amendment, Congress may enforce by "appropriate legislation."

This leads us to inquire whether the act now under consideration is "appropriate legislation" for that purpose. . . .

The statute contemplates a most important change in the election laws. Previous to its adoption, the States, as a general rule, regulated in their own way all the details of all elections. They prescribed the qualifications of voters, and the manner in which those offering to vote at an election should make known their qualifications to the officers in charge. This act interferes with this practice, and prescribes rules not provided by the laws of the States. It substitutes, under certain circumstances, performance wrongfully prevented for performance itself. If the elector makes and presents his affidavit in the form and to the effect prescribed, the inspectors are to treat this as the equivalent of the specified requirement of the State law. This is a radical change in the practice, and the statute which creates it should be explicit in its terms. Nothing should be left to construction, if it can be avoided. The law ought not to be in such a condition that the elector may act upon one idea of its meaning, and the inspector upon another. . . .

If the legislature undertakes to define by statute a new offence, and provide for its punishment, it should express its will in language that need not deceive the common mind. Every man should be able to know with certainty when he is committing a crime.

But . . . we find . . . no words of limitation, or reference even, that can be construed as manifesting any intention to confine its provisions to the terms of the Fifteenth Amendment. That section has for its object the punishment of all persons, who, by force, bribery, &c., hinder, delay, &c., any person from qualifying or voting. In view of all these facts, we feel compelled to say, that, in our opinion, the language of the third and fourth sections does not confine their operation to unlawful discriminations on account of race, &c. If Congress had the power to provide generally for the punishment of those who unlawfully interfere to prevent the exercise of the elective franchise without regard to such discrimination, the language of these sections would be broad enough for that purpose.

It remains now to consider whether a statute, so general as this in its provisions, can be made available for the punishment of those who may be guilty of unlawful discrimination against citizens of the United States, while exercising the elective franchise, on account of their race, &c.

There is no attempt in the sections now under consideration to provide specifically for such an offence. If the case is provided for at all, it is because it comes under the general prohibition against any wrongful act or unlawful obstruction in this particular. . . .

It would certainly be dangerous if the legislature could set a net large enough to catch all possible offenders, and leave it to the courts to step inside and say who could be rightfully detained, and who should be set at large. This would, to some extent, substitute the judicial for the legislative department of the government. The courts enforce the legislative will when ascertained, if within the constitutional grant of power. Within its legitimate sphere, Congress is supreme, and beyond the control of the courts; but if it steps outside of its constitutional limitations, and attempts that which is beyond its reach, the courts are authorized to, and when called upon in due course of legal proceedings must, annul its encroachments upon the reserved power of the States and the people. . . .

To limit this statute in the manner now asked for would be to make a new law, not to enforce an old one. This is no part of our duty.

We must, therefore, decide that Congress has not as yet provided by "appropriate legislation" for the punishment of the offence charged in the indictment. . . .

Civil Rights Cases

This decision effectively quashed federal civil rights legislation for the next eighty years and legitimated discrimination on a grand scale. At issue was the Civil Rights Act of 1875 which forbade racial segregation in transportation, inns, and theaters and required racial equality in selecting juries. Aside from the latter, the legislation was directed primarily against private individuals and their actions. Congress had acted on the basis of the equal protection of the laws clause and the enforcement provision of the Fourteenth Amendment. At stake, then, was whether Congress could implement the amendment with positive legislation to prevent discrimination on the grounds that the state denied equal protection when it tolerated or ignored such practices by its citizens. Justice Harlan again wrote a lonely dissent from what he called the Court's "subtle and ingenious verbal criticism" which subverted the "substance and spirit" of the Fourteenth Amendment.

Justice Bradley delivered the opinion of the Court.

The first section of the Fourteenth Amendment (which is the one relied on), after declaring who shall be citizens of the United States, and of the several States, is prohibitory in its character, and prohibitory upon the States. It declares that:

> "No State shall make or enforce any law which shall abridge the privileges or immunities of citizens of the United States; nor shall any State deprive any person of life, liberty, or property without due process of law; nor deny to any person within its jurisdiction the equal protection of the laws."

It is State action of a particular character that is prohibited. Individual invasion of individual rights is not the subject-matter of the amendment. It has a deeper and broader scope. It nullifies and makes void all State legislation, and State action of every kind, which impairs the privileges and immunities of citizens of the United States, or which injures them in life, liberty or property without due process of law, or which denies to any of them the equal protection of the laws. It not only does this, but, in order that the national will, thus declared, may not be a mere *brutum fulmen*, the last section of the amendment invests Con-

---

109 U.S. 3 (1883)

gress with power to enforce it by appropriate legislation. To enforce what? To enforce the prohibition. To adopt appropriate legislation for correcting the effects of such prohibited State laws and State acts, and thus to render them effectually null, void, and innocuous. This is the legislative power conferred upon Congress, and this is the whole of it. It does not invest Congress with power to legislate upon subjects which are within the domain of State legislation; but **to** provide modes of relief against State legislation, or State action, of the kind referred to. It does not authorize Congress to create a code of municipal law for the regulation of private rights; but to provide modes of redress against the operation of State laws, and the action of State officers executive or judicial, when these are subversive of the fundamental rights specified in the amendment. Positive rights and privileges are undoubtedly secured by the Fourteenth Amendment; but they are secured by way of prohibition against State laws and State proceedings affecting those rights and privileges, and by power given to Congress to legislate for the purpose of carrying such prohibition into effect: and such legislation must necessarily be predicated upon such supposed State laws or State proceedings, and be directed to the correction of their operation and effect. . . .

And so in the present case, until some State law has been passed, or some State action through its officers or agents has been taken, adverse to the rights of citizens sought to be protected by the Fourteenth Amendment, no legislation of the United States under said amendment, nor any proceeding under such legislation, can be called into activity: for the prohibitions of the amendment are against State laws and acts done under State authority. Of course, legislation may, and should be, provided in advance to meet the exigency when it arises; but it should be adapted to the mischief and wrong which the amendment was intended to provide against; and that is, State laws, or State action of some kind, adverse to the rights of the citizen secured by the amendment. Such legislation cannot properly cover the whole domain of rights appertaining to life, liberty and property, defining them and providing for their vindication. That would be to establish a code of municipal law regulative of all private rights between man and man in society. It would be to make Congress take the place of the State legislatures and to supersede them. . . .

If this legislation is appropriate for enforcing the prohibitions of the amendment, it is difficult to see where it is to stop. Why may not Congress with equal show of authority enact a code of laws for the enforcement and vindication of all rights of life, liberty, and property? If it is supposable that the States may deprive persons of life, liberty, and property without due process of law (and the amendment itself does suppose this), why should not Congress proceed at once to prescribe due process of law for the protection of every one of these fundamental rights, in every possible case, as well as to prescribe equal privileges in inns, public conveyances, and theatres? The truth is, that the implication of a power to legislate in this manner is based upon the assumption that if the States are forbidden to legislate or act in a particular way on a particular subject, and power is conferred upon Congress to enforce the prohibition, this gives Congress power to legislate generally upon that subject, and not merely power to provide modes of redress against such State legislation or action. The assumption is certainly unsound. It is repugnant to the Tenth Amendment of the Constitution, which declares that powers not delegated to the United States by the Constitution, nor prohibited by it to the States, are reserved to the States respectively or to the people. . . .

In this connection it is proper to state that civil rights, such as are guaranteed by the Constitution against State aggression, cannot be impaired by the wrongful acts of individuals, unsupported by State authority in the shape of laws, customs, or judicial or executive proceedings. The wrongful act of an individual, unsupported by any such authority, is simply a private wrong, or a crime of that individual; an invasion of the rights of the injured party, it is true, whether they affect his person, his property, or his reputation; but if not sanctioned in some way by the State, or not done under State authority, his rights remain in full force, and may presumably be vindicated by resort to the laws of the State for redress. An individual cannot deprive a man of his right to vote, to hold property, to buy and sell, to sue in the courts, or to be a witness or a juror; he may, by force or fraud, interfere with the enjoyment of the right in a particular case; he may commit an assault against the person, or commit murder, or use ruffian violence at the polls, or slander the good name of a fellow citizen; but, unless protected in these wrongful acts by some shield of State law or State authority, he cannot destroy or injure the right; he will only render himself amenable to satisfaction or punishment; and amenable therefor to the laws of the State where the wrongful acts are committed. Hence, in all those cases where the Constitution seeks to protect the rights of the citizen against discriminative and unjust laws of the State by prohibiting such laws, it is not individual offences, but abrogation and denial of rights, which it denounces, and for which it clothes the Congress with power to provide a remedy. This abrogation and denial of rights, for which the States alone were or could be responsible, was the great seminal and fundamental wrong which was intended to be remedied. And the remedy to be provided must necessarily be predicated upon that wrong. It must assume that in the cases provided for, the evil or wrong actually committed rests upon some State law or State authority for its excuse and perpetration. . . .

It may be that by the Black Code (as it was called), in the times when slavery prevailed, the proprietors of inns and public conveyances were forbidden to receive persons of the African race, because it might assist slaves to escape from the control of their masters. This was merely a means of preventing such escapes, and was no part of the servitude itself. A law of that kind could not have any such object now, however justly it might be deemed an invasion of the party's legal right as a citizen, and amenable to the prohibitions of the Fourth Amendment.

The long existence of African slavery in this country gave us very distinct notions of what it was, and what were its necessary incidents. Compulsory service of the slave for the benefit of the master, restraint of his movements except by the master's will, disability to hold property, to make contracts, to have a standing in court, to be a witness against a white person, and such like burdens and incapacities, were the inseparable incidents of the institution. Severer punishments for crimes were imposed on the slave than on free persons guilty of the same offences. Congress, as we have seen, by the Civil Rights Bill of 1866, passed in view of the Thirteenth Amendment, before the Fourteenth was adopted, undertook to wipe out these burdens and disabilities, the necessary incidents of slavery, constituting its substance and visible form; and to secure to all citizens of every race and color, and without regard to previous servitude, those fundamental rights which are the essence of civil freedom, namely, the same right to make and enforce contracts, to sue, be parties, give evidence, and to inherit, purchase, lease, sell and convey property, as is enjoyed by white citizens. Whether this legislation was fully authorized by the Thirteenth Amendment alone, without the support which it afterward received from the Fourteenth Amendment, after the adoption of which it was re-enacted with some additions, it is not necessary to inquire. It is referred to for the purpose of showing that at that time (in 1866) Congress did not assume, under the authority given by the Thirteenth Amendment, to adjust what may be called the social rights of men and races in the community; but only to declare and vindicate those fundamental rights which appertain to the essence of citizenship, and the enjoyment or deprivation of which constitutes the essential distinction between freedom and slavery. . . .

When a man has emerged from slavery, and by the aid of beneficent legislation has shaken off the inseparable concomitants of that state, there must be some stage in the progress of his elevation when he takes the rank of a mere citizen, and ceases to be the special favorite of the laws, and when his rights as a citizen, or a man, are to be protected in the ordinary modes by which other men's rights are protected. There were thousands of free colored people in this country before the abolition of slavery, enjoying all the essential rights of life, liberty and property the same as white citizens; yet no one, at that time, thought that it was any invasion of his personal status as a freeman because he was not admitted to all the privileges enjoyed by white citizens, or because he was subjected to discriminations in the enjoyment of accommodations in inns, public conveyances and places of amusement. Mere discriminations on account of race or color were not regarded as badges of slavery. If, since that time, the enjoyment of equal rights in all these respects has become established by constitutional enactment, it is not by force of the Thirteenth Amendment (which merely abolishes slavery), but by force of the Thirteenth and Fifteenth Amendments.

On the whole we are of opinion, that no countenance of authority for the passage of the law in question can be found in either the Thirteenth or Fourteenth Amendment of the Constitution; and no other ground of authority for its passage being suggested, it must necessarily be declared void, at least so far as its operation in the several States is concerned. . . .

Justice Harlan dissenting.

The opinion in these cases proceeds, it seems to me, upon grounds entirely too narrow and artificial. I cannot resist the conclusion that the substance and spirit of the recent amendments of the Constitution have been sacrificed by a subtle and ingenious verbal criticism. "It is not the words of the law but the internal sense of it that makes the law: the letter of the law is the body; the sense and reason of the law is the soul." Constitutional provisions, adopted in the interest of liberty, and for the purpose of securing, through national legislation, if need be, rights inhering in a state of freedom, and belonging to American citizenship, have been so construed as to defeat the ends the people desired to accomplish, which they attempted to accomplish, and which they supposed they had accomplished by changes in their fundamental law. By this I do not mean that the determination of these cases should have been materially controlled by considerations of mere expediency or policy. I mean only, in this form, to express an earnest conviction that the court has departed from the familiar rule requiring, in the interpretation of constitutional provisions, that full effect be given to the intent with which they were adopted. . . .

That there are burdens and disabilities which constitute badges of slavery and servitude, and that the power to enforce by appropriate legislation the Thirteenth Amendment may be exerted by legislation of a direct and primary character, for the eradication, not simply of the institution, but of its badges and incidents, are propositions which ought to be deemed indisputable. They lie at the foundation of the Civil Rights Act of 1866. Whether that act was authorized by the Thirteenth Amendment alone, without the support which it subsequently received from the

Fourteenth Amendment, after the adoption of which it was re-enacted with some additions, my brethren do not consider it necessary to inquire. But I submit, with all respect to them, that its constitutionality is conclusively shown by their opinion. They admit, as I have said, that the Thirteenth Amendment established freedom; that these are burdens and disabilities, the necessary incidents of slavery, which constitute its substance and visible form; that Congress, by the act of 1866, passed in view of the Thirteenth Amendment, before the Fourteenth was adopted, undertook to remove certain burdens and disabilities, the necessary incidents of slavery, and to secure to all citizens of every race and color, and without regard to previous servitude, those fundamental rights which are the essence of civil freedom, namely, the same right to make and enforce contracts, to sue, be parties, give evidence, and to inherit, purchase, lease, sell, and convey property as is enjoyed by white citizens; that under the Thirteenth Amendment, Congress has to do with slavery and its incidents; and that legislation, so far as necessary or proper to eradicate all forms and incidents of slavery and involuntary servitude, may be direct and primary, operating upon the acts of individuals, whether sanctioned by State legislation or not. These propositions being conceded, it is impossible, as it seems to me, to question the constitutional validity of the Civil Rights Act of 1866. I do not contend that the Thirteenth Amendment invests Congress with authority, by legislation, to define and regulate the entire body of the civil rights which citizens enjoy, or may enjoy, in the several States. But I hold that since slavery, as the court has repeatedly declared, *Slaughter-House Cases*, 16 Wall. 36; *Strauder* v. *West Virginia*, 100 U.S. 303, was the moving or principal cause of the adoption of that amendment, and since that institution rested wholly upon the inferiority, as a race, of those held in bondage, their freedom necessarily involved immunity from, and protection against, all discrimination against them, because of their race, in respect of such civil rights as belong to freemen of other races. Congress, therefore, under its express power to enforce that amendment, by appropriate legislation, may enact laws to protect that people against the deprivation, *because of their race*, of any civil rights granted to other freemen in the same State; and such legislation may be of a direct and primary character, operating upon States, their officers and agents, and, also, upon, at least, such individuals and corporations as exercise public functions and wield power and authority under the State. . . .

Congress has not, in these matters, entered the domain of State control and supervision. It does not, as I have said, assume to prescribe the general conditions and limitations under which inns, public conveyances, and places of public amusement, shall be conducted or managed. It simply declares, in effect, that since the nation has established universal freedom in this country, for all time, there shall be no discrimination, based merely upon race or color, in respect of the accommodations and advantages of public conveyances, inns, and places of public amusement.

I am of the opinion that such discrimination practised by corporations and individuals in the exercise of their public or quasi-public functions is a badge of servitude the imposition of which Congress may prevent under its power, by appropriate legislation, to enforce the Thirteenth Amendment; and, consequently, without reference to its enlarged power under the Fourteenth Amendment, the act of March 1, 1875, is not, in my judgment, repugnant to the Constitution.

It remains now to consider these cases with reference to the power Congress has possessed since the adoption of the Fourteenth Amendment. Much that has been said as to the power of Congress under the Thirteenth Amendment is applicable to this branch of the discussion, and will not be repeated.

Before the adoption of the recent amendments, it had become, as we have seen, the established doctrine of this court that negroes, whose ancestors had been imported and sold as slaves, could not become citizens of a State, or even of the United States, with the rights and privileges guaranteed to citizens by the national Constitution; further, that one might have all the rights and privileges of a citizen of a State without being a citizen in the sense in which that word was used in the national Constitution, and without being entitled to the privileges and immunities of citizens of the several States. Still, further, between the adoption of the Thirteenth Amendment and the proposal by Congress of the Fourteenth Amendment, on June 16, 1866, the statute books of several of the States, as we have seen, had become loaded down with enactments which, under the guise of Apprentice, Vagrant, and Contract regulations, sought to keep the colored race in a condition, practically, of servitude. It was openly announced that whatever might be the rights which persons of that race had, as freemen, under the guarantees of the national Constitution, they could not become citizens of a State, with the privileges belonging to citizens, except by the consent of such State; consequently, that their civil rights, as citizens of the State, depended entirely upon State legislation. To meet this new peril to the black race, that the purposes of the nation might not be doubted or defeated, and by way of further enlargement of the power of Congress, the Fourteenth Amendment was proposed for adoption. . . .

But what was secured to colored citizens of the United States — as between them and their respective States — by the national grant to them of State citizenship? With what rights, privileges, or immunities did this grant invest them? There is one, if there be no other — exemption from race discrimination in respect of any civil right belonging to citizens of the white race in the same State. That, surely, is their constitutional privilege when within the jurisdiction of other States. And such must be their constitutional right, in their own State, unless the recent amendments be splendid baubles, thrown out to delude those who deserved fair and generous treatment at the hands of the nation. Citizenship in this country necessarily imports at least equality of civil rights among citizens of every race in the same State. It is fundamental in American citizenship that, in respect of such rights, there shall be no discrimination by the State, or its officers, or by individuals or corporations exercising public functions or authority, against any citizen because of his race or previous condition of servitude. . . .

But if it were conceded that the power of Congress could not be brought into activity until the rights specified in the act of 1875 had been abridged or denied by some State law or State action, I maintain that the decision of the court is erroneous. . . .

In every material sense applicable to the practical enforcement of the Fourteenth Amendment, railroad corporations, keepers of inns, and managers of places of public amusement are agents or instrumentalities of the State, because they are charged with duties to the public, and are amenable, in respect of their duties and functions, to governmental regulation. . . .

My brethren say, that when a man has emerged from slavery, and by the aid of beneficent legislation has shaken off the inseparable concomitants of that state, there must be some stage in the progress of his elevation when he takes the rank of a mere citizen, and ceases to be the special favorite of the laws, and when his rights as a citizen, or a man, are to be protected in the ordinary modes by which other men's rights are protected. It is, I submit, scarcely just to say that the colored race has been the special favorite of the laws. The statute of 1875, now adjudged to be unconstitutional, is for the benefit of citizens of every race and color. What the nation, through Congress, has sought to accomplish in reference to that race, is — what had already been done in every State of the Union for the white race — to secure and protect rights belonging to them as freemen and citizens; nothing more. It was not deemed enough "to help the feeble up, but to support him after." The one underlying purpose of congressional legislation has been to enable the black race to take the rank of mere citizens. The difficulty has been to compel a recognition of the legal right of the black race to take the rank of citizens, and to secure the enjoyment of privileges belonging, under the law, to them as a component part of the people for whose welfare and happiness government is ordained. At every step, in this direction, the nation has been confronted with class tyranny, which a contemporary English historian says is, of all tyrannies, the most intolerable, "for it is ubiquitous in its operation, and weighs, perhaps, most heavily on those whose obscurity or distance would withdraw them from the notice of a single despot." To-day, it is the colored race which is denied, by corporations and individuals wielding public authority, rights fundamental in their freedom and citizenship. At some future time, it may be that some other race will fall under the ban of race discrimination. If the constitutional amendments be enforced, according to the intent with which, as I conceive, they were adopted, there cannot be, in this republic, any class of human beings in practical subjection to another class, with power in the latter to dole out to the former just such privileges as they may choose to grant. The supreme law of the land has decreed that no authority shall be exercised in this country upon the basis of discrimination, in respect of civil rights, against freemen and citizens because of their race, color, or previous condition of servitude. To that decree — for the due enforcement of which, by appropriate legislation, Congress has been invested with express power — every one must bow, whatever may have been, or whatever now are, his individual views as to the wisdom or policy, either of the recent changes in the fundamental law, or of the legislation which has been enacted to give them effect.

For the reasons stated I feel constrained to withhold my assent to the opinion of the court.

Virginia *v.* Rives

In Strauder *v.* West Virginia *(100 U.S. 303), a companion case to this one, the Negro won a rare postwar court victory. The Supreme Court found a state statute requiring all-white juries invalid as a denial of the equal protection of the laws. But it was a Pyrrhic victory. The Virginia case below was more significant in long-term impact as it sanctioned a practice which otherwise would have been invalid if formalized in law. While Virginia did not have a statute similar to West Virginia's, Negroes were generally excluded from juries. Without a specific statute, however, the Court refused to act, thus placing the burden upon Negroes to prove systematic and deliberate exclusion. That, of course, proved difficult.*

Justice Strong delivered the opinion of the Court.

Section 641 of the Revised Statutes provides for a removal "when any civil suit or prosecution is commenced in any State court, for any cause whatsoever, against any person who is denied or cannot enforce in the judicial tribunals of the State, or in the part of the State where such suit or prosecution is pending, any right secured to him by any law providing for the equal civil rights of citizens of the United States," &c. It declares that such a case may be removed before trial or final hearing. . . .

It rests upon the Fourteenth Amendment of the Constitution and the legislation to enforce its provisions. That amendment declares that no State shall make or enforce any law which shall abridge the privileges or immunities of citizens of the United States, nor shall any State deprive any person of life, liberty, or property, without due process of law, nor deny to any person within its jurisdiction the equal protection of the laws. It was in pursuance of these constitutional provisions that the civil rights statutes were enacted. . . .

The provisions of the Fourteenth Amendment of the Constitution we have quoted all have reference to State action exclusively, and not to any action of private individuals. It is the State which is prohibited from denying to any person within its jurisdiction the equal protection of the laws, and consequently the statutes partially enumerating what civil rights colored men shall enjoy equally with white persons, founded as they are upon the amendment, are intended for protection against

100 U.S. 313 (1880)

State infringement of those rights. Sect. 641 was also intended for their protection against State action, and against that alone. . . .

The statute authorizes a removal of the case only before trial, not after a trial has commenced. It does not, therefore, embrace many cases in which a colored man's right may be denied. It does not embrace a case in which a right may be denied by judicial action during the trial, or by discrimination against him in the sentence, or in the mode of executing the sentence. But the violation of the constitutional provisions, when made by the judicial tribunals of a State, may be, and generally will be, after the trial has commenced. It is then, during or after the trial, that denials of a defendant's right by judicial tribunals occur. Not often until then. Nor can the defendant know until then that the equal protection of the laws will not be extended to him. Certainly until then he cannot affirm that it is denied, or that he cannot enforce it, in the judicial tribunals.

It is obvious, therefore, that to such a case — that is, a judicial infraction of the constitutional inhibitions, after trial or final hearing has commenced — sect. 641 has no applicability. It was not intended to reach such cases. It left them to the revisory power of the higher courts of the State, and ultimately to review of this court. We do not say that Congress could not have authorized the removal of such a case into the Federal courts at any stage of its proceeding, whenever a ruling should be made in it denying the equal protection of the laws to the defendant. Upon that subject it is unnecessary to affirm any thing. It is sufficient to say now that sect. 641 does not.

It is evident, therefore, that the denial or inability to enforce in the judicial tribunals of a State, rights secured to a defendant by any law providing for the equal civil rights of all persons citizens of the United States, of which sect. 641 speaks, is primarily, if not exclusively, a denial of such rights, or an inability to enforce them, resulting from the Constitution or laws of the State, rather than a denial first made manifest at the trial of the case. In other words, the statute has reference to a legislative denial or an inability resulting from it. Many such cases of denial might have been apprehended, and some existed. Colored men might have been, as they had been, denied a trial by jury. They might have been excluded by law from any jury summoned to try persons of their race, or the law might have denied to them the testimony of colored men in their favor, or process for summoning witnesses. Numerous other illustrations might be given. In all such cases a defendant can affirm, on oath, before trial, that he is denied the equal protection of the laws or equality of civil rights. But in the absence of constitutional or legislative impediments he cannot swear before his case comes to trial that his enjoyment of all his civil rights is denied to him. When he has only an apprehension that such rights will be withheld from him when his case shall come to trial, he cannot affirm that they are actually denied, or that he cannot enforce them. Yet such an affirmation is essential to his right to remove his case. By the express requirement of the statute his petition must set forth the facts upon which he bases his claim to have his case removed, and not merely his belief that he cannot enforce his rights at a subsequent stage of the proceedings. The statute was not, therefore, intended as a corrective of errors or wrongs committed by judicial tribunals in the administration of the law at the trial.

The petition of the two colored men for the removal of their case into the Federal court does not appear to have made any case for removal, if we are correct in our reading of the act of Congress. It did not assert, nor is it claimed now, that the Constitution or laws of Virginia denied to them any civil right, or stood in the way of their enforcing the equal protection of the laws. The law made no discrimination against them because of their color, nor any discrimination at all. The complaint is that there were no colored men in the jury that indicted them, nor in the petit jury summoned to try them. The petition expressly admitted that by the laws of the State all male citizens twenty-one years of age and not over sixty, who are entitled to vote and hold office under the Constitution and laws thereof, are made liable to serve as jurors. And it affirms (what is undoubtedly true) that this law allows the right, as well as requires the duty, of the race to which the petitioners belong to serve as jurors. It does not exclude colored citizens.

Now, conceding as we do, and as we endeavored to maintain in the case of *Strauder* v. *West Virginia*, that discrimination by law against the colored race, because of their color, in the selection of jurors, is a denial of the equal protection of the laws to a negro when he is put upon trial for an alleged criminal offence against a State, the laws of Virginia make no such discrimination. . . . If, as in this case, the subordinate officer whose duty it is to select jurors fails to discharge that duty in the true spirit of the law; if he excludes all colored men solely because they are colored; or if the sheriff to whom a *venire* is given, composed of both white and colored citizens, neglects to summon the colored jurors only because they are colored; or if a clerk whose duty it is to take the twelve names from the box rejects all the colored jurors for the same reason, — it can with no propriety be said the defendant's right is denied by the State and cannot be enforced in the judicial tribunals. . . . We cannot think such cases are within the provisions of sect. 641. . . .

The assertions in the petition for removal, that the grand jury by which the petitioners were indicted, as well as the jury summoned to try them, were composed wholly of the white race, and that their race had never been allowed to serve as jurors in the county of Patrick in any case in which a colored man was interested, fall short of showing that any civil right was denied, or that there had been any discrimination against the defendants because of their color or race. The facts may have been as stated, and yet the jury which indicted them, and the panel summoned to try them, may have been impartially selected.

Nor did the refusal of the court and of the counsel for the prosecution allow a modification of the *venire*, by which one-third of the jury, or a portion of it, should be composed of persons of the petitioners' own race, amount to any denial of a right secured to them by any law providing for the equal civil rights of citizens of the United States. The privilege for which they moved, and which they also asked from the prosecution, was not a right given or secured to them, or to any person, by the law of the State, or by any act of Congress, or by the Fourteenth Amendment of the Constitution. It *is* a right to which every colored man is entitled, that, in the selection of jurors to pass upon his life, liberty, or property, there shall be no exclusion of his race, and no discrimination against them because of their color. But this is a different thing from the right which it is asserted was denied to the petitioners by the State Court, viz. a right to have the jury composed in part of colored men. A mixed jury in a particular case is not essential to the equal protection of the laws, and the right to it is not given by any law of Virginia, or by any Federal statute. It is not, therefore, guaranteed by the Fourteenth Amendment, or within the purview of sect. 641.

It follows that the petition for a removal stated no facts that brought the case within the provisions of this section, and, consequently, no jurisdiction of the case was acquired by the Circuit Court of the United States. . . .

Hall *v.* DeCuir

In 1869 the Louisiana legislature, under Republican control, pro-
hibited racial discrimination in any form of transportation. Iron-
ically, the statute was attacked as an interference with interstate
commerce. The Court accepted this argument and voided the state
law in the case below. But as segregation statutes developed
throughout the South, they were attacked with the same logic;
that is, that segregation requirements similarly interfered with in-
terstate commerce. In Louisiana, N. Orleans, & Texas R.R. Co. *v.*
Mississippi (*133 U.S. 587* [*1890*]), *however, the Court sustained such*
laws as they allegedly applied only to intrastate commerce. It took
the Court more than a half century to discover — or rather, to ack-
nowledge — the inherent, illogical contradiction between the two
cases (Morgan v. Virginia, *328 U.S. 373* [*1946*]).

Chief Justice Waite delivered the opinion of the Court.

For the purposes of this case, we must treat the act of Louisiana of
Feb. 23, 1869, as requiring those engaged in inter-state commerce
to give all persons travelling in that State, upon the public conveyances
employed in such business, equal rights and privileges in all parts of the
conveyance, without distinction or discrimination on account of race or
color. Such was the construction given to that act in the courts below,
and it is conclusive upon us as the construction of a State law by the
State courts. It is with this provision of the statute alone that we have to
deal. We have nothing whatever to do with it as a regulation of internal
commerce, or as affecting any thing else than commerce among the States.

There can be no doubt but that exclusive power has been conferred
upon Congress in respect to the regulation of commerce among the
several States. The difficulty has never been as to the existence of this
power, but as to what is to be deemed an encroachment upon it; for,
as has been often said, "legislation may in a great variety of ways affect
commerce and persons engaged in it without constituting a regulation of
it within the meaning of the Constitution." . . . By such statutes the
States regulate, as a matter of domestic concern, the instruments of commerce situated wholly within their own jurisdictions, and over which
they have exclusive governmental control, except when employed in

95 U.S. 485 (1878)

foreign or inter-state commerce. As they can only be used in the State, their regulation for all purposes may properly by assumed by the State, until Congress acts in reference to their foreign or inter-state relations. When Congress does act, the State laws are superseded only to the extent that they affect commerce outside the State as it comes within the State. It has also been held that health and inspection laws may be passed by the States. . . . The line which separates the powers of the States from this exclusive power of Congress is not always distinctly marked, and oftentimes it is not easy to determine on which side a particular case belongs. Judges not unfrequently differ in their reasons for a decision in which they concur. Under such circumstances it would be a useless task to undertake to fix an arbitrary rule by which the line must in all cases be located. It is far better to leave a matter of such delicacy to be settled in each case upon a view of the particular rights involved.

But we think it may safely be said that State legislation which seeks to impose a direct burden upon inter-state commerce, or to interfere directly with its freedom, does encroach upon the exclusive power of Congress. The statute now under consideration, in our opinion, occupies that position. It does not act upon the business through the local instruments to be employed after coming within the State, but directly upon the business as it comes into the State from without or goes out from within. While it purports only to control the carrier when engaged within the State, it must necessarily influence his conduct to some extent in the management of his business throughout his entire voyage. His disposition of passengers taken up and put down within the State, or taken up within to be carried without, cannot but affect in a greater or less degree those taken up without and brought within, and sometimes those taken up and put down without. A passenger in the cabin set apart for the use of whites without the State must, when the boat comes within, share the accommodations of that cabin with such colored persons as may come on board afterwards, if the law is enforced.

It was to meet just such a case that the commercial clause in the Constitution was adopted. The river Mississippi passes through or along the borders of ten different States, and its tributaries reach many more. The commerce upon these waters is immense, and its regulation clearly a matter of national concern. If each State was at liberty to regulate the conduct of carriers while within its jurisdiction, the confusion likely to follow could not but be productive of great inconvenience and unnecessary hardship. Each State could provide for its own passengers and regulate the transportation of its own freight, regardless of the interests of others. Nay more, it could prescribe rules by which the carrier must be governed within the State in respect to passengers and property brought from without. On one side of the river or its tributaries he might be required to observe one set of rules, and on the other another.

Commerce cannot flourish in the midst of such embarrassments. No carrier of passengers can conduct his business with satisfaction to himself, or comfort to those employing him, if on one side of a State line his passengers, both white and colored, must be permitted to occupy the same cabin, and on the other be kept separate. Uniformity in the regulations by which he is to be governed from one end to the other of his route is a necessity in his business, and to secure it Congress, which is untrammelled by State lines, has been invested with the exclusive legislative power of determining what such regulations shall be. If this statute can be enforced against those engaged in inter-state commerce, it may be as well against those engaged in foreign; and the master of a ship clearing from New Orleans for Liverpool, having passengers on board, would be compelled to carry all, white and colored, in the same cabin during his passage down the river, or be subject to an action for damages, "exemplary as well as actual," by any one who felt himself aggrieved because he had been excluded on account of his color.

This power of regulation may be exercised without legislation as well as with it. By refraining from action, Congress, in effect, adopts as its own regulations those which the common law or the civil law, where that prevails, has provided for the government of such business, and those which the States, in the regulation of their domestic concerns, have established affecting commerce, but not regulating it within the meaning of the Constitution. In fact, congressional legislation is only necessary to cure defects in existing laws, as they are discovered, and to adapt such laws to new developments of trade. As was said by Mr. Justice Field, speaking for the court in *Welton* v. *The State of Missouri*, 91 U.S. 282, "inaction [by Congress] . . . is equivalent to a declaration that inter-state commerce shall remain free and untrammelled." Applying that principle to the circumstances of this case, congressional inaction left [the boatowner] . . . at liberty to adopt such reasonable rules and regulations for the disposition of passengers upon his boat, while pursuing her voyage within Louisiana or without, as seemed to him most for the interest of all concerned. The statute under which this suit is brought, as construed by the State court, seeks to take away from him that power so long as he is within Louisiana; and while recognizing to the fullest extent the principle which sustains a statute, unless its unconstitutionality is clearly established, we think this statute, to the extent that it requires those engaged in the transportation of passengers among the States to carry colored passengers in Louisiana in the same cabin with whites, is unconstitutional and void. If the public good requires such legislation, it must come from Congress and not from the States. . . .

Plessy *v.* Ferguson

By the 1890's, the tide was running strongly against the Negro in the southern states. Disfranchisement was widespread, and the legislatures enacted the whole apparatus supporting segregation as a means of social separation and control. In 1890, Louisiana came full circle from its Reconstruction position and required separate railroad accommodations for the races. Plessy, an octoroon, challenged the law as a violation of the Thirteenth and Fourteenth Amendments. In the case which followed, the Supreme Court in effect put its imprimatur upon the "separate but equal" doctrine, and its opinion became the basic precedent for sustaining and justifying similar legislation. Informally, the justices acknowledged "sociological" considerations as readily as their successors sixty years later. As before, ex-slaveholder Justice Harlan alone protested against the Court's legalization of racism.

Justice Brown delivered the opinion of the Court.

This case turns upon the constitutionality of an act of the General Assembly of the State of Louisiana, passed in 1890, providing for separate railway carriages for the white and colored races. . . .

The first section of the statute enacts "that all railway companies carrying passengers in their coaches in this State, shall provide equal but separate accommodations for the white, and colored races, by providing two or more passenger coaches for each passenger train, or by dividing the passenger coaches by a partition so as to secure separate accommodations: *Provided,* That this section shall not be construed to apply to street railroads. No person or persons, shall be admitted to occupy seats in coaches, other than, the ones, assigned, to them on account of the race they belong to." . . .

The information filed in the criminal District Court charged in substance that Plessy, being a passenger between two stations within the State of Louisiana, was assigned by officers of the company to the coach used for the race to which he belonged, but he insisted upon going into a coach used by the race to which he did not belong. Neither in the information nor plea was his particular race or color averred.

The petition for the writ of prohibition averred that petitioner was seven eighths Caucasian and one eighth African blood; that the mixture of

163 U.S. 537 (1896)

colored blood was not discernible in him, and that he was entitled to every right, privilege and immunity secured to citizens of the United States of the white race; and that, upon such theory, he took possession of a vacant seat in a coach where passengers of the white race were accommodated, and was ordered by the conductor to vacate said coach and take a seat in another assigned to persons of the colored race, and having refused to comply with such demand he was forcibly ejected with the aid of a police officer, and imprisoned in the parish jail to answer a charge of having violated the above act.

The constitutionality of this act is attacked upon the ground that it conflicts both with the Thirteenth Amendment of the Constitution, abolishing slavery, and the Fourteenth Amendment, which prohibits certain restrictive legislation on the part of the States.

1. That it does not conflict with the Thirteenth Amendment, which abolished slavery and involuntary servitude, except as a punishment for crime, is too clear for argument. . . .

. . . The proper construction of the 14th amendment was first called to the attention of this court in the *Slaughter-house cases,* 16 Wall. 36, which involved, however, not a question of race, but one of exclusive privileges. The case did not call for any expression of opinion as to the exact rights it was intended to secure to the colored race, but it was said generally that its main purpose was to establish the citizenship of the negro; to give definitions of citizenship of the United States and of the States, and to protect from the hostile legislation of the States the privileges and immunities of citizens of the United States, as distinguished from those of citizens of the States.

The object of the amendment was undoubtedly to enforce the absolute equality of the two races before the law, but in the nature of things it could not have been intended to abolish distinctions based upon color, or to enforce social, as distinguished from political equality, or a commingling of the two races upon terms unsatisfactory to either. Laws permitting, and even requiring, their separation in places where they are liable to be brought into contact do not necessarily imply the inferiority of either race to the other, and have been generally, if not universally, recognized as within the competency of the state legislatures in the exercise of their police power. The most common instance of this is connected with the establishment of separate schools for white and colored children, which has been held to be a valid exercise of the legislative power even by courts of States where the political rights of the colored race have been longest and most earnestly enforced.

One of the earliest of these cases is that of *Roberts* v. *City of Boston,* 5 Cush. 198 [1849], in which the Supreme Judicial Court of Massachusetts held that the general school committee of Boston had power to make provision for the instruction of colored children in separate schools established exclusively for them, and to prohibit their attendance upon the other schools. "The great principle," said Chief Justice Shaw, p. 206, "advanced by the learned and eloquent advocate for the plaintiff," (Mr. Charles Sumner,) "is, that by the constitution and laws of Massachusetts, all persons without distinction of age or sex, birth or color, origin or condition, are equal before the law. . . . But, when this great principle comes to be applied to the actual and various conditions of persons in society, it will not warrant the assertion, that men and women are legally clothed with the same civil and political powers, and that children and adults are legally to have the same functions and be subject to the same treatment; but only that the rights of all, as they are settled and regulated by law, are equally entitled to the paternal consideration and protection of the law for their maintenance and security." It was held that the powers of the committee extended to the establishment of separate schools for children of different ages, sexes and colors, and that they might also establish special schools for poor and neglected children, who have become too old to attend the primary school, and yet have not acquired the rudiments of learning, to enable them to enter the ordinary schools. Similar laws have been enacted by Congress under its general power of legislation over the District of Columbia . . . as well as by the legislatures of many of the States, and have been generally, if not uniformly, sustained by the courts. . . .

So far, then, as a conflict with the Fourteenth Amendment is concerned, the case reduces itself to the question whether the statute of Louisiana is a reasonable regulation, and with respect to this there must necessarily be a large discretion on the part of the legislature. In determining the question of reasonableness it is at liberty to act with reference to the established usages, customs and traditions of the people, and with a view to the promotion of their comfort, and the preservation of the public peace and good order. Gauged by this standard, we cannot say that a law which authorizes or even requires the separation of the two races in public conveyances is unreasonable, or more obnoxious to the Fourteenth Amendment than the acts of Congress requiring separate schools for colored children in the District of Columbia, the constitutionality of which does not seem to have been questioned, or the corresponding acts of state legislatures.

We consider the underlying fallacy of the plaintiff's argument to consist in the assumption that the enforced separation of the two races stamps the colored race with a badge of inferiority. If this be so, it is not by reason of anything found in the act, but solely because the colored race chooses to put that construction upon it. The argument necessarily assumes that if, as has been more than once the case, and is not unlikely to be so again, the colored race should become the dominant power in the state legislature, and should enact a law in precisely similar terms, it would thereby relegate the white race to an inferior position. We imagine that the white race, at least, would not acquiesce in this assumption. The argument also assumes that social prejudices may be overcome by legislation, and that equal rights cannot be secured to the negro except by an enforced commingling of the two races. We cannot accept this proposition. If the two races are to meet upon terms of social equality, it must be the result of natural affinities, a mutual appreciation of each other's merits and a voluntary consent of individuals. . . . Legislation is powerless to eradicate racial instincts or to abolish distinctions based upon physical differences, and the attempt to do so can only result in accentuating the difficulties of the present situation. If the civil and political rights of both races be equal one cannot be inferior to the other civilly or politically. If one race be inferior to the other socially, the Constitution of the United States cannot put them upon the same plane. . . .

Justice Harlan dissenting.

While there may be in Louisiana persons of different races who are not citizens of the United States, the words in the act, "white and colored races," necessarily include all citizens of the United States of both races residing in that State. So that we have before us a state enactment that compels, under penalties, the separation of the two races in railroad passenger coaches, and makes it a crime for a citizen of either race to enter a coach that has been assigned to citizens of the other race.

Thus the State regulates the use of a public highway by citizens of the United States solely upon the basis of race.

However apparent the injustice of such legislation may be, we have only to consider whether it is consistent with the Constitution of the United States. . . .

In respect of civil rights, common to all citizens, the Constitution of the United States does not, I think, permit any public authority to know the race of those entitled to be protected in the enjoyment of such rights. Every true man has pride of race, and under appropriate circumstances when the rights of others, his equals before the law, are not to be affected, it is his privilege to express such pride and to take such action based upon it as to him seems proper. But I deny that any legislative body or judicial tribunal may have regard to the race of citizens when the civil rights of those citizens are involved. Indeed, such legislation, as that here in question, is inconsistent not only with that equality of rights which pertains to citizenship, National and State, but with the personal liberty enjoyed by every one within the United States. . . .

The white race deems itself to be the dominant race in this country. And so it is, in prestige, in achievements, in education, in wealth and in power. So, I doubt not, it will continue to be for all time, if it remains true to its great heritage and holds fast to the principles of constitutional liberty. But in view of the Constitution, in the eye of the law, there is in this country no superior, dominant, ruling class of citizens. There is no caste here. Our Constitution is color-blind, and neither knows nor tolerates classes among citizens. In respect of civil rights, all citizens are equal before the law. The humblest is the peer of the most powerful. The law regards man as man, and takes no account of his surroundings or of his color when his civil rights as guaranteed by the supreme law of the land are involved. It is, therefore, to be regretted that this high tribunal, the final expositor of the fundamental law of the land, has reached the conclusion that it is competent for a State to regulate the enjoyment by citizens of their civil rights solely upon the basis of race.

In my opinion, the judgment this day rendered will, in time, prove to be quite as pernicious as the decision made by this tribunal in the *Dred Scott case.* It was adjudged in that case that the descendants of Africans who were imported into this country and sold as slaves were not included nor intended to be included under the word "citizens" in the Constitution, and could not claim any of the rights and privileges which that instrument provided for and secured to citizens of the United States; that at the time of the adoption of the Constitution they were "considered as a subordinate and inferior class of beings, who had been subjugated by the dominant race, and, whether emancipated or not, yet remained subject to their authority, and had no rights or privileges but such as those who held the power and the government might choose to grant them." 19 How. 393, 404. The recent amendments of the Constitution, it was supposed, had eradicated these principles from our institutions. But it seems that we have yet, in some of the States, a dominant race — a superior class of citizens, which assumes to regulate the enjoyment of civil rights, common to all citizens, upon the basis of race. The present decision, it may well be apprehended, will not only stimulate aggressions, more or less brutal and irritating, upon the admitted rights of colored citizens, but will encourage the belief that it is possible, by means of state enactments, to defeat the beneficent purposes which the people of the United States had in view when they adopted the recent amendments of the Constitution, by one of which the blacks of this country were made citizens of the United States and of the States in which they respectively reside, and whose privileges and immunities, as citizens, the States are forbidden to abridge. Sixty millions of whites are in no danger from the presence here of eight millions of blacks. The destinies of the two races, in this country, are indissolubly linked together, and the interests of both require that the common government of all shall not permit the seeds of race hate to be planted under the sanction of law. What can more certainly arouse race hate, what more certainly create and perpetuate a feeling of distrust between these races, than state enactments, which, in fact, proceed on the ground that colored citizens are so inferior and degraded that they cannot be allowed to sit in public coaches occupied by white citizens? That, as all will admit, is the real meaning of such legislation as was enacted in Louisiana. . . .

If evils will result from the commingling of the two races upon public highways established for the benefit of all, they will be infinitely less than those that will surely come from state legislation regulating the enjoyment of civil rights upon the basis of race. We boast of the freedom enjoyed by our people above all other peoples. But it is difficult to reconcile that boast with a state of the law which, practically, puts the brand of servitude and degradation upon a large class of our fellow-citizens, our equals before the law. The thin disguise of "equal" accommodations for passengers in railroad coaches will not mislead any one, nor atone for the wrong this day done. . . .

I am of opinion that the statute of Louisiana is inconsistent with the personal liberty of citizens, white and black, in that State, and hostile to both the spirit and letter of the Constitution of the United States. If laws of like character should be enacted in the several States of the Union, the effect would be in the highest degree mischievous. Slavery, as an institution tolerated by law would, it is true, have disappeared from our country, but there would remain a power in the States, by sinister legislation, to interfere with the full enjoyment of the blessings of freedom; to regulate civil rights, common to all citizens upon the basis of race; and to place in a condition of legal inferiority a large body of American citizens, now constituting a part of the political community called the People of the United States, for whom, and by whom through representatives, our government is administered. Such a system is inconsistent with the guarantee given by the Constitution to each State of a republican form of government, and may be stricken down by Congressional action, or by the courts in the discharge of their solemn duty to maintain the supreme law of the land, anything in the constitution or laws of any State to the contrary notwithstanding. . . .

V

The Constitution
and the Economy:

1873–1917

State Rate Regulation and Due Process

Slaughter-House Cases

In 1869, the Louisiana legislature passed an act regulating slaughter-houses in New Orleans, ostensibly as a health measure. It declared that one company would have exclusive privileges for the live-stock landing and the slaughtering business in the city. Led by ex-Justice John A. Campbell as counsel, the companies excluded by the new law contended that it violated the Fourteenth Amendment for it abridged their privileges and immunities, denied them equal protection of the laws, and deprived them of their property without due process of law. The majority of the Court seemed genuinely shocked by the use of the new amendment. They believed that it had been passed solely for the benefit of the new freedman, and they summarily dismissed the butchers' argument. Justice Miller's majority opinion reaffirmed traditional ideas sustaining state regulatory powers. But the dissents of Justices Field and Bradley were more relevant for the future course of constitutional law.

Justice Miller delivered the opinion of the Court.

This statute is denounced not only as creating a monopoly and conferring odious and exclusive privileges upon a small number of persons at the expense of the great body of the community of New Orleans, but it is asserted that it deprives a large and meritorious class of citizens — the whole of the butchers of the city — of the right to exercise their trade, the business to which they have been trained and on which they depend for the support of themselves and their families; and that the unrestricted exercise of the business of butchering is necessary to the daily subsistence of the population of the city.

But a critical examination of the act hardly justifies these assertions. . . .

It is not, and cannot be successfully controverted, that it is both the right and the duty of the legislative body — the supreme power of the

16 Wallace 36 (1873)

State or municipality — to prescribe and determine the localities where the business of slaughtering for a great city may be conducted. To do this effectively it is indispensable that all persons who slaughter animals for food shall do it in those places *and nowhere else.*

The statute under consideration defines these localities and forbids slaughtering in any other. It does not, as has been asserted, prevent the butcher from doing his own slaughtering. On the contrary, the Slaughter-House Company is required, under a heavy penalty, to permit any person who wishes to do so, to slaughter in their houses; and they are bound to make ample provision for the convenience of all the slaughtering for the entire city. The butcher then is still permitted to slaughter, to prepare, and to sell his own meats; but he is required to slaughter at a specified place and to pay a reasonable compensation for the use of the accommodations furnished him at that place.

The wisdom of the monopoly granted by the legislature may be open to question, but it is difficult to see a justification for the assertion that the butchers are deprived of the right to labor in their occupation, or the people of their daily service in preparing food, or how this statute, with the duties and guards imposed upon the company, can be said to destroy the business of the butcher, or seriously interfere with its pursuit.

The power here exercised by the legislature of Louisiana is, in its essential nature, one which has been, up to the present period in the constitutional history of this country, always conceded to belong to the States, however it may *now* be questioned in some of its details. . . .

It may . . . be considered as established, that the authority of the legislature of Louisiana to pass the present statute is ample, unless some restraint in the exercise of that power be found in the constitution of that State or in the amendments to the Constitution of the United States, adopted since the date of the decisions we have already cited.

If any such restraint is supposed to exist in the constitution of the State, the Supreme Court of Louisiana having necessarily passed on that question, it would not be open to review in this court.

The plaintiffs in error accepting this issue, allege that the statute is a violation of the Constitution of the United States in these several particulars:

That it creates an involuntary servitude forbidden by the thirteenth article of amendment;

That it abridges the privileges and immunities of citizens of the United States;

That it denies to the plaintiffs the equal protection of the laws; and,

That it deprives them of their property without due process of law; contrary to the provisions of the first section of the fourteenth article of amendment.

This court is thus called upon for the first time to give construction to these articles. . . .

The most cursory glance at these articles discloses a unity of purpose, when taken in connection with the history of the times, which cannot fail to have an important bearing on any question of doubt concerning their true meaning. Nor can such doubts, when any reasonably exist, be safely and rationally solved without a reference to that history; for in it is found the occasion and the necessity for recurring again to the great source of power in this country, the people of the States, for additional guarantees of human rights; additional powers to the Federal government; additional restraints upon those of the States. Fortunately that history is fresh within the memory of us all, and its leading features, as they bear upon the matter before us, free from doubt.

The institution of African slavery, as it existed in about half the States of the Union, and the contests pervading the public mind for many years, between those who desired its curtailment and ultimate extinction and those who desired additional safeguards for its security and perpetuation, culminated in the effort, on the part of most of the States in which slavery existed, to separate from the Federal government, and to resist its authority. This constituted the war of the rebellion, and whatever auxiliary causes may have contributed to bring about this war, undoubtedly the overshadowing and efficient cause was African slavery.

In that struggle slavery, as a legalized social relation, perished. It perished as a necessity of the bitterness and force of the conflict. . . . Hence the thirteenth article of amendment of that instrument. Its two short sections seem hardly to admit of construction, so vigorous is their expression and so appropriate to the purpose we have indicated.

"1. Neither slavery nor involuntary servitude, except as a punishment for crime, whereof the party shall have been duly convicted, shall exist within the United States or any place subject to their jurisdiction.

"2. Congress shall have power to enforce this article by appropriate legislation."

To withdraw the mind from the contemplation of this grand yet simple declaration of the personal freedom of all the human race within the jurisdiction of this government — a declaration designed to establish the freedom of four millions of slaves — and with a microscopic search endeavor to find in it a reference to servitudes, which may have been attached to property in certain localities, requires an effort, to say the least of it.

That a personal servitude was meant is proved by the use of the word "involuntary," which can only apply to human beings. The exception of servitude as a punishment for crime gives an idea of the class of servitude that is meant. The word servitude is of larger meaning than slavery, as the latter is popularly understood in this country, and the obvious purpose was to forbid all shades and conditions of African slavery. It was very well understood that in the form of apprenticeship for long terms, as it had been practiced in the West India Islands, on the abolition of slavery by the English government, or by reducing the slaves to the condition of serfs attached to the plantation, the purpose of the article might have been evaded, if only the word slavery had been used. . . .

The process of restoring to their proper relations with the Federal government and with the other States those which had sided with the rebellion, undertaken under the proclamation of President Johnson in 1865, and before the assembling of Congress, developed the fact that, notwithstanding the formal recognition by those States of the abolition of slavery, the condition of the slave race would, without further protection of the Federal government, be almost as bad as it was before. Among the first acts of legislation adopted by several of the States in the legislative bodies which claimed to be in their normal relations with the Federal government, were laws which imposed upon the colored race onerous disabilities and burdens, and curtailed their rights in the pursuit of life, liberty, and property to such an extent that their freedom was of little value, while they had lost the protection which they had received from their former owners from motives both of interest and humanity. . . .

These circumstances, whatever of falsehood or misconception may have been mingled with their presentation, forced upon the statesmen who had conducted the Federal government in safety through the crisis of the rebellion, and who supposed that by the thirteenth article of amendment they had secured the result of their labors, the conviction that something more was necessary in the way of constitutional protection to the unfortunate race who had suffered so much. They accordingly passed through Congress the proposition for the fourteenth amendment, and they declined to treat as restored to their full participation in the government of the Union the States which had been in insurrection, until they ratified that article by a formal vote of their legislative bodies. . . .

The first section of the fourteenth article, to which our attention is more specially invited, opens with a definition of citizenship — not only citizenship of the United States, but citizenship of the States. No such definition was previously found in the Constitution, nor had any attempt been made to define it by act of Congress. It had been the occasion of much discussion in the courts, by the executive departments, and in the public journals. It had been said by eminent judges that no man was a citizen of the United States, except as he was a citizen of one of the States composing the Union. Those, therefore, who had been born and resided always in the District of Columbia or in the Territories, though within the United States, were not citizens. Whether this proposition was sound or not had never been judicially decided. But it had been held by this court, in the celebrated Dred Scott case, only a few years before the outbreak of the civil war, that a man of African descent, whether a slave or not, was not and could not be a citizen of a State or of the United States. This decision, while it met the condemnation of some of the ablest statesmen and constitutional lawyers of the country, had never been overruled; and if it was to be accepted as a constitutional limitation of the right of citizenship, then all the negro race who had recently been made freemen, were still, not only not citizens, but were incapable of becoming so by anything short of an amendment to the Constitution.

To remove this difficulty primarily, and to establish a clear and comprehensive definition of citizenship which should declare what should constitute citizenship of the United States, and also citizenship of a State, the first clause of the first section was framed.

"All persons born or naturalized in the United States, and subject to the jurisdiction thereof, are citizens of the United States and of the State wherein they reside."

The first observation we have to make on this clause is, that it puts at rest both the questions which we stated to have been the subject of differences of opinion. It declares that persons may be citizens of the United States without regard to their citizenship of a particular State, and it overturns the Dred Scott decision by making *all persons* born within the United States and subject to its jurisdiction citizens of the United States. That its main purpose was to establish the citizenship of the negro can admit of no doubt. The phrase, "subject to its jurisdiction" was intended to exclude from its operation children of ministers, consuls, and citizens or subjects of foreign States born within the United States.

The next observation is more important in view of the arguments of counsel in the present case. It is, that the distinction between citizenship of the United States and citizenship of a State is clearly recognized and established. Not only may a man be a citizen of the United States without being a citizen of a State, but an important element is necessary to convert the former into the latter. He must reside within the State to make him a citizen of it, but it is only necessary that he should be born or naturalized in the United States to be a citizen of the Union.

It is quite clear, then, that there is a citizenship of the United States, and a citizenship of a State, which are distinct from each other, and which depend upon different characteristics or circumstances in the individual.

We think this distinction and its explicit recognition in this amendment of great weight in this argument, because the next paragraph of this same section, which is the one mainly relied on by the plaintiffs in error, speaks only of privileges and immunities of citizens of the United States, and does not speak of those of citizens of the several States. The argument, however, in favor of the plaintiffs rests wholly on the assumption that the citizenship is the same, and the privileges and immunities guaranteed by the clause are the same.

The language is, "No State shall make or enforce any law which shall abridge the privileges or immunities of citizens of *the United States*." It is a little remarkable, if this clause was intended as a protection to the citizen of a State against the legislative power of his own State, that the word citizen of the State should be left out when it is so carefully used, and used in contradistinction to citizens of the United States, in the very sentence which precedes it. It is too clear for argument that the change in phraseology was adopted understandingly and with a purpose.

Of the privileges and immunities of the citizen of the United States, and of the privileges and immunities of the citizen of the State, and what they respectively are, we will presently consider; but we wish to state here that it is only the former which are placed by this clause under the protection of the Federal Constitution, and that the latter, whatever they may be, are not intended to have any additional protection by this paragraph of the amendment.

If, then, there is a difference between the privileges and immunities belonging to a citizen of the United States as such, and those belonging to the citizen of the State as such the latter must rest for their security and protection where they have heretofore rested; for they are not embraced by this paragraph of the amendment.

The first occurrence of the words "privileges and immunities" in our constitutional history, is to be found in the fourth of the articles of the old Confederation.

It declares

"that the better to secure and perpetuate mutual friendship and intercourse among the people of the different States in this Union, the free inhabitants of each of these States, paupers, vagabonds, and fugitives from justice excepted, shall be entitled to all the privileges and immunities of free citizens in the several States; and the people of each State shall have free ingress and regress to and from any other State, and shall enjoy therein all the privileges of trade and commerce, subject to the same duties, impositions, and restrictions as the inhabitants thereof respectively."

In the Constitution of the United States, which superseded the Articles of Confederation, the corresponding provision is found in section two of the fourth article, in the following words: "The citizens of each State shall be entitled to all the privileges and immunities of citizens of the several States."

There can be but little question that the purpose of both these provisions is the same, and that the privileges and immunities intended are the same in each. In the article of the Confederation we have some of these specifically mentioned, and enough perhaps to give some general idea of the class of civil rights meant by the phrase.

Fortunately we are not without judicial construction of this clause of the Constitution. The first and the leading case on the subject is that of *Corfield* v. *Coryell*, decided by Mr. Justice Washington in the Circuit Court for the District of Pennsylvania in 1823.

> "The inquiry," he says, "is, what are the privileges and immunities of citizens of the several States? We feel no hesitation in confining these expressions to those privileges and immunities which are *fundamental;* which belong of right to the citizens of all free governments, and which have at all times been enjoyed by citizens of the several States which compose this Union, from the time of their becoming free, independent, and sovereign. What these fundamental principles are, it would be more tedious than difficult to enumerate. They may all, however, be comprehended under the following general heads: protection by the government, with the right to acquire and possess property of every kind, and to pursue and obtain happiness and safety, subject, nevertheless, to such restraints as the government may prescribe for the general good of the whole." . . .

The constitutional provision there alluded to did not create those rights, which it called privileges and immunities of citizens of the States. It threw around them in that clause no security for the citizen of the State in which they were claimed or exercised. Nor did it profess to control the power of the State governments over the rights of its own citizens.

Its sole purpose was to declare to the several States, that whatever those rights, as you grant or establish them to your own citizens, or as you limit or qualify, or impose restrictions on their exercise, the same, neither more nor less, shall be the measure of the rights of citizens of other States within your jurisdiction.

It would be the vainest show of learning to attempt to prove by citations of authority, that up to the adoption of the recent amendments, no claim or pretence was set up that those rights depended on the Federal government for their existence or protection, beyond the very few express limitations which the Federal Constitution imposed upon the States — such, for instance, as the prohibition against ex post facto laws, bills of attainder, and laws impairing the obligation of contracts. But with the exception of these and a few other restrictions, the entire domain of the privileges and immunities of citizens of the States, as above defined, lay within the constitutional and legislative power of the States, and without that of the Federal government. Was it the purpose of the fourteenth amendment, by the simple declaration that no State should make or enforce any law which shall abridge the privileges and immunities of *citizens of the United States*, to transfer the security and protection of all the civil rights which we have mentioned, from the States to the Federal government? And where it is declared that Congress shall have the power to enforce that article, was it intended to bring within the power of Congress the entire domain of civil rights heretofore belonging exclusively to the States?

All this and more must follow, if the proposition of the plaintiffs in error be sound. For not only are these rights subject to the control of Congress whenever in its discretion any of them are supposed to be abridged by State legislation, but that body may also pass laws in advance, limiting and restricting the exercise of legislative power by the States, in their most ordinary and usual functions, as in its judgment it may think proper on all such subjects. And still further, such a construction followed by the reversal of the judgments of the Supreme Court of Louisiana in these cases, would constitute this court a perpetual censor upon all legislation of the States, on the civil rights of their own citizens, with authority to nullify such as it did not approve as consistent with those rights, as they existed at the time of the adoption of this amendment. The argument we admit is not always the most conclusive which is drawn from the consequences urged against the adoption of a particular construction of an instrument. But when, as in the case before us, these consequences are so serious, so far-reaching and pervading, so great a departure from the structure and spirit of our institutions; when the effect is to fetter and degrade the State governments by subjecting them to the control of Congress, in the exercise of powers heretofore universally conceded to them of the most ordinary and fundamental character; when in fact it radically changes the whole theory of the relations of the State and Federal governments to each other and of both these governments to the people; the argument has a force that is irresistible, in the absence of language which expresses such a purpose too clearly to admit of doubt.

We are convinced that no such results were intended by the Congress which proposed these amendments, nor by the legislatures of the States which ratified them.

Having shown that the privileges and immunities relied on in the argument are those which belong to citizens of the States as such, and that they are left to the State governments for security and protection, and not by this article placed under the special care of the Federal government, we may hold ourselves excused from defining the privileges and immunities of citizens of the United States which no State can abridge, until some case involving those privileges may make it necessary to do so.

But lest it should be said that no such privileges and immunities are to be found if those we have been considering are excluded, we venture to suggest some which owe their existence to the Federal government, its National character, its Constitution, or its laws.

One of these is well described in the case of *Crandall* v. *Nevada* [1868]. It is said to be the right of the citizen of this great country, protected by implied guarantees of its Constitution, "to come to the seat of government to assert any claim he may have upon that government, to transact any business he may have with it, to seek its protection, to share its offices, to engage in administering its functions. He has the right of free access to its seaports, through which all operations of foreign commerce are conducted, to the subtreasuries, land offices, and courts of justice in the several States." And quoting from the language of Chief Justice Taney in another case, it is said "that *for all the great purposes for which the Federal government* was established, we are one people, with one common country, *we are all citizens of the United States;*" and it is, as such citizens, that their rights are supported in this court in *Crandall* v. *Nevada.*

Another privilege of a citizen of the United States is to demand the care and protection of the Federal government over his life, liberty, and property when on the high seas or within the jurisdiction of a foreign government. Of this there can be no doubt, nor that the right depends upon his character as a citizen of the United States. The right to peaceably assemble and petition for redress of grievances, the privilege of the writ of *habeas corpus,* are rights of the citizen guaranteed by the Federal Constitution. The right to use the navigable waters of the United States, however they may penetrate the territory of the several States, all rights secured to our citizens by treaties with foreign nations, are dependent upon citizenship of the United States, and not citizenship of a State. One of these privileges is conferred by the very article under consideration. It is that a citizen of the United States can, of his own volition, become a citizen of any State of the Union by a *bona fide* residence therein, with the same rights as other citizens of that State. To these may be added the rights secured by the thirteenth and fifteenth articles of amendment, and by the other clause of the fourteenth, next to be considered.

But it is useless to pursue this branch of the inquiry, since we are of opinion that the rights claimed by these plaintiffs in error, if they have any existence, are not privileges and immunities of citizens of the United States within the meaning of the clause of the fourteenth amendment under consideration. . . .

The argument has not been much pressed in these cases that the defendant's charter deprives the plaintiffs of their property without due process of law, or that it denies to them the equal protection of the law. The first of these paragraphs has been in the Constitution since the adoption of the fifth amendment, as a restraint upon the Federal power. It is also to be found in some form of expression in the constitutions of nearly all the States, as a restraint upon the power of the States. This law, then, has practically been the same as it now is during the existence of the government, except so far as the present amendment may place the restraining power over the States in this matter in the hands of the Federal government.

We are not without judicial interpretation, therefore, both State and National, of the meaning of this clause. And it is sufficient to say that under no construction of that provision that we have ever seen, or any that we deem admissible, can the restraint imposed by the State of Louisiana upon the exercise of their trade by the butchers of New Orleans be held to be a deprivation of property within the meaning of that provision:

"Nor shall any State deny to any person within its jurisdiction the equal protection of the laws."

In the light of the history of these amendments, and the pervading purpose of them, which we have already discussed, it is not difficult to give a meaning to this clause. The existence of laws in the States where the newly emancipated negroes resided, which discriminated with gross injustice and hardship against them as a class, was the evil to be remedied by this clause, and by it such laws are forbidden.

If, however, the States did not conform their laws to its requirements, then by the fifth section of the article of amendment Congress was authorized to enforce it by suitable legislation. We doubt very much whether any action of a State not directed by way of discrimination against the negroes as a class, or on account of their race, will ever be held to come within the purview of this provision. It is so clearly a provision for that race and that emergency, that a strong case would be necessary for its application to any other. But as it is a State that is to be dealt with, and not alone the validity of its laws, we may safely leave that matter until Congress shall have exercised its power, or some case of State oppression, by denial of equal justice in its courts, shall have claimed a decision at our hands. We find no such case in the one before us, and do not deem it necessary to go over the argument again, as it may have relation to this particular clause of the amendment.

In the early history of the organization of the government, its statesmen seem to have divided on the line which should separate the powers of the National government from those of the State governments, and though this line has never been very well defined in public opinion, such a division has continued from that day to this.

The adoption of the first eleven amendments to the Constitution so soon after the original instrument was accepted, shows a prevailing sense of danger at that time from the Federal power. And it cannot be denied that such a jealousy continued to exist with many patriotic men until the breaking out of the late civil war. It was then discovered that the true danger to the perpetuity of the Union was in the capacity of the State organizations to combine and concentrate all the powers of the State, and of contiguous States, for a determined resistance to the General Government.

Unquestionably this has given great force to the argument, and added largely to the number of those who believe in the necessity of a strong National government.

But, however pervading this sentiment, and however it may have contributed to the adoption of the amendments we have been considering, we do not see in those amendments any purpose to destroy the main features of the general system. Under the pressure of all the excited feeling growing out of the war, our statesmen have still believed that the existence of the States with powers for domestic and local government, including the regulation of civil rights — the rights of person and of property — was essential to the perfect working of our complex form of government, though they have thought proper to impose additional limitations on the States, and to confer additional power on that of the Nation.

But whatever fluctuations may be seen in the history of public opinion on this subject during the period of our national existence, we think it will be found that this court, so far as its functions required, has always held with a steady and an even hand the balance between State and Federal power, and we trust that such may continue to be the history of its relation to that subject so long as it shall have duties to perform which demand of it a construction of the Constitution, or of any of its parts.

The judgments of the Supreme Court of Louisiana in these cases are
AFFIRMED.

Justice Field, dissenting.

I am unable to agree with the majority of the court in these cases, and will proceed to state the reasons of my dissent from their judgment. . . .

The question presented is . . . one of the gravest importance, not merely to the parties here, but to the whole country. It is nothing less than the question whether the recent amendments to the Federal Constitution protect the citizens of the United States against the deprivation of their common rights by State legislation. In my judgment the fourteenth amendment does afford such protection, and was so intended by the Congress which framed and the States which adopted it. . . .

The first clause of this amendment determines who are citizens of the

United States, and how their citizenship is created. Before its enactment there was much diversity of opinion among jurists and statesmen whether there was any such citizenship independent of that of the State, and, if any existed, as to the manner in which it originated. With a great number the opinion prevailed that there was no such citizenship independent of the citizenship of the State. . . .

The first clause of the fourteenth amendment changes this whole subject, and removes it from the region of discussion and doubt. It recognizes in express terms, if it does not create, citizens of the United States, and it makes their citizenship dependent upon the place of their birth, or the fact of their adoption, and not upon the constitution or laws of any State or the condition of their ancestry. A citizen of a State is now only a citizen of the United States residing in that State. The fundamental rights, privileges, and immunities which belong to him as a free man and a free citizen, now belong to him as a citizen of the United States, and are not dependent upon his citizenship of any State. . . .

The terms, privileges and immunities, are not new in the amendment; they were in the Constitution before the amendment was adopted. They are found in the second section of the fourth article, which declares that "the citizens of each State shall be entitled to all privileges and immunities of citizens in the several States," and they have been the subject of frequent consideration in judicial decisions. In *Corfield* v. *Coryell*, Mr. Justice Washington said he had

> "no hesitation in confining these expressions to those privileges and immunities which were, in their nature, fundamental; which belong of right to citizens of all free governments, and which have at all times been enjoyed by the citizens of the several States which compose the Union, from the time of their becoming free, independent, and sovereign;"

and, in considering what those fundamental privileges were, he said that perhaps it would be more tedious than difficult to enumerate them, but that they might be

> "all comprehended under the following general heads: protection by the government; the enjoyment of life and liberty, with the right to acquire and possess property of every kind, and to pursue and obtain happiness and safety, subject, nevertheless, to such restraints as the government may justly prescribe for the general good of the whole."

This appears to me to be a sound construction of the clause in question. The privileges and immunities designated are those *which of right belong to the citizens of all free governments.* Clearly among these must be placed the right to pursue a lawful employment in a lawful manner, without other restraint than such as equally affects all persons. In the discussions in Congress upon the passage of the Civil Rights Act repeated reference was made to this language of Mr. Justice Washington. It was cited by Senator Trumbull with the observation that it enumerated the very rights belonging to a citizen of the United States set forth in the first section of the act, and with the statement that all persons born in the United States, being declared by the act citizens of the United States, would thenceforth be entitled to the rights of citizens, and that these were the great fundamental rights set forth in the act; and that they were set forth "as appertaining to every freeman."

The privileges and immunities designated in the second section of the fourth article of the Constitution are, then, according to the decision cited, those which of right belong to the citizens of all free governments, and they can be enjoyed under that clause by the citizens of each State in the several States upon the same terms and conditions as they are enjoyed by the citizens of the latter States. No discrimination can be made by one State against the citizens of other States in their enjoyment, nor can any greater imposition be levied than such as is laid upon its own citizens. It is a clause which insures equality in the enjoyment of these rights between citizens of the several States whilst in the same State. . . .

This equality of right, with exemption from all disparaging and partial enactments, in the lawful pursuits of life, throughout the whole country, is the distinguishing privilege of citizens of the United States. To them, everywhere, all pursuits, all professions, all avocations are open without other restrictions than such as are imposed equally upon all others of the same age, sex, and condition. The State may prescribe such regulations for every pursuit and calling of life as will promote the public health, secure the good order and advance the general prosperity of society, but when once prescribed, the pursuit or calling must be free to be followed by every citizen who is within the conditions designated, and will conform to the regulations. This is the fundamental idea upon which our institutions rest, and unless adhered to in the legislation of the country our government will be a republic only in name. The fourteenth amendment, in my judgment, makes it essential to the validity of the legislation of every State that this equality of right should be respected. How widely this equality has been departed from, how entirely rejected and trampled upon by the act of Louisiana, I have already shown. And it is to me a matter of profound regret that its validity is recognized by a majority of this court, for by it the right of free labor, one of the most sacred and imprescriptible rights of man, is violated. . . .

I am authorized by the Chief Justice, Mr. Justice Swayne, and Mr. Justice Bradley, to state that they concur with me in this dissenting opinion.

Mr. Justice Bradley dissenting.

I concur in the opinion which has just been read by Mr. Justice Field; but desire to add a few observations for the purpose of more fully illustrating my views on the important question decided in these cases, and the special grounds on which they rest. . . .

First. Is it one of the rights and privileges of a citizen of the United States to pursue such civil employment as he may choose to adopt, subject to such reasonable regulations as may be prescribed by law?

Secondly. Is a monopoly, or exclusive right, given to one person to the exclusion of all others, to keep slaughter-houses, in a district of nearly twelve hundred square miles, for the supply of meat for a large city, a reasonable regulation of that employment which the legislature has a right to impose?

The first of these questions is one of vast importance, and lies at the very foundations of our government. The question is now settled by the fourteenth amendment itself, that citizenship of the United States is the primary citizenship in this country; and that State citizenship is secondary and derivative, depending upon citizenship of the United States and the citizen's place of residence. The States have not now, if they ever had, any power to restrict their citizenship to any classes or persons. A citizen of the United States has a perfect constitutional right to go to and reside in any State he chooses, and to claim citizenship therein, and an equality of rights with every other citizen; and the whole power of the nation is pledged to sustain him in that right. He is not bound to cringe to any superior, or to pray for any act of grace, as a means of enjoying all the rights and privileges enjoyed by other citizens. And when the spirit of lawlessness, mob violence, and sectional hate can be so completely repressed as to give full practical effect to this right, we shall be a happier nation, and a more prosperous one than we now are. Citizenship of the United States ought to be, and, according to the Constitution, is, a sure and undoubted title to equal rights in any and every State in this Union, subject to such regulations as the legislature may rightfully prescribe. If a man be denied full equality before the law, he is denied one of the essential rights of citizenship as a citizen of the United States.

Every citizen, then, being primarily a citizen of the United States, and, secondarily, a citizen of the State where he resides, what, in general, are the privileges and immunities of a citizen of the United States? Is the right, liberty, or privilege of choosing any lawful employment one of them? . . .

The right of a State to regulate the conduct of its citizens is undoubtedly a very broad and extensive one, and not to be lightly restricted.

But there are certain fundamental rights which this right of regulation cannot infringe. It may prescribe the manner of their exercise, but it cannot subvert the rights themselves. I speak now of the rights of citizens of any free government. Granting for the present that the citizens of one government cannot claim the privileges of citizens in another government; that prior to the union of our North American States the citizens of one State could not claim the privileges of citizens in another State; or, that after the union was formed the citizens of the United States, as such, could not claim the privileges of citizens in any particular State; yet the citizens of each of the States and the citizens of the United States would be entitled to certain privileges and immunities as citizens, at the hands of their own government — privileges and immunities which their own governments respectively would be bound to respect and maintain. In this free country, the people of which inherited certain traditionary rights and privileges from their ancestors, citizenship means something. It has certain privileges and immunities attached to it which the government, whether restricted by express or implied limitations, cannot take away or impair. It may do so temporarily by force, but it cannot do so by right. And these privileges and immunities attach as well to citizenship of the United States as to citizenship of the States. . . .

[P]ersonal rights were . . . claimed by the very first Congress of the Colonies, assembled in 1774, as the undoubted inheritance of the people of this country; and the Declaration of Independence, which was the first political act of the American people in their independent sovereign capacity, lays the foundation of our National existence upon this broad proposition: "That all men are created equal; that they are endowed by their Creator with certain inalienable rights; that among these are life, liberty, and the pursuit of happiness." Here again we have the great threefold division of the rights of freemen, asserted as the rights of man. Rights to life, liberty, and the pursuit of happiness are equivalent to the rights of life, liberty, and property. These are the fundamental rights which can only be taken away by due process of law, and which can only be interfered with, or the enjoyment of which can only be modified, by lawful regulations necessary or proper for the mutual good of all; and these rights, I contend, belong to the citizens of every free government.

For the preservation, exercise, and enjoyment of these rights the individual citizen, as a necessity, must be left free to adopt such calling, profession, or trade as may seem to him most conducive to that end. Without this right he cannot be a freeman. This right to choose one's calling is an essential part of that liberty which it is the object of government to protect; and a calling, when chosen, is a man's property and right. Liberty and property are not protected where these rights are arbitrarily assailed. . . .

But we are not bound to resort to implication, or to the constitutional history of England, to find an authoritative declaration of some of the most important privileges and immunities of citizens of the United States. It is in the Constitution itself. The Constitution, it is true, as it stood prior to the recent amendments, specifies, in terms, only a few of the personal privileges and immunities of citizens, but they are very comprehensive in their character. The States were merely prohibited from passing bills of attainder, *ex post facto* laws, laws impairing the obligation of contracts, and perhaps one or two more. But others of the greatest consequence were enumerated, although they were only secured, in express terms, from invasion by the Federal government; such as the right of *habeas corpus*, the right of trial by jury, of free exercise of religious worship, the right of free speech and a free press, the right peaceably to assemble for the discussion of public measures, the right to be secure against unreasonable searches and seizures, and above all, and including almost all the rest, the right of *not being deprived of life, liberty, or property, without due process of law*. These, and still others are specified in the original Constitution, or in the early amendments of it, as among the privileges and immunities of citizens of the United States, or, what is still stronger for the force of the argument, the rights of all persons, whether citizens or not. . . .

The next question to be determined in this case is: Is a monopoly or exclusive right, given to one person, or corporation, to the exclusion of all others, to keep slaughter-houses in a district of nearly twelve hundred square miles, for the supply of meat for a great city, a reasonable regulation of that employment which the legislature has a right to impose?

The keeping of a slaughter-house is part of, and incidental to, the trade of a butcher — one of the ordinary occupations of human life. To compel a butcher, or rather all the butchers of a large city and an extensive district, to slaughter their cattle in another person's slaughter-house and pay him a toll therefor, is such a restriction upon the trade as materially to interfere with its prosecution. It is onerous, unreasonable, arbitrary, and unjust. It has none of the qualities of a police regulation. If it were really a police regulation, it would undoubtedly be within the power of the legislature. That portion of the act which requires all slaughter-houses to be located below the city, and to be subject to inspection, &c., is clearly a police regulation. That portion which allows no one but the favored company to build, own, or have slaughter-houses is not a police regulation, and has not the faintest semblance of one. It is one of those arbitrary and unjust laws made in the interest of a few scheming individuals, by which some of the Southern States have, within the past few years, been so deplorably oppressed and impoverished. It seems to me strange that it can be viewed in any other light. . . .

In my view, a law which prohibits a large class of citizens from adopting a lawful employment, or from following a lawful employment previously adopted, does deprive them of liberty as well as property, without due process of law. Their right of choice is a portion of their liberty; their occupation is their property. Such a law also deprives those citizens of the equal protection of the laws, contrary to the last clause of the section. . . .

The mischief to be remedied was not merely slavery and its incidents and consequences; but that spirit of insubordination and disloyalty to the National government which had troubled the country for so many years in some of the States, and that intolerance of free speech and free discussion which often rendered life and property insecure, and led to much unequal legislation. The amendment was an attempt to give voice to the strong National yearning for that time and that condition of things, in which American citizenship should be a sure guaranty of safety, and in which every citizen of the United States might stand erect on every portion of its soil, in the full enjoyment of every right and privilege belonging to a freeman, without fear of violence or molestation. . . .

The great question is, What is the true construction of the amendment? When once we find that, we shall find the means of giving it effect. The argument from inconvenience ought not to have a very controlling influence in questions of this sort. The National will and National interest are of far greater importance.

In my opinion the judgment of the Supreme Court of Louisiana ought to be reversed.

Munn *v.* Illinois

Munn *v.* Illinois *was one of several so-called Granger Cases which dealt with state regulations of railroads and grain warehouses. This particular case involved a state statute fixing maximum charges for the storage of grain in the Chicago area. As in the* Slaughter-House Cases, *corporate lawyers again denounced such regulations as tantamount to a deprivation of property without due process of law, and in addition, as unwarranted interferences with interstate commerce. The traditionally oriented majority upheld the Illinois law as a valid regulation of a business affected with a public interest. Still in a minority position, Justice Field again urged his colleagues to acknowledge the due process argument and assume a more activist judicial role in striking down such legislation.*

Chief Justice Waite delivered the opinion of the Court.

The question to be determined in this case is whether the general assembly of Illinois can, under the limitations upon the legislative power of the States imposed by the Constitution of the United States, fix by law the maximum of charges for the storage of grain in warehouses at Chicago and other places in the State having not less than one hundred thousand inhabitants, "in which grain is stored in bulk, and in which the grain of different owners is mixed together, or in which grain is stored in such a manner that the identity of different lots or parcels cannot be accurately preserved."

It is claimed that such a law is repugnant —

1. To that part of sect. 8, art. 1, of the Constitution of the United States which confers upon Congress the power "to regulate commerce with foreign nations and among the several States;"

2. To that part of sect. 9 of the same article which provides that "no preference shall be given by any regulation of commerce or revenue to the ports of one State over those of another;" and

3. To that part of amendment 14 which ordains that no State shall "deprive any person of life, liberty, or property, without due process of law, nor deny to any person within its jurisdiction the equal protection of the laws."

We will consider the last of these objections first. . . .

The Constitution contains no definition of the word "deprive," as used

---

94 U.S. 113 (1877)

in the Fourteenth Amendment. To determine its signification, therefore, it is necessary to ascertain the effect which usage has given it, when employed in the same or a like connection.

While this provision of the amendment is new in the Constitution of the United States, as a limitation upon the powers of the States, it is old as a principle of civilized government. It is found in Magna Charta, and, in substance if not in form, in nearly or quite all the constitutions that have been from time to time adopted by the several States of the Union. By the Fifth Amendment, it was introduced into the Constitution of the United States as a limitation upon the powers of the national government, and by the Fourteenth, as a guaranty against any encroachment upon an acknowledged right of citizenship by the legislature of the States. . . .

When one becomes a member of society, he necessarily parts with some rights or privileges which, as an individual not affected by his relations to others, he might retain. "A body politic," as aptly defined in the preamble of the Constitution of Massachusetts, "is a social compact by which the whole people covenants with each citizen, and each citizen with the whole people, that all shall be governed by certain laws for the common good." This does not confer power upon the whole people to control rights which are purely and exclusively private, . . . but it does authorize the establishment of laws requiring each citizen to so conduct himself, and so use his own property, as not unnecessarily to injure another. This is the very essence of government. . . . From this source come the police powers. . . . Under these powers the government regulates the conduct of its citizens one towards another, and the manner in which each shall use his own property, when such regulation becomes necessary for the public good. In their exercise it has been customary in England from time immemorial, and in this country from its first colonization, to regulate ferries, common carriers, hackmen, bakers, millers, wharfingers, innkeepers, &c., and in so doing to fix a maximum of charge to be made for services rendered, accommodations furnished, and articles sold. To this day, statutes are to be found in many of the States upon some or all these subjects; and we think it has never yet been successfully contended that such legislation came within any of the constitutional prohibitions against interference with private property. . . .

From this it is apparent that, down to the time of the adoption of the Fourteenth Amendment, it was not supposed that statutes regulating the use, or even the price of the use, of private property necessarily deprived an owner of his property without due process of law. Under some circumstances they may, but not under all. The amendment does not change the law in this particular: it simply prevents the States from doing that which will operate as such a deprivation.

This brings us to inquire as to the principles upon which this power of regulation rests, in order that we may determine what is within and what without its operative effect. Looking, then, to the common law, from whence came the right which the Constitution protects, we find that when private property is "affected with a public interest, it ceases to be *juris privati* only." This was said by Lord Chief Justice Hale more than two hundred years ago, . . . and has been accepted without objection as an essential element in the law of property ever since. Property does become clothed with a public interest when used in a manner to make it of public consequence, and affect the community at large. When, therefore, one devotes his property to a use in which the public has an interest, he, in effect, grants to the public an interest in that use, and must submit to be controlled by the public for the common good, to the extent of the interest he has thus created. He may withdraw his grant by discontinuing the use; but, so long as he maintains the use, he must submit to the control. . . .

But we need not go further. Enough has already been said to show that, when private property is devoted to a public use, it is subject to public regulation. It remains only to ascertain whether the warehouses of these plaintiffs in error, and the business which is carried on there, come within the operation of this principle. . . .

In this connection it must also be borne in mind that, although in 1874 there were in Chicago fourteen warehouses adapted to this particular business, and owned by about thirty persons, nine business firms controlled them, and that the prices charged and received for storage were such "as have been from year to year agreed upon and established by the different elevators or warehouses in the city of Chicago, and which rates have been annually published in one or more newspapers printed in said city, in the month of January in each year, as the established rates for the year then next ensuing such publication." Thus it is apparent that all the elevating facilities through which these vast productions "of seven or eight great States of the West" must pass on the way "to four or five of the States on the seashore" may be a "virtual" monopoly.

Under such circumstances it is difficult to see why, if the common carrier, or the miller, or the ferryman, or the innkeeper, or the wharfinger, or the baker, or the cartman, or the hackney-coachman, pursues a public employment and exercises "a sort of public office," these plaintiffs in error do not. They stand, to use again the language of their counsel, in the very "gateway of commerce," and take toll from all who pass. Their business most certainly "tends to a common charge, and is become a thing of public interest and use." . . . Certainly, if any business can be clothed "with a public interest, and cease to be *juris privati* only," this has been. It may not be made so by the operation of the Constitution of Illinois or this statute, but it is by the facts. . . .

For our purposes we must assume that, if a state of facts could exist that would justify such legislation, it actually did exist when the statute now under consideration was passed. For us the question is one of power, not of expediency. If no state of circumstances could exist to justify such a statute, then we may declare this one void, because [it is] in excess of the legislative power of the State. But if it could, we must presume it did. Of the propriety of legislative interference within the scope of legislative power, the legislature is the exclusive judge.

Neither is it a matter of any moment that no precedent can be found for a statute precisely like this. It is conceded that the business is one of recent origin, that its growth has been rapid, and that it is already of great importance. And it must also be conceded that it is a business in which the whole public has a direct and positive interest. It presents, therefore, a case for the application of a long-known and well-established principle in social science, and this statute simply extends the law so as to meet this new development of commercial progress. There is no attempt to compel these owners to grant the public an interest in their property, but to declare their obligations, if they use it in this particular manner.

It matters not in this case that these plaintiffs in error had built their warehouses and established their business before the regulations complained of were adopted. What they did was from the beginning subject to the power of the body politic to require them to conform to such regulations as might be established by the proper authorities for the common good. They entered upon their business and provided themselves with the means to carry it on subject to this condition. If they did not wish to submit themselves to such interference, they should not have clothed the public with an interest in their concerns. The same principle applies to them that does to the proprietor of a hackney-carriage, and as to him it has never been supposed that he was exempt from regulating statutes or ordinances because he had purchased his horses and carriage and established his business before the statute or the ordinance was adopted.

It is insisted, however, that the owner of property is entitled to a reasonable compensation for its use, even though it be clothed with a public interest, and that what is reasonable is a judicial and not a legislative question.

As has already been shown, the practice has been otherwise. In countries where the common law prevails, it has been customary from time immemorial for the legislature to declare what shall be a reasonable compensation under such circumstances, or, perhaps more properly speaking, to fix a maximum beyond which any charge made would be unreasonable. Undoubtedly, in mere private contracts, relating to matters in which the public has no interest, what is reasonable must be ascertained judicially. But this is because the legislature has no control over such a contract. So, too, in matters which do affect the public interest, and as to which legislative control may be exercised, . . . the courts must determine what is reasonable. The controlling fact is the power to regulate at all. If that exists, the right to establish the maximum of charge, as one of the means of regulation, is implied. . . .

We know that this is a power which may be abused; but that is no argument against its existence. For protection against abuses by legislatures the people must resort to the polls, not to the courts. . . .

We come now to consider the effect upon this statute of the power of Congress to regulate commerce. . . .

The warehouses of these plaintiffs in error are situated and their business carried on exclusively within the limits of the State of Illinois. They are used as instruments by those engaged in State as well as those engaged in inter-state commerce, but they are no more necessarily a part of commerce itself than the dray or the cart by which, but for them, grain would be transferred from one railroad station to another. Incidentally they may become connected with inter-state commerce, but not necessarily so. Their regulation is a thing of domestic concern, and, certainly, until Congress acts in reference to their inter-state relations, the State may exercise all the powers of government over them, even though in so doing it may indirectly operate upon commerce outside its immediate jurisdiction. . . .

Mr. Justice Field and Mr. Justice Strong dissented.

Justice Field

I am compelled to dissent from the decision of the court in this case, and from the reasons upon which that decision is founded. The principle upon which the opinion of the majority proceeds is, in my judgment, subversive of the rights of private property, heretofore believed to be protected by constitutional guaranties against legislative interference. . . .

Wabash, St. Louis & Pacific Ry. Co.

v.

Illinois

*In Piek v. Chicago & Northwestern Ry. Co. (94 U.S. 164 [1877]),
one of the Granger Cases, Chief Justice Waite had said that in the
absence of congressional legislation, the states might continue to
regulate railroads even though their activities might be interstate
in character. By the next decade, however, the crazy-quilt pattern
of state regulation was obviously burdensome to the development
of an effective and profitable national railway system. In the case
below, the Court reconsidered its earlier position. In question
was an Illinois prohibition of long-short haul rate discriminations,
a regulation which mostly affected interstate charges.*

Mr. Justice Miller delivered the opinion of the Court.

T he question of the right of the State to regulate the rate of fares
and tolls on railroads, and how far that right was affected by the
commerce clause of the Constitution of the United States, was presented
to the court in [the Granger] cases. And it must be admitted that, in a
general way, the court treated the cases then before it as belonging to
that class of regulations of commerce which, like pilotage, bridging navigable rivers, and many others, could be acted upon by the States in
the absence of any legislation by Congress on the same subject.

By the slightest attention to the matter it will be readily seen that
the circumstances under which a bridge may be authorized across a
navigable stream within the limits of a State, for the use of a public
highway, and the local rules which shall govern the conduct of the pilots
of each of the varying harbors of the coasts of the United States, depend
upon principles far more limited in their application and importance
than those which should regulate the transportation of persons and
property across the half or the whole of the continent, over the territories
of half a dozen States, through which they are carried without change of
car or breaking bulk. . . .

[T]he great question to be decided, and which was decided, and
which was argued in all those cases, was the right of the State within

118 U.S. 557 (1886)

which a railroad company did business to regulate or limit the amount of any of these traffic charges.

The importance of that question overshadowed all others; and the case of *Munn* v. *Illinois* was selected by the court as the most appropriate one in which to give its opinion on that subject, because that case presented the question of a private citizen, or unincorporated partnership, engaged in the warehousing business in Chicago, free from any claim of right or contract under an act of incorporation of any State whatever, and free from the question of continuous transportation through several States. And in that case the court was presented with the question, which it decided, whether any one engaged in a public business, in which all the public had a right to require his service, could be regulated by acts of the legislature in the exercise of this public function and public duty, so far as to limit the amount of charges that should be made for such services.

The railroad companies set up another defence, apart from denying the general right of the legislature to regulate transportation charges, namely, that in their charters from the States they each had a contract, express or implied, that they might regulate and establish their own fares and rates of transportation. These two questions were of primary importance; and though it is true that, as incidental or auxiliary to these, the question of the exclusive right of Congress to make such regulations of charges as any legislative power had the right to make, to the exclusion of the States, was presented, it received but little attention at the hands of the court, and was passed over with the remarks in the opinions of the court which have been cited. . . .

It cannot be too strongly insisted upon that the right of continuous transportation from one end of the country to the other is essential in modern times to that freedom of commerce from the restraints which the State might choose to impose upon it, that the commerce clause was intended to secure. This clause, giving to Congress the power to regulate commerce among the States and with foreign nations, as this court has said before, was among the most important of the subjects which prompted the formation of the Constitution. . . . And it would be a very feeble and almost useless provision, but poorly adapted to secure the entire freedom of commerce among the States which was deemed essential to a more perfect union by the framers of the Constitution, if, at every stage of the transportation of goods and chattels through the country, the State within whose limits a part of this transportation must be done could impose regulations concerning the price, compensation, or taxation, or any other restrictive regulation interfering with and seriously embarrassing this commerce.

The argument on this subject can never be better stated than it is by Chief Justice Marshall in *Gibbons* v. *Ogden*. . . . He there demonstrates that commerce among the States, like commerce with foreign nations, is necessarily a commerce which crosses State lines, and extends into the States, and the power of Congress to regulate it exists wherever that commerce is found. Speaking of navigation as an element of commerce, which it is, only, as a means of transportation, now largely superseded by railroads, he says: "The power of Congress, then, comprehends navigation within the limits of every State in the Union, so far as that navigation may be, in any manner, connected with 'commerce with foreign nations, or among the several States, or with the Indian tribes.' It may, of consequence, pass the jurisdictional line of New York and act upon the very waters [the Hudson River] to which the prohibition now under consideration applies. . . ." So the same power may pass the line of the State of Illinois and act upon its restriction upon the right of transportation extending over several States, including that one. . . .

We must, therefore, hold that it is not, and never has been, the deliberate opinion of a majority of this court that a statute of a State which attempts to regulate the fares and charges by railroad companies within its limits, for a transportation which constitutes a part of commerce among the States, is a valid law.

Let us see precisely what is the degree of interference with transportation of property or persons from one State to another which this statute proposes. A citizen of New York has goods which he desires to have transported by the railroad companies from that city to the interior of the State of Illinois. A continuous line of rail over which a car loaded with these goods can be carried, and is carried habitually, connects the place of shipment with the place of delivery. He undertakes to make a contract with a person engaged in the carrying business at the end of this route from whence the goods are to start, and he is told by the carrier,

> "I am free to make a fair and reasonable contract for this carriage to the line of the State of Illinois, but when the car which carries these goods is to cross the line of that State, pursuing at the same time this continuous tract, I am met by a law of Illinois which forbids me to make a free contract concerning this transportation within that State, and subjects me to certain rules by which I am to be governed as to the charges which the same railroad company in Illinois may make, or has made, with reference to other persons and other places of delivery."

So that while that carrier might be willing to carry these goods from the city of New York to the city of Peoria at the rate of fifteen cents per hundred pounds, he is not permitted to do so because the Illinois railroad company has already charged at the rate of twenty-five cents per hundred pounds for carriage to Gilman, in Illinois, which is eighty-six miles shorter than the distance to Peoria.

So, also, in the present case, the owner of corn, the principal product of the country, desiring to transport it from Peoria, in Illinois, to New York, finds a railroad company willing to do this at the rate of fifteen cents per hundred pounds for a car-load, but is compelled to pay at the rate of twenty-five cents per hundred pounds, because the railroad company has received from a person residing at Gilman twenty-five cents per hundred pounds for the transportation of a car-load of the same class of freight over the same line of road from Gilman to New York. This is the result of the statute of Illinois, in its endeavor to prevent unjust discrimination, as construed by the Supreme Court of that State. The effect of it is, that whatever may be the rate of transportation per mile charged by the railroad company from Gilman to Sheldon, a distance of twenty-three miles, in which the loading and the unloading of the freight is the largest expense incurred by the railroad company, the same rate per mile must be charged from Peoria to the city of New York.

The obvious injustice of such a rule as this, which railroad companies are by heavy penalties compelled to conform to, in regard to commerce among the States, when applied to transportation which includes Illinois in a long line of carriage through several States, shows the value of the constitutional provision which confides the power of regulating inter-state commerce to the Congress of the United States, whose enlarged view of the interests of all the States, and of the railroads concerned, better fits it to establish just and equitable rules.

Of the justice or propriety of the principle which lies at the foundation of the Illinois statute it is not the province of this court to speak. . . . But when it is attempted to apply to transportation through an entire series of States a principle of this kind, and each one of the States shall attempt to establish its own rates of transportation, its own methods to prevent discrimination in rates, or to permit it, the deleterious influence upon the freedom of commerce among the States and upon the transit of goods through those States cannot be overestimated. That this species of regulations is one which must be, if established at all, of a general and national character, and cannot be safely and wisely remitted to local rules and local regulations, we think is clear from what has already been said. And if it be a regulation of commerce, as we think we have demonstrated it is, and as the Illinois court concedes it to be, it must be of that national character, and the regulation can only appropriately exist by general rules and principles, which demand that it should be done by Congress of the United States under the commerce clause of the Constitution. . . .

Chicago, Milw. & St. Paul Ry. Co.

v.

Minnesota

*In 1886, Chief Justice Waite reflected the change in the Court since
Munn v. Illinois when he acknowledged that the "power of limitation
or regulation is [not] itself without limit." He warned specifically
that excessive regulation without regard for corporate profits
"amounts to a taking of private property for public use without just
compensation, or without due process of law." (Stone v. Farmers'
Loan & Trust Co., 116 U.S. 307.) Four years later, in this Minnesota
case, only three members of the 1877 court survived. Justice Field's
long-standing views on due process and judicial review now tri-
umphed completely. At issue was a state law which established a
railroad commission to fix rates without necessarily requiring a
notice and hearing for the carriers. Justice Bradley, who had worked
closely with Waite on the* Munn *opinion, vigorously dissented from
the majority's bold assumption of power.*

Justice Blatchford delivered the opinion of the Court.

The construction put upon the statute by the Supreme Court of
Minnesota must be accepted by this court, for the purpose of the
present case, as conclusive and not to be reëxamined here as to its propriety or accuracy. The Supreme Court authoritatively declares that it
is the expressed intention of the legislature of Minnesota, by the statute,
that the rates recommended and published by the commission, if it proceeds in the manner pointed out by the act, are not simply advisory, nor
merely *prima facie* equal and reasonable, but final and conclusive as to
what are equal and reasonable charges; that the law neither contemplates
nor allows any issue to be made or inquiry to be had as to their equality
or reasonableness in fact; that, under the statute, the rates published by
the commission are the only ones that are lawful, and, therefore, in contemplation of law the only ones that are equal and reasonable; and
that, in a proceeding for a mandamus under the statute, there is no fact
to traverse except the violation of law in not complying with the recommendations of the commission. In other words, although the railroad

134 U.S. 418 (1890)

company is forbidden to establish rates that are not equal and reasonable, there is no power in the courts to stay the hands of the commission, if it chooses to establish rates that are unequal and unreasonable.

This being the construction of the statute by which we are bound in considering the present case, we are of opinion that, so construed, it conflicts with the Constitution of the United States in the particulars complained of by the railroad company. It deprives the company of its right to a judicial investigation, by due process of law, under the forms and with the machinery provided by the wisdom of successive ages for the investigation judicially of the truth of a matter in controversy, and substitutes therefore, as an absolute finality, the action of a railroad commission which, in view of the powers conceded to it by the state court, cannot be regarded as clothed with judicial functions or possessing the machinery of a court of justice. . . .

By the second section of the statute in question, it is provided that all charges made by a common carrier for the transportation of passengers or property shall be equal and reasonable. Under this provision, the carrier has a right to make equal and reasonable charges for such transportation. In the present case, the return alleged that the rate of charge fixed by the commission was not equal or reasonable, and the Supreme Court held that the statute deprived the company of the right to show that judicially. The question of the reasonableness of a rate of charge for transportation by a railroad company, involving as it does the element of reasonableness both as regards the company and as regards the public, is eminently a question for judicial investigation, requiring due process of law for its determination. If the company is deprived of the power of charging reasonable rates for the use of its property, and such deprivation takes place in the absence of an investigation by judicial machinery, it is deprived of the lawful use of its property, and thus, in substance and effect, of the property itself, without due process of law and in violation of the Constitution of the United States; and in so far as it is thus deprived, while other persons are permitted to receive reasonable profits upon their invested capital, the company is deprived of the equal protection of the laws. . . .

Justice Bradley, with whom concurred Justice Gray and Justice Lamar, dissenting.

I cannot agree to the decision of the court in this case. It practically overrules *Munn* v. *Illinois,* 94 U.S. 113, and the several railroad cases that were decided at the same time. The governing principle of those cases was that the regulation and settlement of the fares of railroads and other public accommodations is a legislative prerogative and not a judicial one. This is a principle which I regard as of great importance. . . .

It is always a delicate thing for the courts to make an issue with the legislative department of the government, and they should never do so if it is possible to avoid it. By the decision now made we declare, in effect, that the judiciary, and not the legislature, is the final arbiter in the regulation of fares and freights of railroads and the charges of other public accommodations. It is an assumption of authority on the part of the judiciary which, it seems to me, with all due deference to the judgment of my brethren, it has no right to make. . . .

It is complained that the decisions of the board are final and without appeal. So are the decisions of the courts in matters within their jurisdiction. There must be a final tribunal somewhere for deciding every question in the world. Injustice may take place in all tribunals. All human institutions are imperfect — courts as well as commissions and legislatures. Whatever tribunal has jurisdiction, its decisions are final and conclusive unless an appeal is given therefrom. The important question always is, what is the lawful tribunal for the particular case? In my judgement, in the present case, the proper tribunal was the legislature, or the board of commissioners which it created for the purpose. . . .

Smyth v. Ames

This case further extended judicial power over railroad and utility rates and virtually established the Supreme Court as a "super-commission." The Court here was concerned not only with the "reasonableness" of rates, but whether the rates fixed permitted a "fair return on a fair valuation" of the property. This in turn involved the Court in complex theories of what constituted fair valuation. Was it to be the original cost or was it to be the cost of reproducing the property? The so-called standard established by the Court in this case was vague enough to thrust the judiciary constantly into rate issues on a case-by-case basis, and in turn made state regulation highly uncertain.

Mr. Justice Harlan delivered the opinion of the Court.

We are now to inquire whether the Nebraska statute is repugnant to the Constitution of the United States.

By the Fourteenth Amendment it is provided that no State shall deprive any person of property without due process of law, nor deny to any person within its jurisdiction the equal protection of the laws. That corporations are persons within the meaning of this Amendment is now settled. . . . What amounts to deprivation of property without due process of law or what is a denial of the equal protection of the laws is often difficult to determine, especially where the question relates to the property of a *quasi* public corporation and the extent to which it may be subjected to public control. But this court, speaking by Chief Justice Waite, has said that, while a State has power to fix the charges by railroad companies for the transportation of persons and property within its own jurisdiction, unless restrained by valid contract, or unless what is done amounts to a regulation of foreign or interstate commerce, such power is not without limit; and that, "under pretence of regulating fares and freights, the State cannot require a railroad corporation to carry persons or property without reward, neither can it do that which in law amounts to the taking of private property for public use without just compensation, or without due process of law." . . .

[T]hese principles must be regarded as settled:

---

169 U.S. 466 (1898)

1. A railroad corporation is a person within the meaning of the Fourteenth Amendment declaring that no State shall deprive any person of property without due process of law, nor deny to any person within its jurisdiction the equal protection of the laws.

2. A state enactment, or regulations made under the authority of a state enactment, establishing rates for the transportation of persons or property by railroad that will not admit of the carrier earning such compensation as under all the circumstances is just to it and to the public, would deprive such carrier of its property without due process of law and deny to it the equal protection of the laws, and would therefore be repugnant to the Fourteenth Amendment of the Constitution of the United States.

3. While rates for the transportation of persons and property within the limits of a State are primarily for its determination, the question whether they are so unreasonably low as to deprive the carrier of its property without such compensation as the Constitution secures, and therefore without due process of law, cannot be so conclusively determined by the legislature of the State or by regulations adopted under its authority, that the matter may not become the subject of judicial inquiry.

The cases before us directly present the important question last stated. . . .

What are the considerations to which weight must be given when we seek to ascertain the compensation that a railroad company is entitled to receive, and a prohibition upon the receiving of which may be fairly deemed a deprivation by legislative decree of property without due process of law? Undoubtedly that question could be more easily determined by a commission composed of persons whose special skill, observation and experience qualifies them to so handle great problems of transportation as to do justice both to the public and to those whose money has been used to construct and maintain highways for the convenience and benefit of the people. But despite the difficulties that confessedly attend the proper solution of such questions, the court cannot shrink from the duty to determine whether it be true, as alleged, that the Nebraska statute invades or destroys rights secured by the supreme law of the land. . . .

[T]he plaintiffs contended that a railroad company is entitled to exact such charges for transportation as will enable it, at all times, not only to pay operating expenses, but also to meet the interest regularly accruing upon all its outstanding obligations, and justify a dividend upon all its stock; and that to prohibit it from maintaining rates or charges for transportation adequate to *all* those ends will deprive it of its property without due process of law, and deny to it the equal protection of the laws. This contention was the subject of elaborate discussion; and, as it bears upon each case in its important aspects, it should not be passed without examination.

In our opinion, the broad proposition advanced by counsel involves some misconception of the relations between the public and a railroad corporation. It is unsound in that it practically excludes from consideration the fair value of the property used, omits altogether any consideration of the right of the public to be exempt from unreasonable exactions, and makes the interests of the corporation maintaining a public highway the sole test in determining whether the rates established by or for it are such as may be rightfully prescribed as between it and the public. . . .

What was said in *Covington & Lexington Turnpike Road Co.* v. *Sandford,* 164 U.S. 578, 596–7, is pertinent to the question under consideration. It was there observed: "It cannot be said that a corporation is entitled, as of right, and without reference to the interests of the public, to realize a given per cent upon its capital stock. When the question arises whether the legislature has exceeded its constitutional power in prescribing rates to be charged by a corporation controlling a public highway, stockholders are not the only persons whose rights or interests are to be considered. The rights of the public are not to be ignored. It is alleged here that the rates prescribed are unreasonable and unjust to the company and its stockholders. But that involves an inquiry as to what is reasonable and just for the public. . . . The public cannot properly be subjected to unreasonable rates in order simply that stockholders may earn dividends. The legislature has the authority, in every case, where its power has not been restrained by contract, to proceed upon the ground that the public may not rightfully be required to submit to unreasonable exactions for the use of a public highway established and maintained under legislative authority. If a corporation can not maintain such a highway and earn dividends for stockholders, it is a misfortune for it and them which the Constitution does not require to be remedied by imposing unjust burdens upon the public.". . .

We hold . . . that the basis of all calculations as to the reasonableness of rates to be charged by a corporation maintaining a highway under legislative sanction must be the fair value of the property being used by it for the convenience of the public. And in order to ascertain that value, the original cost of construction, the amount expended in permanent improvements, the amount and market value of its bonds and stock, the present as compared with the original cost of construction, the probable earning capacity of the property under particular rates prescribed by statute, and the sum required to meet operating expenses, are all matters for consideration, and are to be given such weight as may be just and right in each case. We did not say that there may not be other matters to be regarded in estimating the value of the property. What the company is entitled to ask is a fair return upon the value of that which it employs for the public convenience. On the other hand, what the public is entitled to demand is that no more be exacted from it for the use of a public highway than the services rendered by it are reasonably worth. . . .

Federal Transportation Regulation

Interstate Commerce Commission

v.

Cinti., New Orleans & Tex. Pac. Ry. Co.

The Wabash *decision spurred the drive for federal regulation of the national railway network, and the following year, Congress enacted the Interstate Commerce Act. Among other things, the law required rail rates to be "reasonable" and "just," and a five man commission was established to enforce the whole law. The commission was not empowered to set rates, but by implication, the commissioners soon assumed the power to issue cease and desist orders against unreasonable rates. But nothing in the act implied any authority for the ICC to fix new rate schedules in place of the suspended ones. In the case below, the Court specifically denied any such "legislative" role for the commission.*

Justice Brewer delivered the opinion of the Court.

Before the passage of the [Interstate Commerce] act it was generally believed that there were great abuses in railroad management and railroad transportation, and the grave question which Congress had to consider was how those abuses should be corrected and what control should be taken of the business of such corporations. The present inquiry is limited to the question as to what it determined should be done with reference to the matter of rates. There were three obvious and dissimilar courses open for consideration. Congress might itself prescribe the rates; or it might commit to some subordinate tribunal this duty; or it might leave with the companies the right to fix rates, subject to regulations and restrictions, as well as to that rule which is as old as the existence of common carriers, to wit, that rates must be reasonable. There is nothing in the act fixing rates. Congress did not attempt to

167 U.S. 479 (1897)

exercise that power, and if we examine the legislative and public history of the day it is apparent that there was no serious thought of doing so.

The question debated is whether it vested in the commission the power and the duty to fix rates; and the fact that this is a debatable question, and has been most strenuously and earnestly debated, is very persuasive that it did not. The grant of such a power is never to be implied. The power itself is so vast and comprehensive, so largely affecting the rights of carrier and shipper, as well as indirectly all commercial transactions, the language by which the power is given had been so often used and was so familiar to the legislative mind and is capable of such definite and exact statement, that no just rule of construction would tolerate a grant of such power by mere implication. . . .

It is one thing to inquire whether the rates which have been charged and collected are reasonable — that is a judicial act; but an entirely different thing to prescribe rates which shall be charged in the future — that is a legislative act. *Chicago, Milwaukee &c. Railway* v. *Minnesota.* . . .

It will be perceived that in this case the Interstate Commerce Commission assumed the right to prescribe rates which should control in the future, and their application to the court was for a mandamus to compel the companies to comply with their decision; that is, to abide by their legislative determination as to the maximum rates to be observed in the future. Now, nowhere in the interstate commerce act do we find words similar to those in the statutes referred to, giving to the commission power to "increase or reduce any of the rates"; "to establish rates of charges"; "to make and fix reasonable and just rates of freight and passenger tariffs"; "to make a schedule of reasonable maximum rates of charges"; "to fix tables of maximum charges"; to compel the carrier "to adopt such rate, charge or classification as said commissioners shall declare to be equitable and reasonable." The power, therefore, is not expressly given. . . . Congress did not intend to give to the commission the power to prescribe any tariff and determine what for the future should be reasonable and just rates. The power given is the power to execute and enforce, not to legislate. The power given is partly judicial, partly executive and administrative, but not legislative. . . .

We have, therefore, these considerations presented: First. The power to prescribe a tariff of rates for carriage by a common carrier is a legislative and not an administrative or judicial function, and, having respect to the large amount of property invested in railroads, the various companies engaged therein, the thousands of miles of road, and the millions of tons of freight carried, the varying and diverse conditions attaching to such carriage, is a power of supreme delicacy and importance. Second. That Congress has transferred such a power to any administrative body is not to be presumed or implied from any doubtful and uncertain language. The words and phrases efficacious to make such a delegation of power are well understood and have been frequently used, and if Congress had intended to grant such a power to the Interstate Commerce Commission it cannot be doubted that it would have used language open to no misconstruction, but clear and direct. Third. Incorporating into a statute the common law obligation resting upon the carrier to make all its charges reasonable and just, and directing the commission to execute and enforce the provisions of the act, does not by implication carry to the commissioner or invest it with the power to exercise the legislative function of prescribing rates which shall control in the future. Fourth. Beyond the inference which irresistibly follows from the omission to grant in express terms to the commission this power of fixing rates, is the clear language of section 6, recognizing the right of the carrier to establish rates, to increase or reduce them, and prescribing the conditions upon which such increase or reduction may be made, and requiring, as the only conditions of its action, first, publication, and, second, the filing of the tariff with the commission. The grant to the commission of the power to prescribe the form of the schedules, and to direct the place and manner of publication of joint rates, thus specifying the scope and limit of its functions in this respect, strengthens the conclusion that the power to prescribe rates or fix any tariff for the future is not among the powers granted to the commission.

These considerations convince us that under the interstate commerce act the commission has no power to prescribe the tariff of rates which shall control in the future, and, therefore, cannot invoke a judgment in mandamus from the courts to enforce any such tariff by it prescribed. . . .

Interstate Commerce Commission

v.

Illinois Central Railroad Co.

In 1897, the Court also struck at the ICC's fact-finding role when it insisted that courts could reverse the Commission on its facts or determine new ones. (Interstate Commerce Commission v. Alabama Midland Ry. Co., 168 U.S. 144). But new legislation in the next decade, such as the Hepburn Act and the Mann-Elkins Act, revitalized the Commission's role and powers and narrowed the scope of judicial review. In 1907, the Court reversed itself and said that it would accept the Commission's findings of fact as conclusive. (Illinois Central Railroad Co. v. Interstate Commerce Commission, 206 U.S. 441). Three years later, in the case below, the Court indicated a new willingness to accept a policy-making role for the Commission.

Justice White delivered the opinion of the Court.

In determining whether an order of the commission shall be suspended or set aside, we must consider, *a,* all relevant questions of constitutional power or right; *b,* all pertinent questions as to whether the administrative order is within the scope of the delegated authority under which it purports to have been made; and, *c,* a proposition which we state independently, although in its essence it may be contained in the previous one, viz., whether, even although the order be in form within the delegated power, nevertheless it must be treated as not embraced therein, because the exertion of authority which is questioned has been manifested in such an unreasonable manner as to cause it, in truth, to be within the elementary rule that the substance, and not the shadow, determines the validity of the exercise of the power. . . . Plain as it is that the powers just stated are of the essence of judicial authority, and which, therefore, may not be curtailed, and whose discharge may not be by us in a proper case avoided, it is equally plain that such perennial powers lend no support whatever to the proposition that we may, under the guise of exerting judicial power, usurp merely administrative functions by setting aside a lawful administrative order upon our conception as to whether the administrative power has been wisely exercised.

215 U.S. 452 (1910)

Power to make the order and not the mere expediency or wisdom of having made it is the question. . . .

We think the issues for decision will be best disposed of by at once considering the contentions advanced by the railroad company to establish that there was a want of power in the commission to make that portion of the order which the court below enjoined. The contentions on this subject are stated in argument in many different forms, and if not in some respects contradictory, are, at all events, confusing since, considered logically, we think they virtually intermingle power and expediency as if they were one and the same thing. . . .

First. That the act to regulate commerce has not delegated to the commission authority to regulate the distribution of company fuel cars in times of car shortage as a means of prohibiting unjust preferences or undue discrimination. . . .

The deduction from the proposition is, as the movement of coal under the conditions stated is not commerce, it is therefore not within the authority delegated to the commission by the act of Congress, as all such acts have relation to the regulation of commerce, and do not, therefore, embrace that which is not commerce. It is to be observed, in passing, that if the proposition be well founded, it not only challenges the authority of the commission, but extends much further, and in effect denies the power of Congress to confer authority upon the commission over the subject. . . .

[W]hen the erroneous assumption upon which the proposition must rest is considered, its unsoundness is readily demonstrable. That assumption is this, that commerce in the constitutional sense only embraces shipment in a technical sense, and does not, therefore, extend to carriers engaged in interstate commerce, certainly in so far as so engaged, and the instrumentalities by which such commerce is carried on, a doctrine the unsoundness of which has been apparent ever since the decision in *Gibbons* v. *Ogden* . . . and which has not since been open to question. It may not be doubted that the equipment of a railroad company engaged in interstate commerce, included in which are its coal cars, are instruments of such commerce. From this it necessarily follows that such cars are embraced within the governmental power of regulation which extends, in time of car shortage, to compelling a just and equal distribution and the prevention of an unjust and discriminatory one.

The corporation as a carrier engaged in interstate commerce being then, as to its interstate commerce business, subject to the control exerted by the act to regulate commerce, and the instrumentalities employed for the purpose of such commerce, being likewise so subject to control, we are brought to consider the remaining proposition, which is,

Second. That even if power has been delegated to the commission by the act to regulate commerce, the order whose continued enforcement

was enjoined by the court below was beyond the authority delegated by the statute.

In view of the facts found by the commission as to preferences and discriminations resulting from the failure to count the company fuel cars in the daily distribution in times of car shortage, and in further view of the far-reaching preferences and discriminations alleged in the answer of the commission in this case, and which must be taken as true as the cause was submitted on bill and answer, it is beyond controversy that the subject with which the order dealt was within the sweeping provisions of § 3 of the act to regulate commerce prohibiting preferences and discriminations. . . .

[T]he arguments just stated, and others of a like character which we do not deem it essential to specially refer to, but assail the wisdom of Congress in conferring upon the commission the power which has been lodged in that body to consider complaints as to violations of the statute and to correct them if found to exist, or attack as crude or inexpedient the action of the commission in performance of the administrative functions vested in it, and upon such assumption invoke the exercise of unwarranted judicial power to correct the assumed evils. . . .

Mr. Justice Brewer dissented.

Houston, East and West Texas Ry. Co.

v.

United States
[The Shreveport Case]

*In addition to judicial acceptance of the ICC's powers, the Supreme
Court significantly expanded the sphere of the Commission's authority. In the Minnesota Rate Cases of 1913, the Court upheld the
right of the states to fix rates for intrastate rail traffic, but added that
if those rates so affected interstate rates, the federal government
could regulate the former (230 U.S. 352). The ICC already had
acted in this direction a year earlier, but the resulting litigation did
not reach the Court until 1914. The background of the case involved
the competition between Shreveport, Louisiana, and the Texas cities
of Dallas and Houston for the east Texas trade. The rates between
the Texas cities, set by the state commission, were substantially less
than that for comparable distances between Shreveport and the same
cities. The Louisiana railroad commission appealed to the ICC to
lower the interstate rate charges to equalize competition. The Commission equalized competition — by ordering an increase in the
intrastate rate structure.*

Justice Hughes delivered the opinion of the Court.

The point of the objection to the order is that, as the discrimination
found by the Commission to be unjust arises out of the relation of
intrastate rates, maintained under state authority, to interstate rates that
have been upheld as reasonable, its correction was beyond the Commission's power. Manifestly the order might be complied with, and the
discrimination avoided, either by reducing the interstate rates from
Shreveport to the level of the competing intrastate rates, or by raising
these intrastate rates to the level of the interstate rates, or by such reduction in the one case and increase in the other as would result in equality.
But it is urged that, so far as the interstate rates were sustained by the
Commission as reasonable, the Commission was without authority to
compel their reduction in order to equalize them with the lower intrastate rates. The holding of the Commerce Court was that the order re-

234 U.S. 342 (1914)

lieved the appellants from further obligation to observe the intrastate
rates and that they were at liberty to comply with the Commission's requirements by increasing these rates sufficiently to remove the forbidden
discrimination. The invalidity of the order in this aspect is challenged
upon two grounds:

(1) That Congress is impotent to control the intrastate charges of an
interstate carrier even to the extent necessary to prevent injurious discrimination against interstate traffic; and

(2) That, if it be assumed that Congress has this power, still it has
not been exercised, and hence the action of the Commission exceeded
the limits of the authority which has been conferred upon it.

First. It is unnecessary to repeat what has frequently been said by this
court with respect to the complete and paramount character of the power
confided to Congress to regulate commerce among the several States.
It is of the essence of this power that, where it exists, it dominates. Interstate trade was not left to be destroyed or impeded by the rivalries of
local governments. The purpose was to make impossible the recurrence
of the evils which had overwhelmed the Confederation and to provide the
necessary basis of national unity by insuring 'uniformity of regulation
against conflicting and discriminating state legislation.' By virtue of
the comprehensive terms of the grant, the authority of Congress is at all
times adequate to meet the varying exigencies that arise and to protect the
national interest by securing the freedom of interstate commerce.

Congress is empowered to regulate, — that is, to provide the law for
the government of interstate commerce. . . . Its authority, extending to
these interstate carriers as instruments of interstate commerce, necessarily
embraces the right to control their operations in all matters having such
a close and substantial relation to interstate traffic that the control is
essential or appropriate to the security of that traffic, to the efficiency of
the interstate service, and to the maintenance of conditions under which
interstate commerce may be conducted upon fair terms and without
molestation or hindrance. As it is competent for Congress to legislate
to these ends, unquestionably it may seek their attainment by requiring
that the agencies of interstate commerce shall not be used in such manner
as to cripple, retard or destroy it. The fact that carriers are instruments of
intrastate commerce, as well as of interstate commerce, does not derogate
from the complete and paramount authority of Congress over the latter
or preclude the Federal power from being exerted to prevent the intrastate operations of such carriers from being made a means of injury to
that which has been confided to Federal care. Wherever the interstate
and intrastate transactions of carriers are so related that the government
of the one involves the control of the other, it is Congress, and not the
State, that is entitled to prescribe the final and dominant rule, for otherwise Congress would be denied the exercise of its constitutional authority

and the State, and not the Nation, would be supreme within the national field. . . .

While these decisions sustaining the Federal power relate to measures adopted in the interest of the safety of persons and property, they illustrate the principle that Congress in the exercise of its paramount power may prevent the common instrumentalities of interstate and intrastate commercial intercourse from being used in their intrastate operations to the injury of interstate commerce. This is not to say that Congress possesses the authority to regulate the internal commerce of a State, as such, but that it does possess the power to foster and protect interstate commerce, and to take all measures necessary or appropriate to that end, although intrastate transactions of interstate carriers may thereby be controlled.

This principle is applicable here. We find no reason to doubt that Congress is entitled to keep the highways of interstate communication open to interstate traffic upon fair and equal terms. That an unjust discrimination in the rates of a common carrier, by which one person or locality is unduly favored as against another under substantially similar conditions of traffic, constitutes an evil is undeniable; and where this evil consists in the action of an interstate carrier in unreasonably discriminating against interstate traffic over its line, the authority of Congress to prevent it is equally clear. It is immaterial, so far as the protecting power of Congress is concerned, that the discrimination arises from intrastate rates as compared with interstate rates. The use of the instrument of interstate commerce in a discriminatory manner so as to inflict injury upon that commerce, or some part thereof, furnishes abundant ground for Federal intervention. . . .

Problems of Monopoly

United States *v.* E. C. Knight Co.

In 1890 Congress passed the Sherman Anti-Trust Act which pro
vided that "every contract, combination in the form of trust or
otherwise, or conspiracy, in restraint of trade or commerce among
the several States, or with foreign nations, is hereby declared to be
illegal." The law was deceptively simple. The Supreme Court soon
determined that Congress did not really mean "every" combination.
But the Court's most far-reaching effort was the doctrine, developed
in the Knight *case, that production had only an incidental effect*
upon commerce and could not be regulated by the federal govern
ment. Until 1937, the Court's distinction between production and
commerce, though sometimes blurred or ignored, stood as a sig
nificant barrier to federal regulation of the national economy. In
the Knight *case, the government had brought suit against the*
American Sugar Refining Company which admittedly controlled
94% of the sugar refining in the United States.

Chief Justice Fuller delivered the opinion of the Court.

The fundamental question is, whether conceding that the existence
of a monopoly in manufacture is established by the evidence, that
monopoly can be directly suppressed under the act of Congress in the
mode attempted by this bill.

It cannot be denied that the power of a State to protect the lives, health,
and property of its citizens, and to preserve good order and the public
morals, "the power to govern men and things within the limits of its
dominion," is a power originally and always belonging to the States, not
surrendered by them to the general government, nor directly restrained
by the Constitution of the United States, and essentially exclusive. The
relief of the citizens of each State from the burden of monopoly and the
evils resulting from the restraint of trade among such citizens was left
with the States to deal with, and this court has recognized their posses-

---

156 *U.S. 1 (1895)*

sion of that power even to the extent of holding that an employment or business carried on by private individuals, when it becomes a matter of such public interest and importance as to create a common charge or burden upon the citizen; in other words, when it becomes a practical monopoly, to which the citizen is compelled to resort and by means of which a tribute can be exacted from the community, is subject to regulation by state legislative power. On the other hand, the power of Congress to regulate commerce among the several States is also exclusive. The Constitution does not provide that interstate commerce shall be free, but, by the grant of this exclusive power to regulate it, it was left free except as Congress might impose restraints. Therefore it has been determined that the failure of Congress to exercise this exclusive power in any case is an expression of its will that the subject shall be free from restrictions or impositions upon it by the several States, and if a law passed by a State in the exercise of its acknowledged powers comes into conflict with that will, the Congress and the State cannot occupy the position of equal opposing sovereignties, because the Constitution declares its supremacy and that of the laws passed in pursuance thereof; and that which is not supreme must yield to that which is supreme. "Commerce, undoubtedly, is traffic," said Chief Justice Marshall, "but it is something more; it is intercourse. It describes the commercial intercourse between nations and parts of nations in all its branches, and is regulated by prescribing rules for carrying on that intercourse." That which belongs to commerce is within the jurisdiction of the United States, but that which does not belong to commerce is within the jurisdiction of the police power of the State. . . .

The argument is that the power to control the manufacture of refined sugar is a monopoly over a necessary of life, to the enjoyment of which by a large part of the population of the United States interstate commerce is indispensable, and that, therefore, the general government in the exercise of the power to regulate commerce may repress such monopoly directly and set aside the instruments which have created it. But this argument cannot be confined to necessaries of life merely, and must include all articles of general consumption. Doubtless the power to control the manufacture of a given thing involves in a certain sense the control of its disposition, but this is a secondary and not the primary sense; and although the exercise of that power may result in bringing the operation of commerce into play, it does not control it, and affects it only incidentally and indirectly. Commerce succeeds to manufacture, and is not a part of it. The power to regulate commerce is the power to prescribe the rule by which commerce shall be governed, and is a power independent of the power to suppress monopoly. But it may operate in repression of monopoly whenever that comes within the rules by which commerce is governed or whenever the transaction is itself a monopoly of commerce.

It is vital that the independence of the commercial power and of the police power, and the delimitation between them, however sometimes perplexing, should always be recognized and observed, for while the one furnishes the strongest bond of union, the other is essential to the preservation of the autonomy of the States as required by our dual form of government; and acknowledged evils, however grave and urgent they may appear to be, had better be borne, than the risk be run, in the effort to suppress them, of more serious consequences by resort to expedients of even doubtful constitutionality. . . .

Contracts, combinations, or conspiracies to control domestic enterprise in manufacture, agriculture, mining, production in all its forms, or to raise or lower prices or wages, might unquestionably tend to restrain external as well as domestic trade, but the restraint would be an indirect result, however inevitable and whatever its extent, and such result would not necessarily determine the object of the contract, combination, or conspiracy.

Again, all the authorities agree that in order to vitiate a contract or combination it is not essential that its result should be a complete monopoly; it is sufficient if it really tends to that end and to deprive the public of the advantages which flow from free competition. Slight reflection will show that if the national power extends to all contracts and combinations in manufacture, agriculture, mining, and other productive industries, whose ultimate result may affect external commerce, comparatively little of business operations and affairs would be left for state control.

It was in the light of well-settled principles that the act of July 2, 1890, was framed. Congress did not attempt thereby to assert the power to deal with monopoly directly as such; or to limit and restrict the rights of corporations created by the States or the citizens of the States in the acquisition, control, or disposition of property; or to regulate or prescribe the price or prices at which such property or the products thereof should be sold; or to make criminal the acts of persons in the acquisition and control of property which the States of their residence or creation sanctioned or permitted. Aside from the provisions applicable where Congress might exercise municipal power, what the law struck at was combinations, contracts, and conspiracies to monopolize trade and commerce among the several States or with foreign nations; but the contracts and acts of the defendants related exclusively to the acquisition of the Philadelphia refineries and the business of sugar refining in Pennsylvania, and bore no direct relation to commerce between the States or with foreign nations. . . . There was nothing in the proofs to indicate any intention to put a restraint upon trade or commerce, and the fact, as we have seen, that trade or commerce might be indirectly affected was not enough to entitle complainants to a decree. . . .

Justice Harlan, dissenting. . . .

In my judgment, the citizens of the several States composing the Union are entitled, of right, to buy goods in the State where they are manufactured, or in any other State, without being confronted by an illegal combination whose business extends throughout the whole country, which by the law everywhere is an enemy to the public interests, and which prevents such buying, except at prices arbitrarily fixed by it. I insist that the free course of trade among the States cannot coexist with such combinations. When I speak of trade I mean the buying and selling of articles of every kind that are recognized articles of interstate commerce. Whatever improperly obstructs the free course of interstate intercourse and trade, as involved in the buying and selling of articles to be carried from one State to another, may be reached by Congress, under its authority to regulate commerce among the States. The exercise of that authority so as to make trade among the States, in all recognized articles of commerce, absolutely free from unreasonable or illegal restrictions imposed by combinations, is justified by an express grant of power to Congress and would redound to the welfare of the whole country. I am unable to perceive that any such result would imperil the autonomy of the States, especially as that result cannot be attained through the action of any one State. . . .

While the opinion of the court in this case does not declare the act of 1890 to be unconstitutional, it defeats the main object for which it was passed. For it is, in effect, held that the statute would be unconstitutional if interpreted as embracing such unlawful restraints upon the purchasing of goods in one State to be carried to another State as necessarily arise from the *existence* of combinations formed for the purpose and with the effect, not only of monopolizing the ownership of all such goods in every part of the country, but of controlling the prices for them in all the States. This view of the scope of the act leaves the public, so far as national power is concerned, entirely at the mercy of combinations which arbitrarily control the prices of articles purchased to be transported from one State to another State. I cannot assent to that view. In my judgment, the general government is not placed by the Constitution in such a condition of helplessness that it must fold its arms and remain inactive while capital combines, under the name of a corporation, to destroy competition, not in one State only, but throughout the entire country, in the buying and selling of articles — especially the necessaries of life — that go into commerce among the States. The doctrine of the autonomy of the States cannot properly be invoked to justify a denial of power in the national government to meet such an emergency, involving as it does that freedom of commercial intercourse among the States which the Constitution sought to attain. . . .

Northern Securities Company

v.

United States

The Knight *decision temporarily discouraged widespread government assaults upon monopolies. But the Roosevelt and Taft administrations in the next decade brought about a renewed interest in federal regulation, including "trustbusting." The* Northern Securities Case *dramatized the new attitude. The Justice Department challenged the legality of a railroad holding company established by the combined Morgan and Harriman interests to control most of the railroad property between Chicago and the Pacific Northwest. The Court divided 5–4 in favor of the government, with Theodore Roosevelt's new appointee, Oliver Wendell Holmes, leading the dissenters. Although Justice Harlan's majority opinion exaggerated the Court's willingness to apply the anti-trust laws to all monopolies, his remarks on federal commerce power offered a vivid contrast to the narrow scope allowed by Chief Justice Fuller in the* Knight *case.*

Justice Harlan

This suit was brought by the United States against the Northern Securities Company, a corporation of New Jersey. . . .

Its general object was to enforce, as against the defendants, the provisions of the statute of July 2, 1890, commonly known as the Anti-Trust Act, and entitled "An act to protect trade and commerce against unlawful restraints and monopolies." . . .

The Government charges that if the combination was held not to be in violation of the act of Congress, then all efforts of the National Government to preserve to the people the benefits of free competition among carriers engaged in interstate commerce will be wholly unavailing, and

193 U.S. 197 (1904)

all transcontinental lines, indeed the entire railway systems of the country, may be absorbed, merged and consolidated, thus placing the public at the absolute mercy of the holding corporation. . . .

In our judgment, the evidence fully sustains the material allegations of the bill, and shows a violation of the act of Congress, in so far as it declares illegal every combination or conspiracy in restraint of commerce among the several States and with foreign nations, and forbids attempts to monopolize such commerce or any part of it. . . .

Is the act to be construed as forbidding every combination or conspiracy in restraint of trade or commerce among the States or with foreign nations? Or, does it embrace only such restraints as are unreasonable in their nature? Is the motive with which a forbidden combination or conspiracy was formed at all material when it appears that the necessary tendency of the particular combination or conspiracy in question is to restrict or suppress free competition between competing railroads engaged in commerce among the States? Does the act of Congress prescribe, as a *rule* for *interstate* or *international* commerce, that the operation of the natural laws of competition between those engaged in *such* commerce shall not be restricted or interfered with by any contract, combination or conspiracy? . . .

We will not incumber this opinion by extended extracts from the former opinions of this court. It is sufficient to say that from the decisions . . . certain propositions are plainly deducible and embrace the present case. Those propositions are:

That although the act of Congress known as the Anti-Trust Act has no reference to the mere manufacture or production of articles or commodities within the limits of the several States, it does embrace and declare to be illegal every contract, combination or conspiracy, in whatever form, of whatever nature, and whoever may be parties to it, which directly or necessarily operates *in restraint* of trade or commerce *among the several States or with foreign nations;*

That the act is not limited to restraints of interstate and international trade or commerce that are unreasonable in their nature, but embraces *all* direct *restraints* imposed by any combination, conspiracy or monopoly upon such trade or commerce;

That railroad carriers engaged in interstate or international trade or commerce are embraced by the act;

That combinations even among *private* manufacturers or dealers whereby *interstate or international commerce* is restrained are equally embraced by the act;

That Congress has the power to establish *rules* by which *interstate and international* commerce shall be governed, and, by the Anti-Trust Act, has prescribed the rule of free competition among those engaged in such commerce;

That *every* combination or conspiracy which would extinguish competition between otherwise competing railroads engaged in *interstate trade or commerce,* and which would *in that way* restrain *such* trade or commerce, is made illegal by the act;

That the natural effect of competition is to increase commerce, and an agreement whose direct effect is to prevent this play of competition restrains instead of promotes trade and commerce;

That to vitiate a combination, such as the act of Congress condemns, it need not be shown that the combination, in fact, results or will result in a total suppression of trade or in a complete monopoly, but it is only essential to show that by its necessary operation it tends to restrain interstate or international trade or commerce or tends to create a monopoly in such trade or commerce and to deprive the public of the advantages that flow from free competition;

That the constitutional guarantee of liberty of contract does not prevent Congress from prescribing the rule of free competition for those engaged in *interstate and international* commerce; and,

That under its power to regulate commerce among the several States and with foreign nations, Congress had authority to enact the statute in question. . . .

The means employed in respect of the combinations forbidden by the Anti-Trust Act, and which Congress deemed germane to the end to be accomplished, was to prescribe as *a rule* for *interstate and international* commerce (not for domestic commerce), that it should not be vexed by combinations, conspiracies or monopolies which restrain commerce by destroying or restricting competition. We say that Congress has prescribed such a rule, because in all the prior cases in this court the Anti-Trust Act has been construed as forbidding any combination which by its necessary operation destroys or restricts free competition among those engaged in interstate commerce; in other words, that to destroy or restrict free competition in interstate commerce was to restrain such commerce. Now, can this court say that such a rule is prohibited by the Constitution or is not one that Congress could appropriately prescribe when exerting its power under the commerce clause of the Constitution? Whether the free operation of the normal laws of competition is a wise and wholesome rule for trade and commerce is an economic question which this court need not consider or determine. Undoubtedly, there are those who think that the general business interests and prosperity of the country will be best promoted if the rule of competition is not applied. But there are others who believe that such a rule is more necessary in these days of enormous wealth than it ever was in any former period of our history. Be all this as it may, Congress has, in effect, recognized the rule of free competition by declaring illegal every combination or conspiracy in restraint of interstate and international commerce.

We cannot agree that Congress may strike down combinations among manufacturers and dealers in iron pipe, tiles, grates and mantels that restrain commerce among the States in such articles, but may not strike down combinations among stockholders of competing railroad carriers, which restrain commerce as involved in the transportation of passengers and property among the several States. If private parties may not, by combination among themselves, restrain interstate and international commerce in violation of an act of Congress, much less can such restraint be tolerated when imposed or attempted to be imposed upon commerce as carried on over public highways. Indeed, if the contentions of the defendants are sound why may not *all* the railway companies in the United States, that are engaged, under state charters, in interstate and international commerce, enter into a combination such as the one here in question, and by the device of a holding corporation obtain the absolute control throughout the entire country of rates for passengers and freight, beyond the power of Congress to protect the public against their exactions? The argument in behalf of the defendants necessarily leads to such results, and places Congress, although invested by the people of the United States with full authority to regulate interstate and international commerce, in a condition of utter helplessness, so far as the protection of the public against such combinations is concerned. . . .

Many suggestions were made in argument based upon the thought that the Anti-Trust Act would in the end prove to be mischievous in its consequences. Disaster to business and wide-spread financial ruin, it has been intimated, will follow the execution of its provisions. Such predictions were made in all the cases heretofore arising under that act. But they have not been verified. It is the history of monopolies in this country and in England that predictions of ruin are habitually made by them when it is attempted, by legislation, to restrain their operations and to protect the public against their exactions. In this, as in former cases, they seek shelter behind the reserved rights of the States and even behind the constitutional guarantee of liberty of contract. But this court has heretofore adjudged that the act of Congress did not touch the rights of the States, and that liberty of contract did not involve a right to deprive the public of the advantages of free competition in trade and commerce. Liberty of contract does not imply liberty in a corporation or individuals to defy the national will, when legally expressed. Nor does the enforcement of a legal enactment of Congress infringe, in any proper sense, the general inherent right of every one to acquire and hold property. That right, like all other rights, must be exercised in subordination to the law. . . .

It was said in argument that the circumstances under which the Northern Securities Company obtained the stock of the constituent companies imported simply an investment in the stock of other corporations, a purchase of that stock; which investment or purchase, it is contended, was not forbidden by the charter of the company and could not be made illegal by any act of Congress. This view is wholly fallacious, and does not comport with the actual transaction. There was no actual investment, in any substantial sense, by the Northern Securities Company in the stock of the two constituent companies. If it was, in form, such a transaction, it was not, in fact, one of that kind. However that company may have acquired for itself any stock in the Great Northern and Northern Pacific Railway companies, no matter how it obtained the means to do so, all the stock it held or acquired in the constituent companies was acquired and held to be used in suppressing competition between those companies. It came into existence only for that purpose. . . .

Guided by these long-established rules of construction, it is manifest that if the Anti-Trust Act is held not to embrace a case such as is now before us, the plain intention of the legislative branch of the Government will be defeated. If Congress has not, by the words used in the act, described this and like cases, it would, we apprehend, be impossible to find words that would describe them. . . .

Swift and Company *v.* United States

The Swift *case more significantly qualified the* Knight *precedent. The government had charged a number of meat packers with a conspiracy to fix livestock prices in the stockyards. The sales had occurred in local stockyards while the animals were at "rest." But the Court refused to consider local transactions as distinctive from the general flow of interstate commerce. Here, as in a few previous cases, the Court distinguished sales from production, but the distinction was vague. Significantly, through the 1920's and 1930's, Holmes's "stream of commerce" doctrine in this opinion became the cutting edge for the ultimate overthrow of the* Knight *doctrine.*

Justice Holmes delivered the opinion of the Court.

The scheme as a whole seems to us to be within reach of the law. The constituent elements, as we have stated them, are enough to give to the scheme a body and, for all that we can say, to accomplish it. Moreover, whatever we may think of them separately when we

196 U.S. 375 (1905)

take them up as distinct charges, they are alleged sufficiently as elements of the scheme. It is suggested that the several acts charged are lawful and that intent can make no difference. But they are bound together as the parts of a single plan. The plan may make the parts unlawful. . . . The statute gives this proceeding against combinations in restraint of commerce among the States and against attempts to monopolize the same. Intent is almost essential to such a combination and is essential to such an attempt. Where acts are not sufficient in themselves to produce a result which the law seeks to prevent — for instance, the monopoly — but require further acts in addition to the mere forces of nature to bring that result to pass, an intent to bring it to pass is necessary in order to produce a dangerous probability that it will happen. *Commonwealth* v. *Peaslee*, 177 Massachusetts, 267, 272. But when that intent and the consequent dangerous probability exist, this statute, like many others and like the common law in some cases, directs itself against that dangerous probability as well as against the completed result. . . .

One further observation should be made. Although the combination alleged embraces restraint and monopoly of trade within a single State, its effect upon commerce among the States is not accidental, secondary, remote or merely probable. On the allegations of the bill the latter commerce no less, perhaps even more, than commerce within a single State is an object of attack. See *Leloup* v. *Port of Mobile*, 127 U.S. 640, 647; *Crutcher* v. *Kentucky*, 141 U.S. 47, 59; *Allen* v. *Pullman Co.*, 191 U.S. 171, 179, 180. Moreover, it is a direct object, it is that for the sake of which the several specific acts and courses of conduct are done and adopted. Therefore the case is not like *United States* v. *E. C. Knight Co.*, 156 U.S. 1, where the subject matter of the combination was manufacture and the direct object monopoly of manufacture within a State. However likely monopoly of commerce among the States in the article manufactured was to follow from the agreement it was not a necessary consequence nor a primary end. Here the subject matter is sales and the very point of the combination is to restrain and monopolize commerce among the States in respect of such sales. The two cases are near to each other, as sooner or later always must happen where lines are to be drawn, but the line between them is distinct. . . .

[W]e are of opinion that the carrying out of the scheme alleged, by the means set forth, properly may be enjoined, and that the bill cannot be dismissed. . . .

It is said that this charge is too vague and that it does not set forth a case of commerce among the States. Taking up the latter objection first, commerce among the States is not a technical legal conception, but a practical one, drawn from the course of business. When cattle are sent for sale from a place in one State, with the expectation that they will end their transit, after purchase, in another, and when in effect they do so, with only the interruption necessary to find a purchaser at the stock yards, and when this is a typical, constantly recurring course, the current thus existing is a current of commerce among the States, and the purchase of the cattle is a part and incident of such commerce. What we say is true at least of such a purchase by residents in another State from that of the seller and of the cattle. And we need not trouble ourselves at this time as to whether the statute could be escaped by any arrangement as to the place where the sale in point of law is consummated. . . .

Standard Oil Co. of New Jersey

v.

United States

In his Northern Securities dissent, Holmes had noted that the majority was not united on Harlan's implication that the anti-trust laws applied to all monopolies. Holmes's warning that the laws could be used to atomize business and reconstruct society became vivid when the Taft administration launched suits against such corporate giants as Standard Oil, American Tobacco, and International Harvester. As early as the 1890's, it was argued that anti-trust laws be applied only to "unreasonable" combinations in restraint of trade which were detrimental to the public interest. Theodore Roosevelt later summed it up by distinguishing between "good" and "bad" monopolies. The so-called "rule of reason" emerged in the following case. In one of his last opinions, Justice Harlan bitterly dissented in tones reminiscent of his opinions on Negro rights. Once again he charged that the Court had subverted the aims of Congress.

Chief Justice White delivered the opinion of the Court.

First. *The text of the* [Sherman Anti-Trust] *act and its meaning.* We quote the text of the first and second sections of the act, as follows:

"SECTION 1. Every contract, combination in the form of trust or otherwise, or conspiracy, in restraint of trade or commerce, among the several

States, or with foreign nations, is hereby declared to be illegal. Every person who shall make any such contract, or engage in any such combination or conspiracy, shall be deemed guilty of a misdemeanor, and, on conviction thereof, shall be punished by fine not exceeding five thousand dollars, or by imprisonment not exceeding one year, or by both said punishments, in the discretion of the court.

"SEC. 2. Every person who shall monopolize, or attempt to monopolize, or combine or conspire with any other person or persons, to monopolize any part of the trade or commerce among the several States, or with foreign nations, shall be deemed guilty of a misdemeanor, and, on conviction thereof, shall be punished by fine not exceeding five thousand dollars, or by imprisonment not exceeding one year, or by both said punishments, in the discretion of the court."

The debates show that doubt as to whether there was a common law of the United States which governed the subject in the absence of legislation was among the influences leading to the passage of the act. They conclusively show, however, that the main cause which led to the legislation was the thought that it was required by the economic condition of the times, that is, the vast accumulation of wealth in the hands of corporations and individuals, the enormous development of corporate organization, the facility for combination which such organizations afforded, the fact that the facility was being used, and that combinations known as trusts were being multiplied, and the widespread impression that their power had been and would be exerted to oppress individuals and injure the public generally. Although debates may not be used as a means for interpreting a statute . . . that rule in the nature of things is not violated by resorting to debates as a means of ascertaining the environment at the time of the enactment of a particular law, that is, the history of the period when it was adopted.

There can be no doubt that the sole subject with which the first section deals is restraint of trade as therein contemplated, and that the attempt to monopolize and monopolization is the subject with which the second section is concerned. It is certain that those terms, at least in their rudimentary meaning, took their origin in the common law, and were also familiar in the law of this country prior to and at the time of the adoption of the act in question. . . .

Without going into detail and but very briefly surveying the whole field, it may be with accuracy said that the dread of enhancement of prices and of other wrongs which it was thought would flow from the undue limitation on competitive conditions caused by contracts or other acts of individuals or corporations, led, as a matter of public policy, to the prohibition or treating as illegal all contracts or acts which were unreasonably restrictive of competitive conditions, either from the nature or character of the contract or act or where the surrounding circumstances were such as to justify the conclusion that they had not been entered into or performed with the legitimate purpose of reasonably forwarding personal interest and developing trade, but on the contrary were of such a character as to give rise to the inference or presumption that they had been entered into or done with the intent to do wrong to the general public and to limit the right of individuals, thus restraining the free flow of commerce and tending to bring about the evils, such as enhancement of prices, which were considered to be against public policy. It is equally true to say that the survey of the legislation in this country on this subject from the beginning will show, depending as it did upon the economic conceptions which obtained at the time when the legislation was adopted or judicial decision was rendered, that contracts or acts were at one time deemed to be of such a character as to justify the inference of wrongful intent which were at another period thought not to be of that character. . . .

In view of the common law and the law in this country as to restraint of trade, which we have reviewed, and the illuminating effect which that history must have under the rule to which we have referred, we think it results:

a. That the context manifests that the statute was drawn in the light of the existing practical conception of the law of restraint of trade, because it groups as within that class, not only contracts which were in restraint of trade in the subjective sense, but all contracts or acts which theoretically were attempts to monopolize, yet which in practice had come to be considered as in restraint of trade in a broad sense.

b. That in view of the many new forms of contracts and combinations which were being evolved from existing economic conditions, it was deemed essential by an all-embracing enumeration to make sure that no form of contract or combination by which an undue restraint of interstate or foreign commerce was brought about could save such restraint from condemnation. The statute under this view evidenced the intent not to restrain the right to make and enforce contracts, whether resulting from combination or otherwise, which did not unduly restrain interstate or foreign commerce, but to protect that commerce from being restrained by methods, whether old or new, which would constitute an interference that is an undue restraint.

c. And as the contracts or acts embraced in the provision were not expressly defined, since the enumeration addressed itself simply to classes of acts, those classes being broad enough to embrace every conceivable contract or combination which could be made concerning trade or commerce or the subjects of such commerce, and thus caused any act done by any of the enumerated methods anywhere in the whole field of human activity to be illegal if in restraint of trade, it inevitably follows that the provision necessarily called for the exercise of judgment which required that some standard should be resorted to for the purpose of determining whether the prohibitions contained in the statute had or had not in any given case been violated. Thus not specifying but indubitably contemplating and requiring a standard, it follows that it was intended that the standard of reason which had been applied at the common law and in this country in dealing with subjects of the character embraced by the statute, was intended to be the measure used for the purpose of determining whether in a given case a particular act had or had not brought about the wrong against which the statute provided. . . .

Undoubtedly, the words "to monopolize" and "monopolize" as used in the section reach every act bringing about the prohibited results. The ambiguity, if any, is involved in determining what is intended by monopolize. But this ambiguity is readily dispelled in the light of the previous history of the law of restraint of trade to which we have referred and the indication which it gives of the practical evolution by which monopoly and the acts which produce the same result as monopoly, that is, an undue restraint of the course of trade, all came to be spoken of as, and to be indeed synonymous with, restraint of trade. In other words, having by the first section forbidden all means of monopolizing trade, that is, unduly restraining it by means of every contract, combination, etc., the second section seeks, if possible, to make the prohibitions of the act all the more complete and perfect by embracing all attempts to reach the end prohibited by the first section, that is, restraints of trade, by any attempt to monopolize, or monopolization thereof, even although the acts by which such results are attempted to be brought about or are brought about be not embraced within the general enumeration of the first section. And, of course, when the second section is thus harmonized with and made as it was intended to be the complement of the first, it becomes obvious that the criteria to be resorted to in any given case for the purpose of ascertaining whether violations of the section have been committed, is the rule of reason guided by the established law and by the plain duty to enforce the prohibitions of the act and thus the public policy which its restrictions were obviously enacted to subserve. . . .

Justice Harlan concurring in part, and dissenting in part.

All who recall the condition of the country in 1890 will remember that there was everywhere, among the people generally, a deep feeling of unrest. The Nation had been rid of human slavery — fortunately, as all now feel — but the conviction was universal that the country was in real danger from another kind of slavery sought to be fastened on the American people, namely, the slavery that would result from aggregations of capital in the hands of a few individuals and corporations. . . .

On reading the opinion just delivered, the first inquiry will be, that as the court is unanimous in holding that the particular things done by the Standard Oil Company and its subsidiary companies, in this case, were illegal under the Anti-trust Act, whether those things were in reasonable or unreasonable restraint of interstate commerce, why was it necessary to make an elaborate argument, as is done in the opinion, to show that according to the "rule of reason" the act as passed by Congress should be interpreted as if it contained the word "unreasonable" or the word "undue"? The only answer which, in frankness, can be given to this question is, that the court intends to decide that its deliberate judgment, fifteen years ago, to the effect that the act permitted no restraint whatever of interstate commerce, whether reasonable or unreasonable, was not in accordance with the "rule of reason." In effect the court says, that it will now, for the first time, bring the discussion under the "light of reason" and apply the "rule of reason" to the questions to be decided. I have the authority of this court for saying that such a course of proceeding on its part would be "judicial legislation." . . .

The disposition of the case under consideration, according to the views of the defendants, will, it is claimed, quiet and give rest to "the business of the country." On the contrary, I have a strong conviction that it will throw the business of the country into confusion and invite widely-extended and harassing litigation, the injurious effects of which will be felt for many years to come. When Congress prohibited *every* contract, combination or monopoly, in restraint of commerce, it prescribed a simple, definite rule that all could understand, and which could be easily applied by everyone wishing to obey the law, and not to conduct their business in violation of law. But now, it is to be feared, we are to have, in cases without number, the constantly recurring inquiry — difficult to solve by proof — whether the particular contract, combination, or trust involved in each case is or is not an "unreasonable" or "undue" restraint of trade. Congress, in effect, said that there should be *no* restraint of trade, *in any form*, and this court solemnly adjudged many years ago that Congress meant what it thus said in clear and explicit words, and that it *could not* add to the words of the act. . . .

The Fourteenth Amendment and Freedom
of Contract

Lochner *v.* New York

The freedom, or liberty, of contract doctrine developed in the state courts in the last three decades of the nineteenth century. The idea was that as part of the liberty guaranteed by the Fourteenth Amendment, no state could interfere with the right to make lawful contracts. It chiefly was applied to the employee-employer relationship. The Supreme Court first accepted the doctrine in a non-labor case in 1897 (Allgeyer v. Louisiana, 165 U.S. 578). The next year, in a 7–2 decision, the Court ignored it and sustained a Utah law limiting miners to an eight hour work day as a proper health measure (Holden v. Hardy, 169 U.S. 366). But the facts and results of the miners' case proved exceptional when seven years later, the Court reversed itself in the Lochner *case. The state had passed a law limiting bakers to a maximum of ten hours per day or sixty hours per week, on the grounds that longer hours were detrimental to the workers' health. The Court divided 5–4 against the law. Holmes typically dissented by berating the majority's economic predilections, but Harlan, speaking for the other dissenters, boldly challenged the majority with factual evidence.*

Justice Peckham delivered the opinion of the Court.

The statute necessarily interferes with the right of contract between the employer and employés, concerning the number of hours in which the latter may labor in the bakery of the employer. The general right to make a contract in relation to his business is part of the liberty of the individual protected by the Fourteenth Amendment of the Federal Constitution. *Allgeyer* v. *Louisiana,* 165 U.S. 578. Under that provision no State can deprive any person of life, liberty or property without due process of law. The right to purchase or to sell labor is part of the liberty

198 U.S. 45 (1905)

protected by this amendment, unless there are circumstances which exclude the right. There are, however, certain powers, existing in the sovereignty of each State in the Union, somewhat vaguely termed police powers, the exact description and limitation of which have not been attempted by the courts. Those powers, broadly stated and without, at present, any attempt at a more specific limitation, relate to the safety, health, morals and general welfare of the public. Both property and liberty are held on such reasonable conditions as may be imposed by the governing power of the State in the exercise of those powers, and with such conditions the Fourteenth Amendment was not designed to interfere. . . .

The State, therefore, has power to prevent the individual from making certain kinds of contracts, and in regard to them the Federal Constitution offers no protection. If the contract be one which the State, in the legitimate exercise of its police power, has the right to prohibit, it is not prevented from prohibiting it by the Fourteenth Amendment. Contracts in violation of a statute, either of the Federal or state government, or a contract to let one's property for immoral purposes, or to do any other unlawful act, could obtain no protection from the Federal Constitution, as coming under the liberty of person or free contract. Therefore, when the State, by its legislature, in the assumed exercise of its police powers, has passed an act which seriously limits the right to labor or the right of contract in regard to their means of livelihood between persons who are *sui juris* (both employer and employé), it becomes of great importance to determine which shall prevail — the right of the individual to labor for such time as he may choose, or the right of the State to prevent the individual from laboring or from entering into any contract to labor, beyond a certain time prescribed by the State.

This court has recognized the existence and upheld the exercise of the police powers of the States in many cases which might fairly be considered as border ones, and it has, in the course of its determination of questions regarding the asserted invalidity of such statutes, on the ground of their violation of the rights secured by the Federal Constitution, been guided by rules of a very liberal nature, the application of which has resulted, in numerous instances, in upholding the validity of state statutes thus assailed. . . .

It must, of course, be conceded that there is a limit to the valid exercise of the police power by the State. There is no dispute concerning this general proposition. . . . In every case that comes before this court, therefore, where legislation of this character is concerned and where the protection of the Federal Constitution is sought, the question necessarily arises: Is this a fair, reasonable and appropriate exercise of the police power of the State, or is it an unreasonable, unnecessary and arbitrary interference with the right of the individual to his personal liberty or to enter into those contracts in relation to labor which may seem to him appropriate or necessary for the support of himself and his family? Of course the liberty of contract relating to labor includes both parties to it. The one has as much right to purchase as the other to sell labor.

This is not a question of substituting the judgment of the court for that of the legislature. If the act be within the power of the State it is valid, although the judgment of the court might be totally opposed to the enactment of such a law. But the question would still remain: Is it within the police power of the State? and that question must be answered by the court.

The question whether this act is valid as a labor law, pure and simple, may be dismissed in a few words. There is no reasonable ground for interfering with the liberty of person or the right of free contract, by determining the hours of labor, in the occupation of a baker. There is no contention that bakers as a class are not equal in intelligence and capacity to men in other trades or manual occupations, or that they are not able to assert their rights and care for themselves without the protecting arm of the State, interfering with their independence of judgment and of action. They are in no sense wards of the State. . . . The law must be upheld, if at all, as a law pertaining to the health of the individual engaged in the occupation of a baker. It does not affect any other portion of the public than those who are engaged in that occupation. Clean and wholesome bread does not depend upon whether the baker works but ten hours per day or only sixty hours a week. The limitation of the hours of labor does not come within the police power on that ground.

It is a question of which of two powers or rights shall prevail — the power of the State to legislate or the right of the individual to liberty of person and freedom of contract. . . .

We think the limit of the police power has been reached and passed in this case. There is, in our judgment, no reasonable foundation for holding this to be necessary or appropriate as a health law to safeguard the public health or the health of the individuals who are following the trade of a baker. If this statute be valid, and if, therefore, a proper case is made out in which to deny the right of an individual, *sui juris*, as employer or employé, to make contracts for the labor of the latter under the protection of the provisions of the Federal Constitution, there would seem to be no length to which legislation of this nature might not go. . . .

We think that there can be no fair doubt that the trade of a baker, in and of itself, is not an unhealthy one to that degree which would authorize the legislature to interfere with the right to labor, and with the right of free contract on the part of the individual, either as employer or employé. In looking through statistics regarding all trades and occupations, it may be true that the trade of a baker does not appear to be as healthy as some other trades, and is also vastly more healthy than still others. To the common understanding the trade of a baker has never been regarded as an unhealthy one. Very likely physicians would not recommend the exercise of that or of any other trade as a remedy for ill health. Some occupations are more healthy than others, but we think there are none which might not come under the power of the legislature to supervise and control the hours of working therein, if the mere fact that the occupation is not absolutely and perfectly healthy is to confer that right upon the legislative department of the Government. It might be safely affirmed that almost all occupations more or less affect the health. . . . But are we all, on that account, at the mercy of legislative majorities? . . .

Statutes of the nature of that under review, limiting the hours in which grown and intelligent men may labor to earn their living, are mere meddlesome interferences with the rights of the individual, and they are not saved from condemnation by the claim that they are passed in the exercise of the police power and upon the subject of the health of the individual whose rights are interfered with, unless there be some fair ground, reasonable in and of itself, to say that there is material danger to the public health or to the health of the employés, if the hours of labor are not curtailed. If this be not clearly the case the individuals, whose rights are thus made the subject of legislative interference, are under the protection of the Federal Constitution regarding their liberty of contract as well as of person; and the legislature of the State has no power to limit their right as proposed in this statute. . . .

It was further urged on the argument that restricting the hours of labor in the case of bakers was valid because it tended to cleanliness on the part of the workers, as a man was more apt to be cleanly when not overworked, and if cleanly then his "output" was also more likely to be so. . . . In our judgment it is not possible in fact to discover the connection between the number of hours a baker may work in the bakery and the healthful quality of the bread made by the workman. The connection, if any exists, is too shadowy and thin to build any argument for the interference of the legislature. If the man works ten hours a day it is all right, but if ten and a half or eleven his health is in danger and his bread may be unhealthful, and, therefore, he shall not be permitted to do it. This, we think, is unreasonable and entirely arbitrary. . . .

It is manifest to us that the limitation of the hours of labor as provided for in this section of the statute under which the indictment was found, and the plaintiff in error convicted, has no such direct relation to and no such substantial effect upon the health of the employé, as to justify us in regarding the section as really a health law. It seems to us that the real object and purpose were simply to regulate the hours of labor between the master and his employés (all being men, *sui juris*), in a private business, not dangerous in any degree to morals or in any real and substantial degree, to the health of the employés. Under such circumstances the freedom of master and employé to contract with each other in relation to their employment, and in defining the same, cannot be prohibited or interfered with, without violating the Federal Constitution. . . .

Justice Harlan, with whom Justice White and Justice Day concurred, dissenting.

While this court has not attempted to mark the precise boundaries of what is called the police power of the State, the existence of the power has been uniformly recognized, both by the Federal and state courts.

All the cases agree that this power extends at least to the protection of the lives, the health and the safety of the public against the injurious exercise by any citizen of his own rights. . . .

It is plain that this statute was enacted in order to protect the physical well-being of those who work in bakery and confectionery establishments. It may be that the statute had its origin, in part, in the belief that employers and employés in such establishments were not upon an equal footing, and that the necessities of the latter often compelled them to submit to such exactions as unduly taxed their strength. Be this as it may, the statute must be taken as expressing the belief of the people of New York that, as a general rule, and in the case of the average man, labor in excess of sixty hours during a week in such establishments may endanger the health of those who thus labor. Whether or not this be wise legislation it is not the province of the court to inquire. Under our systems of government the courts are not concerned with the wisdom or policy of legislation. So that in determining the question of power to interfere with liberty of contract, the court may inquire whether the means devised by the State are germane to an end which may be lawfully accomplished and have a real or substantial relation to the protection of health, as involved in the daily work of the persons, male and female, engaged in bakery and confectionery establishments. . . . I submit that this court will transcend its functions if it assumes to annul the statute of New York. It must be remembered that this statute does not apply to all kinds of business. It applies only to work in bakery and confectionery establishments, in which, as all know, the air constantly breathed by workmen is not as pure and healthful as that to be found in some other establishments or out of doors.

Professor Hirt in his treatise on the "Diseases of the Workers" has said:

"The labor of the bakers is among the hardest and most laborious imaginable, because it has to be performed under conditions injurious to the health of those engaged in it. It is hard, very hard work, not only because it requires a great deal of physical exertion in an overheated workshop and during unreasonably long hours, but more so because of the erratic demands of the public, compelling the baker to perform the greater part of his work at night, thus depriving him of an opportunity to enjoy the necessary rest and sleep, a fact which is highly injurious to his health."

Another writer says:

"The constant inhaling of flour dust causes inflammation of the lungs and of the bronchial tubes. The eyes also suffer through this dust, which is responsible for the many cases of running eyes among the bakers. The long hours of toil to which all bakers are subjected produce rheumatism, cramps and swollen legs. . . ."

In the Eighteenth Annual Report by the New York Bureau of Statistics of Labor it is stated that among the occupations involving exposure to conditions that interfere with nutrition is that of a baker. . . .

There are many reasons of a weighty, substantial character, based upon the experience of mankind, in support of the theory that, all things considered, more than ten hours' steady work each day, from week to week, in a bakery or confectionery establishment, may endanger the health, and shorten the lives of the workmen, thereby diminishing their physical and mental capacity to serve the State, and to provide for those dependent upon them.

If such reasons exist that ought to be the end of this case, for the State is not amenable to the judiciary, in respect of its legislative enactments, unless such enactments are plainly, palpably, beyond all question, inconsistent with the Constitution of the United States. We are not to presume that the State of New York has acted in bad faith. Nor can we assume that its legislature acted without due deliberation, or that it did not determine this question upon the fullest attainable information, and for the common good. We cannot say that the State has acted without reason nor ought we to proceed upon the theory that its action is a mere sham. Our duty, I submit, is to sustain the statute as not being in conflict with the Federal Constitution, for the reason — and such is an all-sufficient reason — it is not shown to be plainly and palpably inconsistent with that instrument. Let the State alone in the management of its purely domestic affairs, so long as it does not appear beyond all question that it has violated the Federal Constitution. This view necessarily results from the principle that the health and safety of the people of a State are primarily for the State to guard and protect.

I take leave to say that the New York statute, in the particulars here involved, cannot be held to be in conflict with the Fourteenth Amendment, without enlarging the scope of the Amendment far beyond its original purpose and without bringing under the supervision of this court matters which have been supposed to belong exclusively to the legislative departments of the several States when exerting their conceded power to guard the health and safety of their citizens by such regulations as they in their wisdom deem best. . . . A decision that the New York statute is void under the Fourteenth Amendment will, in my opinion, involve consequences of a far-reaching and mischievous character; for such a decision would seriously cripple the inherent power of the States to care for the lives, health and well-being of their citizens. . . .

Justice Holmes dissenting. . . .

This case is decided upon an economic theory which a large part of the country does not entertain. If it were a question whether I agreed with that theory, I should desire to study it further and long before making up my mind. But I do not conceive that to be my duty, because I strongly believe that my agreement or disagreement has nothing to do with the right of a majority to embody their opinions in law. . . . The Fourteenth Amendment does not enact Mr. Herbert Spencer's Social Statics. . . . [A] constitution is not intended to embody a particular economic theory, whether of paternalism and the organic relation of the citizen to the State or of *laissez faire.* It is made for people of fundamentally differing views, and the accident of our finding certain opinions natural and familiar or novel and even shocking ought not to conclude our judgment upon the question whether statutes embodying them conflict with the Constitution of the United States.

General propositions do not decide concrete cases. The decision will depend on a judgment or intuition more subtle than any articulate major premise. But I think that the proposition just stated, if it is accepted, will carry us far toward the end. Every opinion tends to become a law. I think that the word liberty in the Fourteenth Amendment is perverted when it is held to prevent the natural outcome of a dominant opinion, unless it can be said that a rational and fair man necessarily would admit that the statute proposed would infringe fundamental principles as they have been understood by the traditions of our people and our law. It does not need research to show that no such sweeping condemnation can be passed upon the statute before us. A reasonable man might think it a proper measure on the score of health. . . .

Muller *v.* Oregon

Harlan's Lochner *dissent anticipated the famous "Brandeis Brief" used in this case. As counsel for the state, Louis D. Brandeis justified an Oregon statute limiting women to a ten hour day by utilizing sociological, economic, and physical data. Brandeis skill-fully avoided asking the Court to specifically overrule* Lochner. *Instead, he built from Justice Peckham's* Lochner *remark that "no law limiting the liberty of contract ought to go beyond necessity" to defend the Oregon law.*

Justice Brewer delivered the opinion of the Court.

The single question is the constitutionality of the statute under which the defendant was convicted so far as it affects the work of a female in a laundry. . . .

We held in *Lochner* v. *New York* . . . that a law providing that no laborer shall be required or permitted to work in a bakery more than sixty hours in a week or ten hours in a day was not as to men a legitimate exercise of the police power of the State, but an unreasonable, unnecessary and arbitrary interference with the right and liberty of the individual to contract in relation to his labor, and as such was in conflict with, and void under, the Federal Constitution. That decision is invoked by plaintiff in error as decisive of the question before us. But this assumes that the difference between the sexes does not justify a different rule respecting a restriction of the hours of labor.

In patent cases counsel are apt to open the argument with a discussion of the state of the art. It may not be amiss, in the present case, before examining the constitutional question, to notice the course of legislation as well as expressions of opinion from other than judicial sources. In the brief filed by Mr. Louis D. Brandeis, for the defendant in error, is a very copious collection of all these matters. . . .

The legislation and opinions referred to . . . may not be, technically speaking, authorities, and in them is little or no discussion of the constitutional question presented to us for determination, yet they are significant of a widespread belief that woman's physical structure, and the functions she performs in consequence thereof, justify special legislation restricting or qualifying the conditions under which she should be permitted to toil. Constitutional questions, it is true, are not settled by even a consensus of present public opinion, for it is the peculiar value of a written constitution that it places in unchanging form limitations upon legislative action, and thus gives a permanence and stability to popular government which otherwise would be lacking. At the same time, when a question of fact is debated and debatable, and the extent to which a special constitutional limitation goes is affected by the truth in respect to that fact, a widespread and long continued belief concerning it is worthy of consideration. We take judicial cognizance of all matters of general knowledge.

It is undoubtedly true, as more than once declared by this court, that the general right to contract in relation to one's business is part of the liberty of the individual, protected by the Fourteenth Amendment to the Federal Constitution; yet it is equally well settled that this liberty is not absolute and extending to all contracts, and that a State may, without conflicting with the provisions of the Fourteenth Amendment, restrict in many respects the individual's power of contract. . . .

That woman's physical structure and the performance of maternal functions place her at a disadvantage in the struggle for subsistence is obvious. This is especially true when the burdens of motherhood are upon her. Even when they are not, by abundant testimony of the medical fraternity continuance for a long time on her feet at work, repeating this from day to day, tends to injurious effects upon the body, and as healthy mothers are essential to vigorous offspring, the physical well-being of woman becomes an object of public interest and care in order to preserve the strength and vigor of the race.

Still again, history discloses the fact that woman has always been dependent upon man. . . . The two sexes differ in structure of body, in the functions to be performed by each, in the amount of physical strength, in the capacity for long-continued labor, particularly when done standing, the influence of vigorous health upon the future well-being of the race, the self-reliance which enables one to assert full rights, and in the capacity to maintain the struggle for subsistence. This difference justifies a difference in legislation and upholds that which is designed to compensate for some of the burdens which rest upon her. . . .

For these reasons, and without questioning in any respect the decision in *Lochner* v. *New York,* we are of the opinion that it cannot be adjudged that the act in question is in conflict with the Federal Constitution, so far as it respects the work of a female in a laundry. . . .

Bunting *v.* Oregon

The Muller *decision sustained the limitation of working hours for women as a valid health measure. A similar limitation for men, however, aroused a different set of values and further controversy. Furthermore, a link between minimum wages and the state's concern for the health of its citizens was obviously more indirect. The* Bunting *case involved a state law which limited the hours of men as well as women, and it also provided for overtime work with time and one-half wages. The law was challenged on the grounds that it had nothing to do with health and was an unwarranted price-fixing measure. Significantly, or so it seemed at the time, the Court completely ignored* Lochner. *But reports of* Lochner's *demise were greatly exaggerated as events of the next decade were to prove.*

Justice McKenna delivered the opinion of the Court.

The consonance of the Oregon law with the Fourteenth Amendment is the question in the case, and this depends upon whether it is a proper exercise of the police power of the State, as the Supreme Court of the State decided that it is.

That the police power extends to health regulations is not denied, but it is denied that the law has such purpose or justification. It is contended that it is a wage law, not a health regulation, and takes the property of plaintiff in error without due process. The contention presents two questions: (1) Is the law a wage law, or an hours of service law? And (2) if the latter, has it equality of operation?

Section 1 of the law expresses the policy that impelled its enactment to be the interest of the State in the physical well-being of its citizens and that it is injurious to their health for them to work "in any mill, factory or manufacturing establishment" more than ten hours in any one day; and § 2, as we have seen, forbids their employment in those places for a longer time. If, therefore, we take the law at its word there can be no doubt of its purpose, and the Supreme Court of the State has added the confirmation of its decision, by declaring that "the aim of the statute is to fix the maximum hours of service in certain industries. The act makes no attempt to fix the standard of wages. No maximum or minimum wage is named. That is left wholly to the contracting parties." . . .

First, as to plaintiff in error's attack upon the law. He says: "The law

243 U.S. 426 (1917)

is not a ten-hour law; it is a thirteen-hour law designed solely for the purpose of compelling the employer of labor in mills, factories and manufacturing establishments to pay more for labor than the actual market value thereof." And further: "It is a ten-hour law for the purpose of taking the employer's property from him and giving it to the employé; it is a thirteen-hour law for the purpose of protecting the health of the employé." To this plaintiff in error adds that he was convicted, not for working an employee during a busy season for more than ten hours, but for not paying him more than the market value of his services. . . .

There is a certain verbal plausibility in the contention that it was intended to permit 13 hours' work if there be 15½ hours' pay, but the plausibility disappears upon reflection. The provision for overtime is permissive, in the same sense that any penalty may be said to be permissive. Its purpose is to deter by its burden and its adequacy for this was a matter of legislative judgment under the particular circumstances. It may not achieve its end, but its insufficiency cannot change its character from penalty to permission. Besides, it is to be borne in mind that the legislature was dealing with a matter in which many elements were to be considered. It might not have been possible, it might not have been wise, to make a rigid prohibition. We can easily realize that the legislature deemed it sufficient for its policy to give to the law an adaptation to occasions different from special cases of emergency for which it provided, occasions not of such imperative necessity, and yet which should have some accommodation — abuses prevented by the requirement of higher wages. Or even a broader contention might be made that the legislature considered it a proper policy to meet the conditions long existent by a tentative restraint of conduct rather than by an absolute restraint, and achieve its purpose through the interest of those affected rather than by the positive fiat of the law.

We cannot know all of the conditions that impelled the law or its particular form. The Supreme Court, nearer to them, describes the law as follows: "It is clear that the intent of the law is to make 10 hours a regular day's labor in the occupations to which reference is made. Apparently the provisions for permitting labor for the overtime on express conditions were made in order to facilitate the enforcement of the law, and in the nature of a mild penalty for employing one not more than three hours overtime. It might be regarded as more difficult to detect violations of the law by an employment for a shorter time than for a longer time. This penalty also goes to the employee in case the employer avails himself of the overtime clause."

But we need not cast about for reasons for the legislative judgment. We are not required to be sure of the precise reasons for its exercise or be convinced of the wisdom of its exercise. . . . It is enough for our decision if the legislation under review was passed in the exercise of an admitted power of government; and that it is not as complete as it might be, not as rigid in its prohibitions as it might be, gives perhaps evasion too much play, is lighter in its penalties than it might be, is no impeachment of its legality. This may be a blemish, giving opportunity for criticism and difference in characterization, but the constitutional validity of legislation cannot be determined by the degree of exactness of its provisions or remedies. New policies are usually tentative in their beginnings, advance in firmness as they advance in acceptance. They do not at a particular moment of time spring full-perfect in extent or means from the legislative brain. Time may be necessary to fashion them to precedent customs and conditions and as they justify themselves or otherwise they pass from militancy to triumph or from question to repeal.

But passing general considerations and coming back to our immediate concern, which is the validity of the particular exertion of power in the Oregon law, our judgment of it is that it does not transcend constitutional limits. . . .

In Re Debs

As early as 1892 the Justice Department sought to apply the Sherman Anti-Trust Act against combinations of labor. A federal district court judge granted an injunction against the activities of a labor union the following year, noting that Congress intended to apply the act against labor as well as capital. In 1894, the government responded to the Pullman strike by securing a sweeping injunction against Eugene V. Debs, president of the American Railway Union, and other leaders of the union on the basis of the Interstate Commerce Act and the Sherman Act. The Circuit Court in Chicago upheld the decree in a contempt proceeding against Debs. Debs thereupon sought a writ of habeas corpus from the Supreme Court. Without disputing the lower court's use of the anti-trust laws, the high court relied on other federal statutes and general equity jurisdiction to deny Debs's petition But the Supreme Court's silent acquiescence opened the floodgates for widespread use of the Sherman Act to secure injunctions against organized labor.

Justice Brewer delivered the opinion of the Court.

Congress has exercised the power granted in respect to interstate commerce in a variety of legislative acts. . . .

Under the power vested in Congress to establish post offices and post roads, Congress has, by a mass of legislation, established the great post office system of the country, with all its detail of organization, its machinery for the transaction of business, defining what shall be carried and what not, and the prices of carriage, and also prescribing penalties for all offences against it.

Obviously these powers given to the national government over interstate commerce and in respect to the transportation of the mails were not dormant and unused. Congress had taken hold of these two matters, and by various and specific acts had assumed and exercised the powers

158 U.S. 564 (1895)

given to it, and was in the full discharge of its duty to regulate interstate commerce and carry the mails. The validity of such exercise and the exclusiveness of its control had been again and again presented to this court for consideration. It is curious to note the fact that in a large proportion of the cases in respect to interstate commerce brought to this court the question presented was of the validity of state legislation in its bearings upon interstate commerce, and the uniform course of decision has been to declare that it is not within the competency of a State to legislate in such a manner as to obstruct interstate commerce. If a State with its recognized powers of sovereignty is impotent to obstruct interstate commerce, can it be that any mere voluntary association of individuals within the limits of that State has a power which the State itself does not possess?

As, under the Constitution, power over interstate commerce and the transportation of the mails is vested in the national government, and Congress by virtue of such grant has assumed actual and direct control, it follows that the national government may prevent any unlawful and forcible interference therewith. But how shall this be accomplished? Doubtless, it is within the competency of Congress to prescribe by legislation that any interference with these matters shall be offences against the United States, and prosecuted and punished by indictment in the proper courts. But is that the only remedy? Have the vast interests of the nation in interstate commerce, and in the transportation of the mails, no other protection than lies in the possible punishment of those who interfere with it? To ask the question is to answer it. . . .

The entire strength of the nation may be used to enforce in any part of the land the full and free exercise of all national powers and the security of all rights entrusted by the Constitution to its care. The strong arm of the national government may be put forth to brush away all obstructions to the freedom of interstate commerce or the transportation of the mails. If the emergency arises, the army of the Nation, and all its militia, are at the service of the Nation to compel obedience to its laws.

But passing to the second question, is there no other alternative than the use of force on the part of the executive authorities whenever obstructions arise to the freedom of interstate commerce or the transportation of the mails? Is the army the only instrument by which rights of the public can be enforced and the peace of the nation preserved? Grant that any public nuisance may be forcibly abated either at the instance of the authorities, or by any individual suffering private damage therefrom, the existence of this right of forcible abatement is not inconsistent with nor does it destroy the right of appeal in an orderly way to the courts for a judicial determination, and an exercise of their powers by writ of injunction and otherwise to accomplish the same result. . . .

Neither can it be doubted that the government has such an interest in the subject-matter as enables it to appear as party plaintiff in this suit. It is said that equity only interferes for the protection of property, and that the government has no property interest. A sufficient reply is that the United States have a property in the mails, the protection of which was one of the purposes of this bill. . . .

We do not care to place our decision upon this ground alone. Every government, entrusted, by the very terms of its being, with powers and duties to be exercised and discharged for the general welfare, has a right to apply to its own courts for any proper assistance in the exercise of the one and the discharge of the other, and it is no sufficient answer to its appeal to one of those courts that it has no pecuniary interest in the matter. The obligations which it is under to promote the interest of all, and to prevent the wrongdoing of one resulting in injury to the general welfare, is often of itself sufficient to give it a standing in court. This proposition in some of its relations has heretofore received the sanction of this court. . . .

Again, it is objected that it is outside of the jurisdiction of a court of equity to enjoin the commission of crimes. This, as a general proposition, is unquestioned. A chancellor has no criminal jurisdiction. Something more than the threatened commission of an offense against the laws of the land is necessary to call into exercise the injunctive powers of the court. There must be some interferences, actual or threatened, with property or rights of a pecuniary nature, but when such interferences appear the jurisdiction of a court of equity arises, and is not destroyed by the fact that they are accompanied by or are themselves violations of the criminal law. . . .

Further, it is said by counsel in their brief:

> "No case can be cited where such a bill in behalf of the sovereign has been entertained against riot and mob violence, though occurring on the highway. It is not such fitful and temporary obstruction that constitutes a nuisance. The strong hand of executive power is required to deal with such lawless demonstrations.
>
> "The courts should stand aloof from them and not invade executive prerogative, nor even at the behest or request of the executive travel out of the beaten path of well-settled judicial authority. A mob cannot be suppressed by injunction; nor can its leaders be tried, convicted, and sentenced in equity.
>
> "It is too great a strain upon the judicial branch of the government to impose this essentially executive and military power upon courts of chancery."

We do not perceive that this argument questions the jurisdiction of the court, but only the expediency of the action of the government in applying for its process. . . . But does not counsel's argument imply too much? Is it to be assumed that these defendants were conducting a rebellion or inaugurating a revolution, and that they and their associates were thus placing themselves beyond the reach of the civil process of the courts? . . .

We enter into no examination of the [Sherman] act . . . upon which the Circuit Court relied mainly to sustain its jurisdiction. It must not be understood from this that we dissent from the conclusions of that court in reference to the scope of the act, but simply that we prefer to rest our judgment on the broader ground which has been discussed in this opinion, believing it of importance that the principles underlying it should be fully stated and affirmed. . . .

Loewe *v.* Lawlor
[Danbury Hatters' Case]

In this case the Court specifically discussed the relation of the anti-trust laws to organized labor. Anti-trust cases against business combinations always provoked a close division within the Court, but in this case, the justices unanimously found the laws applicable against a labor combination. The case arose from a national boycott instituted by the United Hatters Union against a Danbury, Connecticut hat manufacturer. The aim was to win recognition for the local union. The company responded with a suit, charging the union with a conspiracy to restrain trade in violation of the Sherman Act, and asked for treble damages from the individual striking union members.

Chief Justice Fuller delivered the opinion of the Court.

In our opinion, the combination described in the declaration is a combination "in restraint of trade or commerce among the several States," in the sense in which those words are used in the act, and the action can be maintained accordingly.

And that conclusion rests on many judgments of this court, to the effect that the act prohibits any combination whatever to secure action which essentially obstructs the free flow of commerce between the States, or restricts, in that regard, the liberty of a trader to engage in business.

The combination charged falls within the class of restraints of trade

aimed at compelling third parties and strangers involuntarily not to
engage in the course of trade except on conditions that the combination imposes; and there is no doubt that (to quote from the well-known
work of Chief Justice Erle on Trade Unions) "at common law every
person has individually, and the public also has collectively, a right to
require that the course of trade should be kept free from unreasonable
obstruction." But the objection here is to the jurisdiction, because, even
conceding that the declaration states a case good at common law, it is
contended that it does not state one within the statute. Thus, it is said,
that the restraint alleged would operate to entirely destroy plaintiffs' business and thereby include intrastate trade as well; that physical obstruction
is not alleged as contemplated; and that defendants are not themselves
engaged in interstate trade.

We think none of these objections are tenable, and that they are
disposed of by previous decisions of this court.

United States v. *Trans-Missouri Freight Association,* 166 U.S. 290;
United States v. *Joint Traffic Association,* 171 U.S. 505; and *Northern
Securities Company* v. *United States,* 193 U.S. 197, hold in effect that the
Anti-Trust law has a broader application than the prohibition of restraints
of trade unlawful at common law. . . .

We do not pause to comment on cases such as *United States* v. *Knight,*
156 U.S. 1 . . . in which the undisputed facts showed that the purpose
of the agreement was not to obstruct or restrain interstate commerce.
The object and intention of the combination determined its legality. . . .

The averments here are that there was an existing interstate traffic
between plaintiffs and citizens of other States, and that for the direct
purpose of destroying such interstate traffic defendants combined not
merely to prevent plaintiffs from manufacturing articles then and there
intended for transportation beyond the State, but also to prevent the
vendees from reselling the hats which they had imported from Connecticut, or from further negotiating with plaintiffs for the purchase and inter-
transportation of such hats from Connecticut to the various places of
destination. So that, although some of the means whereby the interstate
traffic was to be destroyed were acts within a State, and some of them
were in themselves as a part of their obvious purpose and effect beyond
the scope of Federal authority, still, as we have seen, the acts must be
considered as a whole, and the plan is open to condemnation, notwithstanding a negligible amount of intrastate business might be affected in
carrying it out. If the purposes of the combination were, as alleged, to
prevent any interstate transportation at all, the fact that the means
operated at one end before physical transportation commenced and at
the other end after the physical transportation ended was immaterial.

Nor can the act in question be held inapplicable because defendants
were not themselves engaged in interstate commerce. The act made no
distinction between classes. It provided that "every" contract, combina-

tion or conspiracy in restraint of trade was illegal. The records of Congress show that several efforts were made to exempt, by legislation, organizations of farmers and laborers from the operation of the act and that all these efforts failed, so that the act remained as we have it before us. . . .

The subject had so broadened in the minds of the legislators that the source of the evil was not regarded as material, and the evil in its entirety is dealt with. They made the interdiction include combinations of labor, as well as of capital; in fact, all combinations in restraint of commerce, without reference to the character of the persons who entered into them. It is true this statute has not been much expounded by judges, but, as it seems to me, its meaning, as far as relates to the sort of combinations to which it is to apply, is manifest, and that it includes combinations which are composed of laborers acting in the interest of laborers. . . .

At the risk of tediousness, we repeat that the complaint averred that plaintiffs were manufacturers of hats in Danbury, Connecticut, having a factory there, and were then and there engaged in an interstate trade in some twenty States other than the State of Connecticut; that they were practically dependent upon such interstate trade to consume the product of their factory, only a small percentage of their entire output being consumed in the State of Connecticut; that at the time the alleged combination was formed they were in the process of manufacturing a large number of hats for the purpose of fulfilling engagements then actually made with consignees and wholesale dealers in States other than Connecticut, and that it prevented from carrying on the work of manufacturing these hats they would be unable to complete their engagements.

That defendants were members of a vast combination called The United Hatters of North America, comprising about 9,000 members and including a large number of subordinate unions, and that they were combined with some 1,400,000 others into another association known as The American Federation of Labor, of which they were members, whose members resided in all the places in the several States where the wholesale dealers in hats and their customers resided and did business; that defendants were "engaged in a combined scheme and effort to force all manufacturers of fur hats in the United States, including the plaintiffs, against their will and their previous policy of carrying on their business, to organize their workmen in the departments of making and finishing, in each of their factories, into an organization, to be part and parcel of the said combination known as The United Hatters of North America, or as the defendants and their confederates term it, to unionize their shops, with the intent thereby to control the employment of labor in and the operation of said factories, and to subject the same to the direction and control of persons, other than the owners of the same, in a manner extremely onerous and distasteful to such owners, and to carry out such scheme, effort and purpose, by restraining and destroying the interstate trade and commerce of such manufacturers, by means of intimidation of and threats made to such manufacturers and their customers in the several States, of boycotting them, their product and their customers, using therefor all the powerful means at their command, as aforesaid, until such time as, from the damage and loss of business resulting therefrom, the said manufacturers should yield to the said demand to unionize their factories." . . .

[T]he defendants proceeded to carry out their combination to restrain and destroy interstate trade and commerce between plaintiffs and their customers in other States by employing the identical means contrived for that purpose; and that by reason of those acts plaintiffs were damaged in their business and property in some $80,000.

We think a case within the [Sherman Act] . . . was set up. . . .

Adair *v.* United States

One of the most widespread and effective business methods to subvert organized labor was the "yellow-dog contract." Employers extracted agreements from workers that they were subject to discharge if they joined a union. In 1898, in the aftermath of the Pullman strike, Congress made it a criminal offense for railroads to discharge workers under such an agreement. The statute was challenged as being beyond Congress's power to regulate interstate commerce and as a violation of the freedom of contract guaranteed by the Fifth Amendment. On the latter point, the Court simply translated its earlier Fourteenth Amendment doctrines and made them applicable against the federal government. In 1915, the Court struck down a similar state law (Coppage *v.* Kansas, 236 U.S. 1). *Harlan's narrow view of federal commerce power in* Adair *offers a striking contrast to his opinions in* Northern Securities *and the* Lottery Case, *discussed below.*

Justice Harlan delivered the opinion of the Court.

May Congress make it a criminal offense against the United States — as by the tenth section of the act of 1898 it does — for an agent or officer of an interstate carrier, having full authority in the

208 *U.S. 161 (1908)*

premises from the carrier, to discharge an employé from service simply because of his membership in a labor organization?

This question is admittedly one of importance, and has been examined with care and deliberation. And the court has reached a conclusion which, in its judgment, is consistent with both the words and spirit of the Constitution and is sustained as well by sound reason.

The first inquiry is whether the part of the tenth section of the act of 1898 upon which the first count of the indictment was based is repugnant to the Fifth Amendment of the Constitution declaring that no person shall be deprived of liberty or property without due process of law. In our opinion that section, in the particular mentioned, is an invasion of the personal liberty, as well as of the right of property, guaranteed by that Amendment. Such liberty and right embraces the right to make contracts for the purchase of the labor of others and equally the right to make contracts for the sale of one's own labor; each right, however, being subject to the fundamental condition that no contract, whatever its subject matter, can be sustained which the law, upon reasonable grounds, forbids as inconsistent with the public interests or as hurtful to the public order or as detrimental to the common good. . . .

In *Lochner* v. *New York* . . . the court said: "The general right to make a contract in relation to his business is part of the liberty of the individual protected by the Fourteenth Amendment of the Federal Constitution." . . .

While, as already suggested, the rights of liberty and property guaranteed by the Constitution against deprivation without due process of law, is subject to such reasonable restraints as the common good or the general welfare may require, it is not within the functions of government — at least in the absence of contract between the parties — to compel any person in the course of his business and against his will to accept or retain the personal services of another, or to compel any person, against his will, to perform personal services for another. The right of a person to sell his labor upon such terms as he deems proper is, in its essence, the same as the right of the purchaser of labor to prescribe the conditions upon which he will accept such labor from the person offering to sell it. So the right of the employé to quit the service of the employer, for whatever reason, is the same as the right of the employer, for whatever reason, to dispense with the services of such employé. It was the legal right of the defendant Adair — however unwise such a course might have been — to discharge Coppage because of his being a member of a labor organization, as it was the legal right of Coppage, if he saw fit to do so — however unwise such a course on his part might have been — to quit the service in which he was engaged, because the defendant employed some persons who were not members of a labor organization. In all such particulars the employer and the employé have equality of

right, and any legislation that disturbs that equality is an arbitrary interference with the liberty of contract which no government can legally
justify in a free land. . . .

But it is suggested that the authority to make it a crime for an agent
or officer of an interstate carrier, having authority in the premises from
his principal, to discharge an employé from service to such carrier, simply
because of his membership in a labor organization, can be referred to the
power of Congress to regulate interstate commerce, without regard to
any question of personal liberty or right of property arising under the
Fifth Amendment. This suggestion can have no bearing in the present
discussion unless the statute, in the particular just stated, is within
the meaning of the Constitution a regulation of commerce among the
States. If it be not, then clearly the Government cannot invoke the
commerce clause of the Constitution as sustaining the indictment against
Adair.

Let us inquire what is commerce, the power to regulate which is given
to Congress?

This question has been frequently propounded in this court, and the
answer has been — and no more specific answer could well have been
given — that commerce among the several States comprehends traffic,
intercourse, trade, navigation, communication, the transit of persons and
the transmission of messages by telegraph — indeed, every species of
commercial intercourse among the several States, but not to that commerce "completely internal, which is carried on between man and man,
in a State, or between different parts of the same State, and which does
not extend to or affect other States." . . . Manifestly, any rule prescribed
for the conduct of interstate commerce, in order to be within the competency of Congress under its power to regulate commerce among the
States, must have some real or substantial relation to or connection with
the commerce regulated. But what possible legal or logical connection is
there between an employé's membership in a labor organization and the
carrying on of interstate commerce? Such relation to a labor organization cannot have, *in itself* and in the eye of the law, any bearing upon the
commerce with which the employé is connected by his labor and services.
Labor associations, we assume, are organized for the general purpose of
improving or bettering the conditions and conserving the interests of its
members as wage-earners — an object entirely legitimate and to be commended rather than condemned. But surely those associations as labor
organizations have nothing to do with interstate commerce as such. One
who engages in the service of an interstate carrier will, it must be assumed, faithfully perform his duty, whether he be a member or not a
member of a labor organization. His fitness for the position in which
he labors and his diligence in the discharge of his duties cannot in law
or sound reason depend in any degree upon his being or not being a

member of a labor organization. It cannot be assumed that his fitness is assured, or his diligence increased, by such membership, or that he is less fit or less diligent because of his not being a member of such an organization. It is the employé as a man and not as a member of a labor organization who labors in the service of an interstate carrier. . . .

It results, on the whole case, that the provision of the statute under which the defendant was convicted must be held to be repugnant to the Fifth Amendment and as not embraced by nor within the power of Congress to regulate interstate commerce, but under the guise of regulating interstate commerce and as applied to this case it arbitrarily sanctions an illegal invasion of the personal liberty as well as the right of property of the defendant Adair. . . .

⋆ F ⋆

Income Tax

Pollock *v.* Farmers' Loan and Trust Co.

A federal income tax was first used during the Civil War but it lapsed by the end of the decade. Few serious constitutional objections were raised at the time. But in 1881, in Springer v. United States, *the Court unanimously sustained the law against a challenge that it was a direct tax which had to be apportioned among the states according to population (102 U.S. 586). The Court then essentially relied on the 1796 case of* Hylton v. United States *for the meaning of direct taxes. Various pressures led to a new income tax law in 1894, but this time constitutional assaults upon the tax were widespread and immediate. A test case was established with a friendly suit against a corporation by a stockholder to prevent payment of the tax. In April, 1895, the eight sitting justices held that taxes on rents derived from land had to be apportioned among the states. Taxes on income from municipal bonds also were voided (*Pollock v. Farmers' Loan and Trust Co., 157 U.S. 429*). The Court, however, was equally divided as to whether taxes on personal property were direct taxes and whether the invalidated sections rendered the whole act void. With the return of the ninth justice, these issues were resolved a month later.*

Chief Justice Fuller delivered the opinion of the Court.

The Constitution divided Federal taxation into two great classes, the class of direct taxes, and the class of duties, imports, and excises; and prescribed two rules which qualified the grant of power as to each class.

The power to lay direct taxes apportioned among the several States in proportion to their representation in the popular branch of Congress, a representation based on population as ascertained by the census, was plenary and absolute; but to lay direct taxes without apportionment was forbidden. The power to lay duties, imposts, and excises was subject to

158 U.S. 601 (1895)

the qualification that the imposition must be uniform throughout the United States.

Our previous decision was confined to the consideration of the validity of the tax on the income from real estate, and on the income from municipal bonds. The question thus limited was whether such taxation was direct or not, in the meaning of the Constitution; and the court went no farther, as to the tax on the income from real estate, than to hold that it fell within the same class as the source whence the income was derived, that is, that a tax upon the realty and a tax upon the receipts therefrom were alike direct; while as to the income from municipal bonds, that could not be taxed because of want of power to tax the source, and no reference was made to the nature of the tax as being direct or indirect.

We are now permitted to broaden the field of inquiry, and to determine to which of the two great classes a tax upon a person's entire income, whether derived from rents, or products, or otherwise, of real estate, or from bonds, stocks, or other forms of personal property, belongs; and we are unable to conclude that the enforced subtraction from the yield of all the owner's real or personal property, in the manner prescribed, is so different from a tax upon the property itself, that it is not a direct, but an indirect tax, in the meaning of the Constitution. . . .

The Constitution prohibits any direct tax, unless in proportion to numbers as ascertained by the census; . . . is it not an evasion of that prohibition to hold that a general unapportioned tax, imposed upon all property owners as a body for or in respect of their property, is not direct, in the meaning of the Constitution, because confined to the income therefrom?

Whatever the speculative views of political economists or revenue reformers may be, can it be properly held that the Constitution, taken in its plain and obvious sense, and with due regard to the circumstances attending the formation of the government, authorizes a general unapportioned tax on the products of the farm and the rents of real estate, although imposed merely because of ownership and with no possible means of escape from payment, as belonging to a totally different class from that which includes the property from whence the income proceeds?

There can be but one answer, unless the constitutional restriction is to be treated as utterly illusory and futile, and the object of its framers defeated. We find it impossible to hold that a fundamental requisition, deemed so important as to be enforced by two provisions, one affirmative and one negative, can be refined away by forced distinctions between that which gives value to property, and the property itself.

Nor can we perceive any ground why the same reasoning does not apply to capital in personalty held for the purpose of income or ordinarily yielding income, and to the income therefrom. All the real estate of the country, and all its invested personal property, are open to the direct operation of the taxing power if an apportionment be made according to the Constitution. The Constitution does not say that no direct tax shall be laid by apportionment on any other property than land; on the contrary, it forbids all unapportioned direct taxes; and we know of no warrant for excepting personal property from the exercise of the power, or any reason why an apportioned direct tax cannot be laid and assessed, as Mr. Gallatin said in his report when Secretary of the Treasury in 1812, "upon the same objects of taxation on which the direct taxes levied under the authority of the State are laid and assessed."

Personal property of some kind is of general distribution; and so are incomes, though the taxable range thereof might be narrowed through large exemptions. . . .

We have unanimously held in this case that, so far as this law operates on the receipts from municipal bonds, it cannot be sustained, because it is a tax on the power of the States, and on their instrumentalities to borrow money, and consequently repugnant to the Constitution. But if, as contended, the interest when received has become merely money in the recipient's pocket, and taxable as such without reference to the source from which it came, the question is immaterial whether it could have been originally taxed at all or not. This was admitted by the Attorney General with characteristic candor; and it follows that, if the revenue derived from municipal bonds cannot be taxed because the source cannot be, the same rule applies to revenue from any other source not subject to the tax; and the lack of power to levy any but an apportioned tax on real and personal property equally exists as to the revenue therefrom.

Admitting that this act taxes the income of property irrespective of its source, still we cannot doubt that such a tax is necessarily a direct tax in the meaning of the Constitution. . . .

Being direct, and therefore to be laid by apportionment, is there any real difficulty in doing so? Cannot Congress, if the necessity exist of raising thirty, forty, or any other number of million dollars for the support of the government, in addition to the revenue from duties, imposts, and excises, apportion the quota of each State upon the basis of the census, and thus advise it of the payment which must be made, and proceed to assess that amount on all the real and personal property and the income of all persons in the State, and collect the same if the State does not in the meantime assume and pay its quota and collect the amount according to its own system and in its own way? Cannot Congress do this, as respects either or all these subjects of taxation, and deal with each in such manner as might be deemed expedient . . . ? Inconveniences might possibly attend the levy of an income tax, notwithstanding the listing of receipts, when adjusted, furnishes its own valuation; but that it is apportionable is hardly denied, although it is asserted that it would operate so unequally as to be undesirable. . . .

We are not here concerned with the question whether an income tax be or be not desirable, nor whether such a tax would enable the government to diminish taxes on consumption and duties on imports, and to enter upon what may be believed to be a reform of its fiscal and commercial system. Questions of that character belong to the controversies of political parties, and cannot be settled by judicial decision. In these cases our province is to determine whether this income tax on the revenue from property does or does not belong to the class of direct taxes. If it does, it is, being unapportioned, in violation of the Constitution, and we must so declare.

Differences have often occurred in this court — differences exist now — but there has never been a time in its history when there has been a difference of opinion as to its duty to announce its deliberate conclusions unaffected by considerations not pertaining to the case in hand. . . .

Our conclusions may, therefore, be summed up as follows:

First. We adhere to the opinion already announced, that, taxes on real estate being indisputably direct taxes, taxes on the rents or income of real estate are equally direct taxes.

Second. We are of opinion that taxes on personal property, or on the income of personal property, are likewise direct taxes.

Third. The tax imposed by sections twenty-seven to thirty-seven, inclusive, of the act of 1894, so far as it falls on the income of real estate and of personal property, being a direct tax within the meaning of the Constitution, and, therefore, unconstitutional and void because not apportioned according to representation, all those sections, constituting one entire scheme of taxation, are necessarily invalid. . . .

Justice Harlan dissenting. . . .

In my judgment — to say nothing of the disregard of the former adjudications of this court, and of the settled practice of the government — this decision may well excite the gravest apprehensions. It strikes at the very foundations of national authority, in that it denies to the general government a power which is, or may become, vital to the very existence and preservation of the Union in a national emergency, such as that of war with a great commercial nation, during which the collection of all duties upon imports will cease or be materially diminished. It tends to reëstablish that condition of helplessness in which Congress found itself during the period of the Articles of Confederation, when it was without authority by laws operating directly upon individuals, to lay and collect, through its own agents, taxes sufficient to pay the debts and defray the expenses of government, but was dependent, in all such matters, upon the good will of the States, and their promptness in meeting requisitions made upon them by Congress.

Why do I say that the decision just rendered impairs or menaces the national authority? The reason is so apparent that it need only be stated. In its practical operation this decision withdraws from national taxation not only all incomes derived from real estate, but tangible personal property, "*invested* personal property, bonds, stocks, investments of all kinds," and the income that may be derived from such property. This results from the fact that by the decision of the court, all such personal property and all incomes from real estate and personal property, are placed beyond national taxation otherwise than by *apportionment* among the States *on the basis* simply *of population*. No such apportionment can possibly be made without doing gross injustice to the many for the benefit of the favored few in particular States. . . .

I cannot assent to an interpretation of the Constitution that impairs and cripples the just powers of the National Government in the essential matter of taxation, and at the same time discriminates against the greater part of the people of our country.

The practical effect of the decision to-day is to give to certain kinds of property a position of favoritism and advantage inconsistent with the fundamental principles of our social organization, and to invest them with power and influence that may be perilous to that portion of the American people upon whom rests the larger part of the burdens of the government, and who ought not to be subjected to the dominion of aggregated wealth any more than the property of the country should be at the mercy of the lawless.

Champion *v.* Ames
[Lottery Case]

At the time when the Court was restricting the scope of the commerce clause in the Knight *case, Congress took a significant step which added a new dimension to the commerce power. In 1895, Congress prohibited the transportation of lottery tickets from state to state. Three years earlier, the Court had upheld the exclusion of such tickets from the mails (In re Rapier, 143 U.S. 110). But the new law obviously presented broader questions such as complete prohibition from interstate traffic and the role of the federal government in policing morality. There was genuine concern that such policy dangerously expanded federal power, however desirable the goals. The Court apparently was troubled by the problem as indicated by the necessity for three hearings of arguments and a narrow 5–4 decision. Harlan's majority opinion contained certain qualifications as to the extent of federal power. But in subsequent cases, for example, the Court sustained federal regulation of adulterated foods (Hipolite Egg Co. v. United States, 220 U.S. 45 [1911]) and interstate traffic in prostitutes (Hoke v. United States, 227 U.S. 308 [1913]) on the basis of this precedent.*

Justice Harlan delivered the opinion of the Court.

It was said in argument that lottery tickets are not of any real or substantial value in themselves, and therefore are not subjects of commerce. If that were conceded to be the only legal test as to what are to be deemed subjects of the commerce that may be regulated by Congress, we cannot accept as accurate the broad statement that such tickets are of no value. Upon their face they showed that the lottery company offered a large capital prize, to be paid to the holder of the ticket winning

---

188 U.S. 321 (1903)

the prize at the drawing advertised to be held at Asuncion, Paraguay. Money was placed on deposit in different banks in the United States to be applied by the agents representing the lottery company to the prompt payment of prizes. These tickets were the subject of traffic; they could have been sold; and the holder was assured that the company would pay to him the amount of the prize drawn. . . . In short, a lottery ticket is a subject of traffic, and is so designated in the act of 1895. . . .

We are of opinion that lottery tickets are subjects of traffic and therefore are subjects of commerce, and the regulation of the carriage of such tickets from State to State, at least by independent carriers, is a regulation of commerce among the several States.

But it is said that the statute in question does not regulate the carrying of lottery tickets from State to State, but by punishing those who cause them to be so carried Congress in effect prohibits such carrying; that in respect of the carrying from one State to another of articles or things that are, in fact, or according to usage in business, the subjects of commerce, the authority given Congress was not to *prohibit*, but only to *regulate*. This view was earnestly pressed at the bar by learned counsel and must be examined. . . .

We have said that the carrying from State to State of lottery tickets constitutes interstate commerce, and that the regulation of such commerce is within the power of Congress under the Constitution. Are we prepared to say that a provision which is, in effect, a *prohibition* of the carriage of such articles from State to State is not a fit or appropriate mode for the *regulation* of that particular kind of commerce? If lottery traffic, *carried on through interstate commerce,* is a matter of which Congress may take cognizance and over which its power may be exerted, can it be possible that it must tolerate the traffic, and simply regulate the manner in which it may be carried on? Or may not Congress, for the protection of the people of all the States, and under the power to regulate interstate commerce, devise such means, within the scope of the Constitution, and not prohibited by it, as will drive that traffic out of commerce among the States?

In determining whether regulation may not under some circumstances properly take the form or have the effect of prohibition, the nature of the interstate traffic which it was sought by the act of May 2, 1895, to suppress cannot be overlooked. . . . In other cases we have adjudged that authority given by legislative enactment to carry on a lottery, although based upon a consideration in money, was not protected by the contract clause of the Constitution; this, for the reason that no State may bargain away its power to protect the public morals, nor excuse it failure to perform a public duty by saying that it had agreed, by legislative enactment, not to do so. . . .

If a State, when considering legislation for the suppression of lotteries within its own limits, may properly take into view the evils that inhere in the raising of money, in that mode, why may not Congress, invested with the power to regulate commerce among the several States, provide that such commerce shall not be polluted by the carrying of lottery tickets from one State to another? . . .

It is said, however, that if, in order to suppress lotteries carried on through interstate commerce, Congress may exclude lottery tickets from such commerce, that principle leads necessarily to the conclusion that Congress may arbitrarily exclude from commerce among the States any article, commodity or thing, of whatever kind or nature, or however useful or valuable, which it may choose, no matter with what motive, to declare shall not be carried from one State to another. It will be time enough to consider the constitutionality of such legislation when we must do so. The present case does not require the court to declare the full extent of the power that Congress may exercise in the regulation of commerce among the States. We may, however, repeat, in this connection, what the court has heretofore said, that the power of Congress to regulate commerce among the States, although plenary, cannot be deemed arbitrary, since it is subject to such limitations or restrictions as are prescribed by the Constitution. This power, therefore, may not be exercised so as to infringe rights secured or protected by that instrument. It would not be difficult to imagine legislation that would be justly liable to such an objection as that stated, and be hostile to the objects for the accomplishment of which Congress was invested with the general power to regulate commerce among the several States. But, as often said, the possible abuse of a power is not an argument against its existence. There is probably no governmental power that may not be exerted to the injury of the public. If what is done by Congress is manifestly in excess of the powers granted to it, then upon the courts will rest the duty of adjudging that its action is neither legal nor binding upon the people. But if what Congress does is within the limits of its power, and is simply unwise or injurious, the remedy is that suggested by Chief Justice Marshall in *Gibbons* v. *Ogden,* when he said: "The wisdom and the discretion of Congress, their identity with the people, and the influence which their constituents possess at elections, are, in this, as in many other instances, as that, for example, of declaring war, the sole restraints on which they have relied, to secure them from its abuse. They are the restraints on which the people must often rely solely, in all representative governments."

The whole subject is too important, and the questions suggested by its consideration are too difficult of solution, to justify any attempt to lay down a rule for determining in advance the validity of every statute. that may be enacted under the commerce clause. We decide nothing more in the present case than that lottery tickets are subjects of traffic among those who choose to sell or buy them; . . . [and] that under its power to regulate commerce among the several States Congress . . . may prohibit the carriage of such tickets from State to State; and that legislation to that end, and of that character, is not inconsistent with any limitation or restriction imposed upon the exercise of the powers granted to Congress. . . .

Chief Justice Fuller, with whom concur Justice Brewer, Justice Shiras and Justice Peckham, dissent.

McCray *v.* United States

A year after the Lottery Case, *the Court approved a similar use of the taxation power, but perhaps in more sweeping and unqualified terms. In 1869, in* Veazie Bank *v.* Fenno *(8 Wallace 533), the Court had sustained a tax on state bank notes which was obviously confiscatory. Nevertheless, the justices refused to inquire into congressional motivation and rendered a broad interpretation of the taxation power. In 1886 and again in 1902, Congress levied taxes upon colored oleomargarine. There was no pretense that these were for revenue; they simply were designed to aid the competitive position of the dairy industry. There were arguments that some colored oleo contained harmful ingredients, but this was immaterial to the Court's consideration as it refused to speculate on congressional motivation.*

Justice White delivered the opinion of the Court.

The summary which follows embodies the propositions contained in the assignments of error, and the substance of the elaborate argument by which those assignments are deemed to be sustained. Not denying the general power of Congress to impose excise taxes, and conceding that the acts in question, on their face, purport to levy taxes of that character, the propositions are these:

(*a*) That the power of internal taxation which the Constitution confers on Congress is given to that body for the purpose of raising revenue, and that the tax on artificially colored oleomargarine is void because it is of such an onerous character as to make it manifest that the purpose of Congress in levying it was not to raise revenue but to suppress the manufacture of the taxed article.

(*b*) The power to regulate the manufacture and sale of oleomargarine being solely reserved to the several States, it follows that the acts in question, enacted by Congress for the purpose of suppressing the manufacture and sale of oleomargarine, when artificially colored, are void, because usurping the reserved power of the States, and therefore exerting an authority not delegated to Congress by the Constitution.

(*c*) Whilst it is true — so the argument proceeds — that Congress in exerting the taxing power conferred upon it may use all means appropriate to the exercise of such power, a tax which is fixed at such a high rate as to suppress the production of the article taxed, is not a legitimate means to the lawful end, and is therefore beyond the scope of the taxing power. . . .

To avoid confusion and repetition we shall consider these distinct contentions separately, and we hence come, first, to ascertain how far, if at all, the motives or purposes of Congress are open to judicial inquiry in considering the power of that body to enact the laws in question. Having determined the question of our right to consider motive or purpose we shall then approach the propositions relied on by the light of the correct rule on the subject of purpose or motive.

Whilst, as a result of our written constitution, it is axiomatic that the judicial department of the government is charged with the solemn duty of enforcing the Constitution, and therefore in cases properly presented, of determining whether a given manifestation of authority has exceeded the power conferred by that instrument, no instance is afforded from the foundation of the government where an act, which was within a power conferred, was declared to be repugnant to the Constitution, because it appeared to the judicial mind that the particular exertion of constitutional power was either unwise or unjust. To announce such a principle would amount to declaring that in our constitutional system the judiciary was not only charged with the duty of upholding the Constitution but also with the responsibility of correcting every possible abuse arising from the exercise by the other departments of their conceded authority. So to hold would be to overthrow the entire distinction between the legislative, judicial and executive departments of the government, upon which our system is founded, and would be a mere act of judicial usurpation. . . .

It is, of course, true, as suggested, that if there be no authority in the judiciary to restrain a lawful exercise of power by another department of the government, where a wrong motive or purpose has impelled to the exertion of the power, that abuses of a power conferred may be temporarily effectual. The remedy for this, however, lies, not in the abuse by the judicial authority of its functions, but in the people, upon whom, after all, under our institutions, reliance must be placed for the correction of abuses committed in the exercise of a lawful power. . . .

It being thus demonstrated that the motive or purpose of Congress in adopting the acts in question may not be inquired into, we are brought to consider the contentions relied upon to show that the acts assailed were beyond the power of Congress, putting entirely out of view all considerations based upon purpose or motive.

1. Undoubtedly, in determining whether a particular act is within a granted power, its scope and effect are to be considered. Applying this rule to the acts assailed, it is self-evident that on their face they levy an excise tax. That being their necessary scope and operation, it follows that the acts are within the grant of power. The argument to the contrary rests on the proposition that, although the tax be within the power, as enforcing it will destroy or restrict the manufacture of artificially colored oleomargarine, therefore the power to levy the tax did not obtain. This, however, is but to say that the question of power depends, not upon the authority conferred by the Constitution, but upon what may be the consequence arising from the exercise of the lawful authority.

Since, as pointed out in all the decisions referred to, the taxing power conferred by the Constitution knows no limits except those expressly stated in that instrument, it must follow, if a tax be within the lawful power, the exertion of that power may not be judicially restrained because of the results to arise from its exercise. The proposition now relied upon was urged in *Knowlton* v. *Moore,* 178 U.S. 41, and was overruled. . . .

2. The proposition that where a tax is imposed which is within the grant of powers, and which does not conflict with any express constitutional limitation, the courts may hold the tax to be void because it is deemed that the tax is too high, is absolutely disposed of by the opinions in the cases hitherto cited, and which expressly hold, to repeat again the language of one of the cases, (*Spencer* v. *Merchant,*) that "The judicial department cannot prescribe to the legislative department limitations upon the exercise of its acknowledged powers. The power to tax may be exercised oppressively upon persons; but the responsibility of the legislature is not to the courts, but to the people by whom its members are elected." . . .

3. Whilst undoubtedly both the Fifth and Tenth Amendments qualify, in so far as they are applicable, all the provisions of the Constitution, nothing in those amendments operates to take away the grant of power to tax conferred by the Constitution upon Congress. The contention on this subject rests upon the theory that the purpose and motive of Congress in exercising its undoubted powers may be inquired into by the courts, and the proposition is therefore disposed of by what has been said on that subject.

The right of Congress to tax within its delegated power being unrestrained, except as limited by the Constitution, it was within the authority conferred on Congress to select the objects upon which an excise should be laid. It therefore follows that, in exerting its power, no want of due process of law could possibly result, because that body chose to impose an excise on artificially colored oleomargarine and not upon natural butter artificially colored. The judicial power may not usurp the functions of the legislative in order to control that branch of the government in the performance of its lawful duties. This was aptly pointed out in the extract heretofore made from the opinion in *Treat* v. *White,* 181 U.S. 264.

But it is urged that artificially colored oleomargarine and artificially colored natural butter are in substance and in effect one and the same thing, and from this it is deduced that to lay an excise tax only on oleomargarine artificially colored and not on butter so colored is violative of the due process clause of the Fifth Amendment, because, as there is no possible distinction between the two, the act of Congress was a mere arbitrary imposition of an excise on the one article and not on the other, although essentially of the same class. Conceding merely for the sake of argument that the due process clause of the Fifth Amendment, would avoid an exertion of the taxing power which, without any basis for classification, arbitrarily taxed one article and excluded an article of the same class, such concession would be wholly inapposite to the case in hand. The distinction between natural butter artificially colored, and oleomargarine artificially colored so as to cause it to look like butter, has been pointed out in previous adjudications of this court. . . . Indeed, in the cases referred to the distinction between the two products was held to be so marked, and the aptitude of oleomargarine when artificially colored, to deceive the public into believing it to be butter, was decided to be so great that it was held no violation of the due process clause of the Fourteenth Amendment was occasioned by state legislation absolutely forbidding the manufacture, within the State, of oleomargarine artifically colored. As it has been thus decided that the distinction between the two products is so great as to justify the absolute prohibition of the manufacture of oleomargarine artificially colored, there is no foundation for the proposition that the difference between the two was not sufficient, under the extremest view, to justify a classification, distinguishing between them.

4. Lastly we come to consider the argument that, even though as a general rule a tax of the nature of the one in question would be within the power of Congress, in this case the tax should be held not to be within such power, because of its effect. This is based on the contention that, as the tax is so large as to destroy the business of manufacturing oleomargarine artificially colored, to look like butter, it thus deprives the manufacturers of that article of their freedom to engage in a lawful pur-

suit, and hence, irrespective of the distribution of powers made by the Constitution, the taxing laws are void, because they violate those fundamental rights which it is the duty of every free government to safeguard, and which, therefore, should be held to be embraced by implied though none the less potential guaranties, or in any event to be within the protection of the due process clause of the Fifth Amendment.

Let us concede, for the sake of argument only, the premise of fact upon which the proposition is based. Moreover, concede for the sake of argument only, that even although a particular exertion of power by Congress was not restrained by any express limitation of the Constitution, if by the perverted exercise of such power so great an abuse was manifested as to destroy fundamental rights which no free government could consistently violate, that it would be the duty of the judiciary to hold such acts to be void upon the assumption that the Constitution by necessary implication forbade them.

Such concession, however, is not controlling in this case. This follows when the nature of oleomargarine, artificially colored to look like butter, is recalled. As we have said, it has been conclusively settled by this court that the tendency of that article to deceive the public into buying it for butter is such that the States may, in the exertion of their police powers, without violating the due process clause of the Fourteenth Amendment, absolutely prohibit the manufacture of the article. It hence results, that even although it be true that the effect of the tax in question is to repress the manufacture of artificially colored oleomargarine, it cannot be said that such repression destroys rights which no free government could destroy, and, therefore, no ground exists to sustain the proposition that the judiciary may invoke an implied prohibition, upon the theory that to do so is essential to save such rights from destruction. And the same considerations dispose of the contention based upon the due process clause of the Fifth Amendment. That provision, as we have previously said, does not withdraw or expressly limit the grant of power to tax conferred upon Congress by the Constitution. From this it follows, as we have also previously declared, that the judiciary is without authority to void an act of Congress exerting the taxing power, even in a case where to the judicial mind it seems that Congress had in putting such power in motion abused its lawful authority by levying a tax which was unwise or oppressive, or the result of the enforcement of which might be to indirectly affect subjects not within the powers delegated to Congress.

Let us concede that if a case was presented where the abuse of the taxing power was so extreme as to be beyond the principles which we have previously stated, and where it was plain to the judicial mind that the power had been called into play not for revenue but solely for the purpose of destroying rights which could not be rightfully destroyed consistently with the principles of freedom and justice upon which the Constitution rests, that it would be the duty of the courts to say that such an arbitrary act was not merely an abuse of a delegated power, but was the exercise of an authority not conferred. This concession, however, like the one previously made, must be without influence upon the decision of this cause for the reasons previously stated; that is, that the manufacture of artificially colored oleomargarine may be prohibited by a free government without a violation of fundamental rights. . . .

Chief Justice, Justice Brown and Justice Peckham dissent.

VI

War, Radicalism,
and Reaction:

1917–1933

⋆ A ⋆

Conscription and the War Power

Selective Draft Law Cases

In a large-scale war effort perhaps no power is more basic than that of raising armed forces. The Constitution (Article I, Section 8) granted Congress such power but nothing was said concerning the power to compel military service. During the Civil War, conscription had caused widespread unrest and some congressional opposition, but there was no test of its constitutionality. However, the Selective Draft Law of May, 1917, was immediately challenged in the courts. It was contended that Congress lacked conscription powers and that the law amounted to involuntary servitude. While the expansion of national powers during World War I often divided the Court, the response in this case was emphatic and unanimous.

Chief Justice White delivered the opinion of the Court.

The possession of authority to enact the statute must be found in the clauses of the Constitution giving Congress power "to declare war; . . . to raise and support armies, but no appropriation of money to that use shall be for a longer term than two years; . . . to make rules for the government and regulation of the land and naval forces." Article I, § 8. And of course the powers conferred by these provisions like all other powers given carry with them as provided by the Constitution the authority "to make all laws which shall be necessary and proper for carrying into execution the foregoing powers." Article I, § 8.

As the mind cannot conceive an army without the men to compose it, on the face of the Constitution the objection that it does not give power to provide for such men would seem to be too frivolous for further notice. It is said, however, that since under the Constitution as originally framed state citizenship was primary and United States citizenship but derivative and dependent thereon, therefore the power conferred upon Congress to raise armies was only coterminous with United States citizenship and could not be exerted so as to cause that citizenship to lose its

245 U.S. 366 (1918)

dependent character and dominate state citizenship. But the proposition simply denies to Congress the power to raise armies which the Constitution gives. That power by the very terms of the Constitution, being delegated, is supreme. Article VI. In truth the contention simply assails the wisdom of the framers of the Constitution in conferring authority on Congress and in not retaining it as it was under the Confederation in the several States. Further it is said, the right to provide is not denied by calling for volunteer enlistments, but it does not and cannot include the power to exact enforced military duty by the citizen. This however but challenges the existence of all power, for a governmental power which has no sanction to it and which therefore can only be exercised provided the citizen consents to its exertion is in no substantial sense a power. It is argued, however, that although this is abstractly true, it is not concretely so because as compelled military service is repugnant to a free government and in conflict with all the great guarantees of the Constitution as to individual liberty, it must be assumed that the authority to raise armies was intended to be limited to the right to call an army into existence counting alone upon the willingness of the citizen to do his duty in time of public need, that is, in time of war. But the premise of this proposition is so devoid of foundation that it leaves not even a shadow of ground upon which to base the conclusion. Let us see if this is not at once demonstrable. It may not be doubted that the very conception of a just government and its duty to the citizen includes the reciprocal obligation of the citizen to render military service in case of need and the right to compel it. Vattel, Law of Nations, Book III, c. 1 & 2. To do more than state the proposition is absolutely unnecessary in view of the practical illustration afforded by the almost universal legislation to that effect now in force. . . .

In the Colonies before the separation from England there cannot be the slightest doubt that the right to enforce military service was unquestioned and that practical effect was given to the power in many cases. Indeed the brief of the Government contains a list of Colonial acts manifesting the power and its enforcement in more than two hundred cases. And this exact situation existed also after the separation. Under the Articles of Confederation it is true Congress had no such power, as its authority was absolutely limited to making calls upon the States for the military forces needed to create and maintain the army, each State being bound for its quota as called. But it is indisputable that the States in response to the calls made upon them met the situation when they deemed it necessary by directing enforced military service on the part of the citizens. In fact the duty of the citizen to render military service and the power to compel him against his consent to do so was expressly sanctioned by the constitutions of at least nine of the States. . . . While it is true that the States were sometimes slow in exerting the power in order to fill their quotas—a condition shown by resolutions of Congress calling upon them to comply by exerting their compulsory power to draft and by earnest requests by Washington to Congress that a demand be made upon the States to resort to drafts to fill their quotas — that fact serves to demonstrate instead a challenge to the existence of the authority. A default in exercising a duty may not be resorted to as a reason for denying its existence.

When the Constitution came to be formed it may not be disputed that one of the recognized necessities for its adoption was the want of power in Congress to raise an army and the dependence upon the States for their quotas. In supplying the power it was manifestly intended to give it all and leave none to the States, since besides the delegation to Congress of authority to raise armies the Constitution prohibited the States, without the consent of Congress, from keeping troops in time of peace or engaging in war. . . .

Thus sanctioned as is the act before us by the text of the Constitution, and by its significance as read in the light of the fundamental principles with which the subject is concerned, by the power recognized and carried into effect in many civilized countries, by the authority and practice of the colonies before the Revolution, of the States under the Confederation and of the Government since the formation of the Constitution, the want of merit in the contentions that the act in the particulars which we have been previously called upon to consider was beyond the constitutional power of Congress, is manifest. . . .

Finally, as we are unable to conceive upon what theory the exaction by government from the citizen of the performance of his supreme and noble duty of contributing to the defense of the rights and honor of the nation, as the result of a war declared by the great representative body of the people, can be said to be the imposition of involuntary servitude in violation of the prohibitions of the Thirteenth Amendment, we are constrained to the conclusion that the contention to that effect is refuted by its mere statement.

Affirmed.

Radicalism and the First Amendment

Schenck *v.* United States

The Court's contribution to the reaction against the so-called "Red Scare" following World War I was comparable to its role in the subversion of Negro rights following Reconstruction. With the exception of a few lonely voices on the bench, the Court emphatically endorsed repressive measures against radical political activities. In future free speech controversies, Holmes's doctrine was utilized for both libertarian and repressive goals. Holmes's opinion for a unanimous bench in the case below tried to reconcile the government's need to guard against subversion with the requirements of the First Amendment. The result was his famous "clear and present danger" test.

Justice Holmes delivered the opinion of the Court.

This is an indictment in three counts. The first charges a conspiracy to violate the Espionage Act of June 15, 1917, . . . by causing and attempting to cause insubordination, &c., in the military and naval forces of the United States, and to obstruct the recruiting and enlistment service of the United States, when the United States was at war with the German Empire, to-wit, that the defendants wilfully conspired to have printed and circulated to men who had been called and accepted for military service under the Act of May 18, 1917, a document set forth and alleged to be calculated to cause such insubordination and obstruction. The count alleges overt acts in pursuance of the conspiracy, ending in the distribution of the document set forth. The second count alleges a conspiracy to commit an offence against the United States, to-wit, to use the mails for the transmission of matter declared to be non-mailable by Title XII, § 2 of the Act of June 15, 1917, to-wit, the above mentioned document, with an averment of the same overt acts. The third count charges an unlawful use of the mails for the transmission of the same matter and otherwise as above. The defendants were found guilty on all the counts. They set up the First Amendment to the Constitution forbidding Congress

249 U.S. 47 (1919)

to make any law abridging the freedom of speech, or of the press, and bringing the case here on that ground have argued some other points also of which we must dispose.

It is argued that the evidence, if admissible, was not sufficient to prove that the defendant Schenck was concerned in sending the documents. According to the testimony Schenck said he was general secretary of the Socialist party and had charge of the Socialist headquarters from which the documents were sent. He identified a book found there as the minutes of the Executive Committee of the party. The book showed a resolution of August 13, 1917, that 15,000 leaflets should be printed on the other side of one of them in use, to be mailed to men who had passed exemption boards, and for distribution. Schenck personally attended to the printing. On August 20 the general secretary's report said "Obtained new leaflets from printer and started work addressing envelopes" &c.; and there was a resolve that Comrade Schenck be allowed $125 for sending leaflets through the mail. He said that he had about fifteen or sixteen thousand printed. There were files of the circular in question in the inner office which he said were printed on the other side of the one sided circular and were there for distribution. Other copies were proved to have been sent through the mails to drafted men. Without going into confirmatory details that were proved, no reasonable man could doubt that the defendant Schenck was largely instrumental in sending the circulars about. As to the defendant Baer there was evidence that she was a member of the Executive Board and that the minutes of its transactions were hers. The argument as to the sufficiency of the evidence that the defendants conspired to send the documents only impairs the seriousness of the real defence. . . .

The document in question upon its first printed side recited the first section of the Thirteenth Amendment, said that the idea embodied in it was violated by the Conscription Act and that a conscript is little better than a convict. In impassioned language it intimated that conscription was despotism in its worst form and a monstrous wrong against humanity in the interest of Wall Street's chosen few. It said "Do not submit to intimidation," but in form at least confined itself to peaceful measures such as a petition for the repeal of the act. The other and later printed side of the sheet was headed "Assert Your Rights." It stated reasons for alleging that any one violated the Constitution when he refused to recognize "your right to assert your opposition to the draft," and went on "If you do not assert and support your rights, you are helping to deny or disparage rights which it is the solemn duty of all citizens and residents of the United States to retain." It described the arguments on the other side as coming from cunning politicians and a mercenary capitalist press, and even silent consent to the conscription law as helping to support an infamous conspiracy. It denied the power to send our citizens away to foreign shores to shoot up the people of other lands, and added that words could not express the condemnation such cold-blooded ruthlessness deserves, &c., &c., winding up "You must do your share to maintain, support and uphold the rights of the people of this country." Of course the document would not have been sent unless it had been intended to have some effect, and we do not see what effect it could be expected to have upon persons subject to the draft except to influence them to obstruct the carrying of it out. The defendants do not deny that the jury might find against them on this point.

But it is said, suppose that was the tendency of this circular, it is protected by the First Amendment to the Constitution. Two of the strongest expressions are said to be quoted respectively from well-known public men. . . . We admit that in many places and in ordinary times the defendants in saying all that was said in the circular would have been within their constitutional rights. But the character of every act depends upon the circumstances in which it is done. . . . The most stringent protection of free speech would not protect a man in falsely shouting fire in a theatre and causing a panic. It does not even protect a man from an injunction against uttering words that may have all the effect of force. . . . The question in every case is whether the words used are used in such circumstances and are of such a nature as to create a clear and present danger that they will bring about the substantive evils that Congress has a right to prevent. It is a question of proximity and degree. When a nation is at war many things that might be said in time of peace are such a hindrance to its effort that their utterance will not be endured so long as men fight and that no Court could regard them as protected by any constitutional right. It seems to be admitted that if an actual obstruction of the recruiting service were proved, liability for words that produced that effect might be enforced. The statute of 1917 in § 4 punishes conspiracies to obstruct as well as actual obstruction. If the act, (speaking, or circulating a paper,) its tendency and the intent with which it is done are the same, we perceive no ground for saying that success alone warrants making the act a crime. . . .

Abrams *v.* United States

Holmes's Schenck *formula of clear and present danger soon proved relative, if not illusory. In the* Abrams *case, the defendants were charged with circulating pamphlets critical of the American intervention in Siberia and calling for a general strike of munitions workers. Basically the pamphlets defended and glorified the Bolshevik Revolution. The defendants were indicted and convicted for violation of the wartime Espionage Acts and the Court sustained the convictions. Speaking for the majority, Justice Clarke expanded the clear and present danger requirement into the so-called "bad tendency" test. "Men must be held to have intended," he wrote, "and to be accountable for, the effects which their acts were likely to produce." In this and similar federal cases, Clarke's reading of the clear and present danger doctrine proved more influential during the next decade. For himself and Justice Brandeis, Holmes delivered an eloquent and moving dissent.*

Justice Holmes dissenting.

I never have seen any reason to doubt that the questions of law that alone were before this Court in the cases of *Schenck, Frohwerk* and *Debs,* 249 U.S. 47, 204, 211, were rightly decided. I do not doubt for a moment that by the same reasoning that would justify punishing persuasion to murder, the United States constitutionally may punish speech that produces or is intended to produce a clear and imminent danger that it will bring about forthwith certain substantive evils that the United States constitutionally may seek to prevent. The power undoubtedly is greater in time of war than in time of peace because war opens dangers that do not exist at other times.

But as against dangers peculiar to war, as against others, the principle of the right to free speech is always the same. It is only the present danger of immediate evil or an intent to bring it about that warrants Congress in setting a limit to the expression of opinion where private rights are not concerned. Congress certainly cannot forbid all effort to change the mind of the country. Now nobody can suppose that the surreptitious publishing of a silly leaflet by an unknown man, without more, would present any immediate danger that its opinions would hinder the success of the government arms or have any appreciable tendency to do

so. Publishing those opinions for the very purpose of obstructing however, might indicate a greater danger and at any rate would have the
quality of an attempt. . . . It is necessary where the success of the attempt depends upon others because if that intent is not present the actor's
aim may be accomplished without bringing about the evils sought to be
checked. An intent to prevent interference with the revolution in Russia
might have been satisfied without any hindrance to carrying on the war
in which we were engaged.

I do not see how anyone can find the intent required by the statute in
any of the defendants' words. The second leaflet is the only one that
affords even a foundation for the charge, and there, without invoking the
hatred of German militarism expressed in the former one, it is evident
from the beginning to the end that the only object of the paper is to help
Russia and stop American intervention there against the popular government — not to impede the United States in the war that it was carrying on.
To say that two phrases taken literally might import a suggestion of conduct that would have interference with the war as an indirect and
probably undesired effect seems to me by no means enough to show an
attempt to produce that effect. . . .

In this case sentences of twenty years imprisonment have been imposed
for the publishing of two leaflets that I believe the defendants had as
much right to publish as the Government has to publish the Constitution
of the United States now vainly invoked by them. Even if I am technically wrong and enough can be squeezed from these poor and puny
anonymities to turn the color of legal litmus paper; I will add, even if
what I think the necessary intent were shown; the most nominal punishment seems to me all that possibly could be inflicted, unless the defendants are to be made to suffer not for what the indictment alleges but for
the creed that they avow — a creed that I believe to be the creed of
ignorance and immaturity when honestly held, as I see no reason to doubt
that it was held here, but which, although made the subject of examination at the trial, no one has a right even to consider in dealing with the
charges before the Court.

Persecution for the expression of opinions seems to me perfectly logical.
If you have no doubt of your premises or your power and want a certain
result with all your heart you naturally express your wishes in law and
sweep away all opposition. To allow opposition by speech seems to indicate that you think the speech impotent, as when a man says that he has
squared the circle, or that you do not care whole-heartedly for the result,
or that you doubt either your power or your premises. But when men
have realized that time has upset many fighting faiths, they may come to
believe even more than they believe the very foundations of their own
conduct that the ultimate good desired is better reached by free trade in
ideas — that the best test of truth is the power of the thought to get itself

accepted in the competition of the market, and that truth is the only ground upon which their wishes safely can be carried out. That at any rate is the theory of our Constitution. It is an experiment, as all life is an experiment. Every year if not every day we have to wager our salvation upon some prophecy based upon imperfect knowledge. While that experiment is part of our system I think that we should be eternally vigilant against attempts to check the expression of opinions that we loathe and believe to be fraught with death, unless they so imminently threaten immediate interference with the lawful and pressing purposes of the law that an immediate check is required to save the country. I wholly disagree with the argument of the Government that the First Amendment left the common law as to seditious libel in force. History seems to me against the notion. I had conceived that the United States through many years had shown its repentance for the Sedition Act of 1798, by repaying fines that it imposed. Only the emergency that makes it immediately dangerous to leave the correction of evil counsels to time warrants making any exception to the sweeping command, "Congress shall make no law . . . abridging the freedom of speech." Of course I am speaking only of expressions of opinion and exhortations, which were all that were uttered here, but I regret that I cannot put into more impressive words my belief that in their conviction upon this indictment the defendants were deprived of their rights under the Constitution of the United States.

Gitlow *v.* New York

During the Red Scare, a number of states passed or expanded diverse measures to quash political radicalism. Benjamin Gitlow was convicted for violation of New York's criminal anarchy statute. Once again, the Court's majority adopted a narrow view of the clear and present danger test and sustained the conviction. Justice Sanford contended that the state could not be expected to measure the danger of every "revolutionary spark" in the "nice balance of a jeweler's scale." But the most significant aspect of this case was the Court's almost casual announcement that the First Amendment guarantees were also applicable against the states by virtue of the Fourteenth Amendment. The Gitlow *case thus marked an important shift from what had been a rigid position since the Court's nineteenth century decisions in the* Slaughter-House Cases *and* Hurtado *v.* California.

Justice Sanford delivered the opinion of the Court.

The precise question presented, and the only question which we can consider under this writ of error, then is, whether the statute, as construed and applied in this case by the state courts, deprived the defendant of his liberty of expression in violation of the due process clause of the Fourteenth Amendment.

The statute does not penalize the utterance or publication of abstract "doctrine" or academic discussion having no quality of incitement to any concrete action. It is not aimed against mere historical or philosophical essays. It does not restrain the advocacy of changes in the form of government by constitutional and lawful means. What it prohibits is language advocating, advising or teaching the overthrow of organized government by unlawful means. These words imply urging to action. Advocacy is defined in the Century Dictionary as: "1. The act of pleading for, supporting, or recommending; active espousal." It is not the abstract "doctrine" of overthrowing organized government by unlawful means which is denounced by the statute, but the advocacy of action for the accomplishment of that purpose. . . .

The Manifesto [published by Gitlow and his co-defendants], plainly, is neither the statement of abstract doctrine nor, as suggested by counsel, mere prediction that industrial disturbances and revolutionary mass strikes

268 U.S. 652 (1925)

will result spontaneously in an inevitable process of evolution in the economic system. It advocates and urges in fervent language mass action which shall progressively foment industrial disturbances and through political mass strikes and revolutionary mass action overthrow and destroy organized parliamentary government. It concludes with a call to action in these words: "The proletariat revolution and the Communist reconstruction of society — *the struggle for these* — is now indispensable. . . . The Communist International calls the proletariat of the world to the final struggle!" This is not the expression of philosophical abstraction, the mere prediction of future events; it is the language of direct incitement.

The means advocated for bringing about the destruction of organized parliamentary government, namely, mass industrial revolts usurping the functions of municipal government, political mass strikes directed against the parliamentary state, and revolutionary mass action for its final destruction, necessarily imply the use of force and violence, and in their essential nature are inherently unlawful in a constitutional government of law and order. That the jury were warranted in finding that the Manifesto advocated not merely the abstract doctrine of overthrowing organized government by force, violence and unlawful means, but action to that end, is clear.

For present purposes we may and do assume that freedom of speech and of the press — which are protected by the First Amendment from abridgment by Congress — are among the fundamental personal rights and "liberties" protected by the due process clause of the Fourteenth Amendment from impairment by the States. We do not regard the incidental statement in *Prudential Ins. Co.* v. *Cheek,* 259 U.S. 530, 543 [1922], that the Fourteenth Amendment imposes no restrictions on the States concerning freedom of speech, as determinative of this question.

It is a fundamental principle, long established, that the freedom of speech and of the press which is secured by the Constitution, does not confer an absolute right to speak or publish, without responsibility, whatever one may choose, or an unrestricted and unbridled license that gives immunity for every possible use of language and prevents the punishment of those who abuse this freedom. . . .

That a State in the exercise of its police power may punish those who abuse this freedom by utterances inimical to the public welfare, tending to corrupt public morals, incite to crime, or disturb the public peace, is not open to question. . . .

And, for yet more imperative reasons, a State may punish utterances endangering the foundations of organized government and threatening its overthrow by unlawful means. These imperil its own existence as a constitutional State. Freedom of speech and press, said [Justice] Story does not protect disturbances to the public peace or the attempt to subvert the government. It does not protect publications or teachings which tend to subvert or imperil the government or to impede or hinder it in the performance of its governmental duties. . . . It does not protect publications prompting the overthrow of government by force; the punishment of those who publish articles which tend to destroy organized society being essential to the security of freedom and the stability of the State. . . . And a State may penalize utterances which openly advocate the overthrow of the representative and constitutional form of government of the United States and the several States, by violence or other unlawful means. . . . In short this freedom does not deprive a State of the primary and essential right of self preservation; which, so long as human governments endure, they cannot be denied. . . .

By enacting the present statute the State has determined, through its legislative body, that utterances advocating the overthrow of organized government by force, violence and unlawful means, are so inimical to the general welfare and involve such danger of substantive evil that they may be penalized in the exercise of its police power. That determination must be given great weight. Every presumption is to be indulged in favor of the validity of the statute. . . . And the case is to be considered "in the light of the principle that the State is primarily the judge of regulations required in the interest of public safety and welfare;" and that its police "statutes may only be declared unconstitutional where they are arbitrary or unreasonable attempts to exercise authority vested in the State in the public interest." *Great Northern Ry.* v. *Clara City,* 246 U.S. 434, 439. That utterances inciting to the overthrow of organized government by unlawful means, present a sufficient danger of substantive evil to bring their punishment within the range of legislative discretion, is clear. Such utterances, by their very nature, involve danger to the public peace and to the security of the State. They threaten breaches of the peace and ultimate revolution. And the immediate danger is none the less real and substantial, because the effect of a given utterance cannot be accurately foreseen. The State cannot reasonably be required to measure the danger from every such utterance in the nice balance of a jeweler's scale. A single revolutionary spark may kindle a fire that, smouldering for a time, may burst into a sweeping and destructive conflagration. It cannot be said that the State is acting arbitrarily or unreasonably when in the exercise of its judgment as to the measures necessary to protect the public peace and safety, it seeks to extinguish the spark without waiting until it has enkindled the flame or blazed into the conflagration. It cannot reasonably be required to defer the adoption of measures for its own peace and safety until the revolutionary utterances lead to actual disturbances of the public peace or imminent and immediate danger of its own destruction; but it may, in the exercise of its judgment, suppress the threatened danger in its incipiency. . . .

We cannot hold that the present statute is an arbitrary or unreasonable exercise of the police power of the State unwarrantably infringing the freedom of speech or press; and we must and do sustain its constitutionality. . . .

[T]he general statement in the *Schenck Case* . . . that the "question in every case is whether the words are used in such circumstances and are of such a nature as to create a clear and present danger that they will bring about the substantive evils," — upon which great reliance is placed in the defendant's argument — was manifestly intended, as shown by the context, to apply only in cases of this class, and has no application to those like the present, where the legislative body itself has previously determined the danger of substantive evil arising from utterances of a specified character. . . .

Whitney *v.* California

Charlotte Anita Whitney, a niece of Justice Field, was convicted of violating California's criminal syndicalism law. She had been charged with assisting in the organization, and being a member of, the state Communist Labor party, a group advocating the overthrow of the existing government. The Court predictably sustained the conviction. But Justice Brandeis, also speaking for Holmes, delivered a concurring opinion which reiterated and expanded the latter's clear and present danger principles. Brandeis accepted the evidence as sufficient for conviction, but he contended that a statute, declaring restrictions on speech and assembly because of alleged danger, was a "rebuttable presumption."

Justice Brandeis, concurring.

Despite arguments to the contrary which had seemed to me persuasive, it is settled that the due process clause of the Fourteenth Amendment applies to matters of substantive law as well as to matters of procedure. Thus all fundamental rights comprised within the term liberty are protected by the Federal Constitution from invasion by the States. The right of free speech, the right to teach and the right of assembly are, of course, fundamental rights. . . . These may not be denied or abridged. But, although the rights of free speech and assembly are fundamental, they are not in their nature absolute. Their exercise is subject to restriction, if the particular restriction proposed is required in order to protect the State from destruction or from serious injury, political, economic or moral. That the necessity which is essential to a valid restriction does not exist unless speech would produce, or is intended to produce, a clear and imminent danger of some substantive evil which the State constitutionally may seek to prevent has been settled. . . .

It is said to be the function of the legislature to determine whether at a particular time and under the particular circumstances the formation of, or assembly with, a society organized to advocate criminal syndicalism constitutes a clear and present danger of substantive evil; and that by enacting the law here in question the legislature of California determined that question in the affirmative. . . . The legislature must obviously decide, in the first instance, whether a danger exists which calls for a particular protective measure. But where a statute is valid only in case certain conditions exist, the enactment of the statute cannot alone establish the facts which are essential to its validity. Prohibitory legislation has repeatedly been held invalid, because unnecessary, where the denial of liberty involved was that of engaging in a particular business. The power of the courts to strike down an offending law is no less when the interests involved are not property rights, but the fundamental personal rights of free speech and assembly.

This Court has not yet fixed the standard by which to determine when a danger shall be deemed clear; how remote the danger may be and yet be deemed present; and what degree of evil shall be deemed sufficiently substantial to justify resort to abridgement of free speech and assembly as the means of protection. To reach sound conclusions on these matters, we must bear in mind why a State is, ordinarily, denied the power to prohibit dissemination of social, economic and political doctrine which a vast majority of its citizens believes to be false and fraught with evil consequence.

Those who won our independence believed that the final end of the State was to make men free to develop their faculties; and that in its government the deliberative forces should prevail over the arbitrary. They valued liberty both as an end and as a means. They believed liberty to be the secret of happiness and courage to be the secret of liberty. They believed that freedom to think as you will and to speak as you think are means indispensable to the discovery and spread of political truth; that without free speech and assembly discussion would be futile; that with them, discussion affords ordinarily adequate protection against the dissemination of noxious doctrine; that the greatest menace to freedom is an inert people; that public discussion is a political duty; and that this should be a fundamental principle of the American government. They recognized the risks to which all human institutions are subject. But they knew that order cannot be secured merely through fear of punishment for

its infraction; that it is hazardous to discourage thought, hope and imagi-
nation; that fear breeds repression; that repression breeds hate; that hate
menaces stable government; that the path of safety lies in the opportunity
to discuss freely supposed grievances and proposed remedies; and that
the fitting remedy for evil counsels is good ones. Believing in the power
of reason as applied through public discussion, they eschewed silence
coerced by law — the argument of force in its worst form. Recognizing
the occasional tyrannies of governing majorities, they amended the Constitution so that free speech and assembly should be guaranteed.

Fear of serious injury cannot alone justify suppression of free speech
and assembly. Men feared witches and burnt women. It is the function
of speech to free men from the bondage of irrational fears. To justify suppression of free speech there must be reasonable ground to fear that serious evil will result if free speech is practiced. There must be reasonable
ground to believe that the danger apprehended is imminent. There must
be reasonable ground to believe that the evil to be prevented is a serious
one. Every denunciation of existing law tends in some measure to increase the probability that there will be violation of it. Condonation of a
breach enhances the probability. Expressions of approval add to the
probability. Propagation of the criminal state of mind by teaching syndicalism increases it. Advocacy of law-breaking heightens it still further.
But even advocacy of violation, however reprehensible morally, is not a
justification for denying free speech where the advocacy falls short of
incitement and there is nothing to indicate that the advocacy would be
immediately acted on. The wide difference between advocacy and incitement, between preparation and attempt, between assembling and conspiracy, must be borne in mind. In order to support a finding of clear and
present danger it must be shown either that immediate serious violence
was to be expected or was advocated, or that the past conduct furnished
reason to believe that such advocacy was then contemplated.

Those who won our independence by revolution were not cowards.
They did not fear political change. They did not exalt order at the cost
of liberty. To courageous, self-reliant men, with confidence in the power
of free and fearless reasoning applied through the processes of popular
government, no danger flowing from speech can be deemed clear and
present, unless the incidence of the evil apprehended is so imminent that
it may befall before there is opportunity for full discussion. If there be
time to expose through discussion the falsehood and fallacies, to avert
the evil by the processes of education, the remedy to be applied is more
speech, not enforced silence. Only an emergency can justify repression.
Such must be the rule if authority is to be reconciled with freedom. Such,
in my opinion, is the command of the Constitution. It is therefore always
open to Americans to challenge a law abridging free speech and assembly
by showing that there was no emergency justifying it.

Moreover, even imminent danger cannot justify resort to prohibition of these functions essential to effective democracy, unless the evil apprehended is relatively serious. Prohibition of free speech and assembly is a measure so stringent that it would be inappropriate as the means for averting a relatively trivial harm to society. A police measure may be unconstitutional merely because the remedy, although effective as means of protection, is unduly harsh or oppressive. Thus, a State might, in the exercise of its police power, make any trespass upon the land of another a crime, regardless of the results or of the intent or purpose of the trespasser. It might, also, punish an attempt, a conspiracy, or an incitement to commit the trespass. But it is hardly conceivable that this Court would hold constitutional a statute which punished as a felony the mere voluntary assembly with a society formed to teach that pedestrians had the moral right to cross unenclosed, unposted, waste lands and to advocate their doing so, even if there was imminent danger that advocacy would lead to a trespass. The fact that speech is likely to result in some violence or in destruction of property is not enough to justify its suppression. There must be the probability of serious injury to the State. Among free men, the deterrents ordinarily to be applied to prevent crime are education and punishment for violations of the law, not abridgment of the rights of free speech and assembly. . . .

Hammer *v.* Dagenhart

This decision heralded the revival of dual federalism and a judicial reaction against some aspects of governmental regulation. A 5–4 majority held the federal child labor law of 1916 unconstitutional. The majority tortuously attempted to distinguish this law from similar ones which were upheld as valid exercises of the federal commerce power. Justice Day insisted that the test was one of "harmfulness"; that is, the things to be excluded from commerce had to be intrinsically harmful. Thus lottery tickets, adulterated foods, prostitutes, and stolen cars were "harmful," but not products manufactured by child labor. Holmes, dissenting, challenged the majority's logic and ironically noted that "civilized countries" had agreed, "far more unanimously than they have with regard to intoxicants and some other matters over which this country is now emotionally aroused," on the "evil of premature and excessive child labor."

Justice Day delivered the opinion of the Court.

I t is insisted that adjudged cases in this court establish the doctrine that the power to regulate given to Congress incidentally includes the authority to prohibit the movement of ordinary commodities and therefore that the subject is not open for discussion. The cases demonstrate the contrary. They rest upon the character of the particular subjects dealt with and the fact that the scope of governmental authority, state or national, possessed over them is such that the authority to prohibit is as to them but the exertion of the power to regulate.

The first of these cases is . . . the so-called *Lottery Case*, in which it was held that Congress might pass a law having the effect to keep the channels of commerce free from use in the transportation of tickets used in the promotion of lottery schemes. In *Hipolite Egg Co.* v. *United States*, . . . this court sustained the power of Congress to pass the Pure Food and Drug Act which prohibited the introduction into the States by

247 U.S. 251 (1918)

means of interstate commerce of impure foods and drugs. In *Hoke* v. *United States,* . . . this court sustained the constitutionality of the so-called "White Slave Traffic Act" whereby the transportation of a woman in interstate commerce for the purpose of prostitution was forbidden. In that case we said, having reference to the authority of Congress, under the regulatory power, to protect the channels of interstate commerce:

> "If the facility of interstate transportation can be taken away from the demoralization of lotteries, the debasement of obscene literature, the contagion of diseased cattle or persons, the impurity of food and drugs, the like facility can be taken away from the systematic enticement to and the enslavement in prostitution and debauchery of women, and, more insistently, of girls." . . .

In each of these instances the use of interstate transportation was necessary to the accomplishment of harmful results. In other words, although the power over interstate transportation was to regulate, that could only be accomplished by prohibiting the use of the facilities of interstate commerce to effect the evil intended.

This element is wanting in the present case. The thing intended to be accomplished by this statute is the denial of the facilities of interstate commerce to those manufacturers in the States who employ children within the prohibited ages. The act in its effect does not regulate transportation among the States, but aims to standardize the ages at which children may be employed in mining and manufacturing within the States. The goods shipped are of themselves harmless. The act permits them to be freely shipped after thirty days from the time of their removal from the factory. When offered for shipment, and before transportation begins, the labor of their production is over, and the mere fact that they were intended for interstate commerce transportation does not make their production subject to federal control under the commerce power. . . .

Over interstate transportation, or its incidents, the regulatory power of Congress is ample, but the production of articles, intended for interstate commerce, is a matter of local regulation. . . .

If it were otherwise, all manufacture intended for interstate shipment would be brought under federal control to the practical exclusion of the authority of the States, a result certainly not contemplated by the framers of the Constitution when they vested in Congress the authority to regulate commerce among the States. . . .

It is further contended that the authority of Congress may be exerted to control interstate commerce in the shipment of child-made goods because of the effect of the circulation of such goods in other States where the evil of this class of labor has been recognized by local legislation, and the right to thus employ child labor has been more rigorously restrained than in the State of production. In other words, that the unfair competition, thus engendered, may be controlled by closing the channels of interstate commerce to manufacturers in those States where the local laws do not meet what Congress deems to be the more just standard of other States.

There is no power vested in Congress to require the States to exercise their police power so as to prevent possible unfair competition. Many causes may coöperate to give one State, by reason of local laws or conditions, an economic advantage over others. The Commerce Clause was not intended to give to Congress a general authority to equalize such conditions. In some of the States laws have been passed fixing minimum wages for women, in others the local law regulates the hours of labor of women in various employments. Business done in such States may be at an economic disadvantage when compared with States which have no such regulations; surely, this fact does not give Congress the power to deny transportation in interstate commerce to those who carry on business where the hours of labor and the rate of compensation for women have not been fixed by a standard in use in other States and approved by Congress.

The grant of power to Congress over the subject of interstate commerce was to enable it to regulate such commerce, and not to give it authority to control the States in their exercise of the police power over local trade and manufacture.

The grant of authority over a purely federal matter was not intended to destroy the local power always existing and carefully reserved to the States in the Tenth Amendment to the Constitution. . . .

That there should be limitations upon the right to employ children in mines and factories in the interest of their own and the public welfare, all will admit. That such employment is generally deemed to require regulation is shown by the fact that the brief counsel states that every State in the Union has a law upon the subject, limiting the right to thus employ children. In North Carolina, the State wherein is located the factory in which the employment was had in the present case, no child under twelve years of age is permitted to work.

It may be desirable that such laws be uniform, but our Federal Government is one of enumerated powers; "this principle," declared Chief Justice Marshall in *McCulloch* v. *Maryland*, . . . "is universally admitted." . . .

In interpreting the Constitution it must never be forgotten that the Nation is made up of States to which are entrusted the powers of local government. And to them and to the people the powers not expressly delegated to the National Government are reserved. . . . The power of the States to regulate their purely internal affairs by such laws as seem wise to the local authority is inherent and has never been surrendered to the general government. . . .

In our view the necessary effect of this act is, by means of a prohibition against the movement in interstate commerce of ordinary commercial commodities, to regulate the hours of labor of children in factories and mines within the States, a purely state authority. Thus the act in a two-fold sense is repugnant to the Constitution. It not only transcends the authority delegated to Congress over commerce but also exerts a power as to a purely local matter to which the federal authority does not extend. The far reaching result of upholding the act cannot be more plainly indicated than by pointing out that if Congress can thus regulate matters entrusted to local authority by prohibition of the movement of commodities in interstate commerce, all freedom of commerce will be at an end, and the power of the States over local matters may be eliminated, and thus our system of government be practically destroyed.

For these reasons we hold that this law exceeds the constitutional authority of Congress. . . .

Bailey *v.* Drexel Furniture Company
[Child Labor Tax Case]

A year after the Court voided the child labor law based on the commerce clause, Congress enacted a measure taxing goods produced by child labor. Congress clearly considered the oleo tax case as ample precedent and justification for its action. But the Court continued to view federal child labor laws with a jaundiced eye, and in 1922, invalidated the new law. It is difficult, however, to discern any serious abridgment of federal police power, on the basis of either the commerce or tax power, in the child labor cases. The decisions proved exceptional and anachronistic.

Chief Justice Taft delivered the opinion of the Court.

The law is attacked on the ground that it is a regulation of the employment of child labor in the States — an exclusively state function under the Federal Constitution and within the reservations of the Tenth Amendment. It is defended on the ground that it is a mere excise tax levied by the Congress of the United States under its broad power of taxation conferred by § 8, Article I, of the Federal Constitution. We must construe the law and interpret the intent and meaning of Congress

259 U.S. 20 (1922)

from the language of the act. The words are to be given their ordinary meaning unless the context shows that they are differently used. Does this law impose a tax with only that incidental restraint and regulation which a tax must inevitably involve? Or does it regulate by the use of the so-called tax as a penalty? If a tax, it is clearly an excise. If it were an excise on a commodity or other thing of value we might not be permitted under previous decisions of this court to infer solely from its heavy burden that the act intends a prohibition instead of a tax. But this act is more. It provides a heavy exaction for a departure from a detailed and specified course of conduct in business. That course of business is that employers shall employ in mines and quarries, children of an age greater than sixteen years; in mills and factories, children of an age greater than fourteen years, and shall prevent children of less than sixteen years in mills and factories from working more than eight hours a day or six days in the week. If an employer departs from this prescribed course of business, he is to pay to the Government one-tenth of his entire net income in the business for a full year. The amount is not to be proportioned in any degree to the extent or frequency of the departures, but is to be paid by the employer in full measure whether he employs five hundred children for a year, or employs only one for a day. Moreover, if he does not know the child is within the named age limit, he is not to pay; that is to say, it is only where he knowingly departs from the prescribed course that payment is to be exacted. Scienter is associated with penalties not with taxes. The employer's factory is to be subject to inspection at any time not only by the taxing officers of the Treasury, the Department normally charged with the collection of taxes, but also by the Secretary of Labor and his subordinates whose normal function is the advancement and protection of the welfare of the workers. In the light of these features of the act, a court must be blind not to see that the so-called tax is imposed to stop the employment of children within the age limits prescribed. Its prohibitory and regulatory effect and purpose are palpable. All others can see and understand this. How can we properly shut our minds to it?

It is the high duty and function of this court in cases regularly brought to its bar to decline to recognize or enforce seeming laws of Congress, dealing with subjects not entrusted to Congress but left or committed by the supreme law of the land to the control of the States. We can not avoid the duty even though it require us to refuse to give effect to legislation designed to promote the highest good. The good sought in unconstitutional legislation is an insidious feature because it leads citizens and legislators of good purpose to promote it without thought of the serious breach it will make in the ark of our covenant or the harm which will come from breaking down recognized standards. In the maintenance of local self government, on the one hand, and the national power, on the other, our country has been able to endure and prosper for near a century and a half.

Out of a proper respect for the acts of a coördinate branch of the Government, this court has gone far to sustain taxing acts as such, even though there has been ground for suspecting from the weight of the tax it was intended to destroy its subject. But, in the act before us, the presumption of validity cannot prevail, because the proof of the contrary is found on the very face of its provisions. Grant the validity of this law, and all that Congress would need to do, hereafter, in seeking to take over to its control any one of the great number of subjects of public interest, jurisdiction of which the States have never parted with, and which are reserved to them by the Tenth Amendment, would be to enact a detailed measure of complete regulation of the subject and enforce it by a so-called tax upon departures from it. To give such magic to the word "tax" would be to break down all constitutional limitation of the powers of Congress and completely wipe out the sovereignty of the States.

The difference between a tax and a penalty is sometimes difficult to define and yet the consequences of the distinction in the required method of their collection often are important. Where the sovereign enacting the law has power to impose both tax and penalty the difference between revenue production and mere regulation may be immaterial, but not so when one sovereign can impose a tax only, and the power of regulation rests in another. Taxes are occasionally imposed in the discretion of the legislature on proper subjects with the primary motive of obtaining revenue from them and with the incidental motive of discouraging them by making their continuance onerous. They do not lose their character as taxes because of the incidental motive. But there comes a time in the extension of the penalizing features of the so-called tax when it loses its character as such and becomes a mere penalty with the characteristics of regulation and punishment. Such is the case in the law before us. Although Congress does not invalidate the contract of employment or expressly declare that the employment within the mentioned ages is illegal, it does exhibit its intent practically to achieve the latter result by adopting the criteria of wrongdoing and imposing its principal consequence on those who transgress its standard.

The case before us can not be distinguished from that of *Hammer* v. *Dagenhart*. . . .

In the case at the bar, Congress in the name of a tax which on the face of the act is a penalty seeks to do the same thing, and the effort must be equally futile.

The analogy of the *Dagenhart Case* is clear. The congressional power over interstate commerce is, within its proper scope, just as complete and unlimited as the congressional power to tax, and the legislative motive in its exercise is just as free from judicial suspicion and inquiry. Yet when Congress threatened to stop interstate commerce in ordinary and necessary commodities, unobjectionable as subjects of transportation, and to deny the same to the people of a State in order to coerce them into compliance with Congress's regulation of State concerns, the court said this was not in fact regulation of interstate commerce, but rather that of State concerns and was invalid. So here the so-called tax is a penalty to coerce people of a State to act as Congress wishes them to act in respect of a matter completely the business of the State government under the Federal Constitution. . . .

For the reasons given, we must hold the Child Labor Tax Law invalid and the judgment of the District Court is

Affirmed. . . .

Justice Clarke dissents.

Truax *v.* Corrigan

During the first two decades of the twentieth century, organized labor launched an all-out attack against court injunctions. Efforts to dissuade judges, however, generally failed and the number of injunctions rapidly increased. In 1914, labor believed that it had secured some relief in the provisions of the Clayton Anti-Trust Act. The law, however, was vague enough to permit a variety of interpretations. In Duplex Printing Press Co. *v.* Deering *(254 U.S. 443) and* American Steel Foundries *v.* Tri-Cities Trades Council *(257 U.S. 184), both in 1921, the Court concluded that the secondary boycott was still illegal and that the equity jurisdiction of the federal courts remained the same. Some states also had attempted to provide relief for labor. A 1913 Arizona statute forbade injunctions against peaceful picketing. In the case below, Truax challenged the law as it denied him an equitable remedy in cases where his property was threatened. He contended that the effect was to deprive him of his property without due process of law and that he was denied equal protection of the laws because injunctions were still available to persons not involved in labor disputes. The confidence and certitude expressed in Taft's opinion are quite misleading, for the Court divided 5–4 in the case. In dissent, Holmes deprecated the majority's use of the Fourteenth Amendment to "prevent the making of social experiments that an important part of the community desires."*

Chief Justice Taft delivered the opinion of the Court.

Plaintiffs' business is a property right (*Duplex Printing Press Co.* v. *Deering*, 254 U.S. 443, 465) and free access for employees, owner and customers to his place of business is incident to such right. Intentional injury caused to either right or both by a conspiracy is a tort. Concert of action is a conspiracy if its object is unlawful or if the means used are unlawful. . . . Intention to inflict the loss and the actual loss caused are clear. The real question here is, were the means used illegal? The . . . recital of what the defendants did, can leave no doubt of that. The libelous attacks upon the plaintiffs, their business, their employees, and their customers, and the abusive epithets applied to them were palpable

257 U.S. 312 (1921)

wrongs. They were uttered in aid of the plan to induce plaintiffs' customers and would-be customers to refrain from patronizing the plaintiffs. The patrolling of defendants immediately in front of the restaurant on the main street and within five feet of plaintiffs' premises continuously during business hours, with the banners announcing plaintiffs' unfairness; the attendance by the picketers at the entrance to the restaurant and their insistent and loud appeals all day long, the constant circulation by them of the libels and epithets applied to employees, plaintiffs and customers, and the threats of injurious consequences to future customers, all linked together in a campaign, were an unlawful annoyance and a hurtful nuisance in respect of the free access to the plaintiffs' place of business. It was not lawful persuasion or inducing. It was not a mere appeal to the sympathetic aid of would-be customers by a simple statement of the fact of the strike and a request to withhold patronage. It was compelling every customer or would-be customer to run the gauntlet of most uncomfortable publicity, aggressive and annoying importunity, libelous attacks and fear of injurious consequences, illegally inflicted, to his reputation and standing in the community. No wonder that a business of $50,000 was reduced to only one-fourth of its former extent. Violence could not have been more effective. It was moral coercion by illegal annoyance and obstruction and it thus was plainly a conspiracy. . . .

A law which operates to make lawful such a wrong as is described in plaintiffs' complaint deprives the owner of the business and the premises of his property without due process, and can not be held valid under the Fourteenth Amendment. . . .

It is to be observed that this is not the mere case of a peaceful secondary boycott as to the illegality of which courts have differed and States have adopted different statutory provisions. A secondary boycott of this kind is where many combine to injure one in his business by coercing third persons against their will to cease patronizing him by threats of similar injury. In such a case the many have a legal right to withdraw their trade from the one, they have the legal right to withdraw their trade from third persons, and they have the right to advise third persons of their intention to do so when each act is considered singly. The question in such cases is whether the moral coercion exercised over a stranger to the original controversy by steps in themselves legal becomes a legal wrong. But here the illegality of the means used is without doubt and fundamental. The means used are the libelous and abusive attacks on the plaintiffs' reputation, like attacks on their employees and customers, threats of such attacks on would-be customers, picketing and patrolling of the entrance to their place of business, and the consequent obstruction of free access thereto — all with the purpose of depriving the plaintiffs of their business. To give operation to a statute whereby serious losses inflicted by such unlawful means are in effect made remediless, is, we think, to disregard fundamental rights of liberty and property and to deprive the person suffering the loss of due process of law. . . .

This brings us to consider the effect in this case of that provision of the Fourteenth Amendment which forbids any State to deny to any person the equal protection of the laws. The clause is associated in the Amendment with the due process clause and it is customary to consider them together. It may be that they overlap, that a violation of one may involve at times the violation of the other, but the spheres of the protection they offer are not coterminous. The due process clause, brought down from Magna Carta, was found in the early state constitutions, and later in the Fifth Amendment to the Federal Constitution as a limitation upon the executive, legislative and judicial powers of the Federal Government, while the equality clause does not appear in the Fifth Amendment and so does not apply to congressional legislation. The due process clause requires that every man shall have the protection of his day in court, and the benefit of the general law, a law which hears before it condemns, which proceeds not arbitrarily or capriciously but upon inquiry, and renders judgment only after trial, so that every citizen shall hold his life, liberty, property and immunities under the protection of the general rules which govern society. *Hurtado* v. *California,* 110 U.S. 516, 535. It, of course, tends to secure equality of law in the sense that it makes a required minimum of protection for every one's right of life, liberty and property, which the Congress or the legislature may not withhold. Our whole system of law is predicated on the general, fundamental principle of equality of application of the law. "All men are equal before the law," "This is a government of laws and not of men," "No man is above the law," are all maxims showing the spirit in which legislatures, executives and courts are expected to make, execute and apply laws. But the framers and adopters of this Amendment were not content to depend on a mere minimum secured by the due process clause, or upon the spirit of equality which might not be insisted on by local public opinion. They therefore embodied that spirit in a specific guaranty.

The guaranty was aimed at undue favor and individual or class privilege, on the one hand, and at hostile discrimination or the oppression of inequality, on the other. It sought an equality of treatment of all persons, even though all enjoyed the protection of due process. . . . Thus the guaranty was intended to secure equality of protection not only for all but against all similarly situated. Indeed, protection is not protection unless it does so. Immunity granted to a class, however limited, having the effect to deprive another class, however limited, of a personal or property right, is just as clearly a denial of equal protection of the laws to the latter class as if the immunity were in favor of, or the deprivation of right permitted worked against, a larger class. . . .

With these views of the meaning of the equality clause, it does not seem possible to escape the conclusion that by the clauses of Paragraph 1464 of the Revised Statutes of Arizona, here relied on by the defendants, as construed by its Supreme Court, the plaintiffs have been deprived of the equal protection of the law. . . .

Adkins *v.* Children's Hospital

Those who thought that the Lochner *decision had been relegated to the ashcan of history received a rude jolt in 1923 when the Court solemnly invoked it and the whole freedom of contract rhetoric to strike down a federal minimum wage law for women in the District of Columbia. No one was more surprised than that impeccable conservative constitutionalist — Chief Justice Taft. As he stated in his dissenting opinion, he believed that* Bunting v. Oregon *had overruled* Lochner. *The* Bunting *case had approved minimum standards for overtime wages only. But an Oregon statute for minimum wages for women was sustained by an equally divided bench the same year (*Stettler v. O'Hara, *243 U.S. 629). Justice Sutherland's majority opinion below labored strenuously to qualitatively distinguish maximum hour and minimum wage legislation. Holmes dissented by typically attacking the Court's prejudices. Taft's dissent, however, was more meaningful for its criticism of the majority's logic and inconsistency.*

Justice Sutherland delivered the opinion of the Court.

The statute now under consideration is attacked upon the ground that it authorizes an unconstitutional interference with the freedom of contract included within the guaranties of the due process clause of the Fifth Amendment. That the right to contract about one's affairs is a part of the liberty of the individual protected by this clause, is settled by the decisions of this Court and is no longer open to question. . . .

Within this liberty are contracts of employment of labor. In making such contracts, generally speaking, the parties have an equal right to obtain from each other the best terms they can as the result of private bargaining. . . .

There is, of course, no such thing as absolute freedom of contract. It is subject to a great variety of restraints. But freedom of contract is, nevertheless, the general rule and restraint the exception; and the exercise of legislative authority to abridge it can be justified only by the existence of exceptional circumstances. Whether these circumstances exist in the present case constitutes the question to be answered. It will be helpful to this end to review some of the decisions where the interference has been upheld and consider the grounds upon which they rest.

(1) *Those dealing with statutes fixing rates and charges to be exacted by businesses impressed with a public interest.* There are many cases, but it is sufficient to cite *Munn* v. *Illinois,* 94 U.S. 113. The power here rests upon the ground that where property is devoted to a public use the owner thereby, in effect, grants to the public an interest in the use which may be controlled by the public for the common good to the extent of the interest thus created. It is upon this theory that these statutes have been upheld and, it may be noted in passing, so upheld even in respect of their incidental and injurious or destructive effect upon preëxisting contracts. . . . In the case at bar the statute does not depend upon the existence of a public interest in any business to be affected, and this class of cases may be laid aside as inapplicable.

(2) *Statutes relating to contracts for the performance of public work.* *Atkin* v. *Kansas,* 191 U.S. 207; *Heim* v. *McCall,* 239 U.S. 175; *Ellis* v. *United States,* 206 U.S. 246. These cases sustain such statutes as depending, not upon the right to condition private contracts, but upon the right of the government to prescribe the conditions upon which it will permit work of a public character to be done for it, or, in the case of a State, for its municipalities. We may, therefore, in like manner, dismiss these decisions from consideration as inapplicable.

(3) *Statutes prescribing the character, methods and time for payment of wages.* Under this head may be included *McLean* v. *Arkansas,* 211 U.S. 539, sustaining a state statute requiring coal to be measured for payment of miners' wages before screening; *Knoxville Iron Co.* v. *Harbison,* 183 U.S. 13, sustaining a Tennessee statute requiring the redemption in cash of store orders issued in payment of wages; *Erie R. R. Co.* v. *Williams,* 233 U.S. 685, upholding a statute regulating the time within which wages shall be paid to employees in certain specified industries; and other cases sustaining statutes of like import and effect. In one of the statutes thus sustained, was the liberty of employer or employee to fix the amount of wages the one was willing to pay and the other willing to receive interfered with. Their tendency and purpose was to prevent unfair and perhaps fraudulent methods in the payment of wages and in no sense can they be said to be, or to furnish a precedent for, wage-fixing statutes.

(4) *Statutes fixing hours of labor.* It is upon this class that the greatest emphasis is laid in argument and therefore, and because such cases ap-

proach most nearly the line of principle applicable to the statute here involved, we shall consider them more at length. In some instances the statute limited the hours of labor for men in certain occupations and in others it was confined in its application to women. No statute has thus far been brought to the attention of this Court which by its terms, applied to all occupations. In *Holden* v. *Hardy*, 169 U.S. 366, the Court considered an act of the Utah legislature, restricting the hours of labor in mines and smelters. This statute was sustained as a legitimate exercise of the police power, on the ground that the legislature had determined that these particular employments, when too long pursued, were injurious to the health of the employees, and that, as there were reasonable grounds for supporting this determination on the part of the legislature, its decision in that respect was beyond the reviewing power of the federal courts.

That this constituted the basis of the decision is emphasized by the subsequent decision in *Lochner* v. *New York*, 198 U.S. 45, reviewing a state statute which restricted the employment of all persons in bakeries to ten hours in any one day. The Court referred to *Holden* v. *Hardy, supra,* and, declaring it to be inapplicable, held the statute unconstitutional as an unreasonable, unnecessary and arbitrary interference with the liberty of contract and therefore void under the Constitution. . . .

Subsequent cases in this Court have been distinguished from that decision [*Lochner*], but the principles therein stated have never been disapproved. . . .

The essential characteristics of the statute now under consideration, which differentiate it from the laws fixing hours of labor, will be made to appear as we proceed. It is sufficient now to point out that the latter as well as the statutes mentioned under paragraph (3), deal with incidents of the employment having no necessary effect upon the heart of the contract, that is, the amount of wages to be paid and received. A law forbidding work to continue beyond a given number of hours leaves the parties free to contract about wages and thereby equalize whatever additional burdens may be imposed upon the employer as a result of the restrictions as to hours, by an adjustment in respect of the amount of wages. Enough has been said to show that the authority to fix hours of labor cannot be exercised except in respect of those occupations where work of long continued duration is detrimental to health. This Court has been careful in every case where the question has been raised, to place its decision upon this limited authority of the legislature to regulate hours of labor and to disclaim any purpose to uphold the legislation as fixing wages, thus recognizing an essential difference between the two. It seems plain that these decisions afford no real support for any form of law establishing minimum wages.

If now, in the light furnished by the foregoing exceptions to the general rule forbidding legislative interference with freedom of contract, we examine and analyze the statute in question, we shall see that it differs from them in every material respect. It is not a law dealing with any business charged with a public interest or with public work, or to meet and tide over a temporary emergency. It has nothing to do with the character, methods or periods of wage payments. It does not prescribe hours of labor or conditions under which labor is to be done. It is not for the protection of persons under legal disability or for the prevention of fraud. It is simply and exclusively a price-fixing law, confined to adult women (for we are not now considering the provisions relating to minors), who are legally as capable of contracting for themselves as men. It forbids two parties having lawful capacity — under penalties as to the employer — to freely contract with one another in respect of the price for which one shall render service to the other in a purely private employment where both are willing, perhaps anxious, to agree, even though the consequence may be to oblige one to surrender a desirable engagement and the other to dispense with the services of a desirable employee. The price fixed by the board need have no relation to the capacity or earning power of the employee, the number of hours which may happen to constitute the day's work, the character of the place where the work is to be done, or the circumstances or surroundings of the employment; and, while it has no other basis to support its validity than the assumed necessities of the employee, it takes no account of any independent resources she may have. It is based wholly on the opinions of the members of the board and their advisers — perhaps an average of their opinions, if they do not precisely agree — as to what will be necessary to provide a living for a woman, keep her in health and preserve her morals. It applies to any and every occupation in the District, without regard to its nature or the character of the work. . . .

The feature of this statute which, perhaps more than any other, puts upon it the stamp of invalidity is that it exacts from the employer an arbitrary payment for a purpose and upon a basis having no causal connection with his business, or the contract or the work the employee engages to do. The declared basis, as already pointed out, is not the value of the service rendered, but the extraneous circumstance that the employee needs to get a prescribed sum of money to insure her subsistence, health and morals. The ethical right of every worker, man or woman, to a living wage may be conceded. One of the declared and important purposes of trade organizations is to secure it. And with that principle and with every legitimate effort to realize it in fact, no one can quarrel; but the fallacy of the proposed method of attaining it is that it assumes that every employer is bound at all events to furnish it. The moral requirement implicit in every contract of employment, viz., that the amount to be paid and the service to be rendered shall bear to each other some relation of just equivalence, is completely ignored. The necessities of the employee are alone considered and these arise outside of the employment, are the same when there is no employment, and as great in one occupation as in another. Certainly the employer by paying a fair equivalent for the service rendered, though not sufficient to support the employee, has neither caused nor contributed to her poverty. On the contrary, to the extent of what he pays he has relieved it. In principle, there can be no difference between the case of selling labor and the case of selling goods. If one goes to the butcher, the baker or grocer to buy food, he is morally entitled to obtain the worth of his money but he is not entitled to more. If what he gets is worth what he pays he is not justified in demanding more simply because he needs more; and the shopkeeper, having dealt fairly and honestly in that transaction, is not concerned in any peculiar sense with the question of his customer's necessities. Should a statute undertake to vest in a commission power to determine the quantity of food necessary for individual support and require the shopkeeper, if he sell to the individual at all, to furnish that quantity at not more than a fixed maximum, it would undoubtedly fall before the constitutional test. The fallacy of any argument in support of the validity of such a statute would be quickly exposed. The argument in support of that now being considered is equally fallacious, though the weakness of it may not be so plain. A statute requiring an employer to pay in money, to pay at pre-scribed and regular intervals, to pay the value of the services rendered, even to pay with fair relation to the extent of the benefit obtained from the service, would be understandable. But a statute which prescribes pay-ment without regard to any of these things and solely with relation to circumstances apart from the contract of employment, the business affected by it and the work done under it, is so clearly the product of a naked, arbitrary exercise of power that it cannot be allowed to stand under the Constitution of the United States.

We are asked, upon the one hand, to consider the fact that several States have adopted similar statutes, and we are invited, upon the other hand, to give weight to the fact that three times as many States, presum-ably as well informed and as anxious to promote the health and morals of their people, have refrained from enacting such legislation. We have also been furnished with a large number of printed opinions approving the policy of the minimum wage, and our own reading has disclosed a large number to the contrary. These are all proper enough for the con-sideration of the lawmaking bodies, since their tendency is to establish the desirability or undesirability of the legislation; but they reflect no legitimate light upon the question of its validity, and that is what we are called upon to decide. The elucidation of that question cannot be aided by counting heads.

It is said that great benefits have resulted from the operation of such statutes, not alone in the District of Columbia but in the several States, where they have been in force. A mass of reports, opinions of special observers and students of the subject, and the like, has been brought before us in support of this statement, all of which we have found interesting but only mildly persuasive. That the earnings of women now are greater than they were formerly and that conditions affecting women have become better in other respects may be conceded, but convincing indications of the logical relation of these desirable changes to the law in question are significantly lacking. They may be, and quite probably are, due to other causes. We cannot close our eyes to the notorious fact that earnings everywhere in all occupations have greatly increased — not alone in States where the minimum wage law obtains but in the country generally — quite as much or more among men as among women and in occupations outside the reach of the law as in those governed by it. No real test of the economic value of the law can be had during periods of maximum employment, when general causes keep wages up to or above the minimum; that will come in periods of depression and struggle for employment when the efficient will be employed at the minimum rate while the less capable may not be employed at all.

Finally, it may be said that if, in the interest of the public welfare, the police power may be invoked to justify the fixing of a minimum wage, it may, when the public welfare is thought to require it, be invoked to justify a maximum wage. The power to fix high wages connotes, by like course of reasoning, the power to fix low wages. If, in the face of the guaranties of the Fifth Amendment, this form of legislation shall be legally justified, the field for the operation of the police power will have been widened to a great and dangerous degree. If, for example, in the opinion of future lawmakers, wages in the building trades shall become so high as to preclude people of ordinary means from building and owning homes, an authority which sustains the minimum wage will be invoked to support a maximum wage for building laborers and artisans, and the same argument which has been here urged to strip the employer of his constitutional liberty of contract in one direction will be utilized to strip the employee of his constitutional liberty of contract in the opposite direction. A wrong decision does not end with itself: it is a precedent, and, with the swing of sentiment, its bad influence may run from one extremity of the arc to the other.

It has been said that legislation of the kind now under review is required in the interest of social justice, for whose ends freedom of contract may lawfully be subjected to restraint. The liberty of the individual to do as he pleases, even in innocent matters, is not absolute. It must frequently yield to the common good, and the line beyond which the power of interference may not be pressed is neither definite nor unalterable but may be made to move, within limits not well defined, with changing need and circumstance. Any attempt to fix a rigid boundary would be unwise as well as futile. But, nevertheless, there are limits to the power, and when these have been passed, it becomes the plain duty of the courts in the proper exercise of their authority to so declare. To sustain the individual freedom of action contemplated by the Constitution, is not to strike down the common good but to exalt it; for surely the good of society as a whole cannot be better served than by the preservation against arbitrary restraint of the liberties of its constituent members. . . .

Chief Justice Taft, dissenting.

I regret much to differ from the Court in these cases.

The boundary of the police power beyond which its exercise becomes an invasion of the guaranty of liberty under the Fifth and Fourteenth Amendments to the Constitution is not easy to mark. Our Court has been laboriously engaged in pricking out a line in successive cases. We must be careful, it seems to me, to follow that line as well as we can and not to depart from it by suggesting a distinction that is formal rather than real.

Legislatures in limiting freedom of contract between employee and employer by a minimum wage proceed on the assumption that employees, in the class receiving least pay, are not upon a full level of equality of choice with their employer and in their necessitous circumstances are prone to accept pretty much anything that is offered. They are peculiarly subject to the overreaching of the harsh and greedy employer. The evils of the sweating system and of the long hours and low wages which are characteristic of it are well known. Now, I agree that it is a disputable question in the field of political economy how far a statutory requirement of maximum hours or minimum wages may be a useful remedy for these evils, and whether it may not make the case of the oppressed employee worse than it was before. But it is not the function of this Court to hold congressional acts invalid simply because they are passed to carry out economic views which the Court believes to be unwise or unsound.

Legislatures which adopt a requirement of maximum hours or minimum wages may be presumed to believe that when sweating employers are prevented from paying unduly low wages by positive law they will continue their business, abating that part of their profits, which were wrung from the necessities of their employees, and will concede the better terms required by the law; and that while in individual cases hardship may result, the restriction will enure to the benefit of the general class of employees in whose interest the law is passed and so to that of the community at large.

The right of the legislature under the Fifth and Fourteenth Amendments to limit the hours of employment on the score of the health of the employee, it seems to me, has been firmly established. As to that, one would think, the line had been pricked out so that it has become a well formulated rule. In *Holden* v. *Hardy*, 169 U.S. 366, it was applied to miners and rested on the unfavorable environment of employment in mining and smelting. In *Lochner* v. *New York*, 198 U.S. 45, it was held that restricting those employed in bakeries to ten hours a day was an arbitrary and invalid interference with the liberty of contract secured by the Fourteenth Amendment. Then followed a number of cases beginning with *Muller* v. *Oregon*, 208 U.S. 412, sustaining the validity of a limit on maximum hours of labor for women . . . , and following these cases came *Bunting* v. *Oregon*, 243 U.S. 426. In that case, this Court sustained a law limiting the hours of labor of any person, whether man or woman, working in any mill, factory or manufacturing establishment to ten hours a day with a proviso as to further hours to which I shall hereafter advert. The law covered the whole field of industrial employment and certainly covered the case of persons employed in bakeries. Yet the opinion in the *Bunting Case* does not mention the *Lochner Case*. No one can suggest any constitutional distinction between employment in a bakery and one in any other kind of a manufacturing establishment which should make a limit of hours in the one invalid, and the same limit in the other permissible. It is impossible for me to reconcile the *Bunting Case* and the *Lochner Case* and I have always supposed that the *Lochner Case* was thus overruled *sub silentio*. Yet the opinion of the Court herein in support of its conclusion quotes from the opinion in the *Lochner Case* as one which has been sometimes distinguished but never overruled. Certainly there was no attempt to distinguish it in the *Bunting Case*.

However, the opinion herein does not overrule the *Bunting Case* in express terms, and therefore I assume that the conclusion in this case rests on the distinction between a minimum of wages and a maximum of hours in the limiting of liberty to contract. I regret to be at variance with the Court as to the substance of this distinction. In absolute freedom of contract the one term is as important as the other, for both enter equally into the consideration given and received, a restriction as to one is not any greater in essence than the other, and is of the same kind. One is the multiplier and the other the multiplicand.

If it be said that long hours of labor have a more direct effect upon the health of the employee than the low wage, there is very respectable authority from close observers, disclosed in the record and in the literature on the subject quoted at length in the briefs, that they are equally harmful in this regard. Congress took this view and we can not say it was not warranted in so doing.

With deference to the very able opinion of the Court and my brethren who concur in it, it appears to me to exaggerate the importance of the wage term of the contract of employment as more inviolate than its other terms. Its conclusion seems influenced by the fear that the concession of the power to impose a minimum wage must carry with it a concession of the power to fix a maximum wage. This, I submit, is a *non sequitur*. A line of distinction like the one under discussion in this case is, as the opinion elsewhere admits, a matter of degree and practical experience and not of pure logic. Certainly the wide difference between prescribing a minimum wage and a maximum wage could as a matter of degree and experience be easily affirmed. . . .

Without, however, expressing an opinion that a minimum wage limitation can be enacted for adult men, it is enough to say that the case before us involves only the application of the minimum wage to women. If I am right in thinking that the legislature can find as much support in experience for the view that a sweating wage has as great and as direct a tendency to bring about an injury to the health and morals of workers, as for the view that long hours injure their health, then I respectfully submit that *Muller* v. *Oregon*, 208 U.S. 412, controls this case. The law which was there sustained forbade the employment of any female in any mechanical establishment or factory or laundry for more than ten hours. This covered a pretty wide field in women's work and it would not seem that any sound distinction between that case and this can be built up on the fact that the law before us applies to all occupations of women with power in the board to make certain exceptions. Mr. Justice Brewer, who spoke for the Court in *Muller* v. *Oregon,* based its conclusion on the natural limit to women's physical strength and the likelihood that long hours would therefore injure her health, and we have had since a series of cases which may be said to have established a rule of decision. . . .

I am not sure from a reading of the opinion whether the Court thinks the authority of *Muller* v. *Oregon* is shaken by the adoption of the Nineteenth Amendment. The Nineteenth Amendment did not change the physical strength or limitations of women upon which the decision in *Muller* v. *Oregon* rests. The Amendment did give women political power and makes more certain that legislative provisions for their protection will be in accord with their interests as they see them. But I don't think we are warranted in varying constitutional construction based on physical differences between men and women, because of the Amendment. . . .

Wolff Packing Co.

v.

Court of Industrial Relations

Despite Taft's comments in Adkins, *he emphatically endorsed Sutherland's view that freedom of contract was the rule and restraint the exception. He merely found minimum wage legislation to be another valid exception. In the case below, Taft used the occasion to formulate definitive guidelines for freedom of contract and to settle precisely which businesses could be regulated on the basis of being affected with a public interest. At issue was a Kansas statute ordering compulsory arbitration for labor disputes in certain industries. For the most part, such laws were equally opposed by business interests and organized labor. Within his definitions of freedom of contract and public interest, Taft, speaking for a unanimous court, found the Kansas law unconstitutional.*

Chief Justice Taft delivered the opinion of the Court.

The necessary postulate of the Industrial Court Act is that the State, representing the people, is so much interested in their peace, health and comfort that it may compel those engaged in the manufacture of food, and clothing, and the production of fuel, whether owners or workers, to continue in their business and employment on terms fixed by an agency of the State if they can not agree. Under the construction adopted by the State Supreme Court the act gives the Industrial Court authority to permit the owner or employer to go out of the business, if he shows that he can only continue on the terms fixed at such heavy loss that collapse will follow; but this privilege under the circumstances is generally illusory. . . . A laborer dissatisfied with his wages is permitted to quit, but he may not agree with his fellows to quit or combine with others to induce them to quit.

These qualifications do not change the essence of the act. It curtails the right of the employer on the one hand, and of the employee on the other, to contract about his affairs. This is part of the liberty of the individual protected by the guaranty of the due process clause of the Fourteenth Amendment. . . . While there is no such thing as absolute free-

262 U.S. 522 (1923)

dom of contract and it is subject to a variety of restraints, they must not be arbitrary or unreasonable. Freedom is the general rule, and restraint the exception. The legislative authority to abridge can be justified only by exceptional circumstances. *Adkins* v. *Children's Hospital.* . . .

It is argued for the State that such exceptional circumstances exist in the present case and that the act is neither arbitrary nor unreasonable. Counsel maintain:

First. The act declares that the preparation of human food is affected by a public interest and the power of the legislature so to declare and then to regulate the business is established in *Munn* v. *Illinois.* . . .

Second. The power to regulate a business affected with a public interest extends to fixing wages and terms of employment to secure continuity of operation. . . .

Businesses said to be clothed with a public interest justifying some public regulation may be divided into three classes:

(1) Those which are carried on under the authority of a public grant of privileges which either expressly or impliedly imposes the affirmative duty of rendering a public service demanded by any member of the public. Such are the railroads, other common carriers and public utilities.

(2) Certain occupations, regarded as exceptional, the public interest attaching to which, recognized from earliest times, has survived the period of arbitrary laws by Parliament or Colonial legislatures for regulating all trades and callings. Such are those of the keepers of inns, cabs and grist mills. . . .

(3) Businesses which though not public at their inception may be fairly said to have risen to be such and have become subject in consequence to some government regulation. They have come to hold such a peculiar relation to the public that this is superimposed upon them. In the language of the cases, the owner by devoting his business to the public use, in effect grants the public an interest in that use and subjects himself to public regulation to the extent of that interest although the property continues to belong to its private owner and to be entitled to protection accordingly. *Munn* v. *Illinois,* 94 U.S. 113. . . .

It is manifest from an examination of the cases cited under the third head that the mere declaration by a legislature that a business is affected with a public interest is not conclusive of the question whether its attempted regulation on that ground is justified. The circumstances of its alleged change from the status of a private business and its freedom from regulation into one in which the public have come to have an interest are always a subject of judicial inquiry. . . .

It has never been supposed, since the adoption of the Constitution, that the business of the butcher, or the baker, the tailor, the wood chopper, the mining operator or the miner was clothed with such a public interest that the price of his product or his wages could be fixed by State regulation. It is true that in the days of the early common law an omnipotent Parliament did regulate prices and wages as it chose, and occasionally a Colonial legislature sought to exercise the same power; but nowadays one does not devote one's property or business to the public use or clothe it with a public interest merely because one makes commodities for, and sells to, the public in the common callings of which those above mentioned are instances. . . .

It is very difficult under the cases to lay down a working rule by which readily to determine when a business has become "clothed with a public interest." All business is subject to some kinds of public regulation; but when the public becomes so peculiarly dependent upon a particular business that one engaging therein subjects himself to a more intimate public regulation is only to be determined by the process of exclusion and inclusion and to gradual establishment of a line of distinction. . . .

To say that a business is clothed with a public interest, is not to determine what regulation may be permissible in view of the private rights of the owner. The extent to which an inn or a cab system may be regulated may differ widely from that allowable as to a railroad or other common carrier. It is not a matter of legislative discretion solely. It depends on the nature of the business, on the feature which touches the public, and on the abuses reasonably to be feared. To say that a business is clothed with a public interest is not to import that the public may take over its entire management and run it at the expense of the owner. (The extent to which regulation may reasonably go varies with different kinds of business.) The regulation of rates to avoid monopoly is one thing. The regulation of wages is another. A business may be of such character that only the first is permissible, while another may involve such a possible danger of monopoly on the one hand, and such disaster from stoppage on the other, that both come within the public concern and power of regulation. . . .

Stafford *v.* Wallace

Under Chief Justice Taft, the Court generally accepted federal regulatory power when predicated on the commerce clause. In a series of decisions, the justices approved the important Transportation Act of 1920, the Grain Futures Act of 1922 regulating the grain exchanges, the Motor Vehicle Theft Act of 1919, and the Packers and Stockyards Act of 1921. Stafford v. Wallace involved the latter and it is a fair summary of the commerce clause views prevailing in the 1920's. From his days as a federal circuit court judge in the 1890's, Taft had consistently favored a liberal interpretation of federal commerce power. Although neither he nor a majority of his colleagues directly refuted the old Knight distinction between production and commerce in this and other cases, they constantly chipped away at its standing as a vital precedent. Taft's expansive views on the commerce clause in fact were a bridge to the decisions of the next decade which ultimately discarded the Knight rule.

Chief Justice Taft delivered the opinion of the Court.

The Packers and Stockyards Act of 1921 seeks to regulate the business of the packers done in interstate commerce and forbids them to engage in unfair, discriminatory or deceptive practices in such commerce, or to subject any person to unreasonable prejudice therein, or to do any of a number of acts to control prices or establish a monopoly in the business. . . .

The object to be secured by the act is the free and unburdened flow of live stock from the ranges and farms of the West and the Southwest through the great stockyards and slaughtering centers on the borders of that region, and thence in the form of meat products to the consuming cities of the country in the Middle West and East, or, still as live stock, to the feeding places and fattening farms in the Middle West or East for further preparation for the market.

The chief evil feared is the monopoly of the packers, enabling them unduly and arbitrarily to lower prices to the shipper who sells, and unduly and arbitrarily to increase the price to the consumer who buys. Congress thought that the power to maintain this monopoly was aided by control of the stockyards. Another evil which it sought to provide

258 U.S. 495 (1922)

against by the act, was exorbitant charges, duplication of commissions, deceptive practices in respect of prices, in the passage of the live stock through the stockyards, all made possible by collusion between the stock- yards management and the commission men, on the one hand, and the packers and dealers on the other. . . .

The stockyards are not a place of rest or final destination. Thousands of head of live stock arrive daily by carload and trainload lots, and must be promptly sold and disposed of and moved out to give place to the constantly flowing traffic that presses behind. The stockyards are but a throat through which the current flows, and the transactions which occur therein are only incident to this current from the West to the East, and from one State to another. Such transactions can not be separated from the movement to which they contribute and necessarily take on its char- acter. The commission men are essential in making the sales without which the flow of the current would be obstructed, and this, whether they are made to packers or dealers. The dealers are essential to the sales to the stock farmers and feeders. The sales are not in this aspect merely local transactions. They create a local change of title, it is true, but they do not stop the flow; they merely change the private interests in the sub- ject of the current, not interfering with, but, on the contrary, being indis- pensable to its continuity. The origin of the live stock is in the West, its ultimate destination known to, and intended by, all engaged in the busi- ness is in the Middle West and East either as meat products or stock for feeding and fattening. This is the definite and well-understood course of business. The stockyards and the sales are necessary factors in the middle of this current of commerce.

The act, therefore, treats the various stockyards of the country as great national public utilities to promote the flow of commerce from the ranges and farms of the West to the consumers in the East. It assumes that they conduct a business affected by a public use of a national character and subject to national regulation. That it is a business within the power of regulation by legislative action needs no discussion. That has been settled since the case of *Munn* v. *Illinois.* . . . The only question here is whether the business done in the stockyards between the receipt of the live stock in the yards and the shipment of them therefrom is a part of interstate commerce, or is so associated with it as to bring it within the power of national regulation. A similar question has been before this court and had great consideration in *Swift & Co.* v. *United States,* 196 U.S. 375 [1905]. The judgment in that case gives a clear and comprehen- sive exposition which leaves to us in this case little but the obvious appli- cation of the principles there declared.

The *Swift Case* presented to this court the sufficiency of a bill in equity brought against substantially the same packing firms as those against whom this legislation is chiefly directed, charging them as a combination of a dominant proportion of the dealers in fresh meat throughout the United States. . . .

[I]n answer to the objection that what was charged did not constitute a case involving commerce among the States, the court said:

> "Commerce among the States is not a technical legal conception, but a practical one, drawn from the course of business. When cattle are sent for sale from a place in one State, with the expectation that they will end their transit, after purchase, in another, and when in effect they do so, with only the interruption necessary to find a purchaser at the stock yards, and when this is a typical, constantly recurring course, the current thus existing is a current of commerce among the States, and the purchase of the cattle is a part and incident of such commerce. What we say is true at least of such a purchase by residents in another State from that of the seller and of the cattle."

The application of the commerce clause of the Constitution in the *Swift Case* was the result of the natural development of interstate commerce under modern conditions. It was the inevitable recognition of the great central fact that such streams of commerce from one part of the country to another which are ever flowing are in their very essence the commerce among the States and with foreign nations which historically it was one of the chief purposes of the Constitution to bring under national protection and control. This court declined to defeat this purpose in respect of such a stream and take it out of complete national regulation by a nice and technical inquiry into the non-interstate character of some of its necessary incidents and facilities when considered alone and without reference to their association with the movement of which they were an essential but subordinate part.

The principles of the *Swift Case* have become a fixed rule of this court in the construction and application of the commerce clause. . . .

If Congress could provide for punishment or restraint of such conspiracies after their formation through the Anti-Trust Law as in the *Swift Case*, certainly it may provide regulation to prevent their formation. The reasonable fear by Congress that such acts, usually lawful and affecting only intrastate commerce when considered alone, will probably and more or less constantly be used in conspiracies against interstate commerce or constitute a direct and undue burden on it, expressed in this remedial legislation, serves the same purpose as the intent charged in the Swift indictment to bring acts of a similar character into the current of interstate commerce for federal restraint. Whatever amounts to more or less constant practice, and threatens to obstruct or unduly to burden the freedom of interstate commerce is within the regulatory power of Congress under the commerce clause, and it is primarily for Congress to consider and decide the fact of the danger and meet it. This court will certainly not substitute its judgment for that of Congress in such a matter unless the relation of the subject to interstate commerce and its effect upon it are clearly non-existent. . . .

VII

*Judicial Power and
Constitutional Change:
1933–1964*

Depression and Constitutional Crisis: 1933–1936

Home Building & Loan Association

v.

Blaisdell

At first, the Court indicated that it would favor vigorous and novel uses of governmental power to combat the ravages of the Great Depression. For example, in the Minnesota case below, the Court narrowly sustained a state mortgage moratorium statute. In 1933, the state legislature had declared the existence of an emergency justifying governmental measures to protect the people and promote the general welfare. To prevent the excessive loss of property by foreclosures for prices much below the mortgage indebtedness of the owners, the state provided that courts could postpone sales and extend the time in which mortgaged property might be redeemed. The law was immediately challenged as a violation of the contract clause, and four members of the Supreme Court agreed. Although Chief Justice Hughes's majority opinion skirted the constitutional requirements on contracts, its guidelines for the uses of emergency power in extraordinary times soon proved ambiguous.

Chief Justice Hughes delivered the opinion of the Court.

Appellant contests the validity of Chapter 339 of the Laws of Minnesota of 1933, p. 514, approved April 18, 1933, called the Minnesota Mortgage Moratorium Law, as being repugnant to the contract clause (Art. I, § 10) and the due process and equal protection clauses of the Fourteenth Amendment, of the Federal Constitution. The statute was sustained by the Supreme Court of Minnesota . . . and the case comes here on appeal.

The Act provides that, during the emergency declared to exist, relief may be had through authorized judicial proceedings with respect to

---
290 U.S. 398 (1934)

foreclosures of mortgages, and execution sales, of real estate; that sales may be postponed and periods of redemption may be extended. The Act does not apply to mortgages subsequently made nor to those made previously which shall be extended for a period ending more than a year after the passage of the Act (Part One, § 8). . . . The Act is to remain in effect "only during the continuance of the emergency and in no event beyond May 1, 1935." . . .

In determining whether the provision for this temporary and conditional relief exceeds the power of the State by reason of the clause in the Federal Constitution prohibiting impairment of the obligations of contracts, we must consider the relation of emergency to constitutional power, the historical setting of the contract clause, the development of the jurisprudence of this Court in the construction of that clause, and the principles of construction which we may consider to be established.

Emergency does not create power. Emergency does not increase granted power or remove or diminish the restrictions imposed upon power granted or reserved. The Constitution was adopted in a period of grave emergency. Its grants of power to the Federal Government and its limitations of the power of the States were determined in the light of emergency and they are not altered by emergency. What power was thus granted and what limitations were thus imposed are questions which have always been, and always will be, the subject of close examination under our constitutional system.

While emergency does not create power, emergency may furnish the occasion for the exercise of power. . . . The constitutional question presented in the light of an emergency is whether the power possessed embraces the particular exercise of it in response to particular conditions. . . . When the provisions of the Constitution, in grant or restriction, are specific, so particularized as not to admit of construction, no question is presented. . . . But where constitutional grants and limitations of power are set forth in general clauses, which afford a broad outline, the process of construction is essential to fill in the details. That is true of the contract clause. . . .

But full recognition of the occasion and general purpose of the clause does not suffice to fix its precise scope. Nor does an examination of the details of prior legislation in the States yield criteria which can be considered controlling. To ascertain the scope of the constitutional prohibition we examine the course of judicial decisions in its application. These put it beyond question that the prohibition is not an absolute one and is not to be read with literal exactness like a mathematical formula. . . .

Not only is the constitutional provision qualified by the measure of control which the State retains over remedial processes, but the State also continues to possess authority to safeguard the vital interests of its people. It does not matter that legislation appropriate to that end "has

the result of modifying or abrogating contracts already in effect." . . .
Not only are existing laws read into contracts in order to fix obligations
as between the parties, but the reservation of essential attributes of sovereign power is also read into contracts as a postulate of the legal order.
The policy of protecting contracts against impairment presupposes the
maintenance of a government by virtue of which contractual relations
are worth while, — a government which retains adequate authority to
secure the peace and good order of society. This principle of harmonizing
the constitutional prohibition with the necessary residuum of state power
has had progressive recognition in the decisions of this Court. . . .

Undoubtedly, whatever is reserved of state power must be consistent
with the fair intent of the constitutional limitation of that power. The
reserved power cannot be construed so as to destroy the limitation, nor
is the limitation to be construed to destroy the reserved power in its
essential aspects. They must be construed in harmony with each other.
This principle precludes a construction which would permit the State
to adopt as its policy the repudiation of debts or the destruction of contracts or the denial of means to enforce them. But it does not follow
that conditions may not arise in which a temporary restraint of enforcement may be consistent with the spirit and purpose of the constitutional
provision and thus be found to be within the range of the reserved power
of the State to protect the vital interests of the community. It cannot be
maintained that the constitutional prohibition should be so construed as
to prevent limited and temporary interpositions with respect to the enforcement of contracts if made necessary by a great public calamity such
as fire, flood, or earthquake. . . . The reservation of state power appropriate to such extraordinary conditions may be deemed to be as much
a part of all contracts, as is the reservation of state power to protect the
public interest in the other situations to which we have referred. And if
state power exists to give temporary relief from the enforcement of contracts in the presence of disasters due to physical causes such as fire, flood
or earthquake, that power cannot be said to be non-existent when the
urgent public need demanding such relief is produced by other and
economic causes. . . .

It is manifest from this review . . . that there has been a growing
appreciation of public needs and of the necessity of finding ground for
a rational compromise between individual rights and public welfare.
The settlement and consequent contraction of the public domain, the
pressure of a constantly increasing density of population, the interrela-
tion of the activities of our people and the complexity of our economic
interests, have inevitably led to an increased use of the organization of
society in order to protect the very bases of individual opportunity.
Where, in earlier days, it was thought that only the concerns of individuals or of classes were involved, and that those of the State itself were

touched only remotely, it has later been found that the fundamental interests of the State are directly affected; and that the question is no longer merely that of one party to a contract as against another, but of the use of reasonable means to safeguard the economic structure upon which the good of all depends.

It is no answer to say that this public need was not apprehended a century ago, or to insist that what the provision of the Constitution meant to the vision of that day it must mean to the vision of our time. If by the statement that what the Constitution meant at the time of its adoption it means to-day, it is intended to say that the great clauses of the Constitution must be confined to the interpretation which the framers, with the conditions and outlook of their time, would have placed upon them, the statement carries its own refutation. It was to guard against such a narrow conception that Chief Justice Marshall uttered the memorable warning — "We must never forget that it is *a constitution* we are expounding" (*McCulloch* v. *Maryland*, 4 Wheat. 316, 407) — "a constitution intended to endure for ages to come, and consequently, to be adapted to the various *crises* of human affairs." *Id.*, p. 415. . . .

Nor is it helpful to attempt to draw a fine distinction between the intended meaning of the words of the Constitution and their intended application. When we consider the contract clause and the decisions which have expounded it in harmony with the essential reserved power of the States to protect the security of their peoples, we find no warrant for the conclusion that the clause has been warped by these decisions from its proper significance or that the founders of our Government would have interpreted the clause differently had they had occasion to assume that responsibility in the conditions of the later day. The vast body of law which has been developed was unknown to the fathers, but it is believed to have preserved the essential content and the spirit of the Constitution. With a growing recognition of public needs and the relation of individual right to public security, the court has sought to prevent the perversion of the clause through its use as an instrument to throttle the capacity of the States to protect their fundamental interests. This development is a growth from the seeds which the fathers planted. . . . The principle of this development is, as we have seen, that the reservation of the reasonable exercise of the protective power of the State is read into all contracts. . . .

Applying the criteria established by our decisions we conclude:

1. An emergency existed in Minnesota which furnished a proper occasion for the exercise of the reserved power of the State to protect the vital interests of the community. . . .

2. The legislation was addressed to a legitimate end, that is, the legislation was not for the mere advantage of particular individuals but for the protection of a basic interest of society.

3. In view of the nature of the contracts in question — mortgages of unquestionable validity — the relief afforded and justified by the emergency, in order not to contravene the constitutional provision, could only be of a character appropriate to that emergency and could be granted only upon reasonable conditions. . . .

We are of the opinion that the Minnesota statute as here applied does not violate the contract clause of the Federal Constitution. Whether the legislation is wise or unwise as a matter of policy is a question with which we are not concerned. . . .

Nebbia *v.* New York

This case also arose out of depression conditions and again apparently indicated the Court's willingness to sustain governmental intervention in the economy. A 5–4 majority approved a New York law establishing a milk control board with the power to fix retail prices of milk. Most importantly, the Court here rejected Chief Justice Taft's rigid categorization of businesses affected with a public interest, as he had specified in the Wolff Packing *case in 1923. The majority now held there was no "closed category" of such businesses, but that government might act where the public interest required intervention. The four dissenters — the familiar bloc of Justices Van Devanter, McReynolds, Sutherland, and Butler — vigorously rejected the idea that this could include price-fixing by government.*

Justice Roberts delivered the opinion of the Court.

The Legislature of New York established, by Chapter 158 of the Laws of 1933, a Milk Control Board with power, among other things, to "fix minimum and maximum . . . retail prices to be charged by . . . stores to consumers for consumption off the premises where sold." The Board fixed nine cents as the price to be charged by a store for a quart of milk. Nebbia, the proprietor of a grocery store in Rochester, sold two quarts and a five cent loaf of bread for eighteen cents; and was convicted for violating the Board's order. At his trial he asserted the statute and order contravene the equal protection clause and the due process clause of the Fourteenth Amendment. . . .

291 U.S. 502 (1934)

The . . . serious question is whether the enforcement of [the act] denied the appellant the due process secured to him by the Fourteenth Amendment. . . .

Under our form of government the use of property and the making of contracts are normally matters of private and not of public concern. The general rule is that both shall be free of governmental interference. But neither property rights nor contract rights are absolute; for government cannot exist if the citizen may at will use his property to the detriment of his fellows, or exercise his freedom of contract to work them harm. Equally fundamental with the private right is that of the public to regulate it in the common interest. . . .

The milk industry in New York has been the subject of long-standing and drastic regulation in the public interest. The legislative investigation of 1932 was persuasive of the fact that for this and other reasons unrestricted competition aggravated existing evils, and the normal law of supply and demand was insufficient to correct maladjustments detrimental to the community. The inquiry disclosed destructive and demoralizing competitive conditions and unfair trade practices which resulted in retail price-cutting and reduced the income of the farmer below the cost of production. We do not understand the appellant to deny that in these circumstances the legislature might reasonably consider further regulation and control desirable for protection of the industry and the consuming public. That body believed conditions could be improved by preventing destructive price-cutting by stores which, due to the flood of surplus milk, were able to buy at much lower prices than the larger distributors and to sell without incurring the delivery costs of the latter. In the order of which complaint is made the Milk Control Board fixed a price of ten cents per quart for sales by a distributor to a consumer, and nine cents by a store to a consumer, thus recognizing the lower costs of the store, and endeavoring to establish a differential which would be just to both. In the light of the facts the order appears not to be unreasonable or arbitrary, or without relation to the purpose to prevent ruthless competition from destroying the wholesale price structure on which the farmer depends for his livelihood, and the community for an assured supply of milk.

But we are told that because the law essays to control prices it denies due process. Notwithstanding the admitted power to correct existing economic ills by appropriate regulation of business, even though an indirect result may be a restriction of the freedom of contract or a modification of charges for services or the price of commodities, the appellant urges that direct fixation of prices is a type of regulation absolutely forbidden. His position is that the Fourteenth Amendment requires us to hold the challenged statute void for this reason alone. The argument runs that the public control of rates or prices is *per se* unreasonable and unconstitutional, save as applied to businesses affected with a public interest; that a business so affected is one in which property is devoted to an enterprise of a sort which the public itself might appropriately undertake, or one whose owner relies on a public grant or franchise for the right to conduct the business, or in which he is bound to serve all who apply; in short, such as is commonly called a public utility; or a business in its nature a monopoly. The milk industry, it is said, possesses none of these characteristics, and, therefore, not being affected with a public interest, its charges may not be controlled by the state. Upon the soundness of this contention the appellant's case against the statute depends.

We may as well say at once that the dairy industry is not, in the accepted sense of the phrase, a public utility. We think the appellant is also right in asserting that there is in this case no suggestion of any monopoly or monopolistic practice. It goes without saying that those engaged in the business are in no way dependent upon public grants or franchises for the privilege of conducting their activities. But if, as must be conceded, the industry is subject to regulation in the public interest, what constitutional principle bars the state from correcting existing maladjustments by legislation touching prices? We think there is no such principle. The due process clause makes no mention of sales or of prices any more than it speaks of business or contracts or buildings or other incidents of property. The thought seems nevertheless to have persisted that there is something peculiarly sacrosanct about the price one may charge for what he makes or sells, and that, however able to regulate other elements of manufacture or trade, with incidental effect upon price, the state is incapable of directly controlling the price itself. This view was negatived many years ago. *Munn* v. *Illinois*. . . .

It is clear that there is no closed class or category of businesses affected with a public interest, and the function of courts in the application of the Fifth and Fourteenth Amendments is to determine in each case whether circumstances vindicate the challenged regulation as a reasonable exertion of governmental authority or condemn it as arbitrary or discriminatory. . . . The phrase "affected with a public interest" can, in the nature of things, mean no more than that an industry, for adequate reason, is subject to control for the public good. In several of the decisions of this court wherein the expressions "affected with a public interest," and "clothed with a public use," have been brought forward as the criteria of the validity of price control, it has been admitted that they are not susceptible of definition and form an unsatisfactory test of the constitutionality of legislation directed at business practices or prices. These decisions must rest, finally, upon the basis that the requirements of due process were not met because the laws were found arbitrary in their operation and effect. But there can be no doubt that upon proper occasion and by appropriate measures the state may regulate a business in any of its aspects, including the prices to be charged for the products or commodities it sells.

So far as the requirement of due process is concerned, and in the absence of other constitutional restriction, a state is free to adopt whatever economic policy may reasonably be deemed to promote public welfare, and to enforce that policy by legislation adapted to its purpose. The courts are without authority either to declare such policy, or, when it is declared by the legislature, to override it. . . .

The Constitution does not secure to anyone liberty to conduct his business in such fashion as to inflict injury upon the public at large, or upon any substantial group of the people. Price control, like any other form of regulation, is unconstitutional only if arbitrary, discriminatory, or demonstrably irrelevant to the policy the legislature is free to adopt, and hence an unnecessary and unwarranted interference with individual liberty. . . .

Schechter Poultry Corp. *v.* United States

Early in 1935, the Court began its all-out assault against the New Deal. First, in Panama Refining Co. *v.* Ryan, *it invalidated the petroleum code established under the National Industrial Recovery Act (293 U.S. 388). By an 8–1 margin, the Court held that the act unduly delegated legislative power to the executive. But in the* Schechter *case a few months later, the Court unanimously condemned the constitutional underpinnings of the NIRA. The "Sick Chicken" case, as it came to be known, hardly reflected the government's concern with basic industries and was, altogether, a poor case for justifying the broad powers encompassed in the NIRA. It involved the live-poultry code which regulated wages, hours, production, and marketing for the poultry industry within the metropolitan New York area. Although this included parts of New Jersey and Connecticut, the regulations mostly covered local transactions. The plaintiffs were charged with selling an "unfit chicken" when they violated the "straight killing" code provision, prohibiting discriminatory selection of fowl. They challenged the act as a regulation of intrastate commerce and also as an excessive delegation of legislative power to the executive branch of government.*

Chief Justice Hughes delivered the opinion of the Court.

First. Two preliminary points are stressed by the Government with respect to the appropriate approach to the important questions presented. We are told that the provision of the statute authorizing the adoption of codes must be viewed in the light of the grave national crisis with which Congress was confronted. Undoubtedly, the conditions to which power is addressed are always to be considered when the exercise of power is challenged. Extraordinary conditions may call for extraordinary remedies. But the argument necessarily stops short of an attempt to justify action which lies outside the sphere of constitutional authority. Extraordinary conditions do not create or enlarge constitutional power. The Constitution established a national government with powers deemed to be adequate, as they have proved to be both in war and peace, but these powers of the national government are limited by the constitutional grants. Those who act under these grants are not at liberty to transcend the imposed limits because they believe that more

295 U.S. 495 (1935)

or different power is necessary. Such assertions of extra-constitutional authority were anticipated and precluded by the explicit terms of the Tenth Amendment, — "The powers not delegated to the United States by the Constitution, nor prohibited by it to the States, are reserved to the States respectively, or to the people." . . .

Second. *The question of the delegation of legislative power.* . . .

Accordingly we turn to the Recovery Act to ascertain what limits have been set to the exercise of the President's discretion. *First,* the President, as a condition of approval, is required to find that the trade or industrial associations or groups which propose a code, "impose no inequitable restrictions on admission to membership" and are "truly representative." That condition, however, relates only to the status of the initiators of the new laws and not to the permissible scope of such laws. *Second,* the President is required to find that the code is not "designed to promote monopolies or to eliminate or oppress small enterprises and will not operate to discriminate against them." And, to this is added a proviso that the code "shall not permit monopolies or monopolistic practices." But these restrictions leave virtually untouched the field of policy envisaged by section one, and, in that wide field of legislative possibilities, the proponents of a code, refraining from monopolistic designs, may roam at will and the President may approve or disapprove their proposals as he may see fit. . . .

Nor is the breadth of the President's discretion left to the necessary implications of this limited requirement as to his findings. As already noted, the President in approving a code may impose his own conditions, adding to or taking from what is proposed, as "in his discretion" he thinks necessary "to effectuate the policy" declared by the Act. Of course, he has no less liberty when he prescribes a code on his own motion or on complaint, and he is free to prescribe one if a code has not been approved. The Act provides for the creation by the President of administrative agencies to assist him, but the action or reports of such agencies, or of his other assistants, — their recommendations and findings in relation to the making of codes — have no sanction beyond the will of the President, who may accept, modify or reject them as he pleases. Such recommendations or findings in no way limit the authority which § 3 undertakes to vest in the President with no other conditions than those there specified. And this authority relates to a host of different trades and industries, thus extending the President's discretion to all the varieties of laws which he may deem to be beneficial in dealing with the vast array of commercial and industrial activities throughout the country.

Such a sweeping delegation of legislative power finds no support in the decisions upon which the Government especially relies. . . .

To summarize and conclude upon this point: Section 3 of the Recovery Act is without precedent. It supplies no standards for any trade, industry or activity. It does not undertake to prescribe rules of conduct to be applied to particular states of fact determined by appropriate administrative procedure. Instead of prescribing rules of conduct, it authorizes the making of codes to prescribe them. For that legislative undertaking, § 3 sets up no standards, aside from the statement of the general aims of rehabilitation, correction and expansion described in section one. In view of the scope of that broad declaration, and of the nature of the few restrictions that are imposed, the discretion of the President in approving or prescribing codes, and thus enacting laws for the government of trade and industry throughout the country, is virtually unfettered. We think that the code-making authority thus conferred is an unconstitutional delegation of legislative power.

Third. *The question of the application of the provisions of the Live Poultry Code to intrastate transactions.* . . .
This aspect of the case presents the question whether the particular provisions of the Live Poultry Code, which the defendants were convicted for violating and for having conspired to violate, were within the regulating power of Congress.

These provisions relate to the hours and wages of those employed by defendants in their slaughterhouses in Brooklyn and to the sales there made to retail dealers and butchers. . . .

The undisputed facts . . . afford no warrant for the argument that the poultry handled by defendants at their slaughterhouse markets was in a *"current"* or *"flow"* of interstate commerce and was thus subject to congressional regulation. The mere fact that there may be a constant flow of commodities into a State does not mean that the flow continues after the property has arrived and has become commingled with the mass of property within the State and is there held solely for local disposition and use. So far as the poultry here in question is concerned, the flow in interstate commerce had ceased. The poultry had come to a permanent rest within the State. It was not held, used, or sold by defendants in relation to any further transactions in interstate commerce and was not destined for transportation to other States. Hence, decisions which deal with a stream of interstate commerce — where goods come to rest within a State temporarily and are later to go forward in interstate commerce — and with the regulations of transactions involved in that practical continuity of movement, are not applicable here. . . .

Did the defendants' transactions directly *"affect"* interstate commerce so as to be subject to federal regulation? The power of Congress extends not only to the regulation of transactions which are part of interstate commerce, but to the protection of that commerce from injury. . . .

In determining how far the federal government may go in controlling intrastate transactions upon the ground that they "affect" interstate commerce, there is a necessary and well-established distinction between direct and indirect effects. The precise line can be drawn only as individual cases arise, but the distinction is clear in principle. Direct effects are illustrated by the railroad cases we have cited, as *e.g.*, the effect of failure to use prescribed safety appliances on railroads which are the highways of both interstate and intrastate commerce, injury to an employee engaged in interstate transportation by the negligence of an employee engaged in an intrastate movement, the fixing of rates for intrastate transportation which unjustly discriminate against interstate commerce. But where the effect of intrastate transactions upon interstate commerce is merely indirect, such transactions remain within the domain of state power. If the commerce clause were construed to reach all enterprises and transactions which could be said to have an indirect effect upon interstate commerce, the federal authority would embrace practically all the activities of the people and the authority of the State over its domestic concerns would exist only by sufferance of the federal government. Indeed, on such a theory, even the development of the State's commercial facilities would be subject to federal control. . . .

The question of chief importance relates to the provisions of the Code as to the hours and wages of those employed in defendants' slaughterhouse markets. It is plain that these requirements are imposed in order to govern the details of defendants' management of their local business. The persons employed in slaughtering and selling in local trade are not employed in interstate commerce. Their hours and wages have no direct relation to interstate commerce. The question of how many hours these employees should work and what they should be paid differs in no essential respect from similar questions in other local businesses which handle commodities brought into a State and there dealt in as a part of its internal commerce. This appears from an examination of the considerations urged by the Government with respect to conditions in the poultry trade. Thus, the Government argues that hours and wages affect prices; that slaughterhouse men sell at a small margin above operating costs; that labor represents 50 to 60 per cent. of these costs; that a slaughterhouse operator paying lower wages or reducing his cost by exacting long hours of work, translates his saving into lower prices; that this results in demands for a cheaper grade of goods; and that the cutting of prices brings about a demoralization of the price structure. Similar conditions may be adduced in relation to other businesses. The argument of the Government proves too much. If the federal government may determine the wages and hours of employees in the internal commerce of a State, because of their relation to cost and prices and their indirect effect upon interstate commerce, it would seem that a similar control might be exerted over other elements of cost, also affecting prices, such as the number of employees, rents, advertising, methods of doing business, etc. All the processes of production and distribution that enter into cost could likewise be controlled. If the cost of doing an intrastate business is in itself the permitted object of federal control, the extent of the regulation of cost would be a question of discretion and not of power. . . .

It is not the province of the Court to consider the economic advantages or disadvantages of such a centralized system. It is sufficient to say that the Federal Constitution does not provide for it. Our growth and development have called for wide use of the commerce power of the federal government in its control over the expanded activities of interstate commerce, and in protecting that commerce from burdens, interferences, and conspiracies to restrain and monopolize it. But the authority of the federal government may not be pushed to such an extreme as to destroy the distinction, which the commerce clause itself establishes, between commerce "among the several States" and the internal concerns of a State. The same answer must be made to the contention that is based upon the serious economic situation which led to the passage of the Recovery Act, — the fall in prices, the decline in wages and employment, and the curtailment of the market for commodities. Stress is laid upon the great importance of maintaining wage distributions which would provide the necessary stimulus in starting "the cumulative forces making for expanding commercial activity." Without in any way disparaging this motive, it is enough to say that the recuperative efforts of the federal government must be made in a manner consistent with the authority granted by the Constitution.

We are of the opinion that the attempt through the provisions of the Code to fix the hours and wages of employees of defendants in their intrastate business was not a valid exercise of federal power. . . .

Carter *v*. Carter Coal Co.

Chief Justice Hughes's Schechter *opinion was vague in its distinction between direct and indirect effects upon interstate commerce. Undoubtedly, he was aware of the decisions since the* Knight *case justifying federal regulation of essentially local matters, thus making an arbitrary exactness of the distinction extremely difficult. But in the* Carter Coal Co. *case, Justice Sutherland unflinchingly offered a more precise definition, chiefly rooted in the* Knight *precedent. Sutherland denounced federal regulation of production, especially as it involved price and labor regulation — that is, labor regulation which was positive and beneficial in its scope. The case involved the constitutionality of the Bituminous Coal Code, regulating prices and wages in the soft coal industry. Although Congress specifically had provided that the price-fixing and labor regulation sections of the code should be considered as separate constitutional problems, the majority boldly ignored the mandate.*

Justice Sutherland delivered the opinion of the Court.

The purposes of the "Bituminous Coal Conservation Act of 1935," involved in these suits, as declared by the title, are to stabilize the bituminous coal-mining industry and promote its interstate commerce; to provide for cooperative marketing of bituminous coal; to levy a tax on such coal and provide for a drawback under certain conditions; to declare the production, distribution, and use of such coal to be affected with a national public interest; to conserve the national resources of such coal; to provide for the general welfare, and for other purposes. . . . The constitutional validity of the act is challenged in each of the suits. . . .

It is very clear that the "excise tax" is not imposed for revenue but exacted as a penalty to compel compliance with the regulatory provisions of the act. The whole purpose of the exaction is to coerce what is called an agreement — which, of course, it is not, for it lacks the essential element of consent. One who does a thing in order to avoid a monetary penalty does not agree; he yields to compulsion precisely the same as though he did so to avoid a term in jail.

The exaction here is a penalty and not a tax within the test laid down by this court in numerous cases. *Child Labor Tax Case*, 259 U.S. 20, 37–39. . . .

298 U.S. 238 (1936)

Certain recitals contained in the act plainly suggest that its makers were of opinion that its constitutionality could be sustained under some general federal power, thought to exist, apart from the specific grants of the Constitution. . . .

The ruling and firmly established principle is that the powers which the general government may exercise are only those specifically enumerated in the Constitution, and such implied powers as are necessary and proper to carry into effect the enumerated powers. Whether the end sought to be attained by an act of Congress is legitimate is wholly a matter of constitutional power and not at all of legislative discretion. Legislative congressional discretion begins with the choice of means and ends with the adoption of methods and details to carry the delegated powers into effect. The distinction between these two things — power and discretion — is not only very plain but very important. For while the powers are rigidly limited to the enumerations of the Constitution, the means which may be employed to carry the powers into effect are not restricted, save that they must be appropriate, plainly adapted to the end, and not prohibited by, but consistent with, the letter and spirit of the Constitution. *McCulloch* v. *Maryland,* 4 Wheat. 316, 421. Thus, it may be said that to a constitutional end many ways are open; but to an end not within the terms of the Constitution, all ways are closed.

The proposition, often advanced and as often discredited, that the power of the federal government inherently extends to purposes affecting the nation as a whole with which the states severally cannot deal or cannot adequately deal, and the related notion that Congress, entirely apart from those powers delegated by the Constitution, may enact laws to promote the general welfare, have never been accepted but always definitely rejected by this court. . . .

Since the validity of the act depends upon whether it is a regulation of interstate commerce, the nature and extent of the power conferred upon Congress by the commerce clause becomes the determinative question in this branch of the case. . . .

We have seen that the word "commerce" is the equivalent of the phrase "intercourse for the purposes of trade." Plainly, the incidents leading up to and culminating in the mining of coal do not constitute such intercourse. The employment of men, the fixing of their wages, hours of labor and working conditions, the bargaining in respect of these things — whether carried on separately or collectively — each and all constitute intercourse for the purposes of production, not of trade. The latter is a thing apart from the relation of employer and employee, which in all producing occupations is purely local in character. Extraction of coal from the mine is the aim and the completed result of local activities. Commerce in the coal mined is not brought into being by force of these activities, but by negotiations, agreements, and circumstances entirely apart from production. Mining brings the subject matter of commerce into existence. Commerce disposes of it.

A consideration of the foregoing, and of many cases which might be added to those already cited, renders inescapable the conclusion that the effect of the labor provisions of the act, including those in respect of minimum wages, wage agreements, collective bargaining, and the Labor Board and its powers, primarily falls upon production and not upon commerce; and confirms the further resulting conclusion that production is a purely local activity. It follows that none of these essential antecedents of production constitutes a transaction in or forms any part of interstate commerce. *Schechter Corp.* v. *United States.* . . . Everything which moves in interstate commerce has had a local origin. Without local production somewhere, interstate commerce, as now carried on, would practically disappear. Nevertheless, the local character of mining, of manufacturing and of crop growing is a fact, and remains a fact, whatever may be done with the products.

The government's contentions in defense of the labor provisions are really disposed of adversely by our decision in the *Schechter* case. . . . The only perceptible difference between that case and this is that in the *Schechter* case the federal power was asserted with respect to commodities which had come to rest after their interstate transportation; while here, the case deals with commodities at rest before interstate commerce has begun. That difference is without significance. The federal regulatory power ceases when interstate commercial intercourse ends; and, correlatively, the power does not attach until interstate commercial intercourse begins. There is no basis in law or reason for applying different rules to the two situations. No such distinction can be found in anything said in the *Schechter* case. On the contrary, the situations were recognized as akin. In the opinion, . . . after calling attention to the fact that if the commerce clause could be construed to reach transactions having an indirect effect upon interstate commerce the federal authority would embrace practically all the activities of the people, and the authority of the state over its domestic concerns would exist only by sufferance of the federal government, we said: "Indeed, on such a theory, even the development of the State's commercial facilities would be subject to federal control." And again, after pointing out that hours and wages have no direct relation to interstate commerce and that if the federal government had power to determine the wages and hours of employees in the internal commerce of a state because of their relation to cost and prices and their indirect effect upon interstate commerce, we said . . . : "All the processes of production and distribution that enter into cost could likewise be controlled. If the cost of doing an intrastate business is in itself the permitted object of federal control, the extent of the regulation of cost would be a question of discretion and not of power." A reading of the entire opinion makes clear, what we now declare, that the want of power on the part of the federal government is the same whether the wages, hours of service, and working conditions, and the bargaining about them, are related to production before interstate commerce has begun, or to sale and distribution after it has ended. . . .

Finally, we are brought to the price-fixing provisions of the code. The necessity of considering the question of their constitutionality will depend upon whether they are separable from the labor provisions so that they can stand independently. Section 15 of the act provides:

"If any provision of this Act, or the application thereof to any person or circumstances, is held invalid, the remainder of the Act and the application of such provisions to other persons or circumstances shall not be affected thereby." . . .

[T]he primary contemplation of the act is stabilization of the industry through the regulation of labor *and* the regulation of prices; for, since both were adopted, we must conclude that both were thought essential. The regulations of labor on the one hand and prices on the other furnish mutual aid and support; and their associated force — not one or the other but both combined — was deemed by Congress to be necessary to achieve the end sought. The statutory mandate for a code upheld by two legs at once suggests the improbability that Congress would have assented to a code supported by only one.

This seems plain enough; for Congress must have been conscious of the fact that elimination of the labor provisions from the act would seriously impair, if not destroy, the force and usefulness of the price provisions. The interdependence of wages and prices is manifest. Approximately two-thirds of the cost of producing a ton of coal is represented by wages. Fair prices necessarily depend upon the cost of production; and since wages constitute so large a proportion of the cost, prices cannot be fixed with any proper relation to cost without taking into consideration this major element. If one of them becomes uncertain, uncertainty with respect to the other necessarily ensues. . . .

The conclusion is unavoidable that the price-fixing provisions of the code are so related to and dependent upon the labor provisions as conditions, considerations or compensations, as to make it clearly probable that the latter being held bad, the former would not have been passed. The fall of the latter, therefore, carries down with it the former. . . .

United States *v.* Butler

It was widely believed that the Court would be more favorably disposed toward governmental regulation under the taxing and spending powers. The Agricultural Adjustment Act of 1933 provided for a processing tax on certain agricultural commodities. The tax was designed to raise money for payments to farmers participating in the government's production control program. Butler challenged the act by primarily attacking the spending, not the taxing, program. The regulation of agriculture, he contended, violated the Tenth Amendment because it interfered with the reserved powers of the states. In addition, he claimed that as the tax was part of an unconstitutional scheme, it, too, was invalid. Justice Roberts's majority opinion was wholly lacking in logic and consistency. Examining the competing constitutional theories of Hamilton and Madison regarding the federal government's spending power, Roberts agreed that Hamilton's broad view had been generally followed, but he nevertheless invoked Madison's ideas. In dissent with Cardozo and Brandeis, Justice Stone bitterly protested the majority's "tortured construction" of the Constitution.

Justice Roberts delivered the opinion of the Court.

I t is inaccurate and misleading to speak of the exaction from processors prescribed by the challenged act as a tax, or to say that as a tax it is subject to no infirmity. A tax, in the general understanding of the term, and as used in the Constitution, signifies an exaction for the support of the Government. The word has never been thought to connote the expropriation of money from one group for the benefit of another. We may concede that the latter sort of imposition is constitutional when imposed to effectuate regulation of a matter in which both groups are interested and in respect of which there is a power of legislative regulation. But manifestly no justification for it can be found unless as an integral part of such regulation. The exaction cannot be wrested out of its setting, denominated an excise for raising revenue and legalized by ignoring its purpose as a mere instrumentality for bringing about a desired end. To do this would be to shut our eyes to what all others than we can see and understand. *Child Labor Tax Case.* . . .

We conclude that the act is one regulating agricultural production;

297 *U.S. 1 (1936)*

that the tax is a mere incident of such regulation and that the respondents have standing to challenge the legality of the exaction. . . .

The Government asserts that even if the respondents may question the propriety of the appropriation embodied in the statute their attack must fail because Article I, § 8 of the Constitution authorizes the contemplated expenditure of the funds raised by the tax. This contention presents the great and the controlling question in the case. . . .

There should be no misunderstanding as to the function of this court in such a case. It is sometimes said that the court assumes a power to overrule or control the action of the people's representatives. This is a misconception. The Constitution is the supreme law of the land ordained and established by the people. All legislation must conform to the principles it lays down. When an act of Congress is appropriately challenged in the courts as not conforming to the constitutional mandate the judicial branch of the Government has only one duty, — to lay the article of the Constitution which is invoked beside the statute which is challenged and to decide whether the latter squares with the former. All the court does, or can do, is to announce its considered judgment upon the question. The only power it has, if such it may be called, is the power of judgment. This court neither approves nor condemns any legislative policy. Its delicate and difficult office is to ascertain and declare whether the legislation is in accordance with, or in contravention of, the provisions of the Constitution; and, having done that, its duty ends.

The question is not what power the Federal Government ought to have but what powers in fact have been given by the people. It hardly seems necessary to reiterate that ours is a dual form of government; that in every state there are two governments, — the state and the United States. Each State has all governmental powers save such as the people, by their Constitution, have conferred upon the United States, denied to the States, or reserved to themselves. The federal union is a government of delegated powers. It has only such as are expressly conferred upon it and such as are reasonably to be implied from those granted. . . .

Article I, § 8, of the Constitution vests sundry powers in the Congress. But two of its clauses have . . . bearing upon the validity of the statute under review. . . .

The clause thought to authorize the legislation, — the first, — confers upon the Congress power "to lay and collect Taxes, Duties, Imposts and Excises, to pay the Debts and provide for the common Defence and general Welfare of the United States. . . ." It is not contended that this provision grants power to regulate agricultural production upon the theory that such legislation would promote the general welfare. The Government concedes that the phrase "to provide for the general welfare" qualifies the power "to lay and collect taxes." . . .

Nevertheless the Government asserts that warrant is found in this clause for the adoption of the Agricultural Adjustment Act. The argument is that Congress may appropriate and authorize the spending of moneys for the "general welfare"; that the phrase should be liberally construed to cover anything conducive to national welfare; that decision as to what will promote such welfare rests with Congress alone, and the courts may not review its determination; and finally that the appropriation under attack was in fact for the general welfare of the United States. . . .

Since the foundation of the Nation sharp differences of opinion have persisted as to the true interpretation of the phrase. Madison asserted it amounted to no more than a reference to the other powers enumerated in the subsequent clauses of the same section; that, as the United States is a government of limited and enumerated powers, the grant of power to tax and spend for the general national welfare must be confined to the enumerated legislative fields committed to the Congress. In this view the phrase is mere tautology, for taxation and appropriation are or may be necessary incidents of the exercise of any of the enumerated legislative powers. Hamilton, on the other hand, maintained the clause confers a power separate and distinct from those later enumerated, is not restricted in meaning by the grant of them, and Congress consequently has a substantive power to tax and to appropriate, limited only by the requirement that it shall be exercised to provide for the general welfare. . . .

We are not now required to ascertain the scope of the phrase "general welfare of the United States" or to determine whether an appropriation in aid of agriculture falls within it. Wholly apart from that question, another principle embedded in our Constitution prohibits the enforcement of the Agricultural Adjustment Act. The act invades the reserved rights of the states. It is a statutory plan to regulate and control agricultural production, a matter beyond the powers delegated to the federal government. The tax, the appropriation of the funds raised, and the direction for their disbursement, are but parts of the plan. They are but means to an unconstitutional end.

From the accepted doctrine that the United States is a government of delegated powers, it follows that those not expressly granted, or reasonably to be implied from such as are conferred, are reserved to the states or to the people. To forestall any suggestion to the contrary, the Tenth Amendment was adopted. The same proposition, otherwise stated, is that powers not granted are prohibited. None to regulate agricultural production is given, and therefore legislation by Congress for that purpose is forbidden.

It is an established principle that the attainment of a prohibited end may not be accomplished under the pretext of the exertion of powers which are granted. . . .

If the taxing power may not be used as the instrument to enforce a regulation of matters of state concern with respect to which the Congress has no authority to interfere, may it, as in the present case, be employed to raise the money necessary to purchase a compliance which the Congress is powerless to command? The Government asserts that whatever might be said against the validity of the plan if compulsory, it is constitutionally sound because the end is accomplished by voluntary cooperation. There are two sufficient answers to the contention. The regulation is not in fact voluntary. The farmer, of course, may refuse to comply, but the price of such refusal is the loss of benefits. The amount offered is intended to be sufficient to exert pressure on him to agree to the proposed regulation. The power to confer or withhold unlimited benefits is the power to coerce or destroy. . . .

Congress has no power to enforce its commands on the farmer to the ends sought by the Agricultural Adjustment Act. It must follow that it may not indirectly accomplish those ends by taxing and spending to purchase compliance. The Constitution and the entire plan of our government negative any such use of the power to tax and to spend as the act undertakes to authorize. It does not help to declare that local conditions throughout the nation have created a situation of national concern; for this is but to say that whenever there is a widespread similarity of local conditions, Congress may ignore constitutional limitations upon its own powers and usurp those reserved to the states. If, in lieu of compulsory regulation of subjects within the states' reserved jurisdiction, which is prohibited, the Congress could invoke the taxing and spending power as a means to accomplish the same end, clause 1 of § 8 of Article I would become the instrument for total subversion of the governmental powers reserved to the individual states. . . .

Until recently no suggestion of the existence of any such power in the Federal Government has been advanced. The expressions of the framers of the Constitution, the decisions of this court interpreting that instrument, and the writings of great commentators will be searched in vain for any suggestion that there exists in the clause under discussion or elsewhere in the Constitution, the authority whereby every provision and every fair implication from that instrument may be subverted, the independence of the individual states obliterated, and the United States converted into a central government exercising uncontrolled police power in every state of the Union, superseding all local control or regulation of the affairs or concerns of the states. . . .

Justice Stone, dissenting. . . .

That the governmental power of the purse is a great one is not now for the first time announced. . . .

The suggestion that it must now be curtailed by judicial fiat because it may be abused by unwise use hardly rises to the dignity of argument. So may judicial power be abused. . . .

A tortured construction of the Constitution is not to be justified by recourse to extreme examples of reckless congressional spending which might occur if courts could not prevent — expenditures which, even if they could be thought to effect any national purpose, would be possible only by action of a legislature lost to all sense of public responsibility. Such suppositions are addressed to the mind accustomed to believe that it is the business of courts to sit in judgment on the wisdom of legislative action. Courts are not the only agency of government that must be assumed to have capacity to govern. Congress and the courts both unhappily may falter or be mistaken in the performance of their constitutional duty. But interpretation of our great charter of government which proceeds on any assumption that the responsibility for the preservation of our institutions is the exclusive concern of any one of the three branches of government, or that it alone can save them from destruction is far more likely, in the long run, "to obliterate the constituent members" of "an indestructible union of indestructible states" than the frank recognition that language, even of a constitution, may mean what it says: that the power to tax and spend includes the power to relieve a nationwide economic maladjustment by conditional gifts of money.

Justice Brandeis and Justice Cardozo join in this opinion.

New Directions in Governmental Regulation

West Coast Hotel Company *v.* Parrish

The Adkins *case in 1923 had invalidated federal regulation of minimum wages for the District of Columbia and it was subsequently used to strike down similar state laws. In his opinion for the Court in 1923, Justice Sutherland had commented that a depression might justify a different attitude toward such laws. But when faced with such a situation in 1936, the Court voided a New York law by invoking the* Adkins *precedent (Morehead* v. *New York ex rel. Tipaldo, 298 U.S. 587). In the* Parrish *case in early 1937, the state of Washington directly challenged the* Adkins *doctrine. The New York state lawyers, for what they thought were good tactical reasons, had avoided a similar challenge the year before. Justice Roberts later claimed that he had never supported* Adkins, *but felt obligated to join the majority in* Tipaldo *because the precedent was not challenged. Now, in 1937, he switched sides and the Court dramatically reversed itself on minimum wages.*

Chief Justice Hughes delivered the opinion of the Court.

This case presents the question of the constitutional validity of the minimum wage law of the State of Washington.

The Act, entitled "Minimum Wages for Women," authorizes the fixing of minimum wages for women and minors. Laws of 1913 (Washington) chap. 174; Remington's Rev. Stat. (1932), §§ 7623 *et seq.* It provides:

"SECTION 1. The welfare of the State of Washington demands that women and minors be protected from conditions of labor which have a pernicious effect on their health and morals. The State of Washington, therefore, exercising herein its police and sovereign power declares that inadequate wages and unsanitary conditions of labor exert such pernicious effect.

"SEC. 2. It shall be unlawful to employ women or minors in any industry or occupation within the State of Washington under conditions

---

300 U.S. 379 (1937)

of labor detrimental to their health or morals; and it shall be unlawful to employ women workers in any industry within the State of Washington at wages which are not adequate for their maintenance.

"SEC. 3. There is hereby created a commission to be known as the 'Industrial Welfare Commission' for the State of Washington, to establish such standards of wages and conditions of labor for women and minors employed within the State of Washington, as shall be held hereunder to be reasonable and not detrimental to health and morals, and which shall be sufficient for the decent maintenance of women."

Further provisions required the Commission to ascertain the wages and conditions of labor of women and minors within the State. . . .

The appellant conducts a hotel. The appellee Elsie Parrish was employed as a chambermaid and (with her husband) brought this suit to recover the difference between the wages paid her and the minimum wage fixed pursuant to the state law. The minimum wage was $14.50 per week of 48 hours. The appellant challenged the act as repugnant to the due process clause of the Fourteenth Amendment of the Constitution of the United States. The Supreme Court of the State, reversing the trial court, sustained the statute and directed judgment for the plaintiffs. . . .

The appellant relies upon the decision of this Court in *Adkins v. Children's Hospital,* 261 U.S. 525, which held invalid the District of Columbia Minimum Wage Act, which was attacked under the due process clause of the Fifth Amendment. . . .

The principle which must control our decision is not in doubt. The constitutional provision invoked is the due process clause of the Fourteenth Amendment governing the States, as the due process clause invoked in the *Adkins* case governed Congress. In each case the violation alleged by those attacking minimum wage regulation for women is deprivation of freedom of contract. What is this freedom? The Constitution does not speak of freedom of contract. It speaks of liberty and prohibits the deprivation of liberty without due process of law. In prohibiting that deprivation the Constitution does not recognize an absolute and uncontrollable liberty. Liberty in each of its phases has its history and connotation. But the liberty safeguarded is liberty in a social organization which requires the protection of law against the evils which menace the health, safety, morals and welfare of the people. Liberty under the Constitution is thus necessarily subject to the restraints of due process, and regulation which is reasonable in relation to its subject and is adopted in the interests of the community is due process.

This essential limitation of liberty in general governs freedom of contract in particular. More than twenty-five years ago we set forth the applicable principle in these words, after referring to the cases where the liberty guaranteed by the Fourteenth Amendment had been broadly described:

"But it was recognized in the cases cited, as in many others, that freedom of contract is a qualified and not an absolute right. There is no absolute freedom to do as one wills or to contract as one chooses. The guaranty of liberty does not withdraw from legislative supervision that wide department of activity which consists of the making of contracts, or deny to government the power to provide restrictive safeguards. Liberty implies the absence of arbitrary restraint, not immunity from reasonable regulations and prohibitions imposed in the interests of the community." *Chicago, B & Q. R. Co.* v. *McGuire,* 219 U.S. 549, 567.

This power under the Constitution to restrict freedom of contract has had many illustrations. That it may be exercised in the public interest with respect to contracts between employer and employee is undeniable. . . .

The point that has been strongly stressed that adult employees should be deemed competent to make their own contracts was decisively met nearly forty years ago in *Holden* v. *Hardy,* . . . where we pointed out the inequality in the footing of the parties. We said . . . :

"The legislature has also recognized the fact, which the experience of legislators in many States has corroborated, that the proprietors of these establishments and their operatives do not stand upon an equality, and that their interests are, to a certain extent, conflicting. The former naturally desire to obtain as much labor as possible from their employes, while the latter are often induced by the fear of discharge to conform to regulations which their judgment, fairly exercised, would pronounce to be detrimental to their health or strength. In other words, the proprietors lay down the rules and the laborers are practically constrained to obey them. In such cases self-interest is often an unsafe guide, and the legislature may properly interpose its authority."

And we added that the fact "that both parties are of full age and competent to contract does not necessarily deprive the State of the power to interfere where the parties do not stand upon an equality, or where the public health demands that one party to the contract shall be protected against himself." . . .

It is manifest that this established principle is peculiarly applicable in relation to the employment of women in whose protection the State has a special interest. That phase of the subject received elaborate consideration in *Muller* v. *Oregon* (1908), 208 U.S. 412, where the constitutional authority of the State to limit the working hours of women was sustained. We emphasized the consideration that "women's physical structure and the performance of maternal functions place her at a disadvantage in the struggle for subsistence" and that her physical well being "becomes an object of public interest and care in order to preserve the strength and vigor of the race." We emphasized the need of protecting women against oppression despite her possession of contractual rights. We said that "though limitations upon personal and contractual rights may be removed by legislation, there is that in her disposition and habits of life which will operate against a full assertion of those rights. She will still be where some legislation to protect her seems necessary to secure a real equality of right."

Hence she was "properly placed in a class by herself, and legislation designed for her protection may be sustained even when like legislation is not necessary for men and could not be sustained." We concluded that the limitations which the statute there in question "placed upon her contractual powers, upon her right to agree with her employer as to the time she shall labor" were "not imposed solely for her benefit, but also largely for the benefit of all." . . .

This array of precedents and the principles they applied were thought by the dissenting Justices in the *Adkins* case to demand that the minimum wage statute be sustained. The validity of the distinction made by the Court between a minimum wage and a maximum of hours in limiting liberty of contract was especially challenged. . . . That challenge persists and is without any satisfactory answer. As Chief Justice Taft observed: "In absolute freedom of contract the one term is as important as the other, for both enter equally into the consideration given and received, a restriction as to the one is not greater in essence than the other and is of the same kind. One is the multiplier and the other the multiplicand." And Mr. Justice Holmes, while recognizing that "the distinctions of the law are distinctions of degree," could "perceive no difference in the kind or degree of interference with liberty, the only matter with which we have any concern, between the one case and the other. The bargain is equally affected whichever half you regulate." . . .

The minimum wage to be paid under the Washington statute is fixed after full consideration by representatives of employers, employees and the public. It may be assumed that the minimum wage is fixed in consideration of the services that are performed in the particular occupations under normal conditions. Provision is made for special licenses at less wages in the case of women who are incapable of full service. The statement of Mr. Justice Holmes in the *Adkins* case is pertinent: "This statute does not compel anybody to pay anything. It simply forbids employment at rates below those fixed as the minimum requirement of health and right living. It is safe to assume that women will not be employed at even the lowest wages allowed unless they earn them, or unless the employer's business can sustain the burden. In short the law in its character and operation is like hundreds of so-called police laws that have been upheld." . . . And Chief Justice Taft forcibly pointed out the consideration which is basic in a statute of this character: "Legislatures which adopt a requirement of maximum hours or minimum wages may be presumed to believe that when sweating employers are prevented from paying unduly low wages by positive law they will continue their business, abating that part of their profits, which were wrung from the necessities of their employees, and will concede the better terms required by the law; and that while in individual cases hardship may result, the restriction will enure to the benefit of the general class of employees in whose interest the law is passed and so to that of the community at large." . . .

We think that the views thus expressed are sound and that the decision in the *Adkins* case was a departure from the true application of the principles governing the regulation by the State of the relation of employer and employed. . . .

With full recognition of the earnestness and vigor which characterize the prevailing opinion in the *Adkins* case, we find it impossible to reconcile that ruling with these well-considered declarations. What can be closer to the public interest than the health of women and their protection from unscrupulous and overreaching employers? And if the protection of women is a legitimate end of the exercise of state power, how can it be said that the requirement of the payment of a minimum wage fairly fixed in order to meet the very necessities of existence is not an admissible means to that end? The legislature of the State was clearly entitled to consider the situation of women in employment, the fact that they are in the class receiving the least pay, that their bargaining power is relatively weak, and that they are the ready victims of those who would take advantage of their necessitous circumstances. The legislature was entitled to adopt measures to reduce the evils of the "sweating system," the exploiting of workers at wages so low as to be insufficient to meet the bare cost of living, thus making their very helplessness the occasion of a most injurious competition. The legislature had the right to consider that its minimum wage requirements would be an important aid in carrying out its policy of protection. The adoption of similar requirements by many States evidences a deepseated conviction both as to the presence of the evil and as to the means adapted to check it. Legislative response to that conviction cannot be regarded as arbitrary or capricious, and that is all we have to decide. Even if the wisdom of the policy be regarded as debatable and its effects uncertain, still the legislature is entitled to its judgment.

There is an additional and compelling consideration which recent economic experience has brought into a strong light. The exploitation of a class of workers who are in an unequal position with respect to bargaining power and are thus relatively defenceless against the denial of a living wage is not only detrimental to their health and well being but casts a direct burden for their support upon the community. What these workers lose in wages the taxpayers are called upon to pay. The bare cost of living must be met. We may take judicial notice of the unparalleled demands for relief which arose during the recent period of depression and still continue to an alarming extent despite the degree of economic recovery which has been achieved. It is unnecessary to cite official statistics to establish what is of common knowledge through the length and breadth of the land. While in the instant case no factual brief has been presented, there is no reason to doubt that the State of Washington has encountered the same social problem that is present elsewhere. The community is not bound to provide what is in effect a subsidy for unconscionable employers. The community may direct its law-making power to correct the abuse which springs from their selfish disregard of the public interest. The argument that the legislation in question constitutes an arbitrary discrimination, because it does not extend to men, is unavailing. This Court has frequently held that the legislative authority, acting within its proper field, is not bound to extend its regulation to all cases which it might possibly reach. The legislature "is free to recognize degrees of harm and it may confine its restrictions to those classes of cases where the need is deemed to be clearest." If "the law presumably hits the evil where it is most felt, it is not to be overthrown because there are other instances to which it might have been applied." There is no "doctrinaire requirement" that the legislation should be couched in all embracing terms. . . .

Our conclusion is that the case of *Adkins* v. *Children's Hospital* . . . should be, and it is, overruled. . . .

Mr. Justice Sutherland, dissenting:

Mr. Justice Van Devanter, Mr. Justice McReynolds, Mr. Justice Butler and I think the judgment of the court below should be reversed. . . .

The suggestion that the only check upon the exercise of the judicial power, when properly invoked, to declare a constitutional right superior to an unconstitutional statute is the judge's own faculty of self-restraint, is both ill considered and mischievous. Self-restraint belongs in the domain of will and not of judgment. The check upon the judge is that imposed by his oath of office, by the Constitution and by his own conscientious and informed convictions; and since he has the duty to make up his own mind and adjudge accordingly, it is hard to see how there could be any other restraint. This court acts as a unit. It cannot act in any other way; and the majority (whether a bare majority or a majority of all but one of its members), therefore, establishes the controlling rule as the decision of the court, binding, so long as it remains unchanged, equally upon those who disagree and upon those who subscribe to it. Otherwise, orderly administration of justice would cease. But it is the right of those in the minority to disagree, and sometimes, in matters of grave importance, their imperative duty to voice their disagreement at such length as the occasion demands — always, of course, in terms which, however forceful, do not offend the proprieties or impugn the good faith of those who think otherwise.

It is urged that the question involved should now receive fresh consideration, among other reasons, because of "the economic conditions which have supervened"; but the meaning of the Constitution does not change with the ebb and flow of economic events. We frequently are told in more general words that the Constitution must be construed in the light of the present. If by that it is meant that the Constitution is made up of living words that apply to every new condition which they include, the statement is quite true. But to say, if that be intended, that the words of the Constitution mean today what they did not mean when written — that is, that they do not apply to a situation now to which they would have applied then — is to rob that instrument of the essential element which continues it in force as the people have made it until they, and not their official agents, have made it otherwise. . . .

The judicial function is that of interpretation; it does not include the power of amendment under the guise of interpretation. To miss the point of difference between the two is to miss all that the phrase "supreme law of the land" stands for and to convert what was intended as inescapable and enduring mandates into mere moral reflections.

If the Constitution, intelligently and reasonably construed in the light of these principles, stands in the way of desirable legislation, the blame must rest upon that instrument, and not upon the court for enforcing it according to its terms. The remedy in that situation — and the only true remedy — is to amend the Constitution. . . .

National Labor Relations Board

v.

Jones & Laughlin Steel Corp.

The Parrish decision did not involve any fundamental shift in judicial attitudes toward governmental power. It simply reversed the Adkins precedent, which was anachronistic even in its own time. But a few weeks later, perhaps under the pressures of Franklin D. Roosevelt's attacks and public opinion, the Court significantly altered its stand on federal regulation of production. In 1935, Congress had passed the National Labor Relations Act, guaranteeing labor the right to organize and bargain collectively. Elaborate federal administrative machinery was established to prevent employers from engaging in unfair labor practices. The law was predictably challenged as a regulation of production. Although Chief Justice Hughes did not specifically overrule the recent and embarrassing Schechter and Carter precedents, he did revive the line of commerce clause decisions from Swift v. United States through the liberal decisions of the 1920's. Following the Jones & Laughlin case, there were a number of unsuccessful attempts by employers to challenge the law where it was applied to smaller, more local industries. (See, for example, N.L.R.B. v. Friedman-Harry Marks Clothing Company, 301 U.S. 58 [1937].)

Chief Justice Hughes delivered the opinion of the Court.

First. *The scope of the Act.* — The Act is challenged in its entirety as an attempt to regulate all industry, thus invading the reserved powers of the States over their local concerns. It is asserted that the references in the Act to interstate and foreign commerce are colorable at best; that the Act is not a true regulation of such commerce or of matters which directly affect it but on the contrary has the fundamental object of placing under the compulsory supervision of the federal government all industrial labor relations within the nation. The argument seeks support in the broad words of the preamble . . . and in the sweep of the provisions of the Act, and it is further insisted that its legislative history shows an essential universal purpose in the light of which its scope cannot be

301 U.S. 1 (1937)

limited by either construction or by the application of the separability clause.

If this conception of terms, intent and consequent inseparability were sound, the Act would necessarily fall by reason of the limitation upon the federal power which inheres in the constitutional grant, as well as because of the explicit reservation of the Tenth Amendment. *Schechter Corp.* v. *United States,* 295 U.S. 495, 549, 550, 554. The authority of the federal government may not be pushed to such an extreme as to destroy the distinction, which the commerce clause itself establishes, between commerce "among the several States" and the internal concerns of a State. That distinction between what is national and what is local in the activities of commerce is vital to the maintenance of our federal system. *Id.* . . . .

We think it clear that the National Labor Relations Act may be construed so as to operate within the sphere of constitutional authority. The jurisdiction conferred upon the Board, and invoked in this instance, is found in § 10 (a), which provides:

> "Sec. 10 (a). The Board is empowered, as hereinafter provided, to prevent any person from engaging in any unfair labor practice (listed in section 8) affecting commerce."

The critical words of this provision, prescribing the limits of the Board's authority in dealing with the labor practices, are "affecting commerce." The Act specifically defines the "commerce" to which it refers (§ 2 (6)):

> "The term 'commerce' means trade, traffic, commerce, transportation, or communication among the several States, or between the District of Columbia or any Territory of the United States and any State or other Territory, or between any foreign country and any State, Territory, or the District of Columbia, or within the District of Columbia or any Territory, or between points in the same State but through any other State or any Territory or the District of Columbia or any foreign country."

There can be no question that the commerce thus contemplated by the Act (aside from that within a Territory or the District of Columbia) is interstate and foreign commerce in the constitutional sense. The Act also defines the term "affecting commerce" (§ 2 (7)):

> "The term 'affecting commerce' means in commerce, or burdening or obstructing commerce or the free flow of commerce, or having led or tending to lead to a labor dispute burdening or obstructing commerce or the free flow of commerce."

This definition is one of exclusion as well as inclusion. The grant of authority to the Board does not purport to extend to the relationship between all industrial employees and employers. Its terms do not impose collective bargaining upon all industry regardless of effects upon interstate or foreign commerce. It purports to reach only what may be deemed to burden or obstruct that commerce and, thus qualified, it must be construed as contemplating the exercise of control within constitutional bounds. It is a familiar principle that acts which directly burden or obstruct interstate or foreign commerce, or its free flow, are within the reach of the congressional power. Acts having that effect are not rendered immune because they grow out of labor disputes. . . . It is the effect upon commerce, not the source of the injury, which is the criterion. . . . Whether or not particular action does affect commerce in such a close and intimate fashion as to be subject to federal control, and hence to lie within the authority conferred upon the Board, is left by the statute to be determined as individual cases arise. We are thus to inquire whether in the instant case the constitutional boundary has been passed.

Second. *The unfair labor practices in question.* — The unfair labor practices found by the Board are those defined in § 8, subdivisions (1) and (3). These provide:

Sec. 8. It shall be an unfair labor practice for an employer —

"(1) To interfere with, restrain, or coerce employees in the exercise of the rights guaranteed in section 7."

"(3) By discrimination in regard to hire or tenure of employment or any term or condition of employment to encourage or discourage membership in any labor organization: . . ."

Section 8, subdivision (1), refers to § 7, which is as follows:

"SEC. 7. Employees shall have the right to self-organization, to form, join, or assist labor organizations, to bargain collectively through representatives of their own choosing, and to engage in concerted activities, for the purpose of collective bargaining or other mutual aid or protection."

Thus, in its present application, the statute goes no further than to safeguard the right of employees to self-organization and to select representatives of their own choosing for collective bargaining or other mutual protection without restraint or coercion by their employer.

That is a fundamental right. Employees have as clear a right to organize and select their representatives for lawful purposes as the respondent has to organize its business and select its own officers and agents. Discrimination and coercion to prevent the free exercise of the right of employees to self-organization and representation is a proper subject for condemnation by competent legislative authority. Long ago we stated the reason for labor organizations. We said that they were organized out of the necessities of the situation; that a single employee was helpless in dealing with an employer; that he was dependent ordinarily on his daily wage for the maintenance of himself and family; that if the employer refused to pay him the wages that he thought fair, he was nevertheless unable to leave the employ and resist arbitrary and unfair treatment; that union was essential to give laborers opportunity to deal on an equality with their employer. . . . Fully recognizing the legality of collective action on the part of employees in order to safeguard their proper interests, we [have] said that Congress was not required to ignore this right but could safeguard it. Congress could seek to make appropriate collective action of employees an instrument of peace rather than of strife. We said that such collective action would be a mockery if representation were made futile by interference with freedom of choice. Hence the prohibition by Congress of interference with the selection of representatives for the purpose of negotiation and conference between employers and employees, "instead of being an invasion of the constitutional right of either, was based on the recognition of the rights of both." . . .

Third. *The application of the Act to employees engaged in production. — The principle involved.* — Respondent says that whatever may be said of employees engaged in interstate commerce, the industrial relations and activities in the manufacturing department of respondent's enterprise are not subject to federal regulation. The argument rests upon the proposition that manufacturing in itself is not commerce. . . . *Schechter Corp.* v. *United States* . . . ; *Carter* v. *Carter Coal Co.* . . .

The Government distinguishes these cases. The various parts of respondent's enterprise are described as interdependent and as thus involving

> "a great movement of iron ore, coal and limestone along well-defined paths to the steel mills, thence through them, and thence in the form of steel products into the consuming centers of the country — a definite and well-understood course of business."

It is urged that these activities constitute a "stream" or "flow" of commerce, of which the Aliquippa manufacturing plant is the focal point, and that industrial strife at that point would cripple the entire movement. Reference is made to our decision sustaining the Packers and Stockyards Act. *Stafford* v. *Wallace*, 258 U.S. 495. The Court found that the stockyards were but a "throat" through which the current of commerce flowed and the transactions which there occurred could not be separated from that movement. Hence the sales at the stockyards were not regarded as merely local transactions, for while they created "a local change of title" they did not "stop the flow," but merely changed the private interests in the subject of the current. Distinguishing the cases which upheld the power of the State to impose a non-discriminatory tax upon property which the owner intended to transport to another State, but which was not in actual transit and was held within the State subject to the disposition of the owner, the Court remarked:

> "The question, it should be observed, is not with respect to the extent of the power of Congress to regulate interstate commerce, but whether a particular exercise of state power in view of its nature and operation must be deemed to be in conflict with this paramount authority." . . .

Respondent contends that the instant case presents material distinctions. Respondent says that the Aliquippa plant is extensive in size and represents a large investment in buildings, machinery and equipment. The raw materials which are brought to the plant are delayed for long periods and, after being subjected to manufacturing processes, "are changed substantially as to character, utility and value." The finished products which emerge "are to a large extent manufactured without reference to pre-existing orders and contracts and are entirely different from the raw materials which enter at the other end." Hence respondent argues that "If importation and exportation in interstate commerce do not singly transfer purely local activities into the field of congressional regulation, it should follow that their combination would not alter the local situation." . . .

We do not find it necessary to determine whether these features of defendant's business dispose of the asserted analogy to the "stream of commerce" cases. The instances in which that metaphor has been used are but particular, and not exclusive, illustrations of the protective power which the Government invokes in support of the present Act. The congressional authority to protect interstate commerce from burdens and obstructions is not limited to transactions which can be deemed to be an essential part of a "flow" of interstate or foreign commerce. Burdens and obstructions may be due to injurious action springing from other sources. The fundamental principle is that the power to regulate commerce is the power to enact "all appropriate legislation" for "its protection and advancement" . . . ; to adopt measures "to promote its growth and insure its safety" . . . ; "to foster, protect, control and restrain." . . . That power is plenary and may be exerted to protect interstate commerce "no matter what the source of the dangers which threaten it." . . . Although activities may be intrastate in character when separately considered, if they have such a close and substantial relation to interstate commerce that their control is essential or appropriate to protect that commerce from burdens and obstructions, Congress cannot be denied the power to exercise that control. . . . Undoubtedly the scope of this power must be considered in the light of our dual system of government and may not be extended so as to embrace effects upon interstate commerce so indirect and remote that to embrace them, in view of our complex society, would effectually obliterate the distinction between what is national and what is local and create a completely centralized government. . . . The question is necessarily one of degree. . . .

That intrastate activities, by reason of close and intimate relation to interstate commerce, may fall within federal control is demonstrated in the case of carriers who are engaged in both interstate and intrastate transportation. There federal control has been found essential to secure the freedom of interstate traffic from interference or unjust discrimination and to promote the efficiency of the interstate service. *Shreveport Case,*

234 U.S. 342, 351, 352. . . . It is manifest that intrastate rates deal *primarily* with a local activity. But in rate-making they bear such a close relation to interstate rates that effective control of the one must embrace some control over the other. . . . Under the Transportation Act, 1920, Congress went so far as to authorize the Interstate Commerce Commission to establish a state-wide level of intrastate rates in order to prevent an unjust discrimination against interstate commerce. . . .

The close and intimate effect which brings the subject within the reach of federal power may be due to activities in relation to productive industry although the industry when separately viewed is local. This has been abundantly illustrated in the application of the federal Anti-Trust Act. In the *Standard Oil* and *American Tobacco* cases, 221 U.S. 1, 106, that statute was applied to combinations of employers engaged in productive industry. . . .

Upon the same principle, the Anti-Trust Act has been applied to the conduct of employees engaged in production. . . .

It is thus apparent that the fact that the employees here concerned were engaged in production is not determinative. The question remains as to the effect upon interstate commerce of the labor practice involved. In the *Schechter* case, *supra,* we found that the effect there was so remote as to be beyond the federal power. To find "immediacy or directness" there was to find it "almost everywhere," a result inconsistent with the maintenance of our federal system. . . .

Fourth. *Effects of the unfair labor practice in respondent's enterprise.* — Giving full weight to respondent's contention with respect to a break in the complete continuity of the "stream of commerce" by reason of respondent's manufacturing operations, the fact remains that the stoppage of those operations by industrial strife would have a most serious effect upon interstate commerce. In view of respondent's far-flung activities, it is idle to say that the effect would be indirect or remote. It is obvious that it would be immediate and might be catastrophic. We are asked to shut our eyes to the plainest facts of our national life and to deal with the question of direct and indirect effects in an intellectual vacuum. Because there may be but indirect and remote effects upon interstate commerce in connection with a host of local enterprises throughout the country, it does not follow that other industrial activities do not have such a close and intimate relation to interstate commerce as to make the presence of industrial strife a matter of the most urgent national concern. When industries organize themselves on a national scale, making their relation to interstate commerce the dominant factor in their activities, how can it be maintained that their industrial labor relations constitute a forbidden field into which Congress may not enter when it is necessary to protect interstate commerce from the paralyzing consequences of industrial war? We have often said that interstate commerce itself is a practical conception. It is equally true that interferences with that commerce must be appraised by a judgment that does not ignore actual experience.

Experience has abundantly demonstrated that the recognition of the right of employees to self-organization and to have representatives of their own choosing for the purpose of collective bargaining is often an essential condition of industrial peace. Refusal to confer and negotiate has been one of the most prolific causes of strife. . . .

These questions have frequently engaged the attention of Congress and have been the subject of many inquiries. The steel industry is one of the great basic industries of the United States, with ramifying activities affecting interstate commerce at every point. The Government aptly refers to the steel strike of 1919–1920 with its far-reaching consequences. The fact that there appears to have been no major disturbance in that industry in the more recent period did not dispose of the possibilities of future and like dangers to interstate commerce which Congress was entitled to foresee and to exercise its protective power to forestall. It is not necessary again to detail the facts as to respondent's enterprise. Instead of being beyond the pale, we think that it presents in a most striking way the close and intimate relation which a manufacturing industry may have to interstate commerce and we have no doubt that Congress had constitutional authority to safeguard the right of respondent's employees to self-organization and freedom in the choice of representatives for collective bargaining.

Fifth. *The means which the Act employs. — Questions under the due process clause and other constitutional restrictions.* — Respondent asserts its right to conduct its business in an orderly manner without being subjected to arbitrary restraints. What we have said points to the fallacy in the argument. Employees have their correlative right to organize for the purpose of securing the redress of grievances and to promote agreements with employers relating to rates of pay and conditions of work. . . . Restraint for the purpose of preventing an unjust interference with that right cannot be considered arbitrary or capricious. . . .

The Act does not compel agreements between employers and employees. It does not compel any agreement whatever. It does not prevent the employer "from refusing to make a collective contract and hiring individuals on whatever terms" the employer "may by unilateral action determine." The Act expressly provides in § 9 (a) that any individual employee or a group of employees shall have the right at any time to present grievances to their employer. The theory of the Act is that free opportunity for negotiation with accredited representatives of employees is likely to promote industrial peace and may bring about the adjustments and agreements which the Act in itself does not attempt to compel. . . . The Act does not interfere with the normal exercise of the right of the employer to select its employees or to discharge them. The employer may not, under cover of that right, intimidate or coerce its employees with respect to their self-organization and representation, and, on the other hand, the Board is not entitled to make its authority a pretext for interference with the right of discharge when that right is exercised for other reasons than such intimidation and coercion. The true purpose is the subject of investigation with full opportunity to show the facts. It would seem that when employers freely recognize the right of their employees to their own organizations and their unrestricted right of representation there will be much less occasion for controversy in respect to the free and appropriate exercise of the right of selection and discharge.

The Act has been criticised as one-sided in its application; that it subjects the employer to supervision and restraint and leaves untouched the abuses for which employees may be responsible; that it fails to provide a more comprehensive plan, — with better assurances of fairness to both sides and with increased chances of success in bringing about, if not compelling, equitable solutions of industrial disputes affecting interstate commerce. But we are dealing with the power of Congress, not with a particular policy or with the extent to which policy should go. We have frequently said that the legislative authority, exerted within its proper field, need not embrace all the evils within its reach. The Constitution does not forbid "cautious advance, step by step," in dealing with the evils which are exhibited in activities within the range of legislative power. . . . The question in such cases is whether the legislature, in what it does prescribe, has gone beyond constitutional limits.

The procedural provisions of the Act are assailed. But these provisions, as we construe them, do not offend against the constitutional requirements governing the creation and action of administrative bodies. . . .

Our conclusion is that the order of the Board was within its competency and that the Act is valid as here applied. The judgment of the Circuit Court of Appeals is reversed and the cause is remanded for further proceedings in conformity with this opinion.

Reversed.

Justice McReynolds delivered a dissenting opinion, concurred in by Justices Van Devanter, Sutherland, and Butler.

United States *v.* Darby Lumber Company

This decision further expanded the Court's new permissiveness toward federal regulation of the economy. At issue was the Fair Labor Standards Act of 1938 establishing national minimum wage standards and regulations for overtime work. In addition, the act virtually repeated the language of the 1916 child labor law prohibiting the shipment in interstate commerce of goods produced by child labor. By 1941, most of the conservative judicial opponents of the New Deal had left the Court, and the justices unanimously rejected all challenges to the 1938 law.

Justice Stone delivered the opinion of the Court.

The two principal questions raised by the record in this case are, *first,* whether Congress has constitutional power to prohibit the shipment in interstate commerce of lumber manufactured by employees whose wages are less than a prescribed minimum or whose weekly hours of labor at that wage are greater than a prescribed maximum, and, *second,* whether it has power to prohibit the employment of workmen in the production of goods "for interstate commerce" at other than prescribed wages and hours. A subsidiary question is whether in connection with such prohibitions Congress can require the employer subject to them to keep records showing the hours worked each day and week by each of his employees including those engaged "in the production and manufacture of goods to-wit, lumber, for 'interstate commerce.'" . . .

The prohibition of shipment of the proscribed goods in interstate commerce. . . .

While manufacture is not of itself interstate commerce, the shipment of manufactured goods interstate is such commerce and the prohibition of such shipment by Congress is indubitably a regulation of the commerce. The power to regulate commerce is the power "to prescribe the rule by which commerce is governed." *Gibbons* v. *Ogden,* 9 Wheat. 1, 196. It extends not only to those regulations which aid, foster and protect the commerce, but embraces those which prohibit it. . . . It is conceded that the power of Congress to prohibit transportation in interstate commerce includes noxious articles, . . . stolen articles, . . . kidnapped persons, . . . and articles such as intoxicating liquor or convict-made goods,

312 U.S. 100 (1941)

traffic in which is forbidden or restricted by the laws of the state of destination. . . .

But it is said that the present prohibition falls within the scope of none of these categories; that while the prohibition is nominally a regulation of the commerce its motive or purpose is regulation of wages and hours of persons engaged in manufacture, the control of which has been reserved to the states and upon which Georgia and some of the states of destination have placed no restriction; that the effect of the present statute is, . . . under the guise of a regulation of interstate commerce, . . . to regulate wages and hours within the state contrary to the policy of the state which has elected to leave them unregulated.

The power of Congress over interstate commerce "is complete in itself, may be exercised to its utmost extent, and acknowledges no limitations other than are prescribed in the Constitution." *Gibbons* v. *Ogden, supra,* 196. That power can neither be enlarged nor diminished by the exercise or non-exercise of state power. . . . Congress, following its own conception of public policy concerning the restrictions which may appropriately be imposed on interstate commerce, is free to exclude from the commerce articles whose use in the states for which they are destined it may conceive to be injurious to the public health, morals or welfare, even though the state has not sought to regulate their use. . . .

Such regulation is not a forbidden invasion of state power merely because either its motive or its consequence is to restrict the use of articles of commerce within the states of destination; and is not prohibited unless by other Constitutional provisions. It is no objection to the assertion of the power to regulate interstate commerce that its exercise is attended by the same incidents which attend the exercise of the police power of the states. . . .

The motive and purpose of the present regulation are plainly to make effective the Congressional conception of public policy that interstate commerce should not be made the instrument of competition in the distribution of goods produced under substandard labor conditions, which competition is injurious to the commerce and to the states from and to which the commerce flows. The motive and purpose of a regulation of interstate commerce are matters for the legislative judgment upon the exercise of which the Constitution places no restriction and over which the courts are given no control. . . . Whatever their motive and purpose, regulations of commerce which do not infringe some constitutional prohibition are within the plenary power conferred on Congress by the Commerce Clause. Subject only to that limitation, presently to be considered, we conclude that the prohibition of the shipment interstate of goods produced under the forbidden substandard labor conditions is within the constitutional authority of Congress.

In the more than a century which has elapsed since the decision of *Gibbons* v. *Ogden,* these principles of constitutional interpretation have been so long and repeatedly recognized by this Court as applicable to the Commerce Clause, that there would be little occasion for repeating them now were it not for the decision of this Court twenty-two years ago in *Hammer* v. *Dagenhart,* 247 U.S. 251. In that case it was held by a bare majority of the Court over the powerful and now classic dissent of Mr. Justice Holmes setting forth the fundamental issues involved, that Congress was without power to exclude the products of child labor from interstate commerce. The reasoning and conclusion of the Court's opinion there cannot be reconciled with the conclusion which we have reached, that the power of Congress under the Commerce Clause is plenary to exclude any article from interstate commerce subject only to the specific prohibitions of the Constitution.

Hammer v. *Dagenhart* has not been followed. The distinction on which the decision was rested that Congressional power to prohibit interstate commerce is limited to articles which in themselves have some harmful or deleterious property — a distinction which was novel when made and unsupported by any provision of the Constitution — has long since been abandoned. . . . The thesis of the opinion that the motive of the prohibition or its effect to control in some measure the use or production within the states of the article thus excluded from the commerce can operate to deprive the regulation of its constitutional authority has long since ceased to have force. . . . And finally we have declared "The authority of the federal government over interstate commerce does not differ in extent or character from that retained by the states over intrastate commerce." . . .

The conclusion is inescapable that *Hammer* v. *Dagenhart* was a departure from the principles which have prevailed in the interpretation of the Commerce Clause both before and since the decision and that such vitality, as a precedent, as it then had has long since been exhausted. It should be and now is overruled.

Validity of the wage and hour requirements. Section 15 (a) (2) and §§ 6 and 7 require employers to conform to the wage and hour provisions with respect to all employees engaged in the production of goods for interstate commerce. . . .

There remains the question whether such restriction on the production of goods for commerce is a permissible exercise of the commerce power. The power of Congress over interstate commerce is not confined to the regulation of commerce among the states. It extends to those activities intrastate which so affect interstate commerce or the exercise of the power of Congress over it as to make regulation of them appropriate means to the attainment of a legitimate end, the exercise of the granted power of Congress to regulate interstate commerce. . . .

Congress, having by the present Act adopted the policy of excluding from interstate commerce all goods produced for the commerce which do not conform to the specified labor standards, it may choose the means reasonably adapted to the attainment of the permitted end, even though they involved control of intrastate activities. . . .

The Sherman Act and the National Labor Relations Act are familiar examples of the exertion of the commerce power to prohibit or control activities wholly intrastate because of their effect on interstate commerce. . . .

The means adopted for the protection of interstate commerce by the suppression of the production of the condemned goods for interstate commerce is so related to the commerce and so affects it as to be within the reach of the commerce power. . . . Congress, to attain its objective in the suppression of nationwide competition in interstate commerce by goods produced under substandard labor conditions, has made no distinction as to the volume or amount of shipments in the commerce or of production for commerce by any particular shipper or producer. It recognized that in present day industry, competition by a small part may affect the whole and that the total effect of the competition of many small producers may be great. . . .

So far as *Carter* v. *Carter Coal Co.*, 298 U.S. 238, is inconsistent with this conclusion, its doctrine is limited in principle by the decisions under the Sherman Act and the National Labor Relations Act, which we have cited and which we follow. . . .

Our conclusion is unaffected by the Tenth Amendment. . . . The amendment states but a truism that all is retained which has not been surrendered. There is nothing in the history of its adoption to suggest that it was more than declaratory of the relationship between the national and state governments as it had been established by the Constitution before the amendment or that its purpose was other than to allay fears that the new national government might seek to exercise powers not granted, and that the states might not be able to exercise fully their reserved powers. . . .

From the beginning and for many years the amendment has been construed as not depriving the national government of authority to resort to all means for the exercise of a granted power which are appropriate and plainly adapted to the permitted end. . . .

Validity of the wage and hour provisions under the Fifth Amendment. Both provisions are minimum wage requirements compelling the payment of a minimum standard wage with a prescribed increased wage for overtime of "not less than one and one-half times the regular rate" at which the worker is employed. Since our decision in *West Coast Hotel Co.* v. *Parrish,* 300 U.S. 379 it is no longer open to question that the fixing of a minimum wage is within the legislative power and that the bare fact of its exercise is not a denial of due process under the Fifth more than under the Fourteenth Amendment. Nor is it any longer open to question that it is within the legislative power to fix maximum hours. . . .

The Act is sufficiently definite to meet constitutional demands. One who employs persons, without conforming to the prescribed wage and hour conditions, to work on goods which he ships or expects to ship across state lines, is warned that he may be subject to the criminal penalties of the Act. No more is required. . . .

Wickard *v.* Filburn

In conjunction with Darby, *this decision marked the complete overthrow of previous judicial restraints on federal commerce power. Following the passage of the Agricultural Adjustment Act of 1938, a referendum of wheat farmers approved the fixing of acreage quotas by the Secretary of Agriculture. Penalties were established for any attempts to market excess production. Filburn, an Ohio farmer, harvested more than double his allotment and was consequently denied the required marketing card by the Secretary. Filburn challenged the law, contending that the excess amount might be consumed on his own farm. For the first time, the Court considered federal regulation of production even when no part of the product was intended for interstate commerce. A few years later, the Court eloquently summed up its commerce clause latitudinarianism when it said that the power is "as broad as the economic needs of the nation"* (American Power & Light *v.* S.E.C., 329 U.S. 90, 104 [1946].)

Justice Jackson delivered the opinion of the Court.

I t is urged that under the Commerce Clause of the Constitution, Article I, § 8, clause 3, Congress does not possess the power it has in this instance sought to exercise. The question would merit little consideration since our decision in *United States* v. *Darby* . . . sustaining the federal power to regulate production of goods for commerce, except for the fact that this Act extends federal regulation to production not intended in any part for commerce but wholly for consumption on the farm. The Act includes a definition of "market" and its derivatives, so that as related to wheat, in addition to its conventional meaning, it also means to dispose of "by feeding (in any form) to poultry or livestock which, or the products of which, are sold, bartered, or exchanged, or to be so disposed of." Hence, marketing quotas not only embrace all that may be sold without penalty but also what may be consumed on the premises. Wheat produced on excess acreage is designated as "available for marketing" as so defined, and the penalty is imposed thereon. Penalties do not depend upon whether any part of the wheat, either within or without the quota, is sold or intended to be sold. The sum of this is that the Federal Government fixes a quota including all that the farmer may harvest for sale or for his own farm needs, and declares that wheat produced on excess acreage may neither be disposed of nor used except upon payment of the penalty, or except it is stored as required by the Act or delivered to the Secretary of Agriculture.

Appellee says that this is a regulation of production and consumption of wheat. Such activities are, he urges, beyond the reach of Congressional power under the Commerce Clause, since they are local in character, and their effects upon interstate commerce are at most "indirect." In answer the Government argues that the statute regulates neither production nor consumption, but only marketing; and, in the alternative, that if the Act does go beyond the regulation of marketing it is sustainable as a "necessary and proper" implementation of the power of Congress over interstate commerce.

The Government's concern lest the Act be held to be a regulation of production or consumption, rather than of marketing, is attributable to a few dicta and decisions of this Court which might be understood to lay it down that activities such as "production," "manufacturing," and "mining" are strictly "local" and, except in special circumstances which are not present here, cannot be regulated under the commerce power because their effects upon interstate commerce are, as matter of law, only "indirect." Even today, when this power has been held to have great latitude, there is no decision of this Court that such activities may be regulated where no part of the product is intended for interstate commerce or intermingled with the subjects thereof. We believe that a review of the course of decision under the Commerce Clause will make plain, however, that questions of the power of Congress are not to be decided by reference to any formula which would give controlling force to nomenclature such as "production" and "indirect" and foreclose consideration of the actual effects of the activity in question upon interstate commerce.

At the beginning Chief Justice Marshall described the federal commerce power with a breadth never yet exceeded. . . . He made emphatic the embracing and penetrating nature of this power by warning that effective restraints on its exercise must proceed from political rather than from judicial processes. . . .

For nearly a century, however, decisions of this Court under the Commerce Clause dealt rarely with questions of what Congress might do in the exercise of its granted power under the Clause, and almost entirely with the permissibility of state activity which it was claimed discriminated against or burdened interstate commerce. During this period there was perhaps little occasion for the affirmative exercise of the commerce power, and the influence of the Clause on American life and law was a negative one, resulting almost wholly from its operation as a restraint upon the powers of the states. In discussion and decision the point of reference, instead of being what was "necessary and proper" to the exercise by Congress of its granted power, was often some concept of sovereignty thought to be implicit in the status of statehood. Certain activities such as "production," "manufacturing," and "mining" were occasionally said to be within the province of state governments and beyond the power of Congress under the Commerce Clause.

It was not until 1887, with the enactment of the Interstate Commerce Act, that the interstate commerce power began to exert positive influence in American law and life. This first important federal resort to the commerce power was followed in 1890 by the Sherman Anti-Trust Act and, thereafter, mainly after 1903, by many others. These statutes ushered in new phases of adjudication, which required the Court to approach the interpretation of the Commerce Clause in the light of an actual exercise by Congress of its power thereunder.

When it first dealt with this new legislation, the Court adhered to its earlier pronouncements, and allowed but little scope to the power of Congress. *United States* v. *Knight Co.* . . . These earlier pronouncements also played an important part in several of the five cases in which this Court later held that Acts of Congress under the Commerce Clause were in excess of its power.

Even while important opinions in this line of restrictive authority were being written, however, other cases called forth broader interpretations of the Commerce Clause destined to supersede the earlier ones, and to bring about a return to the principles first enunciated by Chief Justice Marshall. . . .

Not long after the decision of *United States* v. *Knight Co.,* . . . Mr. Justice Holmes, in sustaining the exercise of national power over intrastate activity, stated for the Court that "commerce among the States is not a technical legal conception, but a practical one, drawn from the course of business." *Swift & Co.* v. *United States* . . . It was soon demonstrated that the effects of many kinds of intrastate activity upon interstate commerce were such as to make them a proper subject of federal regulation. In some cases sustaining the exercise of federal power over intrastate matters the term "direct" was used for the purpose of stating, rather than of reaching, a result; in others it was treated as synonymous with "substantial" or "material"; and in others it was not used at all. Of late its use has been abandoned in cases dealing with questions of federal power under the Commerce Clause.

In the *Shreveport Rate Cases,* . . . the Court held that railroad rates of an admittedly intrastate character and fixed by authority of the state might, nevertheless, be revised by the Federal Government because of the economic effects which they had upon interstate commerce. The opinion of Mr. Justice Hughes found federal intervention constitutionally authorized because of "matters having such a close and substantial relation to interstate traffic that the control is essential or appropriate to the security of that traffic, to the efficiency of the interstate service, and to the maintenance of conditions under which interstate commerce may be conducted upon fair terms and without molestation or hindrance." . . .

The Court's recognition of the relevance of the economic effects in the application of the Commerce Clause, exemplified by this statement, has made the mechanical application of legal formulas no longer feasible. Once an economic measure of the reach of the power granted to Congress in the Commerce Clause is accepted, questions of federal power cannot be decided simply by finding the activity in question to be "production," nor can consideration of its economic effects be foreclosed by calling them "indirect." The present Chief Justice [Stone] has said in summary of the present state of the law:

> "The commerce power is not confined in its exercise to the regulation of commerce among the states. It extends to those activities intrastate which so affect interstate commerce, or the exertion of the power of Congress over it, as to make regulation of them appropriate means to the attainment of a legitimate end, the effective execution of the granted power to regulate interstate commerce. . . . The power of Congress over interstate commerce is plenary and complete in itself, may be exercised to its utmost extent, and acknowledges no limitations other than are prescribed in the Constitution. . . . It follows that no form of state activity can constitutionally thwart the regulatory power granted by the commerce clause to Congress. Hence the reach of that power extends to those intrastate activities which in a substantial way interfere with or obstruct the exercise of the granted power." . . .

Whether the subject of the regulation in question was "production," "consumption," or "marketing" is, therefore, not material for purposes of deciding the question of federal power before us. That an activity is of local character may help in a doubtful case to determine whether Congress intended to reach it. The same consideration might help in determining whether in the absence of Congressional action it would be permissible for the state to exert its power on the subject matter, even though in so doing it to some degree affected interstate commerce. But even if appellee's activity be local and though it may not be regarded as commerce, it may still, whatever its nature, be reached by Congress if it exerts a substantial economic effect on interstate commerce, and this irrespective of whether such effect is what might at some earlier time have been defined as "direct" or "indirect."

The parties have stipulated a summary of the economics of the wheat industry. Commerce among the states in wheat is large and important. Although wheat is raised in every state but one, production in most states is not equal to consumption. Sixteen states on average have had a surplus of wheat above their own requirements for feed, seed, and food. Thirty-two states and the District of Columbia, where production has been below consumption, have looked to these surplus-producing states for their supply as well as for wheat for export and carry-over.

The wheat industry has been a problem industry for some years. Largely as a result of increased foreign production and import restrictions, annual exports of wheat and flour from the United States during the ten-year period ending in 1940 averaged less than 10 per cent of total production, while during the 1920's they averaged more than 25 per cent. The decline in the export trade has left a large surplus in production which, in connection with an abnormally large supply of wheat and other grains in recent years, caused congestion in a number of markets; tied up railroad cars; and caused elevators in some instances to turn away grains, and railroads to institute embargoes to prevent further congestion.

Many countries, both importing and exporting, have sought to modify the impact of the world market conditions on their own economy. Importing countries have taken measures to stimulate production and self-sufficiency. The four large exporting countries of Argentina, Australia, Canada, and the United States have all undertaken various programs for the relief of growers. Such measures have been designed, in part at least, to protect the domestic price received by producers. Such plans have generally evolved towards control by the central government.

In the absence of regulation, the price of wheat in the United States would be much affected by world conditions. During 1941, producers who coöperated with the Agricultural Adjustment program received an average price on the farm of about $1.16 a bushel, as compared with the world market price of 40 cents a bushel.

Differences in farming conditions, however, make these benefits mean different things to different wheat growers. There are several large areas of specialization in wheat, and the concentration on this crop reaches 27 per cent of the crop land, and the average harvest runs as high as 155 acres. Except for some use of wheat as stock feed and for seed, the practice is to sell the crop for cash. Wheat from such areas constitutes the bulk of the interstate commerce therein.

On the other hand, in some New England states less than one per cent of the crop land is devoted to wheat, and the average harvest is less than five acres per farm. In 1940 the average percentage of the total wheat production that was sold in each state, as measured by value, ranged from 29 per cent thereof in Wisconsin to 90 per cent in Washington. Except in regions of large-scale production, wheat is usually grown in rotation with other crops; for a nurse crop for grass seeding; and as a cover crop to prevent soil erosion and leaching. Some is sold, some kept for seed, and a percentage of the total production much larger than in areas of specialization is consumed on the farm and grown for such purpose. Such farmers, while growing some wheat, may even find the balance of their interest on the consumer's side.

The effect of consumption of home-grown wheat on interstate commerce is due to the fact that it constitutes the most variable factor in the disappearance of the wheat crop. Consumption on the farm where grown appears to vary in an amount greater than 20 per cent of average production. The total amount of wheat consumed as food varies but relatively little, and use as seed is relatively constant.

The maintenance by government regulation of a price for wheat undoubtedly can be accomplished as effectively by sustaining or increasing the demand as by limiting the supply. The effect of the statute before us is to restrict the amount which may be produced for market and the extent as well to which one may forestall resort to the market by producing to meet his own needs. That appellee's own contribution to the demand for wheat may be trivial by itself is not enough to remove him from the scope of federal regulation where, as here, his contribution, taken together with that of many others similarly situated, is far from trivial. . . .

It is well established by decisions of this Court that the power to regulate commerce includes the power to regulate the prices at which commodities in that commerce are dealt in and practices affecting such prices. One of the primary purposes of the Act in question was to increase the market price of wheat, and to that end to limit the volume thereof that could affect the market. It can hardly be denied that a factor of such volume and variability as home-consumed wheat would have a substantial influence on price and market conditions. This may arise because being in marketable condition such wheat overhangs the market and, if induced by rising prices, tends to flow into the market and check price increases. But if we assume that it is never marketed, it supplies a need of the man who grew it which would otherwise be reflected by purchases in the open market. Home-grown wheat in this sense competes with wheat in commerce. The stimulation of commerce is a use of the regulatory function quite as definitely as prohibitions or restrictions thereon. This record leaves us in no doubt that Congress may properly have considered that wheat consumed on the farm where grown, if wholly outside the scheme of regulation, would have a substantial effect in defeating and obstructing its purpose to stimulate trade therein at increased prices.

It is said, however, that this Act, forcing some farmers into the market to buy what they could provide for themselves, is an unfair promotion of the markets and prices of specializing wheat growers. It is of the essence of regulation that it lays a restraining hand on the self-interest of the regulated and that advantages from the regulation commonly fall to others. The conflicts of economic interest between the regulated and those who advantage by it are wisely left under our system to resolution by the Congress under its more flexible and responsible legislative process. Such conflicts rarely lend themselves to judicial determination. And with the wisdom, workability, or fairness, of the plan of regulation we have nothing to do. . . .

Steward Machine Company *v.* Davis

The Butler *decision of 1936 also proved to be only a temporary diversion from the Court's usual tolerant attitude toward federal taxing and spending powers. As part of its general acceptance of New Deal legislation, the Court sustained the taxing provisions of the 1935 Social Security Act in the spring of 1937. The case below concerned a federal tax on employers to provide contributions for unemployment compensation. If employers paid a similar tax for a satisfactory state compensation plan, however, they were given credit against federal payments. The act was challenged as an invasion of state powers and as an attempt to coerce the states into passage of certain legislation. In the companion case of* Helvering *v.* Davis, *the Court approved the social security tax for old-age benefits. It concluded that Congress might determine proper subjects for taxing and spending for general welfare purposes. Both cases were decided by a narrow 5–4 majority.*

Justice Cardozo delivered the opinion of the Court.

The validity of the tax imposed by the Social Security Act on employers of eight or more is here to be determined. . . .

The Social Security Act . . . is divided into eleven separate titles, of

301 U.S. 548 (1937)

which only Titles IX and III are so related to this case as to stand in need of summary.

The caption of Title IX is "Tax on Employers of Eight or More." Every employer (with stated exceptions) is to pay for each calendar year "an excise tax, with respect to having individuals in his employ," the tax to be measured by prescribed percentages of the total wages payable by the employer during the calendar year with respect to such employment. . . . One is not, however, an "employer" within the meaning of the act unless he employs eight persons or more. . . . There are also other limitations of minor importance. The term "employment" too has its special definition, excluding agricultural labor, domestic service in a private home and some other smaller classes. . . . The tax begins with the year 1936, and is payable for the first time on January 31, 1937. During the calendar year 1936 the rate is to be one per cent, during 1937 two per cent, and three per cent thereafter. The proceeds, when collected, go into the Treasury of the United States like internal-revenue collections generally. . . . They are not earmarked in any way. In certain circumstances, however, credits are allowable. . . . If the taxpayer has made contributions to an unemployment fund under a state law, he may credit such contributions against the federal tax, provided, however, that the total credit allowed to any taxpayer shall not exceed 90 per centum of the tax against which it is credited, and provided also that the state law shall have been certified to the Secretary of the Treasury by the Social Security Board as satisfying certain minimum criteria. . . . Some of the conditions thus attached to the allowance of a credit are designed to give assurance that the state unemployment compensation law shall be one in substance as well as name. Others are designed to give assurance that the contributions shall be protected against loss after payment to the state. To this last end there are provisions that before a state law shall have the approval of the Board it must direct that the contributions to the state fund be paid over immediately to the Secretary of the Treasury to the credit of the "Unemployment Trust Fund." . . . For the moment it is enough to say that the Fund is to be held by the Secretary of the Treasury, who is to invest in government securities any portion not required in his judgment to meet current withdrawals. He is authorized and directed to pay out of the Fund to any competent state agency such sums as it may duly requisition from the amount standing to its credit. . . .

Title III, which is also challenged as invalid, has the caption "Grants to States for Unemployment Compensation Administration." Under this title, certain sums of money are "authorized to be appropriated" for the purpose of assisting the states in the administration of their unemployment compensation laws, the maximum for the fiscal year ending June 30, 1936 to be $4,000,000, and $49,000,000 for each fiscal year thereafter. . . . No present appropriation is made to the extent of a single dollar. All that the title does is to authorize future appropriations. . . . The appropriations when made were not specifically out of the proceeds of the employment tax, but out of any moneys in the Treasury. Other sections of the title . . . are designed to give assurance to the Federal Government that the moneys granted by it will not be expended for purposes alien to the grant, and will be used in the administration of genuine unemployment compensation laws.

The assault on the statute proceeds on an extended front. Its assailants take the ground that the tax is not an excise; that it is not uniform throughout the United States as excises are required to be; that its exceptions are so many and arbitrary as to violate the Fifth Amendment; that its purpose was not revenue, but an unlawful invasion of the reserved powers of the states; and that the states in submitting to it have yielded to coercion and have abandoned governmental functions which they are not permitted to surrender.

The objections will be considered seriatim with such further explanation as may be necessary to make their meaning clear.

First. The tax, which is described in the statute as an excise, is laid with uniformity throughout the United States as a duty, an impost or an excise upon the relation of employment.

1. We are told that the relation of employment is one so essential to the pursuit of happiness that it may not be burdened with a tax. Appeal is made to history. From the precedents of colonial days we are supplied with illustrations of excises common in the colonies. They are said to have been bound up with the enjoyment of particular commodities. Appeal is also made to principle or the analysis of concepts. An excise, we are told, imports a tax upon a privilege; employment, it is said, is a right, not a privilege, from which it follows that employment is not subject to an excise. Neither the one appeal nor the other leads to the desired goal.

As to the argument from history: Doubtless there were many excises in colonial days and later that were associated, more or less intimately, with the enjoyment or the use of property. This would not prove, even if no others were then known, that the forms then accepted were not subject to enlargement. . . .

But in truth other excises *were* known, and known since early times. . . .

The historical prop failing, the prop or fancied prop of principle remains. We learn that employment for lawful gain is a "natural" or "inherent" or "inalienable" right, and not a "privilege" at all. But natural rights, so called, are as much subject to taxation as rights of less importance. An excise is not limited to vocations or activities that may be prohibited altogether. It is not limited to those that are the outcome of a franchise. It extends to vocations or activities pursued as of common right. What the individual does in the operation of a business is amenable to taxation just as much as what he owns, at all events if the classification is not tyrannical or arbitrary. "Business is as legitimate an object of the taxing powers as property." . . .

The statute books of the states are strewn with illustrations of taxes laid on occupations pursued of common right. We find no basis for a holding that the power in that regard which belongs by accepted practice to the legislatures of the states, has been denied by the Constitution to the Congress of the nation.

2. The tax being an excise, its imposition must conform to the canon of uniformity. There has been no departure from this requirement. According to the settled doctrine the uniformity exacted is geographical, not intrinsic. . . .

Second. The excise is not invalid under the provisions of the Fifth Amendment by force of its exemptions.

The statute does not apply, as we have seen, to employers of less than eight. It does not apply to agricultural labor, or domestic service in a private home or to some other classes of less importance. Petitioner contends that the effect of these restrictions is an arbitrary discrimination vitiating the tax.

The Fifth Amendment unlike the Fourteenth has no equal protection clause. . . . But even the states, though subject to such a clause, are not confined to a formula of rigid uniformity in framing measures of taxation. . . . They may tax some kinds of property at one rate, and others at another, and exempt others altogether. . . . They may lay an excise on the operations of a particular kind of business, and exempt some other kind of business closely akin thereto. . . . If this latitude of judgment is lawful for the states, it is lawful, *a fortiori,* in legislation by the Congress, which is subject to restraints less narrow and confining. . . .

The classifications and exemptions directed by the statute now in controversy have support in considerations of policy and practical convenience that cannot be condemned as arbitrary. The classifications and exemptions would therefore be upheld if they had been adopted by a state and the provisions of the Fourteenth Amendment were invoked to annul them. . . . The act of Congress is therefore valid, so far at least as its system of exemptions is concerned, and this though we assume that discrimination, if gross enough, is equivalent to confiscation and subject under the Fifth Amendment to challenge and annulment.

Third. The excise is not void as involving the coercion of the States in contravention of the Tenth Amendment or of restrictions implicit in our federal form of government.

The proceeds of the excise when collected are paid into the Treasury at Washington, and thereafter are subject to appropriation like public moneys generally. . . . No presumption can be indulged that they will be misapplied or wasted. Even if they were collected in the hope or expectation that some other and collateral good would be furthered as an incident, that without more would not make the act invalid. . . . This indeed is hardly questioned. The case for the petitioner is built on the contention that here an ulterior aim is wrought into the very structure of the act, and what is even more important that the aim is not only ulterior, but essentially unlawful. In particular, the 90 per cent credit is relied upon as supporting that conclusion. But before the statute succumbs to an assault upon these lines, two propositions must be made out by the assailant. . . . There must be a showing in the first place that separated from the credit the revenue provisions are incapable of standing by themselves. There must be a showing in the second place that the tax and the credit in combination are weapons of coercion, destroying or impairing the autonomy of the states. The truth of each proposition being essential to the success of the assault, we pass for convenience to a consideration of the second, without pausing to inquire whether there has been a demonstration of the first.

To draw the line intelligently between duress and inducement there is need to remind ourselves of facts as to the problem of unemployment that are now matters of common knowledge. *West Coast Hotel Co.* v. *Parrish,* 300 U.S. 379. The relevant statistics are gathered in the brief of counsel for the Government. Of the many available figures a few only will be mentioned. During the years 1929 to 1936, when the country was passing through a cyclical depression, the number of the unemployed mounted to unprecedented heights. Often the average was more than 10 million; at times a peak was attained of 16 million or more. Disaster to the breadwinner meant disaster to dependents. Accordingly the roll of the unemployed, itself formidable enough, was only a partial roll of the destitute or needy. The fact developed quickly that the states were unable to give the requisite relief. The problem had become national in area and dimensions. There was need of help from the nation if the people were not to starve. It is too late today for the argument to be heard with tolerance that in a crisis so extreme the use of the moneys of the nation to relieve the unemployed and their dependents is a use for any purpose narrower than the promotion of the general welfare. . . .

In the presence of this urgent need for some remedial expedient, the question is to be answered whether the expedient adopted has overlept the bounds of power. The assailants of the statute say that its dominant end and aim is to drive the state legislatures under the whip of economic pressure into the enactment of unemployment compensation laws at the bidding of the central government. Supporters of the statute say that its operation is not constraint, but the creation of a larger freedom, the states and the nation joining in a coöperative endeavor to avert a common evil. . . .

The Social Security Act is an attempt to find a method by which all these public agencies may work together to a common end. Every dollar of the new taxes will continue in all likelihood to be used and needed by the nation as long as states are unwilling, whether through timidity or for other motives, to do what can be done at home. At least the inference is permissible that Congress so believed, though retaining undiminished freedom to spend the money as it pleased. On the other hand fulfilment of the home duty will be lightened and encouraged by crediting the tax-payer upon his account with the Treasury of the nation to the extent that his contributions under the laws of the locality have simplified or diminished the problem of relief and the probable demand upon the resources of the fisc. Duplicated taxes, or burdens that approach them, are recognized hardships that government, state or national, may properly avoid. . . . If Congress believed that the general welfare would better be promoted by relief through local units than by the system then in vogue, the coöperating localities ought not in all fairness to pay a second time.

Who then is coerced through the operation of this statute? Not the taxpayer. He pays in fulfilment of the mandate of the local legislature. Not the state. Even now she does not offer a suggestion that in passing the unemployment law she was affected by duress. . . . For all that appears she is satisfied with her choice, and would be sorely disappointed if it were now to be annulled. The difficulty with the petitioner's contention is that it confuses motive with coercion. "Every tax is in some measure regulatory. To some extent it interposes an economic impediment to the activity taxed as compared with others not taxed." . . . In like manner every rebate from a tax when conditioned upon conduct is in some measure a temptation. But to hold that motive or temptation is equivalent to coercion is to plunge the law in endless difficulties. The outcome of such a doctrine is the acceptance of a philosophical determinism by which choice becomes impossible. Till now the law has been guided by a robust common sense which assumes the freedom of the will as a working hypothesis in the solution of its problems. The wisdom of the hypothesis has illustration in this case. Nothing in the case suggests the exertion of a power akin to undue influence, if we assume that such a concept can ever be applied with fitness to the relations between state and nation. Even on that assumption the location of the point at which pressure turns into compulsion, and ceases to be inducement, would be a question of degree, — at times, perhaps, of fact. The point had not been reached when Alabama made her choice. We cannot say that she was acting, not of her unfettered will, but under the strain of a persuasion equivalent to undue influence, when she chose to have relief administered under laws of her own making, by agents of her own selection, instead of under federal laws, administered by federal officers, with all the ensuing evils, at least to many minds, of federal patronage and power. There would be a strange irony, indeed, if her choice were now to be annulled on the basis of an assumed duress in the enactment of a statute which her courts have accepted as a true expression of her will. . . . We think the choice must stand.

In ruling as we do, we leave many questions open. We do not say that a tax is valid, when imposed by act of Congress, if it is laid upon the condition that a state may escape its operation through the adoption of a statute unrelated in subject matter to activities fairly within the scope of national policy and power. No such question is before us. In the tender of this credit Congress does not intrude upon fields foreign to its function. The purpose of its intervention, as we have shown, is to safeguard its own treasury and as an incident to that protection to place the states upon a footing of equal opportunity. Drains upon its own resources are to be checked; obstructions to the freedom of the states are to be leveled. It is one thing to impose a tax dependent upon the conduct of the taxpayers, or of the state in which they live, where the conduct to be stimulated or discouraged is unrelated to the fiscal need subserved by the tax in its normal operation, or to any other end legitimately national. . . . It is quite another thing to say that a tax will be abated upon the doing of an act that will satisfy the fiscal need, the tax and the alternative being approximate equivalents. In such circumstances, if in no others, inducement or persuasion does not go beyond the bounds of power. We do not fix the outermost line. Enough for present purposes that wherever the line may be, this statute is within it. Definition more precise must abide the wisdom of the future. . . .

Ferguson *v.* Skrupa

After 1937 the Court regularly turned aside challenges to either federal or state regulation of business and the economy. Occasionally, there were challenges reminiscent of an earlier age which had viewed such legislation as a deprivation of due process or freedom of contract. In 1949 the Court turned down a labor union's argument, ironically based on the Lochner *and* Adair *decisions, that a North Carolina law and a Nebraska constitutional amendment forbidding the closed shop, violated freedom of speech, equal protection of the laws, and due process of law. (Lincoln Federal Labor Union v. Northwestern Iron & Metal Co., 335 U.S. 525). In the more recent case below, a Kansas statute making it a misdemeanor for persons to engage "in the business of debt adjusting" except as an incident to the "lawful practice of law," was challenged as a violation of the due process and equal protection clauses of the Fourteenth Amendment. Justice Black's opinion offers a useful historical survey of the devolution of the substantive due process doctrine.*

Justice Black delivered the opinion of the Court.

The complaint . . . alleged that Skrupa was engaged in the business of "debt adjusting" as defined by the statute, that his business was a "useful and desirable" one, that his business activities were not "inherently immoral or dangerous" or in any way contrary to the public welfare, and that therefore the business could not be "absolutely prohibited" by Kansas. The three-judge court heard evidence by Skrupa tending to show the usefulness and desirability of his business and . . . concluded . . . that the Act was prohibitory, not regulatory, but that even if construed in part as regulatory it was an unreasonable regulation of a "lawful business," which the court held amounted to a violation of the Due Process Clause of the Fourteenth Amendment. The court accordingly enjoined enforcement of the statute.

The only case discussed by the court below as support for its invalidation of the statute was *Commonwealth* v. *Stone* . . . (1959), in which the Superior Court of Pennsylvania struck down a statute almost identical to the Kansas act involved here. . . . In doing so, the Pennsylvania court

372 U.S. 726 (1963)

relied heavily on *Adams* v. *Tanner*, 244 U.S. 590 (1917), which held that the Due Process Clause forbids a State to prohibit a business which is "useful" and not "inherently immoral or dangerous to public welfare."

Both the District Court in the present case and the Pennsylvania court in *Stone* adopted the philosophy of *Adams* v. *Tanner*, and cases like it, that it is the province of courts to draw on their own views as to the morality, legitimacy, and usefulness of a particular business in order to decide whether a statute bears too heavily upon that business and by so doing violates due process. Under the system of government created by our Constitution, it is up to legislatures, not courts, to decide on the wisdom and utility of legislation. There was a time when the Due Process Clause was used by this Court to strike down laws which were thought unreasonable, that is, unwise or incompatible with some particular economic or social philosophy. In this manner the Due Process Clause was used, for example, to nullify laws prescribing maximum hours for work in bakeries, *Lochner* v. *New York*, 198 U.S. 45 (1905), outlawing "yellow dog" contracts, *Coppage v. Kansas*, 236 U.S. 1 (1915), setting minimum wages for women, *Adkins* v. *Children's Hospital*, 261 U.S. 525 (1923), and fixing the weight of loaves of bread, *Jay Burns Baking Co.* v. *Bryan*, 264 U.S. 504 (1924). This intrusion by the judiciary into the realm of legislative value judgments was strongly objected to at the time, particularly by Mr. Justice Holmes and Mr. Justice Brandeis. . . .

The doctrine that prevailed in *Lochner, Coppage, Adkins, Burns,* and like cases — that due process authorizes courts to hold laws unconstitutional when they believe the legislature has acted unwisely — has long since been discarded. We have returned to the original constitutional proposition that courts do not substitute their social and economic beliefs for the judgment of legislative bodies, who are elected to pass laws. As this Court stated in a unanimous opinion in 1941, "We are not concerned . . . with the wisdom, need, or appropriateness of the legislation." Legislative bodies have broad scope to experiment with economic problems, and this Court does not sit to "subject the State to an intolerable supervision hostile to the basic principles of our Government and wholly beyond the protection which the general clause of the Fourteenth Amendment was intended to secure." It is now settled that States "have power to legislate against what are found to be injurious practices in their internal commercial and business affairs, so long as their laws do not run afoul of some specific federal constitutional prohibition, or of some valid federal law."

In the face of our abandonment of the use of the "vague contours" of the Due Process Clause to nullify laws which a majority of the Court believed to be economically unwise, reliance on *Adams* v. *Tanner* is as mistaken as would be adherence to *Adkins* v. *Children's Hospital*, overruled by *West Coast Hotel Co.* v. *Parrish*, 300 U.S. 379 (1937). . . . We conclude that the Kansas Legislature was free to decide for itself that legislation was needed to deal with the business of debt adjusting. Unquestionably, there are arguments showing that the business of debt adjusting has social utility, but such arguments are properly addressed to the legislature, not to us. We refuse to sit as a "superlegislature to weigh the wisdom of legislation," and we emphatically refuse to go back to the time when courts used the Due Process Clause "to strike down state laws, regulatory of business and industrial conditions, because they may be unwise, improvident, or out of harmony with a particular school of thought." Nor are we able or willing to draw lines by calling a law "prohibitory" or "regulatory." Whether the legislature takes for its textbook Adam Smith, Herbert Spencer, Lord Keynes, or some other is no concern of ours. The Kansas debt adjusting statute may be wise or unwise. But relief, if any be needed, lies not with us but with the body constituted to pass laws for the State of Kansas.

Nor is the statute's exception of lawyers a denial of equal protection of the laws to nonlawyers. Statutes create many classifications which do not deny equal protection; it is only "invidious discrimination" which offends the Constitution. The business of debt adjusting gives rise to a relationship of trust in which the debt adjuster will, in a situation of insolvency, be marshalling assets in the manner of a proceeding in bankruptcy. The debt adjuster's client may need advice as to the legality of the various claims against him, remedies existing under state laws governing debtor-creditor relationships, or provisions of the Bankruptcy Act — advice which a nonlawyer cannot lawfully give him. If the State of Kansas wants to limit debt adjusting to lawyers, the Equal Protection Clause does not forbid it. We also find no merit in the contention that the Fourteenth Amendment is violated by the failure of the Kansas statute's title to be as specific as appellee thinks it ought to be under the Kansas Constitution.

Katzenbach *v.* McClung

This was a companion case to Heart of Atlanta Motel *v.* United States *(see Chap. VIII, Sec. D.), sustaining the public accommodations sections of the 1964 Civil Rights Act. Both cases involved the use of the federal commerce power to secure equal access to public accommodations. The* Heart of Atlanta *case was obvious for the motel was adjacent to interstate highways and 75% of its customers were from out-of-state. But* McClung *involved a family-owned restaurant engaged in essentially local business. The federal government nevertheless argued that it had a substantial relation to interstate commerce for nearly half of its food supplies came from outside the state. Civil rights considerations aside, in the* McClung *case the Court continued to allow Congress broad latitude in its determination of what subjects were proper for regulation.*

Justice Clark delivered the opinion of the Court.

Ollie's Barbecue is a family-owned restaurant in Birmingham, Alabama, specializing in barbecued meats and homemade pies, with a seating capacity of 220 customers. It is located on a state highway 11 blocks from an interstate one and a somewhat greater distance from railroad and bus stations. The restaurant caters to a family and white-collar trade with a take-out service for Negroes. It employs 36 persons, two-thirds of whom are Negroes.

In the 12 months preceding the passage of the Act, the restaurant purchased locally approximately $150,000 worth of food, $69,683 or 46% of which was meat that it bought from a local supplier who had procured it from outside the State. The District Court expressly found that a substantial portion of the food served in the restaurant had moved in interstate commerce. The restaurant has refused to serve Negroes in its dining accommodations since its original opening in 1927, and since July 2, 1964, it has been operating in violation of the Act. The court below concluded that if it were required to serve Negroes it would lose a substantial amount of business.

On the merits, the District Court held that the Act could not be applied under the Fourteenth Amendment because it was conceded that the State of Alabama was not involved in the refusal of the restaurant to serve Negroes. It was also admitted that the Thirteenth Amendment was author-

379 U.S. 294 (1964)

ity neither for validating nor for invalidating the Act. As to the Commerce Clause, the court found that it was "an express grant of power to Congress to regulate interstate commerce, which consists of the movement of persons, goods or information from one state to another"; and it found that the clause was also a grant of power "to regulate intrastate activities, but only to the extent that action on its part is necessary or appropriate to the effective execution of its expressly granted power to regulate interstate commerce." There must be, it said, a close and substantial relation between local activities and interstate commerce which requires control of the former in the protection of the latter. The court concluded, however, that the Congress, rather than finding facts sufficient to meet this rule, had legislated a conclusive presumption that a restaurant affects interstate commerce if it serves or offers to serve interstate travelers or if a substantial portion of the food which it serves has moved in commerce. This, the court held, it could not do because there was no demonstrable connection between food purchased in interstate commerce and sold in a restaurant and the conclusion of Congress that discrimination in the restaurant would affect that commerce.

The basic holding in *Heart of Atlanta Motel* . . . answers many of the contentions made by the appellees. There we outlined the overall purpose and operational plan of Title II and found it a valid exercise of the power to regulate interstate commerce insofar as it requires hotels and motels to serve transients without regard to their race or color. In this case we consider its application to restaurants which serve food a substantial portion of which has moved in commerce.

3. *The Act As Applied.* . . .

The Government makes no contention that the discrimination at the restaurant was supported by the State of Alabama. There is no claim that interstate travelers frequented the restaurant. The sole question, therefore, narrows down to whether Title II, as applied to a restaurant receiving about $70,000 worth of food which has moved in commerce, is a valid exercise of the power of Congress. The Government has contended that Congress had ample basis upon which to find that racial discrimination at restaurants which receive from out of state a substantial portion of the food served does, in fact, impose commercial burdens of national magnitude upon interstate commerce. The appellees' major argument is directed to this premise. They urge that no such basis existed. It is to that question that we now turn. . . .

5. *The Power of Congress to Regulate Local Activities.* . . .

The appellees contend that Congress has arbitrarily created a conclusive presumption that all restaurants meeting the criteria set out in the

Act "affect commerce." Stated another way, they object to the omission of a provision for a case-by-case determination — judicial or administrative — that racial discrimination in a particular restaurant affects commerce.

But Congress' action in framing this Act was not unprecedented. In *United States* v. *Darby,* 312 U.S. 100 (1941), this Court held constitutional the Fair Labor Standards Act of 1938. There Congress determined that the payment of substandard wages to employees engaged in the production of goods for commerce, while not itself commerce, so inhibited it as to be subject to federal regulation. The appellees in that case argued, as do the appellees here, that the Act was invalid because it included no provision for an independent inquiry regarding the effect on commerce of substandard wages in a particular business. . . . But the Court rejected the argument. . . .

Here, as there, Congress has determined for itself that refusals of service to Negroes have imposed burdens both upon the interstate flow of food and upon the movement of products generally. Of course, the mere fact that Congress has said when particular activity shall be deemed to affect commerce does not preclude further examination by this Court. But where we find that the legislators, in light of the facts and testimony before them, have a rational basis for finding a chosen regulatory scheme necessary to the protection of commerce, our investigation is at an end. The only remaining question — one answered in the affirmative by the court below — is whether the particular restaurant either serves or offers to serve interstate travelers or serves food a substantial portion of which has moved in interstate commerce. . . .

Confronted as we are with the facts laid before Congress, we must conclude that it had a rational basis for finding that racial discrimination in restaurants had a direct and adverse effect on the free flow of interstate commerce. Insofar as the sections of the Act here relevant are concerned, §§ 201 (b) (2) and (c), Congress prohibited discrimination only in those establishments having a close tie to interstate commerce, *i.e.,* those, like the McClungs', serving food that has come from out of the State. We think in so doing that Congress acted well within its power to protect and foster commerce in extending the coverage of Title II only to those restaurants offering to serve interstate travelers or serving food, a substantial portion of which has moved in interstate commerce.

The absence of direct evidence connecting discriminatory restaurant service with the flow of interstate food, a factor on which the appellees place much reliance, is not, given the evidence as to the effect of such practices on other aspects of commerce, a crucial matter.

The power of Congress in this field is broad and sweeping; where it keeps within its sphere and violates no express constitutional limitation it has been the rule of this Court, going back almost to the founding days of the Republic, not to interfere. The Civil Rights Act of 1964, as here applied, we find to be plainly appropriate in the resolution of what the Congress found to be a national commercial problem of the first magnitude. We find it in no violation of any express limitations of the Constitution and we therefore declare it valid.

The judgment is therefore

Reversed.

VIII

Authority and Liberty: Modern Constitutional Tensions

⋆ A ⋆

The First Amendment: Freedom of Expression, Association, and Assembly

De Jonge *v.* Oregon

There were significant new developments in civil liberties as well as economic regulation in 1937. In the case below, the Supreme Court overruled a conviction for violation of a state syndicalism law. De Jonge, a Communist, had participated in a meeting called by the party. Though the meeting was peaceful, and no unlawful acts were advocated, De Jonge's membership in a group allegedly advocating syndicalism was considered adequate for conviction. The Supreme Court unanimously reversed the verdict, treating his party membership as irrelevant. Whatever the objectives of the party, Chief Justice Hughes said, De Jonge still retained his "personal right of free speech" and his right to participate in a peaceful assembly. Hughes noted that the indictment did not specify that De Jonge's party membership constituted a crime, but he nevertheless had been convicted for this reason. "Conviction upon a charge not made," Hughes commented, "would be sheer denial of due process."

Chief Justice Hughes delivered the opinion of the Court.

It thus appears that, while defendant was a member of the Communist Party, he was not indicted for participating in its organization, or for joining it, or for soliciting members or for distributing its literature. He was not charged with teaching or advocating criminal syndicalism or sabotage or any unlawful acts, either at the meeting or elsewhere. He was accordingly deprived of the benefit of evidence as to the orderly and lawful conduct of the meeting and that it was not called or used for the advocacy of criminal syndicalism or sabotage or any unlawful action. His sole offense as charged, and for which he was convicted and

299 U.S. 353 (1937)

sentenced to imprisonment for seven years, was that he had assisted in the conduct of a public meeting, albeit otherwise lawful, which was held under the auspices of the Communist Party.

The broad reach of the statute as thus applied is plain. While defendant was a member of the Communist Party, that membership was not necessary to conviction on such a charge. A like fate might have attended any speaker, although not a member, who "assisted in the conduct" of the meeting. However innocuous the object of the meeting, however lawful the subjects and tenor of the addresses, however reasonable and timely the discussion, all those assisting in the conduct of the meeting would be subject to imprisonment as felons if the meeting were held by the Communist Party. This manifest result was brought out sharply at this bar by the concessions which the Attorney General made, and could not avoid, in the light of the decision of the state court. Thus if the Communist Party had called a public meeting in Portland to discuss the tariff, or the foreign policy of the Government, or taxation, or relief, or candidacies for the offices of President, members of Congress, Governor, or state legislators, every speaker who assisted in the conduct of the meeting would be equally guilty with the defendant in this case, upon the charge as here defined and sustained. The list of illustrations might be indefinitely extended to every variety of meetings under the auspices of the Communist Party although held for the discussion of political issues or to adopt protests and pass resolutions of an entirely innocent and proper character.

While the States are entitled to protect themselves from the abuse of the privileges of our institutions through an attempted substitution of force and violence in the place of peaceful political action in order to effect revolutionary changes in government, none of our decisions go to the length of sustaining such a curtailment of the right of free speech and assembly as the Oregon statute demands in its present application. . . .

Freedom of speech and of the press are fundamental rights which are safeguarded by the due process clause of the Fourteenth Amendment of the Federal Constitution. . . . The right of peaceable assembly is a right cognate to those of free speech and free press and is equally fundamental. As this Court said in *United States* v. *Cruikshank*, 92 U.S. 542, 552: "The very idea of a government, republican in form, implies a right on the part of its citizens to meet peaceably for consultation in respect to public affairs and to petition for a redress of grievances." The First Amendment of the Federal Constitution expressly guarantees that right against abridgment by Congress. But explicit mention there does not argue exclusion elsewhere. For the right is one that cannot be denied without violating those fundamental principles of liberty and justice which lie at the base of all civil and political institutions, — principles which the Fourteenth Amendment embodies in the general terms of its due process clause. . . .

These rights may be abused by using speech or press or assembly in order to incite to violence and crime. The people through their legislatures may protect themselves against that abuse. But the legislative intervention can find constitutional justification only by dealing with the abuse. The rights themselves must not be curtailed. The greater the importance of safeguarding the community from incitements to the overthrow of our institutions by force and violence, the more imperative is the need to preserve inviolate the constitutional rights of free speech, free press and free assembly in order to maintain the opportunity for free political discussion, to the end that government may be responsive to the will of the people and that changes, if desired, may be obtained by peaceful means. Therein lies the security of the Republic, the very foundation of constitutional government.

It follows from these considerations that, consistently with the Federal Constitution, peaceable assembly for lawful discussion cannot be made a crime. The holding of meetings for peaceable political action cannot be proscribed. Those who assist in the conduct of such meetings cannot be branded as criminals on that score. The question, if the rights of free speech and peaceable assembly are to be preserved, is not as to the auspices under which the meeting is held but as to its purpose; not as to the relations of the speakers, but whether their utterances transcend the bounds of the freedom of speech which the Constitution protects. If the persons assembling have committed crimes elsewhere, if they have formed or are engaged in a conspiracy against the public peace and order, they may be prosecuted for their conspiracy or other violation of valid laws. But it is a different matter when the State, instead of prosecuting them for such offenses, seizes upon mere participation in a peaceable assembly and a lawful public discussion as the basis for a criminal charge.

We are not called upon to review the findings of the state court as to the objectives of the Communist Party. Notwithstanding those objectives, the defendant still enjoyed his personal right of free speech and to take part in a peaceable assembly having a lawful purpose, although called by that Party. The defendant was none the less entitled to discuss the public issues of the day and thus in a lawful manner, without incitement to violence or crime, to seek redress of alleged grievances. That was of the essence of his guaranteed personal liberty.

We hold that the Oregon statute as applied to the particular charge as defined by the state court is repugnant to the due process clause of the Fourteenth Amendment. . . .

Dennis *v.* United States

Throughout the 1930's and 1940's, the Court steadfastly resisted attempts to secure convictions on the basis of guilt by association. In a number of cases, the Court treated membership in the Communist Party as irrelevant to individual guilt. Holmes's clear and present danger concept generally received the liberal construction he had intended, and sometimes a narrow majority was able to advance an even more absolutist protection for free speech. The pressures and burdens of the Cold War, however, were soon felt in the high court. In the Dennis *case, the government had secured convictions of eleven top Communist Party leaders, after a lengthy and acrimonious district court trial. The convictions were based upon the 1940 Smith Act, making it a crime to teach or advocate the overthrow of the government by force. It also was unlawful to belong to any organization advocating such doctrine. Chief Justice Vinson's majority opinion sustaining the convictions redefined the clear and present danger test to one of clear and "probable" danger. Black and Douglas dissented, finding the law and convictions unwarranted invasions of free speech.*

Chief Justice Vinson delivered the opinion of the Court.

I.

It will be helpful in clarifying the issues to treat . . . the contention that the trial judge improperly interpreted the statute by charging that the statute required an unlawful intent before the jury could convict. . . .

The structure and purpose of the statute demand the inclusion of intent as an element of the crime. Congress was concerned with those who advocate and organize for the overthrow of the Government. Certainly those who recruit and combine for the purpose of advocating overthrow intend to bring about that overthrow. We hold that the statute requires as an essential element of the crime proof of the intent of those who are charged with its violation to overthrow the Government by force and violence. . . .

341 U.S. 494 (1951)

II.

The obvious purpose of the statute is to protect existing Government, not from change by peaceable, lawful and constitutional means, but from change by violence, revolution and terrorism. That it is within the *power* of the Congress to protect the Government of the United States from armed rebellion is a proposition which requires little discussion. Whatever theoretical merit there may be to the argument that there is a "right" to rebellion against dictatorial governments is without force where the existing structure of the government provides for peaceful and orderly change. We reject any principle of governmental helplessness in the face of preparation for revolution, which principle, carried to its logical conclusion, must lead to anarchy. No one could conceive that it is not within the power of Congress to prohibit acts intended to overthrow the Government by force and violence. The question with which we are concerned here is not whether Congress has such *power,* but whether the *means* which it has employed conflict with the First and Fifth Amendments to the Constitution.

One of the bases for the contention that the means which Congress has employed are invalid takes the form of an attack on the face of the statute on the grounds that by its terms it prohibits academic discussion of the merits of Marxism-Leninism, that it stifles ideas and is contrary to all concepts of a free speech and a free press. Although we do not agree that the language itself has that significance, we must bear in mind that it is the duty of the federal courts to interpret federal legislation in a manner not inconsistent with the demands of the Constitution. . . . This is a federal statute which we must interpret as well as judge. . . .

The very language of the Smith Act negates the interpretation which petitioners would have us impose on that Act. It is directed at advocacy, not discussion. Thus, the trial judge properly charged the jury that they could not convict if they found that petitioners did "no more than pursue peaceful studies and discussions or teaching and advocacy in the realm of ideas." He further charged that it was not unlawful "to conduct in an American college or university a course explaining the philosophical theories set forth in the books which have been placed in evidence." Such a charge is in strict accord with the statutory language, and illustrates the meaning to be placed on those words. Congress did not intend to eradicate the free discussion of political theories, to destroy the traditional rights of Americans to discuss and evaluate ideas without fear of governmental sanction. Rather Congress was concerned with the very kind of activity in which the evidence showed these petitioners engaged.

III.

But although the statute is not directed at the hypothetical cases which petitioners have conjured, its application in this case has resulted in convictions for the teaching and advocacy of the overthrow of the Government by force and violence, which, even though coupled with the intent to accomplish that overthrow, contains an element of speech. For this reason, we must pay special heed to the demands of the First Amendment marking out the boundaries of speech.

We pointed out in [*American Communication Assn.* v. *Douds* (1950)] that the basis of the First Amendment is the hypothesis that speech can rebut speech, propaganda will answer propaganda, free debate of ideas will result in the wisest governmental policies. It is for this reason that this Court has recognized the inherent value of free discourse. An analysis of the leading cases in this Court which have involved direct limitations on speech, however, will demonstrate that both the majority of the Court and the dissenters in particular cases have recognized that this is not an unlimited, unqualified right, but that the societal value of speech must, on occasion, be subordinated to other values and considerations.

No important case involving free speech was decided by this Court prior to *Schenck* v. *United States,* 249 U.S. 47 (1919). . . . Writing for a unanimous Court, Justice Holmes stated that the "question in every case is whether the words used are used in such circumstances and are of such a nature as to create a clear and present danger that they will bring about the substantive evils that Congress has a right to prevent." . . . The fact is inescapable, too, that the phrase bore no connotation that the danger was to be any threat to the safety of the Republic. The charge was causing and attempting to cause insubordination in the military forces and obstruct recruiting. The objectionable document denounced conscription and its most inciting sentence was, "You must do your share to maintain, support and uphold the rights of the people of this country." . . . Fifteen thousand copies were printed and some circulated. This insubstantial gesture toward insubordination in 1917 during war was held to be a clear and present danger of bringing about the evil of military insubordination.

In several later cases involving convictions under the Criminal Espionage Act, the nub of the evidence . . . [was] held sufficient to meet the "clear and present danger" test enuniciated in *Schenck.* . . . [I]n *American Communications Assn.* v. *Douds* . . . we . . . pointed out that Congress did not intend to punish belief, but rather intended to regulate the conduct of union affairs. We therefore held that any indirect sanction on speech which might arise from the oath requirement did not present a proper case for the "clear and present danger" test, for the regulation was aimed at conduct rather than speech. In discussing the proper measure of evaluation of this kind of legislation, we suggested that the Holmes-Brandeis philosophy insisted that where there was a direct restriction upon speech, a "clear and present danger" that the substantive evil would be caused was necessary before the statute in question could be constitutionally applied. And we stated, "[The First] Amendment requires that one be permitted to believe what he will. It requires that one be permitted to advocate what he will unless there is a clear and present danger that a substantial public evil will result therefrom." . . . But we further suggested that neither Justice Holmes nor Justice Brandeis ever envisioned that a shorthand phrase should be crystallized into a rigid rule to be applied inflexibly without regard to the circumstances of each case. Speech is not an absolute, above and beyond control by the legislature when its judgment, subject to review here, is that certain kinds of speech are so undesirable as to warrant criminal sanction. Nothing is more certain in modern society than the principle that there are no absolutes, that a name, a phrase, a standard has meaning only when associated with the considerations which gave birth to the nomenclature. . . . To those who would paralyze our Government in the face of impending threat by encasing it in a semantic straitjacket we must reply that all concepts are relative.

In this case we are squarely presented with the application of the "clear and present danger" test, and must decide what that phrase imports. We first note that many of the cases in which this Court has reversed convictions by use of this or similar tests have been based on the fact that the interest which the State was attempting to protect was itself too insubstantial to warrant restriction of speech. . . . Overthrow of the Government by force and violence is certainly a substantial enough interest for the Government to limit speech. Indeed, this is the ultimate value of any society, for if a society cannot protect its very structure from armed internal attack, it must follow that no subordinate value can be protected. If, then, this interest may be protected, the literal problem which is presented is what has been meant by the use of the phrase "clear and present danger" of the utterances bringing about the evil within the power of Congress to punish.

Obviously, the words cannot mean that before the Government may act, it must wait until the *putsch* is about to be executed, the plans have been laid and the signal is awaited. If Government is aware that a group aiming at its overthrow is attempting to indoctrinate its members and to commit them to a course whereby they will strike when the leaders feel the circumstances permit, action by the Government is required. The argument that there is no need for Government to concern itself, for Government is strong, it possesses ample powers to put down a rebellion, it may defeat the revolution with ease needs no answer. For that is not the question. Certainly an attempt to overthrow the Government by force, even though doomed from the outset because of inadequate numbers or power of the revolutionists, is a sufficient evil for Congress to prevent. The damage which such attempts create both physically and politically to a nation makes it impossible to measure the validity in terms of the probability of success, or the immediacy of a successful attempt. In the instant case the trial judge charged the jury that they could not convict unless they found that petitioners intended to overthrow the Government "as speedily as circumstances would permit." This does not mean, and could not properly mean, that they would not strike until there was certainty of success. What was meant was that the revolutionists would strike when they thought the time was ripe. We must therefore reject the contention that success or probability of success is the criterion.

The situation with which Justices Holmes and Brandeis were concerned in *Gitlow* was a comparatively isolated event, bearing little relation in their minds to any substantial threat to the safety of the community. . . . They were not confronted with any situation comparable to the instant one — the development of an apparatus designed and dedicated to the overthrow of the Government, in the context of world crisis after crisis.

Chief Judge Learned Hand, writing for the majority below, interpreted the phrase as follows: "In each case [courts] must ask whether the gravity of the 'evil,' discounted by its improbability, justifies such invasion of free speech as is necessary to avoid the danger." . . . We adopt this statement of the rule. As articulated by Chief Judge Hand, it is as succinct and inclusive as any other we might devise at this time. It takes into consideration those factors which we deem relevant, and relates their significances. More we cannot expect from words.

Likewise, we are in accord with the court below, which affirmed the trial court's finding that the requisite danger existed. The mere fact that from the period 1945 to 1948 petitioners' activities did not result in an attempt to overthrow the Government by force and violence is of course no answer to the fact that there was a group that was ready to make the attempt. The formation by petitioners of such a highly organized conspiracy, with rigidly disciplined members subject to call when the leaders, these petitioners, felt that the time had come for action, coupled with the inflammable nature of world conditions, similar uprisings in other countries, and the touch-and-go nature of our relations with countries with whom petitioners were in the very least ideologically attuned, convince us that their convictions were justified on this score. And this analysis disposes of the contention that a conspiracy to advocate, as distinguished from the advocacy itself, cannot be constitutionally restrained, because it comprises only the preparation. It is the existence of the conspiracy which creates the danger. . . . If the ingredients of the reaction are present, we cannot bind the Government to wait until the catalyst is added. . . .

V.

There remains to be discussed the question of vagueness — whether the statute as we have interpreted it is too vague, not sufficiently advising those who would speak of the limitations upon their activity. It is urged that such vagueness contravenes the First and Fifth Amendments. This argument is particularly nonpersuasive when presented by petitioners, who, the jury found, intended to overthrow the Government as speedily as circumstances would permit. . . .

We agree that the standard as defined is not a neat, mathematical formulary. Like all verbalizations it is subject to criticism on the score of indefiniteness. But petitioners themselves contend that the verbalization "clear and present danger" is the proper standard. We see no difference, from the standpoint of vagueness, whether the standard of "clear and present danger" is one contained *in haec verba* within the statute, or whether it is the judicial measure of constitutional applicability. . . .

We hold that § § 2 (a) (1), 2 (a) (3) and 3 of the Smith Act do not inherently, or as construed or applied in the instant case, violate the First Amendment and other provisions of the Bill of Rights, or the First and Fifth Amendments because of indefiniteness. Petitioners intended to overthrow the Government of the United States as speedily as the circumstances would permit. Their conspiracy to organize the Communist Party and to teach and advocate the overthrow of the Government of the United States by force and violence created a "clear and present danger" of an attempt to overthrow the Government by force and violence. They were properly and constitutionally convicted for violation of the Smith Act. The judgments of conviction are

Affirmed.

Justice Black, dissenting. . . .

At the outset I want to emphasize what the crime involved in this case is, and what it is not. These petitioners were not charged with an attempt to overthrow the Government. They were not charged with overt acts of any kind designed to overthrow the Government. They were not even charged with saying anything or writing anything designed to overthrow the Government. The charge was that they agreed to assemble and to talk and publish certain ideas at a later date: The indictment is that they conspired to organize the Communist Party and to use speech or newspapers and other publications in the future to teach and advocate the forcible overthrow of the Government. No matter how it is worded, this is a virulent form of prior censorship of speech and press, which I believe the First Amendment forbids. I would hold § 3 of the Smith Act authorizing this prior restraint unconstitutional on its face and as applied. . . .

Public opinion being what it now is, few will protest the conviction of these Communist petitioners. There is hope, however, that in calmer times, when present pressures, passions and fears subside, this or some later Court will restore the First Amendment liberties to the high preferred place where they belong in a free society.

Yates *v.* United States

The Dennis *decision encouraged the federal government to seek similar convictions of lower echelon Communist Party leaders and members. But by 1957 there were important membership changes in the Supreme Court. In the* Yates *case, the Court reviewed and reversed the convictions of fourteen so-called "second string" Communists. While the majority did not repudiate the* Dennis *upholding of the Smith Act, it established more restrictive standards for securing convictions. Harlan's majority opinion emphasized the difference between advocating an abstract doctrine and advocating unlawful action. Basically following the* Dennis *holding, the trial judge had instructed the jury that the doctrinal justification of overthrowing the government, if intended to accomplish that end, was punishable under the Smith Act. The Court now held that the mere advocacy of ideas was "too remote from concrete action" to justify conviction.*

Justice Harlan delivered the opinion of the Court.

We brought these cases here to consider certain questions arising under the Smith Act which have not heretofore been passed upon by this Court, and otherwise to review the convictions of these petitioners for conspiracy to violate that Act. Among other things, the convictions are claimed to rest upon an application of the Smith Act which is hostile to the principles upon which its constitutionality was upheld in *Dennis* v. *United States*. . . .

These 14 petitioners stand convicted, after a jury trial in the United States District Court for the Southern District of California, upon a single count indictment charging them with conspiring (1) to advocate and teach the duty and necessity of overthrowing the Government of the United States by force and violence, and (2) to organize, as the Communist Party of the United States, a society of persons who so advocate and teach, all with the intent of causing the overthrow of the Government by force and violence as speedily as circumstances would permit. . . .

Upon conviction each of the petitioners was sentenced to five years' imprisonment and a fine of $10,000. . . .

In the view we take of this case, it is necessary for us to consider only the following of petitioners' contentions: (1) that the term "organize" as used in the Smith Act was erroneously construed by the two lower courts; (2) that the trial court's instructions to the jury erroneously excluded from the case the issue of "incitement to action"; (3) that the evidence was so insufficient as to require this Court to direct the acquittal of these petitioners. . . . For reasons given hereafter, we conclude that these convictions must be reversed and the case remanded to the District Court with instructions to enter judgments of acquittal as to certain of the petitioners, and to grant a new trial as to the rest.

I. The Term "Organize."

One object of the conspiracy charged was to violate the third paragraph of 18 U.S.C. § 2385, which provides:

> Whoever organizes or helps or attempts to organize any society, group, or assembly of persons who teach, advocate, or encourage the overthrow or destruction of any [government in the United States] by force or violence . . . [s]hall be fined not more than $10,000 or imprisoned not more than ten years, or both . . . .

Petitioners claim that "organize" means to "establish," "found," or "bring into existence," and that in this sense the Communist Party was organized by 1945 at the latest. On this basis petitioners contend that this part of the indictment, returned in 1951, was barred by the three-year statute of limitations. The Government, on the other hand, says that "organize" connotes a continuing process which goes on throughout the life of an organization, and that, in the words of the trial court's instructions to the jury, the term includes such things as "the recruiting of new members and the forming of new units, and the regrouping or expansion of existing clubs, classes and other units of any society, party, group or other organization." The two courts below accepted the Government's position. We think, however, that petitioners' position must prevail, upon principles stated by Chief Justice Marshall more than a century ago in *United States* v. *Wiltberger.* . . .

> The rule that penal laws are to be construed strictly, is perhaps not much less old than construction itself. It is founded on the tenderness of the law for the rights of individuals; and on the plain principle that the power of punishment is vested in the legislative, not in the judicial department. It is the legislature, not the Court, which is to define a crime, and ordain its punishment . . .

We conclude, therefore, that since the Communist Party came into being in 1945, and the indictment was not returned until 1951, the three-year statute of limitations had run on the "organizing" charge, and required the withdrawal of that part of the indictment from the jury's consideration. . . .

II. Instructions to the Jury.

Petitioners contend that the instructions to the jury were fatally defective in that the trial court refused to charge that, in order to convict, the jury must find that the advocacy which the defendants conspired to promote was of a kind calculated to "incite" persons to action for the forcible overthrow of the Government. It is argued that advocacy of forcible overthrow as mere *abstract doctrine* is within the free speech protection of the First Amendment; that the Smith Act, consistently with that constitutional provision, must be taken as proscribing only the sort of advocacy which incites to illegal *action;* and that the trial court's charge, by permitting conviction for mere advocacy, unrelated to its tendency to produce forcible action, resulted in an unconstitutional application of the Smith Act. The Government, which at the trial also requested the court to charge in terms of "incitement," now takes the position, however, that the true constitutional dividing line is not between inciting and abstract advocacy of forcible overthrow, but rather between advocacy as such, irrespective of its inciting qualities, and the mere discussion or exposition of violent overthrow as an abstract theory. . . .

There can be no doubt from the record that in so instructing the jury the court regarded as immaterial, and intended to withdraw from the jury's consideration, any issue as to the character of the advocacy in terms of its capacity to stir listeners to forcible action. Both the petitioners and the Government submitted proposed instructions which would have required the jury to find that the proscribed advocacy was not of a mere abstract doctrine of forcible overthrow, but of action to that end, by the use of language reasonably and ordinarily calculated to incite persons to such action. The trial court rejected these proposed instructions on the ground that any necessity for giving them which may have existed at the time the *Dennis* case was tried was removed by this Court's subsequent decision in that case. The court made it clear in colloquy with counsel that in its view the illegal advocacy was made out simply by showing that what was said dealt with forcible overthrow and that it was uttered with a specific intent to accomplish that purpose, insisting that all such advocacy was punishable "whether it is language of incitement or not." . . .

We are thus faced with the question whether the Smith Act prohibits advocacy and teaching of forcible overthrow as an abstract principle, divorced from any effort to instigate action to that end, so long as such advocacy or teaching is engaged in with evil intent. We hold that it does not.

The distinction between advocacy of abstract doctrine and advocacy directed at promoting unlawful action is one that has been consistently recognized in the opinions of this Court. . . .

We need not, however, decide the issue before us in terms of constitutional compulsion, for our first duty is to construe this statute. In doing so we should not assume that Congress chose to disregard a constitutional danger zone so clearly marked, or that it used the words "advocate" and "teach" in their ordinary dictionary meanings when they had already been construed as terms of art carrying a special and limited connotation. . . . The legislative history of the Smith Act and related bills shows beyond all question that Congress was aware of the distinction between the advocacy or teaching of abstract doctrine and the advocacy or teaching of action, and that it did not intend to disregard it. The statute was aimed at the advocacy and teaching of concrete action for the forcible overthrow of the Government, and not of principles divorced from action.

The Government's reliance on this Court's decision in *Dennis* is misplaced. . . .

In failing to distinguish between advocacy of forcible overthrow as an abstract doctrine and advocacy of action to that end, the District Court appears to have been led astray by the holding in *Dennis* that advocacy of violent action to be taken at some future time was enough. It seems to have considered that, since "inciting" speech is usually thought of as something calculated to induce immediate action, and since *Dennis* held advocacy of action for future overthrow sufficient, this meant that advocacy, irrespective of its tendency to generate action, is punishable, provided only that it is uttered with a specific intent to accomplish overthrow. In other words, the District Court apparently thought that *Dennis* obliterated the traditional dividing line between advocacy of abstract doctrine and advocacy of action.

This misconceives the situation confronting the Court in *Dennis* and what was held there. Although the jury's verdict, interpreted in light of the trial court's instructions, did not justify the conclusion that the defendants' advocacy was directed at, or created any danger of, immediate overthrow, it did establish that the advocacy was aimed at building up a seditious group and maintaining it in readiness for action at a propitious time. In such circumstances, said Chief Justice Vinson, the Government need not hold its hand "until the *putsch* is about to be executed, the plans have been laid and the signal is awaited. If Government is aware that a group aiming at its overthrow is attempting to indoctrinate its members and to commit them to a course whereby they will strike when the leaders feel the circumstances permit, action by the Government is required." . . . The essence of the *Dennis* holding was that indoctrination of a group in preparation for future violent action, as well as exhortation to immediate action, by advocacy found to be directed to "action for the accomplishment" of forcible overthrow, to violence as "a rule or principle of action," and employing "language of incitement," . . . is not constitutionally protected when the group is of sufficient size and cohesiveness, is sufficiently oriented towards action, and other circumstances are such as reasonably to justify apprehension that action will occur. This is quite a different thing from the view of the District Court here that mere doctrinal justification of forcible overthrow, if engaged in with the intent to accomplish overthrow, is punishable *per se* under the Smith Act. That sort of advocacy, even though uttered with the hope that it may ultimately lead to violent revolution, is too remote from concrete action to be regarded as the kind of indoctrination preparatory to action which was condemned in *Dennis*. As one of the concurring opinions in *Dennis* put it:

> "Throughout our decisions there has recurred a distinction between the statement of an idea which may prompt its hearers to take unlawful action, and advocacy that such action be taken." . . .

There is nothing in *Dennis* which makes that historic distinction obsolete. . . .

In light of the foregoing we are unable to regard the District Court's charge upon this aspect of the case as adequate. The jury was never told that the Smith Act does not denounce advocacy in the sense of preaching abstractly the forcible overthrow of the Government. We think that the trial court's statement that the proscribed advocacy must include the "urging," "necessity," and "duty" of forcible overthrow, and not merely its "desirability" and "propriety," may not be regarded as a sufficient substitute for charging that the Smith Act reaches only advocacy of action for the overthrow of government by force and violence. The essential distinction is that those to whom the advocacy is addressed must be urged to *do* something, now or in the future, rather than merely to *believe* in something. At best the expressions used by the trial court were equivocal, since in the absence of any instructions differentiating advocacy of abstract doctrine from advocacy of action, they were as consistent with the former as they were with the latter. Nor do we regard their ambiguity as lessened by what the trial court had to say as to the right of the defendants to announce their beliefs as to the inevitability of violent revolution, or to advocate other unpopular opinions. Especially when it is unmistakable that the court did not consider the urging of action for forcible overthrow as being a necessary element of the proscribed advocacy, but rather considered the crucial question to be whether the advocacy was uttered with a specific intent to accomplish such overthrow, we would not be warranted in assuming that the jury drew from these instructions more than the court itself intended them to convey. . . .

We recognize that distinctions between advocacy or teaching of abstract doctrines, with evil intent, and that which is directed to stirring people to action, are often subtle and difficult to grasp, for in a broad sense, as Mr. Justice Holmes said in his dissenting opinion in *Gitlow,* . . . "Every idea is an incitement." But the very subtlety of these distinctions required the most clear and explicit instructions with reference to them, for they concerned an issue which went to the very heart of the charges against these petitioners. The need for precise and understandable instructions on this issue is further emphasized by the equivocal character of the evidence in this record, with which we deal in Part III of this opinion. Instances of speech that could be considered to amount to "advocacy of action" are so few and far between as to be almost completely overshadowed by the hundreds of instances in the record in which overthrow, if mentioned at all, occurs in the course of doctrinal disputation so remote from action as to be almost wholly lacking in probative value. Vague references to "revolutionary" or "militant" action of an unspecified character, which are found in the evidence, might in addition be given too great weight by the jury in the absence of more precise instructions. Particularly in light of this record, we must regard the trial court's charge in this respect as furnishing wholly inadequate guidance to the jury on this central point in the case. We cannot allow a conviction to stand on such "an equivocal direction to the jury on a basic issue." . . .

III. THE EVIDENCE.

The determinations already made require a reversal of these convictions. Nevertheless, in the exercise of our power under 28 U.S.C. § 2106 to "direct the entry of such appropriate judgment . . . as may be just under the circumstances," we have conceived it to be our duty to scrutinize this lengthy record with care, in order to determine whether the way should be left open for a new trial of all or some of these petitioners. Such a judgment, we think, should, on the one hand, foreclose further proceedings against those of the petitioners as to whom the evidence in this record would be palpably insufficient upon a new trial, and should, on the other hand, leave the Government free to retry the other petitioners under proper legal standards, especially since it is by no means clear that certain aspects of the evidence against them could not have been clarified to the advantage of the Government had it not been under a misapprehension as to the burden cast upon it by the Smith Act. . . .

Watkins *v.* United States

In the same year as the Yates *case, the Court turned its attention to the investigatory powers of the House Un-American Activities Committee. Enveloped in controversy since its origins as a sub-committee in 1938, HUAC had become synonymous with "witch-hunts" and abuse of witnesses. In a 1927 decision, the Court had given wide latitude to congressional investigating activities, holding that the creation of a committee by Congress presumed a legislative purpose (McGrain v. Daugherty, 273 U.S. 135). But in the case below, the Court declared that investigatory powers were not unlimited. Watkins had been cited and convicted for contempt when he refused to identify other persons as members of the Communist party, although he had admitted his own membership. Specifically, the Court overruled the conviction on due process grounds. But Chief Justice Warren's majority opinion also was concerned with the First Amendment and a "right to privacy."*

Chief Justice Warren delivered the opinion of the Court.

We start with several basic premises on which there is general agreement. The power of the Congress to conduct investigations is inherent in the legislative process. That power is broad. It encompasses inquiries concerning the administration of existing laws as well as proposed or possibly needed statutes. It includes surveys of defects in our social, economic or political system for the purpose of enabling the Congress to remedy them. It comprehends probes into departments of the Federal Government to expose corruption, inefficiency or waste. But, broad as is this power of inquiry, it is not unlimited. There is no general authority to expose the private affairs of individuals without justification in terms of the functions of the Congress. This was freely conceded by the Solicitor General in his argument of this case. Nor is the Congress a law enforcement or trial agency. These are functions of the executive and judicial departments of government. No inquiry is an end in itself; it must be related to, and in furtherance of, a legitimate task of the Congress. Investigations conducted solely for the personal aggrandizement of the investigators or to "punish" those investigated are indefensible.

It is unquestionably the duty of all citizens to cooperate with the Con-

354 U.S. 178 (1957)

gress in its efforts to obtain the facts needed for intelligent legislative action. It is their unremitting obligation to respond to subpoenas, to respect the dignity of the Congress and its committees and to testify fully with respect to matters within the province of proper investigation. This, of course, assumes that the constitutional rights of witnesses will be respected by the Congress as they are in a court of justice. The Bill of Rights is applicable to investigations as to all forms of governmental action. Witnesses cannot be compelled to give evidence against themselves. They cannot be subjected to unreasonable search and seizure. Nor can the First Amendment freedoms of speech, press, religion, or political belief and association be abridged. . . .

In the decade following World War II, there appeared a new kind of congressional inquiry unknown in prior periods of American history. Principally this was the result of the various investigations into the threat of subversion of the United States Government, but other subjects of congressional interest also contributed to the changed scene. This new phase of legislative inquiry involved a broad-scale intrusion into the lives and affairs of private citizens. It brought before the courts novel questions of the appropriate limits of congressional inquiry. Prior cases . . . had defined the scope of investigative power in terms of the inherent limitations of the sources of that power. In the more recent cases, the emphasis shifted to problems of accommodating the interest of the Government with the rights and privileges of individuals. The central theme was the application of the Bill of Rights as a restraint upon the assertion of governmental power in this form.

It was during this period that the Fifth Amendment privilege against self-incrimination was frequently invoked and recognized as a legal limit upon the authority of a committee to require that a witness answer its questions. Some early doubts as to the applicability of that privilege before a legislative committee never matured. When the matter reached this Court, the Government did not challenge in any way that the Fifth Amendment protection was available to the witness, and such a challenge could not have prevailed. It confined its argument to the character of the answers sought and to the adequacy of the claim of privilege. . . .

A far more difficult task evolved from the claim by witnesses that the committees' interrogations were infringements upon the freedoms of the First Amendment. Clearly, an investigation is subject to the command that the Congress shall make no law abridging freedom of speech or press or assembly. While it is true that there is no statute to be reviewed, and that an investigation is not a law, nevertheless an investigation is part of lawmaking. It is justified solely as an adjunct to the legislative process. The First Amendment may be invoked against infringement of the protected freedoms by law or by lawmaking.

Abuses of the investigative process may imperceptibly lead to abridgment of protected freedoms. The mere summoning of a witness and compelling him to testify, against his will, about his beliefs, expressions or associations is a measure of governmental interference. And when those forced revelations concern matters that are unorthodox, unpopular, or even hateful to the general public, the reaction in the life of the witness may be disastrous. This effect is even more harsh when it is past beliefs, expressions or associations that are disclosed and judged by current standards rather than those contemporary with the matters exposed. Nor does the witness alone suffer the consequences. Those who are identified by witnesses and thereby placed in the same glare of publicity are equally subject to public stigma, scorn and obloquy. Beyond that, there is the more subtle and immeasurable effect upon those who tend to adhere to the most orthodox and uncontroversial views and associations in order to avoid a similar fate at some future time. That this impact is partly the result of non-governmental activity by private persons cannot relieve the investigators of their responsibility for initiating the reaction. . . .

Accommodation of the congressional need for particular information with the individual and personal interest in privacy is an arduous and delicate task for any court. We do not underestimate the difficulties that would attend such an undertaking. It is manifest that despite the adverse effects which follow upon compelled disclosure of private matters, not all such inquiries are barred. . . . The critical element is the existence of, and the weight to be ascribed to, the interest of the Congress in demanding disclosures from an unwilling witness. We cannot simply assume, however, that every congressional investigation is justified by a public need that overbalances any private rights affected. To do so would be to abdicate the responsibility placed by the Constitution upon the judiciary to insure that the Congress does not unjustifiably encroach upon an individual's right to privacy nor abridge his liberty of speech, press, religion or assembly.

Petitioner has earnestly suggested that the difficult questions of protecting these rights from infringement by legislative inquiries can be surmounted in this case because there was no public purpose served in his interrogation. His conclusion is based upon the thesis that the Subcommittee was engaged in a program of exposure for the sake of exposure. . . .

We have no doubt that there is no congressional power to expose for the sake of exposure. The public is, of course, entitled to be informed concerning the workings of its government. That cannot be inflated into a general power to expose where the predominant result can only be an invasion of the private rights of individuals. But a solution to our problem is not to be found in testing the motives of committee members for this purpose. Such is not our function. Their motives alone would not vitiate an investigation which had been instituted by a House of Congress if that assembly's legislative purpose is being served. . . .

The theory of a committee inquiry is that the committee members are serving as the representatives of the parent assembly in collecting information for a legislative purpose. Their function is to act as the eyes and ears of the Congress in obtaining facts upon which the full legislature can act. . . .

An essential premise in this situation is that the House or Senate shall have instructed the committee members on what they are to do with the power delegated to them. It is the responsibility of the Congress, in the first instance, to insure that compulsory process is used only in furtherance of a legislative purpose. That requires that the instructions to an investigating committee spell out that group's jurisdiction and purpose with sufficient particularity. Those instructions are embodied in the authorizing resolution. That document is the committee's charter. Broadly drafted and loosely worded, however, such resolutions can leave tremendous latitude to the discretion of the investigators. The more vague the committee's charter is, the greater becomes the possibility that the committee's specific actions are not in conformity with the will of the parent House of Congress.

The authorizing resolution of the Un-American Activities Committee was adopted in 1938 when a select committee, under the chairmanship of Representative Dies, was created. Several years later, the Committee was made a standing organ of the House with the same mandate. It defines the Committee's authority as follows:

> The Committee on Un-American Activities, as a whole or by subcommittee, is authorized to make from time to time investigations of (1) the extent, character, and objects of un-American propaganda activities in the United States, (2) the diffusion within the United States of subversive and un-American propaganda that is instigated from foreign countries or of a domestic origin and attacks the principle of the form of government as guaranteed by our Constitution, and (3) all other questions in relation thereto that would aid Congress in any necessary remedial legislation.

It would be difficult to imagine a less explicit authorizing resolution. Who can define the meaning of "un-American"? What is that single, solitary "principle of the form of government as guaranteed by our Constitution"? There is no need to dwell upon the language, however. At one time, perhaps, the resolution might have been read narrowly to confine the Committee to the subject of propaganda. The events that have transpired in the fifteen years before the interrogation of petitioner make such a construction impossible at this date.

The members of the Committee have clearly demonstrated that they did not feel themselves restricted in any way to propaganda in the narrow sense of the word. Unquestionably the Committee conceived of its task in the grand view of its name. Un-American activities were its target, no matter how or where manifested. Notwithstanding the broad purview of the Committee's experience, the House of Representatives repeatedly approved its continuation. . . .

Combining the language of the resolution with the construction it has been given, it is evident that the preliminary control of the Committee exercised by the House of Representatives is slight or non-existent. No one could reasonably deduce from the charter the kind of investigation that the Committee was directed to make. As a result, we are asked to engage in a process of retroactive rationalization. Looking backward from the events that transpired, we are asked to uphold the Committee's actions unless it appears that they were clearly not authorized by the charter. As a corollary to this inverse approach, the Government urges that we must view the matter hospitably to the power of the Congress — that if there is any legislative purpose which might have been furthered by the kind of disclosure sought, the witness must be punished for withholding it. No doubt every reasonable indulgence of legality must be accorded to the actions of a coordinate branch of our Government. But such deference cannot yield to an unnecessary and unreasonable dissipation of precious constitutional freedoms.

The Government contends that the public interest at the core of the investigations of the Un-American Activities Committee is the need by the Congress to be informed of efforts to overthrow the Government by force and violence so that adequate legislative safeguards can be erected. From this core, however, the Committee can radiate outward infinitely to any topic thought to be related in some way to armed insurrection. The outer reaches of this domain are known only by the content of "un-American activities." . . .

The consequences that flow from this situation are manifold. . . . The Committee is allowed, in essence, to define its own authority, to choose the direction and focus of its activities. In deciding what to do with the power that has been conferred upon them, members of the Committee may act pursuant to motives that seem to them to be the highest. Their decisions, nevertheless, can lead to ruthless exposure of private lives in order to gather data that is neither desired by the Congress nor useful to it. Yet it is impossible in this circumstance, with constitutional freedoms in jeopardy, to declare that the Committee has ranged beyond the area committed to it by its parent assembly because the boundaries are so nebulous.

More important and more fundamental than that, however, it insulates the House that has authorized the investigation from the witnesses who are subjected to the sanctions of compulsory process. There is a wide gulf between the responsibility for the use of investigative power and the actual exercise of that power. This is an especially vital consideration in assuring respect for constitutional liberties. Protected freedoms should not be placed in danger in the absence of a clear determination by the House or the Senate that a particular inquiry is justified by a specific legislative need.

It is, of course, not the function of this Court to prescribe rigid rules for the Congress to follow in drafting resolutions establishing investigating committees. . . . An excessively broad charter, like that of the House Un-American Activities Committee, places the courts in an untenable position if they are to strike a balance between the public need for a particular interrogation and the right of citizens to carry on their affairs free from unnecessary governmental interference. It is impossible in such a situation to ascertain whether any legislative purpose justifies the disclosures sought and, if so, the importance of that information to the Congress in furtherance of its legislative function. The reason no court can make this critical judgment is that the House of Representatives itself has never made it. Only the legislative assembly initiating an investigation can assay the relative necessity of specific disclosures.

Absence of the qualitative consideration of petitioner's questioning by the House of Representatives aggravates a serious problem, revealed in this case, in the relationship of congressional investigating committees and the witnesses who appear before them. Plainly these committees are restricted to the missions delegated to them, *i.e.*, to acquire certain data to be used by the House or the Senate in coping with a problem that falls within its legislative sphere. No witness can be compelled to make disclosures on matters outside that area. This is a jurisdictional concept of pertinency drawn from the nature of a congressional committee's source of authority. It is not wholly different from nor unrelated to the element of pertinency embodied in the criminal statute under which petitioner was prosecuted. When the definition of of jurisdictional pertinency is as uncertain and wavering as in the case of the Un-American Activities Committee, it becomes extremely difficult for the Committee to limit its inquiries to statutory pertinency.

Since World War II, the Congress has practically abandoned its original practice of utilizing the coercive sanction of contempt proceedings at the bar of the House. The sanction there imposed is imprisonment by the House until the recalcitrant witness agrees to testify or disclose the matters sought, provided that the incarceration does not extend beyond adjournment. The Congress has instead invoked the aid of the federal judicial system in protecting itself against contumacious conduct. It has become customary to refer these matters to the United States Attorneys for prosecution under criminal law.

The appropriate statute is found in 2 U.S.C. § 192. It provides:

Every person who having been summoned as a witness by the authority of either House of Congress to give testimony or to produce papers upon any matter under inquiry before either House, or any joint committee established by a joint or concurrent resolution of the two Houses of Congress, or any committee of either House of Congress, will-fully makes default, or who, having appeared, refuses to answer any question pertinent to the question under inquiry, shall be deemed guilty of a misdemeanor, punishable by a fine of not more than $1,000 nor less than $100 and imprisonment in a common jail for not less than one month nor more than twelve months.

In fulfillment of their obligation under this statute, the courts must accord to the defendants every right which is guaranteed to defendants in all other criminal cases. Among these is the right to have available, through a sufficiently precise statute, information revealing the standard of criminality before the commission of the alleged offense. Applied to persons prosecuted under § 192, this raises a special problem in that the statute defines the crime as refusal to answer "any question pertinent to the question under inquiry." Part of the standard of criminality, there-fore, is the pertinency of the questions propounded to the witness.

The problem attains proportion when viewed from the standpoint of the witness who appears before a congressional committee. He must decide at the time the questions are propounded whether or not to answer. . . . An erroneous determination on his part, even if made in the utmost good faith, does not exculpate him if the court should later rule that the questions were pertinent to the question under inquiry.

It is obvious that a person compelled to make this choice is entitled to have knowledge of the subject to which the interrogation is deemed pertinent. That knowledge must be available with the same degree of explicitness and clarity that the Due Process Clause requires in the ex-pression of any element of a criminal offense. The "vice of vagueness" must be avoided here as in all other crimes. There are several sources that can outline the "question under inquiry" in such a way that the rules against vagueness are satisfied. The authorizing resolution, the remarks of the chairman or members of the committee, or even the nature of the proceedings themselves, might sometimes make the topic clear. This case demonstrates, however, that these sources often leave the matter in grave doubt.

The first possibility is that the authorizing resolution itself will so clearly declare the "question under inquiry" that a witness can under-stand the pertinency of questions asked him. The Government does not contend that the authorizing resolution of the Un-American Activities Committee could serve such a purpose. Its confusing breadth is amply illustrated by the innumerable and diverse questions into which the

Committee has inquired under this charter since 1938. If the "question under inquiry" were stated with such sweeping and uncertain scope, we doubt that it would withstand an attack on the ground of vagueness. . . .

The Government believes that the topic of inquiry before the Subcommittee concerned Communist infiltration in labor. In his introductory remarks, the Chairman made reference to a bill, then pending before the Committee, which would have penalized labor unions controlled or dominated by persons who were, or had been, members of a "Communist-action" organization, as defined in the Internal Security Act of 1950. The Subcommittee, it is contended, might have been endeavoring to determine the extent of such a problem. . . .

Looking at the entire hearings, however, there is strong reason to doubt that the subject revolved about labor matters. . . .

Having exhausted the several possible indicia of the "question under inquiry," we remain unenlightened as to the subject to which the questions asked petitioner were pertinent. Certainly, if the point is that obscure after trial and appeal, it was not adequately revealed to petitioner when he had to decide at his peril whether or not to answer. Fundamental fairness demands that no witness be compelled to make such a determination with so little guidance. Unless the subject matter has been made to appear with undisputable clarity, it is the duty of the investigative body, upon objection of the witness on grounds of pertinency, to state for the record the subject under inquiry at that time and the manner in which the propounded questions are pertinent thereto. To be meaningful, the explanation must describe what the topic under inquiry is and the connective reasoning whereby the precise questions asked relate to it.

The statement of the Committee Chairman in this case, in response to petitioner's protest, was woefully inadequate to convey sufficient information as to the pertinency of the questions to the subject under inquiry. Petitioner was thus not accorded a fair opportunity to determine whether he was within his rights in refusing to answer, and his conviction is necessarily invalid under the Due Process Clause of the Fifth Amendment. . . .

The conclusions we have reached in this case will not prevent the Congress, through its committees, from obtaining any information it needs for the proper fulfillment of its role in our scheme of government. The legislature is free to determine the kinds of data that should be collected. It is only those investigations that are conducted by use of compulsory process that give rise to a need to protect the rights of individuals against illegal encroachment. That protection can be readily achieved through procedures which prevent the separation of power from responsibility and which provide the constitutional requisites of fairness for witnesses. A measure of added care on the part of the House and the Senate in authorizing the use of compulsory process and by their committees in exercising that power would suffice. That is a small price to pay if it serves to uphold the principles of limited, constitutional government without constricting the power of the Congress to inform itself. . . .

Barenblatt *v.* United States

The wide-ranging Watkins *opinion aroused vigorous criticism in Congress and sparked a nearly-successful drive to limit the Court's powers. Whether because of congressional pressures, or merely because of internal dissatisfaction with the language of* Watkins, *the Court generally sustained congressional investigatory powers. The* Barenblatt *case below, was a typical example of a majority's insistence that the judiciary lacked authority to intervene against Congress's constitutional power, even when the motive merely was to expose a witness's political beliefs. The majority also resorted to the so-called "balancing" test to resolve the conflict between the rights of the individual and the interests of the government. Justice Black in dissent, with Warren and Douglas concurring, bitterly criticized the formula. He charged that it simply meant the First Amendment would not be followed "unless the Court believes it reasonable to do so."*

Justice Harlan delivered the opinion of the Court.

Once more the Court is required to resolve the conflicting constitutional claims of congressional power and of an individual's right to resist its exercise. . . .

Broad as it is, the power is not, however, without limitations. Since Congress may only investigate into those areas in which it may potentially legislate or appropriate, it cannot inquire into matters which are within the exclusive province of one of the other branches of the Government. Lacking the judicial power given to the Judiciary, it cannot inquire into matters that are exclusively the concern of the Judiciary. Neither can it supplant the Executive in what exclusively belongs to the Executive. And the Congress, in common with all branches of the Government, must exercise its powers subject to the limitations placed by the Constitution on governmental action, more particularly in the context of this case the relevant limitations of the Bill of Rights. . . .

Our function, at this point, is purely one of constitutional adjudication

---

360 U.S. 109 (1959)

in the particular case and upon the particular record before us, not to pass judgment upon the general wisdom or efficacy of the activities of this Committee in a vexing and complicated field.

The precise constitutional issue confronting us is whether the Subcommittee's inquiry into petitioner's past or present membership in the Communist Party transgressed the provisions of the First Amendment, which of course reach and limit congressional investigations. . . .

The Court's past cases establish sure guides to decision. Undeniably, the First Amendment in some circumstances protects an individual from being compelled to disclose his associational relationships. However, the protections of the First Amendment, unlike a proper claim of the privilege against self-incrimination under the Fifth Amendment, do not afford a witness the right to resist inquiry in all circumstances. Where First Amendment rights are asserted to bar governmental interrogation resolution of the issue always involves a balancing by the courts of the competing private and public interests at stake in the particular circumstances shown. These principles were recognized in the *Watkins* case, where, in speaking of the First Amendment in relation to congressional inquiries, we said . . . : "It is manifest that despite the adverse effects which follow upon compelled disclosure of private matters, not all such inquiries are barred. . . . The critical element is the existence of, and the weight to be ascribed to, the interest of the Congress in demanding disclosures from an unwilling witness." . . . More recently in *National Association for the Advancement of Colored People* v. *Alabama,* 357 U.S. 449, 463–466, we applied the same principles in judging state action claimed to infringe rights of association assured by the Due Process Clause of the Fourteenth Amendment, and stated that the " 'subordinating interest of the State must be compelling' " in order to overcome the individual constitutional rights at stake. . . . In light of these principles we now consider petitioner's First Amendment claims.

The first question is whether this investigation was related to a valid legislative purpose, for Congress may not constitutionally require an individual to disclose his political relationships or other private affairs except in relation to such a purpose. . . .

That Congress has wide power to legislate in the field of Communist activity in this Country, and to conduct appropriate investigations in aid thereof, is hardly debatable. The existence of such power has never been questioned by this Court, and it is sufficient to say, without particularization, that Congress has enacted or considered in this field a wide range of legislative measures, not a few of which have stemmed from recommendations of the very Committee whose actions have been drawn in question here. In the last analysis this power rests on the right of self-preservation, "the ultimate value of any society," *Dennis* v. *United States,* 341 U.S. 494, 509. Justification for its exercise in turn rests on the long and widely accepted view that the tenets of the Communist Party include the ultimate overthrow of the Government of the United States by force and violence, a view which has been given formal expression by the Congress.

On these premises, this Court in its constitutional adjudications has consistently refused to view the Communist Party as an ordinary political party, and has upheld federal legislation aimed at the Communist problem which in a different context would certainly have raised constitutional issues of the gravest character. . . . On the same premises this Court has upheld under the Fourteenth Amendment state legislation requiring those occupying or seeking public office to disclaim knowing membership in any organization advocating overthrow of the Government by force and violence, which legislation none can avoid seeing was aimed at membership in the Communist Party. . . . Similarly, in other areas, this Court has recognized the close nexus between the Communist Party and violent overthrow of government. . . . To suggest that because the Communist Party may also sponsor peaceable political reforms the constitutional issues before us should now be judged as if that Party were just an ordinary political party from the standpoint of national security, is to ask this Court to blind itself to world affairs which have determined the whole course of our national policy since the close of World War II, affairs to which Judge Learned Hand gave vivid expression in his opinion in *United States* v. *Dennis*, . . . and to the vast burdens which these conditions have entailed for the entire Nation. . . .

In our opinion this position rests on a too constricted view of the nature of the investigatory process, and is not supported by a fair assessment of the record before us. An investigation of advocacy of or preparation for overthrow certainly embraces the right to identify a witness as a member of the Communist Party . . . and to inquire into the various manifestations of the Party's tenets. The strict requirements of a prosecution under the Smith Act . . . are not the measure of the permissible scope of a congressional investigation into "overthrow," for of necessity the investigatory process must proceed step by step. Nor can it fairly be concluded that this investigation was directed at controlling what is being taught at our universities rather than at overthrow. The statement of the Subcommittee Chairman at the opening of the investigation evinces no such intention, and so far as this record reveals nothing thereafter transpired which would justify our holding that the thrust of the investigation later changed. The record discloses considerable testimony concerning the foreign domination and revolutionary purposes and efforts of the Communist Party. That there was also testimony on the abstract philosophical level does not detract from the dominant theme of this investigation — Communist infiltration furthering the alleged ultimate purpose of overthrow. And certainly the conclusion would not be justified that the questioning of petitioner would have exceeded permissible bounds had he not shut off the Subcommittee at the threshold. . . .

Finally, the record is barren of other factors which in themselves might sometimes lead to the conclusion that the individual interests at stake were not subordinate to those of the state. There is no indication in this record that the Subcommittee was attempting to pillory witnesses. Nor did petitioner's appearance as a witness follow from indiscriminate dragnet procedures, lacking in probable cause for belief that he possessed information which might be helpful to the Subcommittee. And the relevancy of the questions put to him by the Subcommittee is not open to doubt.

We conclude that the balance between the individual and the governmental interests here at stake must be struck in favor of the latter, and that therefore the provisions of the First Amendment have not been offended. . . .

Justice Black, with whom The Chief Justice and Justice Douglas concur, dissent.

National Association for the Advancement of Colored People

v.

Alabama

Like most states, Alabama required out-of-state corporations to register their charters before doing business in the state. The NAACP, chartered in New York, had failed to comply with the requirement, ostensibly because it was a non-profit corporation. In an obvious attempt at harassment, the state brought suit to enjoin the Association's activities within Alabama. Furthermore, the trial court ordered the Association to produce its membership lists for the state. The Association refused and was subsequently fined $100,000 for contempt of court. In its appeal to the Supreme Court, the NAACP claimed that the demand for the membership lists violated the First Amendment's right of free speech and association, which were protected by the Fourteenth against state action.

Justice Harlan delivered the opinion of the Court.

The Association both urges that it is constitutionally entitled to resist official inquiry into its membership lists, and that it may assert, on behalf of its members, a right personal to them to be protected from compelled disclosure by the State of their affiliation with the Association as revealed by the membership lists. We think that petitioner argues more appropriately the rights of its members, and that its nexus with them is sufficient to permit that it act as their representative before this Court. In so concluding, we reject respondent's argument that the Association lacks standing to assert here constitutional rights pertaining to the members, who are not of course parties to the litigation. . . .

If petitioner's rank-and-file members are constitutionally entitled to withhold their connection with the Association despite the production order, it is manifest that this right is properly assertable by the Association. To require that it be claimed by the members themselves would result in nullification of the right at the very moment of its assertion. Petitioner is the appropriate party to assert these rights, because it and

357 U.S. 449 (1958)

its members are in every practical sense identical. The Association, which provides in its constitution that "[a]ny person who is in accordance with [its] principles and policies . . ." may become a member, is but the medium through which its individual members seek to make more effective the expression of their own views. The reasonable likelihood that the Association itself through diminished financial support and membership may be adversely affected if production is compelled is a further factor pointing towards our holding that petitioner has standing to complain of the production order on behalf of its members. . . .

We thus reach petitioner's claim that the production order in the state litigation trespasses upon fundamental freedoms protected by the due process clause of the Fourteenth Amendment. Petitioner argues that in view of the facts and circumstances shown in the record, the effect of compelled disclosure of the membership lists will be to abridge the rights of its rank-and-file members to engage in lawful association in support of their common beliefs. It contends that governmental action which, although not directly suppressing association, nevertheless carries this consequence, can be justified only upon some overriding valid interest of the State.

Effective advocacy of both public and private points of view, particularly controversial ones, is undeniably enhanced by group association, as this Court has more than once recognized by remarking upon the close nexus between the freedoms of speech and assembly. *De Jonge v. Oregon,* 299 U.S. 353, 364. . . . It is beyond debate that freedom to engage in association for the advancement of beliefs and ideas is an inseparable aspect of the "liberty" assured by the due process clause of the Fourteenth Amendment, which embraces freedom of speech. See *Gitlow* v. *New York,* 268 U.S. 652, 666. . . . Of course, it is immaterial whether the beliefs sought to be advanced by association pertain to political, economic, religious, or cultural matters, and state action which may have the effect of curtailing the freedom to associate is subject to the closest scrutiny.

The fact that Alabama, so far as is relevant to the validity of the contempt judgment presently under review, has taken no direct action, cf. *De Jonge* v. *Oregon, supra; Near* v. *Minnesota,* 283 U.S. 697, to restrict the right of petitioner's members to associate freely, does not end inquiry into the effect of the production order. See *American Communications Assn.* v. *Douds,* 339 U.S. 382, 402. In the domain of these indispensable liberties, whether of speech, press, or association, the decisions of this Court recognize that abridgment of such rights, even though unintended, may inevitably follow from varied forms of governmental action. Thus in *Douds,* the Court stressed that the legislation there challenged, which on its face sought to regulate labor unions and to secure stability in interstate commerce, would have the practical effect "of discouraging" the exercise of constitutionally protected political rights, 339 U.S., at 393, and it upheld the statute only after concluding that the reasons advanced for its enactment were constitutionally sufficient to justify its possible deterrent effect upon such freedoms. Similar recognition of possible unconstitutional intimidation of the free exercise of the right to advocate underlay this Court's narrow construction of the authority of a congressional committee investigating lobbying and of an Act regulating lobbying, although in neither case was there an effort to suppress speech. *United States* v. *Rumely,* 345 U.S. 41, 46–47. . . . The governmental action challenged may appear to be totally unrelated to protected liberties. Statutes imposing taxes upon rather than prohibiting particular activity have been struck down when perceived to have the consequence of unduly curtailing the liberty of freedom of press assured under the Fourteenth Amendment. *Grosjean* v. *American Press Co.,* 297 U. S. 233. . . .

It is hardly a novel perception that compelled disclosure of affiliation with groups engaged in advocacy may constitute as effective a restraint on freedom of association as the forms of governmental action in the cases above were thought likely to produce upon the particular constitutional rights there involved. This Court has recognized the vital relationship between freedom to associate and privacy in one's associations. When referring to the varied forms of governmental action which might interfere with freedom of assembly, it said in *American Communications Assn.* v. *Douds, supra,* at 402: "A requirement that adherents of particular religious faiths or political parties wear identifying arm-bands, for example, is obviously of this nature." Compelled disclosure of membership in an organization engaged in advocacy of particular beliefs is of the same order. Inviolability of privacy in group association may in many circumstances be indispensable to preservation of freedom of association, particularly where a group espouses dissident beliefs. . . .

We think that the production order, in the respects here drawn in question, must be regarded as entailing the likelihood of a substantial restraint upon the exercise by petitioner's members of their right to freedom of association. Petitioner has made an uncontroverted showing that on past occasions revelation of the identity of its rank-and-file members has exposed these members to economic reprisal, loss of employment, threat of physical coercion, and other manifestations of public hostility. Under these circumstances, we think it apparent that compelled disclosure of petitioner's Alabama membership is likely to affect adversely the ability of petitioner and its members to pursue their collective effort to foster beliefs which they admittedly have the right to advocate, in that it may induce members to withdraw from the Association and dissuade others from joining it because of fear of exposure of their beliefs shown through their associations and of the consequences of this exposure.

It is not sufficient to answer, as the state does here, that whatever repressive effect compulsory disclosure of names of petitioner's members may have upon participation by Alabama citizens in petitioner's activities follows not from *state* action but from *private* community pressures. The crucial factor is the interplay of governmental and private action, for it is only after the initial exertion of state power represented by the production order that private action takes hold.

We turn to the final question whether Alabama has demonstrated an interest in obtaining the disclosures it seeks from petitioner which is sufficient to justify the deterrent effect which we have concluded these disclosures may well have on the free exercise by petitioner's members of their constitutionally protected right of association. . . .

It is important to bear in mind that petitioner asserts no right to absolute immunity from state investigation, and no right to disregard Alabama's laws. As shown by its substantial compliance with the production order, petitioner does not deny Alabama's right to obtain from it such information as the state desires concerning the purposes of the Association and its activities within the state. Petitioner has not objected to divulging the identity of its members who are employed by or hold official positions with it. It has urged the rights solely of its ordinary rank-and-file members. This is therefore not analogous to a case involving the interest of a state in protecting its citizens in their dealings with paid solicitors or agents of foreign corporations by requiring identification. . . .

Whether there was "justification" in this instance turns solely on the substantiality of Alabama's interest in obtaining the membership lists. During the course of a hearing before the Alabama Circuit Court on a motion of petitioner to set aside the production order, the State Attorney General presented at length, under examination by petitioner, the state's reason for requesting the membership lists. The exclusive purpose was to determine whether petitioner was conducting intrastate business in violation of the Alabama foreign corporation registration statute, and the membership lists were expected to help resolve this question. The issues in the litigation commenced by Alabama by its bill in equity were whether the character of petitioner and its activities in Alabama had been such as to make petitioner subject to the registration statute, and whether the extent of petitioner's activities without qualifying suggested its permanent ouster from the state. Without intimating the slightest view upon the merits of these issues, we are unable to perceive that the disclosure of the names of petitioner's rank-and-file members has a substantial bearing on either of them. . . .

From what has already been said, we think it apparent that *Bryant*

v. *Zimmerman*, 278 U.S. 63, cannot be relied on in support of the state's position, for that case involved markedly different considerations in terms of the interest of the state in obtaining disclosure. There, this Court upheld, as applied to a member of a local chapter of the Ku Klux Klan, a New York statute requiring any unincorporated association which demanded an oath as a condition to membership to file with state officials copies of its ". . . constitution, by-laws, rules, regulations and oath of membership, together with a roster of its membership and a list of its officers for the current year." N.Y. Laws 1923, c. 664, § § 53, 56. In its opinion, the Court took care to emphasize the nature of the organization which New York sought to regulate. The decision was based on the particular character of the Klan's activities, involving acts of unlawful intimidation and violence, which the Court assumed was before the state legislature when it enacted the statute, and of which the Court itself took judicial notice. Furthermore, the situation before us is significantly different from that in *Bryant*, because the organization there had made no effort to comply with any of the requirements of New York's statute but rather had refused to furnish the state with *any* information as to its local activities.

We hold that the immunity from state scrutiny of membership lists which the Association claims on behalf of its members is here so related to the right of the members to pursue their lawful private interest privately and to associate freely with others in so doing as to come within the protection of the Fourteenth Amendment. And we conclude that Alabama has fallen short of showing a controlling justification for the deterrent effect on the free enjoyment of the right to associate which disclosure of membership lists is likely to have. Accordingly, the judgment of civil contempt and the $100,000 fine which resulted from petitioner's refusal to comply with the production order in this respect must fall. . . .

A Book Named [Fanny Hill]

v.

Attorney General of Massachusetts
Ginzburg *v.* United States
Mishkin *v.* New York

In recent years, no First Amendment question has divided the Court more than the censorship and suppression of allegedly obscene literature or art. Although the Court attempted a definitive interpretation of obscenity in Roth v. *United States (354 U.S. 476 [1957]), state and local zealots continued to harass booksellers and movie theater operators with their own diverse standards of purity. In the three cases below, decided the same day, the Court again tried to establish workable guidelines. But as Justice Black noted, despite fourteen separate opinions in the three cases, neither the most learned judge nor the layman could have a clear understanding of what constituted obscenity. The first case was an appeal from a Massachusetts state court decision holding that books patently offensive and appealing to prurient interest, need not be absolutely worthless before being deemed obscene. Ginzburg's case was an appeal from a five year sentence for sending allegedly obscene material in the mails. Mishkin had been convicted for violating a state statute prohibiting the publication of "sadistic" and "masochistic" books.*

Justice Brennan announced the judgment of the Court [in the Fanny Hill *case]. . . .*

The sole question before the state courts was whether *Memoirs* satisfies the test of obscenity established in *Roth* v. *United States,* 354 U.S. 476.

We defined obscenity in *Roth* in the following terms: "[W]hether to the average person, applying contemporary community standards, the dominant theme of the material taken as a whole appeals to prurient interest." . . . Under this definition, as elaborated in subsequent cases, three elements must coalesce: it must be established that (a) the

---

383 U.S. 413 (1966); 383 U.S. 463 (1966); 383 U.S. 502 (1966).

dominant theme of the material taken as a whole appeals to a prurient interest in sex; (b) the material is patently offensive because it affronts contemporary community standards relating to the description or representation of sexual matters; and (c) the material is utterly without redeeming social value.

The Supreme Judicial Court purported to apply the *Roth* definition of obscenity and held all three criteria satisfied. We need not consider the claim that the court erred in concluding that *Memoirs* satisfied the prurient appeal and patent offensiveness criteria; for reversal is required because the court misinterpreted the social value criterion. . . .

The Supreme Judicial Court erred in holding that a book need not be "unqualifiedly worthless before it can be deemed obscene." A book cannot be proscribed unless it is found to be *utterly* without redeeming social value. This is so even though the book is found to possess the requisite prurient appeal and to be patently offensive. Each of the three federal constitutional criteria is to be applied independently; the social value of the book can neither be weighed against nor canceled by its prurient appeal or patent offensiveness. Hence, even on the view of the court below that *Memoirs* possessed only a modicum of social value, its judgment must be reversed as being founded on an erroneous interpretation of a federal constitutional standard.

It does not necessarily follow from this reversal that a determination that *Memoirs* is obscene in the constitutional sense would be improper under all circumstances. On the premise, which we have no occasion to assess, that *Memoirs* has the requisite prurient appeal and is patently offensive, but has only a minimum of social value, the circumstances of production, sale, and publicity are relevant in determining whether or not the publication or distribution of the book is constitutionally protected. Evidence that the book was commercially exploited for the sake of prurient appeal, to the exclusion of all other values, might justify the conclusion that the book was utterly without redeeming social importance. It is not that in such a setting the social value test is relaxed so as to dispense with the requirement that a book be *utterly* devoid of social value, but rather that, as we elaborate in *Ginzburg* v. *United States*, . . . where the purveyor's sole emphasis is on the sexually provocative aspects of his publications, a court could accept his evaluation at its face value. In this proceeding, however, the courts were asked to judge the obscenity of *Memoirs* in the abstract, and the declaration of obscenity was neither aided nor limited by a specific set of circumstances of production, sale, and publicity. All possible uses of the book must therefore be considered, and the mere risk that the book might be exploited by panderers because it so pervasively treats sexual matters cannot alter the fact — given the view of the Massachusetts court attributing to *Memoirs* a modicum of literary and historical value — that the book will have redeeming social importance in the hands of those who publish or distribute it on the basis of that value.

Justice Brennan delivered the opinion of the Court [in the Ginzburg case]. . . .

In the cases in which this Court has decided obscenity questions since *Roth*, it has regarded the materials as sufficient in themselves for the determination of the question. In the present case, however, the prosecution charged the offense in the context of the circumstances of production, sale, and publicity and assumed that, standing alone, the publications themselves might not be obscene. We agree that the question of obscenity may include consideration of the setting in which the publications were presented as an aid to determining the question of obscenity, and assume without deciding that the prosecution could not have succeeded otherwise. As in *Mishkin* v. *New York*, . . . and as did the courts below, . . . we view the publications against a background of commercial exploitation of erotica solely for the sake of their prurient appeal. The record in that regard amply supports the decision of the trial judge that the mailing of all three publications offended the statute. . . .

This evidence, in our view, was relevant in determining the ultimate question of obscenity and, in the context of this record, serves to resolve all ambiguity and doubt. The deliberate representation of petitioners' publications as erotically arousing, for example, stimulated the reader to accept them as prurient; he looks for titillation, not for saving intellectual content. Similarly, such representation would tend to force public confrontation with the potentially offensive aspects of the work; the brazenness of such an appeal heightens the offensiveness of the publications to those who are offended by such material. And the circumstances of presentation and dissemination of material are equally relevant to determining whether social importance claimed for material in the courtroom was, in the circumstances, pretense or reality — whether it was the basis upon which it was traded in the marketplace or a spurious claim for litigation purposes. Where the purveyor's sole emphasis is on the sexually provocative aspects of his publications, that fact may be decisive in the determination of obscenity. Certainly in a prosecution which, as here, does not necessarily imply suppression of the materials involved, the fact that they originate or are used as a subject of pandering is relevant to the application of the *Roth* test. . . .

It is important to stress that this analysis simply elaborates the test by which the obscenity vel non of the material must be judged. Where an exploitation of interests in titillation by pornography is shown with respect to material lending itself to such exploitation through pervasive treatment or description of sexual matters, such evidence may support the determination that the material is obscene even though in other contexts the material would escape such condemnation. . . .

Justice Black dissenting [in the Ginzburg *case].*

Only one stark fact emerges with clarity out of the confusing welter of opinions and thousands of words written in this and two other cases today. That fact is that Ginzburg, petitioner here, is now finally and authoritatively condemned to serve five years in prison for distributing printed matter about sex which neither Ginzburg nor anyone else could possibly have known to be criminal. . . .

My conclusion is that certainly after the fourteen separate opinions handed down in these three cases today no person, not even the most learned judge much less a layman, is capable of knowing in advance of an ultimate decision in his particular case by this Court whether certain material comes within the area of "obscenity" as that term is confused by the Court today. For this reason even if, as appears from the result of the three cases today, this country is far along the way to a censorship of the subjects about which the people can talk or write, we need not commit further constitutional transgressions by leaving people in the dark as to what literature or what words or what symbols if distributed through the mails make a man a criminal. As bad and obnoxious as I believe governmental censorship is in a Nation that has accepted the First Amendment as its basic ideal for freedom, I am compelled to say that censorship that would stamp certain books and literature as illegal in advance of publication or conviction would in some ways be preferable to the unpredictable book-by-book censorship into which we have now drifted.

I close this part of my dissent by saying once again that I think the First Amendment forbids any kind or type or nature of governmental censorship over views as distinguished from conduct. . . .

Justice Brennan delivered the opinion of the Court [in the Mishkin *case]. . . .*

The First Amendment prohibits criminal prosecution for the publication and dissemination of allegedly obscene books that do not satisfy the *Roth* definition of obscenity. States are free to adopt other definitions of obscenity only to the extent that those adopted stay within the bounds set by the constitutional criteria of the *Roth* definition, which restrict the regulation of the publication and sale of books to that traditionally and universally tolerated in our society. . . . [A]ppellant's sole contention regarding the nature of the material is that some of the books involved in this prosecution, those depicting various deviant sexual practices, such as flagellation, fetishism, and lesbianism, do not satisfy the prurient-appeal requirement because they do not appeal to a prurient interest of the "average person" in sex, that "instead of stimulating the erotic, they disgust and sicken." We reject this argument as being founded on an unrealistic interpretation of the prurient-appeal requirement.

Where the material is designed for and primarily disseminated to a clearly defined deviant sexual group, rather than the public at large, the prurient-appeal requirement of the *Roth* test is satisfied if the dominant theme of the material taken as a whole appeals to the prurient interest in sex of the members of that group. The reference to the "average" or "normal" person in *Roth,* . . . does not foreclose this holding. In regard to the prurient-appeal requirement, the concept of the "average" or "normal" person was employed in *Roth* to serve the essentially negative purpose of expressing our rejection of that aspect of the *Hicklin* test, *Regina* v. *Hicklin,* [1868] L.R. 3 Q.B. 360, that made the impact on the most susceptible person determinative. We adjust the prurient-appeal requirement to social realities by permitting the appeal of this type of material to be assessed in terms of the sexual interests of its intended and probable recipient group; and since our holding requires that the recipient group be defined with more specificity than in terms of sexually immature persons, it also avoids the inadequacy of the most-susceptible-person facet of the *Hicklin* test. . . .

Justice Black, dissenting [*in the* Mishkin *case*]. . . .

I dissent from affirmance of this three-year state sentence imposed on Mishkin. Neither in this case nor in *Ginzburg* have I read the alleged obscene matter. This is because I believe for reasons stated in my dissent in *Ginzburg* and in many other prior cases that this Court is without constitutional power to censor speech or press regardless of the particular subject discussed. I think the federal judiciary because it is appointed for life is the most appropriate tribunal that could be selected to interpret the Constitution and thereby mark the boundaries of what government agencies can and cannot do. But because of life tenure as well as other reasons, the federal judiciary is the least appropriate branch of government to take over censorship responsibilities by deciding what pictures and writings people throughout the land can be permitted to see and read. When this Court makes particularized rules on what people can see and read, it determines which policies are reasonable and right, thereby performing the classical function of legislative bodies directly responsible to the people. Accordingly, I wish once more to express my objections to saddling this Court with the irksome and inevitably unpopular and unwholesome task of finally deciding by a case-by-case, sight-by-sight personal judgment of the members of this Court what pornography (whatever that means) is too hard core for people to see or read. If censorship of views about sex or any other subject is constitutional then I am reluctantly compelled to say that I believe the tedious, time-consuming and unwelcome responsibility for finally deciding what particular discussions or opinions must be suppressed in this country, should, for the good of this Court and of the Nation, be vested in some governmental institution or institutions other than this Court.

I would reverse these convictions . . . and announce that the First and Fourteenth Amendments taken together command that neither Congress nor the States shall pass laws which in any manner abridge freedom of speech and press — whatever the subjects discussed. . . .

Miller *v.* California

The "intractable obscenity problem," as Justice John Marshall
Harlan characterized it in 1968 (Interstate Circuit, Inc. v. Dallas,
390 U.S. 676, 704), developed another dimension in the Burger
Court. Once again, the desire for certitude, public concern for
morality, as well as shifting values among the Justices themselves,
promoted the Court's search for firm guidelines in the determination
of obscenity. In this 1973 case, the Court reaffirmed the basic princi-
ple of the Roth *case that obscene material is not protected by the*
First Amendment. But now, the Court applied the Roth *principle of*
"community standards" in a far more literal, focused manner to
enable differing communities throughout the nation to exercise their
own discretion. In a companion case, Paris Adult Theatre I *v.* Slaton
(413 U.S. 49 [1973]), Justice William Brennan, who had written
the Court's opinion in the Roth *case, and had applied it in* Ginzburg,
Mishkin, *and* Fanny Hill, *now maintained that neither the Court,*
Congress, or the states could properly distinguish obscene material
as either protected or unprotected by the First Amendment. Perhaps
most significantly, the Miller *case represented an attempt by the*
Court to relieve itself from an ever-increasing load of obscenity
cases, and similarly relieve itself from having to resolve the "intrac-
table problem." The Court also displayed further tolerance of local
self-determination when it sustained the use of zoning ordinances to
*prohibit "adult" theatres in certain areas (*Young *v.* American Mini
Theatres, Inc. *[1976]).*

Chief Justice Burger delivered the opinion of the Court.

Appellant conducted a mass mailing campaign to advertise the sale of
illustrated books, euphemistically called "adult" material. After a
jury trial, he was convicted of violating California Penal Code § 311.2(a),
a misdemeanor, by knowingly distributing obscene matter, and the Appellate Department, Superior Court of California, County of Orange, summarily affirmed the judgment without opinion. Appellant's conviction was
specifically based on his conduct in causing five unsolicited advertising
brochures to be sent through the mail in an envelope addressed to a restaurant in Newport Beach, California. The envelope was opened by the

---

413 U.S. 15 (1973)

manager of the restaurant and his mother. They had not requested the brochures; they complained to the police.

The brochures advertise four books entitled "Intercourse," "Man-Woman," "Sex Orgies Illustrated," and "An Illustrated History of Pornography," and a film entitled "Marital Intercourse." While the brochures contain some descriptive printed material, primarily they consist of pictures and drawings very explicitly depicting men and women in groups of two or more engaging in a variety of sexual activities, with genitals often prominently displayed.

I

This case involves the application of a State's criminal obscenity statute to a situation in which sexually explicit materials have been thrust by aggressive sales action upon unwilling recipients who had in no way indicated any desire to receive such materials. This Court has recognized that the States have a legitimate interest in prohibiting dissemination or exhibition of obscene material when the mode of dissemination carries with it a significant danger of offending the sensibilities of unwilling recipients or of exposure to juveniles. . . . It is in this context that we are called on to define the standards which must be used to identify obscene material that a State may regulate without infringing on the First Amendment as applicable to the States through the Fourteenth Amendment.

The dissent of MR. JUSTICE BRENNAN reviews the background of the obscenity problem, but since the Court now undertakes to formulate standards more concrete than those in the past, it is useful for us to focus on two of the landmark cases in the somewhat tortured history of the Court's obscenity decisions. In *Roth* v. *United States*, . . . the Court sustained a conviction under a federal statute punishing the mailing of "obscene, lewd, lascivious or filthy . . ." materials. The key to that holding was the Court's rejection of the claim that obscene materials were protected by the First Amendment. . . .

Nine years later, in *Memoirs* v. *Massachusetts*, . . . the Court veered sharply away from the *Roth* concept and, with only three Justices in the plurality opinion, articulated a new test of obscenity. The plurality held that under the *Roth* definition

> "as elaborated in subsequent cases, three elements must coalesce: it must be established that (a) the dominant theme of the material taken as a whole appeals to a prurient interest in sex; (b) the material is patently offensive because it affronts contemporary community standards relating to the description or representation of sexual matters; and (c) the material is utterly without redeeming social value." . . .

Apart from the initial formulation in the *Roth* case, no majority of the Court has at any given time been able to agree on a standard to determine what constitutes obscene, pornographic material subject to regulation under the States' police power. . . . We have seen "a variety of views among the members of the Court unmatched in any other course of constitutional adjudication." *Interstate Circuit, Inc.* v. *Dallas*, 390 U. S., at 704–705. . . . This is not remarkable, for in the area of freedom of speech and press the courts must always remain sensitive to any infringement on genuinely serious literary, artistic, political, or scientific expression. This is an area in which there are few eternal verities. . . .

II

This much has been categorically settled by the Court, that obscene material is unprotected by the First Amendment. . . . We acknowledge, however, the inherent dangers of undertaking to regulate any form of expression. State statutes designed to regulate obscene materials must be carefully limited. . . . As a result, we now confine the permissible scope of such regulation to works which depict or describe sexual conduct. That conduct must be specifically defined by the applicable state law, as written or authoritatively construed. A state offense must also be limited to works which, taken as a whole, appeal to the prurient interest in sex, which portray sexual conduct in a patently offensive way, and which, taken as a whole, do not have serious literary, artistic, political, or scientific value.

The basic guidelines for the trier of fact must be: (a) whether "the average person, applying contemporary community standards" would find that the work, taken as a whole, appeals to the prurient interest . . .; (b) whether the work depicts or describes, in a patently offensive way, sexual conduct specifically defined by the applicable state law; and (c) whether the work, taken as a whole, lacks serious literary, artistic, political, or scientific value. We do not adopt as a constitutional standard the *"utterly without redeeming social value"* test of *Memoirs* v. *Massachusetts* . . .; that concept has never commanded the adherence of more than three Justices at one time. . . . If a state law that regulates obscene material is thus limited, as written or construed, the First Amendment values applicable to the States through the Fourteenth Amendment are adequately protected by the ultimate power of appellate courts to conduct an independent review of constitutional claims when necessary. . . .

We emphasize that it is not our function to propose regulatory schemes for the States. That must await their concrete legislative efforts. . . .

In resolving the inevitably sensitive questions of fact and law, we must continue to rely on the jury system, accompanied by the safeguards that judges, rules of evidence, presumption of innocence, and other protective features provide, as we do with rape, murder, and a host of other offenses against society and its individual members.

Mr. Justice Brennan . . . has abandoned his former position and now maintains that no formulation of this Court, the Congress, or the States can adequately distinguish obscene material unprotected by the First Amendment from protected expression. . . . Paradoxically, Mr. JUSTICE BRENNAN indicates that suppression of unprotected obscene material is permissible to avoid exposure to unconsenting adults, as in this case, and to juveniles, although he gives no indication of how the division between protected and nonprotected materials may be drawn with greater precision for these purposes than for regulation of commercial exposure to consenting adults only. Nor does he indicate where in the Constitution he finds the authority to distinguish between a willing "adult" one month past the state law age of majority and a willing "juvenile" one month younger.

Under the holdings announced today, no one will be subject to prosecution for the sale or exposure of obscene materials unless these materials depict or describe patently offensive "hard core" sexual conduct specifically defined by the regulating state law, as written or construed. We are satisfied that these specific prerequisites will provide fair notice to a dealer in such materials that his public and commercial activities may bring prosecution. . . .

MR. JUSTICE BRENNAN also emphasizes "institutional stress" in justification of his change of view. Noting that "[t]he number of obscenity cases on our docket gives ample testimony to the burden that has been placed upon this Court," he quite rightly remarks that the examination of contested materials "is hardly a source of edification to the members of this Court." . . . He also notes, and we agree, that "uncertainty of the standards creates a continuing source of tension between state and federal courts. . . ." "The problem is . . . that one cannot say with certainty that material is obscene until at least five members of this Court, applying inevitably obscure standards, have pronounced it so." . . .

It is certainly true that the absence, since *Roth*, of a single majority view of this Court as to proper standards for testing obscenity has placed a strain on both state and federal courts. But today, for the first time since *Roth* was decided in 1957, a majority of this Court has agreed on concrete guidelines to isolate "hard core" pornography from expression protected by the First Amendment. . . .

This may not be an easy road, free from difficulty. But no amount of "fatigue" should lead us to adopt a convenient "institutional" rationale—an absolutist, "anything goes" view of the First Amendment—because it will lighten our burdens. . . . Nor should we remedy "tension between state and federal courts" by arbitrarily depriving the States of a power reserved to them under the Constitution, a power which they have enjoyed and exercised continuously from before the adoption of the First Amendment to this day. . . .

III

Under a National Constitution, fundamental First Amendment limitations on the powers of the States do not vary from community to community, but this does not mean that there are, or should or can be, fixed, uniform national standards of precisely what appeals to the "prurient interest" or is "patently offensive." These are essentially questions of fact, and our Nation is simply too big and too diverse for this Court to reasonably expect that such standards could be articulated for all 50 States in a single formulation, even assuming the prerequisite consensus exists. When triers of fact are asked to decide whether "the average person, applying contemporary community standards" would consider certain materials "prurient," it would be unrealistic to require that the answer be based on some abstract formulation. The adversary system, with lay jurors as the usual ultimate factfinders in criminal prosecutions, has historically permitted triers of fact to draw on the standards of their community, guided always by limiting instructions on the law. To require a State to structure obscenity proceedings around evidence of a *national* "community standard" would be an exercise in futility.

As noted before, this case was tried on the theory that the California obscenity statute sought to incorporate the tripartite test of *Memoirs*. This, a "national" standard of First Amendment protection enumerated by a plurality of this Court, was correctly regarded at the time of trial as limiting state prosecution under the controlling case law. The jury, however, was explicitly instructed that, in determining whether the "dominant theme of the material as a whole . . . appeals to the prurient interest" and in determining whether the material "goes substantially beyond customary limits of candor and affronts contemporary community standards of decency," it was to apply "contemporary community standards of the State of California." . . .

We conclude that neither the State's alleged failure to offer evidence of "national standards," nor the trial court's charge that the jury consider state community standards, were constitutional errors. Nothing in the First Amendment requires that a jury must consider hypothetical and unascertainable "national standards" when attempting to determine whether certain materials are obscene as a matter of fact. . . .

It is neither realistic nor constitutionally sound to read the First Amendment as requiring that the people of Maine or Mississippi accept public depiction of conduct found tolerable in Las Vegas, or New York City. . . . People in different States vary in their tastes and attitudes, and this diversity is not to be strangled by the absolutism of imposed uniformity. As the Court made clear in *Mishkin* v. *New York*, 383 U. S., at 508–509, the primary concern with requiring a jury to apply the standard of "the average person, applying contemporary community standards" is to be certain that, so far as material is not aimed at a deviant group, it will be judged by its impact on an average person, rather than a particularly susceptible or sensitive person—or indeed a totally insensitive one. . . . We hold that the requirement that the jury evaluate the materials with reference to "contemporary standards of the State of California" serves this protective purpose and is constitutionally adequate.

IV

The dissenting Justices sound the alarm of repression. But, in our view, to equate the free and robust exchange of ideas and political debate with commercial exploitation of obscene material demeans the grand conception of the First Amendment and its high purposes in the historic struggle for freedom. . . . The First Amendment protects works which, taken as a whole, have serious literary, artistic, political, or scientific value, regardless of whether the government or a majority of the people approve of the ideas these works represent. . . .

But the public portrayal of hard-core sexual conduct for its own sake, and for the ensuing commercial gain, is a different matter.

There is no evidence, empirical or historical, that the stern 19th century American censorship of public distribution and display of material relating to sex . . . in any way limited or affected expression of serious literary, artistic, political, or scientific ideas. On the contrary, it is beyond any question that the era following Thomas Jefferson to Theodore Roosevelt was an "extraordinarily vigorous period," not just in economics and politics, but in *belles lettres* and in "the outlying fields of social and political philosophies." We do not see the harsh hand of censorship of ideas—good or bad—sound or unsound—and "repression" of political liberty lurking in every state regulation of commercial exploitation of human interest in sex.

MR. JUSTICE BRENNAN finds "it is hard to see how state-ordered regimentation of our minds can ever be forestalled." . . . These doleful anticipations assume that courts cannot distinguish commerce in ideas, protected by the First Amendment, from commercial exploitation of obscene material. Moreover, state regulation of hard-core pornography so as to make it unavailable to nonadults, a regulation which MR. JUSTICE BRENNAN finds constitutionally permissible, has all the elements of "censorship" for adults; indeed even more rigid enforcement techniques may be called for with such dichotomy of regulation. . . . One can concede that the "sexual revolution" of recent years may have had useful byproducts in striking layers of prudery from a subject long irrationally kept from needed ventilation. But it does not follow that no regulation of patently offensive "hard core" materials is needed or permissible; civilized people do not allow unregulated access to heroin because it is a derivative of medicinal morphine.

In sum, we (a) reaffirm the *Roth* holding that obscene material is not protected by the First Amendment; (b) hold that such material can be regulated by the States, subject to the specific safeguards enunciated above, without a showing that the material is "*utterly* without redeeming social value"; and (c) hold that obscenity is to be determined by applying "contemporary community standards." . . .

Cox *v.* Louisiana

During the 1960's, mass demonstrations became the chief weapon of both the civil rights and peace movements. The "sit-in" was a particularly useful tactic. Public officials, however, often retaliated by applying broadly-drawn statutes against "disturbing the peace" and "obstructing public buildings." In the Cox *case, the appellant had led a march of 2,000 students on the Baton Rouge courthouse in protest against segregation and the earlier arrest of some students. Cox was arrested and convicted for obstructing public passages and picketing the courthouse. In a separate opinion, the Court held the local anti-picketing ordinance constitutional, but reversed the conviction since Cox had received police permission. In the opinion below, the Court was concerned with the conflict between the right of assembly and the broad, discretionary powers of public officials to keep "order."*

Justice Goldberg delivered the opinion of the Court.

In upholding appellant's conviction under this statute, the Louisiana Supreme Court thus construed the statute so as to apply to public assemblies which do not have as their specific purpose the obstruction of traffic. There is no doubt from the record in this case that this . . . sidewalk was obstructed, and thus, as so construed, appellant violated the statute.

Appellant, however, contends that as so construed and applied in this case, the statute is an unconstitutional infringement on freedom of speech and assembly. This contention on the facts here presented raises an issue with which this Court has dealt in many decisions, that is, the right of a State or municipality to regulate the use of city streets and other facilities to assure the safety and convenience of the people in their use and the concomitant right of the people of free speech and assembly. . . .

---

379 U.S. 536 (1965)

From these decisions certain clear principles emerge. The rights of free speech and assembly, while fundamental in our democratic society, still do not mean that everyone with opinions or beliefs to express may address a group at any public place and at any time. The constitutional guarantee of liberty implies the existence of an organized society maintaining public order, without which liberty itself would be lost in the excesses of anarchy. The control of travel on the streets is a clear example of governmental responsibility to insure this necessary order. A restriction in that relation, designed to promote the public convenience in the interest of all, and not susceptible to abuses of discriminatory application, cannot be disregarded by the attempted exercise of some civil right which, in other circumstances, would be entitled to protection. One would not be justified in ignoring the familiar red light because this was thought to be a means of social protest. Nor could one, contrary to traffic regulations, insist upon a street meeting in the middle of Times Square at the rush hour as a form of freedom of speech or assembly. Governmental authorities have the duty and responsibility to keep their streets open and available for movement. A group of demonstrators could not insist upon the right to cordon off a street, or entrance to a public or private building, and allow no one to pass who did not agree to listen to their exhortations. . . .

We emphatically reject the notion urged by appellant that the First and Fourteenth Amendments afford the same kind of freedom to those who would communicate ideas by conduct such as patrolling, marching, and picketing on streets and highways, as these amendments afford to those who communicate ideas by pure speech. . . . We reaffirm . . . that "it has never been deemed an abridgement of freedom of speech or press to make a course of conduct illegal merely because the conduct was in part initiated, evidenced, or carried out by means of language, either spoken, written or printed."

We have no occasion in this case to consider the constitutionality of the uniform, consistent, and nondiscriminatory application of a statute forbidding all access to streets and other public facilities for parades and meetings. Although the statute here involved on its face precludes all street assemblies and parades, it has not been so applied and enforced by the Baton Rouge authorities. City officials who testified for the State clearly indicated that certain meetings and parades are permitted in Baton Rouge, even though they have the effect of obstructing traffic, provided prior approval is obtained. . . .

The situation is thus the same as if the statute itself expressly provided that there could only be peaceful parades or demonstrations in the unbridled discretion of the local officials. The pervasive restraint on freedom of discussion by the practice of the authorities under the statute is not any less effective than a statute expressly permitting such selective enforcement. A long line of cases in this Court makes it clear that a State or municipality cannot "require all who wish to disseminate ideas to present them first to police authorities for their consideration and approval, with a discretion in the police to say some ideas may, while others may not, be . . . disseminate[d]. . . ."

This Court has recognized that the lodging of such broad discretion in a public official allows him to determine which expressions of view will be permitted and which will not. This thus sanctions a device for the suppression of the communication of ideas and permits the official to act as a censor. . . . Also inherent in such a system allowing parades or meetings only with the prior permission of an official is the obvious danger to the right of a person or group not to be denied equal protection of the laws. . . . It is clearly unconstitutional to enable a public official to determine which expressions of view will be permitted and which will not or to engage in invidious discrimination among persons or groups either by use of a statute providing a system of broad discretionary licensing power or, as in this case, the equivalent of such a system by selective enforcement of an extremely broad prohibitory statute.

It is, of course, undisputed that appropriate, limited discretion, under properly drawn statutes or ordinances, concerning the time, place, duration, or manner of use of the streets for public assemblies may be vested in administrative officials, provided that such limited discretion is "exercised with 'uniformity of method of treatment upon the facts of each application, free from improper or inappropriate considerations and from unfair discrimination' . . . [and with] a 'systematic, consistent and just order of treatment, with reference to the convenience of public use of the highways. . . .'"

But here it is clear that the practice in Baton Rouge allowing unfettered discretion in local officials in the regulation of the use of the streets for peaceful parades and meetings is an unwarranted abridgment of appellant's freedom of speech and assembly secured to him by the First Amendment, as applied to the States by the Fourteenth Amendment. It follows, therefore, that appellant's conviction for violating the statute as so applied and enforced must be reversed.

For the reasons discussed above the judgment of the Supreme Court of Louisiana is reversed.

Virginia State Board of Pharmacy *v.* Virginia Citizens Consumer Council

First Amendment free speech questions in the 1960's and 1970's developed from a wide variety of considerations, such as in obscenity, symbolic speech, and political protest cases. The conclusion of the Supreme Court's 1975 term witnessed the opening of a rather new area with potentially significant economic consequences. In the case below, a nearly-unanimous bench ruled that "commercial speech" is protected by the First and Fourteenth Amendments. The Virginia Consumer Council had challenged a state statute prohibiting licensed pharmacists from advertising prescription drug prices. In declaring the statute void, the Court held that individual consumers and the general society had a vital interest in the unimpeded flow of commercial information, analogous in some ways to the societal stake in an open marketplace for political discourse and information. The Court's decision raised speculation that similar public and private association bans on advertising, such as for lawyers and physicians, also might be unconstitutional. Nearly a month later, the Justice Department filed an anti-trust suit against such restrictions by the American Bar Association. But the results were by no means certain. In a final footnote to its opinion in this case, the Court observed: "Although we express no opinion as to other professions, the distinctions, historical and functional, between professions [such as lawyers and physicians], may require consideration of quite different factors."

Justice Blackmun delivered the opinion of the Court.

The present . . . attack on the statute is one made not by one directly subject to its prohibition, that is, a pharmacist, but by prescription drug consumers who claim that they would greatly benefit if the prohibition were lifted and advertising freely allowed. The plaintiffs are an individual Virginia resident who suffers from diseases that require her to take prescription drugs on a daily basis, and two nonprofit organizations. Their claim is that the First Amendment entitles the user of prescription drugs to receive information, that pharmacists wish to communicate to them

96 S. Ct. 1817 (1976)

through advertising and other promotional means, concerning the prices of such drugs.

Certainly that information may be of value. Drug prices in Virginia, for both prescription and nonprescription items, strikingly vary from outlet to outlet even within the same locality. It is stipulated, for example, that in Richmond "the cost of 40 Achromycin tablets ranges from $2.59 to $6.00, a difference of 140% [*sic*]," and that in the Newport News-Hampton area the cost of tetracycline ranges from $1.20 to $9.00, a difference of 650%....

Here . . . the question whether there is a First Amendment exception for "commercial speech" is squarely before us. Our pharmacist does not wish to editorialize on any subject, cultural, philosophical, or political. He does not wish to report any particularly newsworthy fact, or to make generalized observations even about commercial matters. The "idea" he wishes to communicate is simply this: "I will sell you the X prescription drug at the Y price." Our question, then, is whether this communication is wholly outside the protection of the First Amendment.

We begin with several propositions that already are settled or beyond serious dispute. It is clear, for example, that speech does not lose its First Amendment protection because money is spent to project it, as in a paid advertisement of one form or another. . . . Speech likewise is protected even though it is carried in a form that is "sold" for profit, . . . and even though it may involve a solicitation to purchase or otherwise pay or contribute money. . . .

If there is a kind of commercial speech that lacks all First Amendment protection, therefore, it must be distinguished by its content. Yet the speech whose content deprives it of protection cannot simply be speech on a commercial subject. No one would contend that our pharmacist may be prevented from being heard on the subject of whether, in general, pharmaceutical prices should be regulated, or their advertisement forbidden. Nor can it be dispositive that a commercial advertisement is uneditorial, and merely reports a fact. Purely factual matter of public interest may claim protection. . . .

Our question is whether speech which does "no more than propose a commercial transaction," . . . is so removed from any "exposition of ideas," . . . and from " 'truth, science, morality, and arts in general, in its diffusion of liberal sentiments on the administration of Government,' " . . . that it lacks all protection. Our answer is that it is not.

Focusing first on the individual parties to the transaction that is proposed in the commercial advertisement, we may assume that the advertiser's interest is a purely economic one. That hardly disqualifies him for protection under the First Amendment. The interests of the contestants in a labor dispute are primarily economic, but it has long been settled that both the employee and the employer are protected by the First Amendment when they express themselves on the merits of the dispute in order to influence its outcome. . . . We know of no requirement that, in order to avail themselves of First Amendment protection, the parties to a labor dispute need address themselves to the merits of unionism in general or to any subject beyond their immediate dispute. . . .

Generalizing, society also may have a strong interest in the free flow of commercial information. Even an individual advertisement, though entirely "commercial," may be of general public interest. The facts of decided cases furnish illustrations: advertisements stating that referral services for legal abortions are available . . .; that a manufacturer of artificial furs promotes his product as an alternative to the extinction by his competitors of fur-bearing mammals . . .; and that a domestic producer advertises his product as an alternative to imports that tend to deprive American residents of their jobs. . . . Obviously, not all commercial messages contain the same or even a very great public interest element. There are few to which such an element, however, could not be added. Our pharmacist, for example, could cast himself as a commentator on store-to-store disparities in drug prices, giving his own and those of a competitor as proof. We see little point in requiring him to do so, and little difference if he does not.

Moreover, there is another consideration that suggests that no line between publicly "interesting" or "important" commercial advertising and the opposite kind could ever be drawn. Advertising, however tasteless and excessive it sometimes may seem, is nonetheless dissemination of information as to who is producing and selling what product, for what reason, and at what price. So long as we preserve a predominantly free enterprise economy, the allocation of our resources in large measure will be made through numerous private economic decisions. It is a matter of public interest that those decisions, in the aggregate, be intelligent and well informed. To this end, the free flow of commercial information is indispensable. . . . And if it is indispensable to the proper allocation of resources in a free enterprise system, it is also indispensable to the formation of intelligent opinions as to how that system ought to be regulated or altered. Therefore, even if the First Amendment were thought to be primarily an instrument to enlighten public decisionmaking in a democracy, we could not say that the free flow of information does not serve that goal. . . .

It appears to be feared that if the pharmacist who wishes to provide low cost, and assertedly low quality, services is permitted to advertise, he will be taken up on his offer by too many unwitting customers. They will choose the low-cost, low-quality service and drive the "professional" pharmacist out of business. They will respond only to costly and excessive advertising, and end up paying the price. They will go from one pharmacist to another, following the discount, and destroy the pharmacist-customer relationship. They will lose respect for the profession because it advertises. All this is not in their best interests, and all this can be avoided if they are not permitted to know who is charging what.

There is, of course, an alternative to this highly paternalistic approach. That alternative is to assume that this information is not in itself harmful, that people will perceive their own best interests if only they are well enough informed, and that the best means to that end is to open the channels of communication rather than to close them. If they are truly open, nothing prevents the "professional" pharmacist from marketing his own assertedly superior product, and contrasting it with that of the low-cost, high-volume prescription drug retailer. But the choice among these alternative approaches is not ours to make or the Virginia General Assembly's. It is precisely this kind of choice, between the dangers of suppressing information, and the dangers of its misuse if it is freely available, that the First Amendment makes for us. Virginia is free to require whatever professional standards it wishes of its pharmacists; it may subsidize them or protect them from competition in other ways. . . . But it may not do so by keeping the public in ignorance of the entirely lawful terms that competing pharmacists are offering. In this sense, the justifications Virginia has offered for suppressing the flow of prescription drug price information, far from persuading us that the flow is not protected by the First Amendment, have re-enforced our view that it is. We so hold.

In concluding that commercial speech, like other varieties, is protected, we of course do not hold that it can never be regulated in any way. Some forms of commercial speech regulation are surely permissible. We mention a few only to make clear that they are not before us and therefore are not foreclosed by this case.

There is no claim, for example, that the prohibition on prescription drug price advertising is a mere time, place, and manner restriction. We have often approved restrictions of that kind provided that they are justified without reference to the content of the regulated speech, that they serve a significant governmental interest, and that in so doing they leave open ample alternative channels for communication of the information. . . . Whatever may be the proper bounds of time, place, and manner restrictions on commercial speech, they are plainly exceeded by this Virginia statute, which singles out speech of a particular content and seeks to prevent its dissemination completely. . . .

Obviously, much commercial speech is not provably false, or even wholly false, but only deceptive or misleading. We foresee no obstacle to a State's dealing effectively with this problem. The First Amendment, as we construe it today, does not prohibit the State from insuring that the stream of commercial information flows cleanly as well as freely. . . .

What is at issue is whether a State may completely suppress the dissemination of concededly truthful information about entirely lawful activity, fearful of that information's effect upon its disseminators and its recipients. Reserving other questions, we conclude that the answer to this one is in the negative. . . .

The First Amendment:
Freedom of the Press

Near *v.* Minnesota

This was the first great censorship case decided by the Supreme Court. A 1925 Minnesota law declared that one who engaged in the business of publishing a "malicious, scandalous and defamatory newspaper, magazine, or other periodical" was guilty of a nuisance, and authorized suits by the state to enjoin such publishers. A Minnesota newspaper which regularly attacked city officials, charging them with allowing "Jewish gangsters" to run the city, was brought into court and ordered to cease publication. On appeal, however, the Supreme Court invalidated the statute because it constituted prior restraint. The entire court, incidentally, accepted the idea that freedom of the press was safeguarded by the Fourteenth Amendment from state action. The four dissenters — Butler, McReynolds, Van Devanter, and Sutherland — argued for a reasonable man rule, something they usually refused to do when state economic regulation was at issue. In his dissenting opinion, Justice Butler maintained that the Court was required to assume that "there exists in Minnesota a state of affairs that justifies this measure."

Chief Justice Hughes delivered the opinion of the Court.

This statute, for the suppression as a public nuisance of a newspaper or periodical, is unusual, if not unique, and raises questions of grave importance transcending the local interests involved in the particular action. It is no longer open to doubt that the liberty of the press, and of speech, is within the liberty safeguarded by the due process clause of the Fourteenth Amendment from invasion by state action. . . .

In maintaining this guaranty, the authority of the State to enact laws

---

283 U.S. 697 (1931)

to promote the health, safety, morals and general welfare of its people is necessarily admitted. The limits of this sovereign power must always be determined with appropriate regard to the particular subject of its exercise. . . . Liberty of speech, and of the press, is also not an absolute right, and the State may punish its abuse. . . . Liberty, in each of its phases, has its history and connotation and, in the present instance, the inquiry is as to the historic conception of the liberty of the press and whether the statute under review violates the essential attributes of that liberty. . . .

If we cut through mere details of procedure, the operation and effect of the statute in substance is that public authorities may bring the owner or publisher of a newspaper or periodical before a judge upon a charge of conducting a business of publishing scandalous and defamatory matter — in particular that the matter consists of charges against public officers of official dereliction — and unless the owner or publisher is able and disposed to bring competent evidence to satisfy the judge that the charges are true and are published with good motives and for justifiable ends, his newspaper or periodical is suppressed and further publication is made punishable as a contempt. This is of the essence of censorship.

The question is whether a statute authorizing such proceedings in restraint of publication is consistent with the conception of the liberty of the press as historically conceived and guaranteed. In determining the extent of the constitutional protection, it has been generally, if not universally, considered that it is the chief purpose of the guaranty to prevent previous restraints upon publication. The struggle in England, directed against the legislative power of the licenser, resulted in renunciation of the censorship of the press. The liberty deemed to be established was thus described by Blackstone:

> The liberty of the press is indeed essential to the nature of a free state; but this consists in laying no *previous* restraints upon publications, and not in freedom from censure for criminal matter when published. Every freeman has an undoubted right to lay what sentiments he pleases before the public; to forbid this, is to destroy the freedom of the press; but if he publishes what is improper, mischievous or illegal, he must take the consequence of his own temerity. . . .

[I]t is recognized that punishment for the abuse of the liberty accorded to the press is essential to the protection of the public, and that the common law rules that subject the libeler to responsibility for the public offense, as well as for the private injury, are not abolished by the protection extended in our constitutions. . . . In the present case, we have no occasion to inquire as to the permissible scope of subsequent punishment. For whatever wrong the appellant has committed or may commit, by his publications, the State appropriately affords both public and private redress by its libel laws. As has been noted, the statute in question does not deal with punishments; it provides for no punishment, except in case of contempt for violation of the court's order, but for suppression and injunction, that is, for restraint upon publication.

The objection has also been made that the principle as to immunity from previous restraint is stated too broadly, if every such restraint is deemed to be prohibited. That is undoubtedly true; the protection even as to previous restraint is not absolutely unlimited. But the limitation has been recognized only in exceptional cases: "When a nation is at war many things that might be said in time of peace are such a hindrance to its effort that their utterance will not be endured so long as men fight and that no Court could regard them as protected by any constitutional right." *Schenck* v. *United States*, 249 U.S. 47, 52. . . .

The exceptional nature of its limitations places in a strong light the general conception that liberty of the press, historically considered and taken up by the Federal Constitution, has meant, principally although not exclusively, immunity from previous restraints or censorship. The conception of the liberty of the press in this country had broadened with the exigencies of the colonial period and with the efforts to secure freedom from oppressive administration. That liberty was especially cherished for the immunity it afforded from previous restraint of the publication of censure of public officers and charges of official misconduct. . . .

The importance of this immunity has not lessened. While reckless assaults upon public men, and efforts to bring obloquy upon those who are endeavoring faithfully to discharge official duties, exert a baleful influence and deserve the severest condemnation in public opinion, it cannot be said that this abuse is greater, and it is believed to be less, than that which characterized the period in which our institutions took shape. Meanwhile, the administration of government has become more complex, the opportunities for malfeasance and corruption have multiplied, crime has grown to most serious proportions, and the danger of its protection by unfaithful officials and of the impairment of the fundamental security of life and property by criminal alliances and official neglect, emphasizes the primary need of a vigilant and courageous press, especially in great cities. The fact that the liberty of the press may be abused by miscreant purveyors of scandal does not make any the less necessary the immunity of the press from previous restraint in dealing with official misconduct. Subsequent punishment for such abuses as may exist is the appropriate remedy, consistent with constitutional privilege.

The statute in question cannot be justified by reason of the fact that the publisher is permitted to show, before injunction issues, that the matter published is true and is published with good motives and for justifiable ends. If such a statute, authorizing suppression and injunction on such a basis, is constitutionally valid, it would be equally permissible for the legislature to provide that at any time the publisher of any newspaper could be brought before a court, or even an administrative officer (as the constitutional protection may not be regarded as resting on mere procedural details) and required to produce proof of the truth of his publication, or of what he intended to publish, and of his motives, or stand enjoined. If this can be done, the legislature may provide machinery for determining in the complete exercise of its discretion what are justifiable ends and restrain publication accordingly. And it would be but a step to a complete system of censorship. The recognition of authority to impose previous restraint upon publication in order to protect the community against the circulation of charges of misconduct, and especially of official misconduct, necessarily would carry with it the admission of the authority of the censor against which the constitutional barrier was erected. The preliminary freedom, by virtue of the very reason for its existence, does not depend, as this Court has said, on proof of truth. . . .

Equally unavailing is the insistence that the statute is designed to prevent the circulation of scandal which tends to disturb the public peace and to provoke assaults and the commission of crime. Charges of reprehensible conduct, and in particular of official malfeasance, unquestionably create a public scandal, but the theory of the constitutional guaranty is that even a more serious public evil would be caused by authority to prevent publication.

> To prohibit the intent to excite those unfavorable sentiments against those who administer the Government, is equivalent to a prohibition of the actual excitement of them; and to prohibit the actual excitement of them is equivalent to a prohibition of discussions having that tendency and effect; which, again, is equivalent to a protection of those who administer the Government, if they should at any time deserve the contempt or hatred of the people, against being exposed to it by free animadversions on their characters and conduct.

There is nothing new in the fact that charges of reprehensible conduct may create resentment and the disposition to resort to violent means of redress, but this well-understood tendency did not alter the determination to protect the press against censorship and restraint upon publication. . . . The danger of violent reactions becomes greater with effective organization of defiant groups resenting exposure, and if this consideration warranted legislative interference with the initial freedom of publication, the constitutional protection would be reduced to a mere form of words.

For these reasons we hold the statute . . . to be an infringement of the liberty of the press guaranteed by the Fourteenth Amendment. We should add that this decision rests upon the operation and effect of the statute, without regard to the question of the truth of the charges contained in the particular periodical. . . .

New York Times Co. *v.* Sullivan

The civil rights struggle of the 1960's raised the question of whether a public official could receive damages for libel from critics of his official conduct. In 1960, the New York Times *published an advertisement, critical of the Montgomery, Alabama city officials and police for their handling of racial incidents. The ad contained some erroneous statements about the background of the city's problems. Though he had not been specifically mentioned in the advertisement, one of the city commissioners, L. B. Sullivan, thereupon filed a libel action against four of the Negro signers and the* Times. *A Montgomery jury awarded him $500,000 in damages, and the* Times *appealed to the Supreme Court.*

Justice Brennan delivered the opinion of the Court.

Under Alabama law as applied in this case, a publication is "libelous per se" if the words "tend to injure a person . . . in his reputation" or to "bring [him] into public contempt"; the trial court stated that the standard was met if the words are such as to "injure him in his public office, or impute misconduct to him in his office, or want of official integrity, or want of fidelity to a public trust. . . ." The jury must find that the words were published "of and concerning" the plaintiff, but where the plaintiff is a public official his place in the governmental hierarchy is sufficient evidence to support a finding that his reputation has been affected by statements that reflect upon the agency of which he is in charge. Once "libel per se" has been established, the defendant has no defense as to stated facts unless he can persuade the jury that they were true in all their particulars. . . . His privilege of "fair comment" for expressions of opinion depends on the truth of the facts upon which the comment is based. . . . Unless he can discharge the burden of proving truth, general damages are presumed, and may be awarded without proof of pecuniary injury. A showing of actual malice is apparently a prerequisite to recovery of punitive damages, and the defendant may in

376 U.S. 254 (1964)

any event forestall a punitive award by a retraction meeting the statutory requirements. Good motives and belief in truth do not negate an inference of malice, but are relevant only in mitigation of punitive damages if the jury chooses to accord them weight. . . .

The question before us is whether this rule of liability, as applied to an action brought by a public official against critics of his official conduct, abridges the freedom of speech and of the press that is guaranteed by the First and Fourteenth Amendments.

Respondent relies heavily, as did the Alabama courts, on statements of this Court to the effect that the Constitution does not protect libelous publications. Those statements do not foreclose our inquiry here. None of the cases sustained the use of libel laws to impose sanctions upon expression critical of the official conduct of public officials. . . .

[W]e consider this case against the background of a profound national commitment to the principle that debate on public issues should be uninhibited, robust, and wide-open, and that it may well include vehement, caustic, and sometimes unpleasantly sharp attacks on government and public officials. . . . The present advertisement, as an expression of grievance and protest on one of the major public issues of our time, would seem clearly to qualify for the constitutional protection. The question is whether it forfeits that protection by the falsity of some of its factual statements and by its alleged defamation of respondent.

Authoritative interpretations of the First Amendment guarantees have consistently refused to recognize an exception for any test of truth — whether administered by judges, juries, or administrative officials — and especially one that puts the burden of proving truth on the speaker. . . . The constitutional protection does not turn upon "the truth, popularity, or social utility of the ideas and beliefs which are offered." . . . As Madison said, "Some degree of abuse is inseparable from the proper use of every thing; and in no instance is this more true than in that of the press." . . . That erroneous statement is inevitable in free debate, and that it must be protected if the freedoms of expression are to have the "breathing space" that they "need . . . to survive, ." . . .

Injury to official reputation affords no more warrant for repressing speech that would otherwise be free than does factual error. Where judicial officers are involved, this Court has held that concern for the dignity and reputation of the courts does not justify the punishment as criminal contempt of criticism of the judge or his decision. . . . This is true even though the utterance contains "half-truths" and "misinformation." . . . Such repression can be justified, if at all, only by a clear and present danger of the obstruction of justice. . . . If judges are to be treated as "men of fortitude, able to thrive in a hardy climate," . . . surely the same must be true of other government officials, such as elected city commissioners. Criticism of their official conduct does not lose its constitutional protection merely because it is effective criticism and hence diminishes their official reputations.

If neither factual error nor defamatory content suffices to remove the constitutional shield from criticism of official conduct, the combination of the two elements is no less inadequate. This is the lesson to be drawn from the great controversy over the Sedition Act of 1798, . . . which first crystallized a national awareness of the central meaning of the First Amendment. See Levy, Legacy of Suppression (1960), at 258. . . .

A rule compelling the critic of official conduct to guarantee the truth of all his factual assertions — and to do so on pain of libel judgments virtually unlimited in amount — leads to a comparable "self-censorship." Allowance of the defense of truth, with the burden of proving it on the defendant, does not mean that only false speech will be deterred. Even courts accepting this defense as an adequate safeguard have recognized the difficulties of adducing legal proofs that the alleged libel was true in all its factual particulars. . . . Under such a rule, would-be critics of official conduct may be deterred from voicing their criticism, even though it is believed to be true and even though it is in fact true, because of doubt whether it can be proved in court or fear of the expense of having to do so. They tend to make only statements which "steer far wider of the unlawful zone." . . . The rule thus dampens the vigor and limits the variety of public debate. It is inconsistent with the First and Fourteenth Amendments.

The constitutional guarantees require, we think, a federal rule that prohibits a public official from recovering damages for a defamatory falsehood relating to his official conduct unless he proves that the statement was made with "actual malice" — that is, with knowledge that it was false or with reckless disregard of whether it was false or not. . . .

New York Times Co. *v.* United States

This case, involving the sensational disclosure by the New York
Times *and the* Washington Post *of the so-called "Pentagon Papers,"
provoked in yet another way the tension between the determination
of national security and the guarantees of the Bill of Rights. After
the newspapers began serialization of the documents, formally entitled "History of U.S. Decision-Making Process on Viet Nam Policy,"
the government successfully moved to enjoin further publication in
the* New York Times. *On appeal, the Supreme Court permitted the
injunction to stand while it heard oral arguments. Within a few
days, the Court ruled in a* per curiam *opinion the government had
not met the "heavy burden of showing justification for the enforcement of such a [prior] restraint," and the order was lifted. In a separate opinion, Justice Hugo Black forcefully recited his familiar
First Amendment views, and criticized his colleagues for allowing
the injunction—that is, a prior restraint—to operate at all. Chief Justice Warren Burger, one of three dissenters, decried the haste of the
proceedings, and he clearly indicated that national security concerns
could mitigate an absolutist view of freedom of the press. Burger
also noted agreement with Justice Byron White, who had concurred
with the majority, that the government could pursue prosecution
under ordinary criminal acts regarding stolen materials.*

Justice Black, with Justice Douglas, concurring.

I adhere to the view that the Government's case against the Washington Post should have been dismissed and that the injunction against
the New York Times should have been vacated without oral argument
when the cases were first presented to this Court. I believe that every
moment's continuance of the injunctions against these newspapers
amounts to a flagrant, indefensible, and continuing violation of the First
Amendment. . . . In my view it is unfortunate that some of my Brethren
are apparently willing to hold that the publication of news may sometimes
be enjoined. Such a holding would make a shambles of the First Amendment. . . .

Now, for the first time in the 182 years since the founding of the
Republic, the federal courts are asked to hold that the First Amendment
does not mean what it says, but rather means that the Government can

403 U.S. 713 (1971)

halt the publication of current news of vital importance to the people of this country.

In seeking injunctions against these newspapers and in its presentation to the Court, the Executive Branch seems to have forgotten the essential purpose and history of the First Amendment. When the Constitution was adopted, many people strongly opposed it because the document contained no Bill of Rights to safeguard certain basic freedoms. They especially feared that the new powers granted to a central government might be interpreted to permit the government to curtail freedom of religion, press, assembly, and speech. . . . The Bill of Rights changed the original Constitution into a new charter under which no branch of government could abridge the people's freedoms of press, speech, religion, and assembly. Yet the Solicitor General argues and some members of the Court appear to agree that the general powers of the Government adopted in the original Constitution should be interpreted to limit and restrict the specific and emphatic guarantees of the Bill of Rights adopted later. I can imagine no greater perversion of history. Madison and the other Framers of the First Amendment, able men that they were, wrote in language they earnestly believed could never be misunderstood: "Congress shall make no law . . . abridging the freedom . . . of the press. . . ." Both the history and language of the First Amendment support the view that the press must be left free to publish news, whatever the source, without censorship, injunctions, or prior restraints.

In the First Amendment the Founding Fathers gave the free press the protection it must have to fulfill its essential role in our democracy. The press was to serve the governed, not the governors. The Government's power to censor the press was abolished so that the press would remain forever free to censure the Government. The press was protected so that it could bare the secrets of government and inform the people. Only a free and unrestrained press can effectively expose deception in government. And paramount among the responsibilities of a free press is the duty to prevent any part of the government from deceiving the people and sending them off to distant lands to die of foreign fevers and foreign shot and shell. In my view, far from deserving condemnation for their courageous reporting, the New York Times, the Washington Post, and other newspapers should be commended for serving the purpose that the Founding Fathers saw so clearly. In revealing the workings of government that led to the Vietnam war, the newspapers nobly did precisely that which the Founders hoped and trusted they would do.

The Government's case here is based on premises entirely different from those that guided the Framers of the First Amendment. The Solicitor General has carefully and emphatically stated:

"Now, Mr. Justice [BLACK], your construction of . . . [the First Amendment] is well known, and I certainly respect it. You say that no law means no law, and that should be obvious. I can only say, Mr. Justice, that to me it is equally obvious that 'no law' does not mean 'no law', and I would seek to persuade the Court that that is true. . . . [T]here are other parts of the Constitution that grant powers and responsibilities to the Executive, and . . . the First Amendment was not intended to make it impossible for the Executive to function or to protect the security of the United States."

And the Government argues in its brief that in spite of the First Amendment, "[t]he authority of the Executive Department to protect the nation against publication of information whose disclosure would endanger the national security stems from two interrelated sources: the constitutional power of the President over the conduct of foreign affairs and his authority as Commander-in-Chief."

In other words, we are asked to hold that despite the First Amendment's emphatic command, the Executive Branch, the Congress, and the Judiciary can make laws enjoining publication of current news and abridging freedom of the press in the name of "national security." The Government does not even attempt to rely on any act of Congress. Instead it makes the bold and dangerously far-reaching contention that the courts should take it upon themselves to "make" a law abridging freedom of the press in the name of equity, presidential power and national security, even when the representatives of the people in Congress have adhered to the command of the First Amendment and refused to make such a law. . . . To find that the President has "inherent power" to halt the publication of news by resort to the courts would wipe out the First Amendment and destroy the fundamental liberty and security of the very people the Government hopes to make "secure." No one can read the history of the adoption of the First Amendment without being convinced beyond any doubt that it was injunctions like those sought here that Madison and his collaborators intended to outlaw in this Nation for all time.

The word "security" is a broad, vague generality whose contours should not be invoked to abrogate the fundamental law embodied in the First Amendment. The guarding of military and diplomatic secrets at the expense of informed representative government provides no real security for our Republic. The Framers of the First Amendment, fully aware of both the need to defend a new nation and the abuses of the English and Colonial governments, sought to give this new society strength and security by providing that freedom of speech, press, religion, and assembly should not be abridged. . . .

CHIEF JUSTICE BURGER, dissenting.

In these cases, the imperative of a free and unfettered press comes into collision with another imperative, the effective functioning of a complex modern government and specifically the effective exercise of certain constitutional powers of the Executive. Only those who view the First Amendment as an absolute in all circumstances—a view I respect, but reject—can find such cases as these to be simple or easy.

These cases are not simple for another and more immediate reason. We do not know the facts of the cases. No District Judge knew all the facts. No Court of Appeals judge knew all the facts. No member of this Court knows all the facts.

Why are we in this posture, in which only those judges to whom the First Amendment is absolute and permits of no restraint in any circumstances or for any reason, are really in a position to act?

I suggest we are in this posture because these cases have been conducted in unseemly haste. . . .

Here, moreover, the frenetic haste is due in large part to the manner in which the Times proceeded from the date it obtained the purloined documents. It seems reasonably clear now that the haste precluded reasonable and deliberate judicial treatment of these cases and was not warranted. The precipitate action of this Court aborting trials not yet completed is not the kind of judicial conduct that ought to attend the disposition of a great issue. . . .

An issue of this importance should be tried and heard in a judicial atmosphere conducive to thoughtful, reflective deliberation, especially when haste, in terms of hours, is unwarranted in light of the long period the Times, by its own choice, deferred publication.[1]

It is not disputed that the Times has had unauthorized possession of the documents for three to four months, during which it has had its expert analysts studying them, presumably digesting them and preparing the material for publication. During all of this time, the Times, presumably in its capacity as trustee of the public's "right to know," has held up publication for purposes it considered proper and thus public knowledge was delayed. No doubt this was for a good reason; the analysis of 7,000 pages of complex material drawn from a vastly greater volume of material would inevitably take time and the writing of good news stories takes time. But why should the United States Government, from whom this information was illegally acquired by someone, along with all the counsel, trial judges, and appellate judges be placed under needless pressure?

---

[1] *As noted elsewhere the Times conducted its analysis of the 47 volumes of Government documents over a period of several months and did so with a degree of security that a government might envy. Such security was essential, of course, to protect the enterprise from others. Meanwhile the Times has copyrighted its material and there were strong intimations in the oral argument that the Times contemplated enjoining its use by any other publisher in violation of its copyright. Paradoxically this would afford it a protection, analogous to prior restraint, against all others—a protection the Times denies the Government of the United States.*

After these months of deferral, the alleged "right to know" has somehow and suddenly become a right that must be vindicated instanter.

Would it have been unreasonable, since the newspaper could anticipate the Government's objections to release of secret material, to give the Government an opportunity to review the entire collection and determine whether agreement could be reached on publication? . . . To me it is hardly believable that a newspaper long regarded as a great institution in American life would fail to perform one of the basic and simple duties of every citizen with respect to the discovery of possession of stolen property or secret government documents. That duty, I had thought—perhaps naively—was to report forthwith, to responsible public officers. This duty rests on taxi drivers, Justices, and the New York Times. The course followed by the Times, whether so calculated or not, removed any possibility of orderly litigation of the issues. If the action of the judges up to now has been correct, that result is sheer happenstance.[2]

Our grant of the writ of certiorari before final judgment in the *Times* case aborted the trial in the District Court before it had made a complete record pursuant to the mandate of the Court of Appeals for the Second Circuit.

The consequence of all this melancholy series of events is that we literally do not know what we are acting on. . . .

I would affirm the Court of Appeals for the Second Circuit and allow the District Court to complete the trial aborted by our grant of certiorari. . . . I would direct that the District Court on remand give priority to the *Times* case to the exclusion of all other business of that court but I would not set arbitrary deadlines.

I should add that I am in general agreement with much of what MR. JUSTICE WHITE has expressed with respect to penal sanctions concerning communication or retention of documents or information relating to the national defense.

We all crave speedier judicial processes but when judges are pressured as in these cases the result is a parody of the judicial function.

---

[2] *Interestingly the Times explained its refusal to allow the Government to examine its own purloined documents by saying in substance this might compromise its sources and informants! The Times thus asserts a right to guard the secrecy of its sources while denying that the Government of the United States has that power.*

The First Amendment:
Freedom of—and from—Religion

West Virginia Board of Education

v.

Barnette

This case climaxed a long dispute between the Jehovah's Witnesses and public school officials regarding compulsory flag-salutes, a practice which the sect equates with the worship of a graven image. In 1940, the Court sustained such a requirement in Minersville School District v. Gobitis (310 U.S. 586). Justice Frankfurter argued that "national unity is the basis of national security," and that the flag salute promoted and symbolized that unity. He also justified the regulation in the context of judicial restraint, arguing that the Court was not competent to intervene in a matter involving "pedagogical and psychological dogma." Although the flag salute was the rule of a local school board, Frankfurter treated it as if it were an action by the state itself. Only Justice Stone dissented, finding that the regulation interfered with the free exercise of religion and freedom of speech. In 1942, three of the majority justices indicated misgivings about the Gobitis decision (Jones v. Opelika, 316 U.S. 584). The following year, the Court completely reversed itself in the Barnette case by a 6–3 margin. Justice Jackson built upon Stone's dissent and challenged Frankfurter's notions of judicial restraint in cases where the Bill of Rights was at stake.

Justice Jackson delivered the opinion of the Court.

Following the decision by this Court on June 3, 1940, in *Minersville School District* v. *Gobitis*, 310 U.S. 586, the West Virginia legislature amended its statutes to require all schools therein to conduct courses of

---

319 U.S. 624 (1943)

instruction in history, civics, and in the Constitutions of the United States and of the State "for the purpose of teaching, fostering and perpetuating the ideals, principles and spirit of Americanism, and increasing the knowledge of the organization and machinery of the government." . . .

The Board of Education on January 9, 1942, adopted a resolution containing recitals taken largely from the Court's *Gobitis* opinion and ordering that the salute to the flag become "a regular part of the program of activities in the public schools," that all teachers and pupils "shall be required to participate in the salute honoring the Nation represented by the Flag; provided, however, that refusal to salute the Flag be regarded as an act of insubordination, and shall be dealt with accordingly."

The resolution originally required the "commonly accepted salute to the Flag" which it defined. Objections to the salute as "being too much like Hitler's" were raised by the Parent and Teachers Association, the Boy and Girl Scouts, the Red Cross, and the Federation of Women's Clubs. Some modification appears to have been made in deference to these objections, but no concession was made to Jehovah's Witnesses. What is now required is the "stiff-arm" salute, the saluter to keep the right hand raised with palm turned up while the following is repeated: "I pledge allegiance to the Flag of the United States of America and to the Republic for which it stands; one Nation, indivisible, with liberty and and justice for all."

Failure to conform is "insubordination" dealt with by expulsion. Readmission is denied by statute until compliance. Meanwhile the expelled child is "unlawfully absent" and may be proceeded against as a delinquent. His parents or guardians are liable to prosecution, and if convicted are subject to fine not exceeding $50 and jail term not exceeding thirty days.

Appellees, citizens of the United States and of West Virginia, brought suit in the United States District Court for themselves and others similarly situated asking its injunction to restrain enforcement of these laws and regulations against Jehovah's Witnesses. The Witnesses are an unincorporated body teaching that the obligation imposed by law of God is superior to that of laws enacted by temporal government. Their religious beliefs include a literal version of Exodus, Chapter 20, verses 4 and 5, which says: "Thou shalt not make unto thee any graven image, or any likeness of anything that is in heaven above, or that is in the earth beneath, or that is in the water under the earth; thou shalt not bow down thyself to them nor serve them." They consider that the flag is an "image" within this command. For this reason they refuse to salute it.

Children of this faith have been expelled from school and are threatened with exclusion for no other cause. Officials threaten to send them to reformatories maintained for criminally inclined juveniles. Parents of such children have been prosecuted and are threatened with prosecutions for causing delinquency. . . .

This case calls upon us to reconsider a precedent decision, as the Court throughout its history often has been required to do. . . .

As the present Chief Justice said in dissent in the *Gobitis* case, the State may "require teaching by instruction and study of all in our history and in the structure and organization of our government, including the guaranties of civil liberty, which tend to inspire patriotism and love of country." 310 U.S. at 604. Here, however, we are dealing with a compulsion of students to declare a belief. They are not merely made acquainted with the flag salute so that they may be informed as to what it is or even what it means. The issue here is whether this slow and easily neglected route to aroused loyalties constitutionally may be short-cut by substituting a compulsory salute and slogan. . . .

There is no doubt that, in connection with the pledges, the flag salute is a form of utterance. Symbolism is a primitive but effective way of communicating ideas. The use of an emblem or flag to symbolize some system, idea, institution, or personality, is a short cut from mind to mind. Causes and nations, political parties, lodges and ecclesiastical groups seek to knit the loyalty of their followings to a flag or banner, a color or design. The State announces rank, function, and authority through crowns and maces, uniforms and black robes; the church speaks through the Cross, the Crucifix, the altar and shrine, and clerical raiment. Symbols of State often convey political ideas just as religious symbols come to convey theological ones. Associated with many of these symbols are appropriate gestures of acceptance or respect: a salute, a bowed or bared head, a bended knee. A person gets from a symbol the meaning he puts into it, and what is one man's comfort and inspiration is another's jest and scorn. . . .

It is also to be noted that the compulsory flag salute and pledge requires affirmation of a belief and an attitude of mind. It is not clear whether the regulation contemplates that pupils forego any contrary convictions of their own and become unwilling converts to the prescribed ceremony or whether it will be acceptable if they simulate assent by words without belief and by a gesture barren of meaning. It is now a commonplace that censorship or suppression of expression of opinion is tolerated by our Constitution only when the expression presents a clear and present danger of action of a kind the State is empowered to prevent and punish. It would seem that involuntary affirmation could be commanded only on even more immediate and urgent grounds than silence. But here the power of compulsion is invoked without any allegation that remaining passive during a flag salute ritual creates a clear and present danger that would justify an effort even to muffle expression. To sustain the compulsory flag salute we are required to say that a Bill of Rights which guards the individual's right to speak his own mind, left it open to public authorities to compel him to utter what is not in his mind.

Whether the First Amendment to the Constitution will permit officials to order observance of ritual of this nature does not depend upon whether as a voluntary exercise we would think it to be good, bad or merely innocuous. Any credo of nationalism is likely to include what some disapprove or to omit what others think essential, and to give off different overtones as it takes on different accents or interpretations. If official power exists to coerce acceptance of any patriotic creed, what it shall contain cannot be decided by courts, but must be largely discretionary with the ordaining authority, whose power to prescribe would no doubt include power to amend. Hence validity of the asserted power to force an American citizen publicly to profess any statement of belief or to engage in any ceremony of assent to one, presents questions of power that must be considered independently of any idea we may have as to the utility of the ceremony in question.

Nor does the issue as we see it turn on one's possession of particular religious views or the sincerity with which they are held. . . .

It was said that the flag-salute controversy confronted the Court with "the problem which Lincoln cast in memorable dilemma: 'Must a government of necessity be too *strong* for the liberties of its people, or too *weak* to maintain its own existence?'" and that the answer must be in favor of strength. *Minersville School District* v. *Gobitis.* . . .

We think these issues may be examined free of pressure or restraint growing out of such considerations.

It may be doubted whether Mr. Lincoln would have thought that the strength of government to maintain itself would be impressively vindicated by our confirming power of the State to expel a handful of children from school. Such oversimplification, so handy in political debate, often lacks the precision necessary to postulates of judicial reasoning. If validly applied to this problem, the utterance cited would resolve every issue of power in favor of those in authority and would require us to override every liberty thought to weaken or delay execution of their policies.

Government of limited power need not be anemic government. Assurance that rights are secure tends to diminish fear and jealousy of strong government, and by making us feel safe to live under it makes for its better support. Without promise of a limiting Bill of Rights it is doubtful if our Constitution could have mustered enough strength to enable its ratification. To enforce those rights today is not to choose weak government over strong government. It is only to adhere as a means of strength to individual freedom of mind in preference to officially disciplined uniformity for which history indicates a disappointing and disastrous end.

The subject now before us exemplifies this principle. Free public education, if faithful to the ideal of secular instruction and political neutrality, will not be partisan or enemy of any class, creed, party, or faction. If it is to impose any ideological discipline, however, each party or denomination must seek to control, or failing that, to weaken the influence of the educational system. Observance of the limitations of the Constitution will not weaken government in the field appropriate for its exercise. . . .

It was also considered in the *Gobitis* case that functions of educational officers in States, counties and school districts were such that to interfere with their authority "would in effect make us the school board for the country." . . .

3. The *Gobitis* opinion reasoned that this is a field "where courts possess no marked and certainly no controlling competence," that it is committed to the legislatures as well as the courts to guard cherished liberties and that it is constitutionally appropriate to "fight out the wise use of legislative authority in the forum of public opinion and before legislative assemblies rather than to transfer such a contest to the judicial arena," since all the "effective means of inducing political changes are left free." *Id.* at 597–598, 600.

The very purpose of a Bill of Rights was to withdraw certain subjects from the vicissitudes of political controversy, to place them beyond the reach of majorities and officials and to establish them as legal principles to be applied by the courts. One's right to life, liberty, and property, to free speech, a free press, freedom of worship and assembly, and other fundamental rights may not be submitted to vote; they depend on the outcome of no elections.

In weighing arguments of the parties it is important to distinguish between the due process clause of the Fourteenth Amendment as an instrument for transmitting the principles of the First Amendment and those cases in which it is applied for its own sake. The test of legislation which collides with the Fourteenth Amendment, because it also collides with the principles of the First, is much more definite than the test when only the Fourteenth is involved. Much of the vagueness of the due process clause disappears when the specific prohibitions of the First become its standard. The right of a State to regulate, for example, a public utility may well include, so far as the due process test is concerned, power to impose all of the restrictions which a legislature may have a "rational basis" for adopting. But freedoms of speech and of press, of assembly, and of worship may not be infringed on such slender grounds. They are susceptible of restriction only to prevent grave and immediate danger to interests which the State may lawfully protect. It is important to note that while it is the Fourteenth Amendment which bears directly upon the State it is the more specific limiting principles of the First Amendment that finally govern this case.

Nor does our duty to apply the Bill of Rights to assertions of official authority depend upon our possession of marked competence in the field where the invasion of rights occurs. True, the task of translating the majestic generalities of the Bill of Rights, conceived as part of the pattern of liberal government in the eighteenth century, into concrete restraints on officials dealing with the problems of the twentieth century, is one to disturb self-confidence. These principles grew in soil which also produced a philosophy that the individual was the center of society, that his liberty was attainable through mere absence of governmental restraints, and that government should be entrusted with few controls and only the mildest supervision over men's affairs. We must transplant these rights to a soil in which the *laissez-faire* concept or principle of non-interference has withered at least as to economic affairs, and social advancements are increasingly sought through closer integration of society and through expanded and strengthened governmental controls. These changed conditions often deprive precedents of reliability and cast us more than we would choose upon our own judgment. But we act in these matters not by authority of our competence but by force of our commissions. We cannot, because of modest estimates of our competence in such specialties as public education, withhold the judgment that history authenticates as the function of this Court when liberty is infringed. . . .

Lastly, and this is the very heart of the *Gobitis* opinion, it reasons that "National unity is the basis of national security," that the authorities have "the right to select appropriate means for its attainment," and hence reaches the conclusion that such compulsory measures toward "national unity" are constitutional. *Id.* at 595. Upon the verity of this assumption depends our answer in this case.

National unity as an end which officials may foster by persuasion and example is not in question. The problem is whether under our Constitution compulsion as here employed is a permissible means for its achievement.

Struggles to coerce uniformity of sentiment in support of some end thought essential to their time and country have been waged by many good as well as by evil men. Nationalism is a relatively recent phenomenon but at other times and places the ends have been racial or territorial security, support of a dynasty or regime, and particular plans for saving souls. As first and moderate methods to attain unity have failed, those bent on its accomplishment must resort to an ever-increasing severity. As governmental pressure toward unity becomes greater, so strife becomes more bitter as to whose unity it shall be. Probably no deeper division of our people could proceed from any provocation than from finding it necessary to choose what doctrine and whose program public educational officials shall compel youth to unite in embracing. Ultimate futility of such attempts to compel coherence is the lesson of every such effort from the Roman drive to stamp out Christianity as a disturber of its pagan unity, the Inquisition, as a means to religious and dynastic unity, the Siberian exiles as a means to Russian unity, down to the fast failing efforts of our present totalitarian enemies. Those who begin coercive elimination of dissent soon find themselves exterminating dissenters. Compulsory unification of opinion achieves only the unanimity of the graveyard.

It seems trite but necessary to say that the First Amendment to our Constitution was designed to avoid these ends by avoiding these beginnings. There is no mysticism in the American concept of the State or of the nature or origin of its authority. We set up government by consent of the governed, and the Bill of Rights denies those in power any legal opportunity to coerce that consent. Authority here is to be controlled by public opinion, not public opinion by authority.

The case is made difficult not because the principles of its decision are obscure but because the flag involved is our own. Nevertheless, we apply the limitations of the Constitution with no fear that freedom to be intellectually and spiritually diverse or even contrary will disintegrate the social organization. To believe that patriotism will not flourish if patriotic ceremonies are voluntary and spontaneous instead of a compulsory routine is to make an unflattering estimate of the appeal of our institutions to free minds. We can have intellectual individualism and the rich cultural diversities that we owe to exceptional minds only at the price of occasional eccentricity and abnormal attitudes. When they are so harmless to others or to the State as those we deal with here, the price is not too great. But freedom to differ is not limited to things that do not matter much. That would be a mere shadow of freedom. The test of its substance is the right to differ as to things that touch the heart of the existing order.

If there is any fixed star in our constitutional constellation, it is that no official, high or petty, can prescribe what shall be orthodox in politics, nationalism, religion, or other matters of opinion or force citizens to confess by word or act their faith therein. If there are any circumstances which permit an exception, they do not now occur to us.

We think the action of the local authorities in compelling the flag salute and pledge transcends constitutional limitations on their power and invades the sphere of intellect and spirit which it is the purpose of the First Amendment to our Constitution to reserve from all official control.

The decision of this Court in *Minersville School District* v. *Gobitis* and the holdings of those few *per curiam* decisions which preceded and foreshadowed it are overruled, and the judgment enjoining enforcement of the West Virginia Regulation is

Affirmed.

Justice Frankfurter, dissenting . . . .

One who belongs to the most vilified and persecuted minority in history is not likely to be insensible to the freedoms guaranteed by our Constitution. Were my purely personal attitude relevant I should wholeheartedly associate myself with the general libertarian views in the Court's opinion, representing as they do the thought and action of a lifetime. But as judges we are neither Jew nor Gentile, neither Catholic nor agnostic. We owe equal attachment to the Constitution and are equally bound by our judicial obligations whether we derive our citizenship from the earliest or the latest immigrants to these shores. As a member of this Court I am not justified in writing my private notions of policy into the Constitution, no matter how deeply I may cherish them or how mischievous I may deem their disregard. The duty of a judge who must decide which of two claims before the Court shall prevail, that of a State to enact and enforce laws within its general competence or that of an individual to refuse obedience because of the demands of his conscience, is not that of the ordinary person. It can never be emphasized too much that one's own opinion about the wisdom or evil of a law should be excluded altogether when one is doing one's duty on the bench. The only opinion of our own even looking in that direction that is material is our opinion whether legislators could in reason have enacted such a law. In the light of all the circumstances, including the history of this question in this Court, it would require more daring than I possess to deny that reasonable legislators could have taken the action which is before us for review. Most unwillingly, therefore, I must differ from my brethren with regard to legislation like this. I cannot bring my mind to believe that the "liberty" secured by the Due Process Clause gives this Court authority to deny to the State of West Virginia the attainment of that which we all recognize as a legitimate legislative end, namely, the promotion of good citizenship, by employment of the means here chosen. . . .

We are not reviewing merely the action of a local school board. . . . Practically we are passing upon the political power of each of the forty-eight states. Moreover, since the First Amendment has been read into the Fourteenth, our problem is precisely the same as it would be if we had before us an Act of Congress for the District of Columbia. To suggest that we are here concerned with the heedless action of some village tyrants is to distort the augustness of the constitutional issue and the reach of the consequences of our decision.

Under our constitutional system the legislature is charged solely with civil concerns of society. If the avowed or intrinsic legislative purpose is either to promote or to discourage some religious community or creed, it is clearly within the constitutional restrictions imposed on legislatures and cannot stand. But it by no means follows that legislative power is wanting whenever a general non-discriminatory civil regulation in fact touches conscientious scruples or religious beliefs of an individual or a group. Regard for such scruples or beliefs undoubtedly presents one of the most reasonable claims for the exertion of legislative accommodation. It is, of course, beyond our power to rewrite the State's requirement, by providing exemptions for those who do not wish to participate in the flag salute or by making some other accommodations to meet their scruples. That wisdom might suggest the making of such accommodations and that school administration would not find it too difficult to make them and yet maintain the ceremony for those not refusing to conform, is outside our province to suggest. Tact, respect, and generosity toward variant views will always commend themselves to those charged with the duties of legislation so as to achieve a maximum of good will and to require a minimum of unwilling submission to a general law. But the real question is, who is to make such accommodations, the courts or the legislature? . . .

Everson

v.

Board of Education of the Township of Ewing

Probably no case better illustrates the Court's historical confusion and ideological difficulties over the First Amendment's religion clauses than Everson. A New Jersey statute authorized local school boards to reimburse parents for transportation of their children to schools, whether public or private. Ewing Township provided such funds for parents of Catholic school children and a taxpayer's suit challenged the action on constitutional grounds. The Court agreed that the Fourteenth Amendment incorporated the establishment clause of the first Amendment but narrowly held the reimbursement arrangement valid. Justice Black's majority opinion at times indicated an absolutist interpretation of separation between church and state, but he finally concluded that the payments were a service to children and not to the Catholic schools. In a biting dissent, Justice Jackson compared Black's reasoning and result to Byron's Julia, who, "whispering 'I will ne'er consent,' — consented."

Justice Black delivered the opinion of the Court.

The only contention here is that the state statute and the resolution, insofar as they authorized reimbursement to parents of children attending parochial schools, violate the Federal Constitution in these two respects, which to some extent overlap. *First.* They authorize the State to take by taxation the private property of some and bestow it upon others, to be used for their own private purposes. This, it is alleged, violates the due process clause of the Fourteenth Amendment. *Second.* The statute and the resolution forced inhabitants to pay taxes to help support and maintain schools which are dedicated to, and which regularly teach, the Catholic Faith. This is alleged to be a use of state power to support church schools contrary to the prohibition of the First Amendment which the Fourteenth Amendment made applicable to the states.

First. . . . It is much too late to argue that legislation intended to

330 *U.S.* 1 (1947)

facilitate the opportunity of children to get a secular education serves no public purpose. . . .

Second. The New Jersey statute is challenged as a "law respecting an establishment of religion." The First Amendment, as made applicable to the states by the Fourteenth . . . commands that a state "shall make no law respecting an establishment of religion, or prohibiting the free exercise thereof. . . ." These words of the First Amendment reflected in the minds of early Americans a vivid mental picture of conditions and practices which they fervently wished to stamp out in order to preserve liberty for themselves and for their posterity. Doubtless their goal has not been entirely reached; but so far has the Nation moved toward it that the expression "law respecting an establishment of religion," probably does not so vividly remind present-day Americans of the evils, fears, and political problems that caused that expression to be written into our Bill of Rights. Whether this New Jersey law is one respecting an "establishment of religion" requires an understanding of the meaning of that language, particularly with respect to the imposition of taxes. Once again, therefore, it is not inappropriate briefly to review the background and environment of the period in which that constitutional language was fashioned and adopted.

A large proportion of the early settlers of this country came here from Europe to escape the bondage of laws which compelled them to support and attend government-favored churches. The centuries immediately before and contemporaneous with the colonization of America had been filled with turmoil, civil strife, and persecutions, generated in large part by established sects determined to maintain their absolute political and religious supremacy. With the power of government supporting them, at various times and places, Catholics had persecuted Protestants, Protestants had persecuted Catholics, Protestant sects had persecuted other Protestant sects, Catholics of one shade of belief had persecuted Catholics of another shade of belief, and all of these had from time to time persecuted Jews. In efforts to force loyalty to whatever religious group happened to be on top and in league with the government of a particular time and place, men and women had been fined, cast in jail, cruelly tortured, and killed. Among the offenses for which these punishments had been inflicted were such things as speaking disrespectfully of the views of ministers of government-established churches, non-attendance at those churches, expressions of non-belief in their doctrine, and failure to pay taxes and tithes to support them.

These practices of the old world were transplanted to and began to thrive in the soil of the new America. The very charters granted by the English Crown to the individuals and companies designated to make the laws which would control the destinies of the colonials authorized these individuals and companies to erect religious establishments which all, whether believers or non-believers, would be required to support and attend. An exercise of this authority was accompanied by a repetition of many of the old-world practices and persecutions. Catholics found themselves hounded and proscribed because of their faith; Quakers who followed their conscience went to jail; Baptists were peculiarly obnoxious to certain dominant Protestant sects; men and women of varied faiths who happened to be in a minority in a particular locality were persecuted because they steadfastly persisted in worshipping God only as their own consciences dictated. And all of these dissenters were compelled to pay tithes and taxes to support government-sponsored churches whose ministers preached inflammatory sermons designed to strengthen and consolidate the established faith by generating a burning hatred against dissenters.

These practices became so commonplace as to shock the freedom-loving colonials into a feeling of abhorrence. The imposition of taxes to pay ministers' salaries and to build and maintain churches and church property aroused their indignation. It was these feelings which found expression in the First Amendment. No one locality and no one group throughout the Colonies can rightly be given entire credit for having aroused the sentiment that culminated in adoption of the Bill of Rights' provisions embracing religious liberty. But Virginia, where the established church had achieved a dominant influence in political affairs and where many excesses attracted wide public attention, provided a great stimulus and able leadership for the movement. The people there, as elsewhere, reached the conviction that individual religious liberty could be achieved best under a government which was stripped of all power to tax, to support, or otherwise to assist any or all religions, or to interfere with the beliefs of any religious individual or group.

The movement toward this end reached its dramatic climax in Virginia in 1785–86 when the Virginia legislative body was about to renew Virginia's tax levy for the support of the established church. Thomas Jefferson and James Madison led the fight against this tax. Madison wrote his great Memorial and Remonstrance against the law. In it, he eloquently argued that a true religion did not need the support of law; that no person, either believer or non-believer, should be taxed to support a religious institution of any kind; that the best interest of a society required that the minds of men always be wholly free; and that cruel persecutions were the inevitable result of government-established religions. Madison's Remonstrance received strong support throughout Virginia, and the Assembly postponed consideration of the proposed tax measure until its next session. When the proposal came up for consideration at that session, it not only died in committee, but the Assembly enacted the famous "Virginia Bill for Religious Liberty" originally written by Thomas Jefferson. . . . And the statute itself enacted

That no man shall be compelled to frequent or support any religious worship, place, or ministry whatsoever, nor shall be enforced, restrained, molested, or burthened in his body or goods, nor shall otherwise suffer on account of his religious opinions or belief . . . .

This Court has previously recognized that the provisions of the First Amendment, in the drafting and adoption of which Madison and Jefferson played such leading roles, had the same objective and were intended to provide the same protection against governmental intrusion on religious liberty as the Virginia statute. . . . Prior to the adoption of the Fourteenth Amendment, the First Amendment did not apply as a restraint against the states. Most of them did soon provide similar constitutional protections for religious liberty. But some states persisted for about half a century in imposing restraints upon the free exercise of religion and in discriminating against particular religious groups. In recent years, so far as the provision against the establishment of a religion is concerned, the question has most frequently arisen in connection with proposed state aid to church schools and efforts to carry on religious teachings in the public schools in accordance with the tenets of a particular sect. Some churches have either sought or accepted state financial support for their schools. Here again the efforts to obtain state aid or acceptance of it have not been limited to any one particular faith. The state courts, in the main, have remained faithful to the language of their own constitutional provisions designed to protect religious freedom and to separate religions and governments. Their decisions, however, show the difficulty in drawing the line between tax legislation which provides funds for the welfare of the general public and that which is designed to support institutions which teach religion. . . .

The "establishment of religion" clause of the First Amendment means at least this: Neither a state nor the Federal Government can set up a church. Neither can pass laws which aid one religion, aid all religions, or prefer one religion over another. Neither can force nor influence a person to go to or to remain away from church against his will or force him to profess a belief or disbelief in any religion. No person can be punished for entertaining or professing religious beliefs or disbeliefs, for church attendance or non-attendance. No tax in any amount, large or small, can be levied to support any religious activities or institutions, whatever they may be called, or whatever form they may adopt to teach or practice religion. Neither a state nor the Federal Government can, openly or secretly, participate in the affairs of any religious organizations or groups and *vice versa*. In the words of Jefferson, the clause against establishment of religion by law was intended to erect "a wall of separation between church and State." . . .

Measured by these standards, we cannot say that the First Amendment prohibits New Jersey from spending tax-raised funds to pay the bus fares of parochial school pupils as a part of a general program under which it pays the fares of pupils attending public and other schools. It is undoubtedly true that children are helped to get to church schools. There is even a possibility that some of the children might not be sent to the church schools if the parents were compelled to pay their children's bus fares out of their own pockets when transportation to a public school would have been paid for by the State. The same possibility exists where the state requires a local transit company to provide reduced fares to school children including those attending parochial schools, or where a municipally owned transportation system undertakes to carry all school children free of charge. Moreover, state-paid policemen, detailed to protect children going to and from church schools from the very real hazards of traffic, would serve much the same purpose and accomplish much the same result as state provisions intended to guarantee free transportation of a kind which the state deems to be best for the school children's welfare. And parents might refuse to risk their children to the serious danger of traffic accidents going to and from parochial schools, the approaches to which were not protected by policemen. Similarly, parents might be reluctant to permit their children to attend schools which the state had cut off from such general government services as ordinary police and fire protection, connections for sewage disposal, public highways and sidewalks. Of course, cutting off church schools from these services, so separate and so indisputably marked off from the religious function, would make it far more difficult for the schools to operate. But such is obviously not the purpose of the First Amendment. That Amendment requires the state to be a neutral in its relations with groups of religious believers and non-believers; it does not require the state to be their adversary. State power is no more to be used so as to handicap religions than it is to favor them.

This Court has said that parents may, in the discharge of their duty under state compulsory education laws, send their children to a religious rather than a public school if the school meets the secular educational requirements which the state has power to impose. See *Pierce* v. *Society of Sisters*, 268 U.S. 510. It appears that these parochial schools meet New Jersey's requirements. The State contributes no money to the schools. It does not support them. Its legislation, as applied, does no more than provide a general program to help parents get their children, regardless of their religion, safely and expeditiously to and from accredited schools.

The First Amendment has erected a wall between church and state. That wall must be kept high and impregnable. We could not approve the slightest breach. New Jersey has not breached it here.

Zorach v. Clauson

A *year after the* Everson *decision, the Court broadly construed the establishment clause to invalidate a "released time" system of religious education in the Champaign, Illinois public schools (McCollum v. Board of Education, 333 U.S. 203). The classes were held in the public schools, during regular hours, and the teachers were under the supervision of the local superintendent. The decision was followed by widespread protests from church groups who were advocating wider uses of the released time program. In the case below, the Court retreated from the McCollum decision and reconsidered the problem under somewhat different circumstances. New York City had a program which allowed students to attend religious classes off school property. Justice Douglas used this feature to distinguish the Champaign case as public funds were not involved and religious instruction did not take place in the schools. In dissent, Justice Jackson, protested that the effect was to have the school system use its power to aid religious sects in instruction. The school, he said, "serves as a temporary jail for a pupil who will not go to Church."*

Justice Douglas delivered the opinion of the Court.

New York City has a program which permits its public schools to release students during the school day so that they may leave the school buildings and school grounds and go to religious centers for religious instruction or devotional exercises. A student is released on written request of his parents. Those not released stay in the classrooms. The churches make weekly reports to the schools, sending a list of children who have been released from public school but who have not reported for religious instruction. . . .

This "released time" program involves neither religious instruction in public school classrooms nor the expenditure of public funds. All costs, including the application blanks, are paid by the religious organizations. The case is therefore unlike *McCollum* v. *Board of Education,* 333 U.S. 203, which involved a "released time" program from Illinois. In that case the classrooms were turned over to religious instructors. We accordingly held that the program violated the First Amendment which (by reason

343 U.S. 306 (1952)

of the Fourteenth Amendment) prohibits the states from establishing religion or prohibiting its free exercise. . . .

It takes obtuse reasoning to inject any issue of the "free exercise" of religion into the present case. No one is forced to go to the religious classroom and no religious exercise or instruction is brought to the classrooms of the public schools. A student need not take religious instruction. He is left to his own desires as to the manner or time of his religious devotions, if any.

There is a suggestion that the system involves the use of coercion to get public school students into religious classrooms. There is no evidence in the record before us that supports that conclusion. The present record indeed tells us that the school authorities are neutral in this regard and do no more than release students whose parents so request. If in fact coercion were used, if it were established that any one or more teachers were using their office to persuade or force students to take the religious instruction, a wholly different case would be presented. . . .

We would have to press the concept of separation of Church and State to . . . extremes to condemn the present law on constitutional grounds. The nullification of this law would have wide and profound effects. A Catholic student applies to his teacher for permission to leave the school during hours on a Holy Day of Obligation to attend a mass. A Jewish student asks his teacher for permission to be excused for Yom Kippur. A Protestant wants the afternoon off for a family baptismal ceremony. In each case the teacher requires parental consent in writing. In each case the teacher, in order to make sure the student is not a truant, goes further and requires a report from the priest, the rabbi, or the minister. The teacher in other words cooperates in a religious program to the extent of making it possible for her students to participate in it. Whether she does it occasionally for a few students, regularly for one, or pursuant to a systematized program designed to further the religious needs of all the students does not alter the character of the act.

We are a religious people whose institutions presuppose a Supreme Being. We guarantee the freedom to worship as one chooses. We make room for as wide a variety of beliefs and creeds as the spiritual needs of man deem necessary. We sponsor an attitude on the part of government that shows no partiality to any one group and that lets each flourish according to the zeal of its adherents and the appeal of its dogma. When the state encourages religious instruction or cooperates with religious authorities by adjusting the schedule of public events to sectarian needs, it follows the best of our traditions. For it then respects the religious nature of our people and accommodates the public service to their spiritual needs. To hold that it may not would be to find in the Constitution a requirement that the government show a callous indifference to religious groups. That would be preferring those who believe in no religion over those who do believe. Government may not finance religious groups nor undertake religious instruction nor blend secular and sectarian education nor use secular institutions to force one or some religion on any person. But we find no constitutional requirement which makes it necessary for government to be hostile to religion and to throw its weight against efforts to widen the effective scope of religious influence. The government must be neutral when it comes to competition between sects. It may not thrust any sect on any person. It may not make a religious observance compulsory. It may not coerce anyone to attend church, to observe a religious holiday, or to take religious instruction. But it can close its doors or suspend its operations as to those who want to repair to their religious sanctuary for worship or instruction. No more than that is undertaken here.

This program may be unwise and improvident from an educational or a community viewpoint. . . . Our individual preferences, however, are not the constitutional standard. . . .

In the *McCollum* case the classrooms were used for religious instruction and the force of the public school was used to promote that instruction. Here, as we have said, the public schools do no more than accommodate their schedules to a program of outside religious instruction. We follow the *McCollum* case. But we cannot expand it to cover the present released time program unless separation of Church and State means that public institutions can make no adjustments of their schedules to accommodate the religious needs of the people. We cannot read into the Bill of Rights such a philosophy of hostility to religion.

Justice Jackson, dissenting. . . .

A number of Justices just short of a majority of the majority that promulgates today's passionate dialectics joined in answering them in *Illinois ex rel. McCollum* v. *Board of Education,* 333 U.S. 203. The distinction attempted between that case and this is trivial, almost to the point of cynicism, magnifying its nonessential details and disparaging compulsion which was the underlying reason for invalidity. A reading of the Court's opinion in that case along with its opinion in this case will show such difference of overtones and undertones as to make clear that the *McCollum* case had passed like a storm in a teacup. The wall which the Court was professing to erect between Church and State has become even more warped and twisted than I expected. Today's judgment will be more interesting to students of psychology and of the judicial processes than to students of constitutional law.

Engel *v*. Vitale

*In the early 1960's, the Court began to hear increasing numbers of
cases dealing with the intervention of religion in secular life. In
Torcaso v. Watkins, for example, the justices struck down a Maryland constitutional requirement that public officials offer a "declaration of belief in the existence of God" (367 U.S. 488 [1961]). The
most perplexing questions still involved the place of religion in the
public schools. For example, there is a widespread practice of beginning the school day with a prayer or Bible reading. In 1952,
the Court had refused to hear a challenge to a New Jersey statute
requiring the daily reading of Old Testament passages. But in the
case below, the Court agreed to review a prayer composed by the
New York Board of Regents. A 6–1 majority held that the prayer
violated the establishment clause of the First Amendment. In dissent, Justice Stewart, provided ample ammunition for an emotional
assault by sectarian and congressional critics of the Court. He
argued that as there was no compulsion to recite the prayer, the
Board had not established an "official religion," and that the Court's
action had the effect of denying a majority of the children "the opportunity of sharing in the spiritual heritage of our Nation."*

Justice Black delivered the opinion of the Court.

The respondent Board of Education of Union Free School District
No. 9, New Hyde Park, New York, acting in its official capacity
under state law, directed the School District's principal to cause the following prayer to be said aloud by each class in the presence of a teacher
at the beginning of each school day:

"Almighty God, we acknowledge our dependence upon Thee, and we
beg Thy blessings upon us, our parents, our teachers and our country."

This daily procedure was adopted on the recommendation of the State
Board of Regents, a governmental agency created by the State Constitution to which the New York Legislature has granted broad supervisory,
executive, and legislative powers over the State's public school system.
These state officials composed the prayer which they recommended and
published as a part of their "Statement on Moral and Spiritual Training
in the Schools," saying: "We believe that this Statement will be sub-

370 U.S. 421 (1962)

scribed to by all men and women of good will, and we call upon all of them to aid in giving life to our program."

Shortly after the practice of reciting the Regents' prayer was adopted by the School District, the parents of ten pupils brought this action in a New York State Court insisting that use of this official prayer in the public schools was contrary to the beliefs, religions, or religious practices of both themselves and their children. Among other things, these parents challenged the constitutionality of both the state law authorizing the School District to direct the use of prayer in public schools and the School District's regulation ordering the recitation of this particular prayer on the ground that these actions of official governmental agencies violate that part of the First Amendment of the Federal Constitution which commands that "Congress shall make no law respecting an establishment of religion" — a command which was "made applicable to the State of New York by the Fourteenth Amendment of the said Constitution." The New York Court of Appeals . . . sustained an order of the lower state courts which had upheld the power of New York to use the Regents' prayer as a part of the daily procedures of its public schools so long as the schools did not compel any pupil to join in the prayer over his or his parents' objection. . . .

We think that by using its public school system to encourage recitation of the Regents' prayer, the State of New York has adopted a practice wholly inconsistent with the Establishment Clause. There can, of course, be no doubt that New York's program of daily classroom invocation of God's blessings as prescribed in the Regents' prayer is a religious activity. It is a solemn avowal of divine faith and supplication for the blessings of the Almighty. The nature of such a prayer has always been religious, none of the respondents has denied this and the trial court expressly so found. . . .

The petitioners contend among other things that the state laws requiring or permitting use of the Regents' prayer must be struck down as a violation of the Establishment Clause because that prayer was composed by governmental officials as a part of a governmental program to further religious beliefs. For this reason, petitioners argue, the State's use of the Regents' prayer in its public school system breaches the constitutional wall of separation between Church and State. We agree with that contention since we think that the constitutional prohibition against laws respecting an establishment of religion must at least mean that in this country it is no part of the business of government to compose official prayers for any group of the American people to recite as a part of a religious program carried on by government.

It is a matter of history that this very practice of establishing governmentally composed prayers for religious services was one of the reasons which caused many of our early colonists to leave England and seek religious freedom in America. . . .

It is an unfortunate fact of history that when some of the very groups which had most strenuously opposed the established Church of England found themselves sufficiently in control of colonial governments in this country to write their own prayers into law, they passed laws making their own religion the official religion of their respective colonies. Indeed, as late as the time of the Revolutionary War, there were established churches in at least eight of the thirteen former colonies and established religions in at least four of the other five. But the successful Revolution against English political domination was shortly followed by intense opposition to the practice of establishing religion by law. This opposition crystallized rapidly into an effective political force in Virginia where the minority religious groups such as Presbyterians, Lutherans, Quakers and Baptists had gained such strength that the adherents to the established Episcopal Church were actually a minority themselves. In 1785–1786, those opposed to the established Church, led by James Madison and Thomas Jefferson, who, though themselves not members of any of these dissenting religious groups, opposed all religious establishments by law on grounds of principle, obtained the enactment of the famous "Virginia Bill for Religious Liberty" by which all religious groups were placed on an equal footing so far as the State was concerned. Similar though less far-reaching legislation was being considered and passed in other States.

By the time of the adoption of the Constitution, our history shows that there was a widespread awareness among many Americans of the dangers of a union of Church and State. . . . The First Amendment was added to the Constitution to stand as a guarantee that neither the power nor the prestige of the Federal Government would be used to control, support or influence the kinds of prayer the American people can say — that the people's religions must not be subjected to the pressures of government for change each time a new political administration is elected to office. Under that Amendment's prohibition against governmental establishment of religion, as reinforced by the provisions of the Fourteenth Amendment, government in this country, be it state or federal, is without power to prescribe by law any particular form of prayer which is to be used as an official prayer in carrying on any program of governmentally sponsored religious activity.

There can be no doubt that New York's state prayer program officially establishes the religious beliefs embodied in the Regents' prayer. The respondents' argument to the contrary, which is largely based upon the contention that the Regents' prayer is "non-denominational" and the fact that the program, as modified and approved by state courts, does not require all pupils to recite the prayer but permits those who wish to do so to remain silent or be excused from the room, ignores the essential nature of the program's constitutional defects. Neither the fact that the prayer may be denominationally neutral, nor the fact that its observance on the part of the students is voluntary can serve to free it from the limitations of the Establishment Clause, as it might from the Free Exercise Clause, of the First Amendment, both of which are operative against the States by virtue of the Fourteenth Amendment. Although these two clauses may in certain instances overlap, they forbid two quite different kinds of governmental encroachment upon religious freedom. The Establishment Clause, unlike the Free Exercise Clause, does not depend upon any showing of direct governmental compulsion and is violated by the enactment of laws which establish an official religion whether those laws operate directly to coerce nonobserving individuals or not. This is not to say, of course, that laws officially prescribing a particular form of religious worship do not involve coercion of such individuals. When the power, prestige and financial support of government is placed behind a particular religious belief, the indirect coercive pressure upon religious minorities to conform to the prevailing officially approved religion is plain. But the purposes underlying the Establishment Clause go much further than that. Its first and most immediate purpose rested on the belief that a union of government and religion tends to destroy government and to degrade religion. The history of governmentally established religion, both in England and in this country, showed that whenever government had allied itself with one particular form of religion, the inevitable result had been that it had incurred the hatred, disrespect and even contempt of those who held contrary beliefs. That same history showed that many people had lost their respect for any religion that had relied upon the support of government to spread its faith. The Establishment Clause thus stands as an expression of principle on the part of the Founders of our Constitution that religion is too personal, too sacred, too holy, to permit its "unhallowed perversion" by a civil magistrate. Another purpose of the Establishment Clause rested upon an awareness of the historical fact that governmentally established religions and religious persecutions go hand in hand. . . . It was in large part to get completely away from this sort of systematic religious persecution that the Founders brought into being our Nation, our Constitution, and our Bill of Rights with its prohibition against any governmental establishment of religion. The New York laws officially prescribing the Regents' prayer are inconsistent both with the purposes of the Establishment Clause and with the Establishment Clause itself.

It has been argued that to apply the Constitution in such a way as to prohibit state laws respecting an establishment of religious services in public schools is to indicate a hostility toward religion or toward prayer. Nothing, of course, could be more wrong. The history of man is inseparable from the history of religion. And perhaps it is not too much to say that since the beginning of that history many people have devoutly believed that "More things are wrought by prayer than this world dreams of." It was doubtless largely due to men who believed this that there grew up a sentiment that caused men to leave the cross-currents of officially established state religions and religious persecution in Europe and come to this country filled with the hope that they could find a place in which they could pray when they pleased to the God of their faith in the language they chose. And there were men of this same faith in the power of prayer who led the fight for adoption of our Constitution and also for our Bill of Rights with the very guarantees of religious freedom that forbid the sort of governmental activity which New York has attempted here. These men knew that the First Amendment, which tried to put an end to governmental control of religion and of prayer, was not written to destroy either. They knew rather that it was written to quiet well-justified fears which nearly all of them felt arising out of an awareness that governments of the past had shackled men's tongues to make them speak only the religious thoughts that government wanted them to speak and to pray only to the God that government wanted them to pray to. It is neither sacrilegious nor antireligious to say that each separate government in this country should stay out of the business of writing or sanctioning official prayers and leave that purely religious function to the people themselves and to those the people choose to look to for religious guidance.

It is true that New York's establishment of its Regents' prayer as an officially approved religious doctrine of that State does not amount to a total establishment of one particular religious sect to the exclusion of all others — that, indeed, the governmental endorsement of that prayer seems relatively insignificant when compared to the governmental encroachments upon religion which were commonplace 200 years ago. To those who may subscribe to the view that because the Regents' official prayer is so brief and general there can be no danger to religious freedom in its governmental establishment, however, it may be appropriate to say in the words of James Madison, the author of the First Amendment:

> [I]t is proper to take alarm at the first experiment on our liberties. . . .
> Who does not see that the same authority which can establish Christianity,
> in exclusion of all other Religions, may establish with the same ease
> any particular sect of Christians, in exclusions of all other Sects? That
> the same authority which can force a citizen to contribute three pence
> only of his property for the support of any one establishment, may force
> him to conform to any other establishment in all cases whatsoever?

The judgment of the Court of Appeals of New York is reversed and the cause remanded for further proceedings not inconsistent with this opinion.

Wisconsin *v.* Yoder

The Burger Court Justices left intact—and in some notable ways, expanded—their predecessors' pronouncements favoring a clear separation between church and state, particularly in the area of educational policy. By the 1970's, soaring schooling costs forced sectarian groups to push even harder for some form of public aid. Some states granted public funds for the busing of parochial school children, the rationale being that the child, and not the religious school, derived the chief benefits. By the early 1970's, over thirty states had implemented some forms of direct financial assistance to religious schools, all under the general rubric of "parochiad." These included state payments for tuition, books, teacher subsidies, or tax credits. But in a number of decisions, most notably Lemon v. Kurtzman *(403 U.S. 602 [1971]) and* Committee for Public Education and Religious Liberty v. Nyquist *(413 U.S. 100 [1973]), the Court consistently held parochial programs as unconstitutional impairments of the Establishment Clause of the First Amendment. The case below seemingly did not involve as emotional or politically-oriented an issue; yet it truly raised the fundamental reasons for the religious liberty clauses of the Constitution and the ability of the law to recognize group behavior divergent from normally-accepted societal goals. The respondents in the case were members of the Old Order Amish religion and had been convicted of violating the state's compulsory school attendance law, as they refused to send their children to school beyond the eighth grade. The Amish claimed that attending high school violated their religious beliefs and threatened the sect's way of life.*

Chief Justice Burger delivered the opinion of the Court.

I

There is no doubt as to the power of a State, having a high responsibility for education of its citizens, to impose reasonable regulations for the control and duration of basic education. See, *e.g., Pierce* v. *Society of Sisters*, 268 U. S. 510, 534 (1925). Providing public schools ranks at the very apex of the function of a State. Yet even this paramount responsibility was, in *Pierce*, made to yield to the right of parents to provide an equiva-

---

406 U.S. 205 (1972)

lent education in a privately operated system. There the Court held that Oregon's statute compelling attendance in a public school from age eight to age 16 unreasonably interfered with the interest of parents in directing the rearing of their offspring, including their education in church-operated schools. As that case suggests, the values of parental direction of the religious upbringing and education of their children in their early and formative years have a high place in our society. . . .

It follows that in order for Wisconsin to compel school attendance beyond the eighth grade against a claim that such attendance interferes with the practice of a legitimate religious belief, it must appear either that the State does not deny the free exercise of religious belief by its requirement, or that there is a state interest of sufficient magnitude to override the interest claiming protection under the Free Exercise Clause. . . .

II

We come then to the quality of the claims of the respondents concerning the alleged encroachment of Wisconsin's compulsory school-attendance statute on their rights and the rights of their children to the free exercise of the religious beliefs they and their forebears have adhered to for almost three centuries. In evaluating those claims we must be careful to determine whether the Amish religious faith and their mode of life are, as they claim, inseparable and interdependent. A way of life, however virtuous and admirable, may not be interposed as a barrier to reasonable state regulation of education if it is based on purely secular considerations; to have the protection of the Religion Clauses, the claims must be rooted in religious belief. Although a determination of what is a "religious" belief or practice entitled to constitutional protection may present a most delicate question, the very concept of ordered liberty precludes allowing every person to make his own standards on matters of conduct in which society as a whole has important interests. Thus, if the Amish asserted their claims because of their subjective evaluation and rejection of the contemporary secular values accepted by the majority, much as Thoreau rejected the social values of his time and isolated himself at Walden Pond, their claims would not rest on a religious basis. Thoreau's choice was philosophical and personal rather than religious, and such belief does not rise to the demands of the Religion Clauses.

Giving no weight to such secular considerations, however, we see that the record in this case abundantly supports the claim that the traditional way of life of the Amish is not merely a matter of personal preference, but one of deep religious conviction, shared by an organized group, and intimately related to daily living. That the Old Order Amish daily life and religious practice stem from their faith is shown by the fact that it is in response to their literal interpretation of the Biblical injunction from the Epistle of Paul to the Romans, "be not conformed to the world. . . ." This command is fundamental to the Amish faith. Moreover, for the Old Order Amish, religion is not simply a matter of theocratic belief. As the expert witnesses explained, the Old Order Amish religion pervades and determines virtually their entire way of life, regulating it with the detail of the Talmudic diet through the strictly enforced rules of the church community.

The record shows that the respondents' religious beliefs and attitude toward life, family, and home have remained constant—perhaps some would say static—in a period of unparalleled progress in human knowledge generally and great changes in education. . . .

As the society around the Amish has become more populous, urban, industrialized, and complex, particularly in this century, government regulation of human affairs has correspondingly become more detailed and pervasive. The Amish mode of life has thus come into conflict increasingly with requirements of contemporary society exerting a hydraulic insistence on conformity to majoritarian standards. So long as compulsory education laws were confined to eight grades of elementary basic education imparted in a nearby rural schoolhouse, with a large proportion of students of the Amish faith, the Old Order Amish had little basis to fear that school attendance would expose their children to the worldly influence they reject. But modern compulsory secondary education in rural areas is now largely carried on in a consolidated school, often remote from the student's home and alien to his daily home life. As the record so strongly shows, the values and programs of the modern secondary school are in sharp conflict with the fundamental mode of life mandated by the Amish religion; modern laws requiring compulsory secondary education have accordingly engendered great concern and conflict. The conclusion is inescapable that secondary schooling, by exposing Amish children to worldly influences in terms of attitudes, goals, and values contrary to beliefs, and by substantially interfering with the religious development of the Amish child and his integration into the way of life of the Amish faith community at the crucial adolescent stage of development contravenes the basic religious tenets and practice of the Amish faith, both as to the parent and the child.

The impact of the compulsory-attendance law on respondents' practice of the Amish religion is not only severe, but inescapable, for the Wisconsin law affirmatively compels them, under threat of criminal sanction, to perform acts undeniably at odds with fundamental tenets of their religious beliefs. . . . Nor is the impact of the compulsory-attendance law confined to grave interference with important Amish religious tenets from a subjective point of view. It carries with it precisely the kind of objective danger to the free exercise of religion that the First Amendment was designed to prevent. As the record shows, compulsory school attendance to age 16 for Amish children carries with it a very real threat of undermining the Amish community and religious practice as they exist today; they must either abandon belief and be assimilated into society at large, or be forced to migrate to some other and more tolerant region. . . .

III

Neither the findings of the trial court nor the Amish claims as to the nature of their faith are challenged in this Court by the State of Wisconsin. Its position is that the State's interest in universal compulsory formal secondary education to age 16 is so great that it is paramount to the undisputed claims of respondents that their mode of preparing their youth for Amish life, after the traditional elementary education, is an essential part of their religious belief and practice. Nor does the State undertake to meet the claim that the Amish mode of life and education is inseparable from and a part of the basic tenets of their religion—indeed, as much a part of their religious belief and practices as baptism, the confessional, or a sabbath may be for others.

Wisconsin concedes that under the Religion Clauses religious beliefs are absolutely free from the State's control, but it argues that "actions," even though religiously grounded, are outside the protection of the First Amendment. But our decisions have rejected the idea that religiously grounded conduct is always outside the protection of the Free Exercise Clause. It is true that activities of individuals, even when religiously based, are often subject to regulation by the States in the exercise of their undoubted power to promote the health, safety, and general welfare, or the Federal Government in the exercise of its delegated powers. . . .

We turn, then, to the State's broader contention that its interest in its system of compulsory education is so compelling that even the established religious practices of the Amish must give way. Where fundamental claims of religious freedom are at stake, however, we cannot accept such a sweeping claim; despite its admitted validity in the generality of cases, we must searchingly examine the interests that the State seeks to promote by its requirement for compulsory education to age 16, and the impediment to those objectives that would flow from recognizing the claimed Amish exemption. . . .

The State advances two primary arguments in support of its system of compulsory education. It notes, as Thomas Jefferson pointed out early in our history that some degree of education is necessary to prepare citizens to participate effectively and intelligently in our open political system if we are to preserve freedom and independence. Further, education prepares individuals to be self-reliant and self-sufficient participants in society. We accept these propositions.

However, the evidence adduced by the Amish in this case is persuasively to the effect that an additional one or two years of formal high school for Amish children in place of their long-established program of informal vocational education would do little to serve those interests. . . .

The State attacks respondents' position as one fostering "ignorance" from which the child must be protected by the State. No one can question the State's duty to protect children from ignorance but this argument does not square with the facts disclosed in the record. Whatever their idiosyncrasies as seen by the majority, this record strongly shows that the Amish community has been a highly successful social unit within our society, even if apart from the conventional "mainstream." Its members are productive and very law-abiding members of society; they reject public welfare in any of its usual modern forms. The Congress itself recognized their self-sufficiency by authorizing exemption of such groups as the Amish from the obligation to pay social security taxes.

It is neither fair nor correct to suggest that the Amish are opposed to education beyond the eighth grade level. What this record shows is that they are opposed to conventional formal education of the type provided by a certified high school because it comes at the child's crucial adolescent period of religious development. . . .

The requirement for compulsory education beyond the eighth grade is a relatively recent development in our history. Less than 60 years ago, the educational requirements of almost all of the States were satisfied by completion of the elementary grades, at least where the child was regularly and lawfully employed. The independence and successful functioning of the Amish community for a period approaching almost three centuries and more than 200 years in this country are strong evidence that there is at best a speculative gain, in terms of meeting the duties of citizenship, from an additional one or two years of compulsory formal education. Against this background it would require a more particularized showing from the State on this point to justify the severe interference with religious freedom such additional compulsory attendance would entail. . . .

IV

Finally, the State . . . argues that a decision exempting Amish children from the State's requirement fails to recognize the substantive right of the Amish child to a secondary education, and fails to give due regard to the power of the State as *parents patriae* to extend the benefit of secondary education to children regardless of the wishes of their parents. . . .

This case, of course, is not one in which any harm to the physical or mental health of the child or to the public safety, peace, order, or welfare has been demonstrated or may be properly inferred. The record is to the contrary, and any reliance on that theory would find no support in the evidence. . . .

V

For the reasons stated we hold, with the Supreme Court of Wisconsin, that the first and Fourteenth Amendments prevent the state from compelling respondents to cause their children to attend formal high school to age 16. . . .

Aided by a history of three centuries as an identifiable religious sect and a long history as a successful and self-sufficient segment of American society, the Amish in this case have convincingly demonstrated the sincerity of their religious beliefs, the interrelationship of belief with their mode of life, the vital role that belief and daily conduct play in the continued survival of Old Order Amish communities and their religious organization, and the hazards presented by the State's enforcement of a statute generally valid as to others. Beyond this, they have carried the even more difficult burden of demonstrating the adequacy of their alternative mode of continuing informal vocational education in terms of precisely those overall interests that the State advances in support of its program of compulsory high school education. In light of this convincing showing, one that probably few other religious groups or sects could make, and weighing the minimal difference between what the State would require and what the Amish already accept, it was incumbent on the State to show with more particularity how its admittedly strong interest in compulsory education would be adversely affected by granting an exemption to the Amish. . . .

Discrimination and the Search for Equality

Brown

v.

Board of Education of Topeka

Beginning in the late 1930's, the Court began to chip away at its own precedents upholding state segregation practices. The decisions at first emphasized the requirement that separate facilities be truly equal. Thus in Missouri ex rel. Gaines v. Canada, the Court rejected a state's practice of providing funds for Negroes to attend law schools outside the state rather than provide facilities itself (305 U.S. 337 [1938]). But in Sweatt v. Painter, in 1950, the Court took a significant new turn and held that a separate law school provided by Texas for Negroes violated the equal protection of the laws clause of the Fourteenth Amendment (339 U.S. 629). Although the Court did not directly condemn segregation, the implication was clear that a separate school, maintained for a small minority, lacked the prestige, quality, and facilities offered by the white school. Inevitably, the assaults upon segregation in education turned to the public schools. The Court began to hear arguments on the issue in 1952. Apparently there was some disagreement within the Court for a time, but on May 17, 1954, a unanimous bench, led by the new Chief Justice, handed down its historic decision in the Brown case. More than two decades later, the Court extended its concern to private schools, holding that federal civil rights statutes prohibited private, non-sectarian schools from denying admission to prospective students because they were black (Runyon v. Mcrary, 44 Law Week 5034 [1976]).

Chief Justice Warren delivered the opinion of the Court.

347 U.S. 483 (1954)

T these cases come to us from the States of Kansas, South Carolina, Virginia, and Delaware. They are premised on different facts and different local conditions, but a common legal question justifies their consideration together in this consolidated opinion.

In each of the cases, minors of the Negro race, through their legal representatives, seek the aid of the courts in obtaining admission to the public schools of their community on a nonsegregated basis. In each instance, they had been denied admission to schools attended by white children under laws requiring or permitting segregation according to race. This segregation was alleged to deprive the plaintiffs of the equal protection of the laws under the Fourteenth Amendment. In each of the cases other than the Delaware case, a three-judge federal district court denied relief to the plaintiffs on the so-called "separate but equal" doctrine announced by this Court in *Plessy* v. *Ferguson,* 163 U.S. 537. . . .

The plaintiffs contend that segregated public schools are not "equal" and cannot be made "equal," and that hence they are deprived of the equal protection of the laws. Because of the obvious importance of the question presented, the Court took jurisdiction. Argument was heard in the 1952 Term, and reargument was heard this Term on certain questions propounded by the Court.

Reargument was largely devoted to the circumstances surrounding the adoption of the Fourteenth Amendment in 1868. It covered exhaustively consideration of the Amendment in Congress, ratification by the states, then existing practices in racial segregation, and the views of proponents and opponents of the Amendment. This discussion and our own investigation convince us that, although these sources cast some light, it is not enough to resolve the problem with which we are faced. At best, they are inconclusive. The most avid proponents of the post-War Amendments undoubtedly intended them to remove all legal distinctions among "all persons born or naturalized in the United States." Their opponents, just as certainly, were antagonistic to both the letter and the spirit of the Amendments and wished them to have the most limited effect. What others in Congress and the state legislatures had in mind cannot be determined with any degree of certainty.

An additional reason for the inconclusive nature of the Amendment's history, with respect to segregated schools, is the status of public education at that time. In the South, the movement toward free common schools, supported by general taxation, had not yet taken hold. Education of white children was largely in the hands of private groups. Education of Negroes was almost non-existent, and practically all of the race were illiterate. In fact, any education of Negroes was forbidden by law in some states. Today, in contrast, many Negroes have achieved outstanding success in the arts and sciences as well as in the business and professional world. It is true that public school education at the time of the Amendment had advanced further in the North, but the effect of the Amendment on Northern States was generally ignored in the congressional debates. Even in the North, the conditions of public education did not approximate those existing today. The curriculum was usually rudimentary; ungraded schools were common in rural areas; the school term was but three months a year in many states; and compulsory school attendance was virtually unknown. As a consequence, it is not surprising that there should be so little in the history of the Fourteenth Amendment relating to its intended effect on public education.

In the first cases in this Court construing the Fourteenth Amendment, decided shortly after its adoption, the Court interpreted it as proscribing all state-imposed discriminations against the Negro race. The doctrine of "separate but equal" did not make its appearance in this Court until 1896 in the case of *Plessy* v. *Ferguson, supra,* involving not education but transportation. American courts have since labored with the doctrine for over half a century. In this Court, there have been six cases involving the "separate but equal" doctrine in the field of public education. In *Cumming* v. *County Board of Education,* 175 U.S. 528, and *Gong Lum* v. *Rice,* 275 U.S. 78, the validity of the doctrine itself was not challenged. In more recent cases, all on the graduate school level, inequality was found in that specific benefits enjoyed by white students were denied to Negro students of the same educational qualifications. *Missouri ex rel. Gaines* v. *Canada,* 305 U.S. 337; *Sipuel* v. *Oklahoma,* 332 U.S. 631; *Sweatt* v. *Painter,* 339 U.S. 629; *McLaurin* v. *Oklahoma State Regents,* 339 U.S. 637. In none of these cases was it necessary to re-examine the doctrine to grant relief to the Negro plaintiff. And in *Sweatt* v. *Painter, supra,* the Court expressly reserved decision on the question whether *Plessy* v. *Ferguson* should be held inapplicable to public education.

In the instant cases, that question is directly presented. Here, unlike *Sweatt* v. *Painter,* there are findings below that the Negro and white schools involved have been equalized, or are being equalized, with respect to buildings, curricula, qualifications and salaries of teachers, and other "tangible" factors. Our decision, therefore, cannot turn on merely a comparison of these tangible factors in the Negro and white schools involved in each of the cases. We must look instead to the effect of segregation itself on public education.

In approaching this problem, we cannot turn the clock back to 1868 when the Amendment was adopted, or even to 1896 when *Plessy* v. *Ferguson* was written. We must consider public education in the light of its full development and its present place in American life throughout the Nation. Only in this way can it be determined if segregation in public schools deprives these plaintiffs of the equal protection of the laws.

Today, education is perhaps the most important function of state and local governments. Compulsory school attendance laws and the great expenditures for education both demonstrate our recognition of the importance of education to our democratic society. It is required in the performance of our most basic public responsibilities, even service in the armed forces. It is the very foundation of good citizenship. Today it is a principal instrument in awakening the child to cultural values, in preparing him for later professional training, and in helping him to adjust normally to his environment. In these days, it is doubtful that any child may reasonably be expected to succeed in life if he is denied the opportunity of an education. Such an opportunity, where the state has undertaken to provide it, is a right which must be made available to all on equal terms.

We come then to the question presented: Does segregation of children in public schools solely on the basis of race, even though the physical facilities and other "tangible" factors may be equal, deprive the children of the minority group of equal educational opportunities? We believe that it does.

In *Sweatt* v. *Painter, supra,* in finding that a segregated law school for Negroes could not provide them equal educational opportunities, this Court relied in large part on "those qualities which are incapable of objective measurement but which make for greatness in a law school." In *McLaurin* v. *Oklahoma State Regents, supra,* the Court, in requiring that a Negro admitted to a white graduate school be treated like all other students, again resorted to intangible considerations: ". . . his ability to study, to engage in discussions and exchange views with other students, and, in general, to learn his profession." Such considerations apply with added force to children in grade and high schools. To separate them from others of similar age and qualifications solely because of their race generates a feeling of inferiority as to their status in the community that may affect their hearts and minds in a way unlikely ever to be undone. The effect of this separation on their educational opportunities was well stated by a finding in the Kansas case by a court which nevertheless felt compelled to rule against the Negro plaintiffs:

Segregation of white and colored children in public schools has a detrimental effect upon the colored children. The impact is greater when it has the sanction of the law; for the policy of separating the races is usually interpreted as denoting the inferiority of the negro group. A sense of inferiority affects the motivation of a child to learn. Segregation with the sanction of law, therefore, has a tendency to [retard] the educational and mental development of negro children and to deprive them of some of the benefits they would receive in a racial[ly] integrated school system.

Whatever may have been the extent of psychological knowledge at the time of *Plessy* v. *Ferguson,* this finding is amply supported by modern authority.[1] Any language in *Plessy* v. *Ferguson* contrary to this finding is rejected.

We conclude that in the field of public education the doctrine of "separate but equal" has no place. Separate educational facilities are inherently unequal. Therefore, we hold that the plaintiffs and others similarly situated for whom the actions have been brought are, by reason of the segregation complained of, deprived of the equal protection of the laws guaranteed by the Fourteenth Amendment. This disposition makes unnecessary any discussion whether such segregation also violates the Due Process Clause of the Fourteenth Amendment.

Because these are class actions, because of the wide applicability of this decision, and because of the great variety of local conditions, the formulation of decrees in these cases presents problems of considerable complexity. On reargument, the consideration of appropriate relief was necessarily subordinated to the primary question — the constitutionality of segregation in public education. We have now announced that such segregation is a denial of the equal protection of the laws. In order that we may have the full assistance of the parties in formulating decrees, the cases will be restored to the docket, and the parties are requested to present further argument on Questions 4 and 5 previously propounded by the Court for the reargument this Term. The Attorney General of the United States is again invited to participate. The Attorneys General of the states requiring or permitting segregation in public education will also be permitted to appear as *amici curiae* upon request to do so by September 15, 1954, and submission of briefs by October 1, 1954.

It is so ordered.

[1] K. B. Clark, Effect of Prejudice and Discrimination on Personality Development (Midcentury White House Conference on Children and Youth, 1950); Witmer and Kotinsky, Personality in the Making (1952), c. VI; Deutscher and Chein, The Psychological Effects of Enforced Segregation: A Survey of Social Science Opinion, 26 J. Psychol. 259 (1948); Chein, What are the Psychological Effects of Segregation Under Conditions of Equal Facilities?, 3 Int. J. Opinion and Attitude Res. 229 (1949); Brameld, Educational Costs, in Discrimination and National Welfare (MacIver, ed., 1949), 44–48; Frazier, The Negro in the United States (1949), 674–681. And see generally Myrdal, An American Dilemma (1944).

Cooper *v.* Aaron

A year after the Brown *decision, the Court delivered its decree setting forth guidelines for implementing its 1954 ruling. It re- manded the various cases to the lower courts which were then to fashion equitable solutions in accordance with "varied local school problems." The lower courts and the local school boards together were to admit children to the public schools "on a racially non- discriminatory basis with all deliberate speed." Given the suscepti- bility of both courts and school boards to increasing local political pressures, the 1955 decree was an invitation to evasion. By that time, political forces were at work in the South which polarized the conflict and "massive resistance" was the dominant mood. In the case below, in 1958, the Court responded to the evasion and resist- ance with a ringing affirmation of the principles of its 1954 decision and the authority of the federal courts. Nevertheless, until the Jus- tice Department began to initiate its own desegregation suits in the mid-1960's, including one in the Chicago area in 1968, and there were threats to withhold federal funds from segregated schools, the impact of the* Brown *case was very slight. In 1963, the U.S. Com- mission on Civil Rights reported that less than one-half of one per cent of southern Negroes attended desegregated schools.*

Opinion of the Court by Chief Justice Warren, Justice Black, Justice Frankfurter, Justice Douglas, Justice Burton, Justice Clark, Justice Harlan, Justice Brennan, and Justice Whittaker.

As this case reaches us it raises questions of the highest importance to the maintenance of our federal system of government. It neces- sarily involves a claim by the Governor and Legislature of a State that there is no duty on state officials to obey federal court orders resting on this Court's considered interpretation of the United States Constitution. Specifically it involves actions by the Governor and Legislature of Arkan- sas upon the premise that they are not bound by our holding in *Brown* v. *Board of Education. . . .* That holding was that the Fourteenth Amend- ment forbids States to use their governmental powers to bar children on racial grounds from attending schools where there is state participation through any arrangement, management, funds or property. We are urged to uphold a suspension of the Little Rock School Board's plan to do away

358 U.S. 1 (1958)

with segregated public schools in Little Rock until state laws and efforts to upset and nullify our holding in *Brown* v. *Board of Education* have been further challenged and tested in the courts. We reject these contentions. . . .

The following are the facts and circumstances so far as necessary to show how the legal questions are presented.

On May 17, 1954, this Court decided that enforced racial segregation in the public schools of a State is a denial of the equal protection of the laws enjoined by the Fourteenth Amendment. *Brown* v. *Board of Education.* . . .

On May 20, 1954, three days after the first *Brown* opinion, the Little Rock District School Board adopted, and on May 23, 1954, made public, a statement of policy entitled "Supreme Court Decision — Segregation in Public Schools." In this statement the Board recognized that "It is our responsibility to comply with Federal Constitutional Requirements and we intend to do so when the Supreme Court of the United States outlines the method to be followed."

Thereafter the Board undertook studies of the administrative problems confronting the transition to a desegregated public school system at Little Rock. It instructed the Superintendent of Schools to prepare a plan for desegregation, and approved such a plan on May 24, 1955, seven days before the second *Brown* opinion. The plan provided for desegregation at the senior high school level (grades 10 through 12) as the first stage. Desegregation at the junior high and elementary levels was to follow. It was contemplated that desegregation at the high school level would commence in the fall of 1957, and the expectation was that complete desegregation of the school system would be accomplished by 1963. . . .

While the School Board was thus going forward with its preparation for desegregating the Little Rock school system, other state authorities, in contrast, were actively pursuing a program designed to perpetuate in Arkansas the system of racial segregation which this Court had held violated the Fourteenth Amendment. First came, in November 1956, an amendment to the State Constitution flatly commanding the Arkansas General Assembly to oppose "in every Constitutional manner the Un-Constitutional desegregation decisions of May 17, 1954 and May 31, 1955 of the United States Supreme Court," . . . and, through the initiative, a pupil assignment law. . . . Pursuant to the constitutional command, a law relieving school children from compulsory attendance at racially mixed schools, . . . and a law establishing a State Sovereignty Commission, . . . were enacted by the General Assembly in February 1957.

The School Board and the Superintendent of Schools nevertheless continued with preparations to carry out the first stage of the desegregation program. Nine Negro children were scheduled for admission in September 1957 to Central High School, which has more than two thousand students. Various administrative measures, designed to assure the smooth transition of this first stage of desegregation, were undertaken.

On September 2, 1957, the day before these Negro students were to enter Central High, the school authorities were met with drastic opposing action on the part of the Governor of Arkansas who dispatched units of the Arkansas National Guard to the Central High School grounds, and placed the school "off limits" to colored students. As found by the District Court in subsequent proceedings, the Governor's action had not been requested by the school authorities, and was entirely unheralded. . . .

The Board's petition for postponement in this proceeding states: "The effect of that action [of the Governor] was to harden the core of opposition to the Plan and cause many persons who theretofore had reluctantly accepted the Plan to believe that there was some power in the State of Arkansas which, when exerted, could nullify the Federal law and permit disobedience of the decree of this [District] Court, and from that date hostility to the Plan was increased and criticism of the officials of the [School] District has become more bitter and unrestrained." The Governor's action caused the School Board to request the Negro students on September 2 not to attend the high school "until the legal dilemma was solved." The next day, September 3, 1957, the Board petitioned the District Court for instructions, and the court, after a hearing, found that the Board's request of the Negro students to stay away from the high school had been made because of the stationing of the military guards by the state authorities. The court determined that this was not a reason for departing from the approved plan, and ordered the School Board and Superintendent to proceed with it.

On the morning of the next day, September 4, 1957, the Negro children attempted to enter the high school but, as the District Court later found, units of the Arkansas National Guard "acting pursuant to the Governor's order, stood shoulder to shoulder at the school grounds and thereby forcibly prevented the 9 Negro students . . . from entering," as they continued to do every school day during the following three weeks.

That same day, September 4, 1957, the United States Attorney for the Eastern District of Arkansas was requested by the District Court to begin an immediate investigation in order to fix responsibility for the interference with the orderly implementation of the District Court's direction to carry out the desegregation program. Three days later, September 7, the District Court denied a petition of the School Board and the Superintendent of Schools for an order temporarily suspending continuance of the program.

Upon completion of the United States Attorney's investigation, he and the Attorney General of the United States, at the District Court's request, entered the proceedings and filed a petition on behalf of the United States, as *amicus curiae*, to enjoin the Governor of Arkansas and officers of the

Arkansas National Guard from further attempts to prevent obedience to the court's order. After hearings on the petition, the District Court found that the School Board's plan had been obstructed by the Governor through the use of National Guard troops, and granted a preliminary injunction on September 20, 1957, enjoining the Governor and the officers of the Guard from preventing the attendance of Negro children at Central High School, and from otherwise obstructing or interfering with the orders of the court in connection with the plan. The National Guard was then withdrawn from the school.

The next school day was Monday, September 23, 1957. The Negro children entered the high school that morning under the protection of the Little Rock Police Department and members of the Arkansas State Police. But the officers caused the children to be removed from the school during the morning because they had difficulty controlling a large and demonstrating crowd which had gathered at the high school. On September 25, however, the President of the United States dispatched federal troops to Central High School and admission of the Negro students to the school was thereby effected. Regular army troops continued at the high school until November 27, 1957. They were then replaced by federalized National Guardsmen who remained throughout the balance of the school year. Eight of the Negro students remained in attendance at the school throughout the school year.

We come now to the aspect of the proceedings presently before us. On February 20, 1958, the School Board and the Superintendent of Schools filed a petition in the District Court seeking a postponement of their program for desegregation. Their position in essence was that because of extreme public hostility, which they stated had been engendered largely by the official attitudes and actions of the Governor and the Legislature, the maintenance of a sound educational program at Central High School, with the Negro students in attendance would be impossible. The Board therefore proposed that the Negro students already admitted to the school be withdrawn and sent to segregated schools, and that all further steps to carry out the Board's desegregation program be postponed for a period later suggested by the Board to be two and one-half years.

After a hearing the District Court granted the relief requested by the Board. Among other things the court found that the past year at Central High School had been attended by conditions of "chaos, bedlam and turmoil." . . .

The District Court's judgment was dated June 20, 1958. The Negro respondents appealed to the Court of Appeals for the Eighth Circuit and also sought there a stay of the District Court's judgment. . . . The Court of Appeals did not act on the petition for a stay but on August 18, 1958, after convening in special session on August 4 and hearing the appeal, reversed the District Court. On August 21, 1958, the Court of Appeals stayed its mandate to permit the School Board to petition this Court for certiorari. . . . Recognizing the vital importance of a decision of the issues in time to permit arrangements to be made for the 1958–1959 school year, we convened in Special Term on August 28, 1958, and heard oral argument on the respondent's motions, and also argument of the Solicitor General who, by invitation, appeared for the United States as *amicus curiae,* and asserted that the Court of Appeals' judgment was clearly correct on the merits, and urged that we vacate its stay forthwith. . . . On September 12, 1958, as already mentioned we unanimously affirmed the judgment of the Court of Appeals. . . .

In affirming the judgment of the Court of Appeals which reversed the District Court we have accepted without reservation the position of the School Board, the Superintendent of Schools, and their counsel that they displayed entire good faith in the conduct of these proceedings and in dealing with the unfortunate and distressing sequence of events which has been outlined. We likewise have accepted the findings of the District Court as to the conditions at Central High School during the 1957–1958 school year, and also the findings that the educational progress of all the students, white and colored, of that school has suffered and will continue to suffer if the conditions which prevailed last year are permitted to continue.

The significance of these findings, however, is to be considered in light of the fact, indisputably revealed by the record before us, that the conditions they depict are directly traceable to the actions of legislators and executive officials of the State of Arkansas, taken in their official capacities, which reflect their own determination to resist this Court's decision in the *Brown* case and which have brought about violent resistance to that decision in Arkansas. In its petition for certiorari filed in this Court, the School Board itself describes the situation in this language: "The legislative, executive, and judicial departments of the state government opposed the desegregation of Little Rock schools by enacting laws, calling out troops, making statements vilifying federal law and federal courts, and failing to utilize state law enforcement agencies and judicial processes to maintain public peace." . . .

The constitutional rights of respondents are not to be sacrificed or yielded to the violence and disorder which have followed upon the actions of the Governor and Legislature. . . . Thus law and order are not here to be preserved by depriving the Negro children of their constitutional rights. The record before us clearly establishes that the growth of the Board's difficulties to a magnitude beyond its unaided power to control is the product of state action. Those difficulties, as counsel for the Board forthrightly conceded on the oral argument in this Court, can also be brought under control by state action.

The controlling legal principles are plain. The command of the Fourteenth Amendment is that no "State" shall deny to any person within its jurisdiction the equal protection of the laws. . . . Thus the prohibitions of the Fourteenth Amendment extend to all action of the State denying equal protection of the laws; whatever the agency of the State taking the action. In short, the constitutional rights of children not to be discriminated against in school admission on grounds of race or color declared by this Court in the Brown case can neither be nullified openly and directly by state legislators or state executive or judicial officers, nor nullified indirectly by them through evasive schemes for segregation whether attempted "ingeniously or ingenuously."

What has been said, in the light of the facts developed, is enough to dispose of the case. However, we should answer the premise of the actions of the Governor and Legislature that they are not bound by our holding in the Brown case. It is necessary only to recall some basic constitutional propositions which are settled doctrine.

Article VI of the Constitution makes the Constitution the "supreme Law of the Land." In 1803, Chief Justice Marshall, speaking for a unanimous Court, referring to the Constitution as "the fundamental and paramount law of the nation," declared in the notable case of *Marbury* v. *Madison* . . . that "It is emphatically the province and duty of the judicial department to say what the law is." This decision declared the basic principle that the federal judiciary is supreme in the exposition of the law of the Constitution, and that principle has ever since been respected by this Court and the Country as a permanent and indispensable feature of our constitutional system. It follows that the interpretation of the Fourteenth Amendment enunciated by this Court in the Brown case is the supreme law of the land, and Art. VI of the Constitution makes it of binding effect on the States "any Thing in the Constitution or Laws of any State to the Contrary notwithstanding." Every state legislator and executive and judicial officer is solemnly committed by oath taken pursuant to Art. VI, ¶3 "to support this Constitution." Chief Justice Taney, speaking for a unanimous Court in 1859, said that this requirement reflected the framers' "anxiety to preserve it [the Constitution] in full force, in all its powers, and to guard against resistance to or evasion of its authority, on the part of a State. . . ." *Ableman* v. *Booth*. . . .

No state legislator or executive or judicial officer can war against the Constitution without violating his undertaking to support it. Chief Justice Marshall spoke for a unanimous Court in saying that: "If the legislatures of the several states may, at will, annul the judgments of the courts of the United States, and destroy the rights acquired under those judgments, the constitution itself becomes a solemn mockery. . . ." *United States* v. *Peters*, 5 Cranch 115. A Governor who asserts a power to nullify a federal court order is similarly restrained. If he had such power, said Chief Justice Hughes, in 1932, also for a unanimous Court, "it is manifest that the fiat of a state Governor, and not the Constitution of the United States, would be the supreme law of the land; that the restrictions of the Federal Constitution upon the exercise of state power would be but impotent phrases. . . ."

It is, of course, quite true that the responsibility for public education is primarily the concern of the States, but it is equally true that such responsibilities, like all other state activity, must be exercised consistently with federal constitutional requirements as they apply to state action. The Constitution created a government dedicated to equal justice under law. The Fourteenth Amendment embodied and emphasized that ideal. State support of segregated schools through any arrangement, management, funds, or property cannot be squared with the Amendment's command that no State shall deny to any person within its jurisdiction the equal protection of the laws. The right of a student not to be segregated on racial grounds in schools so maintained is indeed so fundamental and pervasive that it is embraced in the concept of due process of law. . . . The basic decision in Brown was unanimously reached by this Court only after the case had been briefed and twice argued and the issues had been given the most serious consideration. Since the first Brown opinion three new Justices have come to the Court. They are at one with the Justices still on the Court who participated in that basic decision as to its correctness, and that decision is now unanimously reaffirmed. The principles announced in that decision and the obedience of the States to them, according to the command of the Constitution, are indispensable for the protection of the freedoms guaranteed by our fundamental charter for all of us. Our constitutional ideal of equal justice under law is thus made a living truth.

Swann *v*. Charlotte-Mecklenburg Board of Education

Two decades after Brown v. Board of Education, *school desegregation remained a volatile political issue, subject to seemingly endless legal entanglements. After* Cooper v. Aaron, *the federal government had to intervene with force again several times in the early 1960's. In 1964, in* Griffin v. *County Board of Prince Edward County, the Supreme Court struck down a state-subsidized private white school system which had been established when the county closed the public schools (377 U.S. 218). In 1969, after several years of hedging, the Court decisively rejected "freedom-of-choice" plans, in reality a guise for preserving the traditional segregated systems (Alexander v.* Holmes County Board of Education, 396 U.S. 19 [1969]). By *then, southern resistance to* de jure *segregation largely had subsided, but* de facto *segregation—both in the North and the South—came under increasing attack. Urban residential mobility had created separate enclaves of whites and blacks who attended schools according to traditional neighborhood patterns. In various cities, courts ordered massive busing to break down the resulting segregated systems. Once again, desegregation became a highly-charged political issue, particularly exploited in 1968 by Richard Nixon and George Wallace. In the case below, the Supreme Court approved a lower court-ordered busing plan for Charlotte, North Carolina, and in a companion case struck down a state prohibition on busing* (North Carolina State Board of Education v. Swann, 402 U.S. 43 [1971]). *But the court subsequently drew significant limits on the* Swann *doctrine, refusing for example to approve a plan for busing between predominantly black Detroit schools and those in basically white suburbs* (Milliken v. Bradley, 418 U.S. 717 [1974]).

Chief Justice Burger delivered the opinion of the Court.

W e granted certiorari in this case to review important issues as to the duties of school authorities and the scope of powers of federal courts under this Court's mandates to eliminate racially separate public schools established and maintained by state action. *Brown* v. *Board of Education,* 347 U. S. 483 (1954) (*Brown I*).

402 U.S. 1 (1971)

This case and those argued with it arose in States having a long history of maintaining two sets of schools in a single school system deliberately operated to carry out a governmental policy to separate pupils in schools solely on the basis of race. That was what *Brown* v. *Board of Education* was all about. These cases present us with the problem of defining in more precise terms than heretofore the scope of the duty of school authorities and district courts in implementing *Brown I* and the mandate to eliminate dual systems and establish unitary systems at once. Meanwhile district courts and courts of appeals have struggled in hundreds of cases with a multitude and variety of problems under this Court's general directive. Understandably, in an area of evolving remedies, those courts had to improvise and experiment without detailed or specific guidelines. This Court, in *Brown I*, appropriately dealt with the large constitutional principles; other federal courts had to grapple with the flinty, intractable realities of day-to-day implementation of those constitutional commands. Their efforts, of necessity, embraced a process of "trial and error," and our effort to formulate guidelines must take into account their experience. . . .

Nearly 17 years ago this Court held, in explicit terms, that state-imposed segregation by race in public schools denies equal protection of the laws. At no time has the Court deviated in the slightest degree from that holding or its constitutional underpinnings. . . .

None of the parties before us questions the Court's 1955 holding in *Brown II*, that

"School authorities have the primary responsibility for elucidating, assessing, and solving these problems; courts will have to consider whether the action of school authorities constitutes good faith implementation of the governing constitutional principles. Because of their proximity to local conditions and the possible need for further hearings, the courts which originally heard these cases can best perform this judicial appraisal. Accordingly, we believe it appropriate to remand the cases to those courts. . . ."

Over the 16 years since *Brown II*, many difficulties were encountered in implementation of the basic constitutional requirement that the State not discriminate between public school children on the basis of their race. Nothing in our national experience prior to 1955 prepared anyone for dealing with changes and adjustments of the magnitude and complexity encountered since then. Deliberate resistance of some to the Court's mandates has impeded the good-faith efforts of others to bring school systems into compliance. The detail and nature of these dilatory tactics have been noted frequently by this Court and other courts. . . .

The objective today remains to eliminate from the public schools all vestiges of state-imposed segregation. Segregation was the evil struck down by *Brown I* as contrary to the equal protection guarantees of the

Constitution. That was the violation sought to be corrected by the remedial measures of *Brown II*. . . .

If school authorities fail in their affirmative obligations under these holdings, judicial authority may be invoked. Once a right and a violation have been shown, the scope of a district court's equitable powers to remedy past wrongs is broad, for breadth and flexibility are inherent in equitable remedies. . . .

This allocation of responsibility once made, the Court attempted from time to time to provide some guidelines for the exercise of the district judge's discretion and for the reviewing function of the courts of appeals. However, a school desegregation case does not differ fundamentally from other cases involving the framing of equitable remedies to repair the denial of a constitutional right. The task is to correct, by a balancing of the individual and collective interests, the condition that offends the Constitution.

In seeking to define even in broad and general terms how far this remedial power extends it is important to remember that judicial powers may be exercised only on the basis of a constitutional violation. Remedial judicial authority does not put judges automatically in the shoes of school authorities whose powers are plenary. Judicial authority enters only when local authority defaults.

School authorities are traditionally charged with broad power to formulate and implement educational policy and might well conclude, for example, that in order to prepare students to live in a pluralistic society each school should have a prescribed ratio of Negro to white students reflecting the proportion for the district as a whole. To do this as an educational policy is within the broad discretionary powers of school authorities; absent a finding of a constitutional violation, however, that would not be within the authority of a federal court. As with any equity case, the nature of the violation determines the scope of the remedy. In default by the school authorities of their obligation to proffer acceptable remedies, a district court has broad power to fashion a remedy that will assure a unitary school system.

The school authorities argue that the equity powers of federal district courts have been limited by Title IV of the Civil Rights Act of 1964, 42 U. S. C. § 2000c. The language and the history of Title IV show that it was enacted not to limit but to define the role of the Federal Government in the implementation of the *Brown I* decision. It authorizes the Commissioner of Education to provide technical assistance to local boards in the preparation of desegregation plans, to arrange "training institutes" for school personnel involved in desegregation efforts, and to make grants directly to schools to ease the transition to unitary systems. It also authorizes the Attorney General, in specified circumstances to initiate federal desegregation units. Section 2000c (b) defines "desegregation" as it is used in Title IV:

" 'Desegregation' means the assignment of students to public schools and within such schools without regard to their race, color, religion, or national origin, but 'desegregation' shall not mean the assignment of students to public schools in order to overcome racial imbalance."

Section 2000c–6, authorizing the Attorney General to institute federal suits, contains the following proviso:

"nothing herein shall empower any official or court of the United States to issue any order seeking to achieve a racial balance in any school by requiring the transportation of pupils or students from one school to another or one school district to another in order to achieve such racial balance, or otherwise enlarge the existing power of the court to insure compliance with constitutional standards."

On their face, the sections quoted purport only to insure that the provisions of Title IV of the Civil Rights Act of 1964 will not be read as granting new powers. The proviso in § 2000c–6 is in terms designed to foreclose any interpretation of the Act as expanding the *existing* powers of federal courts to enforce the Equal Protection Clause. There is no suggestion of an intention to restrict those powers or withdraw from courts their historic equitable remedial powers. The legislative history of Title IV indicates that Congress was concerned that the Act might be read as creating a right of action under the Fourteenth Amendment in the situation of so-called "de facto segregation," where racial imbalance exists in the schools but with no showing that this was brought about by discriminatory action of state authorities. In short, there is nothing in the Act that provides us material assistance in answering the question of remedy for state-imposed segregation in violation of *Brown I*. The basis of our decision must be the prohibition of the Fourteenth Amendment that no State shall "deny to any person within its jurisdiction the equal protection of the laws." . . .

The central issue in this case is that of student assignment, and there are essentially four problem areas:

(1) to what extent racial balance or racial quotas may be used as an implement in a remedial order to correct a previously segregated system;

(2) whether every all-Negro and all-white school must be eliminated as an indispensable part of a remedial process of desegregation;

(3) what the limits are, if any, on the rearrangement of school districts and attendance zones, as a remedial measure; and

(4) what the limits are, if any, on the use of transportation facilities to correct state-enforced racial school segregation.

(1) *Racial Balances or Racial Quotas.*

The constant theme and thrust of every holding from *Brown I* to date is that state-enforced separation of races in public schools is discrimination that violates the Equal Protection Clause. The remedy commanded was to dismantle dual school systems.

We are concerned in these cases with the elimination of the discrimination inherent in the dual school systems, not with myriad factors of human existence which can cause discrimination in a multitude of ways on racial, religious, or ethnic grounds. The target of the cases from *Brown I* to the present was the dual school system. The elimination of racial discrimination in public schools is a large task and one that should not be retarded by efforts to achieve broader purposes lying beyond the jurisdiction of school authorities. One vehicle can carry only a limited amount of baggage. It would not serve the important objective of *Brown I* to seek to use school desegregation cases for purposes beyond their scope, although desegregation of schools ultimately will have impact on other forms of discrimination. . . .

Our objective in dealing with the issues presented by these cases is to see that school authorities exclude no pupil of a racial minority from any school, directly or indirectly, on account of race; it does not and cannot embrace all the problems of racial prejudice, even when those problems contribute to disproportionate racial concentrations in some schools.

In this case it is urged that the District Court has imposed a racial balance requirement of 71%–29% on individual schools. . . .

If we were to read the holding of the District Court to require, as a matter of substantive constitutional right, any particular degree of racial balance or mixing, that approach would be disapproved and we would be obliged to reverse. The constitutional command to desegregate schools does not mean that every school in every community must always reflect the racial composition of the school system as a whole.

As the voluminous record in this case shows, the predicate for the District Court's use of the 71%–29% ratio was twofold: first, its express finding, approved by the Court of Appeals and not challenged here, that a dual school system had been maintained by the school authorities at least until 1969; second, its finding, also approved by the Court of Appeals, that the school board had totally defaulted in its acknowledged duty to come forward with an acceptable plan of its own, notwithstanding the patient efforts of the District Judge who, on at least three occasions urged the board to submit plans. . . .

We see therefore that the use made of mathematical ratios was no more than a starting point in the process of shaping a remedy, rather than an inflexible requirement. From that starting point the District Court proceeded to frame a decree that was within its discretionary powers, as an equitable remedy for the particular circumstances. As we said in *Green,* a school authority's remedial plan or a district court's remedial decree is to be judged by its effectiveness. Awareness of the racial composition of the whole school system is likely to be a useful starting point in shaping a remedy to correct past constitutional violations. In sum, the very limited use made of mathematical ratios was within the equitable remedial discretion of the District Court.

(2) *One-race Schools.*

The record in this case reveals the familiar phenomenon that in metropolitan areas minority groups are often found concentrated in one part of the city. In some circumstances certain schools may remain all or largely of one race until new schools can be provided or neighborhood patterns change. Schools all or predominately of one race in a district of mixed population will require close scrutiny to determine that school assignments are not part of state-enforced segregation.

In light of the above, it should be clear that the existence of some small number of one-race, or virtually one-race, schools within a district is not in and of itself the mark of a system that still practices segregation by law. The district judge or school authorities should make every effort to achieve the greatest possible degree of actual desegregation and will thus necessarily be concerned with the elimination of one-race schools. No *per se* rule can adequately embrace all the difficulties of reconciling the competing interests involved; but in a system with a history of segregation the need for remedial criteria of sufficient specificity to assure a school authority's complaince with its constitutional duty warrants a presumption against schools that are substantially disproportionate in their racial composition. Where the school authority's proposed plan for conversion from a dual to a unitary system contemplates the continued existence of some schools that are all or predominately of one race, they have the burden of showing that such school assignments are genuinely nondiscriminatory. The court should scrutinize such schools, and the burden upon the school authorities will be to satisfy the court that their racial composition is not the result of present or past discriminatory action on their part. . . .

(3) *Remedial Altering of Attendance Zones.*

The maps submitted in these cases graphically demonstrate that one of the principal tools employed by school planners and by courts to break up the dual school system has been a frank—and sometimes drastic—gerrymandering of school districts and attendance zones. An additional step was pairing, "clustering," or "grouping" of schools with attendance assignments made deliberately to accomplish the transfer of Negro students out of formerly segregated Negro schools and transfer of white students to formerly all-Negro schools. More often than not, these zones are neither compact nor contiguous; indeed they may be on opposite ends of the city. As an interim corrective measure, this cannot be said to be beyond the broad remedial powers of a court.

Absent a constitutional violation there would be no basis for judicially ordering assignment of students on a racial basis. All things being equal, with no history of discrimination, it might well be desirable to assign pupils to schools nearest their homes. But all things are not equal in a system that has been deliberately constructed and maintained to enforce racial segregation. The remedy for such segregation may be administratively awkward, inconvenient, and even bizarre in some situations and may impose burdens on some; but all awkwardness and inconvenince cannot be avoided in the interim period when remedial adjustments are being made to eliminate the dual school systems.

No fixed or even substantially fixed guidelines can be established as to how far a court can go, but it must be recognized that there are limits. The objective is to dismantle the dual school system. "Racially neutral" assignment plans proposed by school authorities to a district court may be inadequate; such plans may fail to counteract the continuing effects of past school segregation resulting from discriminatory location of school sites or distortion of school size in order to achieve or maintain an artificial racial separation. . . .

We hold that the pairing and grouping of noncontiguous school zones is a permissible tool and such action is to be considered in light of the objectives sought. . . .

(4) *Transportation of Students.*

The scope of permissible transportation of students as an implement of a remedial decree has never been defined by this court and by the very nature of the problem it cannot be defined with precision. No rigid guidelines as to student transportation can be given for application to the infinite variety of problems presented in thousands of situations. Bus transportation has been an integral part of the public education system for years, and was perhaps the single most important factor in the transition from the one-room schoolhouse to the consolidated school. Eighteen million of the Nation's public school children, approximately 39%, were transported to their schools by bus in 1969–1970 in all parts of the country. The importance of bus transportation as a normal and accepted tool of educational policy is readily discernible. . . . The Charlotte school authorities did not purport to assign students on the basis of geographically drawn zones until 1965 and then they allowed almost unlimited transfer privileges. The District Court's conclusion that assignment of children to the school nearest their home serving their grade would not produce an effective dismantling of the dual system is supported by the record.

Thus the remedial techniques used in the District Court's order were within that court's power to provide equitable relief; implementation of the decree is well within the capacity of the school authority.

The decree provided that the buses used to implement the plan would operate on direct routes. Students would be picked up at schools near their homes and transported to the schools they were to attend. The trips for elementary school pupils average about seven miles and the District Court found that they would take "not over 35 minutes at the most." This system compares favorably with the transportation plan previously operated in Charlotte under which each day 23,600 students on all grade levels were transported an average of 15 miles one way for an average trip requiring over an hour. In these circumstances, we find no basis for holding that the local school authorities may not be required to employ bus transportation as one tool of school desegregation. Desegregation plans cannot be limited to the walk-in school.

An objection to transportation of students may have validity when the time or distance of travel is so great as to either risk the health of the children or significantly impinge on the educational process. . . .

On the facts of this case, we are unable to conclude that the order of the District Court is not reasonable, feasible and workable. However, in seeking to define the scope of remedial power or the limits on remedial power of courts in an area as sensitive as we deal with here, words are poor instruments to convey the sense of basic fairness inherent in equity. Substance, not semantics, must govern, and we have sought to suggest the nature of limitations without frustrating the appropriate scope of equity.

At some point, these school authorities and others like them should have achieved full compliance with this Court's decision in *Brown I*. The systems would then be "unitary" in the sense required by our decisions in *Green* and *Alexander*.

It does not follow that the communities served by such systems will remain demographically stable, for in a growing, mobile society, few will do so. Neither school authorities nor district courts are constitutionally required to make year-by-year adjustments of the racial composition of student bodies once the affirmative duty to desegregate has been accomplished and racial discrimination through official action is eliminated from the system. This does not mean that federal courts are without power to deal with future problems; but in the absence of a showing that either the school authorities or some other agency of the State has deliberately attempted to fix or alter demographic patterns to affect the racial composition of the schools, further intervention by a district court should not be necessary. . . .

Burton

v.

Wilmington Parking Authority

After eight decades, the basic principles of the Civil Rights Cases
*of 1883, distinguishing state and private action in discrimination,
technically remained the law of the land. But the Supreme Court's
persistent assault upon segregation steadily weakened what once
seemed a simple, discernible dichotomy. Furthermore, the mixing
of state and private activity in modern institutions, had made it increasingly difficult to make a clear-cut distinction between them.
The case below involved the refusal of a privately owned restaurant
to serve a Negro. The restaurant was located in a building owned
and operated by a state agency. Although the Court refused to overrule the* Civil Rights Cases *directly, it did indicate a willingness to
broadly construe the public-private relationship within the particular
facts of each situation.*

Justice Clark delivered the opinion of the Court.

In this action for declaratory and injunctive relief it is admitted that
the Eagle Coffee Shoppe, Inc., a restaurant located within an off-
street automobile parking building in Wilmington, Delaware, has refused
to serve appellant food or drink solely because he is a Negro. The parking
building is owned and operated by the Wilmington Parking Authority, an
agency of the State of Delaware, and the restaurant is the Authority's
lessee. Appellant claims that such refusal abridges his rights under the
Equal Protection Clause of the Fourteenth Amendment to the United
States Constitution. The Supreme Court of Delaware has held that Eagle
was acting in "a purely private capacity" under its lease; that its action
was not that of the Authority and was not, therefore, state action within
the contemplation of the prohibitions contained in that Amendment. It
also held that under 24 Del. Code, § 1501, Eagle was a restaurant, not
an inn, and that as such it "is not required [under Delaware law] to serve
any and all persons entering its place of business." . . .

The *Civil Rights Cases,* 109 U.S. 3 (1883), "embedded in our constitu-

365 U.S. 715 (1961)

tional law" the principle "that the action inhibited by the first section [Equal Protection Clause] of the Fourteenth Amendment is only such action as may fairly be said to be that of the States. That Amendment erects no shield against merely private conduct, however discriminatory or wrongful." Chief Justice Vinson in *Shelley* v. *Kraemer,* 334 U.S. 1, 13 (1948). It was language in the opinion in the *Civil Rights Cases, supra,* that phrased the broad test of state responsibility under the Fourteenth Amendment, predicting its consequence upon "State action of every kind . . . which denies . . . the equal protection of the laws." At p. 11. And only two Terms ago, some 75 years later, the same concept of state responsibility was interpreted as necessarily following upon "state participation through any arrangement, management, funds or property." *Cooper* v. *Aaron,* 358 U.S. 1, 4 (1958). It is clear, as it always has been since the *Civil Rights Cases, supra,* that "Individual invasion of individual rights is not the subject-matter of the amendment," at p. 11, and that private conduct abridging individual rights does no violence to the Equal Protection Clause unless to some significant extent the State in any of its manifestations has been found to have become involved in it. Because the virtue of the right to equal protection of the laws could lie only in the breadth of its application, its constitutional assurance was reserved in terms whose imprecision was necessary if the right were to be enjoyed in the variety of individual-state relationships which the Amendment was designed to embrace. For the same reason, to fashion and apply a precise formula for recognition of state responsibility under the Equal Protection Clause is an "impossible task" which "This Court has never attempted." *Kotch* v. *Pilot Comm'rs,* 330 U.S. 552, 556. Only by sifting facts and weighing circumstances can the nonobvious involvement of the State in private conduct be attributed its true significance. . . .

In this connection the Delaware Supreme Court seems to have placed controlling emphasis on its conclusion, as to the accuracy of which there is doubt, that only some 15% of the total cost of the facility was "advanced" from public funds; that the cost of the entire facility was allocated three-fifths to the space for commercial leasing and two-fifths to parking space; that anticipated revenue from parking was only some 30.5% of the total income, the balance of which was expected to be earned by the leasing; that the Authority had no original intent to place a restaurant in the building, it being only a happenstance resulting from the bidding; that Eagle expended considerable moneys on furnishings; that the restaurant's main and marked public entrance is on Ninth Street without any public entrance direct from the parking area; and that "the only connection Eagle has with the public facility . . . is the furnishing of the sum of $28,700 annually in the form of rent which is used by the Authority to defray a portion of the operating expense of an otherwise unprofitable enterprise." . . . While these factual considerations are indeed validly accountable aspects of the enterprise upon which the State has embarked, we cannot say that they lead inescapably to the conclusion that state action is not present. Their persuasiveness is diminished when evaluated in the context of other factors which must be acknowledged.

The land and building were publicly owned. As an entity, the building was dedicated to "public uses" in performance of the Authority's "essential governmental functions." . . . The costs of land acquisition, construction, and maintenance are defrayed entirely from donations by the City of Wilmington, from loans and revenue bonds and from the proceeds of rentals and parking services out of which the loans and bonds were payable. Assuming that the distinction would be significant, . . . the commercially leased areas were not surplus state property, but constituted a physically and financially integral and, indeed, indispensable part of the State's plan to operate its project as a self-sustaining unit. Upkeep and maintenance of the building, including necessary repairs, were responsibilities of the Authority and were payable out of public funds. It cannot be doubted that the peculiar relationship of the restaurant to the parking facility in which it is located confers on each an incidental variety of mutual benefits. Guests of the restaurant are afforded a convenient place to park their automobiles, even if they cannot enter the restaurant directly from the parking area. Similarly, its convenience for diners may well provide additional demand for the Authority's parking facilities. Should any improvements effected in the leasehold by Eagle become part of the realty, there is no possibility of increased taxes being passed on to it since the fee is held by a tax-exempt government agency. Neither can it be ignored, especially in view of Eagle's affirmative allegation that for it to serve Negroes would injure its business, that profits earned by discrimination not only contribute to, but also are indispensable elements in, the financial success of a governmental agency.

Addition of all these activities, obligations and responsibilities of the Authority, the benefits mutually conferred, together with the obvious fact that the restaurant is operated as an integral part of a public building devoted to a public parking service, indicates that degree of state participation and involvement in discriminatory action which it was the design of the Fourteenth Amendment to condemn. It is irony amounting to grave injustice that in one part of a single building, erected and maintained with public funds by an agency of the State to serve a public purpose, all persons have equal rights, while in another portion, also serving the public, a Negro is a second-class citizen, offensive because of his race, without rights and unentitled to service, but at the same time fully enjoys equal access to nearby restaurants in wholly privately owned buildings. As the Chancellor pointed out, in its lease with Eagle the Authority could have affirmatively required Eagle to discharge the responsibilities under the Fourteenth Amendment imposed upon the private enterprise as a consequence of state participation. But no State may effectively abdicate its responsibilities by either ignoring them or by merely failing to discharge them whatever the motive may be. It is of no consolation to an individual denied the equal protection of the laws that it was done in good faith. . . . By its inaction, the Authority, and through it the State, has not only made itself a party to the refusal of service, but has elected to place its power, property and prestige behind the admitted discrimination. The State has so far insinuated itself into a position of interdependence with Eagle that it must be recognized as a joint participant in the challenged activity, which, on that account, cannot be considered to have been so "purely private" as to fall without the scope of the Fourteenth Amendment.

Because readily applicable formulae may not be fashioned, the conclusions drawn from the facts and circumstances of this record are by no means declared as universal truths on the basis of which every state leasing agreement is to be tested. Owing to the very "largeness" of government, a multitude of relationships might appear to some to fall within the Amendment's embrace, but that, it must be remembered, can be determined only in the framework of the peculiar facts or circumstances present. . . .

The judgment of the Supreme Court of Delaware is reversed and the cause remanded for further proceedings consistent with this opinion. . . .

Moose Lodge No. 107 *v.* Irvis

A decade after Burton *v.* Wilmington Parking Authority, *the Court had undergone significant changes in personnel. In the decision below, four new Justices joined two holdovers to uphold some discriminatory practices in private clubs. A Pennsylvania Moose lodge had refused dining and bar service to a black man who came as a guest of a member. The appellee, Irvis, contended that the discrimination constituted state action in that the club operated with a state liquor permit. Speaking for the majority, Justice William Rehnquist, whose views on segregation had been an object of prolonged inquiry at his confirmation hearings, distinguished the* Burton *decision and held that the state was not sufficiently implicated to create a cause of "state action."*

Justice Rehnquist delivered the opinion of the Court.

Moose Lodge is a private club in the ordinary meaning of that term. It is a local chapter of a national fraternal organization having well-defined requirements for membership. It conducts all of its activities in a building that is owned by it. It is not publicly funded. Only members and guests are permitted in any lodge of the order; one may become a guest only by invitation of a member or upon invitation of the house committee.

Appellee, while conceding the right of private clubs to choose members upon a discriminatory basis, asserts that the licensing of Moose Lodge to serve liquor by the Pennsylvania Liquor Control Board amounts to such state involvement with the club's activities as to make its discriminatory practices forbidden by the Equal Protection Clause of the Fourteenth Amendment. The relief sought and obtained by appellee in the District Court was an injunction forbidding the licensing by the liquor authority of Moose Lodge until it ceased its discriminatory practices. We conclude that Moose Lodge's refusal to serve food and beverages to a guest by reason of the fact that he was a Negro does not, under the circumstances here presented, violate the Fourteenth Amendment.

In 1883, this Court in *The Civil Rights Cases,* 109 U. S. 3, set forth the essential dichotomy between discriminatory action by the State, which is prohibited by the Equal Protection Clause, and private conduct, "how-

407 U.S. 163 (1972)

ever discriminatory or wrongful," against which the clause "erects no shield," *Shelley* v. *Kraemer*, 334 U. S. 1, 13 (1948). That dichotomy has been subsequently reaffirmed in *Shelley* v. *Kraemer, supra,* and in *Burton* v. *Wilmington Parking Authority*, 365 U. S. 715 (1961).

While the principle is easily stated, the question of whether particular discriminatory conduct is private, on the one hand, or amounts to "state action," on the other hand, frequently admits of no easy answer. "Only by sifting facts and weighing circumstances can the nonobvious involvement of the State in private conduct be attributed its true significance." *Burton* v. *Wilmington Parking Authority, supra,* at 722.

Our cases make clear that the impetus for the forbidden discrimination need not originate with the State if it is state action that enforces privately originated discrimination. *Shelley* v. *Kraemer, supra.* The Court held in *Burton* v. *Wilmington Parking Authority, supra,* that a private restaurant owner who refused service because of a customer's race violated the Fourteenth Amendment, where the restaurant was located in a building owned by a state-created parking authority and leased from the authority. The Court, after a comprehensive review of the relationship between the lessee and the parking authority concluded that the latter had "so far insinuated itself into a position of interdependence with Eagle [the restaurant owner] that it must be recognized as a joint participant in the challenged activity, which, on that account, cannot be considered to have been so 'purely private' as to fall without the scope of the Fourteenth Amendment." . . .

The Court has never held, of course, that discrimination by an otherwise private entity would be violative of the Equal Protection Clause if the private entity receives any sort of benefit or service at all from the State, or if it is subject to state regulation in any degree whatever. Since state-furnished services include such necessities of life as electricity, water, and police and fire protection, such a holding would utterly emasculate the distinction between private as distinguished from state conduct set forth in *The Civil Rights Cases, supra,* and adhered to in subsequent decisions. Our holdings indicate that where the impetus for the discrimination is private, the State must have "significantly involved itself with invidious discriminations," *Reitman* v. *Mulkey*, 387 U. S. 369, 380 (1967), in order for the discriminatory action to fall within the ambit of the constitutional prohibition.

Our prior decisions dealing with discriminatory refusal of service in public eating places are significantly different factually from the case now before us. *Peterson* v. *City of Greenville*, 373 U. S. 244 (1963), dealt with the trespass prosecution of persons who "sat in" at a restaurant to protest its refusal of service to Negroes. There the Court held that although the ostensible initiative for the trespass prosecution came from the proprietor, the existence of a local ordinance requiring segregation of races in such places was tantamount to the State having "commanded a particular result," 373 U. S. at 248. With one exception, which is discussed *infra*, at 178–179, there is no suggestion in this record that the Pennsylvania statutes and regulations governing the sale of liquor are intended either overtly or covertly to encourage discrimination. . . .

With the exception hereafter noted, the Pennsylvania Liquor Control Board plays absolutely no part in establishing or enforcing the membership or guest policies of the club that it licenses to serve liquor. There is no suggestion in this record that Pennsylvania law, either as written or as applied, discriminates against minority groups either in their right to apply for club licenses themselves or in their right to purchase and be served liquor in places of public accommodation. The only effect that the state licensing of Moose Lodge to serve liquor can be said to have on the right of any other Pennsylvanian to buy or be served liquor on premises other than those of Moose Lodge is that for some purposes club licenses are counted in the maximum number of licenses that may be issued in a given municipality. . . .

The District Court found that the regulations of the Liquor Control Board adopted pursuant to statute affirmatively require that "[e]very club licensee shall adhere to all the provisions of its Constitution and By-Laws." Appellant argues that the purpose of this provision "is purely and simply and plainly the prevention of subterfuge," pointing out that the *bona fides* of a private club, as opposed to a place of public accommodation masquerading as a private club, is a matter with which the State Liquor Control Board may legitimately concern itself. Appellee concedes this to be the case, and expresses disagreement with the District Court on this point. There can be no doubt that the label "private club" can be and has been used to evade both regulations of state and local authorities, and statutes requiring places of public accommodation to serve all persons without regard to race, color, religion, or national origin. . . .

The effect of this particular regulation on Moose Lodge under the provisions of the constitution placed in the record in the court below would be to place state sanctions behind its discriminatory membership rules, but not behind its guest practices, which were not embodied in the constitution of the lodge. Had there been no change in the relevant circumstances since the making of the record in the District Court, our holding in Part I of this opinion that appellee has standing to challenge only the guest practices of Moose Lodge would have a bearing on our disposition of this issue. Appellee stated upon oral argument, though, and Moose Lodge conceded in its brief that the bylaws of the Supreme Lodge have been altered since the lower court decision to make applicable to guests the same sort of racial restrictions as are presently applicable to members.

Even though the Liquor Control Board regulation in question is neutral in its terms, the result of its application in a case where the constitution and bylaws of a club required racial discrimination would be to invoke the sanctions of the State to enforce a concededly discriminatory private rule. State action, for purposes of the Equal Protection Clause, may emanate from rulings of administrative and regulatory agencies as well as from legislative or judicial action. . . . Although the record before us is not as clear as one would like, appellant has not persuaded us that the District Court should have denied any and all relief. . . .

Heart of Atlanta Motel, Inc.
v.
United States

Title II of the Civil Rights Act of 1964 prohibited racial discrimination in public accommodations. The legislation marked a return to the national policy expressed in the Civil Rights Act of 1875, which the Court had struck down in the Civil Rights Cases *of 1883. That decision's interpretation of the Fourteenth Amendment still posed a formidable barrier. Accordingly, Congress resorted to the commerce clause as the basis for its action, reflecting greater confidence in its authority. The Heart of Atlanta Motel offered an ideal case for the government, for it was located at the intersection of two interstate highways.*

Justice Clark delivered the opinion of the Court.

1. *The Factual Background and Contentions of the Parties.*

The case comes here on admissions and stipulated facts. Appellant owns and operates the Heart of Atlanta Motel which has 216 rooms available to transient guests. The motel is located on Courtland Street, two blocks from downtown Peachtree Street. It is readily accessible to interstate highways 75 and 85 and state highways 23 and 41. Appellant solicits patronage from outside the State of Georgia through various national advertising media, including magazines of national circulation; it

---

379 U.S. 241 (1964)

maintains over 50 billboards and highway signs within the State, soliciting patronage for the motel; it accepts convention trade from outside Georgia and approximately 75% of its registered guests are from out of State. Prior to passage of the Act the motel had followed a practice of refusing to rent rooms to Negroes, and it alleged that it intended to continue to do so. In an effort to perpetuate that policy this suit was filed.

The appellant contends that Congress in passing this Act exceeded its power to regulate commerce under Art. I, § 8, cl. 3, of the Constitution of the United States; that the Act violates the Fifth Amendment because appellant is deprived of the right to choose its customers and operate its business as it wishes, resulting in a taking of its liberty and property without due process of law and a taking of its property without just compensation; and, finally, that by requiring appellant to rent available rooms to Negroes against its will, Congress is subjecting it to involuntary servitude in contravention of the Thirteenth Amendment.

The appellees counter that the unavailability to Negroes of adequate accommodations interferes significantly with interstate travel, and that Congress, under the Commerce Clause, has power to remove such obstructions and restraints; that the Fifth Amendment does not forbid reasonable regulation and that consequential damage does not constitute a "taking" within the meaning of that amendment; that the Thirteenth Amendment claim fails because it is entirely frivolous to say that an amendment directed to the abolition of human bondage and the removal of widespread disabilities associated with slavery places discrimination in public accommodations beyond the reach of both federal and state law. . . .

The Act as finally adopted was most comprehensive, undertaking to prevent through peaceful and voluntary settlement discrimination in voting, as well as in places of accommodation and public facilities, federally secured programs and in employment. Since Title II is the only portion under attack here, we confine our consideration to those public accommodation provisions.

3. *Title II of the Act.*

This Title is divided into seven sections beginning with § 201 (a) which provides that:

> All persons shall be entitled to the full and equal enjoyment of the goods, services, facilities, privileges, advantages, and accommodations of any place of public accommodation, as defined in this section, without discrimination or segregation on the ground of race, color, religion, or national origin.

There are listed in § 201 (b) four classes of business establishments, each of which "serves the public" and "is a place of public accommodation" within the meaning of § 201 (a) "if its operations affect commerce, or if discrimination or segregation by it is supported by State action." The covered establishments are:

(1) any inn, hotel, motel, or other establishment which provides lodging to transient guests, other than an establishment located within a building which contains not more than five rooms for rent or hire and which is actually occupied by the proprietor of such establishment as his residence;

(2) any restaurant, cafeteria . . . [not here involved];

(3) any motion picture house . . . [not here involved];

(4) any establishment . . . which is physically located within the premises of any establishment otherwise covered by this subsection, or . . . within the premises of which is physically located any such covered establishment . . . [not here involved].

Section 201 (c) defines the phrase "affect commerce" as applied to the above establishments. It first declares that "any inn, hotel, motel, or other establishment which provides lodging to transient guests" affects commerce *per se.* . . .

Finally, § 203 prohibits the withholding or denial, etc., of any right or privilege secured by § 201 . . . or the intimidation, threatening or coercion of any person with the purpose of interfering with any such right or the punishing, etc., of any person for exercising or attempting to exercise any such right.

The remaining sections of the Title are remedial ones for violations of any of the previous sections. Remedies are limited to civil actions for preventive relief. The Attorney General may bring suit where he has "reasonable cause to believe that any person or group of persons is engaged in a pattern or practice of resistance to the full enjoyment of any of the rights secured by this title, and that the pattern or practice is of such a nature and is intended to deny the full exercise of the rights herein described. . . ." § 206 (a). . . .

4. *Application of Title II to Heart of Atlanta Motel.*

It is admitted that the operation of the motel brings it within the provisions of § 201 (a) of the Act and that appellant refused to provide lodging for transient Negroes because of their race or color and that it intends to continue that policy unless restrained.

The sole question posed is, therefore, the constitutionality of the Civil Rights Act of 1964 as applied to these facts. The legislative history of the Act indicates that Congress based the Act on § 5 and the Equal Protection

Clause of the Fourteenth Amendment as well as its power to regulate interstate commerce under Art. I, § 8, cl. 3 of the Constitution.

The Senate Commerce Committee made it quite clear that the fundamental object of Title II was to vindicate "the deprivation of personal dignity that surely accompanies denials of equal access to public establishments." At the same time, however, it noted that such an objective has been and could be readily achieved "by congressional action based on the commerce power of the Constitution." S. Rep. No. 872, *supra,* at 16–17. Our study of the legislative record, made in the light of prior cases, has brought us to the conclusion that Congress possessed ample power in this regard, and we have therefore not considered the other grounds relied upon. This is not to say that the remaining authority upon which it acted was not adequate, a question upon which we do not pass, but merely that since the commerce power is sufficient for our decision here we have considered it alone. . . .

5. *The Civil Rights Cases, 109 U.S. 3 (1883), and their Application.*

In light of our ground for decision, it might be well at the outset to discuss the *Civil Rights Cases, supra,* which declared provisions of the Civil Rights Act of 1875 unconstitutional. 18 Stat. 335, 336. We think that decision inapposite, and without precedential value in determining the constitutionality of the present Act. Unlike Title II of the present legislation, the 1875 Act broadly proscribed discrimination in "inns, public conveyances on land or water, theaters, and other places of public amusement," without limiting the categories of affected businesses to those impinging upon interstate commerce. In contrast, the applicability of Title II is carefully limited to enterprises having a direct and substantial relation to the interstate flow of goods and people, except where state action is involved. Further, the fact that certain kinds of businesses may not in 1875 have been sufficiently involved in interstate commerce to warrant bringing them within the ambit of the commerce power is not necessarily dispositive of the same question today. Our populace had not reached its present mobility, nor were facilities, goods and services circulating as readily in interstate commerce as they are today. Although the principles which we apply today are those first formulated by Chief Justice Marshall in *Gibbons* v. *Ogden,* 9 Wheat. 1 (1824), the conditions of transportation and commerce have changed dramatically, and we must apply those principles to the present state of commerce. The sheer increase in volume of interstate traffic alone would give discriminatory practices which inhibit travel a far larger impact upon the Nation's commerce than such practices had on the economy of another day. Finally, there is language in the *Civil Rights Cases* which indicates that the Court did not fully consider whether the 1875 Act could be sustained as an exercise of the commerce power. . . .

6. *The Basis of Congressional Action.*

While the Act as adopted carried no congressional findings the record of its passage through each house is replete with evidence of the burdens that discrimination by race or color places upon interstate commerce. . . .

This testimony included the fact that our people have become increasingly mobile with millions of people of all races traveling from State to State; that Negroes in particular have been the subject of discrimination in transient accommodations, having to travel great distances to secure the same; that often they have been unable to obtain accommodations and have had to call upon friends to put them up overnight, . . . and that these conditions had become so acute as to require the listing of available lodging for Negroes in a special guidebook which was itself "dramatic testimony to the difficulties" Negroes encounter in travel. . . . These exclusionary practices were found to be nationwide, the Under Secretary of Commerce testifying that there is "no question that this discrimination in the North still exists to a large degree" and in the West and Midwest as well. . . . This testimony indicated a qualitative as well as quantitative effect on interstate travel by Negroes. The former was the obvious impairment of the Negro traveler's pleasure and convenience that resulted when he continually was uncertain of finding lodging. As for the latter, there was evidence that this uncertainty stemming from racial discrimination had the effect of discouraging travel on the part of a substantial portion of the Negro community. . . . This was the conclusion not only of the Under Secretary of Commerce but also of the Administrator of the Federal Aviation Agency who wrote the Chairman of the Senate Commerce Committee that it was his "belief that air commerce is adversely affected by the denial to a substantial segment of the traveling public of adequate and desegregated public accommodations." . . . We shall not burden this opinion with further details since the voluminous testimony presents overwhelming evidence that discrimination by hotels and motels impedes interstate travel.

7. *The Power of Congress Over Interstate Travel.*

The power of Congress to deal with these obstructions depends on the meaning of the Commerce Clause. . . .

[T]he determinative test of the exercise of power by the Congress under the Commerce Clause is simply whether the activity sought to be regulated is "commerce which concerns more States than one" and has a real and substantial relation to the national interest. . . .

The Court here reviewed one hundred years of precedents justifying congressional legislation of commerce, especially those laws which touched on intrastate commerce.

Thus the power of Congress to promote interstate commerce also includes the power to regulate the local incidents thereof, including local activities in both the States of origin and destination, which might have a substantial and harmful effect upon that commerce. One need only examine the evidence which we have discussed above to see that Congress may — as it has — prohibit racial discrimination by motels serving travelers, however "local" their operations may appear.

Nor does the Act deprive appellant of liberty or property under the Fifth Amendment. The commerce power invoked here by the Congress is a specific and plenary one authorized by the Constitution itself. The only questions are: (1) whether Congress had a rational basis for finding that racial discrimination by motels affected commerce, and (2) if it had such a basis, whether the means it selected to eliminate that evil are reasonable and appropriate. If they are, appellant has no "right" to select its guests as it sees fit, free from governmental regulation.

There is nothing novel about such legislation. Thirty-two States now have it on their books either by statute or executive order and many cities provide such regulation. Some of these Acts go back fourscore years. It has been repeatedly held by this Court that such laws do not violate the Due Process Clause of the Fourteenth Amendment. . . .

We, therefore, conclude that the action of the Congress in the adoption of the Act as applied here to a motel which concededly serves interstate travelers is within the power granted it by the Commerce Clause of the Constitution, as interpreted by this Court for 140 years. It may be argued that Congress could have pursued other methods to eliminate the obstructions it found in interstate commerce caused by racial discrimination. But this is a matter of policy that rests entirely with the Congress not with the courts. How obstructions in commerce may be removed — what means are to be employed — is within the sound and exclusive discretion of the Congress. It is subject only to one caveat — that the means chosen by it must be reasonably adapted to the end permitted by the Constitution. We cannot say that its choice here was not so adapted. The Constitution requires no more.

Affirmed.

Jones *v.* Alfred H. Mayer Co.

The assault against discrimination in the sale and rental of housing encountered stiff resistance throughout the postwar years. The defenders of the status quo regularly responded with emotional appeals in behalf of private rights and slogans like "a man's house is his castle." Community and state-wide referenda aroused bitter divisions, often resulting in a rejection of "open housing" legislation, or inconsequential policies hedged with a multitude of exceptions. California, for example, nullified its existing legislation with the passage of a constitutional amendment in a 1964 referendum. Both the state and the United States Supreme Courts, however, overturned the election result, holding that the new amendment violated the Fourteenth Amendment (Reitman v. Mulkey, 387 U.S. 369 [1967].) Early in 1968, a lower federal court enjoined a proposed Milwaukee referendum which would have prohibited passage of an open housing ordinance for two years on the grounds that the public had no "right" to vote on a measure that would be unconstitutional if adopted. Various attempts for a federal open housing law were blocked until April 1968 when, in the wake of the assassination of Martin Luther King, Congress passed such a law, although excepting transactions by private homeowners. Two months later, in the case below, the high court turned to the 1866 Civil Rights Act to support a prohibition of racial discrimination in apparently all sales and rental transactions of property. Emphasizing the 1866 law as it did, the Court boldly reminded the nation of its century-old commitment to full freedom for the black, as well as the white, man.

Justice Stewart delivered the opinion of the Court.

In this case we are called upon to determine the scope and the constitutionality of an Act of Congress, 42 U. S. C. § 1982, which provides that:

All citizens of the United States shall have the same right, in every State and Territory, as is enjoyed by white citizens thereof to inherit, purchase, lease, sell, hold, and convey real and personal property.

On September 2, 1965, the petitioners filed a complaint in the District Court for the Eastern District of Missouri, alleging that the respondents

392 U.S. 409 (1968).

had refused to sell them a home in the Paddock Woods community of St. Louis County for the sole reason that petitioner Joseph Lee Jones is a Negro. Relying in part upon § 1982, the petitioners sought injunctive and other relief. The District Court sustained the respondents' motion to dismiss the complaint, and the Court of Appeals for the Eighth Circuit affirmed, concluding that § 1982 applies only to state action and does not reach private refusals to sell. We granted certiorari to consider the questions thus presented. For the reasons that follow, we reverse the judgment of the Court of Appeals. We hold that § 1982 bars *all* racial discrimination, private as well as public, in the sale or rental of property, and that the statute, thus construed, is a valid exercise of the power of Congress to enforce the Thirteenth Amendment.

At the outset, it is important to make clear precisely what this case does *not* involve. Whatever else it may be, 42 U. S. C. § 1982 is not a comprehensive open housing law. In sharp contrast to the Fair Housing Title (Title VIII) of the Civil Rights Act of 1968, Pub. L. 90–284, 82 Stat. 73, the statute in this case deals only with racial discrimination and does not address itself to discrimination on grounds of religion or national origin. It does not deal specifically with discrimination in the provision of services or facilities in connection with the sale or rental of a dwelling. It does not prohibit advertising or other representations that indicate discriminatory preferences. It does not refer explicitly to discrimination in financing arrangements or in the provision of brokerage services. It does not empower a federal administrative agency to assist aggrieved parties. It makes no provision for intervention by the Attorney General. And, although it can be enforced by injunction, it contains no provision expressly authorizing a federal court to order the payment of damages.

Thus, although § 1982 contains none of the exemptions that Congress included in the Civil Rights Act of 1968, it would be a serious mistake to suppose that § 1982 in any way diminishes the significance of the law recently enacted by Congress. Indeed, the Senate Subcommittee on Housing and Urban Affairs was informed in hearings held after the Court of Appeals had rendered its decision in this case that § 1982 might well be "a presently valid federal statutory ban against discrimination by private persons in the sale or lease of real property." The Subcommittee was told, however, that even if this Court should so construe § 1982, the existence of that statute would not "eliminate the need for congressional action" to spell out "responsibility on the part of the federal government to enforce the rights it protects." The point was made that, in light of the many difficulties confronted by private litigants seeking to enforce such rights on their own, "legislation is needed to establish federal machinery for enforcement of the rights guaranteed under Section 1982 of Title 42 even if the plaintiffs in Jones v. Alfred H. Mayer Company should prevail in the United States Supreme Court."

On April 10, 1968 . . . the House passed the Civil Rights Act of 1968. Its enactment had no effect upon § 1982 and no effect upon this litigation, but it underscored the vast differences between, on the one hand, a general statute applicable only to racial discrimination in the rental and sale of property and enforceable only by private parties acting on their own initiative, and, on the other hand, a detailed housing law, applicable to a broad range of discriminatory practices and enforceable by a complete arsenal of federal authority. Having noted these differences, we turn to a consideration of §1982 itself. . . .

We begin with the language of the statute itself. In plain and unambiguous terms, § 1982 grants to all citizens, without regard to race or color, "the same right" to purchase and lease property "as is enjoyed by white citizens." As the Court of Appeals in this case evidently recognized, that right can be impaired as effectively by "those who place property on the market" as by the State itself. For, even if the State and its agents lend no support to those who wish to exclude persons from their communities on racial grounds, the fact remains that, whenever property "is placed on the market for whites only, whites have a right denied to Negroes." So long as a Negro citizen who wants to buy or rent a home can be turned away simply because he is not white, he cannot be said to enjoy "the *same* right . . . as is enjoyed by white citizens . . . to . . . purchase [and] lease . . . real and personal property." 42 U. S. C. § 1982. (Emphasis added.)

On its face, therefore, § 1982 appears to prohibit *all* discrimination against Negroes in the sale or rental of property — discrimination by private owners as well as discrimination by public authorities. Indeed, even the respondents seem to concede that, if § 1982 "means what it says" — to use the words of the respondents' brief — then it must encompass every racially motivated refusal to sell or rent and cannot be confined to officially sanctioned segregation in housing. Stressing what they consider to be the revolutionary implications of so literal a reading of § 1982, the respondents argue that Congress cannot possibly have intended any such result. Our examination of the relevant history, however, persuades us that Congress meant exactly what it said.

In its original form, 42 U. S. C. § 1982 was part of § 1 of the Civil Rights Act of 1866. . . . The crucial language for our purposes was that which guaranteed all citizens "the same right, in every State and Territory in the United States, . . . to inherit, purchase, lease, sell, hold, and convey real and personal property . . . as is enjoyed by white citizens. . . ." To the Congress that passed the Civil Rights Act of 1866, it was clear that the right to do these things might be infringed not only by "State or local law" but also by "custom, or prejudice." Thus, when Congress provided in § 1 of the Civil Rights Act that the right to purchase and lease property was to be enjoyed equally throughout the United States by Negro and white citizens alike, it plainly meant to secure that right against interference from any source whatever, whether governmental or private.

Indeed, if § 1 had been intended to grant nothing more than an immunity from *governmental* interference, then much of § 2 would have made no sense at all. For that section, which provided fines and prison terms for certain individuals who deprived others of rights "secured or protected" by § 1, was carefully drafted to exempt private violations of § 1 from the criminal sanctions it imposed. There would, of course, have been no private violations to exempt if the only "right" granted by § 1 had been a right to be free of discrimination by public officials. Hence the structure of the 1866 Act, as well as its language, points to the conclusion urged by the petitioners in this case — that § 1 was meant to prohibit *all* racially motivated deprivations of the rights enumerated in the statute, although only those deprivations perpetrated "under color of law" were to be criminally punishable under § 2.

In attempting to demonstrate the contrary, the respondents rely heavily upon the fact that the Congress which approved the 1866 statute wished to eradicate the recently enacted Black Codes — laws which had saddled Negroes with "onerous disabilities and burdens, and curtailed their rights . . . to such an extent that their freedom was of little value. . . ." *Slaughter-House Cases,* 16 Wall. 36, 70. The respondents suggest that the only evil Congress sought to eliminate was that of racially discriminatory laws in the former Confederate States. But the Civil Rights Act was drafted to apply throughout the country, and its language was far broader than would have been necessary to strike down discriminatory statutes.

That broad language, we are asked to believe, was a mere slip of the legislative pen. We disagree. For the same Congress that wanted to do away with the Black Codes *also* had before it an imposing body of evidence pointing to the mistreatment of Negroes by private individuals and unofficial groups, mistreatment unrelated to any hostile state legislation. "Accounts in newspapers North and South, Freedmen's Bureau and other official documents, private reports and correspondence were all adduced" to show that "private outrage and atrocity" was "daily inflicted on freedmen. . . ." The congressional debates are replete with references to private injustices against Negroes — references to white employers who refused to pay their Negro workers, white planters who agreed among themselves not to hire freed slaves without the permission of their former masters, white citizens who assaulted Negroes or who combined to drive them out of their communities. . . .

The remaining question is whether Congress has power under the Constitution to do what § 1982 purports to do: to prohibit all racial discrimination, private and public, in the sale and rental of property. Our starting point is the Thirteenth Amendment, for it was pursuant to that constitutional provision that Congress originally enacted what is now § 1982. The Amendment consists of two parts. Section 1 states:

Neither slavery nor involuntary servitude, except as a punishment for a crime whereof the party shall have been duly convicted, shall exist within the United States, or any place subject to their jurisdiction.

Section 2 provides:

Congress shall have power to enforce this article by appropriate legislation.

As its text reveals, the Thirteenth Amendment "is not a mere prohibition of State laws establishing or upholding slavery, but an absolute declaration that slavery or involuntary servitude shall not exist in any part of the United States." *Civil Rights Cases,* 109 U.S. 3, 20. It has never been doubted, therefore, "that the power vested in Congress to enforce the article by appropriate legislation," *ibid.,* includes the power to enact laws "direct and primary, operating upon the acts of individuals, whether sanctioned by State legislation or not." *Id.,* at 23.

Thus, the fact that § 1982 operates upon the unofficial acts of private individuals, whether or not sanctioned by state law, presents no constitutional problem. If Congress has power under the Thirteenth Amendment to eradicate conditions that prevent Negroes from buying and renting property because of their race or color, then no federal statute calculated to achieve that objective can be thought to exceed the constitutional power of Congress simply because it reaches beyond state action to regulate the conduct of private individuals. The constitutional question in this case, therefore, comes to this: Does the authority of Congress to enforce the Thirteenth Amendment "by appropriate legislation" include the power to eliminate all racial barriers to the acquisition of real and personal property? We think the answer to that question is plainly yes.

"By its own unaided force and effect," the Thirteenth Amendment "abolished slavery, and established universal freedom." *Civil Rights Cases,* 109 U.S. 3, 20. Whether or not the Amendment *itself* did any more than that — a question not involved in this case — it is at least clear that the Enabling Clause of that Amendment empowered Congress to do much more. For that clause clothed "Congress with power to pass *all laws necessary and proper for abolishing all badges and incidents of slavery in the United States." Ibid.* (Emphasis added.)

Those who opposed passage of the Civil Rights Act of 1866 argued in effect that the Thirteenth Amendment merely authorized Congress to dissolve the legal bond by which the Negro slave was held to his master. Yet many had earlier opposed the Thirteenth Amendment on the very ground that it would give Congress virtually unlimited power to enact

laws for the protection of Negroes in every State. And the majority
leaders in Congress — who were, after all, the authors of the Thirteenth
Amendment — had no doubt that its Enabling Clause contemplated the
sort of positive legislation that was embodied in the 1866 Civil Rights Act.
Their chief spokesman, Senator Trumbull of Illinois, the Chairman of
the Judiciary Committee, had brought the Thirteenth Amendment to the
floor of the Senate in 1864. In defending the constitutionality of the 1866
Act, he argued that, if the narrower construction of the Enabling Clause
were correct, then

> "the trumpet of freedom that we have been blowing throughout the
> land has given an 'uncertain sound,' and the promised freedom is a
> delusion. Such was not the intention of Congress, which proposed the
> constitutional amendment, nor is such the fair meaning of the amendment
> itself. . . . I have no doubt that under this provision . . . we may
> destroy all these discriminations in civil rights against the black man;
> and if we cannot, our constitutional amendment amounts to nothing. It
> was for that purpose that the second clause of that amendment was
> adopted, which says that Congress shall have authority, by appropriate
> legislation, to carry into effect the article prohibiting slavery. Who is
> to decide what that appropriate leglislation is to be? The Congress of
> the United States; and it is for Congress to adopt such appropriate
> leglislation as it may think proper, so that it be a means to accomplish
> the end."

Surely Senator Trumbull was right. Surely Congress has the power
under the Thirteenth Amendment rationally to determine what are the
badges and the incidents of slavery, and the authority to translate that
determination into effective legislation. . . .

Negro citizens North and South, who saw in the Thirteenth Amendment a promise of freedom — freedom to "go and come at pleasure" and
to "buy and sell when they please" — would be left with "a mere paper
guarantee" if Congress were powerless to assure that a dollar in the hands
of a Negro will purchase the same thing as a dollar in the hands of a
white man. At the very least, the freedom that Congress is empowered to
secure under the Thirteenth Amendment includes the freedom to buy
whatever a white man can buy, the right to live wherever a white man can
live. If Congress cannot say that being a free man means at least this
much, then the Thirteenth Amendment made a promise the Nation
cannot keep.

Representative Wilson of Iowa was the floor manager in the House for
the Civil Rights Act of 1866. In urging that Congress had ample authority to pass the pending bill, he recalled the celebrated words of Chief
Justice Marshall in *McCulloch* v. *Maryland*. . . . "The end is legitimate,"
the Congressman said, "because it is defined by the Constitution itself.
The end is the maintenance of freedom. . . . A man who enjoys the civil

rights mentioned in this bill cannot be reduced to slavery. . . . This settles the appropriateness of this measure, and that settles its constitutionality."

We agree. . . .

Justice Harlan, whom Justice White joins, dissenting.

Reed *v.* Reed, Administrator

The drive for equality in the 1960's and 1970's eventually encompassed long-standing discrimination against the status and rights of women. Women's rights attracted a broad spectrum of activism and political support, with, it should be added, a militant, organized effort on the other side. Much of the battle involved removing legal impediments and discrimination that restrained women from equal opportunities and control of their own lives. The drive for the Equal Rights Amendment to the U.S. Constitution, along with federal, state, and local affirmative action programs, represented the most prominent and significant goals of the women's movement. Inevitably, the Supreme Court confronted cases of sex discrimination that presented issues similar to those involving race. A number of them involved statutory or administrative practices requiring discrimination. A typical case, for example, concerned a school board's requirement that pregnant teachers take a five-month unpaid maternity leave before childbirth. In addition, the teacher was not guaranteed reemployment but merely given priority in reassignment to a position for which she was qualified. The Court struck down this practice on the grounds that it violated the due process clause of the Fourteenth Amendment (Cleveland Board of Education v. LeFleur, 414 U.S. 632 [1974]). The case below, with its use of the equal protection doctrine, perhaps represents the fundamental thrust of decisions dealing with blatant sex discrimination.

Chief Justice Burger delivered the opinion of the Court.

R ichard Lynn Reed, a minor, died intestate in Ada County, Idaho, on March 29, 1967. His adoptive parents, who had separated sometime prior to his death, are the parties to this appeal. Approximately seven months after Richard's death, his mother, appellant Sally Reed, filed a petition in the Probate Court of Ada County, seeking appointment as administratrix of her son's estate. Prior to the date set for a hearing on the mother's petition, appellee Cecil Reed, the father of the decedent, filed a competing petition seeking to have himself appointed administrator of the son's estate. The probate court held a joint hearing on the two petitions and thereafter ordered that letters of administration be issued to appellee Cecil Reed upon his taking the oath and filing the bond required by law. The court treated §§ 15–312 and 15–314 of the Idaho Code as the controlling statutes and read those sections as compelling a preference for Cecil Reed because he was a male.

Section 15–312 designates the persons who are entitled to administer the estate of one who dies intestate. In making these designations, that section lists 11 classes of persons who are so entitled and provides, in substance, that the order in which those classes are listed in the section shall be determinative of the relative rights of competing applicants for letters of administration. One of the 11 classes so enumerated is "[t]he father or mother" of the person dying intestate. Under this section, then, appellant and appellee, being members of the same entitlement class, would seem to have been equally entitled to administer their son's estate. Section 15–314 provides, however, that

"[o]f several persons claiming and equally entitled [under § 15–312] to administer, males must be preferred to females, and relatives of the whole to those of the half blood."

In issuing its order, the probate court implicitly recognized the equality of entitlement of the two applicants under § 15–312 and noted that neither of the applicants was under any legal disability; the court ruled, however, that appellee, being a male, was to be preferred to the female appellant "by reason of Section 15–314 of the Idaho Code." In stating this conclusion, the probate judge gave no indication that he had attempted to determine the relative capabilities of the competing applicants to perform the functions incident to the administration of an estate. It seems clear the probate judge considered himself bound by statute to give preference to the male candidate over the female, each being otherwise "equally entitled."

Sally Reed appealed from the probate court order, and her appeal was treated by the District Court of the Fourth Judicial District of Idaho as a constitutional attack on § 15–314. In dealing with the attack, that court held that the challenged section violated the Equal Protection Clause of the Fourteenth Amendment and was, therefore void; the matter was ordered "returned to the Probate Court for its determination of which of the two parties" was better qualified to administer the estate.

This order was never carried out, however, for Cecil Reed took a further appeal to the Idaho Supreme Court, which reversed the District Court and reinstated the original order naming the father administrator of the estate. In reaching this result, the Idaho Supreme Court first dealt with the governing statutory law and held that under § 15–312 "a father and mother are 'equally entitled' to letters of administration," but the preference given to males by § 15–314 is "mandatory" and leaves no room for the exercise of a probate court's discretion in the appointment of administrators. Having thus definitively and authoritatively interpreted the statutory provisions involved, the Idaho Supreme Court then proceeded to examine, and reject, Sally Reed's contention that § 15–314 violates the Equal Protection Clause by giving a mandatory preference to males over females, without regard to their individual qualifications as potential estate administrators. . . .

Sally Reed thereupon appealed for review by this court. . . . Having examined the record and considered the briefs and oral arguments of the parties, we have concluded that the arbitrary preference established in favor of males by § 15–314 of the Idaho Code cannot stand in the face of the Fourteenth Amendment's command that no State deny the equal protection of the laws to any person within its jurisdiction.

Idaho does not, of course, deny letters of administration to women altogether. Indeed, under § 15–312, a woman whose spouse dies intestate has a preference over a son, father, brother, or any other male relative of the decedent. Moreover, we can judicially notice that in this country, presumably due to the greater longevity of women, a large proportion of estates, both intestate and under wills of decedents, are administered by surviving widows.

Section 15–314 is restricted in its operation to those situations where competing applications for letters of administration have been filed by both male and female members of the same entitlement class established by § 15–312. In such situations, § 15–314 provides that different treatment be accorded to the applicants on the basis of their sex; it thus establishes a classification subject to scrutiny under the Equal Protection Clause.

In applying that clause, this Court has consistently recognized that the Fourteenth Amendment does not deny to States the power to treat different classes of persons in different ways. . . . The Equal Protection Clause of that amendment does, however, deny to States the power to legislate that different treatment be accorded to persons placed by a statute into different classes on the basis of criteria wholly unrelated to the objective of that statute. A classification "must be reasonable, not arbitrary, and must rest upon some ground of difference having a fair and substantial relation to the object of the legislation, so that all persons similarly circumstanced shall be treated alike." *Royster Guano Co.* v. *Virginia*, 253 U. S. 412, 415 (1920). The question presented by this case, then, is whether a difference in the sex of competing applicants for letters of administration bears a rational relationship to a state objective that is sought to be advanced by the operation of §§ 15–312 and 15–314.

In upholding the latter section, the Idaho Supreme Court concluded that its objective was to eliminate one area of controversy when two or more persons, equally entitled under § 15–312, seek letters of administration and thereby present the probate court "with the issue of which one should be named." The court also concluded that where such persons are not of the same sex, the elimination of females from consideration "is neither an illogical nor arbitrary method devised by the legislature to resolve an issue that would otherwise require a hearing as to the relative merits . . . of the two or more petitioning relatives. . . . "

Clearly the objective of reducing the workload on probate courts by eliminating one class of contests is not without some legitimacy. The crucial question, however, is whether § 15–314 advances that objective in a manner consistent with the command of the Equal Protection Clause. We hold that it does not. To give a mandatory preference to members of either sex over members of the other, merely to accomplish the elimination of hearings on the merits, is to make the very kind of arbitrary legislative choice forbidden by the Equal Protection Clause of the Fourteenth Amendment; and whatever may be said as to the positive values of avoiding intrafamily controversy, the choice in this context may not lawfully be mandated solely on the basis of sex.

We note finally that if § 15–314 is viewed merely as a modifying appendage to § 15–312 and as aimed at the same objective, its constitutionality is not thereby saved. The objective of § 15–312 clearly is to establish degrees of entitlement of various classes of persons in accordance with their varying degrees and kinds of relationship to the intestate. Regardless of their sex, persons within any one of the enumerated classes of that section are similarly situated with respect to that objective. By providing dissimilar treatment for men and women who are thus similarly situated, the challenged section violates the Equal Protection Clause. . . .

McDonald *v.* Santa Fe Trail Transportation Co.

"Affirmative Action" and quota programs designed to favor specific racial, ethnic, or sex groups ultimately raised legal questions regarding the rights of those disregarded or excluded from jobs or opportunities because of the demands of the new programs. Admission to law school involved a typical example. In an attempt to promote opportunities for blacks and women, special admission standards, programs, and financial aids were offered. These endeavors, however, sometimes excluded individuals from admission even though their qualifications were either superior or conformed to the norm. In De Funis v. Odegaard (416 U.S. 312 [1974]) the Court refused to confront such an issue on its merits because De Funis had gained admission and nearly completed his studies as a result of lower court proceedings. Dissenting, Justice Douglas warned that "the consideration of race as a measure of an applicant's qualification normally introduces a capricious and irrelevant factor working an invidious discrimination. . . ." The Constitution, he said, offered no right of racial preference; rather, the problems of discrimination or opportunity must be confronted "in a racially neutral way." Two years later, in this case below, the Court indicated its willingness to grapple with certain types of "reverse discrimination." The petitioners, who were white, had been charged with stealing some of their employer's property. A fellow black employee was similarly accused, but the company discharged only the two white men. The latter appealed unsuccessfully to their union and to the Equal Employment Opportunity Commission, claiming their dismissal violated the Civil Rights Act of 1964.

Justice Marshall delivered the opinion of the Court.

Title VII of the Civil Rights of 1964 prohibits the discharge of "any individual" because of "such individual's race." . . . Its terms are not limited to discrimination against members of any particular race. Thus, although we were not there confronted with racial discrimination against whites, we described the Act in *Griggs v. Duke Power Co.*, 401 U. S. 424, 431 (1971), as prohibiting "[d]iscriminatory preference for *any* [racial]

44 Law Week 5067 (1976)

group, *minority* or *majority*" (emphasis added). Similarly the EEOC, whose interpretations are entitled to great deference, *Griggs* v. *Duke Power Co.,* 401 U. S., at 433–434, has consistently interpreted Title VII to proscribe racial discrimination in private employment against whites on the same terms as racial discrimination against non-whites, holding that to proceed otherwise would.

> "constitute a dereliction of the Congressional mandate to eliminate all practices which operate to disadvantage the employment opportunities of any group protected by Title VII, including Caucasians." . . .

This conclusion is in accord with uncontradicted legislative history to the effect that Title VII was intended to "cover all white men and white women and all Americans," . . . and create an "obligation not to discriminate against whites," . . . We therefore hold today that Title VII prohibits racial discrimination against the white petitioners in this case upon the same standards as would be applicable were they Negroes and Jackson white.

Respondents contend that, even though generally applicable to white persons, Title VII affords petitioners no protection in this case, because their dismissal was based upon their commission of a serious criminal offense against their employer. We think this argument is foreclosed by our decision in *McDonnell Douglas Corp.* v. *Green,* [411 U. S. 791 (1973)]. . . .

In *McDonnell Douglas,* a laid-off employee took part in an illegal "stall-in" designed to block traffic into his former employer's plant, and was arrested, convicted, and fined for obstructing traffic. At a later date, the former employee applied for an open position with the company, for which he was apparently otherwise qualified, but the employer turned down the application, assertedly because of the former employee's illegal activities against it. Charging that he was denied re-employment because he was a Negro, a claim the company denied, the former employee sued under Title VII. Reviewing the case on certiorari, we concluded that the rejected employee had adequately stated a claim under Title VII. . . . Although agreeing with the employer that "[n]othing in Title VII compels an employer to resolve and rehire one who has engaged in such deliberate, unlawful activity against it," . . . we also recognized that

> "the inquiry must not end there. While Title VII does not, without more, compel rehiring of [the former employee], neither does it permit [the employer] to use [the former employee's] conduct as a pretext for the sort of discrimination prohibited by [the Act]. On remand, [the former employee] must . . . be afforded a fair opportunity to show that [the employer's] stated reason for [the former employee's] rejection was in fact pretext. Especially relevant to such a showing would be evidence that white employees involved in acts against [the employer] of comparable seriousness to the 'stall-in' were

nevertheless retained or rehired. [The employer] may justifiably refuse to rehire one who has engaged in unlawful, disruptive acts against it, but only if this criterion is applied alike to members of all races." . . .

We find this case indistinguishable from *McDonnell Douglas*. Fairly read, the complaint asserted that petitioners were discharged for their alleged participation in a misappropriation of cargo entrusted to Santa Fe, but that a fellow employee, likewise implicated, was not so disciplined, and that the reason for the discrepancy in discipline was that the favored employee is Negro while petitioners are white. . . . While Santa Fe may decide that participation in a theft of cargo may render an employee unqualified for employment, this criterion must be "applied, alike to members of all races," and Title VII is violated if, as petitioners alleged, it was not.

We cannot accept respondent's argument that the principles of *McDonnell Douglas* are inapplicable where the discharge was based, as petitioners' complaint admitted, on participation in serious misconduct or crime directed against the employer. The Act prohibits *all* racial discrimination in employment, without exception for any group of particular employees, and while crime or other misconduct may be a legitimate basis for discharge, it is hardly one for racial discrimination. Indeed, the Title VII plaintiff in *McDonnell Douglas* had been convicted for a nontrivial offense against his former employer. It may be that theft of property entrusted to an employer for carriage is a more compelling basis for discharge than obstruction of an employer's traffic arteries, but this does not diminish the illogic in retaining guilty employees of one color while discharging those of another color.

At this stage of the litigation the claim against Local 988 must go with the claim against Santa Fe, for in substance the complaint alleges that the Union shirked its duty properly to represent McDonald, but instead "acquiesced and/or joined in" Santa Fe's alleged racial discrimination against him. Local 988 argues that as a matter of law it should not be subject to liability under Title VII in a situation, such as this, where some but not all culpable employees are ultimately discharged on account of joint misconduct, because in representing all the affected employees in their relations with the employer, the Union may necessarily have to compromise by securing retention of only some. We reject the argument. The same reasons which prohibit an employer from discriminating on the basis of race among the culpable employees apply equally to the Union; and whatever factors the mechanisms of compromise may legitimately take into account in mitigating discipline of some employees, under Title VII race may not be among them.

Thus, we conclude that the District Court erred in dismissing both petitioners' Title VII claims against Santa Fe, and petitioner McDonald's Title VII claim against Local 988. . . .

[W]e cannot accept the view that the terms of § 1981 exclude its application to racial discrimination against white persons. On the contrary, the statute explicitly applies to *"all* persons" (emphasis added), including white persons. . . . While a mechanical reading of the phrase "as is enjoyed by white citizens" would seem to lend support to respondents' reading of the statute, we have previously described this phrase simply as emphasizing "the racial character of the rights being protected," . . . In any event, whatever ambiguity there may be in the language of § 1981, . . . is clarified by an examination of the legislative history of § 1981's language as it was originally forged in the Civil Rights Act of 1866. . . .

The bill ultimately enacted as the Civil Rights Act of 1866 was introduced by Senator Trumbull of Illinois as a "Bill to protect *all* persons in the United States in their civil rights . . ." (emphasis added), and was initially described by him as applying to "every race and color." . . . Consistent with the views of its draftsman, and the prevailing view in the Congress as to the reach of its powers under the enforcement section of the Thirteenth Amendment, the terms of the bill prohibited any racial discrimination in the making and enforcement of contracts against whites as well as non-whites. . . .

This cumulative evidence of congressional intent makes clear, we think, that the 1866 statute, designed to protect the "same right . . . to make and enforce contracts" of "citizens of every race and color" was not understood or intended to be reduced by Congressman Wilson's amendment, or any other provision, to the protection solely of nonwhites. Rather, the Act was meant, by its broad terms, to proscribe discrimination in the making or enforcement of contracts against, or in favor of, any race. Unlikely as it might have appeared in 1866 that white citizens would encounter substantial racial discrimination of the sort proscribed under the Act, the statutory structure and legislative history persuades us that the Thirty-ninth Congress was intent upon establishing in the federal law a broader principle than would have been necessary simply to meet the particular and immediate plight of the newly freed Negro slaves. And while the statutory language has been somewhat streamlined in re-enactment and codification, there is no indication that § 1981 is intended to provide any less than the Congress enacted in 1866 regarding racial discrimination against white persons. . . . Thus, we conclude that the District Court erred in dismissing petitioners' claims under § 1981 on the ground that the protection of that provision are unavailable to white persons. . . .

Shapiro *v.* Thompson

As part of the "Privileges and Immunities" clauses of the Constitution (Article IV & the Fourteenth Amendment), American citizens had a well-established "right to travel" among the various states. At the same time, transients or new residents traditionally had been subjected to special treatment as a result of various, often divergent, residency requirements. Such laws favored established residents in a wide number of areas such as voting, access to institutions of higher education, and assorted other public benefits. If residing in a state constituted citizenship, then did state residency requirements in these matters deprive individuals of equal protection of the laws? In the case below, the Court determined that the constitutional guarantee of the right to interstate movement could not be diminished or deterred by discrimination and unequal treatment toward new migrants. The Shapiro *case involved Connecticut's refusal to grant welfare payments to persons who had resided within the state less than one year and again reflected the Warren Court's concern with public discrimination against disadvantaged groups. In the years since this decision, the courts have struck down or severely restricted residency requirements in other cases involving indigents or voting rights. But the* Shapiro *doctrine also has been distinguished to maintain state or local residency requirements for divorce, admission to the bar, election as a state senator, and for employment by a municipality.*

Justice Brennan delivered the opinion of the Court.

There is no dispute that the effect of the waiting-period requirement in each case is to create two classes of needy resident families indistinguishable from each other except that one is composed of residents who have resided a year or more, and the second of residents who have resided less than a year, in the jurisdiction. On the basis of this sole difference the first class is granted and the second class is denied welfare aid upon which may depend the ability of the families to obtain the very means to subsist—food, shelter, and other necessities of life. In each case, the District Court found that appellees met the test for residence in their jurisdictions, as well as all other eligibility requirements except the

394 U.S. 618 (1969)

requirement of residence for a full year prior to their applications. On reargument, appellees' central contention is that the statutory prohibition of benefits to residents of less than a year creates a classification which constitutes an invidious discrimination denying them equal protection of the laws. We agree. The interests which appellants assert are promoted by the classification either may not constitutionally be promoted by government or are not compelling governmental interests.

Primarily, appellants justify the waiting-period requirement as a protective device to preserve the fiscal integrity of state public assistance programs. It is asserted that people who require welfare assistance during their first year of residence in a State are likely to become continuing burdens on state welfare programs. Therefore, the argument runs, if such people can be deterred from entering the jurisdiction by denying them welfare benefits during the first year, state programs to assist long-time residents will not be impaired by a substantial influx of indigent newcomers.

There is weighty evidence that exclusion from the jurisdiction of the poor who need or may need relief was the specific objective of these provisions. In the Congress, sponsors of federal legislation to eliminate all residence requirements have been consistently opposed by representatives of state and local welfare agencies who have stressed the fears of the States that elimination of the requirements would result in a heavy influx of individuals into States providing the most generous benefits. . . .

We do not doubt that the one-year waiting-period device is well suited to discourage the influx of poor families in need of assistance. An indigent who desires to migrate, resettle, find a new job, and start a new life will doubtless hesitate if he knows that he must risk making the move without the possibility of falling back on state welfare assistance during his first year of residence, when his need may be most acute. But the purpose of inhibiting migration by needy persons into the State is constitutionally impermissible.

This Court long ago recognized that the nature of our Federal Union and our constitutional concepts of personal liberty unite to require that all citizens be free to travel throughout the length and breadth of our land uninhibited by statutes, rules, or regulations which unreasonably burden or restrict this movement. That proposition was early stated by Chief Justice Taney in the *Passenger Case,* 7 How. 283, 492 (1849):

"For all the great purposes for which the Federal government was formed, we are one people, with one common country. We are all citizens of the United States; and, as members of the same community, must have the right to pass and repass through every part of it without interruption, as freely as in our own States."

We have no occasion to ascribe the source of this right to travel inter-state to a particular constitutional provision. It suffices that, as MR. JUS-TICE STEWART said for the Court in *United States* v. *Guest*, 383 U. S. 745, 757–758 (1966):

"The constitutional right to travel from one State to another . . . occupies a position fundamental to the concept of our Federal Union. It is a right that has been firmly established and repeatedly recognized.

". . . [T]he right finds no explicit mention in the Constitution. The reason, it has been suggested, is that a right so elementary was conceived from the beginning to be a necessary concomitant of the stronger Union the Constitution created. In any event, freedom to travel throughout the United States has long been recognized as a basic right under the Constitution."

Thus, the purpose of deterring the in-migration of indigents cannot serve as justification for the classification created by the one-year waiting period, since that purpose is constitutionally impermissible. If a law has "no other purpose . . . than to chill the assertion of constitutional rights by penalizing those who choose to exercise them, then it [is] patently uncon-stitutional." . . .

Alternatively, appellants argue that even if it is impermissible for a State to attempt to deter the entry of all indigents, the challenged classifi-cation may be justified as a permissible state attempt to discourage those indigents who would enter the State solely to obtain larger benefits. We observe first that none of the statutes before us is tailored to serve that objective. Rather, the class of barred newcomers is all-inclusive, lumping the great majority who come to the State for other purposes with those who come for the sole purpose of collecting higher benefits. In actual operation, therefore, the three statutes enact what in effect are nonrebut-table presumptions that every applicant for assistance in his first year of residence came to the jurisdiction solely to obtain higher benefits. Nothing whatever in any of these records supplies any basis in fact for such a presumption.

More fundamentally, a State may no more try to fence out those indi-gents who seek higher welfare benefits than it may try to fence out in-digents generally. Implicit in any such distinction is the notion that indi-gents who enter a State with the hope of securing higher welfare benefits are somehow less deserving than indigents who do not take this consider-ation into account. But we do not perceive why a mother who is seeking to make a new life for herself and her children should be regarded as less deserving because she considers, among other factors, the level of a State's public assistance. Surely such a mother is no less deserving than a mother who moves into a particular State in order to take advantage of its better educational facilities.

Appellants argue further that the challenged classification may be sustained as an attempt to distinguish between new and old residents on the basis of the contribution they have made to the community through the payment of taxes. We have difficulty seeing how long-term residents who qualify for welfare are making a greater present contribution to the State in taxes than indigent residents who have recently arrived. . . . But we need not rest on the particular facts of these cases. Appellants' reasoning would logically permit the State to bar new residents from schools, parks, and libraries or deprive them of police and fire protection. Indeed it would permit the State to apportion all benefits and services according to the past tax contributions of its citizens. The Equal Protection Clause prohibits such an apportionment of state services.

We recognize that a State has a valid interest in preserving the fiscal integrity of its programs. It may legitimately attempt to limit its expenditures, whether for public assistance, public education, or any other program. But a State may not accomplish such a purpose by invidious distinctions between classes of its citizens. It could not, for example, reduce expenditures for education by barring indigent children from its schools. Similarly, in the cases before us, appellants must do more than show that denying welfare benefits to new residents saves money. The saving of welfare costs cannot justify an otherwise invidious classification.

In sum, neither deterrence of indigents from migrating to the State nor limitation of welfare benefits to those regarded as contributing to the State is a constitutionally permissible state objective.

Appellants next advance as justification certain administrative and related governmental objectives allegedly served by the waiting-period requirement. They argue that the requirement (1) facilitates the planning of the welfare budget; (2) provides an objective test of residency; (3) minimizes the opportunity for recipients fraudulently to receive payments from more than one jurisdiction; and (4) encourages early entry of new residents into the labor force.

At the outset, we reject appellants' argument that a mere showing of a rational relationship between the waiting period and these four admittedly permissible state objectives will suffice to justify the classification. . . . The waiting-period provision denies welfare benefits to otherwise eligible applicants solely because they have recently moved into the jurisdiction. But in moving from State to State or to the District of Columbia appellees were exercising a constitutional right, and any classification which serves to penalize the exercise of that right, unless shown to be necessary to promote a *compelling* governmental interest, is unconstitutional. . . .

The argument that the waiting-period requirement facilitates budget predictability is wholly unfounded. The records in all three cases are utterly devoid of evidence that either State or the District of Columbia in fact uses the one-year requirement as a means to predict the number of people who will require assistance in the budget year. . . .

Similarly, there is no need for a State to use the one-year waiting period as a safeguard against fraudulent receipt of benefits; for less drastic means are available, and are employed, to minimize that hazard. Of course, a State has a valid interest in preventing fraud by any applicant, whether a newcomer or a long-time resident. . . .

We conclude therefore that appellants in these cases do not use and have no need to use the one-year requirement for the governmental purposes suggested. Thus, even under traditional equal protection tests a classification of welfare applicants according to whether they have lived in the State for one year would seem irrational and unconstitutional. But, of course, the traditional criteria do not apply in these cases. Since the classification here touches on the fundamental right of interstate movement, its constitutionality must be judged by the stricter standard of whether it promotes a *compelling* state interest. Under this standard, the waiting-period requirement clearly violates the Equal Protection Clause. . . .

Smith *v.* Allwright

In 1935, the Court unanimously upheld the right of the Texas Democratic party to restrict its membership to whites only. This effectively excluded Negroes from the primaries. As the decision was made by the party alone, the Court ruled that there was no violation of the Fourteenth Amendment (Grovey v. Townsend, 295 U.S. 45). But in United States v. Classic in 1941, the Court ignored the Grovey decision and held that congressional primaries were an "integral part" of the electoral process, and the federal government could intervene if fraud were alleged (313 U.S. 299). Then, in the case below, which again involved Texas primary practices, the Court directly overruled Grovey. Although the "whites only" practice was a party rule, the Court noted that primaries and parties alike were regulated in many ways by state laws. Therefore, the party was in effect an agency of the state and its discriminatory practices were the same as state action.

Justice Reed delivered the opinion of the Court.

This writ of certiorari brings here for review a claim for damages in the sum of $5,000 on the part of the petitioner, a Negro citizen of the 48th precinct of Harris County, Texas, for the refusal of respondents, election and associate election judges respectively of that precinct, to give petitioner a ballot or to permit him to cast a ballot in the primary election of July 27, 1940, for the nomination of Democratic candidates for the United States Senate and House of Representatives, and Governor and other state officers. The refusal is alleged to have been solely because of the race and color of the proposed voter. . . .

Texas is free to conduct her elections and limit her electorate as she may deem wise, save only as her action may be affected by the prohibi-

---

321 U.S. 649 (1944)

tions of the United States Constitution or in conflict with powers delegated to and exercised by the National Government. The Fourteenth
Amendment forbids a state from making or enforcing any law which
abridges the privileges or immunities of citizens of the United States and
the Fifteenth Amendment specifically interdicts any denial or abridgement by a state of the right of citizens to vote on account of color.
Respondents appeared in the District Court and the Circuit Court of
Appeals and defended on the ground that the Democratic party of Texas
is a voluntary organization with members banded together for the purpose
of selecting individuals of the group representing the common political
beliefs as candidates in the general election. As such a voluntary organization, it was claimed, the Democratic party is free to select its own
membership and limit to whites participation in the party primary. Such
action, the answer asserted, does not violate the Fourteenth, Fifteenth or
Seventeenth Amendment as officers of government cannot be chosen at
primaries and the Amendments are applicable only to general elections
where governmental officers are actually elected. Primaries, it is said, are
political party affairs, handled by party, not governmental, officers. No
appearance for respondents is made in this Court. Arguments presented
here by the Attorney General of Texas and the Chairman of the State
Democratic Executive Committee of Texas, as amici curiae, urged substantially the same grounds as those advanced by the respondents. . . .

In *Grovey* v. *Townsend* [1935] . . . this Court had before it another
suit for damages for the refusal in a primary of a county clerk, a Texas
officer with only public functions to perform, to furnish petitioner, a
Negro, an absentee ballot. The refusal was solely on the ground of
race. . . . This Court went on to announce that to deny a vote in a
primary was a mere refusal of party membership with which "the state
need have no concern," . . . while for a state to deny a vote in a general
election on the ground of race or color violated the Constitution. Consequently, there was found no ground for holding that the county clerk's
refusal of a ballot because of racial ineligibility for party membership
denied the petitioner any right under the Fourteenth or Fifteenth Amendments.

Since *Grovey* v. *Townsend* and prior to the present suit, no case from
Texas involving primary elections has been before this Court. We did
decide, however, *United States* v. *Classic* [1941]. . . . We there held that
§ 4 of Article I of the Constitution authorized Congress to regulate primary as well as general elections, . . . "where the primary is by law
made an integral part of the election machinery." . . . The fusing by the
Classic case of the primary and general elections into a single instrumentality for choice of officers has a definite bearing on the permissibility
under the Constitution of excluding Negroes from primaries. This is not
to say that the *Classic* case cuts directly into the rationale of *Grovey* v.

Townsend. This latter case was not mentioned in the opinion. *Classic* bears upon *Grovey* v. *Townsend* not because exclusion of Negroes from primaries is any more or less state action by reason of the unitary character of the electoral process but because the recognition of the place of the primary in the electoral scheme makes clear that state delegation to a party of the power to fix the qualifications of primary elections is delegation of a state function that may make the party's action the action of the state. When *Grovey* v. *Townsend* was written, the Court looked upon the denial of a vote in a primary as a mere refusal by a party of party membership. . . . As the Louisiana statutes for holding primaries are similar to those of Texas, our ruling in *Classic* as to the unitary character of the electoral process calls for a re-examination as to whether or not the exclu-'sion of Negroes from a Texas party primary was state action. . . .

It may now be taken as a postulate that the right to vote in such a primary for the nomination of candidates without discrimination by the State, like the right to vote in a general election, is a right secured by the Constitution. . . . By the terms of the Fifteenth Amendment that right may not be abridged by any state on account of race. Under our Constitution the great privilege of the ballot may not be denied a man by the State because of his color. . . .

Primary elections are conducted by the party under state statutory authority. The county executive committee selects precinct election officials and the county, district or state executive committees, respectively, canvass the returns. These party committees or the state convention certify the party's candidates to the appropriate officers for inclusion on the official ballot for the general election. No name which has not been so certified may appear upon the ballot for the general election as a candidate of a political party. No other name may be printed on the ballot which has not been placed in nomination by qualified voters who must take oath that they did not participate in a primary for the selection of a candidate for the office for which the nomination is made.

The state courts are given exclusive original jurisdiction of contested elections and of mandamus proceedings to compel party officers to perform their statutory duties. . . .

The United States is a constitutional democracy. Its organic law grants to all citizens a right to participate in the choice of elected officials without restriction by any state because of race. This grant to the people of the opportunity for choice is not to be nullified by a state through casting its electoral process in a form which permits a private organization to practice racial discrimination in the election. Constitutional rights would be of little value if they could be thus indirectly denied. . . .

The privilege of membership in a party may be, as this Court said in *Grovey* v. *Townsend,* . . . no concern of a state. But when, as here, that privilege is also the essential qualification for voting in a primary to select nominees for a general election, the state makes the action of the party the action of the state. In reaching this conclusion we are not unmindful of the desirability of continuity of decision in constitutional questions. However, when convinced of former error, this Court has never felt constrained to follow precedent. In constitutional questions, where correction depends upon amendment and not upon legislative action, this Court throughout its history has freely exercised its power to re-examine the basis of its constitutional decisions. This has long been accepted practice, and this practice has continued to this day. This is particularly true when the decision believed erroneous is the application of a constitutional principle rather than in interpretation of the Constitution to extract the principle itself. Here we are applying, contrary to the recent decision in *Grovey* v. *Townsend,* the well established principle of the Fifteenth Amendment, forbidding the abridgement by a state of a citizen's right to vote. *Grovey* v. *Townsend* is overruled. . . .

South Carolina

v.

Katzenbach, Attorney General

The Voting Rights Act of 1965 marked the culmination of a series of congressional statutes to utilize federal power against voting discrimination on the basis of color. Legislation passed in 1957, 1960, and 1964, however, failed to cope adequately with ingenious devices imposed by southern states designed to keep Negro voting at a minimum. Finally, in response to massive demonstrations and presidential pressures, Congress acted to increase federal authority to break down state discriminatory barriers. The 1965 act abolished literacy tests, waived accumulated poll taxes, and gave the Attorney General vast discretionary powers to deal with areas suspected of discriminating against Negro voters. The Attorney General, for example, could send federal examiners to any county in which 50% or more of the voting age population was not registered, and they then could list all qualified voters and declare them eligible to participate in elections. Although the entire act was not challenged in the case below, Chief Justice Warren's opinion clearly and emphatically endorsed the basic philosophy of massive federal intervention in behalf of voting rights.

Chief Justice Warren delivered the opinion of the Court.

By leave of the Court, . . . South Carolina has filed a bill of complaint, seeking a declaration that selected provisions of the Voting Rights Act of 1965 violate the Federal Constitution, and asking for an injunction against enforcement of these provisions by the Attorney General. . . .

The Voting Rights Act was designed by Congress to banish the blight of racial discrimination in voting, which has infected the electoral process in parts of our country for nearly a century. The Act creates stringent new remedies for voting discrimination where it persists on a pervasive scale, and in addition the statute strengthens existing remedies for pockets of voting discrimination elsewhere in the country. Congress assumed the

---

383 U.S. 301 (1966)

power to prescribe these remedies from § 2 of the Fifteenth Amendment, which authorizes the National Legislature to effectuate by "appropriate" measures the constitutional prohibition against racial discrimination in voting. We hold that the sections of the Act which are properly before us are an appropriate means for carrying out Congress' constitutional responsibilities and are consonant with all other provisions of the Constitution. We therefore deny South Carolina's request that enforcement of these sections of the Act be enjoined.

The constitutional propriety of the Voting Rights Act of 1965 must be judged with reference to the historical experience which it reflects. . . .

Two points emerge vividly from the voluminous legislative history of the Act contained in the committee hearings and floor debates. First: Congress felt itself confronted by an insidious and pervasive evil which had been perpetuated in certain parts of our country through unremitting and ingenious defiance of the Constitution. Second: Congress concluded that the unsuccessful remedies which it had prescribed in the past would have to be replaced by sterner and more elaborate measures in order to satisfy the clear commands of the Fifteenth Amendment. . . .

The Voting Rights Act of 1965 reflects Congress' firm intention to rid the country of racial discrimination in voting. The heart of the Act is a complex scheme of stringent remedies aimed at areas where voting discrimination has been most flagrant. Section 4 (a)–(d) lays down a formula defining the States and political subdivisions to which these new remedies apply. The first of the remedies, contained in § 4 (a), is the suspension of literacy tests and similar voting qualifications for a period of five years from the last occurrence of substantial voting discrimination. Section 5 prescribes a second remedy, the suspension of all new voting regulations pending review by federal authorities to determine whether their use would perpetuate voting discrimination. The third remedy, covered in §§ 6 (b), 7, 9, and 13 (a), is the assignment of federal examiners on certification by the Attorney General to list qualified applicants who are thereafter entitled to vote in all elections.

Other provisions of the Act prescribe subsidiary cures for persistent voting discrimination. Section 8 authorizes the appointment of federal poll-watchers in places to which federal examiners have already been assigned. Section 10 (d) excuses those made eligible to vote in sections of the country covered by § 4 (b) of the Act from paying accumulated past poll taxes for state and local elections. Section 12 (e) provides for balloting by persons denied access to the polls in areas where federal examiners have been appointed.

The remaining remedial portions of the Act are aimed at voting discrimination in any area of the country where it may occur. Section 2 broadly prohibits the use of voting rules to abridge exercise of the franchise on racial grounds. Sections 3, 6 (a), and 13 (b) strengthen

existing procedures for attacking voting discrimination by means of litigation. Section 4 (e) excuses citizens educated in American schools conducted in a foreign language from passing English-language literacy tests.
Section 10 (a)–(c) facilitates constitutional litigation challenging the
imposition of all poll taxes for state and local elections. Sections 11 and
12 (a)–(d) authorize civil and criminal sanctions against interference
with the exercise of rights guaranteed by the Act. . . .

These provisions of the Voting Rights Act of 1965 are challenged on the
fundamental ground that they exceed the powers of Congress and encroach on an area reserved to the States by the Constitution. . . . Has
Congress exercised its power under the Fifteenth Amendment in an
appropriate manner with relation to the States?

The ground rules for resolving this question are clear. The language
and purpose of the Fifteenth Amendment, the prior decisions construing
its several provisions, and the general doctrine of constitutional interpretation, all point to one fundamental principle. As against the reserved
powers of the States, Congress may use any rational means to effectuate
the constitutional prohibition of racial discrimination in voting. . . .

Section 1 of the Fifteenth Amendment declares that "[t]he right of
citizens of the United States to vote shall not be denied or abridged by
the United States or by any State on account of race, color, or previous
condition of servitude." This declaration has always been treated as self-
executing and has repeatedly been construed, without further legislative
specification, to invalidate state voting qualifications or procedures which
are discriminatory on their face or in practice. . . .

§ 2 of the Fifteenth Amendment expressly declares that "Congress shall
have power to enforce this article by appropriate legislation." By adding
this authorization, the Framers indicated that Congress was to be chiefly
responsible for implementing the rights created in § 1. . . .

Congress has repeatedly exercised these powers in the past, and its
enactments have repeatedly been upheld. For recent examples, see the
Civil Rights Act of 1957, which was sustained in *United States* v.
Raines. . . .

Congress exercised its authority under the Fifteenth Amendment in an
inventive manner when it enacted the Voting Rights Act of 1965. First:
The measure prescribes remedies for voting discrimination which go into
effect without any need for prior adjudication. This was clearly a legitimate response to the problem, for which there is ample precedent under
other constitutional provisions. . . . Congress had found that case-by-
case litigation was inadequate to combat widespread and persistent discrimination in voting, because of the inordinate amount of time and
energy required to overcome the obstructionist tactics invariably encountered in these lawsuits. After enduring nearly a century of systematic
resistance to the Fifteenth Amendment, Congress might well decide to

shift the advantage of time and inertia from the perpetrators of the evil to its victims. The question remains, of course, whether the specific remedies prescribed in the Act were an appropriate means of combatting the evil, and to this question we shall presently address ourselves.

Second: The Act intentionally confines these remedies to a small number of States and political subdivisions which in most instances were familiar to Congress by name. This, too, was a permissible method of dealing with the problem. Congress had learned that substantial voting discrimination presently occurs in certain sections of the country, and it knew no way of accurately forecasting whether the evil might spread elsewhere in the future. In acceptable legislative fashion, Congress chose to limit its attention to the geographic areas where immediate action seemed necessary. . . . The doctrine of the equality of States, invoked by South Carolina, does not bar this approach, for that doctrine applies only to the terms upon which States are admitted to the Union, and not to the remedies for local evils which have subsequently appeared. . . .

Coverage formula.

We now consider the related question of whether the specific States and political subdivisions within § 4 (b) of the Act were an appropriate target for the new remedies. South Carolina contends that the coverage formula is awkwardly designed in a number of respects and that it disregards various local conditions which have nothing to do with racial discrimination. . . .

The areas. . . . for which there was evidence of actual voting discrimination, share two characteristics incorporated by Congress into the coverage formula: the use of tests and devices for voter registration, and a voting rate in the 1964 presidential election at least 12 points below the national average. Tests and devices are relevant to voting discrimination because of their long history as a tool for perpetrating the evil; a low voting rate is pertinent for the obvious reason that widespread disenfranchisement must inevitably affect the number of actual voters. Accordingly, the coverage formula is rational in both practice and theory. . . .

Suspension of tests.

We now arrive at consideration of the specific remedies prescribed by the Act for areas included within the coverage formula. . . . The record shows that in most of the States covered by the Act, including South Carolina, various tests and devices have been instituted with the purpose of disenfranchising Negroes, have been framed in such a way as to facilitate this aim, and have been administered in a discriminatory fashion for many years. Under these circumstances, the Fifteenth Amendment has clearly been violated. . . .

The Act suspends literacy tests and similar devices for a period of five years from the last occurrence of substantial voting discrimination. **This** was a legitimate response to the problem, for which there is ample precedent in Fifteenth Amendment cases. . . . Underlying the response was the feeling that States and political subdivisions which had been allowing white illiterates to vote for years could not sincerely complain about "dilution" of their electorates through the registration of Negro illiterates. Congress knew that continuance of the tests and devices in use at the present time, no matter how fairly administered in the future, would freeze the effect of past discrimination in favor of unqualified white registrants. Congress permissibly rejected the alternative of requiring a complete re-registration of all voters, believing that this would be too harsh on many whites who had enjoyed the franchise for their entire adult lives.

Review of new rules.

The Act suspends new voting regulations pending scrutiny by federal authorities to determine whether their use would violate the Fifteenth Amendment. This may have been an uncommon exercise of congressional power, as South Carolina contends, but the Court has recognized that exceptional conditions can justify legislative measures not otherwise appropriate. . . . Congress knew that some of the States covered by § 4 (b) of the Act had resorted to the extraordinary stratagem of contriving new rules of various kinds for the sole purpose of perpetuating voting discrimination in the face of adverse federal court decrees. Congress had reason to suppose that these States might try similar maneuvers in the future in order to evade the remedies for voting discrimination contained in the Act itself. Under the compulsion of these unique circumstances, Congress responded in a permissibly decisive manner. . . .

Federal examiners.

The Act authorizes the appointment of federal examiners to list qualified applicants who are thereafter entitled to vote, subject to an expeditious challenge procedure. This was clearly an appropriate response to the problem, closely related to remedies authorized in prior cases. . . . In many of the political subdivisions covered by § 4 (b) of the Act, voting officials have persistently employed a variety of procedural tactics to deny Negroes the franchise, often in direct defiance or evasion of federal court decrees. Congress realized that merely to suspend voting rules which have been misused or are subject to misuse might leave this localized evil undisturbed. As for the briskness of the challenge procedure, Congress knew that in some of the areas affected, challenges had been persistently employed to harass registered Negroes. It chose to forestall this abuse, at the same time providing alternative ways for removing persons listed through error or fraud. In addition to the judicial challenge procedure, § 7 (d) allows for the removal of names by the examiner himself, and § 11 (c) makes it a crime to obtain a listing through fraud. . . .

After enduring nearly a century of widespread resistance to the Fifteenth Amendment, Congress has marshalled an array of potent weapons against the evil, with authority in the Attorney General to employ them effectively. Many of the areas directly affected by this development have indicated their willingness to abide by any restraints legitimately imposed upon them. We here hold that the portions of the Voting Rights Act properly before us are a valid means for carrying out the commands of the Fifteenth Amendment. Hopefully, millions of non-white Americans will now be able to participate for the first time on an equal basis in the government under which they live. We may finally look forward to the day when truly "[t]he right of citizens of the United States to vote shall not be denied or abridged by the United States or by any State on account of race, color, or previous condition of servitude."

The bill of complaint is

Dismissed.

Baker *v*. Carr

Racial discrimination was only one cause of inequity in American voting patterns. Malapportionment of representative districts — local, state, and federal — prevailed throughout the nation, and effectively diluted the voting power of new interest groups and, in many cases, numerical majorities. The "political questions" doctrine of Luther v. Borden had long barred the way for judicial action in such cases. In Colegrove v. Green, for example, the Supreme Court had refused to intervene against malapportioned congressional districts in Illinois (328 U.S. 549 [1946]). Justice Frankfurter contended that the question was political and "therefore not meet for judicial determination." The courts, he warned, should not involve themselves in the "political thicket" surrounding apportionment problems. But, speaking for a unanimous bench in 1960, Frankfurter accepted jurisdiction in a redistricting case which involved the political annihilation of almost all Negro voters from Tuskegee, Alabama (Gomillion v. Lightfoot, 364 U.S. 399). Finally, in the landmark case below, the Court announced its intention to allow the judicial process to work its will when the political process failed to respond.

Justice Brennan delivered the opinion of the Court.

This civil action was brought under 42 U. S. C. §§ 1983 and 1988 to redress the alleged deprivation of federal constitutional rights. The complaint, alleging that by means of a 1901 statute of Tennessee apportioning the members of the General Assembly among the State's 95 counties, "these plaintiffs and others similarly situated, are denied the equal protection of the laws accorded them by the Fourteenth Amendment to the Constitution of the United States by virtue of the debasement of their votes," was dismissed by a three-judge court convened under 28 U. S. C. § 2281 in the Middle District of Tennessee. The court held that it lacked jurisdiction of the subject matter and also that no claim was stated upon which relief could be granted. . . . We noted probable jurisdiction of the appeal. . . . We hold that the dismissal was error, and remand the cause to the District Court for trial and further proceedings consistent with this opinion. . . .

Tennessee's standard for allocating legislative representation among her counties is the total number of qualified voters resident in the respective

369 U.S. 186 (1962)

counties, subject only to minor qualifications. Decennial reapportionment in compliance with the constitutional scheme was effected by the General Assembly each decade from 1871 to 1901. The 1871 apportionment was preceded by an 1870 statute requiring an enumeration. The 1881 apportionment involved three statutes, the first authorizing an enumeration, the second enlarging the Senate from 25 to 33 members and the House from 75 to 99 members, and the third apportioning the membership of both Houses. In 1891 there were both an enumeration and an apportionment. In 1901 the General Assembly abandoned separate enumeration in favor of reliance upon the Federal Census and passed the Apportionment Act here in controversy. In the more than 60 years since that action, all proposals in both Houses of the General Assembly for reapportionment have failed to pass. . . .

Jurisdiction of the Subject Matter

The District Court was uncertain whether our cases withholding federal judicial relief rested upon a lack of federal jurisdiction or upon the inappropriateness of the subject matter for judicial consideration — what we have designated "nonjusticiability." The distinction between the two grounds is significant. In the instance of nonjusticiability, consideration of the cause is not wholly and immediately foreclosed; rather, the Court's inquiry necessarily proceeds to the point of deciding whether the duty asserted can be judicially identified and its breach judicially determined, and whether protection for the right asserted can be judicially molded. In the instance of lack of jurisdiction the cause either does not "arise under" the Federal Constitution, laws or treaties (or fall within one of the other enumerated categories of Art. III, § 2), or is not a "case or controversy" within the meaning of that section; or the cause is not one described by any jurisdictional statute. Our conclusion . . . that this cause presents no nonjusticiable "political question" settles the only possible doubt that it is a case or controversy. Under the present heading of "Jurisdiction of the Subject Matter" we hold only that the matter set forth in the complaint does arise under the Constitution and is within 28 U. S. C. § 1343.

Article III, § 2, of the Federal Constitution provides that "The judicial Power shall extend to all Cases, in Law and Equity, arising under this Constitution, the Laws of the United States, and Treaties made, or which shall be made, under their Authority. . . ." It is clear that the cause of action is one which "arises under" the Federal Constitution. The complaint alleges that the 1901 statute effects an apportionment that deprives the appellants of the equal protection of the laws in violation of the Fourteenth Amendment. . . .

The appellees refer to *Colegrove* v. *Green*, 328 U.S. 549, as authority that the District Court lacked jurisdiction of the subject matter. Appellees misconceive the holding of that case. The holding was precisely contrary to their reading of it. Seven members of the Court participated in the decision. Unlike many other cases in this field which have assumed without discussion that there was jurisdiction, all three opinions filed in *Colegrove* discussed the question. Two of the opinions expressing the views of four of the Justices, a majority, flatly held that there was jurisdiction of the subject matter. MR. JUSTICE BLACK joined by MR. JUSTICE DOUGLAS and Mr. Justice Murphy stated: "It is my judgment that the District Court had jurisdiction. . . ." Mr. Justice Rutledge, writing separately, expressed agreement with this conclusion. . . .

We hold that the District Court has jurisdiction of the subject matter of the federal constitutional claim asserted in the complaint.

JUSTICIABILITY

In holding that the subject matter of this suit was not justiciable, the District Court relied on *Colegrove* v. *Green, supra,* and subsequent *per curiam* cases. The court stated: "From a review of these decisions there can be no doubt that the federal rule . . . is that the federal courts . . . will not intervene in cases of this type to compel legislative reapportionment." 179 F. Supp., at 826. We understand the District Court to have read the cited cases as compelling the conclusion that since the appellants sought to have a legislative apportionment held unconstitutional, their suit presented a "political question" and was therefore nonjusticiable. We hold that this challenge to an apportionment presents no nonjusticiable "political question." The cited cases do not hold the contrary.

Of course the mere fact that the suit seeks protection of a political right does not mean it presents a political question. Such an objection "is little more than a play upon words." *Nixon* v. *Herndon,* 273 U.S. 536, 540. . . .

Our discussion, even at the price of extending this opinion, requires review of a number of political question cases, in order to expose the attributes of the doctrine — attributes which, in various settings, diverge, combine, appear, and disappear in seeming disorderliness. Since that review is undertaken solely to demonstrate that neither singly nor collectively do these cases support a conclusion that this apportionment case is nonjusticiable, we of course do not explore their implications in other contexts. That review reveals that in the Guaranty Clause cases and in the other "political question" cases, it is the relationship between the judiciary and the coordinate branches of the Federal Government, and not the federal judiciary's relationship to the States, which gives rise to the "political question."

We have said that "In determining whether a question falls within [the political question] category, the appropriateness under our system of

government of attributing finality to the action of the political departments and also the lack of satisfactory criteria for a judicial determination
are dominant considerations." *Coleman* v. *Miller*, 307 U.S. 433, 454–455.
The nonjusticiability of a political question is primarily a function of the
separation of powers. Much confusion results from the capacity of the
"political question" label to obscure the need for case-by-case inquiry.
Deciding whether a matter has in any measure been committed by the
Constitution to another branch of government, or whether the action of
that branch exceeds whatever authority has been committed, is itself a
delicate exercise in constitutional interpretation, and is a responsibility
of this Court as ultimate interpreter of the Constitution. To demonstrate
this requires no less than to analyze representative cases and to infer from
them the analytical threads that make up the political question doctrine. . . .

We come, finally, to the ultimate inquiry whether our precedents as to
what constitutes a nonjusticiable "political question" bring the case before
us under the umbrella of that doctrine. A natural beginning is to note
whether any of the common characteristics which we have been able to
identify and label descriptively are present. We find none: The question
here is the consistency of state action with the Federal Constitution. We
have no question decided, or to be decided, by a political branch of government coequal with this Court. Nor do we risk embarrassment of our
government abroad, or grave disturbance at home if we take issue with
Tennessee as to the constitutionality of her action here challenged. Nor
need the appellants, in order to succeed in this action, ask the Court to
enter upon policy determinations for which judicially manageable standards are lacking. Judicial standards under the Equal Protection Clause
are well developed and familiar, and it has been open to courts since the
enactment of the Fourteenth Amendment to determine, if on the particular facts they must, that a discrimination reflects *no* policy, but simply
arbitrary and capricious action. . . .

When challenges to state action respecting matters of "the administration of the affairs of the State and the officers through whom they are
conducted" have rested on claims of constitutional deprivation which are
amenable to judicial correction, this Court has acted upon its view of the
merits of the claim. For example, in *Boyd* v. *Nebraska ex rel. Thayer*,
143 U.S. 135, we reversed the Nebraska Supreme Court's decision that
Nebraska's Governor was not a citizen of the United States or of the State
and therefore could not continue in office. In *Kennard* v. *Louisiana ex
rel. Morgan*, 92 U.S. (2 Otto) 480, and *Foster* v. *Kansas ex rel. Johnston*,
112 U.S. 201, we considered whether persons had been removed from
public office by procedures consistent with the Fourteenth Amendment's
due process guaranty, and held on the merits that they had. And only last
Term, in *Gomillion* v. *Lightfoot*, 364 U.S. 339, we applied the Fifteenth

Amendment to strike down a redrafting of municipal boundaries which effected a discriminatory impairment of voting rights, in the face of what a majority of the Court of Appeals thought to be a sweeping commitment to state legislatures of the power to draw and redraw such boundaries.

Gomillion was brought by a Negro who had been a resident of the City of Tuskegee, Alabama, until the municipal boundaries were so recast by the State Legislature as to exclude practically all Negroes. The plaintiff claimed deprivation of the right to vote in municipal elections. The District Court's dismissal for want of jurisdiction and failure to state a claim upon which relief could be granted was affirmed by the Court of Appeals. This Court unanimously reversed. . . .

We have already noted that the District Court's holding that the subject matter of this complaint was nonjusticiable relied upon *Colegrove* v. *Green, supra,* and later cases. Some of those concerned the choice of members of a state legislature, as in this case; others, like *Colegrove* itself and earlier precedents, *Smiley* v. *Holm,* 285 U.S. 355, *Koenig* v. *Flynn,* 285 U.S. 375, and *Carroll* v. *Becker,* 285 U.S. 380, concerned the choice of Representatives in the Federal Congress. *Smiley, Koenig* and *Carroll* settled the issue in favor of justiciability of questions of congressional redistricting. The Court followed these precedents in *Colegrove* although over the dissent of three of the seven Justices who participated in that decision. On the issue of justiciability, all four Justices comprising a majority relied upon *Smiley* v. *Holm,* but in two opinions, one for three Justices, 328 U.S., at 566, 568, and a separate one by Mr. Justice Rutledge, 328 U.S., at 564. . . .

Article I, §§ 2, 4, and 5, and Amendment XIV, § 2, relate only to congressional elections and obviously do not govern apportionment of state legislatures. However, our decisions in favor of justiciability even in light of those provisions plainly afford no support for the District Court's conclusion that the subject matter of this controversy presents a political question. Indeed, the refusal to award relief in *Colegrove* resulted only from the controlling view of a want of equity. Nor is anything contrary to be found in those *per curiams* that came after *Colegrove.* . . .

We conclude that the complaint's allegations of a denial of equal protection present a justiciable constitutional cause of action upon which appellants are entitled to a trial and a decision. The right asserted is within the reach of judicial protection under the Fourteenth Amendment.

The judgment of the District Court is reversed and the cause is remanded for further proceedings consistent with this opinion.

Justice Frankfurter, whom Justice Harlan joins, dissenting.

The Court today reverses a uniform course of decision established by a dozen cases, including one by which the very claim now sustained was unanimously rejected only five years ago. The impressive body of rulings thus cast aside reflected the equally uniform course of our political history regarding the relationship between population and legislative representation — a wholly different matter from denial of the franchise to individuals because of race, color, religion or sex. Such a massive repudiation of the experience of our whole past in asserting destructively novel judicial power demands a detailed analysis of the role of this Court in our constitutional scheme. Disregard of inherent limits in the effective exercise of the Court's "judicial Power" not only presages the futility of judicial intervention in the essentially political conflict of forces by which the relation between population and representation has time out of mind been and now is determined. It may well impair the Court's position as the ultimate organ of "the supreme Law of the Land" in that vast range of legal problems, often strongly entangled in popular feeling, on which this Court must pronounce. The Court's authority — possessed neither of the purse nor the sword — ultimately rests on sustained public confidence in its moral sanction. Such feeling must be nourished by the Court's complete detachment, in fact and in appearance, from political entanglements and by abstention from injecting itself into the clash of political forces in political settlements.

A hypothetical claim resting on abstract assumptions is now for the first time made the basis for affording illusory relief for a particular evil even though it foreshadows deeper and more pervasive difficulties in consequence. The claim is hypothetical and the assumptions are abstract because the Court does not vouchsafe the lower courts — state and federal — guide-lines for formulating specific, definite, wholly unprecedented remedies for the inevitable litigations that today's unbrageous disposition is bound to stimulate in connection with politically motivated reapportionments in so many States. In such a setting, to promulgate jurisdiction in the abstract is meaningless. It is devoid of reality as "a brooding omnipresence in the sky" for it conveys no intimation what relief, if any, a District Court is capable of affording that would not invite legislatures to play ducks and drakes with the judiciary. For this Court to direct the District Court to enforce a claim to which the Court has over the years consistently found itself required to deny legal enforcement and at the same time to find it necessary to withhold any guidance to the lower court how to enforce this turnabout, new legal claim, manifests an odd — indeed an esoteric — conception of judicial propriety. One of the Court's supporting opinions, as elucidated by commentary, unwittingly affords a disheartening preview of the mathematical quagmire (apart from divers judicially inappropriate and elusive determinants), into which this Court today catapults the lower courts of the country without so much as adumbrating the basis for a legal calculus as a means of extrication. Even assuming the indispensable intellectual disinterestedness on the part of judges in such matters, they do not have accepted legal standards or criteria or even reliable analogies to draw upon for making judicial judgments. To charge courts with the task of accommodating the incommensurable factors of policy that underlie these mathematical puzzles is to attribute, however flatteringly, omnicompetence to judges. The Framers of the Constitution persistently rejected a proposal that embodied this assumption and Thomas Jefferson never entertained it.

Recent legislation, creating a district appropriately described as "an atrocity of ingenuity," is not unique. Considering the gross inequality among legislative electoral units within almost every State, the Court naturally shrinks from asserting that in districting at least substantial equality is a constitutional requirement enforceable by courts. Room continues to be allowed for weighting. This of course implies that geography, economics, urban-rural conflict, and all the other non-legal factors which have throughout our history entered into political districting are to some extent not to be ruled out in the undefined vista now opened up by review in the federal courts of state reapportionments. To some extent — aye, there's the rub. In effect, today's decision empowers the courts of the country to devise what should constitute the proper composition of the legislatures of the fifty States. If state courts should for one reason or another find themselves unable to discharge this task, the duty of doing so is put on the federal courts or on this Court, if State views do not satisfy this Court's notion of what is proper districting.

We were soothingly told at the bar of this Court that we need not worry about the kind of remedy a court could effectively fashion once the abstract constitutional right to have courts pass on a state-wide system of electoral districting is recognized as a matter of judicial rhetoric, because legislatures would heed the Court's admonition. This is not only an euphoric hope. It implies a sorry confession of judicial impotence in place of a frank acknowledgment that there is not under our Constitution a judicial remedy for every political mischief, for every undesirable exercise of legislative power. The Framers carefully and with deliberate forethought refused so to enthrone the judiciary. In this situation, as in others of like nature, appeal for relief does not belong here. Appeal must be to an informed, civically militant electorate. In a democratic society like ours, relief must come through an aroused popular conscience that sears the conscience of the people's representatives. In any event there is nothing judicially more unseemly nor more self-defeating than for this Court to make *in terrorem* pronouncements, to indulge in merely empty rhetoric, sounding a word of promise to the ear, sure to be disappointing to the hope. . . .

In sustaining appellants' claim, based on the Fourteenth Amendment, that the District Court may entertain this suit, this Court's uniform course of decision over the years is overruled or disregarded. Explicitly it begins with *Colegrove* v. *Green, supra,* decided in 1946, but its roots run deep in the Court's historic adjudicatory process.

Colegrove held that a federal court should not entertain an action for declaratory and injunctive relief to adjudicate the constitutionality, under the Equal Protection Clause and other federal constitutional and statutory provisions, of a state statute establishing the respective districts for the State's election of Representatives to the Congress. Two opinions were written by the four Justices who composed the majority of the seven sitting members of the Court. Both opinions joining in the result in *Colegrove* v. *Green* agreed that considerations were controlling which dictated denial of jurisdiction though not in the strict sense of want of power. While the two opinions show a divergence of view regarding some of these considerations, there are important points of concurrence. Both opinions demonstrate a predominant concern, first, with avoiding federal judicial involvement in matters traditionally left to legislative policy-making; second, with respect to the difficulty — in view of the nature of the problems of apportionment and its history in this country — of drawing on or devising judicial standards for judgment, as opposed to legislative determinations, of the part which mere numerical equality among voters should play as a criterion for the allocation of political power; and, third, with problems of finding appropriate modes of relief — particularly, the problem of resolving the essentially political issue of the relative merits of at-large elections and elections held in districts of unequal population.

The broad applicability of these considerations — summarized in the loose shorthand phrase, "political question" — in cases involving a State's apportionment of voting power among its numerous localities has led the Court, since 1946, to recognize their controlling effect in a variety of situations. . . .

[In *Luther* v. *Borden*] it was recognized that the compulsion to follow state law would not apply in a federal court in the face of a superior command found in the federal constitution, . . . but no such command was found. The Constitution, the Court said — referring to the Guarantee Clause of the Fourth Article — ". . . as far as it has provided for an emergency of this kind, and authorized the general government to interfere in the domestic concerns of a State, has treated the subject as political in its nature, and placed the power in the hands of that department." . . .

In determining this issue non-justiciable, the Court was sensitive to the same considerations to which its later decisions have given the varied applications already discussed. It adverted to the delicacy of judicial intervention into the very structure of government. It acknowledged that tradition had long entrusted questions of this nature to non-judicial processes, and that judicial processes were unsuited to their decision. The absence of guiding standards for judgment was critical, for the question whether the Dorr constitution has been rightfully adopted depended, in part, upon the extent of the franchise to be recognized — the very point of contention over which rebellion had been fought. . . .

The present case involves all of the elements that have made the Guarantee Clause cases non-justiciable. It is, in effect, a Guarantee Clause claim masquerading under a different label. But it cannot make the case more fit for judicial action that appellants invoke the Fourteenth Amendment rather than Art. IV, § 4, where, in fact, the gist of their complaint is the same — unless it can be found that the Fourteenth Amendment speaks with greater particularity to their situation. We have been admonished to avoid "the tyranny of labels." *Snyder* v. *Massachusetts*, 291 U.S. 97, 114. Art. IV, § 4, is not committed by express constitutional terms to Congress. It is the nature of the controversies arising under it, nothing else, which has made it judicially unenforceable. . . .

What, then, is this question of legislative apportionment? Appellants invoke the right to vote and to have their votes counted. But they are permitted to vote and their votes are counted. They go to the polls they cast their ballots, they send their representatives to the state councils. Their complaint is simply that the representatives are not sufficiently numerous or powerful — in short, that Tennessee has adopted a basis of representation with which they are dissatisfied. Talk of "debasement" or "dilution" is circular talk. One cannot speak of "debasement" or "dilution" of the value of a vote until there is first defined a standard of reference as to what a vote should be worth. What is actually asked of the Court in this case is to choose among competing bases of representation — ultimately, really, among competing theories of political philosophy — in order to establish an appropriate frame of government for the State of Tennessee and thereby for all the States of the Union. . . .

The notion that representation proportioned to the geographic spread of population is so universally accepted as a necessary element of equality between man and man that it must be taken to be the standard of a political equality preserved by the Fourteenth Amendment — that it is, in appellants' words "the basic principles of representative government" — is, to put it bluntly, not true. However desirable and however desired by some among the great political thinkers and framers of our government, it has never been generally practiced, today or in the past. It was not the English system, it was not the colonial system, it was not the system chosen for the national government by the Constitution, it was not the system exclusively or even predominantly practiced by the States at the time of adoption of the Fourteenth Amendment, it is not predominantly practiced by the States today. Unless judges, the judges of this Court, are to make their private views of political wisdom the measure of the Constitution — views which in all honesty cannot but give the appearance, if not reflect the reality, of involvement with the business of partisan politics so inescapably a part of apportionment controversies — the Fourteenth Amendment, "itself a historical product," *Jackman* v. *Rosenbaum Co.*, 260 U.S. 22, 31, provides no guide for judicial oversight of the representation problem. . . .

Detailed recent studies are available to describe the present-day constitutional and statutory status of apportionment in the fifty States. They demonstrate a decided twentieth-century trend away from population as the exclusive base of representation. Today, only a dozen state constitutions provide for periodic legislative reapportionment of both houses by a substantially unqualified application of the population standard, and only about a dozen more prescribe such reapportionment for even a single chamber. "Specific provision for county representation in at least one house of the state legislature has been increasingly adopted since the end of the 19th century. . . ." More than twenty States now guarantee each county at least one seat in one of their houses regardless of population, and in nine others county or town units are given equal representation in one legislative branch, whatever the number of each unit's inhabitants. Of course, numerically considered, "These provisions invariably result in over-representation of the least populated areas. . . ." And in an effort to curb the political dominance of metropolitan regions, at least ten States now limit the maximum entitlement of any single county (or, in some cases, city) in one legislative house — another source of substantial numerical disproportion.

Moreover, it is common knowledge that the legislatures have not kept reapportionment up to date, even where state constitutions in terms require it. In particular, the pattern of according greater per capita representation to rural, relatively sparsely populated areas — the same pattern which finds expression in various state constitutional provisions, and which has been given effect in England and elsewhere — has, in some of the States, been made the law by legislative inaction in the face of population shifts. Throughout the country, urban and suburban areas tend to be given higher representation ratios than do rural areas.

The stark fact is that if among the numerous widely varying principles and practices that control state legislative apportionment today there is any generally prevailing feature, that feature is geographic inequality in relation to the population standard. Examples could be endlessly multiplied. . . .

Manifestly, the Equal Protection Clause supplies no clearer guide for judicial examination of apportionment methods than would the Guarantee Clause itself. Apportionment, by its character, is a subject of extraordinary complexity, involving — even after the fundamental theoretical issues concerning what is to be represented in a representative legislature have been fought out or compromised — considerations of geography, demography, electoral convenience, economic and social cohesions or diver-

gencies among particular local groups, communications, the practical
effects of political institutions like the lobby and the city machine, ancient
traditions and ties of settled usage, respect for proven incumbents of long
experience and senior status, mathematical mechanics, censuses compil-
ing relevant data, and a host of others. Legislative responses throughout the country to the reapportionment demands of the 1960 Census
have glaringly confirmed that these are not factors that lend themselves to
evaluations of a nature that are the staple of judicial determinations or
for which judges are equipped to adjudicate by legal training or experience or native wit. And this is the more so true because in every
strand of this complicated, intricate web of values meet the contending
forces of partisan politics. The practical significance of apportionment
is that the next election results may differ because of it. Apportionment
battles are overwhelmingly party or "intra-party contests. It will add a
virulent source of friction and tension in federal-state relations to embroil
the federal judiciary in them. . . .

Reynolds *v.* Sims

Baker *v.* Carr *opened the floodgates for litigation, and the federal
courts were soon swamped with reapportionment suits in virtually
every state. The decision also cast the mean light of publicity upon
an often unrecognized situation, with the result that some state
legislatures voluntarily reapportioned their representative districts.
In 1964, in* Wesberry *v.* Sanders, *the Court ruled that Article I of
the federal constitution required equality of congressional districts
(376 U.S. 1). During the same term, in the case below, the Court
struck down the traditional system of one state legislative house
being based on considerations other than population. The case involved Alabama's upper house, which contained one senator from
each of thirty-five counties, ranging in population from 15,000 to
more than 600,000 persons.*

Chief Justice Warren delivered the opinion of the Court.

In *Baker* v. *Carr* we . . . held that a claim asserted under the Equal
Protection Clause challenging the constitutionality of a State's apportionment of seats in its legislature, on the ground that the right to vote

of certain citizens was effectively impaired since debased and diluted, in effect presented a justiciable controversy subject to adjudication by federal courts. The spate of similar cases filed and decided by lower courts since our decision in *Baker* amply shows that the problem of state legislative malapportionment is one that is perceived to exist in a large number of the States. . . .

In *Gray* v. *Sanders,* 372 U.S. 368, we held that the Georgia county unit system, applicable in statewide primary elections, was unconstitutional since it resulted in a dilution of the weight of the votes of certain Georgia voters merely because of where they resided. . . . [W]e stated that "there is no indication in the Constitution that homesite or occupation affords a permissible basis for distinguishing between qualified voters within the State." And, finally, we concluded: "The conception of political equality from the Declaration of Independence, to Lincoln's Gettysburg Address, to the Fifteenth, Seventeenth, and Nineteenth Amendments can mean only one thing — one person, one vote." . . .

We stated in *Gray,* however, that that case,

> unlike *Baker* v. *Carr,* . . . does not involve a question of the degree to which the Equal Protection Clause of the Fourteenth Amendment limits the authority of a State Legislature in designing the geographical districts from which representatives are chosen either for the State Legislature or for the Federal House of Representatives. . . . Nor does it present the question, inherent in the bicameral form of our Federal Government, whether a State may have one house chosen without regard to population.

Of course, in these cases we are faced with the problem not presented in *Gray* — that of determining the basic standards and stating the applicable guidelines for implementing our decision in *Baker* v. *Carr.*

In *Wesberry* v. *Sanders,* 376 U.S. 1, decided earlier this Term, we held that attacks on the constitutionality of congressional districting plans enacted by state legislatures do not present nonjusticiable questions and should not be dismissed generally for "want of equity." We determined that the constitutional test for the validity of congressional districting schemes was one of substantial equality of population among the various districts established by a state legislature for the election of members of the Federal House of Representatives.

In that case we decided that an apportionment of congressional seats which "contracts the value of some votes and expands that of others" is unconstitutional, since "the Federal Constitution intends that when qualified voters elect members of Congress each vote be given as much weight as any other vote. . . ." We concluded that the constitutional prescription for election of members of the House of Representatives "by the People," construed in its historical context, "means that as nearly as is practicable one man's vote in a congressional election is to be worth as much as another's." . . .

[T]he fundamental principle of representative government in this country is one of equal representation for equal numbers of people, without regard to race, sex, economic status, or place of residence within a State. Our problem, then, is to ascertain, in the instant cases, whether there are any constitutionally cognizable principles which would justify departures from the basic standard of equality among voters in the apportionment of seats in state legislatures. . . .

Legislators represent people, not trees or acres. Legislators are elected by voters, not farms or cities or economic interests. As long as ours is a representative form of government, and our legislatures are those instruments of government elected directly by and directly representative of the people, the right to elect legislators in a free and unimpaired fashion is a bedrock of our political system. It could hardly be gainsaid that a constitutional claim had been asserted by an allegation that certain otherwise qualified voters had been entirely prohibited from voting for members of their state legislature. And, if a State should provide that the votes of citizens in one part of the State should be given two times, or five times, or 10 times the weight of votes of citizens in another part of the State, it could hardly be contended that the right to vote of those residing in the disfavored areas had not been effectively diluted. It would appear extraordinary to suggest that a State could be constitutionally permitted to enact a law providing that certain of the State's voters could vote two, five, or 10 times for their legislative representatives, while voters living elsewhere could vote only once. And it is inconceivable that a state law to the effect that, in counting votes for legislators, the votes of citizens in one part of the State would be multiplied by two, five, or 10, while the votes of persons in another area would be counted only at face value, could be constitutionally sustainable. Of course, the effect of state legislative districting schemes which give the same number of representatives to unequal numbers of constituents is identical. Overweighting and overvaluation of the votes of those living here has the certain effect of dilution and undervaluation of the votes of those living there. The resulting discrimination against those individual voters living in disfavored areas is easily demonstrable mathematically. Their right to vote is simply not the same right to vote as that of those living in a favored part of the State. Two, five, or 10 of them must vote before the effect of their voting is equivalent to that of their favored neighbor. Weighting the votes of citizens differently, by any method or means, merely because of where they happen to reside, hardly seems justifiable. One must be ever aware that the Constitution forbids "sophisticated as well as simple-minded modes of discrimination." . . .

Logically, in a society ostensibly grounded on representative government, it would seem reasonable that a majority of the people of a State could elect a majority of that State's legislators. To conclude differently, and to sanction minority control of state legislative bodies, would appear to deny majority rights in a way that far surpasses any possible denial of minority rights that might otherwise be thought to result. Since legislatures are responsible for enacting laws by which all citizens are to be governed, they should be bodies which are collectively responsive to the popular will. And the concept of equal protection has been traditionally viewed as requiring the uniform treatment of persons standing in the same relation to the governmental action questioned or challenged. With respect to the allocation of legislative representation, all voters, as citizens of a State, stand in the same relation regardless of where they live. Any suggested criteria for the differentiation of citizens are insufficient to justify any discrimination, as to the weight of their votes, unless relevant to the permissible purposes of legislative apportionment. Since the achieving of fair and effective representation for all citizens is concededly the basic aim of legislative apportionment, we conclude that the Equal Protection Clause guarantees the opportunity for equal participation by all voters in the election of state legislators. . . . Our constitutional system amply provides for the protection of minorities by means other than giving them majority control of state legislatures. And the democratic ideals of equality and majority rule, which have served this Nation so well in the past, are hardly of any less significance for the present and the future.

We are told that the matter of apportioning representation in a state legislature is a complex and many-faceted one. We are advised that States can rationally consider factors other than population in apportioning legislative representation. We are admonished not to restrict the power of the States to impose differing views as to political philosophy on their citizens. We are cautioned about the dangers of entering into political thickets and mathematical quagmires. Our answer is this: a denial of constitutionally protected rights demands judicial protection; our oath and our office require no less of us. . . . To the extent that a citizen's right to vote is debased, he is that much less a citizen. The fact that an individual lives here or there is not a legitimate reason for overweighting or diluting the efficacy of his vote. The complexions of societies and civilizations change, often with amazing rapidity. A nation once primarily rural in character becomes predominantly urban. Representation schemes once fair and equitable become archaic and outdated. But the basic principle of representative government remains, and must remain, unchanged — the weight of a citizen's vote cannot be made to depend on where he lives. Population is, of necessity, the starting point for consideration and the controlling criterion for judgment in legislative apportionment controversies. . . .

We hold that, as a basic constitutional standard, the Equal Protection Clause requires that the seats in both houses of a bicameral state legislature must be apportioned on a population basis. Simply stated, an individual's right to vote for state legislators is unconstitutionally impaired when its weight is in a substantial fashion diluted when compared with votes of citizens living in other parts of the State. . . .

We find the federal analogy inapposite and irrelevant to state legislative districting schemes. Attempted reliance on the federal analogy appears often to be little more than an after-the-fact rationalization offered in defense of maladjusted state apportionment arrangements. The original constitutions of 36 of our States provided that representation in both houses of the state legislatures would be based completely, or predominantly, on population. And the Founding Fathers clearly had no intention of establishing a pattern or model for the apportionment of seats in state legislatures when the system of representation in the Federal Congress was adopted. Demonstrative of this is the fact that the Northwest Ordinance, adopted in the same year, 1787, as the Federal Constitution, provided for the apportionment of seats in territorial legislatures solely on the basis of population.

The system of representation in the two Houses of the Federal Congress is one ingrained in our Constitution, as part of the law of the land. It is one conceived out of compromise and concession indispensable to the establishment of our federal republic. Arising from unique historical circumstances, it is based on the consideration that in establishing our type of federalism a group of formerly independent States bound themselves together under one national government. . . .

Political subdivisions of States — counties, cities, or whatever — never were and never have been considered as sovereign entities. Rather, they have been traditionally regarded as subordinate governmental instrumentalities created by the State to assist in the carrying out of state governmental functions. . . .

Since we find the so-called federal analogy inapposite to a consideration of the constitutional validity of state legislative apportionment schemes, we necessarily hold that the Equal Protection Clause requires both houses of a state legislature to be apportioned on a population basis. The right of a citizen to equal representation and to have his vote weighted equally with those of all other citizens in the election of members of one house of a bicameral state legislature would amount to little if States could effectively submerge the equal-population principle in the apportionment of seats in the other house. . . .

By holding that as a federal constitutional requisite both houses of a state legislature must be apportioned on a population basis, we mean that the Equal Protection Clause requires that a State make an honest and good faith effort to construct districts, in both houses of its legislature, as nearly of equal population as is practicable. We realize that it is a practical impossibility to arrange legislative districts so that each one has an identical number of residents, or citizens, or voters. Mathematical exactness or precision is hardly a workable constitutional requirement. . . .

Somewhat more flexibility may therefore be constitutionally permissible with respect to state legislative apportionment than in congressional districting. Lower courts can and assuredly will work out more concrete and specific standards for evaluating state legislative apportionment schemes in the context of actual litigation. For the present, we deem it expedient not to attempt to spell out any precise constitutional tests. What is marginally permissible in one State may be unsatisfactory in another, depending on the particular circumstances of the case. Developing a body of doctrine on a case-by-case basis appears to us to provide the most satisfactory means of arriving at detailed constitutional requirements in the area of state legislative apportionment. . . .

Justice Harlan dissenting.

⋆ F ⋆

Rights of the Accused

Mapp *v.* Ohio

In 1949, the Supreme Court had held that the Fourteenth Amendment was not applicable against the use of evidence, obtained in an unreasonable search and seizure, in a state court proceeding (Wolf v. Colorado, 338 U.S. 25). But in the 1960's, as part of its new position that the Fourteenth Amendment incorporated various procedural rights of the accused, the Court began to apply federal constitutional standards of searches and seizures to state practices. The Mapp case below directly overruled Wolf. A year later, in Ker v. California, the Court flatly stated that the guarantee against unreasonable search and seizure "is the same under the Fourth and Fourteenth Amendments" (374 U.S. 23).

Justice Clark delivered the opinion of the Court.

Appellant stands convicted of knowingly having had in her possession and under her control certain lewd and lascivious books, pictures, and photographs in violation of § 2905.34 of Ohio's Revised Code. As officially stated in the syllabus to its opinion, the Supreme Court of Ohio found that her conviction was valid though "based primarily upon the introduction in evidence of lewd and lascivious books and pictures unlawfully seized during an unlawful search of defendant's home. . . ."

At the trial no search warrant was produced by the prosecution, nor was the failure to produce one explained or accounted for. . . .

The State says that even if the search were made without authority, or otherwise unreasonably, it is not prevented from using the unconstitutionally seized evidence at trial, citing *Wolf v. Colorado*, 338 U.S. 25 (1949), in which this Court did indeed hold "that in a prosecution in a State court for a State crime the Fourteenth Amendment does not

---

367 U.S. 643 (1961)

forbid the admission of evidence obtained by an unreasonable search and seizure." . . .

Since the Fourth Amendment's right of privacy has been declared enforceable against the States through the Due Process Clause of the Fourteenth, it is enforceable against them by the same sanction of exclusion as is used against the Federal Government. Were it otherwise, . . . the assurance against unreasonable federal searches and seizures would be "a form of words," valueless and undeserving of mention in a perpetual charter of inestimable human liberties, so too, . . . the freedom from state invasions of privacy would be so ephemeral and so neatly severed from its conceptual nexus with the freedom from all brutish means of coercing evidence as not to merit this Court's high regard as a freedom "implicit in the concept of ordered liberty." At the time that the Court held in *Wolf* that the Amendment was applicable to the States through the Due Process Clause, the cases of this Court, as we have seen, had steadfastly held that as to federal officers the Fourth Amendment included the exclusion of evidence seized in violation of its provisions. Even *Wolf* "stoutly adhered" to that proposition. . . . Therefore, in extending the substantive protections of due process to all constitutionally unreasonable searches — state or federal — it was logically and constitutionally necessary that the exclusion doctrine — an essential part of the right to privacy — be also insisted upon as an essential ingredient of the right newly recognized by the *Wolf* case. In short, the admission of the new constitutional right by *Wolf* could not consistently tolerate denial of its most important constitutional privilege, namely, the exclusion of the evidence which an accused had been forced to give by reason of the unlawful seizure. To hold otherwise is to grant the right but in reality to withhold its privilege and enjoyment. . . .

Moreover, our holding that the exclusionary rule is an essential part of both the Fourth and Fourteenth Amendments is not only the logical dictate of prior cases, but it also makes very good sense. There is no war between the Constitution and common sense. Presently, a federal prosecutor may make no use of evidence illegally seized, but a State's attorney across the street may, although he supposedly is operating under the enforceable prohibitions of the same Amendment. Thus the State, by admitting evidence unlawfully seized, serves to encourage disobedience to the Federal Constitution which it is bound to uphold. . . . Moreover, "[t]he very essence of a healthy federalism depends upon the avoidance of needless conflict between state and federal courts." Yet the double standard recognized until today hardly put such a thesis into practice. In nonexclusionary States, federal officers, being human, were by it invited to and did, as our cases indicate, step across the street to the State's attorney with their unconstitutionally seized evidence. Prosecution on the basis of that evidence was then had in a state court in utter disregard of the enforceable Fourth Amendment. If the fruits of an unconstitutional search had been inadmissible in both state and federal courts, this inducement to evasion would have been sooner eliminated. . . .

Federal-state cooperation in the solution of crime under constitutional standards will be promoted, if only by recognition of their now mutual obligation to respect the same fundamental criteria in their approaches. "However much in a particular case insistence upon such rules may appear as a technicality that inures to the benefit of a guilty person, the history of the criminal law proves that tolerance of shortcut methods in law enforcement impairs its enduring effectiveness." . . . Denying shortcuts to only one of two cooperating law enforcement agencies tends naturally to breed legitimate suspicion.

The ignoble shortcut to conviction left open to the State tends to destroy the entire system of constitutional restraints on which the liberties of the people rest. Having once recognized that the right to privacy embodied in the Fourth Amendment is enforceable against the States, and that the right to be secure against rude invasions of privacy by state officers is, therefore, constitutional in origin, we can no longer permit that right to remain an empty promise. Because it is enforceable in the same manner and to like effect as other basic rights secured by the Due Process Clause, we can no longer permit it to be revocable at the whim of any police officer who, in the name of law enforcement itself, chooses to suspend its enjoyment. Our decision, founded on reason and truth, gives to the individual no more than that which the Constitution guarantees him, to the police officer no less than that to which honest law enforcement is entitled, and, to the courts, that judicial integrity so necessary in the true administration of justice. . . .

Malloy v. Hogan, Sheriff

In this case, the Court again reversed its stand on incorporation of procedural guarantees. At issue was the question of whether the privilege against self-incrimination was safeguarded against state action by the Fourteenth Amendment. In Twining v. New Jersey *(211 U.S. 78 [1908]), and in subsequent cases, the Court had held consistently that it was not. In a companion case to the one below, the Court also overturned the rule that an immunity statute applied to a witness protected that person only in the jurisdiction which granted it* (Murphy v. Waterfront Commission of New York, 378 U.S. 52). *A year later, in* Griffin v. California *(381 U.S. 957), the Court further expanded self-incrimination privileges by reversing a state conviction in which the judge had made unfavorable remarks concerning the defendant's refusal to testify.*

Justice Brennan delivered the opinion of the Court.

We hold that the Fourteenth Amendment guaranteed the petitioner the protection of the Fifth Amendment's privilege against self-incrimination, and that under the applicable federal standard, the Connecticut Supreme Court of Errors erred in holding that the privilege was not properly invoked.

The extent to which the Fourteenth Amendment prevents state invasion of rights enumerated in the first eight Amendments has been considered in numerous cases in this Court since the Amendment's adoption in 1868. Although many Justices have deemed the Amendment to incorporate all eight of the Amendments, the view which has thus far prevailed dates from the decision in 1897 in *Chicago, B. & Q.R. Co.* v. *Chicago,* 166 U.S. 226, which held that the Due Process Clause requires the States to pay just compensation for private property taken for public use. It was on the authority of that decision that the Court said in 1908 in *Twining* v. *New Jersey* . . . that "it is possible that some of the personal rights safeguarded by the first eight Amendments against National action may also be safeguarded against state action, because a denial of them would be a denial of due process of law." 211 U.S., at 99.

The Court has not hesitated to re-examine past decisions according the Fourteenth Amendment a less central role in the preservation of basic liberties than that which was contemplated by its Framers when they added the Amendment to our constitutional scheme. Thus, although the Court as late as 1922 said that "neither the Fourteenth Amendment nor any other provision of the Constitution of the United States imposes upon the States any restrictions about 'freedom of speech' . . . ," *Prudential Ins. Co.* v. *Cheek*, 259 U.S. 530, 543, three years later *Gitlow* v. *New York*, 268 U.S. 652, initiated a series of decisions which today hold immune from state invasion every First Amendment protection for the cherished rights of mind and spirit — the freedoms of speech, press, religion, assembly, association, and petition for redress of grievances. . . .

Brown v. *Mississippi*, 297 U.S. 278, was the first case in which the Court held that the Due Process Clause prohibited the States from using the accused's coerced confessions against him. The Court in *Brown* felt impelled, in light of *Twining*, to say that its conclusion did not involve the privilege against self-incrimination. "Compulsion by torture to extort a confession is a different matter." 297 U.S., at 285. But this distinction was soon abandoned, and today the admissibility of a confession in a state criminal prosecution is tested by the same standard applied in federal prosecutions since 1897, when, in *Bram* v. *United States*, 168 U.S. 532, the Court held that "[i]n criminal trials, in the courts of the United States, wherever a question arises whether a confession is incompetent because not voluntary, the issue is controlled by that portion of the Fifth Amendment to the Constitution of the United States, commanding that no person 'shall be compelled in any criminal case to be a witness against himself.'" *Id.*, at 542. Under this test, the constitutional inquiry is not whether the conduct of state officers in obtaining the confession was shocking, but whether the confession was "free and voluntary: that is, [it] must not be extracted by any sort of threats or violence, nor obtained by any direct or implied promises, however slight, nor by the exertion of any improper influence. . . ." *Id.*, at 542–543. . . . In other words the person must not have been compelled to incriminate himself. We have held inadmissible even a confession secured by so mild a whip as the refusal, under certain circumstances, to allow a suspect to call his wife until he confessed. . . .

The marked shift to the federal standard in state cases began with *Lisenba* v. *California*, 314 U.S. 219, where the Court spoke of the accused's "free choice to admit, to deny, or to refuse to answer." . . . The shift reflects recognition that the American system of criminal prosecution is accusatorial, not inquisitorial, and that the Fifth Amendment privilege is its essential mainstay. . . . Governments, state and federal, are thus constitutionally compelled to establish guilt by evidence independently and freely secured, and may not by coercion prove a charge against an accused out of his own mouth. Since the Fourteenth Amendment prohibits the States from inducing a person to confess through "sympathy falsely aroused," . . . or other like inducement far short of "compulsion by torture," . . . it follows *a fortiori* that it also forbids the States to resort to imprisonment, as here, to compel him to answer questions that might incriminate him. The Fourteenth Amendment secures against state invasion the same privilege that the Fifth Amendment guarantees against federal infringement — the right of a person to remain silent unless he chooses to speak in the unfettered exercise of his own will, and to suffer no penalty, as held in *Twining*, for such silence.

This conclusion is fortified by our recent decision in *Mapp* v. *Ohio*, . . . overruling *Wolf* v. *Colorado*, . . . which had held "that in a prosecution in a State court for a State crime the Fourteenth Amendment does not forbid the admission of evidence obtained by an unreasonable search and seizure," . . . . *Mapp* held that the Fifth Amendment privilege against self-incrimination implemented the Fourth Amendment in such cases, and that the two guarantees of personal security conjoined in the Fourteenth Amendment to make the exclusionary rule obligatory upon the States. . . .

The respondent Sheriff concedes in his brief that under our decisions, particularly those involving coerced confessions, "the accusatorial system has become a fundamental part of the fabric of our society and, hence, is enforceable against the States." The State urges, however, that the availability of the federal privilege to a witness in a state inquiry is to be determined according to a less stringent standard than is applicable in a federal proceeding. We disagree. We have held that the guarantees of the First Amendment, . . . the prohibition of unreasonable searches and seizures of the Fourth Amendment, . . . and the right to counsel guaranteed by the Sixth Amendment, . . . are all to be enforced against the States under the Fourteenth Amendment according to the same standards that protect those personal rights against federal encroachment. In the coerced confession cases, involving the policies of the privilege itself, there has been no suggestion that a confession might be considered coerced if used in a federal but not a state tribunal. The Court thus has rejected the notion that the Fourteenth Amendment applies to the States only a "watered-down, subjective version of the individual guarantees of the Bill of Rights," . . . . What is accorded is a privilege of refusing to incriminate one's self, and the feared prosecution may be by either federal or state authorities. . . . It would be incongruous to have different standards determine the validity of a claim of privilege based on the same feared prosecution, depending on whether the claim was asserted in a state or federal court. Therefore, the same standards must determine whether an accused's silence in either a federal or state proceeding is justified. . . .

The investigation in the course of which petitioner was questioned began when the Superior Court in Hartford County appointed the

Honorable Ernest A. Inglis, formerly Chief Justice of Connecticut, to conduct an inquiry into whether there was reasonable cause to believe that crimes, including gambling, were being committed in Hartford County. Petitioner appeared on January 16 and 25, 1961, and in both instances he was asked substantially the same questions about the circumstances surrounding his arrest and conviction for pool selling in late 1959. The questions which petitioner refused to answer may be summarized as follows: (1) for whom did he work on September 11, 1959; (2) who selected and paid his counsel in connection with his arrest on that date and subsequent conviction; (3) who selected and paid his bondsman; (4) who paid his fine; (5) what was the name of the tenant of the apartment in which he was arrested; and (6) did he know John Bergoti. The Connecticut Supreme Court of Errors ruled that the answers to these questions could not tend to incriminate him because the defenses of double jeopardy and the running of the one-year statute of limitations on misdemeanors would defeat any prosecution growing out of his answers to the first five questions. As for the sixth question, the court held that petitioner's failure to explain how a revelation of his relationship with Bergoti would incriminate him vitiated his claim to the protection of the privilege afforded by state law.

The conclusions of the Court of Errors, tested by the federal standard, fail to take sufficient account of the setting in which the questions were asked. The interrogation was part of a wide-ranging inquiry into crime, including gambling, in Hartford. It was admitted on behalf of the State at oral argument — and indeed it is obvious from the questions themselves — that the State desired to elicit from the petitioner the identity of the person who ran the pool-selling operation in connection with which he had been arrested in 1959. It was apparent that petitioner might apprehend that if this person were still engaged in unlawful activity, disclosure of his name might furnish a link in a chain of evidence sufficient to connect the petitioner with a more recent crime for which he might still be prosecuted. . . .

Gideon *v.* Wainwright

*In 1942, the Court had held that states were not bound by the
Sixth Amendment guarantee that "in all criminal prosecutions" the
accused was entitled to the right of counsel. The decision in
Betts v. Brady (316 U.S. 455), re-affirmed the prevailing view
that "the due process clause of the Fourteenth Amendment does
not incorporate . . . the specific guarantees found in the Sixth
Amendment." But perhaps mindful of its earlier decision in Powell
v. Alabama (287 U.S. 45 [1932]), one of the Scottsboro cases, the
Court added that "certain circumstances," "shocking to the universal sense of justice," might constitute a denial of the Fourteenth
Amendment's due process clause. The case below abandoned the
selective, non-incorporation arguments of Betts v. Brady, and
adopted what Justice Black called the "noble ideal" that "every
defendant stands equal before the law."*

*Although the Burger Court Justices significantly diminished the
rights of the accused as established by their predecessors, the
Gideon doctrine was expanded. In Argersinger v. Hamlin (407 U.S.
25 [1972]), the Court held that, however petty the offense, the
accused was entitled to counsel in all trials involving possible
imprisonment.*

Justice Black delivered the opinion of the Court.

Petitioner was charged in a Florida state court with having broken
[into] and entered a poolroom with intent to commit a misdemeanor.
This offense is a felony under Florida law. Appearing in court without
funds and without a lawyer, petitioner asked the court to appoint counsel
for him, whereupon the following colloquy took place:

> The COURT: Mr. Gideon, I am sorry, but I cannot appoint Counsel
> to represent you in this case. Under the laws of the State of Florida,
> the only time the Court can appoint Counsel to represent a Defendant
> is when that person is charged with a capital offense. I am sorry, but I
> will have to deny your request to appoint Counsel to defend you in this
> case.
>
> The DEFENDANT: The United States Supreme Court says I am en-
> titled to be represented by Counsel.

Put to trial before a jury, Gideon conducted his defense about as well
as could be expected from a layman. He made an opening statement

372 U.S. 335 (1963)

to the jury, cross-examined the State's witnesses, presented witnesses in his own defense, declined to testify himself, and made a short argument "emphasizing his innocence to the charge contained in the Information filed in this case." The jury returned a verdict of guilty, and petitioner was sentenced to serve five years in the state prison. Later, petitioner filed in the Florida Supreme Court this habeas corpus petition attacking his conviction and sentence on the ground that the trial court's refusal to appoint counsel for him denied him rights "guaranteed by the Constitution and the Bill of Rights by the United States Government." Treating the petition for habeas corpus as properly before it, the State Supreme Court, "upon consideration thereof" but without an opinion, denied all relief. Since 1942, when *Betts* v. *Brady* . . . was decided by a divided Court, the problem of a defendant's federal constitutional right to counsel in a state court has been a continuing source of controversy and litigation in both state and federal courts. To give this problem another review here, we granted certiorari. . . . Since Gideon was proceeding *in forma pauperis*, we appointed counsel to represent him and requested both sides to discuss in their briefs and oral arguments the following: "Should this Court's holding in *Betts* v. *Brady*, 316 U.S. 455, be reconsidered?"

I.

The facts upon which Betts claimed that he had been unconstitutionally denied the right to have counsel appointed to assist him are strikingly like the facts upon which Gideon here bases his federal constitutional claim. Betts was indicted for robbery in a Maryland state court. On arraignment, he told the trial judge of his lack of funds to hire a lawyer and asked the court to appoint one for him. Betts was advised that is was not the practice in that county to appoint counsel for indigent defendants except in murder and rape cases. He then pleaded not guilty, had witnesses summoned, cross-examined the State's witnesses, examined his own, and chose not to testify himself. He was found guilty by the judge, sitting without a jury, and sentenced to eight years in prison. Like Gideon, Betts sought release by habeas corpus, alleging that he had been denied the right to assistance of counsel in violation of the Fourteenth Amendment. Betts was denied any relief, and on review this Court affirmed. It was held that a refusal to appoint counsel for an indigent defendant charged with a felony did not necessarily violate the Due Process Clause of the Fourteenth Amendment, which for reasons given the Court deemed to be the only applicable federal constitutional provision. The Court said:

> Asserted denial [of due process] is to be tested by an appraisal of the totality of facts in a given case. That which may, in one setting, con-

stitute a denial of fundamental fairness, shocking to the universal sense
of justice, may, in other circumstances, and in the light of other considerations, fall short of such denial. . . .

Treating due process as "a concept less rigid and more fluid than those
envisaged in other specific and particular provisions of the Bill of Rights,"
the Court held that refusal to appoint counsel under the particular facts
and circumstances in the *Betts* case was not so "offensive to the common
and fundamental ideas of fairness" as to amount to a denial of due
process. Since the facts and circumstances of the two cases are so
nearly indistinguishable, we think the *Betts* v. *Brady* holding if left
standing would require us to reject Gideon's claim that the Constitution
guarantees him the assistance of counsel. Upon full reconsideration we
conclude that *Betts* v. *Brady* should be overruled.

II.

The Sixth Amendment provides, "In all criminal prosecutions, the
accused shall enjoy the right . . . to have the Assistance of Counsel for
his defence." We have construed this to mean that in federal courts
counsel must be provided for defendants unable to employ counsel
unless the right is competently and intelligently waived. Betts argued
that this right is extended to indigent defendants in state courts by the
Fourteenth Amendment. In response the Court stated that, while the
Sixth Amendment laid down "no rule for the conduct of the States, the
question recurs whether the constraint laid by the Amendment upon
the national courts expresses a rule so fundamental and essential to a fair
trial, and so, to due process of law, that it is made obligatory upon the
States by the Fourteenth Amendment." . . . In order to decide whether
the Sixth Amendment's guarantee of counsel is of this fundamental
nature, the Court in *Betts* set out and considered "[r]elevant data on the
subject . . . afforded by constitutional and statutory provisions sub-
sisting in the colonies and the States prior to the inclusion of the Bill of
Rights in the national Constitution, and in the constitutional, legislative,
and judicial history of the States to the present date." . . . On the basis
of this historical data the Court concluded that "appointment of counsel
is not a fundamental right, essential to a fair trial." . . . It was for this
reason the *Betts* Court refused to accept the contention that the Sixth
Amendment's guarantee of counsel for indigent federal defendants
was extended to or, in the words of that Court, "made obligatory upon
the States by the Fourteenth Amendment." Plainly, had the Court concluded that appointment of counsel for an indigent criminal defendant
was "a fundamental right, essential to a fair trial," it would have held that
the Fourteenth Amendment requires appointment of counsel in a state
court, just as the Sixth Amendment requires in a federal court.

We think the Court in *Betts* had ample precedent for acknowledging that those guarantees of the Bill of Rights which are fundamental safeguards of liberty immune from federal abridgment are equally protected against state invasion by the Due Process Clause of the Fourteenth Amendment. This same principle was recognized, explained, and applied in *Powell* v. *Alabama*, 287 U.S. 45 (1932), a case upholding the right of counsel, where the Court held that despite sweeping language to the contrary in *Hurtado* v. *California*, 110 U.S. 516 (1884), the Fourteenth Amendment "embraced" those " 'fundamental principles of liberty and justice which lie at the base of all our civil and political institutions,' " even though they had been "specifically dealt with in another part of the federal Constitution." 287 U.S., at 67. In many cases other than *Powell* and *Betts*, this Court has looked to the fundamental nature of original Bill of Rights guarantees to decide whether the Fourteenth Amendment makes them obligatory on the States. Explicitly recognized to be of this "fundamental nature" and therefore made immune from state invasion by the Fourteenth, or some part of it, are the First Amendment's freedoms of speech, press, religion, assembly, association, and petition for redress of grievances. For the same reason, though not always in precisely the same terminology, the Court has made obligatory on the States the Fifth Amendment's command that private property shall not be taken for public use without just compensation, the Fourth Amendment's prohibition of unreasonable searches and seizures, and the Eighth's ban on cruel and unusual punishment. On the other hand, this Court in *Palko* v. *Connecticut*, 302 U.S. 319 (1937), refused to hold that the Fourteenth Amendment made the double jeopardy provision of the Fifth Amendment obligatory on the States. In so refusing, however, the Court, speaking through Mr. Justice Cardozo, was careful to emphasize that "immunities that are valid as against the federal government by force of the specific pledges of particular amendments have been found to be implicit in the concept of ordered liberty, and thus, through the Fourteenth Amendment, become valid as against the states" and that guarantees "in their origin . . . effective against the federal government alone" had by prior cases "been taken over from the earlier articles of the federal bill of rights and brought within the Fourteenth Amendment by a process of absorption." . . .

We accept *Betts* v. *Brady*'s assumption, based as it was on our prior cases, that a provision of the Bill of Rights which is "fundamental and essential to a fair trial" is made obligatory upon the States by the Fourteenth Amendment. We think the Court in *Betts* was wrong, however, in concluding that the Sixth Amendment's guarantee of counsel is not one of these fundamental rights. . . .

The fact is that in deciding as it did — that "appointment of counsel is not a fundamental right, essential to a fair trial" — the Court in *Betts* v. *Brady* made an abrupt break with its own well-considered precedents. In returning to these old precedents, sounder we believe than the new, we but restore constitutional principles established to achieve a fair system of justice. Not only these precedents but also reason and reflection require us to recognize that in our adversary system of criminal justice, any person haled into court, who is too poor to hire a lawyer, cannot be assured a fair trial unless counsel is provided for him. This seems to us to be an obvious truth. Governments, both state and federal, quite properly spend vast sums of money to establish machinery to try defendants accused of crime. Lawyers to prosecute are everywhere deemed essential to protect the public's interest in an orderly society. Similarly, there are few defendants charged with crime, few indeed, who fail to hire the best lawyers they can get to prepare and present their defenses. That government hires lawyers to prosecute and defendants who have the money hire lawyers to defend are the strongest indications of the widespread belief that lawyers in criminal courts are necessities, not luxuries. The right of one charged with crime to counsel may not be deemed fundamental and essential to fair trials in some countries, but it is in ours. From the very beginning, our state and national constitutions and laws have laid great emphasis on procedural and substantive safeguards designed to assure fair trials before impartial tribunals in which every defendant stands equal before the law. This noble ideal cannot be realized if the poor man charged with crime has to face his accusers without a lawyer to assist him. . . . The Court in *Betts* v. *Brady* departed from the sound wisdom upon which the Court's holding in *Powell* v. *Alabama* rested. Florida, supported by two other States, has asked that *Betts* v. *Brady* be left intact. Twenty-two States, as friends of the Court, argue that *Betts* was "an anachronism when handed down" and that it should now be overruled. We agree.

The judgment is reversed and the cause is remanded to the Supreme Court of Florida for further action not inconsistent with this opinion.

Reversed.

In Re Gault

The application of constitutional procedural guarantees to juveniles accused of delinquency or crime signified further expansion of the Warren Court's concern for individual liberties. In its origins, the juvenile court system represented an attempt to separate youthful offenders from ordinary criminal processes, and thereby avoid stigmatizing minor children as criminals. Such proceedings, however, were done in camera, and the accused subject to arbitrary decisions and care by judges and juvenile authorities. Traditional guarantees such as the right to counsel, notice of hearing, and privilege against self-incrimination simply did not prevail in the juvenile court system. In the case below, Gault sought release for his fifteen-year old son, Gerald, who had been declared delinquent by an Arizona juvenile court and sentenced to a state industrial school. The boy had been charged with making an obscene telephone call and had been arrested without his parents' knowledge. The detention home informed the parents there would be a hearing the following day. At that hearing, the judge refused to show the complaint to the parents, no transcript was made, and the judge directly examined the boy. Gerald admitted making the call but insisted that his companion made the obscene remarks. The complainant did not appear and had been contacted only once by the arresting officer. At the end of the hearing, the judge sentenced Gerald to the state school until the age of twenty-one. Arizona law prohibited appeals in juvenile cases.

Justice Fortas delivered the opinion of the Court.

I t is claimed that juveniles obtain benefits from the special procedures applicable to them which more than offset the disadvantages of denial of the substance of normal due process. As we shall discuss, the observance of due process standards, intelligently and not ruthlessly administered, will not compel the States to abandon or displace any of the substantive benefits of the juvenile process. But it is important, we think, that the claimed benefits of the juvenile process should be candidly appraised. Neither sentiment nor folklore should cause us to shut our eyes, for example, to such startling findings as that reported in an exceptionally reliable study of repeaters or recidivism conducted by the Stanford Research

387 U.S. 1 (1967)

Institute for the President's Commission on Crime in the District of Columbia. This Commission's Report states:

> "In fiscal 1966 approximately 66 percent of the 16- and 17-year-old juveniles referred to the court by the Youth Aid Division had been before the court previously. In 1965, 56 percent of those in the Receiving Home were repeaters. The SRI study revealed that 61 percent of the sample Juvenile Court referrals in 1965 had been previously referred at least once and that 42 percent had been referred at least twice before." *Id.* at 773.

Certainly, these figures and the high crime rates among juveniles to which we have referred . . . could not lead us to conclude that the absence of constitutional protections reduces crime, or that the juvenile system, functioning free of constitutional inhibitions as it has largely done, is effective to reduce crime or rehabilitate offenders. We do not mean by this to denigrate the juvenile court process or to suggest that there are not aspects of the juvenile system relating to offenders which are valuable. But the features of the juvenile system which its proponents have asserted are of unique benefit will not be impaired by constitutional domestication. For example, the commendable principles relating to the processing and treatment of juveniles separately from adults are in no way involved or affected by the procedural issues under discussion. Further, we are told that one of the important benefits of the special juvenile court procedures is that they avoid classifying the juvenile as a "criminal." The juvenile offender is now classed as a "delinquent." There is, of course, no reason why this should continue. It is disconcerting, however, that this term has come to involve only slightly less stigma than the term "criminal" applied to adults. It is also emphasized that in practically all jurisdictions, statutes provide that an adjudication of the child as a delinquent shall not operate as a civil disability or disqualify him for civil service appointment. There is no reason why the application of due process requirements should interfere with such provisions. . . .

Ultimately, however, we confront the reality of that portion of the Juvenile Court process with which we deal in this case. A boy is charged with misconduct. The boy is committed to an institution where he may be restrained of liberty for years. It is of no constitutional consequence—and of limited practical meaning—that the institution to which he is committed is called an Industrial School. The fact of the matter is that, however euphemistic the title, a "receiving home" or an "industrial school" for juveniles is an institution of confinement in which the child is incarcerated for a greater or lesser time. . . .

In view of this, it would be extraordinary if our Constitution did not require the procedural regularity and the exercise of care implied in the phrase "due process." Under our Constitution, the condition of being a boy does not justify a kangaroo court. The traditional ideas of Juvenile

Court procedure, indeed, contemplated that time would be available and care would be used to establish precisely what the juvenile did and why he did it—was it a prank of adolescence or a brutal act threatening serious consequences to himself or society unless corrected? Under traditional notions, one would assume that in a case like that of Gerald Gault, where the juvenile appears to have a home, a working mother and father, and an older brother, the Juvenile Judge would have made a careful inquiry and judgment as to the possibility that the boy could be disciplined and dealt with at home, despite his previous transgressions. Indeed, so far as appears in the record before us, except for some conversation with Gerald about his school work and his "wanting to go to . . . Grand Canyon with his father," the points to which the judge directed his attention were little different from those that would be involved in determining any charge of violation of a penal statute. The essential difference between Gerald's case and a normal criminal case is that safeguards available to adults were discarded in Gerald's case. The summary procedure as well as the long commitment was possible because Gerald was 15 years of age instead of over 18.

If Gerald had been over 18, he would not have been subject to Juvenile Court proceedings. For the particular offense immediately involved, the maximum punishment would have been a fine of $5 to $50, or imprisonment in jail for not more than two months. Instead, he was committed to custody for a maximum of six years. If he had been over 18 and had committed an offense to which such a sentence might apply, he would have been entitled to substantial rights under the Constitution of the United States as well as under Arizona's laws and constitution. The United States Constitution would guarantee him rights and protections with respect to arrest, search and seizure, and pretrial interrogation. It would assure him of specific notice of the charges and adequate time to decide his course of action and to prepare his defense. He would be entitled to clear advice that he could be represented by counsel, and, at least if a felony were involved, the State would be required to provide counsel if his parents were unable to afford it. If the court acted on the basis of his confession, careful procedures would be required to assure its voluntariness. If the case went to trial, confrontation and opportunity for cross-examination would be guaranteed. So wide a gulf between the State's treatment of the adult and of the child requires a bridge sturdier than mere verbiage, and reasons more persuasive than cliché can provide. . . .

Notice of Charges

Appellants allege that the Arizona Juvenile Code is unconstitutional or alternatively that the proceedings before the Juvenile Court were constitutionally defective because of failure to provide adequate notice of the hearings. No notice was given to Gerald's parents when he was taken into custody on Monday, June 8. On that night, when Mrs. Gault went to the Detention Home, she was orally informed that there would be a hearing the next afternoon and was told the reason why Gerald was in custody. . . .

We cannot agree . . . that adequate notice was given in this case. Notice, to comply with due process requirements must be given sufficiently in advance of scheduled court proceedings so that reasonable opportunity to prepare will be afforded, and it must "set forth the alleged misconduct with particularity." . . .

RIGHT TO COUNSEL.

Appellants charge that the Juvenile Court proceedings were fatally defective because the court did not advise Gerald or his parents of their right to counsel, and proceeded with the hearing, the adjudication of delinquency and the order of commitment in the absence of counsel for the child and his parents or an express waiver of the right thereto. . . .

We conclude that the Due Process Clause of the Fourteenth Amendment requires that in respect of proceedings to determine delinquency which may result in commitment to an institution in which the juvenile's freedom is curtailed, the child and his parents must be notified of the child's right to be represented by counsel retained by them, or if they are unable to afford counsel, that counsel will be appointed to represent the child. . . .

CONFRONTATION, SELF-INCRIMINATION CROSS-EXAMINATION.

Appellants urge that the writ of habeas corpus should have been granted because of the denial of the rights of confrontation and cross-examination in the Juvenile Court hearings, and because the privilege against self-incrimination was not observed. The Juvenile Court Judge testified at the habeas corpus hearing that he had proceeded on the basis of Gerald's admissions at the two hearings. Appellants attack this on the ground that the admissions were obtained in disregard of the privilege against self-incrimination. . . .

We conclude that the constitutional privilege against self-incrimination is applicable in the case of juveniles as it is with respect to adults. We appreciate that special problems may arise with respect to waiver of the privilege by or on behalf of children, and that there may well be some differences in technique—but not in principle—depending upon the age of the child and the presence and competence of parents. The participation of counsel will, of course, assist the police, Juvenile Courts and appellate tribunals in administering the privilege. If counsel was not present for some permissible reason when an admission was obtained, the greatest care must be taken to assure that the admission was voluntary, in the sense not only that it was not coerced or suggested, but also that it was not the product of ignorance of rights or of adolescent fantasy, fright or despair.

The "confession" of Gerald Gault was first obtained by Officer Flagg, out of the presence of Gerald's parents, without counsel and without advising him of his right to silence, as far as appears. The judgment of the Juvenile Court was stated by the judge to be based on Gerald's admissions in court. Neither "admission" was reduced to writing, and, to say the least, the process by which the "admissions" were obtained and received must be characterized as lacking the certainty and order which are required of proceedings of such formidable consequences. Apart from the "admissions," there was nothing upon which a judgment or finding might be based. There was no sworn testimony. Mrs. Cook, the complainant, was not present. The Arizona Supreme Court held that "sworn testimony must be required of all witnesses including police officers, probation officers and others who are part of or officially related to the juvenile court structure." We hold that this is not enough. . . .

Miranda *v.* Arizona

In Escobedo *v.* Illinois, *the Supreme Court reversed a state murder conviction because the accused had been denied the right of counsel during his interrogation, and because the police had failed to advise him of his constitutional rights (378 U.S. 478 [1964]). During the interrogation, Escobedo had made numerous damaging statements which subsequently led to his conviction when they were used in his trial. The Court expanded its* Gideon *ruling and applied rigid standards against self-incrimination to overturn the conviction. The* Escobedo *decision naturally aroused criticism that the Court was "coddling" criminals. In addition, there was a more valid body of criticism which took the Court to task for its failure to establish proper guidelines for interrogation procedures by law enforcement officials. In the* Miranda *case below, the Court responded to both points.*

Chief Justice Warren delivered the opinion of the Court.

The cases before us raise questions which go to the roots of our concepts of American criminal jurisprudence: the restraints society must observe consistent with the Federal Constitution in prosecuting individuals for crime. More specifically, we deal with the admissibility of statements obtained from an individual who is subjected to custodial police interrogation and the necessity for procedures which assure that the individual is accorded his privilege under the Fifth Amendment to the Constitution not to be compelled to incriminate himself. . . .

The constitutional issue we decide in each of these cases is the admissibility of statements obtained from a defendant questioned while in custody or otherwise deprived of his freedom of action in any significant way. In each, the defendant was questioned by police officers, detectives, or a prosecuting attorney in a room in which he was cut off from the outside world. In none of these cases was the defendant given a full and effective warning of his rights at the outset of the interrogation process. In all the cases, the questioning elicited oral admissions, and in three of them, signed statements as well which were admitted at their trials. They all thus share salient features — incommunicado interrogation of individuals in a police-dominated atmosphere, resulting in self-incriminating statements without full warnings of constitutional rights. . . . The denial of the defendant's request for his attorney thus undermined his ability to exercise the privilege — to remain silent if he chose to speak without any intimidation, blatant or subtle. The presence of counsel in all the cases before us today, would be the adequate protective device necessary to make the process of police interrogation conform to the dictates of the privilege. His presence would insure that statements made in the government-established atmosphere are not the product of compulsion.

It was in this manner that *Escobedo* explicated another facet of the pre-trial privilege, noted in many of the Court's prior decisions: the protection of rights at trial. That counsel is present when statements are taken from an individual during interrogation obviously enhances the integrity of the fact-finding processes in court. The presence of an attorney, and the warnings delivered to the individual, enable the defendant under otherwise compelling circumstances to tell his story without fear, effectively, and in a way that eliminates the evils in the interrogation process. . . .

Today . . . there can be no doubt that the Fifth Amendment privilege is available outside of criminal court proceedings and serves to protect persons in all settings in which their freedom of action is curtailed in any significant way from being compelled to incriminate themselves. We have concluded that without proper safeguards the process of in-custody interrogation of persons suspected or accused of crime contains inherently compelling pressures which work to undermine the individual's will to resist and to compel him to speak where he would not otherwise do so freely. In order to combat these pressures and to permit a full opportunity to exercise the privilege against self-incrimination, the accused must be adequately and effectively apprised of his rights and the exercise of those rights must be fully honored. . . .

The Fifth Amendment privilege is so fundamental to our system of constitutional rule and the expedient of giving an adequate warning as to the availability of the privilege so simple, we will not pause to inquire in individual cases whether the defendant was aware of his rights without a warning being given. Assessments of the knowledge the defendant possessed, based on information as to his age, education, intelligence, or prior contact with authorities, can never be more than speculation; a warning is a clearcut fact. More important, whatever the background of the person interrogated, a warning at the time of the interrogation is indispensable to overcome its pressures and to insure that the individual knows he is free to exercise the privilege. . . .

If an individual indicates that he wishes the assistance of counsel before any interrogation occurs, the authorities cannot rationally ignore or deny his request on the basis that the individual does not have or cannot afford a retained attorney. The financial ability of the individual has no relationship to the scope of the rights involved here. The privilege against self-incrimination secured by the Constitution applies to all individuals. The need for counsel in order to protect the privilege exists for the indigents as well as the affluent. In fact, were we to limit these constitutional rights to those who can retain an attorney, our decisions today would be of little significance. The cases before us as well as the vast majority of confession cases with which we have dealt in the past involve those unable to retain counsel. While authorities are not required to relieve the accused of his poverty, they have the obligation not to take advantage of indigence in the administration of justice. Denial of counsel to the indigent at the time of interrogation while allowing an attorney to those who can afford one would be no more supportable by reason or logic than the similar situation at trial and on appeal struck down in *Gideon* v. *Wainwright*. . . .

In order fully to apprise a person interrogated of the extent of his rights under this system then, it is necessary to warn him not only that he has the right to consult with an attorney, but also that if he is indigent a lawyer will be appointed to represent him. Without this additional warning, the admonition of the right to consult with counsel would often be understood as meaning only that he can consult with a lawyer if he has one or has the funds to obtain one. The warning of a right to counsel would be hollow if not couched in terms that would convey to the indigent — the person most often subjected to interrogation — the knowledge that he too has a right to have counsel present. As with the warnings of the right to remain silent and of the general right to counsel, only by effective and express explanation to the indigent of this right can there be assurance that he was truly in a position to exercise it. . . .

This does not mean, as some have suggested, that each police station must have a "station house lawyer" present at all times to advise prisoners. It does mean, however, that if police propose to interrogate a person they must make known to him that he is entitled to a lawyer and that if he cannot afford one, a lawyer will be provided for him prior to any interrogation. If authorities conclude that they will not provide counsel during a reasonable period of time in which investigation in the field is carried out, they may refrain from doing so without violating the person's Fifth Amendment privilege so long as they do not question him during that time. . . .

The principles announced today deal with the protection which must be given to the privilege against self-incrimination when the individual is first subjected to police interrogation while in custody at the station or otherwise deprived of his freedom of action in any significant way. It is at this point that our adversary system of criminal proceedings commences, distinguishing itself at the outset from the inquisitorial system recognized in some countries. Under the system of warnings we delineate today or under any other system which may be devised and found effective, the safeguards to be erected about the privilege must come into play at this point.

Our decision is not intended to hamper the traditional function of police officers in investigating crime. . . . When an individual is in custody on probable cause, the police may, of course, seek out evidence in the field to be used at trial against him. Such investigation may include inquiry of persons not under restraint. General on-the-scene questioning as to facts surrounding a crime or other general questioning of citizens in the fact-finding process is not affected by our holding. It is an act of responsible citizenship for individuals to give whatever information they may have to aid in law enforcement. In such situations the compelling atmosphere inherent in the process of in-custody interrogation is not necessarily present.

In dealing with statements obtained through interrogation, we do not purport to find all confessions inadmissible. Confessions remain a proper element in law enforcement. Any statement given freely and voluntarily without any compelling influences is, of course, admissible in evidence. The fundamental import of the privilege while an individual is in custody is not whether he is allowed to talk to the police without the benefit of warnings and counsel, but whether he can be interrogated. There is no requirement that police stop a person who enters a police station and states that he wishes to confess to a crime, or a person who calls the police to offer a confession or any other statement he desires to make. Volunteered statements of any kind are not barred by the First Amendment and their admissibility is not affected by our holding today.

To summarize, we hold that when an individual is taken into custody or otherwise deprived of his freedom by the authorities in any significant way and is subjected to questioning, the privilege against self-incrimination is jeopardized. Procedural safeguards must be employed to protect the privilege, and unless other fully effective means are adopted to notify the person of his right of silence and to assure that the exercise of the right will be scrupulously honored, the following measures are required. He must be warned prior to any questioning that he has the right to remain silent, that anything he says can be used against him in a court of law, that he has the right to the presence of an attorney, and that if he cannot afford an attorney one will be appointed for him prior to any questioning if he so desires. Opportunity to exercise these rights must be afforded to him throughout the interrogation. After such warnings have been given, and such opportunity afforded him, the individual may knowingly and intelligently waive these rights and agree to answer questions or make a statement. But unless and until such warnings and waiver are demonstrated by the prosecution at trial, no evidence obtained as a result of interrogation can be used against him. . . .

Harris *v.* New York

The Miranda *ruling, while clarifying some problems of the* Escobedo *decision, only heightened police and prosecutorial criticism
that courts were "soft" on criminals. A facile, unproved correlation
was drawn between a soaring crime rate and decisions such as*
Miranda. *In the presidential campaign of 1968, Richard Nixon
promised a restoration of "law and order" and that he would
appoint Supreme Court Justices who would reverse the decisions of
the Warren Court. Those Justices, he charged, were "seriously
hamstringing the peace forces in our society and strengthening the
criminal forces." By 1971, after Nixon had named two new Justices,
the case below signalled a noteworthy dilution of the* Miranda *doctrine.* Harris *v.* New York *involved the admissibility of a pre-trial
confession obtained without* Miranda *guarantees. The close division
within the Court soon changed when, a few months later, the confirmation of two new Nixon nominees, Lewis Powell and William
Rehnquist, contributed to the further erosion of* Miranda. *For example, in* Kirby *v.* Illinois *(406 U.S. 682 [1972]) and* United
States *v.* Ash *(413 U.S. 300 [1973]), the Court held that the
presence of counsel was not necessary in pre-trial police identification lineups.*

Chief Justice Burger delivered the opinion of the Court.

We granted the writ in this case to consider petitioner's claim that a
statement made by him to police under circumstances rendering
it inadmissible to establish the prosecution's case in chief under *Miranda
v. Arizona,* 384 U. S. 436 (1966), may not be used to impeach his credibility.

The State of New York charged petitioner in a two-count indictment
with twice selling heroin to an undercover police officer. At a subsequent
jury trial the officer was the State's chief witness, and he testified as to
details of the two sales. A second officer verified collateral details of the
sales, and a third offered testimony about the chemical analysis of the
heroin.

Petitioner took the stand in his own defense. He admitted knowing the
undercover police officer but denied a sale on January 4, 1966. He admitted making a sale of contents of a glassine bag to the officer on January 6

401 U.S. 222 (1971)

but claimed it was baking powder and part of a scheme to defraud the purchaser.

On cross-examination petitioner was asked seriatim whether he had made specified statements to the police immediately following his arrest on January 7—statements that partially contradicted petitioner's direct testimony at trial. In response to the cross-examination, petitioner testified that he could not remember virtually any of the questions or answers recited by the prosecutor. At the request of petitioner's counsel the written statement from which the prosecutor had read questions and answers in his impeaching process was placed in the record for possible use on appeal; the statement was not shown to the jury.

The trial judge instructed the jury that the statements attributed to petitioner by the prosecution could be considered only in passing on petitioner's credibility and not as evidence of guilt. In closing summations both counsel argued the substance of the impeaching statements. The jury then found petitioner guilty on the second count of the indictment. The New York Court of Appeals affirmed. . . .

At trial the prosecution made no effort in its case in chief to use the statements allegedly made by petitioner, conceding that they were inadmissible under *Miranda* v. *Arizona,* 384 U. S. 436 (1966). The transcript of the interrogation used in the impeachment, but not given to the jury, shows that no warning of a right to appointed counsel was given before questions were put to petitioner when he was taken into custody. Petitioner makes no claim that the statements made to the police were coerced or involuntary.

Some comments in the *Miranda* opinion can indeed be read as indicating a bar to use of an uncounseled statement for any purpose, but discussion of that issue was not at all necessary to the Court's holding and cannot be regarded as controlling. *Miranda* barred the prosecution from making its case with statements of an accused made while in custody prior to having or effectively waiving counsel. It does not follow from *Miranda* that evidence inadmissible against an accused in the prosecution's case in chief is barred for all purposes, provided of course that the trustworthiness of the evidence satisfies legal standards.

In *Walder* v. *United States,* 347 U. S. 62 (1954), the Court permitted physical evidence, inadmissible in the case in chief, to be used for impeachment purposes.

"It is one thing to say that the Government cannot make an affirmative use of evidence unlawfully obtained. It is quite another to say that the defendant can turn the illegal method by which evidence in the Government's possession was obtained to his own advantage, and provide himself with a shield against contradiction of his untruths. Such an extension of the *Weeks* doctrine would be a perversion of the Fourth Amendment.

"[T]here is hardly justification for letting the defendant affirmatively resort to perjurious testimony in reliance on the Government's disability to challenge his credibility." . . .

It is true that Walder was impeached as to collateral matters included in his direct examination, whereas petitioner here was impeached as to testimony bearing more directly on the crimes charged. We are not persuaded that there is a difference in principle that warrants a result different from that reached by the Court in *Walder*. Petitioner's testimony in his own behalf concerning the events of January 7 contrasted sharply with what he told the police shortly after his arrest. The impeachment process here undoubtedly provided valuable aid to the jury in assessing petitioner's credibility, and the benefits of this process should not be lost, in our view, because of the speculative possibility that impermissible police conduct will be encouraged thereby. Assuming that the exclusionary rule has a deterrent effect on proscribed police conduct, sufficient deterrence flows when the evidence in question is made unavailable to the prosecution in its case in chief.

Every criminal defendant is privileged to testify in his own defense, or to refuse to do so. But that privilege cannot be construed to include the right to commit perjury. . . . Having voluntarily taken the stand, petitioner was under an obligation to speak truthfully and accurately, and the prosecution here did no more than utilize the traditional truth-testing devices of the adversary process. Had inconsistent statements been made by the accused to some third person, it could hardly be contended that the conflict could not be laid before the jury by way of cross-examination and impeachment.

The shield provided by *Miranda* cannot be perverted into a license to use perjury by way of a defense, free from the risk of confrontation with prior inconsistent utterances. We hold, therefore, that petitioner's credibility was appropriately impeached by use of his earlier conflicting statements.

MR. JUSTICE BLACK dissents.

MR. JUSTICE BRENNAN, with whom MR. JUSTICE DOUGLAS and MR. JUSTICE MARSHALL join, dissenting.

It is conceded that the question-and-answer statement used to impeach petitioner's direct testimony was, under *Miranda* v. *Arizona*, 384 U. S. 436 (1966), constitutionally inadmissible as part of the State's direct case against petitioner. I think that the Constitution also denied the State the use of the statement on cross-examination to impeach the credibility of petitioner's testimony given in his own defense. . . .

The objective of deterring improper police conduct is only part of the larger objective of safeguarding the integrity of our adversary system. The "essential mainstay" of that system, *Miranda* v. *Arizona*, 384 U. S., at 460, is the privilege against self-incrimination, which for that reason has occupied a central place in our jurisprudence since before the Nation's birth. Moreover, "we may view the historical development of the privilege as one which groped for the proper scope of governmental power over the citizen. . . . All these policies point to one overriding thought: the constitutional foundation underlying the privilege is the respect a government . . . must accord to the dignity and integrity of its citizens." *Ibid.* These values are plainly jeopardized if an exception against admission of tainted statements is made for those used for impeachment purposes. Moreover, it is monstrous that courts should aid or abet the law-breaking police officer. It is abiding truth that "[n]othing can destroy a government more quickly than its failure to observe its own laws, or worse, its disregard of the charter of its own existence." *Mapp* v. *Ohio*, 367 U. S. 643, 659 (1961). Thus, even to the extent that *Miranda* was aimed at deterring police practices in disregard of the Constitution, I fear that today's holding will seriously undermine the achievement of that objective. The Court today tells the police that they may freely interrogate an accused incommunicado and without counsel and know that although any statement they obtain in violation of *Miranda* cannot be used on the State's direct case, it may be introduced if the defendant has the temerity to testify in his own defense. This goes far toward undoing much of the progress made in conforming police methods to the Constitution. I dissent.

Gregg *v.* Georgia

A *movement for abolition of the death penalty in the United States extended back to the nineteenth century. By the mid-twentieth century, the number of capital crimes had diminished to include only first-degree homicide, kidnapping, rape, and treason cases. The abolition drive traditionally had been conducted in the separate states, but the rapid nationalization of civil rights in the 1960's led to numerous challenges that the death penalty violated the Eighth Amendment sanction against the imposition of "cruel and unusual" punishment. Equally important was clear statistical evidence that the poor and racial minorities received a disproportionate share of death sentences. The proponents of the death penalty countered with deterrent arguments, insisting that maintenance of law and order required "tough" penalties. In* Furman v. Georgia *(408 U.S. 238 [1972]), a closely-divided court declared the state's death penalty unconstitutional. But the five Justices who joined in that judgment disagreed sharply among themselves, with only two—Brennan and Marshall—arguing that all death penalties violated the Eighth Amendment. Significantly, all four Nixon appointees dissented, and two other Justices (Stewart and White) joined the majority only because they opposed the capricious and irrational manner in which courts imposed death penalties. Within four years, however, over thirty-five states and Congress enacted new statutes providing for capital punishment. Public opinion polls showed an overwhelming majority in favor of such laws. The new legislative standards and the public sentiment combined in July 1976 to produce a fairly decisive reversal of the* Furman *decision. In a cluster of five cases, the Court clearly held that the death penalty was not* per se *cruel and unusual punishment. But in two cases (*Woodson v. North Carolina, *44 L.W. 5267;* Roberts v. Louisiana, *44 L.W. 5281), a majority refused to accept mandatory death sentences for certain crimes. In the Georgia case below, along with companion cases from Florida and Texas (*Proffitt v. Florida, *44 L.W. 5256;* Jurek v. Texas *44 L.W. 5256), a swing group of three Justices joined those who favored deferring to legislative determination in all such cases to find that the state had provided for reasonable and fair standards of imposing the death penalty. There was no majority opinion, but Justice Stewart spoke for himself and the other two swing judges who clearly held the balance of power in the five cases.*

> *Justice Stewart announced the judgment of the Court.*

---

44 *Law Week* 5230 (1976)

The imposition of the death penalty for the crime of murder has a long history of acceptance both in the United States and in England. The common-law rule imposed a mandatory death sentence on all convicted murderers. . . . And the penalty continued to be used into the 20th century by most American States, although the breadth of the common-law rule was diminished, initially by narrowing the class of murders to be punished by death and subsequently by widespread adoption of laws expressly granting juries the discretion to recommend mercy. . . .

It is apparent from the text of the Constitution itself that the existence of capital punishment was accepted by the Framers. At the time the Eighth Amendment was ratified, capital punishment was a common sanction in every State. Indeed, the First Congress of the United States enacted legislation providing death as the penalty for specified crimes. . . .

For nearly two centuries, this Court, repeatedly and often expressly, has recognized that capital punishment is not invalid *per se*. In *Wilkerson* v. *Utah*, 99 U. S., at 134–135, where the Court found no constitutional violation in inflicting death by public shooting, it said:

> "Cruel and unusual punishments are forbidden by the Constitution, but the authorities referred to are quite sufficient to show that the punishment of shooting as a mode of executing the death penalty for the crime of murder in the first degree is not included in that category, within the meaning of the eighth amendment."

Rejecting the contention that death by electrocution was "cruel and unusual," the Court in *In re Kemmler*, 136 U. S., at 447, reiterated:

> ". . . the punishment of death is not cruel, within the meaning of that word as used in the Constitution. It implies there something inhuman and barbarous, something more than the mere extinguishment of life." . . .

The petitioners in the capital cases before the Court today renew the "standards of decency" argument, but developments during the four years since *Furman* have undercut substantially the assumptions upon which their argument rested. Despite the continuing debate, dating back to the 19th century, over the morality and utility of capital punishment, it is now evident that a large proportion of American society continues to regard it as an appropriate and necessary criminal sanction.

The most marked indication of society's endorsement of the death penalty for murder is the legislative response to *Furman*. The legislatures of at least 35 States have enacted new statutes that provide for the death penalty for at least some crimes that result in the death of another person. And the Congress of the United States in 1974, enacted a statute providing the death penalty for aircraft piracy that results in death. . . .

In the only statewide referendum occurring since *Furman* and brought to our attention, the people of California adopted a constitutional amendment that authorized capital punishment, in effect negating a prior ruling by the Supreme Court of California . . . that the death penalty violated the California Constitution. . . .

The death penalty is said to serve two principal social purposes: retribution and deterrence of capital crimes by prospective offenders.

In part, capital punishment is an expression of society's moral outrage at particularly offensive conduct. This function may be unappealing to many, but it is essential in an ordered society that asks its citizens to rely on legal processes rather than self-help to vindicate their wrongs. . . .

Statistical attempts to evaluate the worth of the death penalty as a deterrent to crimes by potential offenders have occasioned a great deal of debate. The results simply have been inconclusive. . . .

The value of capital punishment as a deterrent of crime is a complex factual issue the resolution of which properly rests with the legislatures, which can evaluate the results of statistical studies in terms of their own local conditions and with a flexibility of approach that is not available to the courts. . . . Indeed, many of the post-*Furman* statutes reflect just such a responsible effort to define those crimes and those criminals for which capital punishment is most probably an effective deterrent.

In sum, we cannot say that the judgment of the Georgia legislature that capital punishment may be necessary in some cases is clearly wrong. Considerations of federalism, as well as respect for the ability of a legislature to evaluate, in terms of its particular state the moral consensus concerning the death penalty and its social utility as a sanction, require us to conclude, in the absence of more convincing evidence, that the infliction of death as a punishment for murder is not without justification and thus is not unconstitutionally severe. . . .

We hold that the death penalty is not a form of punishment that may never be imposed, regardless of the circumstances of the offense, regardless of the character of the offender, and regardless of the procedure followed in reaching the decision to impose it.

We now consider whether Georgia may impose the death penalty on the petitioner in this case.

While *Furman* did not hold that the infliction of the death penalty *per se* violates the Constitution's ban on cruel and unusual punishments, it did recognize that the penalty of death is different in kind from any other punishment imposed under our system of criminal justice. Because of the uniqueness of the death penalty, *Furman* held that it could not be imposed under sentencing procedures that created a substantial risk that it would be inflicted in an arbitrary and capricious manner. . . .

Furman mandates that where discretion is afforded a sentencing body on a matter so grave as the determination of whether a human life should be taken or spared, that discretion must be suitably directed and limited so as to minimize the risk of wholly arbitrary and capricious action. . . .

We now turn to consideration of the constitutionality of Georgia's capital-sentencing procedures. In the wake of *Furman*, Georgia amended its capital punishment statute, but chose not to narrow the scope of its murder provisions. See Part II, *supra*. Thus, now as before *Furman*, in Georgia "[a] person commits murder when he unlawfully and with malice aforethought, either express or implied, causes the death of another human being." Ga. Code Ann., § 26–1101 (a) (1972). All persons convicted of murder "shall be punished by death or by imprisonment for life." § 26–1101 (c) (1972).

Georgia did act, however, to narrow the class of murderers subject to capital punishment by specifying 10 statutory aggravating circumstances, one of which must be found by the jury to exist beyond a reasonable doubt before a death sentence can ever be imposed. In addition, the jury is authorized to consider any other appropriate aggravating or mitigating circumstances. § 27.2534.1 (b) (Supp. 1975). The jury is not required to find any mitigating circumstance in order to make a recommendation of mercy that is binding on the trial court, see § 27–2302 (Supp. 1975), but it must find a *statutory* aggravating circumstance before recommending a sentence of death.

These procedures require the jury to consider the circumstances of the crime and the criminal before it recommends sentence. No longer can a Georgia jury do as Furman's jury did: reach a finding of the defendant's guilt and then, without guidance or direction, decide whether he should live or die. Instead, the jury's attention is directed to the specific circumstances of the crime: Was it committed in the course of another capital felony? Was it committed for money? Was it committed upon a peace officer or judicial officer? Was it committed in a particularly heinous way or in a manner that endangered the lives of many persons? In addition, the jury's attention is focused on the characteristics of the person who committed the crime: Does he have a record of prior convictions for capital offenses? Are there any special facts about this defendant that mitigate against imposing capital punishment (*e.g.*, his youth, the extent of his cooperation with the police, his emotional state at the time of the crime). As a result, while some jury discretion still exists, "the discretion to be exercised is controlled by clear and objective standards so as to produce non-discriminatory application." . . .

As an important additional safeguard against arbitrariness and caprice, the Georgia statutory scheme provides for automatic appeal of all death sentences to the State's supreme court. That court is required by statute to review each sentence of death and determine whether it was imposed under the influence of passion or prejudice, whether the evidence supports the jury's finding of a statutory aggravating circumstance, and whether the sentence is disproportionate compared to those sentences imposed in similar cases. . . .

In short, Georgia's new sentencing procedures require as a prerequisite to the imposition of the death penalty, specific jury findings as to the circumstances of the crime or the character of the defendant. Moreover to guard further against a situation comparable to that presented in *Furman*, the Supreme Court of Georgia compares each death sentence with the sentences imposed on similarly situated defendants to ensure that the sentence of death in a particular case is not disproportionate. On their face these procedures seem to satisfy the concerns of *Furman*. . . .

The basic concern of *Furman* centered on those defendants who were being condemned to death capriciously and arbitrarily. Under the procedures before the Court in that case, sentencing authorities were not directed to give attention to the nature or circumstances of the crime committed or to the character or record of the defendant. Left unguided, juries imposed the death sentence in a way that could only be called freakish. The new Georgia sentencing procedures, by contrast, focus the jury's attention on the particularized characteristics of the individual defendant. While the jury is permitted to consider any aggravating or mitigating circumstances, it must find and identify at least one statutory aggravating factor before it may impose a penalty of death. In this way the jury's discretion is channeled. No longer can a jury wantonly and freakishly impose the death sentence; it is always circumscribed by the legislative guidelines. In addition, the review function of the Supreme Court of Georgia affords additional assurance that the concerns that prompted our decision in *Furman* are not present to any significant degree in the Georgia procedure applied here.

For the reasons expressed in this opinion, we hold that the statutory system under which Gregg was sentenced to death does not violate the Constitution. Accordingly, the judgment of the Georgia Supreme Court is affirmed.

It is so ordered.

Privacy and Personal Relations

Griswold *v.* Connecticut

The notion of a constitutional right to "privacy" matured in a wide variety of cases in the 1960's and 1970's. Decisions involving the Fourth Amendment, "right of association," among others, all touched on the subject. The new libertarianism of the period particularly stressed the right of privacy in matters involving personal relations between consenting individuals and vigorously opposed governmental intrusion in such matters. Obviously, influences other than abstract constitutional doctrine figured prominently in this concern. In Griswold v. Connecticut, for example, the growing awareness of overpopulation and the need for birth control measures stimulated the drive for privacy. The case involved officials of the Planned Parenthood League who had given married couples advice on birth control and contraceptive prescriptions. An 1879 state act—"an uncommonly silly law," as even one of the dissenters in the case, Justice Potter Stewart, described it—prohibited such practices. In a concurring opinion, Justice Arthur Goldberg sought to locate the "right to privacy" in the seldom-invoked Ninth Amendment. But in the following decade, Goldberg's opinion gained little support among the other Justices or legal commentators, and subsequent privacy cases were decided on more traditional grounds.

Justice Douglas delivered the opinion of the Court.

We think that appellants have standing to raise the constitutional rights of the married people with whom they had a professional relationship. . . .

The case is more akin to *Truax* v. *Raich*, 239 U. S. 33, where an employee was permitted to assert the rights of his employer; to *Pierce* v. *Society of Sisters*, 268 U. S. 510, where the owners of private schools were

---

381 U.S. 479 1965)

entitled to assert the rights of potential pupils and their parents; and to *Barrows* v. *Jackson*, 346 U. S. 249, where a white defendant, party to a racially restrictive covenant, who was being sued for damages by the covenantors because she had conveyed her property to Negroes, was allowed to raise the issue that enforcement of the covenant violated the rights of prospective Negro purchasers to equal protection, although no Negro was a party to the suit. . . . The rights of husband and wife, pressed here, are likely to be diluted or adversely affected unless those rights are considered in a suit involving those who have this kind of confidential relation to them. . . .

The association of people is not mentioned in the Constitution nor in the Bill of Rights. The right to educate a child in a school of the parents' choice—whether public or private or parochial—is also not mentioned. Nor is the right to study any particular subject or any foreign language. Yet the First Amendment has been construed to include certain of those rights.

By *Pierce* v. *Society of Sisters, supra*, the right to educate one's children as one chooses is made applicable to the States by the force of the First and Fourteenth Amendments. . . . In other words, the State may not, consistently with the spirit of the First Amendment, contract the spectrum of available knowledge. The right of freedom of speech and press includes not only the right to utter or to print, but the right to distribute, the right to receive, the right to read (*Martin* v. *Struthers*, 319 U. S. 141, 143) and freedom of inquiry, freedom of thought, and freedom to teach (see *Wieman* v. *Updegraff*, 344 U. S. 183, 195)—indeed the freedom of the entire university community. *Sweezy* v. *New Hampshire*, 354 U. S. 234, 249–250, 261–263. . . . Without those peripheral rights the specific rights would be less secure. . . .

In *NAACP* v. *Alabama*, 357 U. S. 449, 462, we protected the "freedom to associate and privacy in one's associations," noting that freedom of association was a peripheral First Amendment right. Disclosure of membership lists of a constitutionally valid association, we held, was invalid "as entailing the likelihood of a substantial restraint upon the exercise by petitioner's members of their right to freedom of association." *Ibid.* In other words, the First Amendment has a penumbra where privacy is protected from governmental intrusion. In like context, we have protected forms of "association" that are not political in the customary sense but pertain to the social, legal, and economic benefit of the members. . . .

The foregoing cases suggest that specific guarantees in the Bill of Rights have penumbras, formed by emanations from those guarantees that help give them life and substance. . . . Various guarantees create zones of privacy. The right of association contained in the penumbra of the First Amendment is one, as we have seen. The Third Amendment in its prohibition against the quartering of soldiers "in any house" in time of peace without the consent of the owner is another facet of that privacy. The Fourth Amendment explicitly affirms the "right of the people to be secure in their persons, houses, papers, and effects, against unreasonable searches and seizures." The Fifth Amendment in its Self-Incrimination Clause enables the citizen to create a zone of privacy which government may not force him to surrender to his detriment. The Ninth Amendment provides: "The enumeration in the Constitution, of certain rights, shall not be construed to deny or disparage others retained by the people." . . .

The present case, then, concerns a relationship lying within the zone of privacy created by several fundamental constitutional guarantees. And it concerns a law which, in forbidding the *use* of contraceptives rather than regulating their manufacture or sale, seeks to achieve its goals by means having a maximum destructive impact upon that relationship. Such a law cannot stand in light of the familiar principle, so often applied by this Court, that a "governmental purpose to control or prevent activities constitutionally subject to state regulation may not be achieved by means which sweep unnecessarily broadly and thereby invade the area of protected freedoms." *NAACP* v. *Alabama*, 377 U. S. 288, 307. Would we allow the police to search the sacred precincts of marital bedrooms for telltale signs of the use of contraceptives? The very idea is repulsive to the notions of privacy surrounding the marriage relationship.

We deal with a right of privacy older than the Bill of Rights—older than our political parties, older than our school system. Marriage is a coming together for better or for worse, hopefully enduring, and intimate to the degree of being sacred. It is an association that promotes a way of life, not causes; a harmony in living, not political faiths; a bilateral loyalty, not commercial or social projects. Yet it is an association for as noble a purpose as any involved in our prior decisions.

Reversed.

Roe *v.* Wade

The Connecticut case aroused vigorous protest from some religious and socially conservative groups. But the issue of abortion produced a much larger split in the society, with even sharper emotional arguments on both sides. Many states had statutes that provided for abortion in very limited or specific circumstances, focused on medical considerations involving the mother. Feminist and reformist groups in the 1960's, however, made a concerted effort to change state laws. In New York, in 1970, the legislature established "abortion on demand" during the first twenty-four weeks of pregnancy. Most states, responding to enormous pressures, refused to alter their laws; indeed, some even strengthened them. In this case, the Court confronted a typical nineteenth century statute, making abortion a criminal offense. Although the Court rather decisively approved liberal abortion rights, the opposition persisted, even to the point where a presidential candidate ran in the 1976 Democratic primaries exclusively on a "Right to Life" platform, and received federal funds. Yet at the same time, the Court significantly expanded its decision by ruling that wives need not secure consent of their husbands for an abortion (Planned Parenthood of Central Missouri *v.* Danforth, 44 Law Week 5197 [1976]).

Justice Blackmun delivered the opinion of the Court.

T hree reasons have been advanced to explain historically the enactment of criminal abortion laws in the 19th century and to justify their continued existence.

It has been argued occasionally that these laws were the product of a Victorian social concern to discourage illicit sexual conduct. Texas, however, does not advance this justification in the present case, and it appears that no court or commentator has taken the argument seriously. . . .

A second reason is concerned with abortion as a medical procedure. When most criminal abortion laws were first enacted, the procedure was a hazardous one for the woman. . . . Thus, it has been argued that a State's real concern in enacting a criminal abortion law was to protect the pregnant woman, that is, to restrain her from submitting to a procedure that placed her life in serious jeopardy.

---

410 U.S. 113 (1973)

Modern medical techniques have altered this situation. Appellants and various *amici* refer to medical data indicating that abortion in early pregnancy, that is, prior to the end of the first trimester, although not without its risk, is now relatively safe. Mortality rates for women undergoing early abortions, where the procedure is legal, appear to be as low as or lower than the rates for normal childbirth. Consequently, any interest of the State in protecting the woman from an inherently hazardous procedure, except when it would be equally dangerous for her to forgo it, has largely disappeared. Of course, important state interests in the areas of health and medical standards do remain. The State has a legitimate interest in seeing to it that abortion, like any other medical procedure, is performed under circumstances that insure maximum safety for the patient. This interest obviously extends at least to the performing physician and his staff, to the facilities involved, to the availability of after-care, and to adequate provision for any complication or emergency that might arise. The prevalence of high mortality rates at illegal "abortion mills" strengthens, rather than weakens, the State's interest in regulating the conditions under which abortions are performed. Moreover, the risk to the woman increases as her pregnancy continues. Thus, the State retains a definite interest in protecting the woman's own health and safety when an abortion is proposed at a late stage of pregnancy.

The third reason is the State's interest—some phase it in terms of duty—in protecting prenatal life. Some of the argument for this justification rests on the theory that a new human life is present from the moment of conception. The State's interest and general obligation to protect life then extends, it is argued, to prenatal life. Only when the life of the pregnant mother herself is at stake, balanced against the life she carries within her, should the interest of the embryo or fetus not prevail. Logically, of course, a legitimate state interest in this area need not stand or fall on acceptance of the belief that life begins at conception or at some other point prior to live birth. In assessing the State's interest, recognition may be given to the less rigid claim that as long as at least *potential* life is involved, the State may assert interests beyond the protection of the pregnant woman alone. . . .

The Constitution does not explicitly mention any right of privacy. In a line of decisions, however, going back perhaps as far as *Union Pacific R. Co.* v. *Botsford*, 141 U. S. 250, 251 (1891), the Court has recognized that a right of personal privacy, or a guarantee of certain areas or zones of privacy, does exist under the Constitution. . . .

This right of privacy, whether it be founded in the Fourteenth Amendment's concept of personal liberty and restrictions upon state action, as we feel it is, or, as the District Court determined, in the Ninth Amendment's reservation of rights to the people, is broad enough to encompass a woman's decision whether or not to terminate her pregnancy. The detriment that the State would impose upon the pregnant woman by denying this choice altogether is apparent. Specific and direct harm medically diagnosable even in early pregnancy may be involved. Maternity, or additional offspring, may force upon the woman a distressful life and future. Psychological harm may be imminent. Mental and physical health may be taxed by child care. There is also the distress, for all concerned, associated with the unwanted child, and there is the problem of bringing a child into a family already unable, psychologically and otherwise, to care for it. In other cases, as in this one, the additional difficulties and continuing stigma of unwed motherhood may be involved. All these are factors the woman and her responsible physician necessarily will consider in consultation.

On the basis of elements such as these, appellant and some *amici* argue that the woman's right is absolute and that she is entitled to terminate her pregnancy at whatever time, in whatever way, and for whatever reason she alone chooses. With this we do not agree. Appellant's arguments that Texas either has no valid interest at all in regulating the abortion decision, or no interest strong enough to support any limitation upon the woman's sole determination, are unpersuasive. The Court's decisions recognizing a right of privacy also acknowledge that some state regulation in areas protected by that right is appropriate. As noted above, a State may properly assert important interests in safeguarding health, in maintaining medical standards, and in protecting potential life. At some point in pregnancy, these respective interests become sufficiently compelling to sustain regulation of the factors that govern the abortion decision. The privacy right involved, therefore, cannot be said to be absolute. In fact, it is not clear to us that the claim asserted by some *amici* that one has an unlimited right to do with one's body as one pleases bears a close relationship to the right of privacy previously articulated in the Court's decisions. The Court has refused to recognize an unlimited right of this kind in the past. *Jacobson* v. *Massachusetts,* 197 U. S. 11 (1905) (vaccination); *Buck* v. *Bell,* 274 U. S. 200 (1927) (sterilization).

We, therefore, conclude that the right of personal privacy includes the abortion decision, but that this right is not unqualified and must be considered against important state interests in regulation. . . .

Although the results are divided, most . . . courts have agreed that the right of privacy, however based, is broad enough to cover the abortion decision; that the right, nonetheless, is not absolute and is subject to some limitations; and that at some point the state interests as to protection of health, medical standards, and prenatal life, become dominant. We agree with this approach. . . .

Those striking down state laws have generally scrutinized the State's interests in protecting health and potential life, and have concluded that neither interest justified broad limitations on the reasons for which a physician and his pregnant patient might decide that she should have an abortion in the early stages of pregnancy. Courts sustaining state laws have held that the State's determinations to protect health or prenatal life are dominant and constitutionally justifiable.

The District Court held that the appellee failed to meet his burden of demonstrating that the Texas statute's infringement upon Roe's rights was necessary to support a compelling state interest, and that, although the appellee presented "several compelling justifications for state presence in the area of abortions," the statutes outstripped these justifications and swept "far beyond any areas of compelling state interest." . . . Appellant and appellee both contest that holding. Appellant, as has been indicated, claims an absolute right that bars any state imposition of criminal penalties in the area. Appellee argues that the State's determination to recognize and protect prenatal life from and after conception constitutes a compelling state interest. As noted above, we do not agree fully with either formulation.

A. The appellee and certain *amici* argue that the fetus is a "person" within the language and meaning of the Fourteenth Amendment. In support of this, they outline at length and in detail the well-known facts of fetal development. If this suggestion of personhood is established, the appellant's case, of course, collapses, for the fetus' right to life would then be guaranteed specifically by the Amendment. The appellant conceded as much on reargument. On the other hand, the appellee conceded on reargument that no case could be cited that holds that a fetus is a person within the meaning of the Fourteenth Amendment.

The Constitution does not define "person" in so many words. Section 1 of the Fourteenth Amendment contains three references to "person." The first, in defining "citizens," speaks of "persons born or naturalized in the United States." The word also appears both in the Due Process Clause and in the Equal Protection Clause. "Person" is used in other places in the Constitution. . . . But in nearly all these instances, the use of the word is such that it has application only postnatally. None indicates, with any assurance, that it has any possible pre-natal application.

All this, together with our observation, *supra*, that throughout the major portion of the 19th century prevailing legal abortion practices were far freer than they are today, persuades us that the word "person," as used in the Fourteenth Amendment, does not include the unborn. . . .

B. The pregnant woman cannot be isolated in her privacy. She carries an embryo and, later, a fetus, if one accepts the medical definitions of the developing young in the human uterus. See Dorland's Illustrated Medical Dictionary 478–479, 547 (24th ed. 1965). The situation therefore is inherently different from marital intimacy, or bedroom possession of obscene material, or marriage, or procreation, or education. . . . As we have intimated above, it is reasonable and appropriate for a State to decide that at some point in time another interest, that of health of the mother or that of potential human life, becomes significantly involved. The woman's privacy is no longer sole and any right of privacy she possesses must be measured accordingly.

Texas urges that, apart from the Fourteenth Amendment, life begins at conception and is present throughout pregnancy, and that, therefore, the State has a compelling interest in protecting that life from and after conception. We need not resolve the difficult question of when life begins. When those trained in the respective disciplines of medicine, philosophy, and theology are unable to arrive at any consensus, the judiciary, at this point in the development of man's knowledge, is not in a position to speculate as to the answer.

It should be sufficient to note briefly the wide divergence of thinking on this most sensitive and difficult question. There has always been strong support for the view that life does not begin until live birth. This was the belief of the Stoics. It appears to be the predominant, though not the unanimous attitude of the Jewish faith. It may be taken to represent also the position of a large segment of the Protestant community, insofar as that can be ascertained; organized groups that have taken a formal position on the abortion issue have generally regarded abortion as a matter for the conscience of the individual and her family. As we have noted, the common law found greater significance in quickening. Physicians and their scientific colleagues have regarded that event with less interest and have tended to focus either upon conception, upon live birth, or upon the interim point at which the fetus becomes "viable," that is, potentially able to live outside the mother's womb, albeit with artificial aid. Viability is usually placed at about seven months (28 weeks) but may occur earlier, even at 24 weeks. The Aristotelian theory of "mediate animation," that held sway throughout the Middle Ages and the Renaissance in Europe, continued to be official Roman Catholic dogma until the 19th century, despite opposition to this "ensoulment" theory from those in the Church who would recognize the existence of life from the moment of conception. The latter is now, of course, the official belief of the Catholic Church. As one brief *amicus* discloses, this is a view strongly held by many non-Catholics as well, and by many physicians. Substantial problems for precise definition of this view are posed, however, by new embryological data that purport to indicate that conception is a "process" over time, rather than an event, and by new medical techniques such as menstrual extraction, the "morning-after" pill, implantation of embryos, artificial insemination, and even artificial wombs.

In areas other than criminal abortion, the law has been reluctant to endorse any theory that life, as we recognize it, begins before live birth or to accord legal rights to the unborn except in narrowly defined situations and except when the rights are contingent upon live birth. For example, the traditional rule of tort law denied recovery for prenatal injuries even though the child was born alive. That rule has been changed in almost every jurisdiction. In most States, recovery is said to be permitted only if the fetus was viable, or at least quick, when the injuries were sustained, though few courts have squarely so held. In a recent development, generally opposed by the commentators, some States permit the parents of a stillborn child to maintain an action for wrongful death because of prenatal injuries. Such an action, however, would appear to be one to vindicate the parents' interest and is thus consistent with the view that the fetus, at most, represents only the potentiality of life. Similarly, unborn children have been recognized as acquiring rights or interests by way of inheritance or other devolution of property, and have been represented by guardians *ad litem*. Perfection of the interests involved, again, has generally been contingent upon live birth. In short, the unborn have never been recognized in the law as persons in the whole sense.

In view of all this, we do not agree that, by adopting one theory of life, Texas may override the rights of the pregnant woman that are at stake. We repeat, however, that the State does have an important and legitimate interest in preserving and protecting the health of the pregnant woman, whether she be a resident of the State or a nonresident who seeks medical consultation and treatment there, and that it has still *another* important and legitimate interest in protecting the potentiality of human life. These interests are separate and distinct. Each grows in substantiality as the woman approaches term and, at a point during pregnancy, each becomes "compelling."

With respect to the State's important and legitimate interest in the health of the mother, the "compelling" point, in the light of present medical knowledge, is at approximately the end of the first trimester. This is so because of the now-established fact, . . . that until the end of the first trimester mortality in abortion may be less than mortality in normal childbirth. It follows that, from and after this point, a State may regulate the abortion procedure to the extent that the regulation reasonably relates to the preservation and protection of maternal health. Examples of permissible state regulation in this area are requirements as to the qualifications of the person who is to perform the abortion; as to the licensure of that person; as to the facility in which the procedure is to be performed, that is, whether it must be a hospital or may be a clinic or some other place of less-than-hospital status; as to the licensing of the facility; and the like.

This means, on the other hand, that, for the period of pregnancy prior to this "compelling" point, the attending physician, in consultation with his patient, is free to determine, without regulation by the State, that, in his medical judgment, the patient's pregnancy should be terminated. If that decision is reached, the judgment may be effectuated by an abortion free of interference by the State.

With respect to the State's important and legitimate interest in potential life, the "compelling" point is at viability. This is so because the fetus then presumably has the capability of meaningful life outside the mother's womb. State regulation protective of fetal life after viability thus has both logical and biological justifications. If the State is interested in protecting fetal life after viability, it may go so far as to proscribe abortion during that period, except when it is necessary to preserve the life or health of the mother.

Measured against these standards, Art. 1196 of the Texas Penal Code, in restricting legal abortions to those "procured or attempted by medical advice for the purpose of saving the life of the mother," sweeps too broadly. The statute makes no distinction between abortions performed early in pregnancy and those performed later, and it limits to a single reason, "saving" the mother's life, the legal justification for the procedure. The statute, therefore, cannot survive the constitutional attack made upon it here. . . .

To summarize and to repeat:

1. A state criminal abortion statute of the current Texas type, that excepts from criminality only a *life-saving* procedure on behalf of the mother, without regard to pregnancy stage and without recognition of the other interests involved, is violative of the Due Process Clause of the Fourteenth Amendment.

(a) For the stage prior to approximately the end of the first trimester, the abortion decision and its effectuation must be left to the medical judgment of the pregnant woman's attending physician.

(b) For the stage subsequent to approximately the end of the first trimester, the State, in promoting its interest in the health of the mother, may, if it chooses, regulate the abortion procedure in ways that are reasonably related to maternal health.

(c) For the stage subsequent to viability, the State in promoting its interest in the potentiality of human life may, if it chooses, regulate, and even proscribe, abortion except where it is necessary, in appropriate medical judgment, for the preservation of the life or health of the mother. . . .

United States *v.* O'Brien

As American involvement in Vietnam intensified in the 1960's, opposition and dissent at home likewise escalated. Mass and individual protests against the war took a variety of forms, both peaceful and violent. Such actions almost inevitably led to a broad range of constitutional challenges to the war. In some cases, individuals sought guarantees for freedom to protest; in others, individuals sought exemption from military service and raised novel questions; finally, there were formalized, concerted challenges to the constitutional validity of the war itself. Most members of the Warren Court, either privately or publicly accepted the government's policy. Accordingly, the Court turned aside cases that challenged large political and foreign policy questions; yet in a number of other cases, the Justices stressed libertarian values in the First Amendment clauses on speech and religion. In the O'Brien case below, however, the Court reflected its long-standing tradition of disapproving conduct that interfered with the process of conscription. Draft-card burning (or often of what purported to be draft-cards) was one of the more dramatic forms of protest at the time. Congress responded with a 1965 amendment to the conscription laws making it a criminal offense for anyone to knowingly destroy or mutilate their certificate. David O'Brien and others were arrested by FBI agents who, with a large crowd, witnessed O'Brien's public burning of his registration card. O'Brien challenged the 1965 amendment as an abridgement of free speech and as having no legitimate legislative purpose.

Chief Justice Warren delivered the opinion of the Court.

O'Brien first argues that the 1965 Amendment is unconstitutional as applied to him because his act of burning his registration certificate was protected "symbolic speech" within the First Amendment. His

---

391 U.S. 367 (1968)

argument is that the freedom of expression which the First Amendment guarantees includes all modes of "communication of ideas by conduct," and that his conduct is within this definition because he did it in "demonstration against the war and against the draft."

We cannot accept the view that an apparently limitless variety of conduct can be labeled "speech" whenever the person engaging in the conduct intends thereby to express an idea. However, even on the assumption that the alleged communicative element in O'Brien's conduct is sufficient to bring into play the First Amendment, it does not necessarily follow that the destruction of a registration certificate is constitutionally protected activity. This Court has held that when "speech" and "nonspeech" elements are combined in the same course of conduct, a sufficiently important governmental interest in regulating the nonspeech element can justify incidental limitations on First Amendment freedoms. To characterize the quality of the governmental interest which must appear, the Court has employed a variety of descriptive terms: compelling; substantial; subordinating; paramount; cogent; strong. Whatever imprecision inheres in these terms, we think it clear that a government regulation is sufficiently justified if it is within the constitutional power of the Government; if it furthers an important or substantial governmental interest; if the governmental interest is unrelated to the suppression of free expression; and if the incidental restriction on alleged First Amendment freedoms is no greater than is essential to the furtherance of that interest. We find that the 1965 Amendment to § 12(b)(3) of the Universal Military Training and Service Act meets all of these requirements, and consequently that O'Brien can be constitutionally convicted for violating it.

The constitutional power of Congress to raise and support armies and to make all laws necessary and proper to that end is broad and sweeping. . . . The power of Congress to classify and conscript manpower for military service is "beyond question." . . . Pursuant to this power, Congress may establish a system of registration for individuals liable for training and service, and may require such individuals within reason to cooperate in the registration system. The issuance of certificates indicating the registration and eligibility classification of individuals is a legitimate and substantial administrative aid in the functioning of this system. And legislation to insure the continuing availability of issued certificates serves a legitimate and substantial purpose in the system's administration.

O'Brien's argument to the contrary is necessarily premised upon his unrealistic characterization of Selective Service certificates. He essentially adopts the position that such certificates are so many pieces of paper designed to notify registrants of their registration or classification, to be retained or tossed in the wastebasket according to the convenience or taste of the registrant. Once the registrant has received notification, according to this view, there is no reason for him to retain the certificates.

O'Brien notes that most of the information on a registration certificate serves no notification purpose at all; the registrant hardly needs to be told his address and physical characteristics. We agree that the registration certificate contains much information of which the registrant needs no notification. This circumstance, however, does not lead to the conclusion that the certificate serves no purpose, but that, like the classification certificate, it serves purposes in addition to initial notification. Many of these purposes would be defeated by the certificates' destruction or multilation. Among these are:

1. The registration certificate serves as proof that the individual described thereon has registered for the draft. The classification certificate shows the eligibility classification of a named but undescribed individual. Voluntarily displaying the two certificates is an easy and painless way for a young man to dispel a question as to whether he might be delinquent in his Selective Service obligations. Correspondingly, the availability of the certificates for such display relieves the Selective Service System of the administrative burden it would otherwise have in verifying the registration and classification of all suspected delinquents. Further, since both certificates are in the nature of "receipts" attesting that the registrant has done what the law requires, it is in the interest of the just and efficient administration of the system that they be continually available, in the event, for example, of a mix-up in the registrant's file. Additionally, in a time of national crisis, reasonable availability to each registrant of the two small cards assures a rapid and uncomplicated means for determining his fitness for immediate induction, no matter how distant in our mobile society he may be from his local board.

2. The information supplied on the certificates facilitates communication between registrants and local boards, simplifying the system and benefiting all concerned. . . .

3. Both certificates carry continual reminders that the registrant must notify his local board of any change of address, and other specified changes in his status. . . .

4. The regulatory scheme involving Selective Service certificates includes clearly valid prohibitions against the alteration, forgery, or similar deceptive misuse of certificates. The destruction or mutilation of certificates obviously increases the difficulty of detecting and tracing abuses such as these. Further, a mutilated certificate might itself be used for deceptive purposes.

The many functions performed by Selective Service certificates establish beyond doubt that Congress has a legitimate and substantial interest in preventing their wanton and unrestrained destruction and assuring their continuing availability by punishing people who knowingly and wilfully destroy or mutilate them. And we are unpersuaded that the preexistence of the nonpossession regulations in any way negates this interest. . . .

We think it apparent that the continuing availability to each registrant of his Selective Service certificates substantially furthers the smooth and proper functioning of the system that Congress has established to raise armies. We think it also apparent that the Nation has a vital interest in having a system for raising armies that functions with maximum efficiency and is capable of easily and quickly responding to continually changing circumstances. For these reasons, the Government has a substantial interest in assuring the continuing availability of issued Selective Service certificates. . . .

In conclusion, we find that because of the Government's substantial interest in assuring the continuing availability of issued Selective Service certificates, because amended § 462(b) is an appropriately narrow means of protecting this interest and condemns only the independent noncommunicative impact of conduct within its reach, and because the noncommunicative impact of O'Brien's act of burning his registration certificate frustrated the Government's interest, a sufficient governmental interest has been shown to justify O'Brien's conviction.

O'Brien finally argues that the 1965 Amendment is unconstitutional as enacted because what he calls the "purpose" of Congress was "to suppress freedom of speech." We reject this argument because under settled principles the purpose of Congress, as O'Brien uses that term, is not a basis for declaring this legislation unconstitutional.

It is a familiar principle of constitutional law that this Court will not strike down an otherwise constitutional statute on the basis of an alleged illicit legislative motive. . . .

Inquiries into congressional motives or purposes are a hazardous matter. When the issue is simply the interpretation of legislation, the Court will look to statements by legislators for guidance as to the purpose of the legislature, because the benefit to sound decision-making in this circumstance is thought sufficient to risk the possibility of misreading Congress' purpose. It is entirely a different matter when we are asked to void a statute that is, under well-settled criteria, constitutional on its face, on the basis of what fewer than a handful of Congressmen said about it. What motivates one legislator to make a speech about a statute is not necessarily what motivates scores of others to enact it, and the stakes are sufficiently high for us to eschew guesswork. We decline to void essentially on the ground that it is unwise legislation which Congress had the undoubted power to enact and which could be reenacted in its exact form if the same or another legislator made a "wiser" speech about it. . . .

Tinker *v.* Des Moines School District

In the case below, three Iowa children had been suspended from public school for wearing black armbands as a protest against the Vietnam war. Their parents sought damages and an injunction against the school board's regulation. A majority of the Court, carefully noting the act as "symbolic" free speech and finding the conduct non-disruptive, found for the petitioners. In dissent, however, Justice Black underlined an important qualification to his usual absolutist free speech views. Black emphasized the petitioners' conduct, finding it disruptive and violative of the proper powers of school authorities.

Justice Fortas delivered the opinion of the Court.

I.

T he District Court recognized that the wearing of an armband for the purpose of expressing certain views is the type of symbolic act that is within the Free Speech Clause of the First Amendment. . . . As we shall discuss, the wearing of armbands in the circumstances of this case was entirely divorced from actually or potentially disruptive conduct by those participating in it. It was closely akin to "pure speech" which we have repeatedly held, is entitled to comprehensive protection under the First Amendment. . . .

II.

The problem posed by the present case does not relate to regulation of the length of skirts or the type of clothing, to hair style, or deportment. . . . It does not concern aggressive, disruptive action or even group demonstrations. Our problem involves direct, primary First Amendment rights akin to "pure speech."

The school officials banned and sought to punish petitioners for a silent, passive expression of opinion, unaccompanied by any disorder or disturbance on the part of petitioners. There is here no evidence whatever of petitioners' interference, actual or nascent, with the schools' work or of collision with the rights of other students to be secure and to be let alone. Accordingly, this case does not concern speech or action that intrudes upon the work of the schools or the rights of other students.

Only a few of the 18,000 students in the school system wore the black

---

393 U.S. 503 (1969)

armbands. Only five students were suspended for wearing them. There is no indication that the work of the schools or any class was disrupted. Outside the classrooms, a few students made hostile remarks to the children wearing armbands, but there were no threats or acts of violence on school premises.

The District Court concluded that the action of the school authorities was reasonable because it was based upon their fear of a disturbance from the wearing of the armbands. But, in our system, undifferentiated fear or apprehension of disturbance is not enough to overcome the right to freedom of expression. Any departure from absolute regimentation may cause trouble. Any variation from the majority's opinion may inspire fear. Any word spoken, in class, in the lunchroom, or on the campus, that deviates from the views of another person may start an argument or cause a disturbance. But our Constitution says we must take this risk, *Terminiello* v. *Chicago*, 337 U. S. 1 (1949); and our history says that it is this sort of hazardous freedom—this kind of openness—that is the basis of our national strength and of the independence and vigor of Americans who grow up and live in this relatively permissive, often disputatious, society.

In order for the State in the person of school officials to justify prohibition of a particular expression of opinion, it must be able to show that its action was caused by something more than a mere desire to avoid the discomfort and unpleasantness that always accompany an unpopular viewpoint. Certainly where there is no finding and no showing that engaging in the forbidden conduct would "materially and substantially interfere with the requirements of appropriate discipline in the operation of the school," the prohibition cannot be sustained. . . .

In the present case, the District Court made no such finding, and our independent examination of the record fails to yield evidence that the school authorities had reason to anticipate that the wearing of the armbands would substantially interfere with the work of the school or impinge upon the rights of other students. Even an official memorandum prepared after the suspension that listed the reasons for the ban on wearing the armbands made no reference to the anticipation of such disruption.

On the contrary, the action of the school authorities appears to have been based upon an urgent wish to avoid the controversy which might result from the expression, even by the silent symbol of armbands, of opposition to this Nation's part in the conflagration in Vietnam. It is revealing, in this respect, that the meeting at which the school principals decided to issue the contested regulation was called in response to a student's statement to the journalism teacher in one of the schools that he wanted to write an article on Vietnam and have it published in the school paper. (The student was dissuaded.)

It is also relevant that the school authorities did not purport to prohibit the wearing of all symbols of political or controversial significance. The record shows the students in some of the schools wore buttons relating to national political campaigns, and some even wore the Iron Cross, traditionally a symbol of Nazism. The order prohibiting the wearing of armbands did not extend to these. Instead, a particular symbol—black armbands worn to exhibit opposition to this Nation's involvement in Vietnam —was singled out for prohibition. Clearly, the prohibition of expression of one particular opinion, at least without evidence that it is necessary to avoid material and substantial interference with schoolwork or discipline, is not constitutionally permissible. . . .

The principal use to which the schools are dedicated is to accommodate students during prescribed hours for the purpose of certain types of activities. Among those activities is personal intercommunication among the students. This is not only an inevitable part of the process of attending school; it is also an important part of the educational process. A student's rights, therefore, do not embrace merely the classroom hours. When he is in the cafeteria, or on the playing field, or on the campus during the authorized hours, he may express his opinions, even on controversial subjects like the conflict in Vietnam, if he does so without "materially and substantially interfer[ing] with the requirements of appropriate discipline in the operation of the school" and without colliding with the rights of others. . . . But conduct by the student, in class or out of it, which for any reason—whether it stems from time, place, or type of behavior—materially disrupts classwork or involves substantial disorder or invasion of the rights of others is, of course, not immunized by the constitutional guarantee of freedom of speech. . . .

Under our Constitution, free speech is not a right that is given only to be so circumscribed that it exists in principle but not in fact. Freedom of expression would not truly exist if the right could be exercised only in an area that a benevolent government has provided as a safe haven for crackpots. The Constitution says that Congress (and the States) may not abridge the right to free speech. This provision means what it says. We properly read it to permit reasonable regulation of speech-connected activities in carefully restricted circumstances. But we do not confine the permissible exercise of First Amendment rights to a telephone booth or the four corners of a pamphlet, or to supervised and ordained discussion in a school classroom.

If a regulation were adopted by school officials forbidding discussion of the Vietnam conflict, or the expression by any student of opposition to it anywhere on school property except as part of a prescribed classroom exercise, it would be obvious that the regulation would violate the constitutional rights of students, at least if it could not be justified by a showing that the students' activities would materially and substantially disrupt the work and discipline of the school. . . . In the circumstances of the present case, the prohibition of the silent, passive "witness of the armbands," as one of the children called it, is no less offensive to the Constitution's guarantees.

As we have discussed, the record does not demonstrate any facts which might reasonably have led school authorities to forecast substantial disruption of or material interference with school activities, and no disturbances or disorders on the school premises in fact occurred. These petitioners merely went about their ordained rounds in school. Their deviation consisted only in wearing on their sleeve a band of black cloth, not more than two inches wide. They wore it to exhibit their disapproval of the Vietnam hostilities and their advocacy of a truce, to make their views known, and, by their example, to influence others to adopt them. They neither interrupted school activities nor sought to intrude in the school affairs or the lives of others. They caused discussion outside of the classrooms, but no interference with work and no disorder. In the circumstances, our Constitution does not permit officials of the State to deny their form of expression. . . .

MR. JUSTICE BLACK, dissenting. . . .

. . . Iowa's public schools . . . are operated to give students an opportunity to learn, not to talk politics by actual speech, or by "symbolic" speech. And, as I have pointed out before, the record amply shows that public protest in the school classes against the Vietnam war "distracted from that singleness of purpose which the State [here Iowa] desired to exist in its public educational institutions." Here the Court should accord Iowa educational institutions the same right to determine for themselves to what extent free expression should be allowed in its schools as it accorded Mississippi with reference to freedom of assembly. But even if the record were silent as to protests against the Vietnam war distracting students from their assigned class work, members of this Court, like all other citizens, know, without being told, that the disputes over the wisdom of the Vietnam war have disrupted and divided this country as few other issues ever have. Of course students, like other people, cannot concentrate on lesser issues when black armbands are being ostentatiously displayed in their presence to call attention to the wounded and dead of the war, some of the wounded and the dead being their friends and neighbors. It was, of course, to distract the attention of other students that some students insisted up to the very point of their own suspension from school that they were determined to sit in school with their symbolic armbands.

Change has been said to be truly the law of life but sometimes the old and the tried and true are worth holding. The schools of this Nation have undoubtedly contributed to giving us tranquility and to making us a more law-abiding people. Uncontrolled and uncontrollable liberty is an enemy to domestic peace. We cannot close our eyes to the fact that some of the country's greatest problems are crimes committed by the youth, too many of school age. School discipline, like parental discipline, is an integral and important part of training our children to be good citizens—to be better citizens. Here a very small number of students have crisply and summarily refused to obey a school order designed to give pupils who want to learn the opportunity to do so. One does not need to be a prophet or the son of a prophet to know that after the Court's holding today some students in Iowa schools and indeed in all schools will be ready, able, and willing to defy their teachers on practically all orders. This is the more unfortunate for the schools since groups of students all over the land are already running loose, conducting break-ins, sit-ins, lie-ins, and smash-ins. Many of these student groups, as is all too familiar to all who read the newspapers and watch the television news programs, have already engaged in rioting, property seizures, and destruction. They have picketed schools to force students not to cross their picket lines and have too often violently attacked earnest but frightened students who wanted an education that the pickets did not want them to get. Students engaged in such activities are apparently confident that they know far more how to operate public school systems than do their parents, teachers, and elected school officials. It is no answer to say that the particular students here have not yet reached such high points in their demands to attend classes in order to exercise their political pressures. Turned loose with lawsuits for damages and injunctions against their teachers as they are here, it is nothing but wishful thinking to imagine that young, immature students will not soon believe it is their right to control the schools rather than the right of the States that collect the taxes to hire the teachers for the benefit of the pupils. This case, therefore, wholly without constitutional reasons in my judgment, subjects all the public schools in the country to the whims and caprices of their loudest-mouthed, but maybe not their brightest, students. I, for one, am not fully persuaded that school pupils are wise enough, even with this Court's expert help from Washington, to run the 23,390 public school systems in our 50 States. I wish, therefore, wholly to disclaim any purpose on my part to hold that the Federal Constitution compels the teachers, parents, and elected school officials to surrender control of the American public school system to public school students. I dissent.

Welsh *v.* United States

The Vietnam conflict provoked new, knotty claims from conscientious objectors. The conscription laws exempted from military service those who by "religious training and belief" conscientiously opposed war in any manner. The act defined that belief as one of "a relation to a Supreme Being involving duties superior to those arising from any human relation"; but it did not include "essentially political, sociological, or philosophical views or a merely personal code." In United States *v.* Seeger *(380 U.S. 163 [1965]), the Court allowed the test of religious belief to include beliefs other than formalized or institutionalized faiths. "A sincere and meaningful belief which occupies in the life of its possessor a place parallel to that filled by the God of those admittedly qualifying for the exemption," the Court said in* Seeger, *"comes within the statutory definition." Elliott Welsh refused to affirm or deny belief in a Supreme Being and claimed that he had deep conscientious scruples against participating in wars. Significantly, he struck the words "my religious training and belief" from his form. His draft board denied his petition and he subsequently was convicted for refusing to submit to induction. Justice Black's opinion below also represented the views of Justices Douglas, Brennan, and Marshall. Justice Harlan joined only in the judgment to form a majority, while Chief Justice Burger, and Justices White and Stewart dissented. Justice Blackmun did not participate.*

Justice Black delivered the judgment of the Court.

F or the reasons to be stated, and without passing upon the constitutional arguments that have been raised, we vote to reverse this conviction because of its fundamental inconsistency with *United States* v. *Seeger, supra.*

The controlling facts in this case are strikingly similar to those in *Seeger.* Both Seeger and Welsh were brought up in religious homes and attended church in their childhood, but in neither case was this church one which taught its members not to engage in war at any time for any reason. Neither Seeger nor Welsh continued his childhood religious ties into his young manhood, and neither belonged to any religious group or

398 U.S. 333 (1970)

adhered to the teachings of any organized religion during the period of his involvement with the Selective Service System. At the time of registration for the draft, neither had yet come to accept pacifist principles. Their views on war developed only in subsequent years, but when their ideas did fully mature both made application to their local draft boards for conscientious objector exemptions from military service under § 6 (j) of the Universal Military Training and Service Act. That section then provided, in part:

> "Nothing contained in this title shall be construed to require any person to be subject to combatant training and service in the armed forces of the United States who, by reason of religious training and belief, is conscientiously opposed to participation in war in any form. Religious training and belief in this connection means an indivdual's belief in a relation to a Supreme Being involving duties superior to those arising from any human relation, but does not include essentially political, sociological, or philosophical views or a merely personal moral code."

In filling out their exemption applications both Seeger and Welsh were unable to sign the statement that, as printed in the Selective Service form, stated "I am, by reason of my religious training and belief, conscientiously opposed to participation in war in any form." Seeger could sign only after striking the words "training and" and putting quotation marks around the word "religious." Welsh could sign only after striking the words "my religious training and." On those same applications, neither could definitely affirm or deny that he believed in a "Supreme Being," both stating that they preferred to leave the question open. But both Seeger and Welsh affirmed on those applications that they held deep conscientious scruples against taking part in wars where people were killed. Both strongly believed that killing in war was wrong, unethical, and immoral, and their consciences forbade them to take part in such an evil practice. Their objection to participating in war in any form could not be said to come from a "still, small voice of conscience"; rather, for them that voice was so loud and insistent that both men preferred to go to jail rather than serve in the Armed Forces. There was never any question about the sincerity and depth of Seeger's convictions as a conscientious objector, and the same is true of Welsh. . . . But in both cases the Selective Service System concluded that the beliefs of these men were in some sense insufficiently "religious" to qualify them for conscientious objector exemptions under the terms of § 6 (j). Seeger's conscientious objector claim was denied "solely because it was not based upon a 'belief in a relation to a Supreme Being' as required by § 6 (j) of the Act," *United States* v. *Seeger*, 380 U. S. 163, 167 (1965), while Welsh was denied the exemption because his Appeal Board and the Department of Justice hearing officer "could find no religious basis for the registrant's beliefs, opinions and convictions." . . .

Both Seeger and Welsh subsequently refused to submit to induction into the military and both were convicted of that offense.

In *Seeger* the Court . . . made it clear that these sincere and meaningful beliefs that prompt the registrant's objection to all wars need not be confined in either source or content to traditional or parochial concepts of religion. It held that § 6 (j) "does not distinguish between externally and internally derived beliefs," . . . and also held that "intensely personal" convictions which some might find "incomprehensible" or "incorrect" come within the meaning of "religious belief" in the Act. . . . What is necessary under *Seeger* for a registrant's conscientious objection to all war to be "religious" within the meaning of § 6 (j) is that this opposition to war stem from the registrant's moral, ethical, or religious beliefs about what is right and wrong and that these beliefs be held with the strength of traditional religious convictions. Most of the great religions of today and of the past have embodied the idea of a Supreme Being or a Supreme Reality—a God—who communicates to man in some way a consciousness of what is right and should be done, of what is wrong and therefore should be shunned. If an individual deeply and sincerely holds beliefs that are purely ethical or moral in source and content but that nevertheless impose upon him a duty of conscience to refrain from participating in any war at any time, those beliefs certainly occupy in the life of that individual "a place parallel to that filled by . . . God" in traditionally religious persons. Because his beliefs function as a religion in his life, such an individual is as much entitled to a "religious" conscientious objector exemption under § 6 (j) as is someone who derives his conscientious opposition to war from traditional religious convictions. . . .

In the case before us the Government seeks to distinguish our holding in *Seeger* on basically two grounds, both of which were relied upon by the Court of Appeals in affirming Welsh's conviction. First, it is stressed that Welsh was far more insistent and explicit than Seeger in denying that his views were religious. For example, in filling out their conscientious objector applications, Seeger put quotation marks around the word "religious," but Welsh struck the word "religious" entirely and later characterized his beliefs as having been formed "by reading in the fields of history and sociology." . . . The Court of Appeals found that Welsh had "denied that his objection to war was premised on religious belief" and concluded that "[t]he Appeal Board was entitled to take him at his word." . . . We think this attempt to distinguish *Seeger* fails for the reason that it places undue emphasis on the registrant's interpretation of his own beliefs. The Court's statement in *Seeger* that a registrant's characterization of his own belief as "religious" should carry great weight, . . . does not imply that his declaration that his views are nonreligious should be treated similarly. When a registrant states that his objections to war are "religious," that information is highly relevant to the question of the function his beliefs have in his life. But very few registrants are fully aware of the broad scope of the word "religious" as used in § 6 (j), and accordingly a registrant's statement that his beliefs are nonreligious is a highly unreliable guide for those charged with administering the exemption. Welsh himself presents a case in point. Although he originally characterized his beliefs as nonreligious, he later upon reflection wrote a long and thoughtful letter to his Appeal Board in which he declared that his beliefs were "certainly religious in the ethical sense of the word." . . .

The Government also seeks to distinguish *Seeger* on the ground that Welsh's views, unlike Seeger's, were "essentially political, sociological, or philosophical views or a merely personal moral code." As previously noted, the Government made the same argument about Seeger, and not without reason, for Seeger's views had a substantial political dimension. . . . In this case, Welsh's conscientious objection to war was undeniably based in part on his perception of world politics. . . .

We certainly do not think that § 6 (j)'s exclusion of those persons with "essentially political, sociological, or philosophical views or a merely personal moral code" should be read to exclude those who hold strong beliefs about our domestic and foreign affairs or even those whose conscientious objection to participation in all wars is founded to a substantial extent upon considerations of public policy. The two groups of registrants that obviously do fall within these exclusions from the exemption are those whose beliefs are not deeply held and those whose objection to war does not rest at all upon moral, ethical, or religious principle but instead rests solely upon considerations of policy, pragmatism, or expediency. In applying § 6 (j)'s exclusion of those whose views are "essentially political, sociological, or philosophical" or of those who have a "merely personal moral code," it should be remembered that these exclusions are definitional and do not therefore restrict the category of persons who are conscientious objectors by "religious training and belief." Once the Selective Service System has taken the first step and determined under the standards set out here and in *Seeger* that the registrant is a "religious" conscientious objector, it follows that his views cannot be "essentially political, sociological, or philosophical." Nor can they be a "merely personal moral code." . . .

Welsh stated that he "believe[d] the taking of life—anyone's life—to be morally wrong." . . . In his original conscientious objector application he wrote the following:

"I believe that human life is valuable in and of itself; in its living; therefore I will not injure or kill another human being. This belief (and the corresponding 'duty' to abstain from violence toward another person) is not 'superior to those arising from any human relation.' On the contrary: *it is essential to every human relation.* I cannot, therefore, conscientiously comply with the

Government's insistence that I assume duties which I feel are immoral and totally repugnant." . . .

Welsh elaborated his beliefs in later communications with Selective Service officials. On the basis of these beliefs and the conclusion of the Court of Appeals that he held them "with the strength of more traditional religious convictions," 404 F. 2d, at 1081, we think Welsh was clearly entitled to a conscientious objector exemption. . . .

Gillette *v.* United States

The following case presented a far more focused question than the generalized "religious" views of the Welsh *and* Seeger *cases.* Gillette *refused induction into the military on the grounds that the Vietnam conflict specifically was an "unjust" war. He also challenged the conscientious objection clause of the Military Selective Service Act as violative of the free exercise and establishment of religion clauses of the First Amendment if construed to cover only objections to all wars.*

Justice Marshall delivered the opinion of the Court.

For purposes of determining the statutory status of conscientious objection to a particular war, the focal language of § 6 (j) is the phrase, "conscientiously opposed to participation in war in any form." This language, on a straightforward reading, can bear but one meaning; that conscientious scruples relating to war and military service must amount to conscientious opposition to participating personally in any war and all war. . . . It matters little for present purposes whether the words, "in any form," are ready to modify "war" or "participation." On the first reading, conscientious scruples must implicate "war in any form," and an objection involving a particular war rather than all war would plainly not be covered by § 6 (j). On the other reading, an objector must oppose "participation in war." It would strain good sense to read this phrase otherwise than to mean "participation in all war." For the word "war" would still be used in an unqualified, generic sense, meaning war as such. Thus, however the statutory clause be parsed, it remains that conscientious objection must run to war in any form. . . .

It should be emphasized that our cases explicating the "religious training and belief" clause of § 6 (j), or cognate clauses of predecessor provisions, are not relevant to the present issue. The question here is not whether these petitioners' beliefs concerning war are "religious" in nature. Thus, petitioners' reliance on *United States* v. *Seeger*, 380 U. S. 163, and *Welsh* v. *United States*, 398 U. S. 333, is misplaced. Nor do we decide that conscientious objection to a particular war necessarily falls within § 6 (j)'s expressly excluded class of "essentially political, sociological, or philosophical views, or a merely personal moral code." Rather, we hold that Congress intended to exempt persons who oppose participating in all war —"participation in war in any form"—and that persons who object solely to participation in a particular war are not within the purview of the exempting section, even though the latter objection may have such roots in a claimant's conscience and personality that it is "religious" in character.

A further word may be said to clarify our statutory holding. Apart from abstract theological reservations, two other sorts of reservations concerning use of force have been thought by lower courts not to defeat a conscientious objector claim. Willingness to use force in self-defense, in defense of home and family, or in defense against immediate acts of aggressive violence toward other persons in the community, has not been regarded as inconsistent with a claim of conscientious objection to war as such. . . . But surely willingness to use force defensively in the personal situations mentioned is quite different from willingness to fight in some wars but not in others. . . . Somewhat more opposite to the instant situation are cases dealing with persons who oppose participating in all wars, but cannot say with complete certainty that their present convictions and existing state of mind are unalterable. . . . Unwillingness to deny the possibility of a change of mind, in some hypothetical future circumstances, may be no more than humble good sense, casting no doubt on the claimant's present sincerity of belief. At any rate there is an obvious difference between present sincere objection to all war, and present opposition to participation in a particular conflict only.

Both petitioners argue that § 6 (j), construed to cover only objectors to all war, violates the religious clauses of the First Amendment. The First Amendment provides that "Congress shall make no law respecting an establishment of religion, or prohibiting the free exercise thereof. . . ." Petitioners contend that Congress interferes with free exercise of religion by failing to relieve objectors to a particular war from military service, when the objection is religious or conscientious in nature. While the two religious clauses—pertaining to "free exercise" and "establishment" of religion—overlap and interact in many ways, . . . it is best to focus first on petitioners' other contention, that § 6 (j) is a law respecting the establishment of religion. For despite free exercise overtones, the gist of the constitutional complaint is that § 6 (j) impermissibly discriminates among types of religious belief and affiliation.

On the assumption that these petitioners' beliefs concerning war have roots that are "religious" in nature, within the meaning of the Amendment as well as this Court's decisions construing § 6 (j), petitioners ask how their claims to relief from military service can be permitted to fail, while other "religious" claims are upheld by the Act. It is a fact that § 6 (j), properly construed, has this effect. Yet we cannot conclude in mechanical fashion, or at all, that the section works an establishment of religion.

An attack founded on disparate treatment of "religious" claims invokes what is perhaps the central purpose of the Establishment Clause—the purpose of ensuring governmental neutrality in matters of religion. . . . Here there is no claim that exempting conscientious objectors to war amounts to an overreaching of secular purposes and an undue involvement of government in affairs of religion. . . . To the contrary, petitioners ask for greater "entanglement" by judicial expansion of the exemption to cover objectors to particular wars. Necessarily the constitutional value at issue is "neutrality." And as a general matter it is surely true that the Establishment Clause prohibits government from abandoning secular purposes in order to put an imprimatur on one religion, or on religion as such, or to favor the adherents of any sect or religious organization. . . . The metaphor of a "wall" or impassable barrier between Church and State, taken too literally, may mislead constitutional analysis. . . . but the Establishment Clause stands at least for the proposition that when government activities touch on the religious sphere, they must be secular in purpose, evenhanded in operation, and neutral in primary impact. . . .

The critical weakness of petitioners' establishment claim arises from the fact that § 6 (j), on its face, simply does not discriminate on the basis of religious affiliation or religious belief, apart of course from beliefs concerning war. The section says that anyone who is conscientiously opposed to all war shall be relieved of military service. The specified objection must have a grounding in "religious training and belief," but no particular sectarian affiliation or theological position is required. . . .

We conclude not only that the affirmative purposes underlying § 6 (j) are neutral and secular, but also that valid neutral reasons exist for limiting the exemption to objectors to all war, and that the section therefore cannot be said to reflect a religious preference.

Apart from the Government's need for manpower, perhaps the central interest involved in the administration of conscription laws is the interest in maintaining a fair system for determining "who serves when not all serve." When the Government exacts so much, the importance of fair, evenhanded, and uniform decisionmaking is obviously intensified. The

Government argues that the interest in fairness would be jeopardized by expansion of § 6 (j) to include conscientious objection to a particular war. The contention is that the claim to relief on account of such objection is intrinsically a claim of uncertain dimensions, and that granting the claim in theory would involve a real danger of erratic or even discriminatory decisionmaking in administrative practice. . . .

For their part, petitioners make no attempt to provide a careful definition of the claim to exemption that they ask the courts to carve out and protect. They do not explain why objection to a particular conflict—much less an objection that focuses on a particular facet of a conflict—should excuse the objector from all military service whatever, even from military operations that are connected with the conflict at hand in remote or tenuous ways. They suggest no solution to the problems arising from the fact that altered circumstances may quickly render the objection to military service moot. . . .

Ours is a Nation of enormous heterogeneity in respect of political views, moral codes, and religious persuasions. It does not bespeak an establishing of religion for Congress to forgo the enterprise of distinguishing those whose dissent has some conscientious basis from those who simply dissent. There is a danger that as between two would-be objectors, both having the same complaint against a war, that objector would succeed who is more articulate, better educated, or better counseled. There is even a danger of unintended religious discrimination—a danger that a claim's chances of success would be greater the more familiar or salient the claim's connection with conventional religiosity could be made to appear. . . .

[S]ome have perceived a danger that exempting persons who dissent from a particular war, albeit on grounds of conscience and religion in part, would "open the doors to a general theory of selective disobedience to law" and jeopardize the binding quality of democratic decisions. Report of the National Advisory Commission on Selective Service, In Pursuit of Equity: Who Serves When Not All Serve? 50 (1967). . . . Other fields of legal obligation aside, it is undoubted that the nature of conscription, much less war itself, requires the personal desires and perhaps the dissenting views of those who must serve to be subordinated in some degree to the pursuit of public purposes. It is also true that opposition to a particular war does depend *inter alia* upon particularistic factual beliefs and policy assessments, beliefs and assessments that presumably were overridden by the government that decides to commit lives and resources to a trial of arms. Further, it is not unreasonable to suppose that some persons who are *not* prepared to assert a conscientious objection, and instead accept the hardships and risks of military service, may well agree at all points with the objector, yet conclude, as a matter of conscience, that they are personally bound by the decision of the democratic process.

The fear of the National Advisory Commission on Selective Service, apparently, is that exemption of objectors to particular wars would weaken the resolve of those who otherwise would feel themselves bound to serve despite personal cost, uneasiness at the prospect of violence, or even serious moral reservations or policy objections concerning the particular conflict.

We need not and do not adopt the view that a categorical, global "interest" in stifling individualistic claims to noncompliance, in respect of duties generally exacted, is the neutral and secular basis of § 6 (j). As is shown by the long history of the very provision under discussion, it is not inconsistent with orderly democratic government for individuals to be exempted by law, on account of special characteristics, from general duties of a burdensome nature. But real dangers—dangers of the kind feared by the Commission—might arise if an exemption were made available that in its nature could not be administered fairly and uniformly over the run of relevant fact situations. Should it be thought that those who go to war are chosen unfairly or capriciously, then a mood of bitterness and cynicism might corrode the spirit of public service and the values of willing performance of a citizen's duties that are the very heart of free government. In short, the considerations mentioned in the previous paragraph, when seen in conjunction with the central problem of fairness, are without question properly cognizable by Congress. In light of these valid concerns, we conclude that it is supportable for Congress to have decided that the objector to all war—to all killing in war—has a claim that is distinct enough and intense enough to justify special status, while the objector to a particular war does not.

Of course, we do not suggest that Congress would have acted irrationally or unreasonably had it decided to exempt those who object to particular wars. Our analysis of the policies of § 6 (j) is undertaken in order to determine the existence *vel non* of a neutral, secular justification for the lines Congress has drawn. We find that justifying reasons exist and therefore hold that the Establishment Clause is not violated. . . .

Massachusetts *v.* Laird,
Secretary of Defense

*As the Vietnam war continued, dissent and protest against the
conflict widened throughout the nation. The expansion of the bombing raids in the North, and the invasion of Cambodia in the spring
of 1970—all at a time when the Nixon administration contended that
the war was ending—brought increased resistance to the American
involvement. Perhaps one of the most dramatic gestures came in
1970, when the Massachusetts legislature directed that a suit be filed
to obtain a determination of the constitutionality of American participation; further, the legislature provided that if Congress did not
formally declare war within ninety days, then an attempt would be
made to enjoin the Secretary of Defense from ordering any inhabitant of Massachusetts to participate. Six of the Supreme Court Justices refused to accept the case. Justices Harlan and Stewart favored
hearing arguments on standing and justiciability. In the remarks
below, Justice Douglas formally dissented against the Court's refusal
to file and hear the complaint. In 1973, the Court resorted again to
its "political questions" doctrine and refused to support a lower
court determination that the presidential bombing of Cambodia was
illegal (Holtzman v. Schlesinger, 414 U.S. 1304 [1973]).*

Justice Douglas dissenting.

I believe that Massachusetts has standing and the controversy is justiciable. At the very least, however, it is apparent that the issues are not
so clearly foreclosed as to justify a summary denial of leave to file.

STANDING

In *Massachusetts* v. *Mellon*, 262 U. S. 447 (hereafter *Mellon*), the
Court held that a State lacked standing to challenge, as *parens patriae*, a
federal grant-in-aid program under which the Federal Government was
allegedly usurping powers reserved to the States. It was said in *Mellon*:

> "[T]he citizens of Massachusetts are also citizens of the United States. It
> cannot be conceded that a State, as *parens patriae*, may institute judicial pro-
> ceedings to protect citizens of the United States from the operation of the

---

400 U.S. 886 (1970)

statutes thereof. While the State, under some circumstances, may sue in that capacity for the protection of its citizens (*Missouri* v. *Illinois*, 180 U. S. 208, 241), it is no part of its duty or power to enforce their rights in respect of their relations with the Federal Government. In that field it is the United States, and not the State, which represents them as *parens patriae*, when such representation becomes appropriate; and to the former, and not to the latter, they must look for such protective measures as flow from that status." *Id.*, at 485–486.

The Solicitor General argues that *Mellon* stands as a bar to this suit.

Yet the ruling of the Court in that case is not dispositive of this one. The opinion states: "We need not go so far as to say that a State may never intervene by suit to protect its citizens against any form of enforcement of unconstitutional acts of Congress; but we are clear that the right to do so does not arise here." *Id.*, at 485. Thus the case did not announce a *per se* rule to bar all suits against the Federal Government as *parens patriae*, and a closer look at the bases of the opinion is necessary to determine the limits on its applicability.

Mellon relates to an Act of Congress signed by the Executive, a distinction noted in other original actions. . . .

Massachusetts attacks no federal statute. In fact, the basis of Massachusetts' complaint is the absence of congressional action.

It is said that the Federal Government "represents" the citizens. Here the complaint is that only one representative of the people, the Executive, has acted and the other representatives of the citizens have not acted, although, it is argued, the Constitution provides that they must act before an overseas "war" can be conducted. . . .

Furthermore, the basis on which *Flast* distinguished *Frothingham* is also present here. The allegation in both *Mellon* and *Frothingham* was that Congress had exceeded the general powers delegated to it by Art. I, § 8, and invaded the reserved powers of the states under the Tenth Amendment. The claim was not specific; but, as *Flast* held, if a taxpayer can allege spending violates a *specific constitutional limitation*, then he has standing. Here Massachusetts points to a specific provision of the Constitution. Congress by Art. I, § 8, has the power "To declare War." Does not that make this case comparable to *Flast?*

It has been settled, at least since 1901, that "if the health and comfort of the inhabitants of a State are threatened, the State is the proper party to represent and defend them," . . . an original action in this Court. Those cases involved injury to inhabitants of one State by water or air pollution of another State, by interference with navigation, by economic losses caused by an out-of-state agency, and the like. The harm to citizens of Massachusetts suffered by being drafted for a war are certainly of no less a magnitude. Massachusetts would clearly seem to have standing as *par-*

ens patriae to represent, as alleged in its complaint, its male citizens being drafted for overseas combat in Indochina.

JUSTICIABILITY

A question that is "political" is opposed to one that is "justiciable." In reviewing the dimensions of the "political" question we said in *Baker* v. *Carr*, 369 U. S. 186, 217:

> "Prominent on the surface of any case held to involve a political question is found a textually demonstrable constitutional commitment of the issue to a coordinate political department; or a lack of judicially discoverable and manageable standards for resolving it; or the impossibility of deciding without an initial policy determination of a kind clearly for nonjudicial discretion; or the impossibility of a court's undertaking independent resolution without expressing lack of the respect due coordinate branches of government; or an unusual need for unquestioning adherence to a political decision already made; or the potentiality of embarrassment from multifarious pronouncements by various departments on one question."

1. *A textually demonstrable constitutional commitment of the issue to a coordinate political department.* At issue here is the phrase in Art. I § 8, cl. 11: "To declare War." Congress definitely has that power. The Solicitor General argues that only Congress can determine whether it has declared war. He states, " 'To declare War' includes a power to determine, free of judicial interference, the form which its authorization of hostilities will take." This may be correct. But, as we stated in *Powell* v. *McCormack*, 395 U. S. 486, the question of a textually demonstrable commitment and "what is the *scope* of such commitment are questions [this Court] must resolve for the first time in this case." *Id.*, at 521 (emphasis added). It may well be that it is for Congress, and Congress alone, to determine the form of its authorization, but if that is the case we should make that determination only after full briefs on the merits and oral argument.

2. *A lack of judicially discoverable and manageable standards for resolving the issue.* The standards that are applicable are not elusive. The case is not one where the Executive is repelling a sudden attack. The present Indochina "war" has gone on for six years. The question is whether the Gulf of Tonkin Resolution was a declaration of war or whether other Acts of Congress were its equivalent.

3. *The impossibility of deciding without an initial policy determination of a kind clearly for nonjudicial discretion.* In *Ex parte Milligan*, 4 *Wall.* 2, 139 (concurring opinion), it was stated that "neither can the President, in war more than in peace, intrude upon the proper authority of Congress. . . ." The issue in this case is not whether we ought to fight a war in Indochina, but whether the Executive can authorize it without congres-

sional authorization. This is not a case where we would have to determine the wisdom of any policy.

4. *The impossibility of a court's undertaking independent resolution without expressing lack of respect due coordinate branches of government.* The Solicitor General argues that it would show disrespect of the Executive to go behind his statements and determine his authority to act in these circumstances. Both *Powell* and the *Steel Seizure Case* (*Youngstown, Sheet & Tube* v. *Sawyer*, 343 U. S. 579), however, demonstrate that the duty of this Court is to interpret the Constitution, and in the latter case we did go behind an executive order to determine his authority. . . .

It is far more important to be respectful to the Constitution than to a coordinate branch of government.

5. *An unusual need for unquestioning adherence to a political decision already made.* This test is essentially a preference to a commitment of a problem and its solution to a coordinate branch of government—a matter not involved here.

6. *The potentiality of embarrassment from multifarious pronouncements by various departments of government on one question.* Once again this relates back to whether the problem and its solution are committed to a given branch of government.

We have never ruled, I believe, that when the Federal Government takes a person by the neck and submits him to punishment, imprisonment, taxation, or to some ordeal, the complaining person may not be heard in court. The rationale in cases such as the present is that government cannot take life, liberty, or property of the individual and escape adjudication by the courts of the legality of its action.

That is the heart of this case. It does not concern the wisdom of fighting in Southeast Asia. Likewise no question of whether the conflict is either just or necessary is present. We are asked instead whether the Executive has power, absent a congressional declaration of war, to commit Massachusetts citizens to armed hostilities on foreign soil. Another way of putting the question is whether under our Constitution presidential wars are permissible. Should that question be answered in the negative we would then have to determine whether Congress has declared war. That question which Massachusetts presents is in my view justiciable. . . .

"The war power of the United States, like its other powers . . . is subject to applicable constitutional limitations." *Hamilton* v. *Kentucky Distilleries & Warehouse Co.*, 251 U. S. 146, 156. No less than the war power—the greatest leveler of them all—is the power of the Commander in Chief subject to constitutional limitations. That was the crux of the *Steel Seizure Case.* Concurring in the judgment in that case, Mr. Justice Clark stated: "I conclude that where Congress has laid down specific procedures to deal with the type of crisis confronting the President, he must follow those procedures in meeting the crisis. . . . I cannot sustain the seizure in question because . . . Congress had [*sic*] prescribed methods to be followed by the President. . . ." . . . If the President must follow procedures prescribed by Congress, it follows *a fortiori* that he must follow procedures prescribed by the Constitution.

This Court has previously faced issues of presidential war making. The legality of Lincoln's blockade was considered in the *Prize Cases*, . . . and although the Court narrowly split in supporting the President's position, the split was on the merits, not on whether the claim was justiciable. And even though that war was the Civil War and not one involving an overseas expedition, the decision was 5 to 4.

In the *Steel Seizure Case* members of this Court wrote seven opinions and each reached the merits of the Executive's seizure. In that case, as here, the issue related to the President's powers as Commander in Chief and the fact that all nine Justices decided the case on the merits and construed the powers of a coordinate branch at a time of extreme emergency should be instructive. . . .

If we determine that the Indochina conflict is unconstitutional because it lacks a congressional declaration of war, the Chief Executive is free to seek one, as was President Truman free to seek congressional approval after our *Steel Seizure* decision.

There is, of course, a difference between this case and the *Prize Cases* and the *Steel Seizure Case*. In those cases a private party was asserting a wrong to him: his *property* was being taken and he demanded a determination of the legality of the taking. Here the *lives* and *liberties* of Massachusetts citizens are in jeopardy. Certainly the Constitution gives no greater protection to *property* than to *life* and *liberty*. It might be argued that the authority in the *Steel Seizure Case* was not textually apparent in the Constitution, while the power of the Commander in Chief to commit troops is obvious and therefore a different determination on justiciability is needed. The *Prize Cases*, however, involved Lincoln's exercise of power in ordering a blockade by virtue of his powers as the Commander in Chief.

Since private parties—represented by Massachusetts as *parens patriae*—are involved in this case, the teaching of the *Prize Cases* and the *Steel Seizure Case* is that their claims are justiciable.

The Solicitor General urges that no effective remedy can be formulated. He correctly points out enforcing or supervising injunctive relief would involve immense complexities and difficulties. But there is no requirement that we issue an injunction. Massachusetts seeks declaratory relief as well as injunctive relief. . . . It may well be that even declaratory relief would be inappropriate respecting many of the numerous issues involved if the Court held that the war were unconstitutional. I restrict this opinion to the question of the propriety of a declaratory judgment that no Massachusetts man can be taken against his will and made to serve in the war. . . .

Today we deny a hearing to a State which attempts to determine whether it is constitutional to require its citizens to fight in a foreign war absent a congressional declaration of war. Three years ago we refused to hear a case involving draftees who sought to prevent their shipment overseas. *Mora* v. *McNamara*, . . . cert. denied, 389 U. S. 934 (1967). The question of an unconstitutional war is neither academic nor "political." This case has raised the question in an adversary setting. It should be settled here and now.

I would set the motion for leave to file down for argument and decide the merits only after full argument.

Executive Power: Prerogatives and Limits

United States *v.* Curtiss-Wright Export Corp.

Beginning with George Washington's tenure, the President generally has been accorded rather broad latitude in the conduct of foreign affairs. The Chief Executive's power in this area derives from his role as Commander-in-Chief and his constitutional right to negotiate treaties. Furthermore, it has been recognized that the fluid, precipitative, sometimes secretive nature of diplomacy has required granting significant discretionary power to the President. In the first years of the republic, for example, Congress on several occasions provided for executive authority to suspend or impose embargoes on trade; in more recent times, however, congressional acquiescence has been less precise as in the Tonkin Gulf resolution of 1964 which authorized the President to use almost unlimited military power in Indochina. The following case in the 1930's arose out of attempts to sell weapons to Bolivia, then involved in the so-called Chaco War with Paraguay. The Curtiss-Wright Corporation had violated an executive order prohibiting such sales, an order issued under authority delegated to the President by a congressional resolution. Justice George Sutherland, who regularly opposed delegated executive power in domestic matters, spoke for the Court and sharply distinguished the practice in the conduct of foreign affairs. For the next three decades, the decision served as a basic legal rationale for presidential dominance and initiative in foreign policy-making.

Justice Sutherland delivered the opinion of the Court

First. It is contended that by the Joint Resolution, the going into effect and continued operation of the resolution was conditioned (a) upon the President's judgment as to its beneficial effect upon the reestablishment of peace between the countries engaged in armed conflict in the Chaco;

299 U.S. 304 (1936)

(b) upon the making of a proclamation, which was left to his unfettered discretion, thus constituting an attempted substitution of the President's will for that of Congress; (c) upon the making of a proclamation putting an end to the operation of the resolution, which again was left to the President's unfettered discretion; and (d) further, that the extent of its operation in particular cases was subject to limitation and exception by the President, controlled by no standard. In each of these particulars, appellees urge that Congress abdicated its essential functions and delegated them to the Executive.

Whether, if the Joint Resolution had related solely to internal affairs it would be open to the challenge that it constituted an unlawful delegation of legislative power to the Executive, we find it unnecessary to determine. The whole aim of the resolution is to affect a situation entirely external to the United States, and falling within the category of foreign affairs. The determination which we are called to make, therefore, is whether the Joint Resolution, as applied to that situation, is vulnerable to attack under the rule that forbids a delegation of the law-making power. In other words, assuming (but not deciding) that the challenged delegation, if it were confined to internal affairs, would be invalid, may it nevertheless be sustained on the ground that its exclusive aim is to afford a remedy for a hurtful condition within foreign territory?

It will contribute to the elucidation of the question if we first consider the differences between the powers of the federal government in respect of foreign or external affairs and those in respect of domestic or internal affairs. That there are differences between them, and that these differences are fundamental, may not be doubted.

The two classes of powers are different, both in respect of their origin and their nature. The broad statement that the federal government can exercise no powers except those specifically enumerated in the Constitution, and such implied powers as are necessary and proper to carry into effect the enumerated powers, is categorically true only in respect of our internal affairs. In that field, the primary purpose of the Constitution was to carve from the general mass of legislative powers *then possessed by the states* such portions as it was thought desirable to vest in the federal government, leaving those not included in the enumeration still in the States. *Carter* v. *Carter Coal Co.*, 298 U. S. 238, 294. That this doctrine applies only to powers which the states had, is self evident. And since the states severally never possessed international powers, such powers could not have been carved from the mass of state powers but obviously were transmitted to the United States from some other source. During the colonial period, those powers were possessed exclusively by and were entirely under the control of the Crown. By the Declaration of Independence, "the Representatives of the United States of America" declared the United (not the several) Colonies to be free and independent states, and as such to have "full Power to levy War, conclude Peace, contract Alliances, establish Commerce and to do all other Acts and Things which Independent States may of right do."

As a result of the separation from Great Britain by the colonies acting as a unit, the powers of external sovereignty passed from the Crown not to the colonies severally, but to the colonies in their collective and corporate capacity as the United States of America. Even before the Declaration, the colonies were a unit in foreign affairs, acting through a common agency—namely the Continental Congress, composed of delegates from the thirteen colonies. That agency exercised the powers of war and peace, raised an army, created a navy, and finally adopted the Declaration of Independence. Rulers come and go; governments end and forms of government change; but sovereignty survives. A political society cannot endure without a supreme will somewhere. Sovereignty is never held in suspense. When, therefore, the external sovereignty of Great Britain in respect of the colonies ceased, it immediately passed to the Union. . . .

It results that the investment of the federal government with the powers of external sovereignty did not depend upon the affirmative grants of the Constitution. The powers to declare and wage war, to conclude peace, to make treaties, to maintain diplomatic relations with other sovereignties, if they had never been mentioned in the Constitution, would have vested in the federal government as necessary concomitants of nationality. Neither the Constitution nor the laws passed in pursuance of it have any force in foreign territory unless in respect of our own citizens; and operations of the nation in such territory must be governed by treaties, international understandings and compacts, and the principles of international law. As a member of the family of nations, the right and power of the United States in that field are equal to the right and power of the other members of the international family. Otherwise, the United States is not completely sovereign. The power to acquire territory by discovery and occupation, the power to expel undesirable aliens, the power to make such international agreements as do not constitute treaties in the constitutional sense; none of which is expressly affirmed by the Constitution, nevertheless exist as inherently inseparable from the conception of nationality. This the court recognized, and in each of the cases cited found the warrant for its conclusions not in the provisions of the Constitution, but in the law of nations. . . .

Not only, as we have shown, is the federal power over external affairs in origin and essential character different from that over internal affairs, but participation in the exercise of the power is significantly limited. In this vast external realm, with its important, complicated, delicate and manifold problems, the President alone has the power to speak or listen as a representative of the nation. He *makes* treaties with the advice and consent of the Senate; but he alone negotiates. Into the field of negotiation the Senate cannot intrude; and Congress itself is powerless to invade it. . . .

It is important to bear in mind that we are here dealing not alone with an authority vested in the President by an exertion of legislative power, but with such an authority plus the very delicate, plenary and exclusive power of the President as the sole organ of the federal government in the field of international relations—a power which does not require as a basis for its exercise an act of Congress, but which, of course, like every other governmental power, must be exercised in subordination to the applicable provisions of the Constitution. It is quite apparent that if, in the maintenance of our international relations, embarrassment—perhaps serious embarrassment—is to be avoided and success for our aims achieved, congressional legislation which is to be made effective through negotiation and inquiry within the international field must often accord to the President a degree of discretion and freedom from statutory restriction which would not be admissible were domestic affairs alone involved. Moreover he, not Congress, has the better opportunity of knowing the conditions which prevail in foreign countries, and especially is this true in time of war. He has his confidential sources of information. He has his agents in the form of diplomatic, consular and other officials. Secrecy in respect of information gathered by them may be highly necessary, and the premature disclosure of it productive of harmful results. Indeed, so clearly is this true that the first President refused to accede to a request to lay before the House of Representatives the instructions, correspondence and documents relating to the negotiation of the Jay Treaty. . . .

In the light of the foregoing observations, it is evident that this court should not be in haste to apply a general rule which will have the effect of condemning legislation like that under review as constituting an unlawful delegation of legislative power. The principles which justify such legislation find overwhelming support in the unbroken legislative practice which has prevailed almost from the inception of the national government to the present day. . . .

The result of holding that the joint resolution here under attack is void and unenforceable as constituting an unlawful delegation of legislative power would be to stamp this multitude of comparable acts and resolutions as likewise invalid. And while this court may not, and should not, hesitate to declare acts of Congress, however many times repeated, to be unconstitutional if beyond all rational doubt it finds them to be so, an impressive array of legislation such as we have just set forth, enacted by nearly every Congress from the beginning of our national existence to the present day, must be given unusual weight in the process of reaching a correct determination of the problem. A legislative practice such as we have here, evidenced not by only occasional instances, but marked by the movement of a steady stream for a century and a half of time, goes a long way in the direction of proving the presence of unassailable ground for the constitutionality of the practice, to be found in the origin and history of the power involved, or in its nature or in both combined. . . .

The uniform, long-continued and undisputed legislative practice just disclosed rests upon an admissible view of the Constitution which, even if the practice found far less support in principle than we think it does, we should not feel at liberty at this late day to disturb. . . .

The judgment of the court below must be reversed and the cause remanded for further proceedings in accordance with the foregoing opinion.

Korematsu *v.* United States

*Unlike World War I, the war fought between 1941 and 1945 did
not create serious internal divisions within the United States. In
turn, there was a minimum of governmental repression of individuals or political groups. The notable exception, of course, involved the government's treatment of the Japanese-Americans. First-
generation Japanese immigrants were excluded from American
citizenship by law; their children and subsequent generations, however, automatically were citizens if born here, as provided for by the
opening words of the Fourteenth Amendment. After the outbreak
of war with Japan, civilian hysteria on the west coast, overreaction
by area military commanders, and, as recent scholarship has demonstrated, active, long-standing presidential enmity toward Japan and
Japanese-Americans, combined and resulted in the segregation, confinement, and ultimately, removal of Japanese-Americans to "relocation camps" further inland from the west coast. This action was
based specifically on Executive Order No. 9066, issued by President
Roosevelt on February 19, 1942. As a result, families were suddenly
uprooted, with little regard shown for property or civil rights. The
case below tested the validity of the exclusion orders and involved
a citizen. The Court divided 6-3 in favor of the government. The
division represented a classic conflict between those who chose to
defer to executive authority in time of crisis and those who insisted
on the maintenance of civil rights for all citizens at all times, as
Justice Murphy stated in dissent. In 1976, President Ford rescinded
the 1942 executive order, with appropriate apologies to the
Japanese; nevertheless, that act alone does not necessarily insure
against a repetition of such executive authority. It is noteworthy
that in an interview shortly before his death, Justice Black maintained that both the President and the Court had been right in their
wartime actions.*

Justice Black delivered the opinion of the Court.

The petitioner, an American citizen of Japanese descent, was convicted in a federal district court for remaining in San Leandro,
California, a "Military Area," contrary to Civilian Exclusion Order No.
34 of the Commanding General of the Western Command, U.S. Army,
which directed that after May 9, 1942, all persons of Japanese ancestry

---

323 U.S. 214 (1944)

should be excluded from that area. No question was raised as to petitioner's loyalty to the United States. . . .

It should be noted, to begin with, that all legal restrictions which curtail the civil rights of a single racial group are immediately suspect. That is not to say that all such restrictions are unconstitutional. It is to say that courts must subject them to the most rigid scrutiny. Pressing public necessity may sometimes justify the existence of such restrictions; racial antagonism never can. . . .

[E]xclusion of those of Japanese origin was deemed necessary because of the presence of an unascertained number of disloyal members of the group, most of whom we have no doubt were loyal to this country. It was because we could not reject the finding of the military authorities that it was impossible to bring about an immediate segregation of the disloyal from the loyal that we sustained the validity of the curfew order as applying to the whole group. In the instant case, temporary exclusion of the entire group was rested by the military on the same ground. The judgment that exclusion of the whole group was for the same reason a military imperative answers the contention that the exclusion was in the nature of group punishment based on antagonism to those of Japanese origin. That there were members of the group who retained loyalties in Japan has been confirmed by investigations made subsequent to the exclusion. Approximately five thousand American citizens of Japanese ancestry refused to swear unqualified allegiance to the United States and to renounce allegiance to the Japanese Emperor, and several thousand evacuees requested repatriation to Japan.

We uphold the exclusion order as of the time it was made and when the petitioner violated it. . . . In doing so, we are not unmindful of the hardships imposed by it upon a large group of American citizens. . . . But hardships are part of war, and war is an aggregation of hardships. All citizens alike, both in and out of uniform, feel the impact of war in greater or lesser measure. Citizenship has its responsibilities as well as its privileges, and in time of war the burden is always heavier. Compulsory exclusion of large groups of citizens from their homes, except under circumstances of direst emergency and peril, is inconsistent with our basic governmental institutions. But when under conditions of modern warfare our shores are threatened by hostile forces, the power to protect must be commensurate with the threatened danger. . . .

It is said that we are dealing here with the case of imprisonment of a citizen in a concentration camp solely because of his ancestry, without evidence or inquiry concerning his loyalty and good disposition towards the United States. Our task would be simple, our duty clear, were this a case involving the imprisonment of a loyal citizen in a concentration camp because of racial prejudice. Regardless of the true nature of the assembly and relocation centers — and we deem it unjustifiable to call them concentration camps with all the ugly connotations that term implies — we are dealing specifically with nothing but an exclusion order. To cast this case into outlines of racial prejudice, without reference to the real military dangers which were presented, merely confuses the issue. Korematsu was not excluded from the Military Area because of hostility to him or his race. He *was* excluded because we are at war with the Japanese Empire, because the properly constituted military authorities feared an invasion of our West Coast and felt constrained to take proper security measures, because they decided that the military urgency of the situation demanded that all citizens of Japanese ancestry be segregated from the West Coast temporarily, and finally, because Congress, reposing its confidence in this time of war in our military leaders — as inevitably it must — determined that they should have the power to do just this. There was evidence of disloyalty on the part of some, the military authorities considered that the need for action was great, and time was short. We cannot — by availing ourselves of the calm perspective of hindsight — now say that at that time these actions were unjustified.

Justice Murphy, dissenting.

This exclusion of "all persons of Japanese ancestry, both alien and non-alien," from the Pacific Coast area on a plea of military necessity in the absence of martial law ought not to be approved. Such exclusion goes over "the very brink of constitutional power" and falls into the ugly abyss of racism.

In dealing with matters relating to the prosecution and progress of a war, we must accord great respect and consideration to the judgments of the military authorities who are on the scene and who have full knowledge of the military facts. The scope of their discretion must, as a matter of necessity and common sense, be wide. And their judgments ought not to be overruled lightly by those whose training and duties ill-equip them to deal intelligently with matters so vital to the physical security of the nation.

At the same time, however, it is essential that there be definite limits to military discretion, especially where martial law has not been declared. Individuals must not be left impoverished of their constitutional rights on a plea of military necessity that has neither substance nor support. . . .

The judicial test of whether the Government, on a plea of military necessity, can validly deprive an individual of any of his constitutional rights is whether the deprivation is reasonably related to a public danger that is so "immediate, imminent, and impending" as not to admit of delay and not to permit the intervention of ordinary constitutional processes to alleviate the danger. . . . Civilian Exclusion Order No. 34, banishing from a prescribed area of the Pacific Coast "all persons of Japanese ancestry, both alien and non-alien," clearly does not meet that test. Being an obvious racial discrimination, the order deprives all those within its scope of the equal protection of the laws as guaranteed by the Fifth Amendment. It further deprives these individuals of their constitutional rights to live and work where they will, to establish a home where they choose and to move about freely. In excommunicating them without benefit of hearings, this order also deprives them of all their constitutional rights to procedural due process. Yet no reasonable relation to an "immediate, imminent, and impending" public danger is evident to support this racial restriction which is one of the most sweeping and complete deprivations of constitutional rights in the history of this nation in the absence of martial law.

It must be conceded that the military and naval situation in the spring of 1942 was such as to generate a very real fear of invasion of the Pacific Coast, accompanied by fears of sabotage and espionage in that area. The military command was therefore justified in adopting all reasonable means necessary to combat these dangers. In adjudging the military action taken in light of the then apparent dangers, we must not erect too high or too meticulous standards; it is necessary only that the action have some reasonable relation to the removal of the dangers of invasion, sabotage and espionage. But the exclusion, either temporarily or permanently, of all persons with Japanese blood in their veins has no such reasonable relation. And that relation is lacking because the exclusion order necessarily must rely for its reasonableness upon the assumption that *all* persons of Japanese ancestry may have a dangerous tendency to commit sabotage and espionage and to aid our Japanese enemy in other ways. It is difficult to believe that reason, logic or experience could be marshalled in support of such an assumption.

That this forced exclusion was the result in good measure of this erroneous assumption of racial guilt rather than bona fide military necessity is evidenced by the Commanding General's Final Report on the evacuation from the Pacific Coast area. In it he refers to all individuals of Japanese descent as "subversive," as belonging to "an enemy race" whose "racial strains are undiluted," and as constituting "over 112,000 potential enemies . . . at large today" along the Pacific Coast. In support of this blanket condemnation of all persons of Japanese descent, however, no reliable evidence is cited to show that such individuals were generally disloyal, or had generally so conducted themselves in this area as to constitute a special menace to defense installations or war industries, or had otherwise by their behavior furnished reasonable ground for their exclusion as a group.

Justification for the exclusion is sought, instead, mainly upon questionable racial and sociological grounds not ordinarily within the realm of expert military judgment, supplemented by certain semi-military conclusions drawn from an unwarranted use of circumstantial evidence. . . .

No one denies, of course, that there were some disloyal persons of Japanese descent on the Pacific Coast who did all in their power to aid their ancestral land. Similar disloyal activities have been engaged in by many persons of German, Italian and even more pioneer stock in our country. But to infer that examples of individual disloyalty prove group disloyalty and justify discriminatory action against the entire group is to deny that under our system of law individual guilt is the sole basis for deprivation of rights. . . . To give constitutional sanction to that inference in this case, however well-intentioned may have been the military command on the Pacific Coast, is to adopt one of the cruelest of the rationales used by our enemies to destroy the dignity of the individual and to encourage and open the door to discriminatory actions against other minority groups in the passions of tomorrow.

No adequate reason is given for the failure to treat these Japanese Americans on an individual basis by holding investigations and hearings to separate the loyal from the disloyal, as was done in the case of persons of German and Italian ancestry. . . . It is asserted merely that the loyalties of this group "were unknown and time was of the essence." Yet nearly four months elapsed after Pearl Harbor before the first exclusion order was issued. . . .

Moreover, there was no adequate proof that the Federal Bureau of Investigation and the military and naval intelligence services did not have the espionage and sabotage situation well in hand during this long period. Nor is there any denial of the fact that not one person of Japanese ancestry was accused or convicted of espionage or sabotage after Pearl Harbor while they were still free. . . .

I dissent, therefore, from this legalization of racism. Racial discrimination in any form and in any degree has no justifiable part whatever in our democratic way of life. It is unattractive in any setting but it is utterly revolting among a free people who have embraced the principles set forth in the Constitution of the United States. All residents of this nation are kin in some way by blood or culture to a foreign land. Yet they are primarily and necessarily a part of the new and distinct civilization of the United States. They must accordingly be treated at all times as the heirs of the American experiment and as entitled to all the rights and freedoms guaranteed by the Constitution.

Youngstown Sheet & Tube Co. *v.* Sawyer

*This case resulted from the steel strike during the Korean War.
Failing to secure agreement from management and labor, the Truman Administration seized the steel plants and operated them pending a settlement of the labor dispute. The President justified his
action on the basis of his "inherent" executive powers and his powers
as commander-in-chief of the armed forces. A 6–3 majority of the
Court, however, rejected the Administration's views. But the decision was only a limited victory for "free enterprise" as the majority
agreed that Congress could authorize seizure. Led by Chief Justice
Vinson, the dissenters advocated a broad view of executive powers,
curiously similar to the spirit of the* Debs *case of 1895.*

Justice Black delivered the opinion of the Court.

We are asked to decide whether the President was acting within his
constitutional power when he issued an order directing the Secretary of Commerce to take possession of and operate most of the Nation's
steel mills. The mill owners argue that the President's order amounts to
lawmaking, a legislative function which the Constitution has expressly
confided to the Congress and not to the President. The Government's
position is that the order was made on findings of the President that his
action was necessary to avert a national catastrophe which would inevitably result from a stoppage of steel production, and that in meeting
this grave emergency the President was acting within the aggregate of
his constitutional powers as the Nation's Chief Executive and the Commander in Chief of the Armed Forces of the United States. . . .

The President's power, if any, to issue the order must stem either from
an act of Congress or from the Constitution itself. There is no statute
that expressly authorizes the President to take possession of property as
he did here. Nor is there any act of Congress to which our attention has
been directed from which such a power can fairly be implied. Indeed, we
do not understand the Government to rely on statutory authorization for
this seizure. . . .

Moreover, the use of the seizure technique to solve labor disputes in
order to prevent work stoppages was not only unauthorized by any congressional enactment; prior to this controversy, Congress had refused to

343 U.S. 579 (1952)

adopt that method of settling labor disputes. When the Taft-Hartley Act was under consideration in 1947, Congress rejected an amendment which would have authorized such governmental seizures in cases of emergency. Apparently it was thought that the technique of seizure, like that of compulsory arbitration, would interfere with the process of collective bargaining. Consequently, the plan Congress adopted in that Act did not provide for seizure under any circumstances. . . .

It is clear that if the President had authority to issue the order he did, it must be found in some provision of the Constitution. And it is not claimed that express constitutional language grants this power to the President. The contention is that presidential power should be implied from the aggregate of his powers under the Constitution. Particular reliance is placed on provisions in Article II which say that "The executive Power shall be vested in a President . . ."; that "he shall take Care that the Laws be faithfully executed"; and that he "shall be Commander in Chief of the Army and Navy of the United States."

The order cannot properly be sustained as an exercise of the President's military power as Commander in Chief of the Armed Forces. The Government attempts to do so by citing a number of cases upholding broad powers in military commanders engaged in day-to-day fighting in a theater of war. Such cases need not concern us here. Even though "theater of war" be an expanding concept, we cannot with faithfulness to our constitutional system hold that the Commander in Chief of the Armed Forces has the ultimate power as such to take possession of private property in order to keep labor disputes from stopping production. This is a job for the Nation's lawmakers, not for its military authorities.

Nor can the seizure order be sustained because of the several constitutional provisions that grant executive power to the President. In the framework of our Constitution, the President's power to see that the laws are faithfully executed refutes the idea that he is to be a lawmaker. The Constitution limits his functions in the lawmaking process to the recommending of laws he thinks wise and the vetoing of laws he thinks bad. And the Constitution is neither silent or equivocal about who shall make laws which the President is to execute. . . .

It is said that other Presidents without congressional authority have taken possession of private business enterprises in order to settle labor disputes. But even if this be true, Congress has not thereby lost its exclusive constitutional authority to make laws necessary and proper to carry out the powers vested by the Constitution "in the Government of the United States, or any Department or Officer thereof."

The Founders of this Nation entrusted the lawmaking power to the Congress alone in both good and bad times. It would do no good to recall the historical events, the fears of power and the hopes for freedom that lay behind their choice. Such a review would but confirm our holding that this seizure order cannot stand. . . .

Chief Justice Vinson, with whom Justice Reed and Justice Minton join, dissenting. . . .

One is not here called upon even to consider the possibility of executive seizure of a farm, a corner grocery store or even a single industrial plant. Such considerations arise only when one ignores the central fact of this case — that the Nation's entire basic steel production would have shut down completely if there had been no Government seizure. Even ignoring for the moment whatever confidential information the President may possess as "the Nation's organ for foreign affairs," the uncontroverted affidavits in this record amply support the finding that "a work stoppage would immediately jeopardize and imperil our national defense." . . . Plaintiffs' counsel tells us that "sooner or later" the mills will operate again. That may satisfy the steel companies and, perhaps, the Union. But our soldiers and our allies will hardly be cheered with the assurance that the ammunition upon which their lives depend will be forthcoming — "sooner or later," or, in other words, "too little and too late." . . .

The absence of a specific statute authorizing seizure of the steel mills as a mode of executing the laws — both the military procurement program and the anti-inflation program — has not until today been thought to prevent the President from executing the laws. Unlike an administrative commission confined to the enforcement of the statute under which it was created, or the head of a department when administering a particular statute, the President is a constitutional officer charged with taking care that a "mass of legislation" be executed. Flexibility as to mode of execution to meet critical situations is a matter of practical necessity. . . .

There is no statute prohibiting seizure as a method of enforcing legislative programs. Congress has in no wise indicated that its legislation is not to be executed by the taking of private property (subject of course to the payment of just compensation) if its legislation cannot otherwise be executed. . . .

Whatever the extent of Presidential power on more tranquil occasions, and whatever the right of the President to execute legislative programs as he sees fit without reporting the mode of execution to Congress, the single Presidential purpose disclosed on this record is to faithfully execute the laws by acting in an emergency to maintain the status quo, thereby preventing collapse of the legislative programs until Congress could act. The President's action served the same purposes as a judicial stay entered to maintain the status quo in order to preserve the jurisdiction of a court.

In his Message to Congress immediately following the seizure, the President explained the necessity of his action in executing the military procurement and anti-inflation legislative programs and expressed his desire to cooperate with any legislative proposals approving, regulating or rejecting the seizure of the steel mills. Consequently, there is no evidence whatever of any Presidential purpose to defy Congress or act in any way inconsistent with the legislative will. . . .

United States *v.* United States District Court for the Eastern District of Michigan

The domestic political discord and a soaring crime rate produced the Omnibus Crime Control and Safe Streets Act of 1968, a provision of which authorized court-approved electronic surveillance for specified crimes. Congress also added a proviso to the effect that "nothing contained in this chapter . . . shall limit the constitutional power of the President to take such measures as he deems necessary to protect the United States against the overthrow of the Government . . ." (18 U.S.C. Sec. 2511[3]). The Nixon Administration used Section 2511 to institute widespread electronic surveillance against domestic political activists. The case below involved defendants charged with bombing a CIA office in Ann Arbor, Michigan. Prior to the trial, the defendants asked the District Court to compel the government to produce any information derived from wiretaps and electronic surveillance. Attorney General John Mitchell acknowledged that such information existed but argued that disclosure "would prejudice the national interest." The District Court nevertheless ruled that the surveillance violated the Fourth Amendment and directed the government to disclose the results to the defendants. On appeal to the Supreme Court, the government argued that such surveillance was a lawful, reasonable exercise of presidential power, despite the lack of prior judicial approval.

Justice Powell delivered the opinion of the Court.

We think the language of § 2511 (3), as well as the legislative history of the statute, refutes this interpretation. The relevant language is that:

"Nothing contained in this chapter . . . shall limit the constitutional power of the President to take such measures as he deems necessary to protect . . ."

against the dangers specified. At most, this is an implicit recognition that the President does have certain powers in the specified areas. Few would doubt this, as the section refers—among other things—to protection

407 U.S. 297 (1972)

"against actual or potential attack or other hostile acts of a foreign power." But so far as the use of the President's electronic surveillance power is concerned, the language is essentially neutral.

Section 2511 (3) certainly confers no power, as the language is wholly inappropriate for such a purpose. It merely provides that the Act shall not be interpreted to limit or disturb such power as the President may have under the Constitution. In short, Congress simply left presidential powers where it found them. . . .

One could hardly expect a clearer expression of congressional neutrality. The debate above explicitly indicates that nothing in § 2511 (3) was intended to *expand* or to *contract* or to *define* whatever presidential surveillance powers existed in matters affecting the national security. If we could accept the Government's characterization of § 2511 (3) as a congressionally prescribed exception to the general requirement of a warrant, it would be necessary to consider the question of whether the surveillance in this case came within the exception and, if so, whether the statutory exception was itself constitutionally valid. But viewing § 2511 (3) as a congressional disclaimer and expression of neutrality, we hold that the statute is not the measure of the executive authority asserted in this case. Rather, we must look to the constitutional powers of the President. . . .

We begin the inquiry by noting that the President of the United States has the fundamental duty, under Art. II, § 1, of the Constitution, to "preserve, protect and defend the Constitution of the United States." Implicit in that duty is the power to protect our Government against those who would subvert or overthrow it by unlawful means. In the discharge of this duty, the President—through the Attorney General—may find it necessary to employ electronic surveillance to obtain intelligence information on the plans of those who plot unlawful acts against the Government. The use of such surveillance in internal security cases has been sanctioned more or less continuously by various Presidents and Attorneys General since July 1946. . . .

Though the Government and respondents debate their seriousness and magnitude, threats and acts of sabotage against the Government exist in sufficient number to justify investigative powers with respect to them. The covertness and complexity of potential unlawful conduct against the Government and the necessary dependency of many conspirators upon the telephone make electronic surveillance an effective investigatory instrument in certain circumstances. The marked acceleration in technological developments and sophistication in their use have resulted in new techniques for the planning, commission, and concealment of criminal activities. It would be contrary to the public interest for Government to deny to itself the prudent and lawful employment of those very techniques which are employed against the Government and its law-abiding citizens. . . .

But a recognition of these elementary truths does not make the employment by Government of electronic surveillance a welcome development—even when employed with restraint and other judicial supervision. There is, understandably, a deep-seated uneasiness and apprehension that this capability will be used to intrude upon cherished privacy of law-abiding citizens. We look to the Bill of Rights to safeguard this privacy. Though physical entry of the home is the chief evil against which the wording of the Fourth Amendment is directed, its broader spirit now shields private speech from unreasonable surveillance. . . .

National security cases, moreover, often reflect a convergence of First and Fourth Amendment values not present in cases of "ordinary" crime. Though the investigative duty of the executive may be stronger in such cases, so also is there greater jeopardy to constitutionally protected speech. "Historically the struggle for freedom of speech and press in England was bound up with the issue of the scope of the search and seizure power," *Marcus* v. *Search Warrant*, 367 U. S. 717, 724 (1961). History abundantly documents the tendency of Government—however benevolent and benign its motives—to view with suspicion those who most fervently dispute its policies. Fourth Amendment protections become the more necessary when the targets of official surveillance may be those suspected of unorthodoxy in their political beliefs. The danger to political dissent is acute where the Government attempts to act under so vague a concept as the power to protect "domestic security." Given the difficulty of defining the domestic security interest, the danger of abuse in acting to protect that interest becomes apparent. . . . The price of lawful public dissent must not be a dread of subjection to an unchecked surveillance power. Nor must the fear of unauthorized official eavesdropping deter vigorous citizen dissent and discussion of Government action in private conversation. For private dissent, no less than open public discourse, is essential to our free society.

As the Fourth Amendment is not absolute in its terms, our task is to examine and balance the basic values at stake in this case: the duty of Government to protect the domestic security, and the potential danger posed by unreasonable surveillance to individual privacy and free expression. If the legitimate need of Government to safeguard domestic security requires the use of electronic surveillance, the question is whether the needs of citizens for privacy and free expression may not be better protected by requiring a warrant before such surveillance is undertaken. We must also ask whether a warrant requirement would unduly frustrate the efforts of Government to protect itself from acts of subversion and overthrow directed against it. . . .

. . . Fourth Amendment freedoms cannot properly be guaranteed if domestic security surveillances may be conducted solely within the discretion of the Executive Branch. The Fourth Amendment does not contemplate the executive officers of Government as neutral and disinterested magistrates. Their duty and responsibility are to enforce the laws, to investigate, and to prosecute. . . . But those charged with this investigative and prosecutorial duty shall not be the sole judges of when to utilize constitutionally sensitive means in pursuing their tasks. The historical judgment, which the Fourth Amendment accepts, is that unreviewed executive discretion may yield too readily to pressures to obtain incriminating evidence and overlook potential invasions of privacy and protected speech.

It may well be that, in the instant case, the Government's surveillance of Plamondon's conversations was a reasonable one which readily would have gained prior judicial approval. But . . . the Fourth Amendment contemplates a prior judicial judgment, not the risk that executive discretion may be reasonably exercised. This judicial role accords with our basic constitutional doctrine that individual freedoms will best be preserved through a separation of powers and division of functions among the different branches and levels of Government. . . . The independent check upon executive discretion is not satisfied, as the Government argues, by "extremely limited" post-surveillance judicial review. Indeed, post-surveillance review would never reach the surveillances which failed to result in prosecutions. Prior review by a neutral and detached magistrate is the time-tested means of effectuating Fourth Amendment rights. . . .

The Government argues that the special circumstances applicable to domestic security surveillances necessitate a further exception to the warrant requirement. It is urged that the requirement of prior judicial review would obstruct the President in the discharge of his constitutional duty to protect domestic security. We are told further that these surveillances are directed primarily to the collecting and maintaining of intelligence with respect to subversive forces, and are not an attempt to gather evidence for specific criminal prosecutions. It is said that this type of surveillance should not be subject to traditional warrant requirements which were established to govern investigation of criminal activity, not ongoing intelligence gathering. . . .

The Government further insists that courts "as a practical matter would have neither the knowledge nor the techniques necessary to determine whether there was probable cause to believe that surveillance was necessary to protect national security." These security problems, the Government contends, involve "a large number of complex and subtle factors" beyond the competence of courts to evaulate. . . .

As a final reason for exemption from a warrant requirement, the Government believes that disclosure to a magistrate of all or even a significant portion of the information involved in domestic security surveillances "would create serious potential dangers to the national security and to the lives of informants and agents. . . . Secrecy is the essential ingredient in intelligence gathering; requiring prior judicial authorization would create a greater 'danger of leaks . . . , because in addition to the judge, you have the clerk, the stenographer and some other officer like a law assistant or bailiff who may be apprised of the nature' of the surveillance." . . .

These contentions in behalf of a complete exemption from the warrant requirement, when urged on behalf of the President and the national security in its domestic implications, merit the most careful consideration. We certainly do not reject them lightly, especially at a time of worldwide ferment and when civil disorders in this country are more prevalent than in the less turbulent periods of our history. There is, no doubt, pragmatic force to the Government's position.

But we do not think a case has been made for the requested departure from Fourth Amendment standards. The circumstances described do not justify complete exemption of domestic security surveillance from prior judicial scrutiny. Official surveillance, whether its purpose be criminal investigation or ongoing intelligence gathering, risks infringement of constitutionally protected privacy of speech. Security surveillances are especially sensitive because of the inherent vagueness of the domestic security concept, the necessarily broad and continuing nature of intelligence gathering, and the temptation to utilize such surveillances to oversee political dissent. We recognize, as we have before, the constitutional basis of the President's domestic security role, but we think it must be exercised in a manner compatible with the Fourth Amendment. In this case we hold that this requires an appropriate prior warrant procedure.

We cannot accept the Government's argument that internal security matters are too subtle and complex for judicial evaluation. Courts regularly deal with the most difficult issues of our society. There is no reason to believe that federal judges will be insensitive to or uncomprehending of the issues involved in domestic security cases. Certainly courts can recognize that domestic security surveillance involves different considerations from the surveillance of "ordinary crime." If the threat is too subtle or complex for our senior law enforcement officers to convey its significance to a court, one may question whether there is probable cause for surveillance.

Nor do we believe prior judicial approval will fracture the secrecy essential to official intelligence gathering. The investigation of criminal activity has long involved imparting sensitive information to judicial officers who have respected the confidentialities involved. Judges may be counted upon to be especially conscious of security requirements in national security cases. Title III of the Omnibus Crime Control and Safe Streets Act already has imposed this responsibility on the judiciary in connection with such crimes as espionage, sabotage, and treason, §§ 2516 (1)(a) and (c), each of which may involve domestic as well as foreign security threats. Moreover, a warrant application involves no public or adversary proceedings: it is an *ex parte* request before a magistrate or judge. Whatever security dangers clerical and secretarial personnel may pose can be minimized by proper administrative measures, possibly to the point of allowing the Government itself to provide the necessary clerical assistance.

Thus, we conclude that the Government's concerns do not justify departure in this case from the customary Fourth Amendment requirement of judicial approval prior to initiation of a search or surveillance. Although some added burden will be imposed upon the Attorney General, this inconvenience is justified in a free society to protect constitutional values. Nor do we think the Government's domestic surveillance powers will be impaired to any significant degree. A prior warrant establishes presumptive validity of the surveillance and will minimize the burden of justification in post-surveillance judicial review. By no means of least importance will be the reassurance of the public generally that indiscriminate wiretapping and bugging of law-abiding citizens cannot occur.

We emphasize, before concluding this opinion, the scope of our decision. As stated at the outset, this case involves only the domestic aspects of national security. We have not addressed, and express no opinion as to, the issues which may be involved with respect to activities of foreign powers or their agents. . . .

United States *v.* Nixon

*This case played a decisive role in the events leading to President
Richard Nixon's resignation in August 1974. As the complex strands
of the Watergate conspiracy unraveled in 1973 and 1974, it soon
became evident that public disclosure of the private presidential
tape recordings was necessary for the process of criminal prosecution of the President's associates—and for a determination of the
President's culpability. The Special Prosecutor, appointed by Nixon
to investigate the affair, secured a subpoena in the District Court
directing Nixon to produce the tapes. The President refused, contending that the Special Prosecutor was an executive subordinate,
with no standing to seek an order. He further maintained that the
tapes could be withheld on the grounds of executive privilege. The
Supreme Court unanimously rejected the President's arguments, yet
acknowledged some legitimacy to the then hotly-disputed doctrine
of executive privilege. After some apparent hesitation, the President
complied with the Court's order. The subsequent tape disclosures
contributed significantly to the almost total erosion of both public
and congressional support for Nixon.*

Chief Justice Burger delivered the opinion of the Court.

On March 1, 1974, a grand jury of the United States District Court for
the District of Columbia returned an indictment charging seven
named individuals with various offenses, including conspiracy to defraud
the United States and to obstruct justice. Although he was not designated
as such in the indictment, the grand jury named the President, among
others, as an unindicted co-conspirator. On April 18, 1974, upon motion of
the Special Prosecutor, . . . a subpoena *duces tecum* was issued pursuant
to Rule 17 (c) to the President by the United States District Court and
made returnable on May 2, 1974. This subpoena required the production,
in advance of the September 9 trial date, of certain tapes, memoranda,
papers, transcripts, or other writings relating to certain precisely identified meetings between the President and others. . . .

The District Court held that the judiciary, not the President, was the
final arbiter of a claim of executive privilege. The court concluded that,
under the circumstances of this case, the presumptive privilege was overcome by the Special Prosecutor's prima facie "demonstration of need sufficiently compelling to warrant judicial examination in chambers. . . ." . . .

---

418 U.S. 683 (1974)

JUSTICIABILITY

In the District Court, the President's counsel argued that the court lacked jurisdiction to issue the subpoena because the matter was an intra-branch dispute between a subordinate and superior officer of the Executive Branch and hence not subject to judicial resolution. That argument has been renewed in this Court with emphasis on the contention that the dispute does not present a "case" or "controversy" which can be adjudicated in the federal courts. The President's counsel argues that the federal courts should not intrude into areas committed to the other branches of Government. He views the present dispute as essentially a "jurisdictional" dispute within the Executive Branch which he analogizes to a dispute between two congressional committees. Since the Executive Branch has exclusive authority and absolute discretion to decide whether to prosecute a case, . . . it is contended that a President's decision is final in determining what evidence is to be used in a given criminal case. Although his counsel concedes that the President has delegated certain specific powers to the Special Prosecutor, he has not "waived nor delegated to the Special Prosecutor the President's duty to claim privilege as to all materials . . . which fall within the President's inherent authority to refuse to disclose to any executive officer." . . .

Our starting point is the nature of the proceeding for which the evidence is sought—here a pending criminal prosecution. It is a judicial proceeding in a federal court alleging violation of federal laws and is brought in the name of the United States as sovereign. . . . Under the authority of Art. II, § 2, Congress has vested in the Attorney General the power to conduct the criminal litigation of the United States Government. . . . It has also vested in him the power to appoint subordinate officers to assist him in the discharge of his duties. . . . Acting pursuant to those statutes, the Attorney General has delegated the authority to represent the United States in these particular matters to a Special Prosecutor with unique authority and tenure. The regulation gives the Special Prosecutor explicit power to contest the invocation of executive privilege in the process of seeking evidence deemed relevant to the performance of these specially delegated duties. . . .

The demands of and the resistance to the subpoena present an obvious controversy in the ordinary sense, but that alone is not sufficient to meet constitutional standards. In the constitutional sense, controversy means more than disagreement and conflict; rather it means the kind of controversy courts traditionally resolve. Here at issue is the production or nonproduction of specified evidence deemed by the Special Prosecutor to be relevant and admissible in a pending criminal case. It is sought by one official of the Executive Branch within the scope of his express authority; it is resisted by the Chief Executive on the ground of his duty to preserve the confidentiality of the communications of the President. Whatever the correct answer on the merits, these issues are "of a type which are traditionally justiciable." *United States* v. *ICC*, 337 U. S., at 430. The independent Special Prosecutor with his asserted need for the subpoenaed material in the underlying criminal prosecution is opposed by the President with his steadfast assertion of privilege against disclosure of the material. This setting assures there is "that concrete adverseness which sharpens the presentation of issues upon which the court so largely depends for illumination of difficult constitutional questions." *Baker* v. *Carr*, 369 U. S., at 204. Moreover, since the matter is one arising in the regular course of a federal criminal prosecution, it is within the traditional scope of Art. III power. *Id.* at 198.

In light of the uniqueness of the setting in which the conflict arises, the fact that both parties are officers of the Executive Branch cannot be viewed as a barrier to justiciability. It would be inconsistent with the applicable law and regulation, and the unique facts of this case to conclude other than that the Special Prosecutor has standing to bring this action and that a justiciable controversy is presented for decision. . . .

THE CLAIM OF PRIVILEGE

A

. . . [W]e turn to the claim that the subpoena should be quashed because it demands "confidential conversations between a President and his close advisors that it would be inconsistent with the public interest to produce." . . . The first contention is a broad claim that the separation of powers doctrine precludes judicial review of a President's claim of privilege. The second contention is that if he does not prevail on the claim of absolute privilege, the court should hold as a matter of constitutional law that the privilege prevails over the subpoena *duces tecum.*

In the performance of assigned constitutional duties each branch of the Government must initially interpret the Constitution, and the interpretation of its powers by any branch is due great respect from the others. The President's counsel, as we have noted, reads the Constitution as providing an absolute privilege of confidentiality for all Presidential communications. Many decisions of this Court, however, have unequivocally reaffirmed the holding of *Marbury* v. *Madison*, 1 Cranch 137 (1803), that "[i]t is emphatically the province and duty of the judicial department to say what the law is." *Id.*, at 177.

No holding of the Court has defined the scope of judicial power specifically relating to the enforcement of a subpoena for confidential Presidential communications for use in a criminal prosecution, but other exercises of power by the Executive Branch and the Legislative Branch have been found invalid as in conflict with the Constitution. *Powell* v. *McCormack*, 395 U. S. 486 (1969); *Youngstown Sheet & Tube Co.* v. *Sawyer*, 343 U. S. 579 (1952). . . .

B

In support of his claim of absolute privilege, the President's counsel urges two grounds, one of which is peculiar to our system of separation of powers. The first ground is the valid need for protection of communications between high Government officials and those who advise and assist them in the performance of their manifold duties; the importance of this confidentiality is too plain to require further discussion. Human experience teaches that those who expect public dissemination of their remarks may well temper candor with a concern for appearances and for their own interests to the detriment of the decisionmaking process. Whatever the nature of the privilege of confidentiality of Presidential communications in the exercise of Art. II powers, the privilege can be said to derive from the supremacy of each branch within its own assigned area of constitutional duties. Certain powers and privileges flow from the nature of enumerated powers; the protection of the confidentiality of Presidential communications has similar constitutional underpinnings.

The second ground asserted by the President's counsel in support of the claim of absolute privilege rests on the doctrine of separation of powers. Here it is argued that the independence of the Executive Branch within its own sphere . . . insulates a President from a judicial subpoena in an ongoing criminal prosecution, and thereby protects confidential Presidential communications.

However, neither the doctrine of separation of powers, nor the need for confidentiality of high-level communications, without more, can sustain an absolute, unqualified Presidential privilege of immunity from judicial process under all circumstances. The President's need for complete candor and objectivity from advisers calls for great deference from the courts. However, when the privilege depends solely on the broad, undifferentiated claim of public interest in the confidentiality of such conversations, a confrontation with other values arises. Absent a claim of need to protect military, diplomatic, or sensitive national security secrets, we find it difficult to accept the argument that even the very important interest in confidentiality of Presidential communications is significantly diminished by production of such material for *in camera* inspection with all the protection that a district court will be obliged to provide.

The impediment that an absolute, unqualified privilege would place in the way of the primary constitutional duty of the Judicial Branch to do justice in criminal prosecutions would plainly conflict with the function of the courts under Art. III. In designing the structure of our Government and dividing and allocating the sovereign power among three co-equal branches, the Framers of the Constitution sought to provide a comprehensive system, but the separate powers were not intended to operate with absolute independence. . . .

C

. . . The expectation of a President to the confidentiality of his conversations and correspondence, like the claim of confidentiality of judicial deliberations, for example, has all the values to which we accord deference for the privacy of all citizens and, added to those values, is the necessity for protection of the public interest in candid, objective, and even blunt or harsh opinions in Presidential decision-making. A President and those who assist him must be free to explore alternatives in the process of shaping policies and making decisions and to do so in a way many would be unwilling to express except privately. These are the considerations justifying a presumptive privilege for Presidential communications. The privilege is fundamental to the operation of Government and inextricably rooted in the separation of powers under the Constitution. In *Nixon* v. *Sirica*, 159 U. S. App. D. C. 58, 487 F. 2d 700 (1973), the Court of Appeals held that such Presidential communications are "presumptively privileged." . . .

But this presumptive privilege must be considered in light of our historic commitment to the rule of law. . . . We have elected to employ an adversary system of criminal justice in which the parties contest all issues before a court of law. The need to develop all relevant facts in the adversary system is both fundamental and comprehensive. The ends of criminal justice would be defeated if judgments were to be founded on a partial or speculative presentation of the facts. The very integrity of the judicial system and public confidence in the system depend on full disclosure of all the facts, within the framework of the rules of evidence. To ensure that justice is done, it is imperative to the function of courts that compulsory process be available for the production of evidence needed either by the prosecution or by the defense. . . .

In this case we must weigh the importance of the general privilege of confidentiality of Presidential communications in performance of the President's responsibilities against the inroads of such a privilege on the fair administration of criminal justice. The interest in preserving confidentiality is weighty indeed and entitled to great respect. However, we cannot conclude that advisers will be moved to temper the candor of their remarks by the infrequent occasions of disclosure because of the possibility that such conversations will be called for in the context of a criminal prosecution.

On the other hand, the allowance of the privilege to withhold evidence that is demonstrably relevant in a criminal trial would cut deeply into the guarantee of due process of law and gravely impair the basic function of the courts. A President's acknowledged need for confidentiality in the communications of his office is general in nature, whereas the constitutional need for production of relevant evidence in a criminal proceeding is specific and central to the fair adjudication of a particular criminal case in the administration of justice. Without access to specific facts a criminal prosecution may be totally frustrated. The President's broad interest in confidentiality of communications will not be vitiated by disclosure of a limited number of conversations preliminarily shown to have some bearing on the pending criminal cases.

We conclude that when the ground for asserting privilege as to subpoenaed materials sought for use in a criminal trial is based only on the generalized interest in confidentiality, it cannot prevail over the fundamental demands of due process of law in the fair administration of criminal justice. The generalized assertion of privilege must yield to the demonstrated, specific need for evidence in a pending criminal trial. . . .

Appendixes

THE CONSTITUTION OF THE UNITED STATES

JUSTICES OF THE UNITED STATES SUPREME COURT

TABLE OF CASES

The Constitution of the United States

We the people of the United States, in order to form a more perfect union, establish justice, insure domestic tranquillity, provide for the common defense, promote the general welfare, and secure the blessings of liberty to ourselves and our posterity, do ordain and establish this Constitution for the United States of America.

ARTICLE I

Section 1. All legislative powers herein granted shall be vested in a Congress of the United States, which shall consist of a Senate and House of Representatives.

Section 2. (1). The House of Representatives shall be composed of members chosen every second year by the people of the several States, and the electors in each State shall have the qualifications requisite for electors of the most numerous branch of the State legislature.

(2). No person shall be a Representative who shall not have attained to the age of twenty five years, and been seven years a citizen of the United States, and who shall not, when elected, be an inhabitant of that State in which he shall be chosen.

(3). Representatives and direct taxes[1] shall be apportioned among the several States which may be included within this Union, according to their respective numbers, which shall be determined by adding to the whole number of free persons, including those bound to service for a term of years, and excluding Indians not taxed, three fifths of all other persons.[2] The actual enumeration shall be made within three years after the first meeting of the Congress of the United States, and within every subsequent term of ten years, in such manner as they shall by law direct. The number of Representatives shall not exceed one for every thirty thousand, but each State shall have at least one Representative; and until such enumeration shall be made, the State of New Hampshire shall be entitled to choose three, Massachusetts eight, Rhode Island and Providence Plantations one, Connecticut five, New York six, New Jersey four, Pennsylvania eight, Delaware one, Maryland six, Virginia ten, North Caroline five, South Carolina five, and Georgia three.

(4). When vacancies happen in the representation from any State, the executive authority thereof shall issue writs of election to fill such vacancies.

[1] Modified by the 16th Amendment.
[2] Nullified by the 14th Amendment.

(5). The House of Representatives shall choose their Speaker and other officers; and shall have the sole power of impeachment.

Section 3. (1). The Senate of the United States shall be composed of two Senators from each State, chosen by the Legislature thereof,[3] for six years; and each Senator shall have one vote.

(2). Immediately after they shall be assembled in consequence of the first election, they shall be divided as equally as may be into three classes. The seats of the Senators of the first class shall be vacated at the expiration of the second year, of the second class at the expiration of the fourth year, and of the third class at the expiration of the sixth year, so that one third may be chosen every second year; and if vacancies happen by resignation, or otherwise, during the recess of the legislature of any State, the executive thereof may make temporary appointments until the next meeting of the legislature, which shall then fill such vacancies.

(3). No person shall be a Senator who shall not have attained to the age of thirty years, and been nine years a citizen of the United States, and who shall not, when elected, be an inhabitant of that State for which he shall be chosen.

(4). The Vice President of the United States shall be president of the Senate, but shall have no vote, unless they be equally divided.

(5). The Senate shall choose their other officers, and also a president pro tempore, in the absence of the Vice President, or when he shall exercise the office of President of the United States.

(6). The Senate shall have the sole power to try all impeachments. When sitting for that purpose, they shall be on oath or affirmation. When the President of the United States is tried, the Chief Justice shall preside: and no person shall be convicted without the concurrence of two thirds of the members present.

(7). Judgment in cases of impeachment shall not extend further than to removal from office, and disqualification to hold and enjoy any office of honor, trust or profit under the United States: but the party convicted shall nevertheless be liable and subject to indictment, trial, judgment and punishment, according to law.

Section 4. (1). The times, places and manner of holding elections for Senators and Representatives, shall be prescribed in each State by the legislature thereof; but the Congress may at any time by law make or alter such regulations, except as to the places of choosing Senators.

(2). The Congress shall assemble at least once in every year, and such meeting shall be on the first Monday in December, unless they shall by law appoint a different day.

Section 5. (1) Each House shall be the judge of the elections, returns and qualifications of its own members, and a majority of each shall constitute a quorum to do business; but a smaller number may adjourn from day to day, and may be authorized to compel the attendance of absent members, in such manner, and under such penalties as each House may provide.

(2) Each House may determine the rules of its proceedings, punish its

---

[3] Modified by the 17th Amendment.

members for disorderly behavior, and, with the concurrence of two thirds, expel a member.

(3). Each House shall keep a journal of its proceedings, and from time to time publish the same, excepting such parts as may in their judgment require secrecy; and the yeas and nays of the members of either House on any question shall, at the desire of one fifth of those present, be entered on the journal.

(4). Neither House, during the session of Congress, shall, without the consent of the other, adjourn for more than three days, nor to any other place than that in which the two Houses shall be sitting.

Section 6. (1). The Senators and Representatives shall receive a compensation for their services, to be ascertained by law, and paid out of the Treasury of the United States. They shall in all cases, except treason, felony and breach of the peace, be privileged from arrest during their attendance at the session of their respective Houses, and in going to and returning from the same; and for any speech or debate in either House, they shall not be questioned in any other place.

(2). No Senator or Representative shall, during the time for which he was elected, be appointed to any civil office under the authority of the United States, which shall have been created, or the emoluments whereof shall have been increased during such time; and no person holding any office under the United States, shall be a member of either House during his continuance in office.

Section 7. (1). All bills for raising revenue shall originate in the House of Representatives; but the Senate may propose or concur with amendments as on other bills.

(2). Every bill which shall have passed the House of Representatives and the Senate, shall, before it become a law, be presented to the President of the United States; if he approve he shall sign it, but if not he shall return it, with his objections to that House in which it shall have originated, who shall enter the objections at large on their journal, and proceed to reconsider it. If after such reconsideration two thirds of that House shall agree to pass the bill, it shall be sent, together with the objections, to the other House, by which it shall likewise be reconsidered, and if approved by two thirds of that House, it shall become a law. But in all such cases the votes of both Houses shall be determined by yeas and nays, and the names of the persons voting for and against the bill shall be entered on the journal of each House respectively. If any bill shall not be returned by the President within ten days (Sundays excepted) after it shall have been presented to him, the same shall be a law, in like manner as if he had signed it, unless the Congress by their adjournment prevent its return, in which case it shall not be a law.

(3). Every order, resolution, or vote to which the concurrence of the Senate and House of Representatives may be necessary (except on a question of adjournment) shall be presented to the President of the United States; and before the same shall take effect, shall be approved by him, or being disapproved by him, shall be repassed by two thirds of the Senate and House of Representatives, according to the rules and limitations prescribed in the case of a bill.

Section 8. The Congress shall have power (1). To lay and collect taxes, duties, imposts and excises, to pay the debts and provide for the common defense and general welfare of the United States; but all duties, imposts and excises shall be uniform throughout the United States;

(2). To borrow money on the credit of the United States;

(3). To regulate commerce with foreign nations, and among the several States, and with the Indian tribes;

(4). To establish an uniform rule of naturalization, and uniform laws on the subject of bankruptcies throughout the United States;

(5). To coin money, regulate the value thereof, and foreign coin, and fix the standard of weights and measures;

(6). To provide for the punishment of counterfeiting the securities and current coin of the United States;

(7). To establish post offices and post roads;

(8). To promote the progress of science and useful arts, by securing for limited times to authors and inventors the exclusive right to their respective writings and discoveries;

(9). To constitute tribunals inferior to the Supreme Court;

(10). To define and punish piracies and felonies committed on the high seas, and offenses against the law of nations;

(11). To declare war, grant letters of marque and reprisal, and make rules concerning captures on land and water;

(12). To raise and support armies, but no appropriation of money to that use shall be for a longer term than two years;

(13). To provide and maintain a navy;

(14.) To make rules for the government and regulation of the land and naval forces;

(15). To provide for calling forth the militia to execute the laws of the Union, suppress insurrections and repel invasions;

(16). To provide for organizing, arming, and disciplining the militia, and for governing such part of them as may be employed in the service of the United States, reserving to the States respectively, the appointment of the officers, and the authority of training the militia according to the discipline prescribed by Congress;

(17). To exercise exclusive legislation in all cases whatsoever, over such district (not exceeding ten miles square) as may, by cession of particular States, and the acceptance of Congress, become the seat of the government of the United States, and to exercise like authority over all places purchased by the consent of the legislature of the State in which the same shall be, for the erection of forts, magazines, arsenals, dock-yards, and other needful buildings;—And

(18). To make all laws which shall be necessary and proper for carrying into excution the foregoing powers, and all other powers vested by this Constitution in the government of the United States, or in any department or officer thereof.

Section 9. (1). The migration or importation of such persons as any of the States now existing shall think proper to admit, shall not be prohibited by the Congress prior to the year one thousand eight hundred and eight, but a tax or duty may be imposed on such importation, not exceeding ten dollars for each person.

(2). The privilege of the writ of habeas corpus shall not be suspended, unless when in cases of rebellion or invasion the public safety may require it.

(3). No bill of attainder or ex post facto law shall be passed.

(4). No capitation, or other direct, tax shall be laid, unless in proportion to the census of enumeration herein before directed to be taken.[4]

(5). No tax or duty shall be laid on articles exported from any State.

(6). No preference shall be given by any regulation of commerce or revenue to the ports of one State over those of another: nor shall vessels bound to, or from, one State, be obliged to enter, clear, or pay duties in another.

(7). No money shall be drawn from the Treasury, but in consequence of appropriations made by law; and a regular statement and account of the receipts and expenditures of all public money shall be published from time to time.

(8). No title of nobility shall be granted by the United States: and no person holding any office of profit or trust under them, shall, without the consent of the Congress, accept of any present, emolument, office, or title, of any kind whatever, from any king, prince, or foreign State.

Section 10. (1). No State shall enter into any treaty, alliance, or confederation; grant letters of marque and reprisal; coin money; emit bills of credit; make anything but gold and silver coin a tender in payment of debts; pass any bill of attainder, ex post facto law, or law impairing the obligation of contracts, or grant any title of nobility.

(2). No State shall, without the consent of the Congress, lay any imposts or duties on imports or exports, except what may be absolutely necessary for executing its inspection laws: and the net produce of all duties and imposts, laid by any State on imports or exports, shall be for the use of the Treasury of the United States; and all such laws shall be subject to the revision and control of the Congress.

(3). No State shall, without the consent of Congress, lay any duty of tonnage, keep troops, or ships of war in time of peace, enter into any agreement or compact with another State, or with a foreign power, or engage in war, unless actually invaded, or in such imminent danger as will not admit of delay.

ARTCLE II

Section 1. (1). The executive power shall be vested in a President of the United States of America. He shall hold his office during the term of four years, and, together with the Vice President, chosen for the same term, be elected, as follows:

(2). Each State shall appoint, in such manner as the legislature thereof may direct, a number of electors, equal to the whole number of Senators and Representatives to which the State may be entitled in the Congress: but no Senator or Representative, or person holding an office of trust or profit under the United States, shall be appointed an elector.

[4] Modified by the 16th Amendment.

The electors[5] shall meet in their respective States, and vote by ballot for two persons, of whom one at least shall not be an inhabitant of the same State with themselves. And they shall make a list of all the persons voted for, and of the number of votes for each; which list they shall sign and certify, and transmit sealed to the seat of the government of the United States, directed to the president of the Senate. The president of the Senate shall, in the presence of the Senate and House of Representatives, open all the certificates, and the votes shall then be counted. The person having the greatest number of votes shall be the President, if such number be a majority of the whole number of electors appointed; and if there be more than one who have such majority, and have an equal number of votes, then the House of Representatives shall immediately choose by ballot one of them for President; and if no person have a majority, then from the five highest on the list the said House shall in like manner choose the President. But in choosing the President, the votes shall be taken by States, the representation from each State having one vote; a quorum for this purpose shall consist of a member or members from two thirds of the States, and a majority of all the States shall be necessary to a choice. In every case, after the choice of the President, the person having the greatest number of votes of the electors shall be the Vice President. But if there should remain two or more who have equal votes, the Senate shall choose from them by ballot the Vice President.

(3). The Congress may determine the time of choosing the electors, and the day on which they shall give their votes; which day shall be the same throughout the United States.

(4). No person except a natural born citizen, or a citizen of the United States, at the time of the adoption of this Constitution, shall be eligible to the office of President; neither shall any person be eligible to that office who shall not have attained to the age of thirty five years, and been fourteen years a resident within the United States.

(5). In case of the removal of the President from office, or of his death, resignation, or inability to discharge the powers and duties of the said office, the same shall devolve on the Vice President, and the Congress may by law provide for the case of removal, death, resignation or inability, both of the President and Vice President, declaring what officer shall then act as President, and such officer shall act accordingly, until the disability be removed, or a President shall be elected.[6]

(6). The President shall, at stated times, receive for his services, a compensation, which shall neither be increased nor diminished during the period for which he shall have been elected, and he shall not receive within that period any other emolument from the United States, or any of them.

(7). Before he enter on the execution of his office, he shall take the following oath or affirmation: — "I do solemnly swear (or affirm) that I will faithfully execute the office of President of the United States, and will to the best of my ability, preserve, protect and defend the Constitution of the United States."

Section 2. (1). The President shall be commander in chief of the army

[5] Replaced by the 12th Amendment.
[6] Altered by the 25th Amendment.

and navy of the United States, and of the militia of the several States, when called into the actual service of the United States; he may require the opinion, in writing, of the principal officer in each of the executive departments, upon any subject relating to the duties of their respective offices, and he shall have power to grant reprieves and pardons for offenses against the United States, except in cases of impeachment.

(2). He shall have power, by and with the advice and consent of the Senate, to make treaties, provided two thirds of the Senators present concur; and he shall nominate, and by and with the advice and consent of the Senate, shall appoint ambassadors, other public ministers and consuls, judges of the Supreme Court, and all other officers of the United States, whose appointments are not herein otherwise provided for, and which shall be established by law: but the Congress may by law vest the appointment of such inferior officers, as they think proper, in the President alone, in the courts of law, or in the heads of departments.

(3). The President shall have power to fill up all vacancies that may happen during the recess of the Senate, by granting commissions which shall expire at the end of their next session.

Section 3. He shall from time to time give to the Congress information of the state of the Union, and recommend to their consideration such measures as he shall judge necessary and expedient; he may, on extraordinary occasions, convene both Houses, or either of them, and in case of disagreement between them, with respect to the time of adjournment, he may adjourn them to such time as he shall think proper; he shall receive ambassadors and other public ministers; he shall take care that the laws be faithfully executed, and shall commission all the officers of the United States.

Section 4. The President, Vice President and all civil officers of the United States, shall be removed from office on impeachment for, and conviction of, treason, bribery, or other high crimes and misdemeanors.

ARTICLE III

Section 1. The judicial power of the United States, shall be vested in one Supreme Court, and in such inferior courts as the Congress may from time to time ordain and establish. The judges, both of the Supreme and inferior courts, shall hold their offices during good behavior, and shall, at stated times, receive for their services, a compensation, which shall not be diminished during their continuance in office.

Section 2. (1). The judicial power shall extend to all cases, in law and equity, arising under this Constitution, the laws of the United States, and treaties made, or which shall be made, under their authority; — to all cases affecting ambassadors, other public ministers and consuls; — to all cases of admiralty and maritime jurisdiction; — to controversies to which the United States shall be a party; — to controversies between two or more States; — between a State and citizens of another State;[7] — between citizens of different States; — between citizens of the same State claiming lands under grants of

[7] Qualified by the 11th Amendment.

different States, and between a State, or the citizens thereof, and foreign States, citizens or subjects.

(2). In all cases affecting ambassadors, other public ministers and consuls, and those in which a State shall be party, the Supreme Court shall have original jurisdiction. In all the other cases before mentioned, the Supreme Court shall have appellate jurisdiction, both as to law and fact, with such exceptions, and under such regulations as the Congress shall make.

(3). The trial of all crimes, except in cases of impeachment, shall be by jury; and such trial shall be held in the State where the said crimes shall have been committed; but when not committed within any State, the trial shall be at such place or places the Congress may by law have directed.

Section 3. (1). Treason against the United States, shall consist only in levying war against them, or in adhering to their enemies, giving them aid and comfort. No person shall be convicted of treason unless on the testimony of two witnesses to the same overt act, or on confession in open court.

(2). The Congress shall have power to declare the punishment of treason, but no attainder of treason shall work corruption of blood, or forfeiture except during the life of the person attainted.

ARTICLE IV

Section 1. Full faith and credit shall be given in each State to the public acts, records, and judicial proceedings of every other State. And the Congress may by general laws prescribe the manner in which such acts, records and proceedings shall be proved, and the effect thereof.

Section 2. (1). The citizens of each State shall be entitled to all privileges and immunities of citizens in the several States.

(2). A person charged in any State with treason, felony, or other crime, who shall flee from justice, and be found in another State, shall on demand of the executive authority of the State from which he fled, be delivered up, to be removed to the State having jurisdiction of the crime.

(3). No person held to service or labor in one State, under the laws thereof, escaping into another, shall, in consequence of any law or regulation therein, be discharged from such service or labor, but shall be delivered up on claim of the party to whom such service or labor may be due.

Section 3. (1). New States may be admitted by the Congress into this Union; but no new State shall be formed or erected within the jurisdiction of any other State; nor any State be formed by the junction of two or more States, or parts of States, without the consent of the legislatures of the States concerned as well as of the Congress.

(2). The Congress shall have power to dispose of and make all needful rules and regulations respecting the territory or other property belonging to the United States; and nothing in this Constitution shall be so construed as to prejudice any claims of the United States or of any particular State.

Section 4. The United States shall guarantee to every State in this Union a republican form of government, and shall protect each of them against invasion; and on application of the legislature, or of the executive (when the legislature cannot be convened) against domestic violence.

ARTICLE V

The Congress, whenever two thirds of both Houses shall deem it necessary, shall propose amendments to this Constitution, or, on the application of the legislatures of two thirds of the several States, shall call a convention for proposing amendments, which, in either case, shall be valid to all intents and purposes, as part of this Constitution, when ratified by the legislatures of three fourths of the several States, or by conventions in three fourths thereof, as the one or the other mode of ratification may be proposed by the Congress; Provided that no amendment which may be made prior to the year one thousand eight hundred and eight shall in any manner affect the first and fourth clauses in the ninth section of the first article; and that no State, without its consent, shall be deprived of its equal suffrage in the Senate.

ARTICLE VI

Section 1. All debts contracted and engagements entered into, before the adoption of this Constitution, shall be as valid against the United States under this Constitution, as under the Confederation.

Section 2. This Constitution, and the laws of the United States which shall be made in pursuance thereof, and all treaties made, or which shall be made, under the authority of the United States, shall be the supreme law of the land; and the judges in every State shall be bound thereby, anything in the constitution or laws of any State to the contrary notwithstanding.

Section 3. The Senators and Representatives before mentioned, and the members of the several State legislatures, and all executive and judicial officers, both of the United States and of the several States, shall be bound by oath or affirmation, to support this Constitution; but no religious test shall ever be required as a qualification to any office or public trust under the United States.

ARTICLE VII

The ratification of the conventions of nine States, shall be sufficient for the establishment of this Constitution between the States so ratifying the same.

Articles in addition to and amendment of the Constitution of the United States of America, proposed by Congress, and ratified by the legislatures of the several States, pursuant to the fifth article of the original Constitution.

ARTICLE I

Congress shall make no law respecting an establishment of religion, or prohibiting the free exercise thereof; or abridging the freedom of speech, or of the press; or the right of the people peaceably to assemble, and to petition the government for a redress of grievances. [1791]

ARTICLE II

A well regulated militia, being necessary to the security of a free State, the right of the people to keep and bear arms, shall not be infringed. [1791]

Article III

No soldier shall, in time of peace be quartered in any house, without the consent of the owner, nor in time of war, but in a manner to be prescribed by law. [1791]

Article IV

The right of the people to be secure in their persons, houses, papers, and effects, against unreasonable searches and seizures, shall not be violated, and no warrants shall issue, but upon probable cause, supported by oath or affirmation, and particularly describing the place to be searched, and the persons or things to be seized. [1791]

Article V

No person shall be held to answer for a capital, or otherwise infamous crime, unless on a presentment or indictment of a grand jury, except in cases arising in the land or naval forces, or in the militia, when in actual service in time of war or public danger; nor shall any person be subject for the same offense to be twice put in jeopardy of life or limb; nor shall be compelled in any criminal case to be a witness against himself, nor be deprived of life, liberty, or property, without due process of law; nor shall private property be taken for public use, without just compensation. [1791]

Article VI

In all criminal prosecutions, the accused shall enjoy the right to a speedy and public trial, by an impartial jury of the State and district wherein the crime shall have been committed, which district shall have been previously ascertained by law, and to be informed of the nature and cause of the accusation; to be confronted with the witnesses against him; to have compulsory process for obtaining witnesses in his favor, and to have the assistance of counsel for his defense. [1791]

Article VII

In suits at common law, where the value in controversy shall exceed twenty dollars, the right of trial by jury shall be preserved, and no fact tried by a jury, shall be otherwise reexamined in any court of the United States, than according to the rules of the common law. [1791]

Article VIII

Excessive bail shall not be required, nor excessive fines imposed, nor cruel and unusual punishments inflicted. [1791]

ARTICLE IX

The enumeration in the Constitution, of certain rights, shall not be construed to deny or disparage others retained by the people. [1791]

ARTICLE X

The powers not delegated to the United States by the Constitution, nor prohibited by it to the States, are reserved to the States respectively, or to the people. [1791]

ARTICLE XI

The judicial power of the United States shall not be construed to extend to any suit in law or equity, commenced or prosecuted against one of the United States by citizens of another State, or by citizens or subjects of any foreign State. [1798]

ARTICLE XII

The electors shall meet in their respective States and vote by ballot for President and Vice-President, one of whom, at least, shall not be an inhabitant of the same State with themselves; they shall name in their ballots the person voted for as President, and in distinct ballots the person voted for as Vice-President, and they shall make distinct lists of all persons voted for as President, and of all persons voted for as Vice-President, and of the number of votes for each, which lists they shall sign and certify, and transmit sealed to the seat of the government of the United States, directed to the president of the Senate; — The president of the Senate shall, in the presence of the Senate and House of Representatives, open all the certificates and the votes shall then be counted; — The person having the greatest number of votes for President, shall be the President, if such number be a majority of the whole number of electors appointed; and if no person have such majority, then from the persons having the highest numbers not exceeding three on the list of those voted for as President, the House of Representatives shall choose immediately, by ballot, the President. But in choosing the President, the votes shall be taken by States, the representation from each State having one vote; a quorum for this purpose shall consist of a member or members from two-thirds of the States, and a majority of all the States shall be necessary to a choice. And if the House of Representatives shall not choose a President whenever the right of choice shall devolve upon them, before the fourth day of March next following, then the Vice-President shall act as President, as in the case of the death or other constitutional disability of the President. — The person having the greatest number of votes as Vice-President, shall be the Vice-President, if such number be a majority of the whole number of electors appointed, and if no person have a majority, then from the two highest numbers on the list, the Senate shall choose the Vice-President; a quorum for the purpose shall consist of two-thirds of the whole number of Senators, and a majority of the whole number shall be necessary to a choice. But no person constitutionally ineligible to the office of President shall be eligible to that of Vice-President of the United States. [1804]

Article XIII

Section 1. Neither slavery nor involuntary servitude, except as a punishment for crime whereof the party shall have been duly convicted, shall exist within the United States, or any place subject to their jurisdiction.

Section 2. Congress shall have power to enforce this article by appropriate legislation. [1865]

Article XIV

Section 1. All persons born or naturalized in the United States, and subject to the jurisdiction thereof, are citizens of the United States and of the State wherein they reside. No State shall make or enforce any law which shall abridge the privileges or immunities of citizens of the United States; nor shall any State deprive any person of life, liberty, or property, without due process of law; nor deny to any person within its jurisdiction the equal protection of the laws.

Section 2. Representatives shall be apportioned among the several States according to their respective numbers, counting the whole number of persons in each State, excluding Indians not taxed. But when the right to vote at any election for the choice of electors for President and Vice President of the United States, Representatives in Congress, the executive and judicial officers of a State, or the members of the legislature thereof, is denied to any of the male inhabitants of such State, being twenty-one years of age, and citizens of the United States, or in any way abridged, except for participation in rebellion, or other crime, the basis of representation therein shall be reduced in the proportion which the number of such male citizens shall bear to the whole number of male citizens twenty-one years of age in such State.

Section 3. No person shall be a Senator or Representative in Congress, or elector of President and Vice President, or hold any office, civil or military, under the United States, or under any State, who, having previously taken an oath, as a member of Congress, or as an officer of the United States, or as a member of any State legislature, or as an executive or judicial officer of any State, to support the Constitution of the United States, shall have engaged in insurrection or rebellion against the same, or given aid or comfort to the enemies thereof. But Congress may by a vote of two-thirds of each House, remove such disability.

Section 4. The validity of the public debt of the United States, authorized by law, including debts incurred for payment of pensions and bounties for services in suppressing insurrection or rebellion, shall not be questioned. But neither the United States nor any State shall assume or pay any debt or obligation incurred in aid of insurrection or rebellion against the United States, or any claim for the loss or emancipation of any slave; but all such debts, obligations and claims shall be held illegal and void.

Section 5. The Congress shall have power to enforce, by appropriate legislation, the provisions of this article. [1868]

ARTICLE XV

Section 1. The right of citizens of the United States to vote shall not be denied or abridged by the United States or by any State on account of race, color, or previous condition of servitude.

Section 2. The Congress shall have power to enforce this article by appropriate legislation. [1870]

ARTICLE XVI

The Congress shall have power to lay and collect taxes on incomes, from whatever source derived, without apportionment among the several States, and without regard to any census or enumeration. [1913]

ARTICLE XVII

The Senate of the United States shall be composed of two Senators from each State, elected by the people thereof, for six years; and each Senator shall have one vote. The electors in each State shall have the qualifications requisite for electors of the most numerous branch of the State legislatures.

When vacancies happen in the representation of any State in the Senate, the executive authority of such State shall issue writs of election to fill such vacancies: *Provided,* That the legislature of any State may empower the executive thereof to make temporary appointments until the people fill the vacancies by election as the legislature may direct.

This amendment shall not be so construed as to affect the election or term of any Senator chosen before it becomes valid as part of the Constitution. [1913]

ARTICLE XVIII

Section 1. After one year from the ratification of this article the manufacture, sale, or transportation of intoxicating liquors within, the importation thereof into, or the exportation thereof from the United States and all territory subject to the jurisdiction thereof for beverage purposes is hereby prohibited.

Section 2. The Congress and the several States shall have concurrent power to enforce this article by appropriate legislation.

Section 3. This article shall be inoperative unless it shall have been ratified as an amendment to the Constitution by the legislatures of the several States, as provided in the Constitution, within seven years from the date of the submission hereof to the States by the Congress. [1919]

ARTICLE XIX

The right of citizens of the United States to vote shall not be denied or abridged by the United States or by any State on account of sex.

The Congress shall have power to enforce this article by appropriate legislation. [1920]

ARTICLE XX

Section 1. The terms of the President and Vice President shall end at noon on the 20th day of January, and the terms of Senators and Representatives at noon on the 3d day of January, of the years in which such terms would have ended if this article had not been ratified; and the terms of their successors shall then begin.

Section 2. The Congress shall assemble at least once in every year, and such meeting shall begin at noon on the 3d day of January, unless they shall by law appoint a different day.

Section 3. If, at the time fixed for the beginning of the term of the President, the President elect shall have died, the Vice President elect shall become President. If a President shall not have been chosen before the time fixed for the beginning of his term, or if the President elect shall have failed to qualify, then the Vice President elect shall act as President until a President shall have qualified; and the Congress may by law provide for the case wherein neither a President elect nor a Vice President elect shall have qualified, declaring who shall then act as President, or the manner in which one who is to act shall be selected, and such person shall act accordingly until a President or Vice President shall have qualified.

Section 4. The Congress may by law provide for the case of the death of any of the persons from whom the House of Representatives may choose a President whenever the right of choice shall have devolved upon them, and for the case of the death of any of the persons from whom the Senate may choose a Vice President whenever the right of choice shall have developed upon them.

Section 5. Sections 1 and 2 shall take effect on the 15th day of October following the ratification of this article.

Section 6. This article shall be inoperative unless it shall have been ratified as an amendment to the Constitution by the legislatures of three-fourths of the several States within seven years from the date of its submission. [1933]

ARTICLE XXI

Section 1. The Eighteenth Article of Amendment to the Constitution of the United States is hereby repealed.

Section 2. The transportation or importation into any State, Territory or possession of the United States for delivery or use therein of intoxicating liquors, in violation of the laws thereof, is hereby prohibited.

Section 3. This article shall be inoperative unless it shall have been ratified as an amendment to the Constitution by conventions in the several States, as provided in the Constitution, within seven years from the date of the submission hereof to the States by the Congress. [1933]

ARTICLE XXII

Section 1. No person shall be elected to the office of the President more than twice, and no person who has held the office of President, or acted as President, for more than two years of a term to which some other person was elected President shall be elected to the office of the President more than once. But this Article shall not apply to any person holding the office of President when this Article was proposed by the Congress, and shall not prevent any person who may be holding the office of President, or acting as President, during the term within which this Article becomes operative from holding the office of President or acting as President during the remainder of such term.

Section 2. This Article shall be inoperative unless it shall have been ratified as an amendment to the Constitution by the legislatures of three-fourths of the several States within seven years from the date of its submission to the States by the Congress. [1951]

ARTICLE XXIII

Section 1. The District constituting the seat of Government of the United States shall appoint in such manner as the Congress may direct:

A number of electors of President and Vice President equal to the whole number of Senators and Representatives in Congress to which the District would be entitled if it were a State, but in no event more than the least populous State; they shall be in addition to those appointed by the States, but they shall be considered, for the purposes of the election of President and Vice President, to be electors appointed by a State; and they shall meet in the District and perform such duties as provided by the twelfth article of amendment.

Section 2. The Congress shall have power to enforce this article by appropriate legislation. [1961]

ARTICLE XXIV

Section 1. The right of citizens of the United States to vote in any primary or other election for President or Vice President, for electors for President or Vice President, or for Senator or Representative in Congress, shall not be denied or abridged by the United States or any State by reason of failure to pay any poll tax or other tax.

Section 2. The Congress shall have power to enforce this article by appropriate legislation. [1964]

ARTICLE XXV

Section 1. In case of the removal of the President from office or of his death or resignation, the Vice President shall become President.

Section 2. Whenever there is a vacancy in the office of the Vice President, the President shall nominate a Vice President who shall take office upon confirmation by a majority vote of both Houses of Congress.

Section 3. Whenever the President transmits to the President Pro Tempore of the Senate and the Speaker of the House of Representatives his written declaration that he is unable to discharge the powers and duties of his office, and until he transmits to them a written declaration to the contrary, such powers and duties shall be discharged by the Vice President as Acting President.

Section 4. Whenever the Vice President and a majority of either the principal officers of the executive departments or of such other body as Congress may by law provide, transmit to the President Pro Tempore of the Senate and the Speaker of the House of Representatives their written declaration that the President is unable to discharge the powers and duties of his office, the Vice President shall immediately assume the powers and duties of the office as Acting President.

Thereafter, when the President transmits to the President Pro Tempore of the Senate and the Speaker of the House of Representatives his written declaration that no inability exists, he shall resume the powers and duties of his office unless the Vice President and a majority of either the principal officers of the executive department or of such other body as Congress may by law provide, transmit within four days to the President Pro Tempore of the Senate and the Speaker of the House of Representatives their written declaration that the President is unable to discharge the powers and duties of his office. Thereupon Congress shall decide the issue, assembling within forty-eight hours for that purpose if not in session. If the Congress, within twenty-one days after receipt of the latter written declaration, or, if Congress is not in session, within twenty-one days after Congress is required to assemble, determines by two-thirds vote of both Houses that the President is unable to discharge the powers and duties of his office, the Vice President shall continue to discharge the same as Acting President; otherwise, the President shall resume the powers and duties of his office.[1967]

Justices of the United States Supreme Court
1789–1977

NAME	TERM	APPOINTED BY
John Jay	1789–1795	Washington
John Rutledge	1789–1791	Washington
William Cushing	1789–1810	Washington
James Wilson	1789–1798	Washington
John Blair	1789–1796	Washington
James Iredell	1790–1799	Washington
Thomas Johnson	1791–1793	Washington
William Paterson	1793–1806	Washington
John Rutledge	1795	Washington
Samuel Chase	1796–1811	Washington
Oliver Ellsworth	1796–1800	Washington
Bushrod Washington	1798–1829	John Adams
Alfred Moore	1799–1804	John Adams
John Marshall	1801–1835	John Adams
William Johnson	1804–1834	Jefferson
H. Brockholst Livingston	1806–1823	Jefferson
Thomas Todd	1807–1826	Jefferson
Gabriel Duval	1811–1835	Madison
Joseph Story	1811–1845	Madison
Smith Thompson	1823–1843	Monroe
Robert Trimble	1826–1828	John Quincy Adams
John McLean	1829–1861	Jackson
Henry Baldwin	1830–1844	Jackson
James M. Wayne	1835–1867	Jackson
Roger B. Taney	1836–1864	Jackson
Philip P. Barbour	1836–1841	Jackson
John Catron	1837–1865	Van Buren
John McKinley	1837–1852	Van Buren
Peter V. Daniel	1841–1860	Van Buren
Samuel Nelson	1845–1872	Tyler
Levi Woodbury	1845–1851	Polk
Robert C. Grier	1846–1870	Polk
Benjamin R. Curtis	1851–1857	Fillmore
John A. Campbell	1853–1861	Pierce
Nathan Clifford	1858–1881	Buchanan
Noah H. Swayne	1862–1881	Lincoln
Samuel F. Miller	1862–1890	Lincoln
David Davis	1862–1877	Lincoln
Stephen J. Field	1863–1897	Lincoln

(Chief Justices in italics)

NAME	TERM	APPOINTED BY
Salmon P. Chase	1864–1873	Lincoln
William Strong	1870–1880	Grant
Joseph P. Bradley	1870–1892	Grant
Ward Hunt	1872–1882	Grant
Morrison R. Waite	1874–1888	Grant
John Marshall Harlan	1877–1911	Hayes
William B. Woods	1880–1887	Hayes
Stanley Matthews	1881–1889	Garfield
Horace Gray	1881–1902	Arthur
Samuel Blatchford	1882–1893	Arthur
Lucius Q. C. Lamar	1888–1893	Cleveland
Melville W. Fuller	1888–1910	Cleveland
David J. Brewer	1889–1910	Benjamin Harrison
Henry B. Brown	1890–1906	Benjamin Harrison
George Shiras	1892–1903	Benjamin Harrison
Howell E. Jackson	1893–1895	Benjamin Harrison
Edward D. White	1894–1910	Cleveland
Rufus W. Peckham	1895–1909	Cleveland
Joseph McKenna	1898–1925	McKinley
Oliver Wendell Holmes	1902–1932	Theodore Roosevelt
William R. Day	1903–1922	Theodore Roosevelt
William H. Moody	1906–1910	Theodore Roosevelt
Horace H. Lurton	1909–1914	Taft
Charles E. Hughes	1910–1916	Taft
Edward D. White	1910–1921	Taft
Willis Van Devanter	1910–1937	Taft
Joseph R. Lamar	1910–1916	Taft
Mahlon Pitney	1912–1922	Taft
James C. McReynolds	1914–1941	Wilson
Louis D. Brandeis	1916–1939	Wilson
John H. Clarke	1916–1922	Wilson
William H. Taft	1921–1930	Harding
George Sutherland	1922–1938	Harding
Pierce Butler	1922–1939	Harding
Edward T. Sanford	1923–1930	Harding
Harlan F. Stone	1925–1941	Coolidge
Charles E. Hughes	1930–1941	Hoover
Owen J. Roberts	1930–1945	Hoover
Benjamin N. Cardozo	1932–1938	Hoover
Hugo L. Black	1937–1971	Franklin D. Roosevelt
Stanley F. Reed	1938–1957	Franklin D. Roosevelt
Felix Frankfurter	1939–1962	Franklin D. Roosevelt
William O. Douglas	1939–1975	Franklin D. Roosevelt
Frank Murphy	1940–1949	Franklin D. Roosevelt
James F. Byrnes	1941–1942	Franklin D. Roosevelt

(Chief Justices in italics)

NAME	TERM	APPOINTED BY
Harlan F. Stone	1941–1946	Franklin D. Roosevelt
Robert H. Jackson	1941–1954	Franklin D. Roosevelt
Wiley B. Rutledge	1943–1949	Franklin D. Roosevelt
Harold H. Burton	1945–1958	Truman
Fred M. Vinson	1946–1953	Truman
Tom C. Clark	1949–1967	Truman
Sherman Minton	1949–1956	Truman
Earl Warren	1953–1969	Eisenhower
John Marshall Harlan	1955–1971	Eisenhower
William J. Brennan, Jr.	1956–	Eisenhower
Charles E. Whittaker	1957–1962	Eisenhower
Potter Stewart	1958–	Eisenhower
Arthur J. Goldberg	1962–1965	Kennedy
Byron R. White	1962–	Kennedy
Abe Fortas	1965–1969	Lyndon B. Johnson
Thurgood Marshall	1967–	Lyndon B. Johnson
Warren E. Burger	1969 –	Nixon
Harry A. Blackmun	1970 –	Nixon
Lewis F. Powell, Jr.	1972 –	Nixon
William H. Rehnquist	1972 –	Nixon
John Paul Stevens	1975 –	Ford

——————

(Chief Justices in italics)

Table of Cases

Ableman v. Booth, 21 Howard 506 (1859) 110–113
Abrams v. United States, 250 U.S. 616 (1919) 327–329
Adair v. United States, 208 U.S. 161 (1908) 300-303, 419
Adkins v. Children's Hospital, 261 U.S. 525 (1923) 347–355, 356, 387, 394
Alexander v. Holmes County Board of Education, 396 U.S. 19 (1969) 534
Allgeyer v. Louisiana, 165 U.S. 578 (1897) 282
American Power & Light v. S. E. C., 329 U.S. 90 (1946) 406
American Steel Foundries v. Tri-Cities Trades Council,
    257 U.S. 184 (1921) 344
Argersinger v. Hamlin, 407 U.S. 25 (1972) 607

Bailey v. Drexel Furniture Co., 259 U.S. 20 (1922) 340–343
Baker v. Carr, 369 U.S. 186 (1962) 584–594
Bank of Augusta v. Earle, 13 Peters 519 (1839) 139–141
Barenblatt v. United States, 360 U.S. 109 (1959) 453–456
Barron v. Baltimore, 7 Peters 243 (1833) 60–62, 192
Betts v. Brady, 316 U.S. 455 (1942) 607
Book Named [Fanny Hill] v. Attorney General of Massachusetts,
    383 U.S. 413 (1966) 462–467, 468
Brown v. Board of Education of Topeka, 347 U.S. 483 (1954) 522–526, 527, 534
Bunting v. Oregon, 243 U.S. 426 (1917) 291–293, 347
Burton v. Wilmington Parking Authority, 365 U.S. 715 (1961) 542–545, 546

Calder v. Bull, 3 Dallas 386 (1798) 13–16
Carter v. Carter Coal Co., 298 U.S. 238 (1936) 378–381, 394
Champion v. Ames, 188 U.S. 321 (1903) 300, 309–312
Chicago, Milwaukee, St. Paul Ry. Co. v. Minnesota, 134 U.S. 418
    (1890) 251–253
Child Labor Tax Case (See Bailey v. Drexel Furniture Co.)
Chisholm v. Georgia, 2 Dallas 419 (1793) 3–6
Civil Rights Cases, 109 U.S. 3 (1883) 200–208, 542, 549
Cleveland Board of Education v. LeFleur, 414 U.S. 632 (1974) 561
Cohens v. Virginia, 6 Wheaton 264 (1821) 41–49, 110
Colegrove v. Green, 328 U.S. 549 (1946) 584
Committee for Public Education and Religious Liberty v. Nyquist,
    413 U.S. 100 (1973) 516
Cooley v. Board of Wardens of the Port of Philadelphia, 12 Howard 299
    (1851) 135–138
Cooper v. Aaron, 358 U.S. 1 (1958) 527–533, 534
Coppage v. Kansas, 236 U.S. 1 (1915) 300
Cox v. Louisiana, 379 U.S. 536 (1965) 474–476
Cummings v. Missouri, 4 Wallace 277 (1867) 170–174

Danbury Hatters' Case (See Loewe v. Lawlor)
Dartmouth College v. Woodward, 4 Wheaton 518 (1819) 72–78, 87
Debs, In re, 158 U.S. 564 (1895) 294–297, 674
De Funis v. Odegaard, 416 U.S. 312 (1974) 565

De Jonge *v.* Oregon, 299 U.S. 353 (1937) — 429–431
Dennis *v.* United States, 341 U.S. 494 (1951) — 432–438
Dodge *v.* Woolsey, 18 Howard 331 (1856) — 124–125
Dred Scott *v.* Sandford, 19 Howard 393 (1857) — 101, 150–157
Duplex Printing Press Co. *v.* Deering, 254 U.S. 443 (1921) — 344

Eakin *v.* Raub, 12 Serg. & Rawle (Penna.) 330 (1825) — 31–35
Engel *v.* Vitale, 370 U.S. 421 (1962) — 511–515
Escobedo *v.* Illinois, 378 U.S. 478 (1964) — 616, 621
Everson *v.* Board of Education of Ewing, 330 U.S. 1 (1947) — 503–507

Fairfax's Devisee *v.* Hunter's Lessee, 7 Cranch 603 (1813) — 36
Ferguson *v.* Skrupa, 372 U.S. 726 (1963) — 419–421
Fletcher *v.* Peck, 6 Cranch 87 (1810) — 63–71
Furman *v.* Georgia, 408 U.S. 238 (1972) — 625

Garland, Ex parte, 4 Wallace 333 (1867) — 170
Gault, In re, 387 U.S. 1 (1967) — 612–616
Georgia *v.* Stanton, 6 Wallace 50 (1868) — 177
Gibbons *v.* Ogden, 9 Wheaton 1 (1824) — 90–96, 97, 126
Gideon *v.* Wainwright, 372 U.S. 335 (1963) — 468, 607–611, 616
Gillette *v.* United States, 401 U.S. 437 (1971) — 653–657
Ginzburg *v.* United States, 383 U.S. 463 (1966) — 462–467
Gitlow *v.* New York, 268 U.S. 652 (1925) — 330–333
Gomillion *v.* Lightfoot, 364 U.S. 399 (1960) — 584
Gregg *v.* Georgia, 44 Law Week 5230 (1976) — 625–629
Griffin *v.* California, 381 U.S. 957 (1965) — 603
Griffin *v.* County Board of Prince Edward County, 377 U.S. 218 (1964) — 534
Griswold *v.* Connecticut, 381 U.S. 479 (1965) — 630–632
Grovey *v.* Townsend, 295 U.S. 45 (1935) — 574

Hall *v.* DeCuir, 95 U.S. 485 (1878) — 213–215
Hammer *v.* Dagenhart, 247 U.S. 251 (1918) — 337–340
Harris *v.* New York, 401 U.S. 222 (1971) — 621–624
Heart of Atlanta Motel, Inc. *v.* United States, 379 U.S. 241 (1964) — 422, 549–554
Helvering *v.* Davis, 301 U.S. 619 (1937) — 412
Hepburn *v.* Griswold, 8 Wallace 603 (1870) — 183–187
Hipolite Egg Co. *v.* United States, 220 U.S. 45 (1911) — 309
Hoke *v.* United States, 227 U.S. 308 (1913) — 309
Holden *v.* Hardy, 169 U.S. 366 (1898) — 282
Holtzman *v.* Schlesinger, 441 U.S. 1304 (1973) — 658
Home Building and Loan Association Co. *v.* Blaisdell, 290 U.S. 398 (1934) — 365–369
Houston, East and West Texas Ry. Co. *v.* United States, 234 U.S. 342 (1914) — 264–266
Hurtado *v.* California, 110 U.S. 516 (1884) — 193–196, 330
Hylton *v.* United States, 3 Dallas 171 (1796) — 20–22, 304

Illinois Central Railroad Co. *v.* Interstate Commerce Commission, 206 U.S. 441 (1907) — 261
Interstate Circuit, Inc. *v.* Dallas, 390 U.S. 676, 704 (1968) — 468
Interstate Commerce Commission *v.* Alabama Midland Ry. Co., 168 U.S. 144 (1897) — 261
Interstate Commerce Commission *v.* Cinti., N. Orl. and Tex. Pac. Ry., 167 U.S. 479 (1897) — 258–260

Interstate Commerce Commission *v.* Illinois Central Railroad Co.,
215 U.S. 452 (1910)   261–263

Jones *v.* Alfred H. Mayer Co., 392 U.S. 409 (1968)   555–561
Jones *v.* Opelika, 316 U.S. 584 (1942)   494
Jurek *v.* Texas, 44 Law Week 5256 (1976)   625

Katzenbach *v.* McClung, 379 U.S. 294 (1964)   422–425
Ker *v.* California, 374 U.S. 23 (1962)   600
Kirby *v.* Illinois, 406 U.S. 682 (1972)   621
Knox *v.* Lee (See Legal Tender Cases)
Korematsu *v.* United States, 323 U.S. 214 (1944)   669–673

Legal Tender Cases, 12 Wallace 457 (1871)   188–191
Lemon *v.* Kurtzman, 403 U.S. 602 (1971)   516
Lincoln Federal Labor Union *v.* Northwestern Iron & Metal Co.,
335 U.S. 525 (1949)   419
Lochner *v.* New York, 198 U.S. 45 (1905)   282–289, 291, 347, 419
Loewe *v.* Lawlor, 208 U.S. 274 (1908)   297–300
Lottery Cases (See Champion *v.* Ames)
Louisiana, N. Orl. & Texas R.R. Co. *v.* Mississippi, 133 U.S. 587 (1890)   213
Louisville, Cincinnati & Charlestown R.R. Co. *v.* Letson,
2 Howard 497 (1844)   142–144
Luther *v.* Borden, 7 Howard 1 (1849)   101–105, 584

Malloy *v.* Hogan, Sheriff, 378 U.S. 1 (1964)   603–606
Mapp *v.* Ohio, 367 U.S. 643 (1961)   600–602
Marbury *v.* Madison, 1 Cranch 137 (1803)   25–31
Martin *v.* Hunter's Lessee, 1 Wheaton 304 (1816)   36–40, 41
Massachusetts *v.* Laird, Secretary of Defense, 400 U.S. 886 (1970)   658–663
McCardle, Ex parte, 7 Wallace 506 (1869)   177–178
McCollum *v.* Board of Education, 333 U.S. 203 (1948)   508
McCray *v.* United States, 195 U.S. 27 (1904)   312–317
McCulloch *v.* Maryland, 4 Wheaton 316 (1819)   50–60
McDonald *v.* Santa Fe Trail Transportation Co., 44 Law Week
5067 (1976)   565–568
McGrain *v.* Daugherty, 273 U.S. 135 (1927)   445
Miller *v.* California, 413 U.S. 15 (1973)   468–474
Milligan, Ex parte, 4 Wallace 2 (1866)   164–169, 174
Milliken *v.* Bradley, 418 U.S. 717 (1974)   534
Minersville School District *v.* Gobitis, 310 U.S. 586 (1940)   494
Minnesota Rate Cases, 230 U.S. 352 (1913)   264
Miranda *v.* Arizona, 383 U.S. 436 (1966)   616–620, 621
Mishkin *v.* New York, 383 U.S. 502 (1966)   462–467, 468
Mississippi *v.* Johnson, 4 Wallace 475 (1867)   174–176, 177
Missouri ex rel. Gaines *v.* Canada, 305 U.S. 337 (1938)   522
Moose Lodge No. 107 *v.* Irvis, 407 U.S. 163 (1972)   546–549
Morehead *v.* New York ex rel. Tipaldo, 298 U.S. 587 (1936)   387
Morgan *v.* Virginia, 328 U.S. 373 (1946)   213
Muller *v.* Oregon, 208 U.S. 412 (1908)   289–290, 291
Munn *v.* Illinois, 94 U.S. 113 (1877)   242–246, 251
Murphy *v.* Waterfront Commission of New York, 378 U.S. 52 (1964)   603

National Association for the Advancement of Colored People *v.* Alabama,
357 U.S. 449 (1958)   457–461

National Labor Relations Board *v.* Friedman-Marks Clothing Co.,
   301 U.S. 58 (1937) — 394
National Labor Relations Board *v.* Jones & Laughlin Steel Corp.,
   301 U.S. 1 (1937) — 394–401
Near *v.* Minnesota, 283 U.S. 697 (1931) — 482–486
Nebbia *v.* New York, 291 U.S. 502 (1934) — 369–372
New York *v.* Miln, 11 Peters 102 (1837) — 126–129
New York Times Co. *v.* Sullivan, 376 U.S. 254 (1964) — 486–488
New York Times Co. *v.* United States, 403 U.S. 713 (1971) — 489–493
North Carolina State Board of Education *v.* Swann, 402 U.S. 43 (1971) — 534
Northern Securities Company *v.* United States,
   193 U.S. 197 (1904) — 271–275, 277, 300

Ogden *v.* Saunders, 12 Wheaton 213 (1827) — 79–86
Ohio Life Insurance & Trust Co. *v.* Debolt, 16 Howard 416 (1854) — 120–123
Osborn *v.* Bank of the United States, 9 Wheaton 738 (1824) — 3

Panama Refining Co. *v.* Ryan, 293 U.S. 388 (1935) — 373
Paris Adult Theatre I *v.* Slaton, 413 U.S. 49 (1973) — 468
Parker *v.* Davis (See Legal Tender Cases)
Passenger Cases, 7 Howard 283 (1849) — 130–134
Peik *v.* Chicago & Northwestern Ry. Co., 94 U.S. 164 (1877) — 247
Planned Parenthood of Central Missouri *v.* Danforth, 44 Law Week
   5197 (1976) — 633
Plessy *v.* Ferguson, 163 U.S. 537 (1896) — 216–221
Pollock *v.* Farmers' Loan and Trust Co., 158 U.S. 601 (1895) — 20, 304–308
Powell *v.* Alabama, 287 U.S. 45 (1932) — 607
Prigg *v.* Pennsylvania, 16 Peters 539 (1842) — 145–149
Prize Cases, 2 Black 635 (1863) — 161–164
Proffitt *v.* Florida, 44 Law Week 5256 (1976) — 625
Propeller Genesee Chief *v.* Fitzhugh, 12 Howard 443 (1851) — 105–109
Proprietors of the Charles River Bridge *v.* Proprietors of the
   Warren Bridge, 11 Peters 420 (1837) — 105, 114–119, 120
Providence Bank *v.* Billings, 4 Peters 516 (1830) — 87–89, 114

Rapier, In re, 143 U.S. 110 (1895) — 309
Reed *v.* Reed, Administrator, 404 U.S. 71 (1971) — 561–564
Reitman *v.* Mulkey, 387 U.S. 369 (1967) — 555
Reynolds *v.* Sims, 377 U.S. 533 (1964) — 594–599
Roberts *v.* Louisiana, 44 Law Week 5281 (1976) — 625
Roe *v.* Wade, 410 U.S. 113 (1973) — 633–639
Roth *v.* United States, 354 U.S. 476 (1957) — 462, 468
Runyon *v.* Mcrary, 44 Law Week 5034 (1976) — 522

Schechter *v.* United States, 295 U.S. 495 (1935) — 373–377, 378, 394
Schenck *v.* United States, 249 U.S. 47 (1919) — 324–326, 327
Selective Draft Law Cases, 245 U.S. 366 (1918) — 321–323
Shapiro *v.* Thompson, 394 U.S. 618 (1969) — 569–573
Shreveport Case (See Houston, East and West Texas Ry. Co.
   v. United States)
Slaughter-House Cases, 16 Wallace 36 (1873) — 192, 193, 197, 225–241, 242, 330
Smith *v.* Allwright, 321 U.S. 649 (1944) — 574–577
Smyth *v.* Ames, 169 U.S. 466 (1898) — 254–257
South Carolina *v.* Katzenbach, Attorney General, 383 U.S. 301 (1966) — 578–583
Springer *v.* United States, 102 U.S. 586 (1881) — 304
Stafford *v.* Wallace, 258 U.S. 495 (1922) — 359–362

Standard Oil Co. of New Jersey *v.* United States, 221 U.S. 1 (1911)   277–281
Steamboat Thomas Jefferson, 10 Wheaton 428 (1825)   105
Stettler *v.* O'Hara, 243 U.S. 629 (1917)   347
Steward Machine Company *v.* Davis, 301 U.S. 548 (1937)   412–418
Stone *v.* Farmers' Loan & Trust Co., 116 U.S. 307 (1886)   251
Strauder *v.* West Virginia, 100 U.S. 303 (1880)   209
Strawbridge *v.* Curtiss, 3 Cranch 267 (1806)   142
Sturges *v.* Crowninshield, 4 Wheaton 122 (1819)   79
Swann *v.* Charlotte-Mecklenburg Board of Education, 402 U.S. 1
    (1971)   534–541
Sweatt *v.* Painter, 339 U.S. 629 (1950)   522
Swift and Co. *v.* United States, 196 U.S. 375 (1905)   275–277, 394

Test Oath Cases (See Cummings *v.* Missouri; Ex parte Garland)
Texas *v.* White, 7 Wallace 700 (1869)   179–182
Tinker *v.* Des Moines School District, 393 U.S. 503 (1969)   644–648
Torcaso *v.* Watkins, 367 U.S. 488 (1961)   511
Truax *v.* Corrigan, 257 U.S. 312 (1921)   344–347
Twining *v.* New Jersey, 211 U.S. 78 (1908)   603

United States *v.* Ash, 413 U.S. 300 (1973)   621
United States *v.* Butler, 297 U.S. 1 (1936)   382–386, 412
United States *v.* Classic, 313 U.S. 299 (1941)   574
United States *v.* Curtiss-Wright Export Corp., 299 U.S. 304 (1936)   664–668
United States *v.* Darby Lumber Company, 312 U.S. 100 (1941)   402–406
United States *v.* E. C. Knight Co.,
    156 U.S. 1 (1895)   267–271, 271, 275, 359, 378
United States *v.* Nixon, 418 U.S. 683 (1974)   684–689
United States *v.* O'Brien, 391 U.S. 367 (1968)   640–643
United States *v.* Reese, 92 U.S. 214 (1876)   197–199
United States *v.* Seeger, 380 U.S. 163 (1965)   649, 653
United States *v.* United States District Court for the Eastern District
    of Michigan, 407 U.S. 297 (1972)   678–683

Vanhorne's Lessee *v.* Dorrance, 2 Dallas 304 (1795)   7–13, 63
Veazie Bank *v.* Fenno, 8 Wallace 533 (1869)   312
Virginia *v.* Rives, 100 U.S. 313 (1880)   209–212
Virginia State Board of Pharmacy *v.* Virginia Citizens Consumer
    Council, 96 S. Ct. 1817 (1976)   477–481

Wabash, St. Louis and Pacific Ry. Co. *v.* Illinois,
    118 U.S. 557 (1886)   247–250, 258
Ware *v.* Hylton, 3 Dallas 199 (1796)   17–19
Watkins *v.* United States, 354 U.S. 178 (1957)   445–453
Welsh *v.* United States, 398 U.S. 333 (1970)   649–653, 653
Wesberry *v.* Sanders, 376 U.S. 1 (1964)   594
West Coast Hotel Company *v.* Parrish, 300 U.S. 379 (1937)   387–393, 394
West Virginia Board of Education *v.* Barnette, 319 U.S. 624 (1943)   494–502
Whitney *v.* California, 274 U.S. 357 (1927)   333–336
Wickard *v.* Filburn, 317 U.S. 111 (1942)   406–412
Willson *v.* Black Bird Creek Marsh Co., 2 Peters 245 (1829)   97–98, 126
Wisconsin *v.* Yoder, 406 U.S. 205 (1972)   516–521
Wolf *v.* Colorado, 338 U.S. 25 (1949)   600
Wolff Packing Co. *v.* Court of Industrial Relations,
    262 U.S. 522 (1923)   356–358, 369
Woodson *v.* North Carolina, 44 Law Week 5267 (1976)   625

Yates *v*. United States, 354 U.S. 298 (1957)   438–444, 445
Yerger, Ex parte, 8 Wallace 85 (1869)   177
Young *v*. American Mini Theatres, Inc. (1976)   468
Youngstown Sheet and Tube Co. *v*. Sawyer, 343 U.S. 579 (1952)   674–677

Zorach *v*. Clauson, 343 U.S. 306 (1952)   508–510